# CCNP Security VPN 642-647

## Official Cert Guide

Howard Hooper, CCIE No. 23470

**Cisco Press**

800 East 96th Street

Indianapolis, IN 46240

# CCNP Security VPN 642-647 Official Cert Guide

Howard Hooper, CCIE No. 23470

Copyright © 2012 Pearson Education, Inc.

Published by:
Cisco Press
800 East 96th Street
Indianapolis, IN 46240 USA

Printed in the United States of America

First Printing July 2011

Library of Congress Cataloging-in-Publication data is on file.

ISBN-13: 978-1-58714-256-7

ISBN-10: 1-58714-256-2

## Warning and Disclaimer

This book is designed to provide information for the Cisco CCNP Security VPN 642-647 exam. Every effort has been made to make this book as complete and as accurate as possible, but no warranty or fitness is implied.

The information is provided on an "as is" basis. The authors, Cisco Press, and Cisco Systems, Inc., shall have neither liability nor responsibility to any person or entity with respect to any loss or damages arising from the information contained in this book or from the use of the discs or programs that may accompany it.

The opinions expressed in this book belong to the author and are not necessarily those of Cisco Systems, Inc.

## Feedback Information

At Cisco Press, our goal is to create in-depth technical books of the highest quality and value. Each book is crafted with care and precision, undergoing rigorous development that involves the unique expertise of members from the professional technical community.

Readers' feedback is a natural continuation of this process. If you have any comments regarding how we could improve the quality of this book, or otherwise alter it to better suit your needs, you can contact us through e-mail at feedback@ciscopress.com. Please make sure to include the book title and ISBN in your message.

We greatly appreciate your assistance.

## Corporate and Government Sales

Cisco Press offers excellent discounts on this book when ordered in quantity for bulk purchases or special sales. For more information, please contact: U.S. Corporate and Government Sales 1-800-382-3419 corpsales@pearsontechgroup.com

For sales outside of the U.S., please contact: International Sales 1-317-581-3793 international@pearsontechgroup.com

We greatly appreciate your assistance.

## Trademark Acknowledgments

All terms mentioned in this book that are known to be trademarks or service marks have been appropriately capitalized. Cisco Press or Cisco Systems, Inc., cannot attest to the accuracy of this information. Use of a term in this book should not be regarded as affecting the validity of any trademark or service mark.

## Corporate and Government Sales

The publisher offers excellent discounts on this book when ordered in quantity for bulk purchases or special sales, which may include electronic versions and/or custom covers and content particular to your business, training goals, marketing focus, and branding interests. For more information, please contact: U.S. Corporate and Government Sales 1-800-382-3419 corpsales@pearsontechgroup.com

For sales outside the United States, please contact: International Sales international@pearsoned.com

| | |
|---|---|
| Publisher: Paul Boger | Manager, Global Certification: Erik Ullanderson |
| Associate Publisher: Dave Dusthimer | Business Operation Manager, Cisco Press: Anand Sundaram |
| Managing Editor: Sandra Schroeder | Technical Editors: James Risler, Cristian Matei |
| Editorial Assistant: Vanessa Evans | Compositor: Mark Shirar |
| Executive Editor: Brett Bartow | Development Editor: Kimberley Debus |
| Book Designer: Gary Adair | Proofreader: Water Crest Publishing, Inc. |
| Indexer: Tim Wright | Senior Project Editor: Tonya Simpson |
| Copy Editor: Keith Cline | |

Americas Headquarters
Cisco Systems, Inc.
San Jose, CA

Asia Pacific Headquarters
Cisco Systems (USA) Pte. Ltd.
Singapore

Europe Headquarters
Cisco Systems International BV
Amsterdam, The Netherlands

Cisco has more than 200 offices worldwide. Addresses, phone numbers, and fax numbers are listed on the Cisco Website at www.cisco.com/go/offices.

CCDE, CCENT, Cisco Eos, Cisco HealthPresence, the Cisco logo, Cisco Lumin, Cisco Nexus, Cisco StadiumVision, Cisco TelePresence, Cisco WebEx, DCE, and Welcome to the Human Network are trademarks; Changing the Way We Work, Live, Play, and Learn and Cisco Store are service marks; and Access Registrar, Aironet, AsyncOS, Bringing the Meeting To You, Catalyst, CCDA, CCDP, CCIE, CCIP, CCNA, CCNP, CCSP, CCVP, Cisco, the Cisco Certified Internetwork Expert logo, Cisco IOS, Cisco Press, Cisco Systems, Cisco Systems Capital, the Cisco Systems logo, Cisco Unity, Collaboration Without Limitation, EtherFast, EtherSwitch, Event Center, Fast Step, Follow Me Browsing, FormShare, GigaDrive, HomeLink, Internet Quotient, IOS, iPhone, iQuick Study, IronPort, the IronPort logo, LightStream, Linksys, MediaTone, MeetingPlace, MeetingPlace Chime Sound, MGX, Networkers, Networking Academy, Network Registrar, PCNow, PIX, PowerPanels, ProConnect, ScriptShare, SenderBase, SMARTnet, Spectrum Expert, StackWise, The Fastest Way to Increase Your Internet Quotient, TransPath, WebEx, and the WebEx logo are registered trademarks of Cisco Systems, Inc. and/or its affiliates in the United States and certain other countries.

All other trademarks mentioned in this document or website are the property of their respective owners. The use of the word partner does not imply a partnership relationship between Cisco and any other company. (0812R)

## About the Author

**Howard Hooper**, CCIE No. 23470, CCNP, CCNA, CCDA, JNCIA, works as a network consultant for his companies SYNCom Ltd. and Transcend Networks Ltd., specializing in network design, installation, and automation for enterprise and government clients. He has worked in the network industry for 10 years, starting his career in the service provider field as a support engineer, before moving on to installations engineer and network architect roles, working on small, medium, enterprise, and service provider networks.

## About the Technical Reviewers

**James Risler**, CCIE No. 15412, is a systems engineer education specialist for Cisco Systems. His focus is on security technology and training development. James has more than 18 years of experience in IP internetworking, including the design and implementation of enterprise networks. Before joining Cisco Systems, James provided Cisco security training and consulting for Fortune 500 companies and government agencies. He holds two Bachelor degrees from University of South Florida and is currently working on his MBA at the University of Tampa.

**Cristian Matei**, CCIE No. 23684, is a senior security consultant for Datanet Systems, Cisco Gold Partner in Romania. He has designed, implemented, and maintained multiple large enterprise networks covering the Cisco security, routing, switching, and wireless portfolio of products. Cristian started this journey back in 2005 with Microsoft technology and finished MCSE Security and MCSE Messaging tracks. He then joined Datanet Systems, where he quickly obtained his Security CCIE among other certifications and specializations such as CCNP, CCSP, and CCDP. Since 2007, Cristian has been a Cisco Certified Systems Instructor (CCSI) teaching CCNA, CCNP, and CCSP curriculum courses. In 2009, he was awarded by Cisco with Cisco Trusted Technical Advisor (TTA) and got certified as Cisco IronPort Certified Security Professional on Email and Web (CICSP). That same year, he started his collaboration with Internetwork Expert as technical editor on the CCIE Routing & Switching and Security Workbook series. In 2010, Cristian earned his ISACA Certified Information Security Manager (CISM) certification. He is currently preparing for Routing & Switching, Service Provider CCIE tracks and can be found as a regular active member on Internetwork Expert and Cisco forums.

# Dedications

I dedicate this book to my family, without whom I would not be in the position that I am and have the opportunities I currently enjoy.

In particular, I want to say special thanks to the following:

My grandfather, Geoffrey, for becoming my father figure and teaching me what I consider to be one of the most important lessons I received early on in my life: that you must work and work hard for what you want. You are forever missed and never forgotten.

My mother, Sally, for providing me with the greatest example of personal strength and determination anyone could ever hope to possess. You scaled mountains to make sure we always had everything we needed and were protected; we are only here because of you.

My son, Ridley, for giving me the reason I need at times to carry on and the drive to become better at everything I do. Even though I cannot be there all the time, Daddy loves you very much.

I hope I have and will always go on to make you proud of me. I would not be the man I am today without you, for that I thank you.

# Acknowledgments

When writing a book, a small army of people back you up and undertake a huge amount of work behind the scenes. I want to thank everyone involved who helped with the writing, reviewing, editing, and production of this book. In particular, I want to acknowledge Brett Bartow for giving me this fantastic opportunity and for his help with the many deadline extensions and obstacles that presented themselves along the way. I also want to acknowledge and thank Kimberley Debus, who transformed my words into human-readable form and kept me on track. I know she worked many late nights and weekends to help complete this book, and I shall miss our "conversations through the comments." I will be forever grateful to both of you.

Thanks must also go out to the two technical reviewers, Cristian Matei and James Risler. Your comments and suggestions have been brilliant throughout the entire book. Your help and input has definitely made this book better.

Last, but by no means least, I want thank my family and co-workers for their support during the writing of this book. Without that support, this would not have been possible, and as soon as I have caught up on sleep again, I will be conscious enough to thank you personally.

# Contents at a Glance

# Contents

# Icons Used in This Book

 Wireless Router

 Router

 ATM/FastGb Eitherswitch

 Access Point

 Switch

 Secure Switch

 Cisco IOS Firewall

 CS-MARS

 IPS

 SSL VPN Gateway

 IP Phone

 AAA Server

 Web Server

 Secure Endpoint

 Database

 PC

 File/ Application Server

 Laptop

 Wireless Connection

 Network Cloud

Ethernet Connection

# Introduction

This book is designed to help you prepare for the Cisco VPN certification exam. The VPN exam is one in a series of exams required for the Cisco Certified Network Professional - Security (CCNP - Security) certification. This exam focuses on the application of security principles with regard to Cisco IOS routers, switches, and virtual private network (VPN) devices.

## Who Should Read This Book

Network security is a complex business. It is important that you have extensive experience in and an in-depth understanding of computer networking before you can begin to apply security principles. The Cisco VPN program was developed to introduce the remote-access and site-to-site VPN products associated with or integrated into the Cisco Adaptive Security Appliance (ASA) and available client software, explain how each product is applied, and explain how it can increase the security of your network. The VPN program is for network administrators, network security administrators, network architects, and experienced networking professionals who are interested in applying security principles to their networks.

## How to Use This Book

The book consists of 23 chapters. Each chapter tends to build upon the chapter that precedes it. The chapters that cover specific commands and configurations include case studies or practice configurations.

The chapters of the book cover the following topics:

- **Chapter 1, "Evaluation of the ASA Architecture":** This chapter reviews the ASA operation and architecture. It is this core of understanding that provides a good base for the other chapters.

- **Chapter 2, "Configuring Policies, Inheritance, and Attributes":** This chapter reviews the different methods used to apply policies and their contained attributes for controlling and ultimately securing our remote users. The policy inheritance model is also introduced to help network security personnel understand the results of having multiple policy types configured.

- **Chapter 3, "Deploying an AnyConnect Remote-Access VPN Solution":** This chapter introduces you to the Cisco AnyConnect remote-access VPN configuration and client software. You learn how to configure a basic AnyConnect remote-access connection, along with the configuration required basic remote user authentication.

- **Chapter 4, "Advanced Authentication and Authorization of AnyConnect VPNs":** This chapter reviews the available mechanisms that can be configured to successfully authenticate your remote users. We take a closer look at Public Key Infrastructure (PKI) technology and its implementation as a standalone authentication mechanism, along with the steps required for successful deployment of PKI and username/password-based authentication (doubling up on authentication).

- **Chapter 5, "Advanced Deployment and Management of the AnyConnect Client":** This chapter reviews the various methods of the AnyConnect client deployment and installation available. In addition, we explore the various modules that are available and their benefits.

- **Chapter 6, "Advanced Authorization Using AAA and DAPs":** This chapter describes the role and implementation of advanced authorization, which enables us to maintain complete control over the resources our remote users can or cannot access before and during their connection to our VPN deployment. In addition, we review the role of DAPs and how their configuration can be used to enhance the authorization process.

- **Chapter 7, "AnyConnect Integration with Cisco Secure Desktop and Optional Modules":** This chapter reviews the Cisco Secure Desktop (CSD) environment and associated modules. We also introduce you to the optional AnyConnect modules that are available for installation either as standalone components or deployed through client profiles.

- **Chapter 8, "AnyConnect High Availability and Performance":** This chapter reviews the different types of redundancy and high availability that can be deployed on the ASA device through configuration of the AnyConnect client or with external hardware.

- **Chapter 9, "Deploying a Clientless SSL VPN Solution":** This chapter introduces you to the Cisco clientless Secure Sockets Layer (SSL) VPN implementation. In addition, we look at the configuration required for a basic deployment of an SSL VPN.

- **Chapter 10, "Advanced Clientless SSL VPN Settings":** This chapter reviews the advanced settings that are available for our clientless SSL VPN deployment and the available application-access methods and their configuration.

- **Chapter 11, "Customizing the Clientless Portal":** This chapter reviews the available customization options we have when approaching the task of customizing our clientless SSL VPN environment for our remote users. We also discuss the implementation PKI and of double-authentication mechanisms.

- **Chapter 12, "Advanced Authorization Using Dynamic Access Policies":** This chapter reviews the implementation and configuration of group policies and the available attributes contained within. We also discuss the available logging and accounting methods on the ASA.

- **Chapter 13, "Clientless SSL VPN with Cisco Secure Desktop":** This chapter reviews the Cisco Secure Desktop environment and associated modules. In addition, we cover how to deploy the CSD with a clientless SSL VPN solution.

- **Chapter 14, "Clientless SSL VPN High Availability and Performance Options":** This chapter reviews the available HA and performance enhancements that can be deployed when working with clientless SSL VPN solutions.

- **Chapter 15, "Deploying and Managing the Cisco VPN Client":** This chapter introduces you to the Cisco IPSec VPN Client and its available methods of installation, configuration, and advanced customization.

- **Chapter 16, "Deploying Easy VPN Solutions":** This chapter introduces you to the Cisco Easy VPN client and server architecture. In addition, we review the configuration steps required for a basic Easy VPN deployment, XAUTH configuration, IP address assignment, and so on

- **Chapter 17, "Advanced Authentication and Authorization Using Easy VPN":** In this chapter, we review the configuration of PKI and its subsequent implementation with Easy VPN deployments. We also cover certificate mappings and their role when used for advanced authentication purposes.

- **Chapter 18, "Advanced Easy VPN Authorization":** This chapter describes the implementation of group policies and the attributes that can be included to provide advanced authorization of our remote users. In addition, this chapter describes logging and accounting methods and their use with Easy VPN deployments.

- **Chapter 19, "High Availability and Performance for Easy VPN":** This chapter describes the mechanisms that can be put in place to provide an HA solution that will protect an organization from outages alongside an Easy VPN deployment.

- **Chapter 20, "Easy VPN Operation Using the ASA 5505 as a Hardware Client":** This chapter introduces you to the Easy VPN hardware client capabilities of the ASA 5505 device and the configuration required for successful deployment.

- **Chapter 21, "Deploying IPsec Site-to-Site VPNs":** This chapter introduces you to the IPsec site-to-site VPN solution available on the ASA devices and the configuration procedures required for a successful deployment.

- **Chapter 22, "High Availability and Performance Strategies for IPSec Site-to-Site VPNs":** In this chapter, we discuss the available HA mechanisms for use when providing hardware- and software-level redundancy with an IPsec site-to-site VPN deployment. We also review the available quality-of-service (QoS) mechanisms on the ASA and their associated configuration.

- **Chapter 23, "Final Exam Preparation":** This short chapter lists the exam preparation tools useful at this point in the study process and provides a suggested study plan now that you have completed all the earlier chapters in this book.

- **Appendix A, "Answers to the "Do I Know This Already?" Quizzes":** This appendix provides the answers to the "Do I Know This Already?" quizzes that you will find at the beginning of each chapter.

- **Appendix B, "642-647 CCNP Security VPN Exam Updates, Version 1.0":** This appendix is intended to provide you with updated information if Cisco makes minor modifications to the exam upon which this book is based. When Cisco releases an entirely new exam, the changes are usually too extensive to provide in a simple update appendix. In those cases, you need to consult the new edition of the book for the updated content. This additional content about the exam will be posted as a PDF document on this book's companion website, at www.ciscopress.com/title/9781587142567.

- **Appendix C, "Memory Tables" (CD only):** This appendix, which you will find in PDF form on the CD accompanying this book, provides a series of tables that highlight some of the key topics in each chapter. Each table provides some cues and clues that will enable you to complete the table and test your knowledge about the table topics.

- **Appendix D, "Memory Tables Answer Key" (CD only):** This appendix, which you will find in PDF form on the CD accompanying this book, provides the completed memory tables from Appendix C so that you can check your answers. In addition, you can use this appendix as a standalone study tool to help you prepare for the exam.

- **Glossary:** This glossary defines the key terms that appear at the end of each chapter, for which you should be able to provide definitions on your own in preparation for the exam.

Each chapter follows the same format and incorporates the following tools to assist you by assessing your current knowledge and emphasizing specific areas of interest within the chapter:

- **"Do I Know This Already?" Quiz:** Each chapter begins with a quiz to help you assess your current knowledge about the subject. The quiz is divided into specific areas of emphasis that enable you to best determine where to focus your efforts when working through the chapter.

- **Foundation Topics:** The foundation topics are the core sections of each chapter. They focus on the specific protocols, concepts, or skills that you must master to successfully prepare for the examination.

- **Exam Preparation:** Near the end of each chapter, the Exam Preparation section highlights the key topics from the chapter and the pages where you can find them for quick review. This section also refers you to the Memory Tables appendixes, and provides a list of key terms that you should be able to define in preparation for the exam. It is unlikely that you will be able to successfully complete the certification exam by just studying the key topics, memory tables, and key terms, although they are a good tool for last-minute preparation just before taking the exam.

- **Practice exam on CD-ROM:** This book includes a CD-ROM containing several interactive practice exams. It is recommended that you continue to test your knowledge and test-taking skills by using these exams. You will find that your test-taking skills will improve by continued exposure to the test format. Remember that the potential range of exam questions is limitless. Therefore, your goal should not be to "know" every possible answer but to have a sufficient understanding of the subject matter so that you can figure out the correct answer with the information provided.

## Certification Exam and This Preparation Guide

The questions for each certification exam are a closely guarded secret. The truth is that if you had the questions and could only pass the exam, you would be in for quite an embarrassment as soon as you arrived at your first job that required these skills. The point is to know the material, not just to successfully pass the exam. We do know which topics you must know to successfully complete this exam, because they are published by Cisco. Coincidentally, these are the same topics required for you to be proficient when configuring Cisco security devices. It is also important to understand that this book is a "static" reference, whereas the exam topics are dynamic. Cisco can and does change the topics covered on certification exams often. This exam guide should not be your only reference when preparing for the certification exam. You can find a wealth of information available at Cisco.com that covers each topic in painful detail. The goal of this book is to prepare you as well as possible for the VPN exam. Some of this is completed by breaking a 600-page (average) implementation guide into a 30-page chapter that is easier to digest. If you think that you need more detailed information about a specific topic, feel free to surf. Table I-1 lists each exam topic along with a reference to the chapter that covers the topic.

**Table I-1**  *VPN Exam Topics and Chapter References*

| Exam Topic | Chapter Where Topic Is Covered |
| --- | --- |
| **Preproduction Design** | |
| Choose ASA VPN technologies to implement high-level design (HLD) based on given requirements | 1, 3, 8, 15, 16, 21 |
| Choose the correct ASA model and license to implement HLD based on given performance requirements | 1, 3, 8, 15, 16, 21 |
| Choose the correct ASA VPN features to implement HLD based on given corporate security policy and network requirements | 1–5, 8–10, 15–17, 20, 21 |
| Integrate ASA VPN solutions with other security technology domains (CSD, ACS, device managers, cert servers, and so on) | 1–5, 8–10, 15–21 |
| **Complex Operations Support** | |
| Optimize ASA VPN performance, functions, and configurations | 3–5, 7–10, 15–22 |
| Configure and verify complex ASA VPN networks using features such as DAP, CSD, smart tunnels, AnyConnect SSL VPN, clientless SSL VPN, site-to-site VPN, RA VPN, certificates, QoS, and so on to meet security policy requirements | 3–10, 15–22 |
| Create complex ASA network security rules using such features as ACLs, DAP, VPN profiles, certificates, MPF, and so on to meet the corporate security policy | 4–6, 10–12, 15, 17, 18, 20 |
| **Advanced Troubleshooting** | |
| Perform advanced ASA VPN configuration and troubleshooting | 4–6, 8, 10–12, 14, 15, 17–19, 22 |

You will notice that not all the chapters map to a specific exam topic. This is because of the selection of evaluation topics for each version of the certification exam. Our goal is to provide the most comprehensive coverage to ensure that you are well prepared for the exam. To do this, we cover all the topics that have been addressed in different versions of this exam (past and present). Network security can (and should) be extremely complex and usually results in a series of interdependencies between systems operating in concert. This book shows you how one system (or function) relies on another, and each chapter of the book provides insight into topics in other chapters. Many of the chapters that do not specifically address exam topics provide a foundation that is necessary for a clear understanding of network security. Your short-term goal might be to pass this exam, but your overall goal is to become a qualified network security professional.

Note that because security vulnerabilities and preventive measures continue apace, Cisco Systems reserves the right to change the exam topics without notice. Although you can refer to the list of exam topics listed in Table I-1, always check the Cisco Systems website to verify the actual list of topics to ensure that you are prepared before taking an exam. You can view the current exam topics on any current Cisco certification exam by visiting its website at Cisco.com, hovering over Training & Events, and selecting from the Certifications list. Note also that, if needed, Cisco Press might post additional preparatory content on the web page associated with this book at www.ciscopress.com/title/9781587142567. It is a good idea to check the website a couple of weeks before taking your exam to be sure that you have up-to-date content.

## Overview of the Cisco Certification Process

The network security market is currently in a position where the demand for qualified engineers vastly surpasses the supply. For this reason, many engineers consider migrating from routing/networking over to network security. Remember that "network security" is just "security" applied to "networks." This sounds like an obvious concept, but it is actually an important one if you are pursuing your security certification. You must be familiar with networking before you can begin to apply the security concepts. For example, the skills required to complete the CCNP Security exam will give you a solid foundation that you can expand upon and use when working in the network security field.

The requirements for and explanation of the CCNP Security certification are outlined at the Cisco Systems website. Go to Cisco.com, hover over Training & Events, and select CCNP Security from the Certifications list.

## Taking the VPN Certification Exam

As with any Cisco certification exam, it is best to be thoroughly prepared before taking the exam. There is no way to determine exactly what questions are on the exam, so the best way to prepare is to have a good working knowledge of all subjects covered on the exam. Schedule yourself for the exam and be sure to be rested and ready to focus when taking the exam.

The best place to find out the latest available Cisco training and certifications is under the Training & Events section at Cisco.com.

## Tracking CCNP Security Status

You can track your certification progress by checking www.cisco.com/go/certifications/login. You must create an account the first time you log in to the site.

## How to Prepare for an Exam

The best way to prepare for any certification exam is to use a combination of the preparation re-sources, labs, and practice tests. This guide has integrated some practice questions and labs to help you better prepare. It is encouraged that you have hands-on experience with the Cisco ASA devices. There is no substitute for experience, and it is much easier to understand the commands and concepts when you can actually work with Cisco ASA devices. If you do not have access to a Cisco ASA device, you can choose from among a variety of simulation packages available for a reasonable price. Last, but certainly not least, Cisco.com provides a wealth of information about the Cisco ASA device, all the products that operate using Cisco ASA software, and the products that interact with Cisco ASA devices. No single source can adequately prepare you for the VPN exam unless you already have extensive experience with Cisco products and a background in networking or network security. At a minimum, you will want to use this book combined with the Technical Support and Documentation site resources (www.cisco.com/cisco/web/support/index.html) to prepare for this exam.

## Assessing Exam Readiness

After completing a number of certification exams, we have found that you do not actually know whether you are adequately prepared for the exam until you have completed about 30 percent of the questions. At this point, if you are not prepared, it is too late. The best way to determine your readiness is to work through the "Do I Know This Already?" quizzes at the beginning of each chapter. It is best to work your way through the entire book unless you can complete each subject without having to do any research or look up any answers.

## Cisco Security Specialist in the Real World

Cisco has one of the most recognized names on the Internet. You cannot go into a data center or server room without seeing some Cisco equipment. Cisco-certified security specialists can bring quite a bit of knowledge to the table because of their deep understanding of the relationship between networking and network security. This is why the Cisco certification carries such clout. Cisco certifications demonstrate to potential employers and contract holders a certain professional-ism and the dedication required to complete a goal. Face it, if these certifications were easy to acquire, everyone would have them.

## Cisco ASA Software Commands

A firewall or router is not normally something to play with. That is to say that after you have it properly configured, you will tend to leave it alone until there is a problem or you need to make some other configuration change. This is the reason that the question mark (?) is probably the most widely used Cisco IOS and Cisco ASA software command. Unless you have constant exposure to this equipment, it can be difficult to remember the numerous commands required to configure devices and troubleshoot problems. Most engineers remember enough to go in the right direction but will use the ? to help them use the correct syntax. This is life in the real world. Unfortunately, the question mark is not always available in the testing environment.

## Rules of the Road

We have always found it confusing when different addresses are used in the examples throughout a technical publication. For this reason, we use the address space defined in RFC 1918. We understand that these addresses are not routable across the Internet and are not normally used on outside interfaces. Even with the millions of IP addresses available on the Internet, there is a slight chance that we could have chosen to use an address that the owner did not want published in this book.

It is our hope that this will assist you in understanding the examples and the syntax of the many commands required to configure and administer Cisco ASA devices.

## Exam Registration

The VPN exam is a computer-based exam, with multiple-choice, fill-in-the-blank, list-in-order, and simulation-based questions. You can take the exam at any Pearson VUE (www.pearsonvue.com) testing center. Your testing center can tell you the exact length of the exam. Be aware that when you register for the exam, you might be told to allow a certain amount of time to take the exam that is longer than the testing time indicated by the testing software when you begin. This discrepancy is because the testing center will want you to allow for some time to get settled and take the tutorial about the test engine.

## Book Content Updates

Because Cisco Systems occasionally updates exam topics without notice, Cisco Press might post additional preparatory content on the web page associated with this book at www.ciscopress.com/title/9781587142567. It is a good idea to check the website a couple of weeks before taking your exam, to review any updated content that might be posted online. We also recommend that you periodically check back to this page on the Cisco Press website to view any errata or supporting book files that may be available.

This chapter covers the following subjects:

- **Examining ASA Control Fundamentals:** In this section, we review interface configuration, Ether-Channels, ACLs, security levels and interface names, MPF, and more.

- **Routing the Environment:** In this section, we review the available routing methods and protocols on the ASA device.

- **Address Translations and Your ASA:** In this section, we discuss the overhaul of NAT commands and naming conventions on the ASA since the introduction of ASA 8.3.

- **AAA for Network-Based Access:** In this section, we review the role of AAA, the available server types for AAA, and some examples of their configuration on the ASA.

- **ASA VPN Technology Comparison:** In this section, we briefly compare the available VPN methods on the ASA, including a look at some of the benefits and drawbacks of each method.

- **Managing Your ASA Device:** In this section, we review the available methods for management of the ASA.

- **ASA Packet Processing:** In this section, we discuss the process that is followed by the ASA device for a packet traveling through it both inbound toward your internal environment and outbound away from it.

- **Controlling VPN Access:** In this section, we build on the earlier ACL discussion and introduce web ACLs, time ranges, split tunneling, portal and VPN selection processes, and more.

- **The Good, the Bad, and the Licensing:** In this section, we discuss the overall licensing model used by the ASA, the implementation of optional features, and licensing requirements they may have.

# CHAPTER 1

# Evaluation of the ASA Architecture

So you just received your first brand-new Adaptive Security Appliance (ASA) device and have unpacked the box. Your heart and mind fill with excitement as you stare at the shining rectangular, rack-mountable beacon of near-endless security possibilities. You let out a faint giggle as the flick of the rear power switch causes a rush of cool air to escape from the built-in fan mechanisms, and the intense flash of the front and rear LEDs suggests that your new friend shares your enthusiasm to start building a new secure future. You decide the first thing you want to do is to give the ASA an IP address so that you and the ASA can start to communicate with each other properly, but how? You then realize that you have purchased the *CCNP Security VPN Certification Guide* and not the ASA all-in-one how-to book you really need.

Yes, the preceding paragraph might provide some of you with the warm feeling of nostalgia and others with a cringe-like sensation. However, you have learned an important piece of information: This book is *not* a how-to-do-everything-on-an-ASA manual. Instead, as we work through the various information, facts, and examples together, I am assuming you already have a good understanding of the various virtual private network (VPN) and ASA architectures.

This chapter serves as a review for much of the ASA and its overall operation. However, as we move through the chapter, we start to explore more VPN-specific information in the form of their security, the protocols used, and their operation. We then finish our discussion with a look at the various licenses available on the ASA device and which ones you might need for the successful deployment and operation of the technologies we explore throughout this book.

## "Do I Know This Already?" Quiz

The "Do I Know This Already?" quiz helps you determine your level of knowledge on this chapter's topics before you begin. Table 1-1 details the major topics discussed in this chapter and their corresponding quiz sections.

**Table 1-1** *"Do I Know This Already?" Section-to-Question Mapping*

| Foundation Topics Section | Questions |
|---|---|
| Examining ASA Control Fundamentals | 4, 5, 6 |
| Routing the Environment | 3 |

**Table 1-1**    *"Do I Know This Already?" Section-to-Question Mapping*

| Foundation Topics Section | Questions |
|---|---|
| Address Translations and Your ASA | 2 |
| ASA VPN Technology Comparison | 1 |
| Managing Your ASA Device | 7 |
| ASA Packet Processing | 8, 9 |

1. Which of the following are available VPN connection methods on the ASA? (Choose all that apply.)

   a. Clientless SSL

   b. AnyConnect IKEv2

   c. Easy VPN IKEv2

   d. AnyConnect SSL

2. Which of the following are valid NAT rule types? (Choose all that apply.)

   a. Twice NAT

   b. Thrice NAT

   c. Host NAT

   d. Object NAT

3. Which of the following is not an available routing method on the ASA?

   a. OSPF

   b. IS-IS

   c. EIGRP

   d. Static routing

4. By default, which rule applies to packets traveling from a high-security interface to a low-security interface?

   a. Packets will be dropped.

   b. Packets will be allowed.

5. What is the maximum number of interfaces that you can configure in an EtherChannel?

   a. 8

   b. 16

**6.** What is the minimum number of interfaces required before you can configure an EtherChannel?

   **a.** 1

   **b.** 2

   **c.** 3

   **d.** 4

**7.** Which of the following are available methods of management access for the ASA? (Choose all that apply.)

   **a.** Telnet

   **b.** SNMP

   **c.** SSH

   **d.** ASDM

**8.** Which of the following is not a valid packet-processing action taken by the ASA for flows traveling from the inside interface to the outside interface?

   **a.** NAT host check

   **b.** Route lookup

   **c.** IP options lookup (MPF)

   **d.** NAT (RPF)

**9.** Which of the following is the recommended tool for viewing the path a packet takes through the ASA device?

   **a.** Traceroute

   **b.** Ping

   **c.** Packet Tracer

   **d.** SNMP

## Foundation Topics

# Examining ASA Control Fundamentals

Welcome to ASA 101... well, not quite. As mentioned earlier, this chapter serves as a review of the key components and operation of the ASA device. It is assumed you have a working knowledge of the ASA and of VPN deployments. This book helps you review those topics that you might be unclear about or for which you require further study. By the time you reach the end, you will be more than adequately prepared for the exam.

The Adaptive Security Appliance device is Cisco's flagship firewall and VPN product, merging the best of its predecessors, the PIX Firewall and the VPN 3000 Concentrator. In addition to the various physical configurations that exist between models (for example, fixed interfaces, 4Gig Ethernet interface modules, filtering, and Intrusion Prevention System [IPS] modules), the ASA software provides a feature-rich platform for both network and security purposes, in addition to a wide variety of VPN deployments, both client and clientless (as covered in later chapters).

At the time of this writing, the current version of ASA being used in the exam environment for simulations and scenarios is 8.2 and Adaptive Security Device Manager (ASDM) 6.3. However, where applicable, we include the updated ASA 8.4(1) information and features, which will prepare you for any future exam upgrades. You might also notice that many of the screenshots taken to guide you through the examples in this chapter and those that follow show the ASDM 6.4. Unless specifically defined, any window/configuration differences that may exist between ASDM 6.3 and ASDM 6.4 are either negligible or do not exist for the topic we are covering.

## Interfaces, Security Levels, and EtherChannels

Depending on the model of ASA you have, some differences might exist between the interface configurations. For example, the ASA 5505 physical interfaces are mapped to internal VLANs. (The ASA 5505 has switchport [Layer 2] interfaces, and the rest of the models have routed ports [Layer 3] interfaces.) However, when working with an ASA 5510 or higher model, you work directly with the devices' physical interfaces when configuring their IP addresses, security levels, and so on. Besides just using the ASA's physical interfaces, when working with external VLANs we can create logical subinterfaces of each physical interface and assign them each to a VLAN, using this method we can trunk the configured VLANs between the ASA and its directly connected neighbor switch (the neighboring switch requires its port connected to the ASA to be configured as a trunk and, preferably, carrying only the necessary VLANs required). The number of subinterfaces that you can configure on your device is model or license specific. Table 1-2 lists the available ASA models and their current physical and logical interface limits as of ASA Version 8.4(1).

**Table 1-2**   *ASA Model-Specific Physical and Logical Interface Limits*

| Model | Physical Interface Limit | Logical (Sub) Interface Limit |
|---|---|---|
| 5505 | 8-port 10/100 switch with 2 Power over Ethernet (PoE) ports | 3/20 (requires Security Plus license) |
| 5510 | 5 10/100/<br>2 10/100/1000<br>3 10/100 | 50/100 (requires Security Plus license) |
| 5520 | +4 10/100/1000<br>4 small form-factor pluggable (SFP) (with 4GE Security Services Module [SSM]) | 150 |
| 5540 | 4 10/100/1000<br>1 10/100 | 200 |
| 5550 | +4 10/100/1000<br>4 SFP (with 4GE SSM) | 400 |
| 5580-20 | 2–10/100/1000 management<br>+4–10/100/1000 (with ASA5580-4 GE-CU)<br>+4 GE SR (with ASA5580-4 GE-FI)<br>+2 10 GE SR (with ASA5580-2X10 GE-SR) | 1024 |
| 5580-40 | 2–10/100/1000 management<br>+4-10/100/1000 (with ASA5580-4 GE-CU)<br>+4 GE SR (with ASA5580-4 GE-FI)<br>+2 10 GE SR (with ASA5580-2X10 GE-SR) | 1024 |
| 5585-X with SSP-10 | 8–10/100/1000<br>2–10 GE SFP+ (with ASA 5585 Security Plus license)<br>2–10/100/1000 management<br>+ 8–10/100/1000<br>2–10 GE SFP+<br>2–10/100/1000 management (with IPS SSP-10) | 1024 |

**Table 1-2** *ASA Model-Specific Physical and Logical Interface Limits*

| Model | Physical Interface Limit | Logical (Sub) Interface Limit |
|---|---|---|
| 5585-X with SSP-20 | 8–10/100/1000<br>2-10 GE SFP+ (with ASA 5585 Security Plus license)<br>2-10/100/1000 management<br>+ 8–10/100/1000<br>2–10 GE SFP+<br>2–10/100/1000 management (with IPS SSP-20) | 1024 |
| 5585-X with SSP-40 | 6–10/100/1000 4-10 GE SFP+<br>2–10/100/1000 management<br>+ 6–10/100/1000<br>4–10 GE SFP+<br>2–10/100/1000 management (with IPS SSP-40) | 1024 |
| 5585-X with SSP-60 | 6–10/100/1000<br>4–10 GE SFP+<br>2–10/100/1000 management<br>+ 6–10/100/1000<br>4–10 GE SFP+<br>2–10/100/1000 management (with IPS SSP-60) | 1024 |

By default, when first powered on, the interfaces on an ASA device are in an administratively shut down state (with the exception of the management0/0 interface and all interfaces on the ASA 5505 device). Before they can be used, we must enable them.

Figure 1-1 shows the configuration of our GigabitEthernet0/0 interface in the Edit Interface window.

Open the interface properties by first choosing an interface in **Configuration > Device Setup > Interfaces** and clicking **Edit**. In the Edit Interface window, enable it by selecting **Enable Interface**. In addition, we can assign our interface an IP address in the IP Address section of the window or choose to retrieve the IP address information for this interface using Dynamic Host Control Protocol (DHCP) or Point-to-Point Protocol over Ethernet (PPPoE) by selecting the **Obtain IP Address via DHCP** or **Use PPPoE** options, respectively.

We have also chosen to configure the media type (where available), duplex, and speed of the physical interface by selecting **Configure Hardware Properties**. In our example, we have set our interface to use **RJ-45**, **Full**, **1000** Mbps, respectively.

In the Edit Interface window, we can also assign our interface a name and security level.

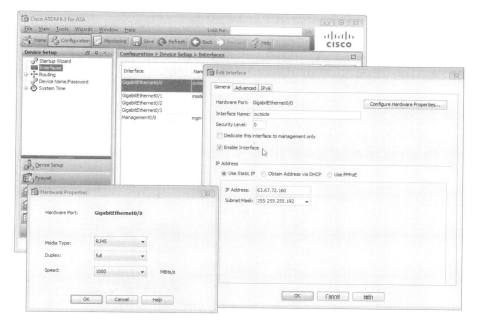

**Figure 1-1**  *ASA Interface Configuration*

## Security Levels

Security levels are used by the ASA to determine the level of trust given to a network that is located behind or directly attached to the respective interface. The security level is configured as a number in the range 0 to 100 (allowing for 101 possible values), with the higher number being trusted and the lower untrusted. By default, the inside interface on every ASA is the only interface to be configured with a name and security level of 100, and any remaining interfaces that are not configured with a security level explicitly are automatically given the security level of 0 (the lowest security level) regardless of their name. If we were to name one interface Outside and another DMZ, for example, the two would automatically be given the security level 0, even though we might trust our DMZ network more than the Outside network we are connected to.

The successful forwarding of packets between interfaces with or without a configured access control list (ACL), the configuration of which we cover in a moment, is also based on the interfaces' security level. By default, the ASA allows packets from a higher (trusted) security interface to a lower (untrusted) security interface without the need for an ACL explicitly allowing the packets. However, for packets that enter a lower (untrusted) security interface destined to a network on a higher (trusted) security interface, an ACL that explicitly allows the incoming packets is required on the incoming (untrusted) interface before communication is successful.

It is common to think of the analogy of a person traveling up and down a hill or the water flowing in a waterfall to remember ASA security level operation. Visualize a waterfall (can you see it yet?) and imagine the top of the waterfall as the higher (trusted) security interface and the bottom of the waterfall as the lower (untrusted) security interface. Now think of the water traveling through the waterfall as the packets flowing through your firewall. Water (your packets) naturally flows from the top (trusted) of the waterfall to the bottom (untrusted) freely and without any interruptions (apart from the odd rock and maybe a stump). However, when the water tries to travel from the bottom (untrusted) of the waterfall to the top (trusted), it is much harder—if not impossible—without help. The help in our ASA's case is the introduction of an ACL on the untrusted/lower security (bottom of the waterfall) interface.

Figure 1-2 shows another example of the behavior between higher and lower security levels with the help of an ACL for packets traveling from a lower to a higher level.

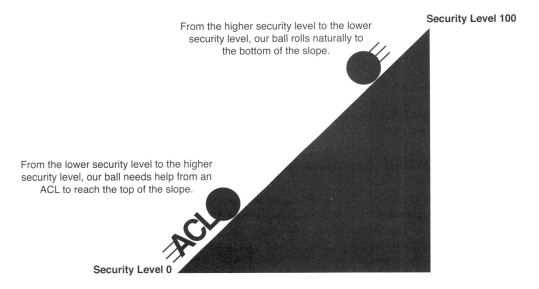

**Figure 1-2**  *ASA Higher and Lower Security Interface Operation*

## Same Security Interface and Intra-Interface Communication

So what happens when we have two or more interfaces with the same security level that want to communicate with each other? Our packets are allowed, right? Wrong. The ASA, by default, denies packets traveling from one interface to another that have the same security levels applied, and it drops packets that come into an interface and need to leave out of the same interface in which they arrived. This behavior is solved with the introduction of the **same-security-traffic permit inter-interface** and **same-security-interface permit intra-interface** CLI commands, respectively. The second scenario (that is, packets must leave the same ASA interface they arrived into) is commonly seen in VPN and hub-and-spoke deployments, as discussed in later chapters of this book.

For now, you just need to know that such a command exists to circumvent the default behavior of dropping our packets in these scenarios. We carry out the configuration of these commands using the ASDM by selecting the **Enable Traffic Between Two or More Interfaces Which Are Configured with the Same Security Levels** and **Enable Traffic Between**

Two or More Hosts Connected to the Same Interface options at the bottom of the Interfaces window (Configuration > Device Setup > Interfaces).

### EtherChannels

EtherChannels are a new addition to the ASA, starting from Version 8.4(1) and available on all ASA devices apart from the 5505. We can now assign up to 16 interfaces to a channel group to create 1 logical connection between our ASA and a switch or multiple switches if we are connecting to a Virtual Switching System (VSS) pair. Note that only eight interfaces can be active in the EtherChannel. Any remaining interfaces act as standby and do not forward packets. If any of our active interfaces fail, the standby interfaces take their place in the EtherChannel and begin forwarding.

The ASA and connecting device dynamically negotiate and enable an EtherChannel using 802.3ad Link Aggregation Control Protocol (LACP). Before we can configure an EtherChannel interface on the ASA, we must have one or more physical interfaces available that has no configuration (that is, name, security level, or IP address) assigned.

Figure 1-3 displays the configuration of a new EtherChannel interface that includes two free physical interfaces of the ASA. The IP address and subnet mask information of the EtherChannel interface have also been configured for connectivity purposes.

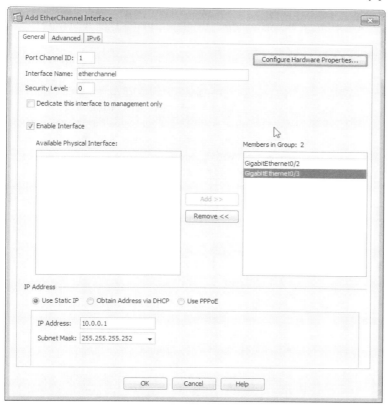

**Figure 1-3**  *ASA EtherChannel Configuration*

After making sure we have the interfaces available, we can create a new EtherChannel interface by navigating to **Configuration > Device Setup > Interfaces** and clicking the **Add > EtherChannel Interface** menu option on the right side of the window. In the Add EtherChannel Interface window, we assign our new logical interface an ID (this is locally specific), name, security level, and IP address. Then select the interfaces that will be used as members of our EtherChannel group by selecting them in the Available Physical Interfaces window and clicking the **Add >>** button to move them to the Members in Group window. We also have the option to configure the speed and duplex settings that will apply to all physical ports we have selected to become members of our EtherChannel by clicking **Configure Hardware Properties.**

As mentioned earlier, the ASA and connecting device use LACP to dynamically negotiate the parameters of the EtherChannel (for example, the physical [active] and standby [interfaces] that will or will not be used for forwarding). The LACP negotiations are based on a master/slave relationship between the ASA and connected device, in which the master assumes the role of managing the negotiations. The master device is elected based on a combination of a 2-byte configurable priority (default 32768) and 6-byte MAC address. Whoever has the highest priority (the lowest combined priority and MAC address value) wins the election and proceeds to take control of the overall communication/negotiation between devices. To make sure the election process between your ASA and connecting device (typically a switch) is deterministic, we configure the LACP priority to either a higher or lower value in the EtherChannel window (**Configuration > Device Setup > EtherChannel**).

### Access Control Lists

ACLs are used on the ASA for management purposes and to control (deny or allow) packets that travel through the ASA device and between interfaces. As mentioned previously, the ASA depends on ACL configuration to allow traffic from a lower security interface to a higher security interface. By default, there is no requirement to explicitly allow packets from a higher to a lower security interface. However, for the purposes of controlling the traffic entering and leaving your organization, it is recommended to apply an ACL to all interfaces of your ASA device. Note that as soon as an ACL is applied inbound to an interface, any traffic inbound to that interface is subject to the ACL rule, and the security level is ignored for traffic in that direction. For example, remember by default, traffic is allowed to flow freely from a higher security level interface (inside of 100) to a lower security level interface (outside of 0). As soon as you apply an ACL inbound to the higher security level interface (inside), however, all inbound traffic reaching the inside interface is restricted per the ACL rules.

The ASA uses both standard and extended ACLs. If you recall, standard ACLs can only be configured to allow access from specific source networks/addresses. These are typically used for management access purposes or for network/subnet lists used by other features, such as split tunneling (which you will see a lot more of in following chapters).

Extended ACLs operate by filtering packets based on criteria held in a five-tuple (quintuple) format. The five criteria used are source IP address, destination IP address, source port, destination port, and the protocol (TCP, UDP, and so on). Extended ACLs are typically configured and assigned to the ASA interfaces for the purposes of controlling the traffic entering and leaving your organization (for example, to secure an internal network).

Extended ACLs are viewable and configured in **Configuration > Firewall > Advanced > ACL Manager** for globally available ACLs, or **Configuration > Firewall > Access Rules**, as shown in Figure 1-4, for interface-specific ACLs.

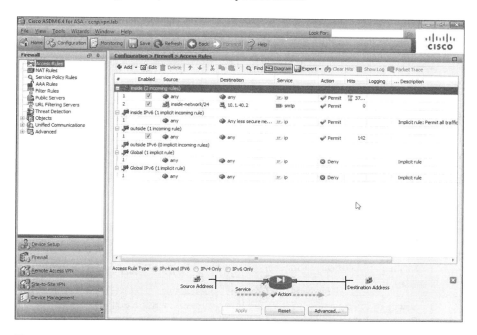

**Figure 1-4**   *ASDM ACL Configuration*

To configure our extended ACL, click **Add** in the Access Rules window, and then select either **Add Access Rule** or **Add IPv6 Access Rule** depending on the version of IP we are using in the network and the IP addresses configured on our ASA interfaces.

In the Add Access Rule window, select the appropriate options or enter the information required into the available fields, as shown in Table 1-3.

**Table 1-3**   *Extended ACL Configuration*

| Field/Option | Value |
| --- | --- |
| Interface | Using the drop-down list, select the interface your ACL entry will apply to. |
| Action | Select either **Permit** or **Deny** to carry out the actions you require to any packets matched by your ACL criteria. |

**Table 1-3**  *Extended ACL Configuration*

| Field/Option | Value |
|---|---|
| Source | Enter the source network, subnet, or host that your ACL will match against either in the form of <IP address>/<prefix>. Select from a preconfigured object available on the ASA or create a new one. |
| Destination | Enter the destination network, subnet, or host that your ACL will match against either in the form of <IP address>/<prefix>. Select from a preconfigured object available on the ASA or create a new one. |
| Service | Enter the service or select from a list of predefined objects on the ASA (for example, TCP, UDP, ICMP, or IP). |
| Description | (Optional) Enter a description for your access control entry (ACE). |
| Enable Logging | Select this option if you want to have packets matching this rule logged by the ASA. Optionally, select a logging level used to define the level of information logged. |
| Enable Rule | (Enabled by default) Uncheck this option to disable your ACL rule. |
| Traffic Direction | Select the direction in which this ACL will be applied to the interface, either **In** or **Out**. |
| Source Service | Enter or select from a predefined list on the ASA the source TCP or UDP service/application for incoming/outgoing packets your ACL will match against. |
| Time Range | Select or create a new time range that your ACL will be enabled for. (By default, the ACL is enabled for all time.) |

Standard ACLs are configured in the Standard ACL window (**Configuration > Firewall > Advanced > Standard ACL**). To configure a standard ACL, click **Add > Add ACL**, and when prompted, enter a name for the new ACL. (You can skip this process if you are configuring an existing ACL.) Then highlight the new or existing ACL and click **Add > Add ACE**. Figure 1-5 shows the Add ACE window that opens.

**Figure 1-5**  *Standard ACL Configuration*

As shown in the figure, the information we are required and able to enter for a standard ACL is a lot less specific than for an extended ACL due to the ACL's (standard/extended) purpose.

You will see many uses and configuration examples of both standard and extended ACLs in later chapters when working with split tunneling, internal resource access, and so on.

## Modular Policy Framework

Modular Policy Framework (MPF) enables us to configure global or interface-level actions or features and apply them to a specific class of traffic (for example, allowing a particular Internet Control Message Protocol [ICMP] packet type and code into the ASA or setting TCP connection timeouts). The MPF, as discussed in later chapters, is also used for the configuration and implementation of quality of service (QoS) and NetFlow policies used for packet classification, prioritization, policing, shaping, and flow-based logging.

If you have worked with QoS policies on an IOS router before, the syntax or behavior might be familiar to you because both a router and ASA use the following to classify packets, perform the actions you specify, and apply the policy (although the exception is the ASA's ability to apply MPF globally to all incoming packets):

■ **Class map:** Used to select packets based on the protocol, ACL, and so on

■ **Policy map:** Used to apply the actions or policies you define to the packets matched by your class map

■ **Service policy:** Used to apply the policy map and associated class maps either to an interface or globally

MPF rules that combine the class maps, policy maps, and service policy criteria we define are configured in **Configuration > Firewall > Service Policy Rules**. Two MPF rule types are available for configuration:

■ **Service policy rule:** Can match and apply criteria/actions to Layer 7 packet information traveling into, out of, and through the ASA

■ **Management service policy rule:** Used to match Layer 3 and 4 packet information for the purposes of controlling management traffic into, through, and out of the ASA (for example, embryonic connection limits and timeouts)

The feature we are enabling or using our MPF rules for can affect the direction in which our MPF rules can apply. Table 1-4 includes the available features and the directions that our configured MPF rule actions can apply to them.

**Table 1-4**   *MPF Feature Directionality*

| Feature | Single-Interface Direction | Global Direction |
|---------|---------------------------|------------------|
| Application inspection | Bidirectional | Ingress |
| Content Security and Control Module (CSC) | Bidirectional | Ingress |
| Intrusion Prevention System (IPS) | Bidirectional | Ingress |

**Table 1-4** *MPF Feature Directionality*

| Feature | Single-Interface Direction | Global Direction |
| --- | --- | --- |
| NetFlow secure event logging filtering | N/A | Ingress |
| QoS input policing | Ingress | Ingress |
| QoS output policing | Egress | Egress |
| Priority queue | Egress | Egress |
| Traffic shaping | Egress | Egress |
| TCP and UDP connection limits and timeouts, and TCP sequence number randomization | Bidirectional | Ingress |
| TCP normalization | Bidirectional | Ingress |
| TCP state bypass | Bidirectional | Ingress |

## Routing the Environment

**Key Topic**

The ASA can perform routing operations using the following methods:

■ Static routes

■ Enhanced Interior Gateway Routing Protocol (EIGRP)

■ Open Shortest Path First (OSPF)

■ RIPv2

Of the available methods listed here, probably the most common implementation on the ASA is static routing. This is partly because static routing is easy to configure and will minimize the overhead on your ASA device, allowing it to concentrate on the security functions it has been implemented for.

However, your own implementation of routing on the ASA will depend largely on your environment. Many small businesses might lack the expertise or might believe that a dynamic routing protocol in their network would be overkill based on the number of devices, available paths, and subsequent routes that are available. Therefore, static routing is usually configured to keep things simple. However, in larger corporations and enterprise networks that have a large amount of internal and or external routing information, in addition to many interfaces taking part in forwarding operations on the ASA, a common dynamic routing protocol such as OSPF may be implemented network-wide, including on the ASA.

In addition to learning routes dynamically from neighboring routers or equipment, the ASA device can forward these routes onto neighboring devices.

We can inspect our current routing configuration and create new static routes or dynamic routing protocol instances in the Routing window (**Configuration > Device Setup > Routing**) of the ASDM. Figure 1-6 shows the configuration of a new static route for entry into our ASA's routing table.

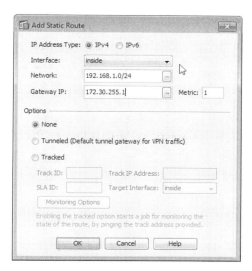

**Figure 1-6**   *ASA Static Route Configuration*

As shown in the figure, we have selected the IP protocol version to which the route applies, the interface on which the traffic is received for this route, the subnet/prefix combination, and the next-hop IP address. This is the minimum amount of information we can enter when creating a new route for entry into our ASA's local routing table. However, as you might have noticed, the following options are available for configuration when creating our new route:

■   **Tunneled:** This option allows for a default route to be added only for use by incoming VPN traffic. After the packets have been decrypted, they follow the new default route instead of any existing default route that might already be present in the routing table and used by other traffic. With this option, we can enter *only* a default route. The typical purpose of the route addition is to be able to direct VPN traffic to a Network Admission Control (NAC) device for advanced authentication and network access purposes. The tunneled default route takes precedence over normal default routes for VPN decrypted packets, but not over specific routes, which are still taken into consideration.

■   **Tracked:** This option allows us to apply an IP service level agreement (IP SLA) monitor to our route that has been configured, for example, to ping a remote address periodically. If the IP SLA object fails (that is, the ASA fails to receive any ICMP echoes in response to its sent ICMP packets), the route is removed from the routing table automatically. This feature is mainly scoped to allow for route redundancy. When you have two possible different paths toward a destination, the exit interface from the ASA perspective is different. This is because the ASA does not support load balancing over multiple interfaces; so, you cannot have two routes to identical prefixes over two different interfaces in the ASA routing table at the same time.

## Address Translations and Your ASA

For those who have been working with Cisco firewall products since the time of the PIX and have become comfortable and proficient in the configuration of Network Address Translation (NAT) and the various commands available, be aware that since the release of Version 8.3(1), everything has changed. For example, the static, global, nat-control, and NAT commands have been deprecated, and new NAT, Object Network, and Object Service commands have been introduced. You will notice the main difference in available configuration commands when working from the command-line interface (CLI). However, in the ASDM, the configuration is still pretty straightforward.

On the ASA, we can configure two main types of NAT:

- Object NAT

- Twice NAT

Object NAT enables you to create a specific NAT statement that applies to a source host, range, or network. Upon creation of an object NAT rule, the NAT statement is now applied in the object group, instead of the object group being applied to the NAT statement. A downside of the new Object NAT is that each NAT statement configured requires a separate object group configured, instead of being able to configure multiple NAT commands within the same object group. As you might guess, this can result in your configuration becoming bloated and many pages longer. For example, if you have many NAT rules that are applied to the same host, range, or network but between different interfaces (that is, Inside to Outside, Inside to DMZ), you are required to create a new object group per NAT command.

As shown in Figure 1-7, we create a new object NAT rule in the NAT Rules window (**Configuration > Firewall > NAT Rules**) by clicking **Add > Add Network Object NAT Rule**.

In the Add Network Object dialog, configure the following details:

- **Name:** Enter a name for the NAT rule.

- **Type:** Select the type of object we are configuring (a host, range of IP addresses, or network).

- **IP Address:** Enter the IP addresses of our host, range, or network (along with the subnet mask where required).

Then, in the NAT section of the window, configure the following:

- **Type:** Select Static, Dynamic (PAT) Hide, or Dynamic as the translation type, depending on whether we are interested in creating a one-to-one NAT or a one-to-many NAT, based on a specific IP address or interface.

- **Translated Addr:** If we select Static or Dynamic, we complete the configuration by entering the IP address or selecting from a list of predefined objects on our ASA.

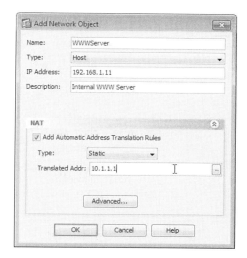

**Figure 1-7**    *Object NAT Creation*

Twice NAT rules are typically configured to achieve policy-based NAT behavior, whereby the source addresses of a conversation are translated to a specific source address if the destination is a particular host or network. Put simply, the twice NAT rules enable us to NAT both the source and destination IP addresses and source and destination ports contained in a packet. The main difference between twice NAT and object NAT rules (apart from not being configured in an object group) is that in a twice NAT rule, everything is explicit; there is no opportunity to add dynamic objects (that is, dynamically NAT your source addresses to an interface IP address), unless the IP address has been configured as a specific object.

We also configure twice NAT rules in the NAT Rules window (**Configuration > Firewall > NAT Rules**) of the ASDM. However, be aware that any twice NAT rules configured are placed at the end of the NAT table, and any object-level NAT rules that have been configured or might be configured in the future are placed before your configured twice NAT rules. This behavior might be undesirable if, for example, you have configured object NAT rules that might prevent your more-specific twice NAT rules from operating because the packets are matched lower down in the table before ever getting to them. We can overcome this problem by clicking **Add > Add NAT Rule Before Network Object Rules** when configuring our twice NAT rules. Figure 1-8 shows the Add NAT Rule window.

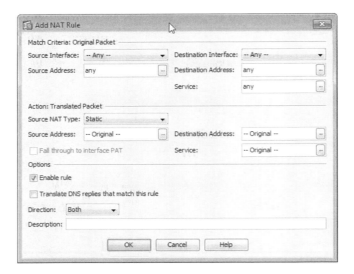

**Figure 1-8**    *Twice NAT Configuration*

When configuring a twice NAT rule, we are given the fields and options listed in Table 1-5.

**Table 1-5**    *Fields and Options for Twice NAT Configuration*

| Field/Option | Value |
|---|---|
| *Match Criteria* | |
| Source Interface | Select the source interface from the drop-down list. |
| Source Address | Enter the source addresses that your NAT rule will apply to. |
| Destination Interface | Select the destination interface from the drop-down list. |
| Destination Address | Enter the destination addresses that your NAT rule will apply to. |
| Service | Select from the list of available service objects or create a new one that your NAT rule will match. |
| *Action* | |
| Source NAT Type | Select the type of NAT to be performed on your packets matched using the criteria entered earlier (Static, Dynamic PAT (Hide), or Dynamic). |
| Source Address | Enter the new mapped address that will replace the original source address in packets this NAT rule will apply to. |
| Destination Address | Enter the new mapped address that will replace the original destination address in packets this NAT rule will apply to. |

**Table 1-5**  *Fields and Options for Twice NAT Configuration*

| Field/Option | Value |
|---|---|
| Service | Enter the new mapped service that will replace the original service in packets this NAT rule will apply to. |
| *Options* | |
| Enable Rule | Selected by default, uncheck this option to enter your rule in a disabled state. |
| Translate DNS Replies That Match This Packet | By default, the IP address entries in DNS answer packets sent to a host that match those configured as the original source addresses in our NAT rule are not translated. To enable the IP addresses to be mapped using the IP address information in this NAT rule for received DNS answer files, select this option. |
| Description | Optionally, enter a description for your NAT rule. |

# AAA for Network-Based Access

Authentication, authorization, and accounting (AAA) network security services enable us to centralize our user and management access policies by storing them on remote AAA servers. We can also provide authentication for both our users and administrators wanting to manage the devices, control network or device access, and restrict the commands that may or may not be available during a device access session. We can also configure extensive accounting options, allowing us to track user and device management actions (for example, the command entered, the mode it was entered in, the device and the user entering the commands, and VPN session accounting).

Based on the two scenarios described here, we can categorize AAA access methods into the following two types:

■ User AAA access (Packet mode)

■ Management AAA access (Character mode)

Although we look at a large number of management access examples throughout this book, we will generally be concentrating on the role of providing user AAA (Packet mode) for our remote users accessing our various VPN deployment scenarios in the chapters that follow.

The following AAA server types can be configured on the ASA for successful user AAA (where available). Note that not all these server types are available for every AAA paradigm:

■ RADIUS

■ TACACS+

- LDAP

- System Diagnostic Interface (SDI)

- NT Domain

- Kerberos

- HTTP Form

To prepare the ASA for use with an external AAA server, the following steps must be performed:

**Step 1.**  Create an AAA server group.

**Step 2.**  Add the servers to the AAA server group.

Begin by creating the AAA server group by navigating in the ASDM to **Configuration > Device Management > Users/AAA > AAA Server Groups** and clicking **Add** in the AAA Server Groups section of the window. The Add AAA Server Group window opens, as shown in Figure 1-9.

**Figure 1-9**  *AAA Server Group Configuration*

In the Add AAA Server Group window, we can enter the following information based on the protocol we choose:

- **Server Group:** Enter a name for the server group.

- **Protocol:** You can choose any from the previously described protocols (LDAP, TACACS, and so on). Based on the selected protocol, further options might or might not be available to configure.

- **Accounting Mode (RADIUS and TACACS+ only):** Choose either **Simultaneous** (the ASA sends accounting data to all servers in the group) or **Single** (the ASA sends accounting data to only one server). This option is not available for LDAP or other protocols.

- **Reactivation Mode (RADIUS and TACACS+ only):** Select either **Depletion** (servers that have failed in the group are reactivated only when all other servers in the group are inactive) or **Timed** (failed servers are reactivated after 30 seconds). If Depletion mode is selected, you can also modify the dead timer (default 10 minutes), which is the time that elapses between disabling the last server in the group and re-enabling of all servers.

- **Max Failed Attempts (available for all protocols):** Enter the maximum number of attempts that will be used to connect to a server configured in the server group before considering it dead (default 3).

- **Enable Interim Accounting Update (RADIUS only):** Select this option to enable multisession accounting for both AnyConnect and clientless SSL VPNs.

- **VPN3K Compatibility (RADIUS only):** Select either **Do Not Merge** (to disable merging of RADIUS downloadable ACLs with received A/V pair ACLs), **Place the downloadable ACL after the Cisco AV-Pair ACL**, or **Place the Downloadable ACL Before the Cisco AV-Pair ACL**.

After creating the AAA server group, we must add the AAA servers we will be using in it. Select the new group we have created from the list shown. Then, in the Servers in the Selected Group section of the window, click **Add**. As shown in Figure 1-10, we enter our server-specific details in the Add AAA Server window.

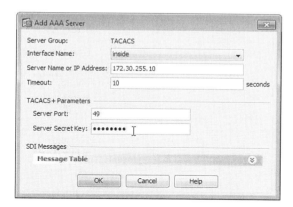

**Figure 1-10**  *Add AAA Server*

We first identify the interface on which the server is available and enter the IP address of the server (and the secret key used for authentication purposes if necessary). Otherwise, the default options (timeout, ports, and so on) should suffice for the majority of the deployments you carry out.

In addition to the values we can enter for AAA server communication and identification on the ASA, we can customize (by expanding the SDI Messages section of the window) the various informational messages that are presented to our remote users if we have deployed an SDI server for the purposes of RSA authentication.

## ASA VPN Technology Comparison

You will see many examples, explanations, and information about the VPN deployments available on the ASA device as you read through this book. However, the following is a brief summary of the available deployment types:

- IPsec remote access (IKEv1)

- Easy VPN remote and server (IKEv1)

- Easy VPN remote hardware client (ASA 5505 Only)

- Clientless SSL

- AnyConnect SSL

- AnyConnect IKEv2

- IPsec site to site (IKEv1)

Table 1-6 lists the methods and their typical deployment scenarios, IP addressing, feature support, and so on.

**Table 1-6**   *Advantages and Limitations of Available ASA VPN Methods*

|  | IPsec Remote Access | Easy VPN | Clientless SSL |
|---|---|---|---|
| Protocol | IPsec/IKEv1 | IPsec/IKEv1 | SSL/TLS |
| Client-based/remote access/site to site | Cisco IPsec VPN client | ASA 5505 hardware client<br><br>Site to site/remote access on supported client device | Clientless Browser based |
| Client IP addressing | Supported | Supported | Not supported<br><br>All traffic tunneled |
| High availability (HA) support | Stateful | Stateful | Stateless |
| Management/deployment overhead | Configuration on the ASA required<br><br>Manual installation and distribution of Cisco IPsec VPN client software | Configuration on the local and remote ASA device<br><br>Basic configuration required on ASA 5505<br><br>Policy deployed during connection | Configuration on the ASA required |

**Table 1-6**  *Advantages and Limitations of Available ASA VPN Methods*

| | **IPsec Remote Access** | **Easy VPN** | **Clientless SSL** |
|---|---|---|---|
| Policy update/configuration change method | Manual configuration for client authentication changes and so on in the Cisco IPsec VPN client | Automatic policy download and update during connection establishment | Requires client to log out and back in to the web interface for updates to portal to take effect |
| Client authentication methods | X-Auth by user AAA or local ASA user based, certificates, hybrid SDI | X-Auth by user AAA or local ASA user based. Additionally for hardware client SUA and IUA. | User AAA or local ASA user based, certificates, SDI |
| LAN extension | Yes | Yes | No |
| Standards-based access method/protocols | Yes | Proprietary | Yes |
| Protocol | SSL/TLS | IKEv2 | IPsec/IKEv1 |
| Client-based/remote access/site to site | AnyConnect secure mobility client | AnyConnect secure mobility client | Remote router, firewall, or concentrator device |
| Client IP addressing | Supported | Supported | N/A |
| HA support | Stateful | Stateful | Stateful |
| Management/deployment overhead | Configuration on the ASA required<br><br>Automatic download and installation/upgrade of AnyConnect client software | Configuration on the ASA required<br><br>Automatic download and installation/upgrade of AnyConnect client software | Configuration on the ASA required and matching configuration on remote devices |

**Table 1-6**  *continued*

|  | **AnyConnect SSL** | **AnyConnect IKEv2** | **IPsec Site to Site** |
|---|---|---|---|
| Policy update/configuration change method | Automatic download and installation of policy updates during connection establishment | Automatic download and installation of policy updates during connection establishment | Remote devices must manually update their policies/settings to match |
| Client authentication methods | User AAA or local ASA user based, certificates, SDI | User AAA or local ASA user based, certificates, Extensible Access Protocol (EAP) methods, Cisco Proprietary EAP | N/A |
| LAN extension | Yes | Yes | Yes |
| Standards-based access method/protocols | Yes | Yes | Yes |

Based on the information shown in the preceding table, we can assume that if you require a site-to-site VPN providing LAN extension services between two Cisco devices, an Easy VPN client/server deployment should meet your requirements. However, if you have the same requirements but the remote endpoint is a checkpoint or other third-party device, a standard IPsec site-to-site VPN connection must be used.

If we concentrate on the remote-access VPN methods, based on ease of deployment and policy update procedures, an AnyConnect VPN deployment or clientless SSL VPN-based deployment may meet the needs of our remote users. However, if our remote users require full LAN extension (that is, to be able to seamlessly access internal resources and servers as though working from in the office), an AnyConnect SSL or IKEv2 VPN should be implemented because of the minimal support for this access method offered with the browser-based Clientless SSL VPN.

You can use the clientless SSL VPN if your remote users operate a number of web-based applications that do not require their remote devices to have an IP address or use complicated dynamic protocols for access to internal resources. However, as discussed in later chapters, we can provide a level of application and server access to our remote users with the implementation of smart tunnels, port forwarding, and plug-ins.

# Managing Your ASA Device

The examples in this book all use the ASDM interface for configuration, troubleshooting, and monitoring purposes. However, it is important to know the other types of management access that exist on the ASA device and how to configure ASDM access using the command line if it has not already been set up.

The following are methods of management access available for the ASA:

■ ASDM

■ Secure Shell (SSH)

■ Telnet

By default, the ASA device ships with its management interface configured with the following IP address details:

■ **IP address:** 192.168.1.1

■ **Subnet mask:** 255.255.255.0

We can telnet to the device using this IP address from a laptop/PC directly connected to the management interface or begin a session using the ASDM by accessing the following URL:

https://192.168.1.1

Because no default SSL VPNs are set up on the ASA, we are directed to the ASDM web page. (As soon as Secure Sockets Layer [SSL] VPN access has been configured on our device, we can access the ASDM by appending **/admin** to the URL of the ASA device.) We can then enter the default **cisco/cisco** password combination to access the ASA.

The ASDM image used for management access is held on the local Disk0 file system of the ASA. However, to tell the ASA the name and location of the image, if our device has not yet been configured to allow management access via the ASDM interface, we use the following command at the CLI:

```
asdm image disk0:/<name>
```

In addition to accessing the ASA using the management interface, we can allow (and it will probably be a requirement in any production network you work on) access to the ASA using the various protocols listed earlier. We carry out this task in the ASDM/HTTPS/Telnet/SSH window (**Configuration > Device Management > Management Access > ASDM/HTTPS/Telnet/SSH**) of the ASDM, shown in Figure 1-11.

In this window, we can configure access to our ASA on any interface by clicking **Add**. In the Add Device Access Configuration window, select the type of access you want to allow (ASDM/HTTPS, Telnet, or SSH), the interface the management sessions will be sourced from, and the IP address and subnet mask of the host or network used to access the ASA from. Note that pure Telnet sessions are not allowed on the outside interface (lowest security interface), even though you may configure it, except if they are coming from an encrypted VPN session.

**Figure 1-11** *Allowing Management Access to Your ASA*

We can also change the HTTP port settings and idle timeout (if we prefer not to have our ASA device visible on the default HTTPS port [443]), change, the Telnet timeout in minutes (default 5), and specify the SSH version allowed from incoming clients and the SSH timeout.

## Packet Processing

When processing incoming and outgoing packets from our internal and external networks, the ASA device goes through a flow of operations in which it performs routing lookups, enforces host limits, inspects the packet against any configured ACLs, and so on.

When configuring available features and settings, it is important to understand the flow of operations that ASA devices engage in on both an incoming and outgoing path. Understanding this information can also save you a great deal of time when troubleshooting a configuration error or even a suspected error on the ASA.

However, depending on the incoming interface (direction of traffic), the ASA processes the operations in a different order. The following list shows the order of operations the ASA goes through upon receiving a packet from an inside interface destined to a host on the outside interface:

- **Received Packet from Interface:** Inside.

- **Flow Lookup:** Does this packet belong to an existing flow entry?

- **Route Lookup:** Perform a longest prefix match route lookup for the destination IP address in the packet against the information held within the ASA's routing table.

- **Access List:** Check the packet against any access lists configured on the incoming path.

- **IP Options (MPF):** Check the packet against MPF configured policies (QoS, embryonic limits, and so on).

- **VPN Crypto Match?:** Is this packet destined for a host through a VPN tunnel?

- **NAT:** Perform NAT translation against the fields in the packet based on any configured NAT rules.

- **NAT Host Limit:** Is this packet subject to any limits imposed that might cause it to be discarded (for example, half-open connections)?

- **IP Options (MPF):** Check the packet against MPF configured policies (QoS, embryonic limits, and so on).

- **Flow Creation:** If this packet is a new flow, create a new flow entry for it here.

- **Send Packet Out of Interface:** Outside.

The following is the order of operations taken by the ASA upon receiving a packet on the outside interface destined for a host connected to a network on the inside interface:

- **Received Packet from Interface:** Outside.

- **Flow Lookup**

- **Route Lookup**

- **Access List**

- **IP Options (MPF)**

- **VPN Crypto Match?**

- **NAT (RPF):** Is the best path in the routing table toward the source IP address in the packet through the interface in which it came into the ASA?

- **NAT Host Limit**

- **NAT Lookup**

- **Send Packet Out of Interface:** Inside.

We can also use the available Packet Tracer tool as a visual guide to how a packet will be treated by our ASA device, by specifying the source and destination IP address, ports, protocol, and the incoming interface the packet may be received on.

Figure 1-12 shows the Packet Tracer utility available from the Tools menu along the top of the ASDM window. This tool can prove invaluable when troubleshooting a problem if, for example, you are experiencing packet loss or drops and suspect the problem might be caused by something configured on your ASA device.

The Packet Tracer tool assesses the IP, port, protocol, and interface information you enter against any configured access lists, MPF, NAT rules, and so on and provides you with the results of its step-by-step check.

# Controlling VPN Access

In addition to access lists, many other methods are available on the ASA for controlling user access. However, for the purposes of this book, we are interested in controlling the access of our remote users only when they are attempting to access our internal resources through a VPN connection.

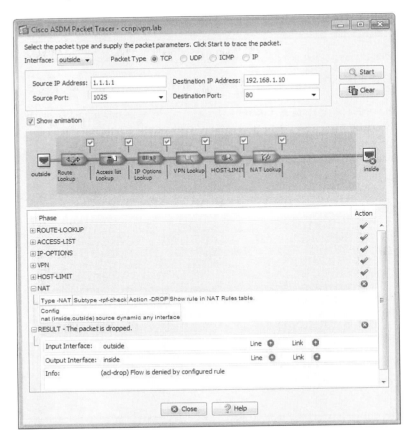

**Figure 1-12**  *ASA Packet Tracer Utility*

As you go through the remaining chapters of this book, you will discover available VPN access control methods and how they interoperate. You will also learn about the policy inheritance model that is applied to users during their connection to the device. Here is a brief list of the available ways to control a VPN user's access:

- Web ACLs
- Split tunneling
- Filtering with access lists
- Remote AAA authorization
- Selective portal/VPN access (using group URLs and aliases)
- Access hours
- Simultaneous logins
- Connection and idle timeouts
- SSL portal customization

The various access control methods can be applied to our users through one of the following methods, as explained further in the chapters that follow:

- DAPs (Dynamic Access Policies)

- Group policies

- Direct user assignment

By default, all VPN traffic bypasses any ACL configurations applied to the incoming interface. However, if we want our VPN traffic to also be subject to our configured ACLs, we can disable the default setting in **Configuration > Remote Access VPN > Network (Client) Access > Advanced > SSL VPN > Bypass Interface Access List**. As shown in Figure 1-13, the ACL bypass option is selected by default. To disable this behavior, we just uncheck the box.

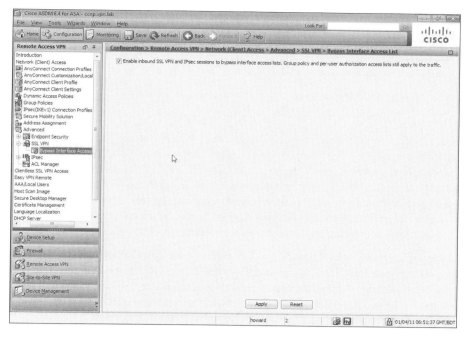

**Figure 1-13**  *Disable VPN ACL Bypass*

We can configure web ACLs for later use in our clientless SSL VPN group policy objects by navigating to **Configuration > Remote Access VPN > Clientless SSL VPN Access > Advanced, Web ACLs**.

The process of creating a web ACL is similar to that of creating an ACL. First click **Add > Add ACL**, and then in the Add ACL window, enter a name for our web ACL. After creating the web ACL entry, we can now add access control entries to either allow or deny access to specific URLs or TCP services.

As shown in Figure 1-14, we have created our web ACL web_acl and are now in the process of adding an ACE to it that will permit access to http://www.cisco.com.

**Figure 1-14**   *Web ACL Configuration*

Time range ACLs are another global object that can play an important part in the security of our VPN connections. For example, we can allow access to our VPN connection only during work hours. Outside of these times, access to the VPN connection is denied, which allows us to accurately know when remote users will be using them. We can even plan change control timeslots around our time ranges by specifying that changes to any of the VPN settings or environments happen only during the time when connections are unavailable to users, thus preventing any potential loss of service and complaints.

We configure time ranges by navigating to **Configuration > Firewall > Objects > Time Ranges** and clicking **Add**. Then, in the Add Time Range window, shown in Figure 1-15, we can give our time range a name and enter the times and dates that our time range will become available from (either now or in the future) and the times and dates that it will be available until. We can also specify a range of recurring times (for example, Monday through Friday 9 a.m to 6 p.m), and for all other times, access will be denied.

## The Good, the Bad, and the Licensing

Now that we have reviewed the basics of the ASA and some of the common ways to control access through it, it is time to take a look at the licensing models available. When it comes to licensing on the ASA, a lot of information is involved. I suggest using the following information as a handy reference instead of trying to memorize all of it. You might be required to know the result of combining two matching licenses—for example, on two devices during a failover configuration. However, the majority of the information provided here is for your information only and will not be included on the exam.

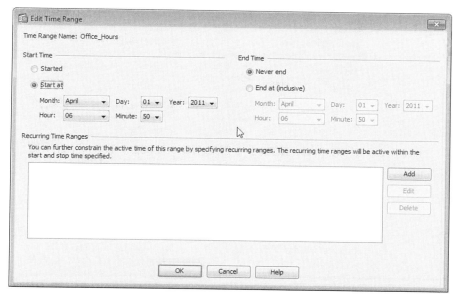

**Figure 1-15**   *Time Range Configuration*

You can view your currently installed and active licenses on the ASA by navigating to **Configuration > Device Management > Licensing > Activation Key.**

The license information available includes the combination of all permanent and time-based licenses. (Time-based licenses are explained in greater detail in the next section.)

Tables 1-7 to 1-12 include the model-specific licensing information available for the ASA 5505 to ASA 5580.

**Table 1-7**   *ASA 5505 License Features*

| ASA 5505 | Base License | Security Plus |
|---|---|---|
| *Firewall Licenses* | | |
| Botnet Traffic Filter | Disabled *(Optional time-based license available)* | Disabled *(Optional time-based license available)* |
| Firewall Conns, Concurrent | 10 K | 25 K |
| GTP/GPRS | No support | No support |
| Intercompany Media Engine | Disabled *(Optional license available)* | Disabled *(Optional license available)* |
| Unified Comm. Sessions | 2 *(Optional license upgrade: 24)* | 2 *(Optional license upgrade: 24)* |

**Table 1-7**  *ASA 5505 License Features*

| ASA 5505 | Base License | Security Plus |
|---|---|---|
| *VPN Licenses* | | |
| Adv. Endpoint Assessment | Disabled *(Optional license available)* | Disabled *(Optional license available)* |
| AnyConnect Essentials | Disabled *(Optional license available)* | Disabled *(Optional license available)* |
| AnyConnect Mobile | Disabled *(Optional license available)* | Disabled *(Optional license available)* |
| AnyConnect Premium SSL VPN Edition (sessions)* | 2 *(Optional permanent or time-based licenses: 10 or 25 sessions)* | 2 *(Optional permanent or time-based licenses: 10 or 25 sessions)* |
| IPsec VPN (sessions) | 10 (max. 25 combined IPsec and SSL VPN) | 25 (max. 25 combined IPsec and SSL VPN) |
| VPN load balancing | No support | No support |
| *General Licenses* | | |
| Encryption | Base (DES) *(Optional license: Strong [3DES/AES])* | Base (DES) *(Optional license: Strong [3DES/AES])* |
| Failover | No support | Active/Standby (no stateful failover) |
| Security contexts | No support | No support |
| Users, concurrent | 10 *(Optional licenses: 50 or unlimited)* | 10 *(Optional licenses: 50 or unlimited)* |
| VLANs/zones, maximum | 3 (2 regular zones and 1 restricted zone) | 20 |
| VLAN trunk, maximum | No support | 8 trunks |

**Table 1-8**  *ASA 5510 License Features*

| ASA 5510 | Base License | Security Plus |
|---|---|---|
| *Firewall Licenses* | | |
| Botnet Traffic Filter | Disabled<br><br>*(Optional time-based license available)* | Disabled<br><br>*(Optional time-based license available)* |
| Firewall Conns, Concurrent | 50 K | 130 K |
| GTP/GPRS | No support | No support |
| Intercompany Media Engine | Disabled<br><br>*(Optional license available)* | Disabled<br><br>*(Optional license available)* |
| Unified Comm. Sessions | 2<br><br>*(Optional licenses available: 24, 50, or 100 sessions)* | 2<br><br>*(Optional licenses available: 24, 50, or 100 sessions)* |
| *VPN Licenses* | | |
| Adv. Endpoint Assessment | Disabled<br><br>*(Optional license available)* | Disabled<br><br>*(Optional license available)* |
| AnyConnect Essentials | Disabled<br><br>*(Optional license available)* | Disabled<br><br>*(Optional license available)* |
| AnyConnect Mobile | Disabled<br><br>*(Optional license available)* | Disabled<br><br>*(Optional license available)* |
| AnyConnect Premium SSL VPN Edition (sessions) | 2<br><br>*(Optional permanent or time-based licenses available: 10, 20, 50, 100, or 250 sessions)*<br><br>*Optional shared licenses: Participant or Server. For the Server, these licenses are available:*<br><br>*500–50,000 in increments of 500*<br><br>*50,000–545,000 in increments of 1,000* | 2<br><br>*(Optional permanent or time-based licenses available: 10, 20, 50, 100, or 250 sessions)*<br><br>*Optional shared licenses: Participant or Server. For the Server, these licenses are available:*<br><br>*500–50,000 in increments of 500*<br><br>*50,000–545,000 in increments of 1,000* |
| IPsec VPN (sessions) | 250 (max. 250 combined IPsec and SSL VPN) | 250 (max. 250 combined IPsec and SSL VPN) |
| VPN Load Balancing | No support | Supported |
| *General Licenses* | | |

**Table 1-8**   *ASA 5510 License Features*

| ASA 5510 | Base License | Security Plus |
|---|---|---|
| Encryption | Base (DES) *Optional license available: Strong (3DES/AES)* | Base (DES) *Optional license available: Strong (3DES/AES)* |
| Failover | No support | Active/Standby or Active/Active |
| Interface Speed | All: Fast Ethernet | Ethernet 0/0 and 0/1: Gigabit Ethernet Ethernet 0/2, 0/3, and 0/4 (and any others): Fast Ethernet |
| Security Contexts | No support | 2 *Optional licenses: 5* |
| VLANs, Maximum | 50 | 100 |

**Table 1-9**   *ASA 5520 License Features*

| ASA 5520 | Base License |
|---|---|
| *Firewall Licenses* | |
| Botnet Traffic Filter | Disabled *(Optional time-based license available)* |
| Firewall Conns, Concurrent | 280 K |
| GTP/GPRS | Disabled *(Optional license available)* |
| Intercompany Media Engine | Disabled *(Optional license available)* |
| Unified Communications Proxy Sessions | 2 *(Optional licenses available: 24, 50, 100, 250, 500, 750, or 1,000 sessions)* |
| *VPN Licenses* | |
| Adv. Endpoint Assessment | Disabled *(Optional license available)* |
| AnyConnect Essentials | Disabled *(Optional license available)* |
| AnyConnect Mobile | Disabled *(Optional license available)* |

**Table 1-9**   *ASA 5520 License Features*

| ASA 5520 | Base License |
| --- | --- |
| AnyConnect Premium SSL VPN Edition (sessions) | 2 |
| | *(Optional permanent or time-based licenses available: 10, 25, 50, 100, 250, 500, or 750 sessions)* |
| | *Optional shared licenses: Participant or Server. For the Server, these licenses are available:* |
| | *500–50,000 in increments of 500* |
| | *50,000–545,000 in increments of 1,000* |
| IPsec VPN (sessions) | 750 (max. 750 combined IPsec and SSL VPN) |
| VPN Load Balancing | Supported |
| *General Licenses* | |
| Encryption | Base (DES) |
| | *Optional license available: Strong (3DES/AES)* |
| Failover | Active/Standby or Active/Active |
| Security Contexts | 2 |
| | *(Optional licenses available: 5, 10, or 20)* |
| VLANs, Maximum | 150 |

**Table 1-10**   *ASA 5540 License Features*

| ASA 5540 | Base License |
| --- | --- |
| *Firewall Licenses* | |
| Botnet Traffic Filter | Disabled |
| | *(Optional time-based license available)* |
| Firewall Conns, Concurrent | 400 K |
| GTP/GPRS | Disabled |
| | *(Optional license available)* |
| Intercompany Media Engine | Disabled |
| | *(Optional license available)* |
| Unified Communications Proxy Sessions | 2 |
| | *(Optional licenses available: 24, 50, 100, 250, 500, 750, 1,000, or 2,000 sessions)* |

**Table 1-10**   *ASA 5540 License Features*

| ASA 5540 | Base License |
|---|---|
| *VPN Licenses* | |
| Adv. Endpoint Assessment | Disabled<br>*(Optional license available)* |
| AnyConnect Essentials | Disabled<br>*(Optional license available)* |
| AnyConnect Mobile | Disabled<br>*(Optional license available)* |
| AnyConnect Premium SSL VPN Edition (sessions) | 2<br>*Optional permanent or time-based licenses available:*<br>*10, 25, 50, 100, 250, 500, 750, 1,000, or 2,500 sessions*<br>*Optional shared licenses: Participant or Server. For*<br>*the Server, these licenses are available:*<br>*500–50,000 in increments of 500*<br>*50,000–545,000 in increments of 1,000* |
| IPsec VPN (sessions) | 5,000 (max. 5,000 combined IPsec and SSL VPN) |
| VPN Load Balancing | Supported |
| *General Licenses* | |
| Encryption | Base (DES)<br>*(Optional license available: Strong [3DES/AES])* |
| Failover | Active/Standby or Active/Active |
| Security Contexts | *2*<br>*(Optional licenses available: 5, 10, 20, or 50)* |
| VLANs, Maximum | 200 |

**Table 1-11**   *ASA 5550 License Features*

| ASA 5550 | Base License |
|---|---|
| *Firewall Licenses* | |
| Botnet Traffic Filter | Disabled<br>*(Optional time-based license available)* |
| Firewall Conns, Concurrent | 650 K |
| GTP/GPRS | Disabled<br>*(Optional license available)* |

**Table 1-11**   *ASA 5550 License Features*

| ASA 5550 | Base License |
|---|---|
| Intercompany Media Engine | Disabled |
| | *(Optional license available)* |
| Unified Communications Proxy Sessions | 2 |
| | *(Optional licenses available: 24, 50, 100, 250, 500, 750, 1,000, 2,000, or 3,000 sessions)* |
| *VPN Licenses* | |
| Adv. Endpoint Assessment | Disabled |
| | *(Optional license available)* |
| AnyConnect Essentials | Disabled |
| | *(Optional license available)* |
| AnyConnect Mobile | Disabled |
| | *(Optional license available)* |
| AnyConnect Premium SSL VPN Edition (sessions) | 2 |
| | *Optional permanent or time-based licenses available: 10, 25, 50, 100, 250, 500, 750, 1,000, 2,500, or 5,000* |
| | *Optional shared licenses: Participant or Server. For the Server, these licenses are available:* |
| | *500–50,000 in increments of 500* |
| | *50,000–545,000 in increments of 1,000* |
| IPsec VPN (sessions) | 5,000 (max. 5,000 combined IPsec and SSL VPN) |
| VPN Load Balancing | Supported |
| *General Licenses* | |
| Encryption | Base (DES) |
| | *(Optional license available: Strong [3DES/AES])* |
| Failover | Active/Standby or Active/Active |
| Security Contexts | 2 |
| | *(Optional licenses available: 5, 10, 20, or 50)* |
| VLANs, Maximum | 250 |

**Table 1-12** *ASA 5580 License Features*

| ASA 5580 | Base License |
| --- | --- |
| *Firewall Licenses* | |
| Botnet Traffic Filter | Disabled<br>*(Optional time-based license available)* |
| Firewall Conns, Concurrent | 5580-20: 1000 K<br>5580-40: 2000 K |
| GTP/GPRS | Disabled<br>*(Optional license available)* |
| Intercompany Media Engine | Disabled<br>*(Optional license available)* |
| Unified Communications Proxy Sessions | 2<br>*Optional licenses available: 24, 50, 100, 250, 500, 750, 1,000, 2,000, 3,000, 5,000, or 10,000 sessions* |
| *VPN Licenses* | |
| Adv. Endpoint Assessment | Disabled<br>*(Optional license available)* |
| AnyConnect Essentials | Disabled<br>*(Optional license available)* |
| AnyConnect Mobile | Disabled<br>*(Optional license available)* |
| AnyConnect Premium SSL VPN Edition (sessions) | 2<br>*Optional permanent or time-based licenses available: 10, 25, 50, 100, 250, 500, 750, 1,000, 2,500, or 5,000*<br>*Optional shared licenses: Participant or Server. For the Server, these licenses are available:*<br>*500–50,000 in increments of 500*<br>*50,000–545,000 in increments of 1,000* |
| IPsec VPN (sessions) | 5,000 (max. 5,000 combined IPsec and SSL VPN) |
| VPN Load Balancing | Supported |
| *General Licenses* | |
| Encryption | Base (DES)<br>*(Optional license available: Strong [3DES/AES])* |
| Failover | Active/Standby or Active/Active |

**Table 1-12**  *ASA 5580 License Features*

| ASA 5580 | Base License |
|---|---|
| Security Contexts | 2 |
| | *Optional licenses available: 5, 10, 20, or 50* |
| VLANs, Maximum | 250 |

Table 1-13 includes the VPN-specific licensing information. By default, the ASA includes two AnyConnect Premium licenses. You cannot mix an AnyConnect Premium and Any-Connect Essentials license on the same device. You can have only one or the other.

**Table 1-13**  *VPN Licensing and Compatibility*

| | Enable One of the Following Licenses | |
|---|---|---|
| Supported With | AnyConnect Essentials | AnyConnect Premium SSL VPN Edition |
| AnyConnect Mobile | Yes | Yes |
| Advanced Endpoint Assessment | No | Yes |
| AnyConnect Premium SSL VPN Edition Shared | No | Yes |
| Client-based SSL VPN | Yes | Yes |
| Browser-based (clientless) SSL VPN | No | Yes |
| IPsec VPN | Yes | Yes |
| VPN load balancing | Yes | Yes |
| Cisco Secure Desktop | No | Yes |

**Note:**  IKEv1 IPsec sessions are not licensed, and the maximum number of sessions available equal the maximum number available for the ASA platform used.
IKEv2 IPsec remote-access VPN sessions are available for use only with the AnyConnect client and as such are licensed using the same AnyConnect Essentials or AnyConnect Premium licenses used with SSL VPNs.

## Time-Based Licenses

You might have noticed in these tables the inclusion of an optional time-based license available from Cisco for the particular feature you are enabling. Time-based licenses are usually purchased from Cisco to allow your device to handle temporary surges of use for a particular feature. For example, if you are performing a failover of your production traffic to a secondary device during a weekend, but your secondary device does not have enough installed licenses to support the number of SSL VPN sessions required, a time-based license could be installed to cover your requirements for the weekend but only last, say, 90 days.

The timer for a time-based license starts to count down as soon as the license has been activated on your ASA and continues to count down even if your device is shut down for a period of time and then turned on again. It is possible to install multiple time-based licenses. However, only one license can be active on your device at any one time. For example, if you were to install a 250 Clientless SSL VPN time-based license and then a 500 Clientless SSL VPN time-based license, only the 250 license would be active.

## When Time-Based and Permanent Licenses Combine

Depending on the feature you are purchasing or have installed, a time-based license for the resulting combination of your permanent and time-based licenses will differ. For example:

- **SSL VPN Sessions (Client and Clientless):** The license with the higher value is used. For example, if you have a time-based license with a 1000-session limit and a permanent license with a 500-session limit, the result will be the time-based license is used and you have 1000 sessions available.

- **Unified Communications Proxy Sessions:** The time-based and permanent licenses are combined up to the platform limit. For example, if you have a time-based license with a 1000-session limit and a permanent license with a 2000-session limit, you have 3000 sessions available.

- **Security Contexts:** The time-based and permanent licenses are combined up to the platform limit. For example, if you have a time-based license with a 20-context limit and a permanent license with a 5-context limit, you have 25 contexts available.

- **Botnet Traffic Filter:** There is no permanent license for this feature. The time-based license is always used.

- **All remaining licensed features:** The license with the higher limit is used.

**Note:** It is not advisable to install a time-based license with a lower license limit than your current permanent licenses, because features that use the license with the higher limit will continue to use your permanent license.

## Shared SSL VPN Licenses

Instead of purchasing device-specific license bundles, it is also possible to set up a shared SSL VPN server if you are running two or more ASA devices (Version 8.2+). Licenses are purchased from Cisco in large numbers and entered onto the ASA and will be configured with the role of the shared SSL VPN License server. The other ASA devices contact the SSL VPN License server running on the ASA and request licenses in blocks of 50 to allow for them to cope with the current connections they have.

The ASA devices can contact the SSL VPN License server and keep requesting licenses. However, they can only install and use up to the platform limit locally.

## Failover Licensing

Beginning with ASA Version 8.3(1), the two devices in a failover pair no longer require matching licenses to operate. Instead, the primary failover device typically has a license installed and the secondary device inherits this license.

If both devices have licenses installed, however, they merge to become one large failover interface, allowing for the combination of licensed VPN session numbers up to the platform-specific maximum.

Both ASA 5505 and ASA 5510 devices require the Security Plus license before they can operate in Failover mode.

## Exam Preparation Tasks

As mentioned in the section "How to Use This Book" in the Introduction, you have a couple of choices for exam preparation: the memory tables in Appendix C, Chapter 23, "Final Exam Preparation," and the exam simulation questions on the CD-ROM.

## Review All Key Topics

Review the most important topics in the chapter, noted with the Key Topic icon in the outer margin of the page. Table 1-14 lists a reference of these key topics and the page numbers on which each is found.

**Table 1-14**   *Key Topics*

| Key Topic Element | Description | Page |
|---|---|---|
| Subtopic | Security levels | 9 |
| Subtopic | EtherChannel configuration | 11 |
| Bulleted List | Available routing methods | 16 |
| Bulleted List | Available NAT rules | 18 |
| Topic | Available VPN methods on the ASA | 24 |
| Topic | ASA internal packet processing | 28 |

## Complete Tables and Lists from Memory

Print a copy of Appendix C, "Memory Tables" (found on the CD), or at least the section for this chapter, and complete the tables and lists from memory. Appendix D, "Memory Tables Answer Key," also on the CD, includes completed tables and lists to check your work.

## Define Key Terms

Define the following key terms from this chapter, and check your answers in the glossary:

ACL, web ACL

This chapter covers the following subjects:

- **Policies and Their Relationships:** In this section, we review the available policies that can be applied during a VPN connection and how they work together to form the overall policy applied to a remote user.

- **Understanding Connection Profiles:** In this section, we discuss the role of connection profiles, their configuration elements, and how they are applied to remote users.

- **Understanding Group Policies:** In this section, we discuss the role of group policies for attribute assignment and control of your remote users.

- **Configure User Attributes:** In this section, we review the creation of a user account and take a look at the available parameters and attributes that can be assigned to an individual remote user.

- **Using External Servers for AAA and Policy Assignment:** In this section, we discuss the role of AAA servers and briefly cover their configuration and how we can deploy policies through them.

# CHAPTER 2

# Configuring Policies, Inheritance, and Attributes

An important part of the deployment of a Secure Sockets Layer (SSL) or IPsec virtual private network (VPN) connection is the use of policies to allow access to resources through the VPN tunnel and the ability to control the access granted to those resources, whether this is based on the user and their internal group membership or department, the site and specific resources they are accessing, or role in the company.

We are given a wide range of options that can be configured and specified using the available policy set in the Adaptive Security Appliance (ASA), allowing us to take a very granular approach to allow or deny access based on a user's attributes. Furthermore, if a user is a member of multiple groups in the business, we can assign multiple policies, resulting in the inheritance of higher-level policies and only the more specific attributes being directly assigned.

In this chapter, we take a look at the methods available for policy assignment both in real-life scenarios and throughout this book. We then review how these policy methods work together if more than one is assigned to a user through the inheritance mode.

## "Do I Know This Already?" Quiz

The "Do I Know This Already?" quiz helps you determine your level of knowledge on this chapter's topics before you begin. Table 2-1 details the major topics discussed in this chapter and their corresponding quiz sections.

**Table 2-1** *"Do I Know This Already?" Section-to-Question Mapping*

| Foundation Topics Section | Questions |
| --- | --- |
| Policies and Their Relationships | 2 |
| Understanding Connection Profiles | 1, 3 |
| Understanding Group Policies | 4, 5 |
| Using External Servers for AAA and Policy Assignment | 6 |

1. Which of the following are available methods of assigning a connection profile? (Choose all that apply.)

   a. User connection profile lock

   b. Certificate to connection profile maps

   c. User choice using a menu in either clientless or full-tunnel VPN

   d. All of the above

2. Which of the following policy types take precedence over all others configured based on the ASA policy hierarchy?

   a. DAPs

   b. Group policy

   c. Connection profile

   d. User attributes

3. Which two of the following are the default connection profiles that exist on the ASA device?

   a. DefaultRAGroup

   b. DefaultWebVPNGroup

   c. DefaultL2LGroup

   d. DefaultAnyConnectGroup

4. Which of the following objects can be used for post-login policy assignment? (Choose all that apply.)

   a. Connection profiles

   b. User attributes

   c. Group policies

   d. DAPs

5. Which of the following are valid group policy types?

   a. External

   b. Internal

   c. Local

   d. Remote

6. When configuring external group policies, which AAA protocols or servers can you use for authorization?

   a. RADIUS

   b. SDI

   c. TACACS+

   d. LDAP

# Foundation Topics

## Policies and Their Relationships

User policy and connection parameter enforcement is an important part of any VPN deployment. Without it, we cannot provide login parameters, authorization methods, or resource access for our users, which control what they can or cannot access and when.

An important part of policy assignment is the ability to provide flexibility and scalability to both administrators configuring them and the remote users using them.

**Key Topic**

- Flexibility is achieved through being able to assign the same security or network settings to any user or group regardless of their connection type.

- Scalability is achieved through modularity and policy inheritance, limiting the amount of duplicate configuration items required by policy reuse among groups or individual users.

All remote users must go through two phases before they can successfully connect and start to access resources made available through your VPN connection:

- **The prelogin phase** is achieved through the use of connection profiles (also known as tunnel groups). In connection profiles, we can carry out the assignment of connection attributes and parameters (for example, authentication, authorization, and accounting [AAA] and IP address assignment) and define the available connection methods (for example, IKEv1 and IKEv2 SSL), allowing our users to start the login process.

- **The post-login phase** is achieved through the use of group policy objects, Dynamic Access Policies (DAPs), and user-specific attributes. These may include such items as IPv4 or IPv6 access lists, Domain Name System (DNS) servers, access hours, split tunneling, and so on. Group policies offer a great deal of flexibility when assigning attributes to users, either individually in a user account or groupwide by assignment to a connection profile. DAPs provide an advanced policy assignment method based on user AAA attributes or client device posture assessment. We discuss DAPs, their configuration, and deployment in later chapters.

Different policy types, although they include their own specific attributes, are really just containers that can be used to hold multiple configuration items that might have been used multiple times already in different policies. For example, we can configure an access control list (ACL) (we'll call it Server_Access) to only allow access between remote client A and corporate server A. We assign it to the group policy object AnyConnect, limiting internal resource access for our AnyConnect users. Later, we create a new group policy for our IPsec VPN users and assign our Server_Access ACL to this group policy, as well.

In our example, we have two groups of users accessing our corporate network through their own protocol-specific connection profiles (AnyConnect and IPsec). Each of the two connection profiles has its own group policy objects, both using our Server_Access ACL.

If we want to reduce the amount of configuration we have to carry out but still allow each connection group to have its specific attributes (for example, IP address pools and DNS servers), we can create a single group policy object using our Server_Access ACL and apply this to each connection profile.

Furthermore, if we want to really minimize the amount of configuration we have on our device, and the only difference between these two groups of users is their connection type (that is, they do not require any further attribute or parameter assignments between them), we can create a single connection profile allowing multiple connectivity types and attach the single group policy that uses our Server_Access ACL. Later, if one of our users requires access to corporate server B, we can create a custom ACL and apply it directly to their user account, or create a user-specific group policy object and assign this directly to our user.

**Key Topic**

We can be as specific as we like or as needs require for our particular environment, either sharing multiple policies between multiple groups, reusing multiple attributes in multiple policies, using multiple groups connecting to one connection profile, or configuring each group to have its own specific connection profiles, policies, and attributes. The choice is, well, yours.

As we create our connection profiles and policies, we might end up with a user who has been assigned the same attributes multiple times by separate policies. These might have been applied because of the user's group or department membership, connection type, or location. Regardless of the reason for these assignments, the result is that our user's policies are merged and assigned in a hierarchical fashion.

The hierarchal policy model shown in Figure 2-1 works from top to bottom with any attributes set within policy assignment methods toward the top of the list (DAPs), taking precedence over any conflicting attributes assigned within methods toward the end of the list (default group policy object).

Each connection entry has its own default group policy object. As shown in Figure 2-1, the default group policy is at the end of the policy hierarchy. As a result, any attributes/settings that have not been configured within policies already assigned to a user are applied using the attribute assignment of the default group policy.

The same applies to other policy types within the policy hierarchy. However, if two policy types contain different values for the same attribute or property, the user is assigned the attribute set within the policy type that is higher in the hierarchy. For example, if IP pool A has been assigned to the group policy applied to the connection profile and IP pool B has been assigned to the user account directly, the user is assigned an IP address from IP pool B.

## Understanding Connection Profiles

As you saw earlier, connection profiles provide our users with the necessary prelogin policies that must successfully establish a connection to our ASA device. We can also use connection profiles to separate our connecting users into the relevant groups that may require separate methods of access (for example, clientless SSL VPN, AnyConnect VPN sessions, or even separate AAA methods).

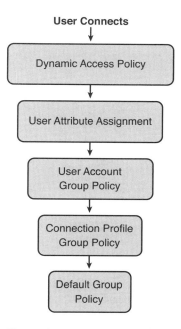

**User Connects**

Dynamic Access Policy

User Attribute Assignment

User Account
Group Policy

Connection Profile
Group Policy

Default Group
Policy

**Figure 2-1** *ASA VPN Policy Enforcement Hierarchy*

Consider the following scenario. You have two groups of users connecting into your environment: guests and corporate employees. Guests connecting into your organization do not require the same level of access as your employees. In fact, they only require access to an internal intranet portal. On the other hand, your corporate employees require access to internal file servers and email. Based on the level of access required by each group, we could create two connection profiles, aptly named Guests and Corporate for our discussion. Our Guests connection profile would only allow access for incoming clientless SSL VPNs and authenticate connecting users with a shared guest internal username and password. A group policy (covered in greater depth during the next section) would be applied to our connection profile containing the relevant bookmarks needed for browsing our company's intranet in the SSL VPN portal. However, our Corporate connection profile would allow access for incoming AnyConnect SSL, IKEv2, and IKEv1 (IPsec VPN clients), and an IP address would be assigned per remote user from an existing IP address pool. Authentication and authorization would be carried out using a combination of a one-time password (OTP) and internal Windows Active Directory server. A group policy would be applied to the connection profile to provide users with split-tunnel lists and access lists, restricting communication to only those internal subnets and devices that are required.

A few methods are available for allowing our users to select/connect to the appropriate connection profile they require. Depending on the authentication scheme we have configured for our users and their chosen login method (clientless SSL VPN, AnyConnect, IPsec client), they can either select a connection profile manually from a list of those available or have it selected for them automatically, based on one of the following methods:

Key
Topic

- Group URL

- Group alias

- Certificate to connection profile mapping

- Per-user connection profile lock

### Group URL

Group URLs allow remote users to select a connection profile by entering the direct URL configured for the profile they require. An example of a configured group URL is either of the following:

https://<ASA IP address>/<connection profile>

https://<ASA FQDN>/<connection profile>

### Group Alias

Group aliases allow clientless SSL VPN users to select the appropriate connection profile from a list at the portal login page and AnyConnect users to select a connection profile in the client software. Both scenarios occur before a user has logged in and are covered in greater detail in Chapter 3, "Deploying an AnyConnect Remote-Access VPN Solution," and Chapter 9, "Deploying a Clientless SSL VPN Solution." As shown in Figure 2-2, the configuration of both a group alias and group URL is carried out in the Group Alias/Group URL pane of a connection profiles properties window. We navigate to **Configuration > Remote Access VPN > Network (Client) Access | Clientless SSL VPN Access > AnyConnect Connection Profiles | Connection Profiles**, select the connection profile, click **Edit**, and then use the menu on the left side to select **Advanced > Group Alias/Group URL**.

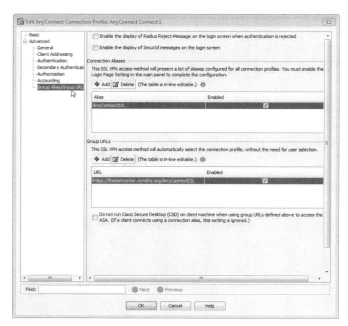

**Figure 2-2**   *Connection Profile Group URL and Alias Configuration*

As you will also see in later chapters, before our remote users can select a connection profile by group alias, we must first enable this feature on the ASA in the respective connection profiles pane of the Adaptive Security Device Manager (ASDM), as shown in Figure 2-3.

For example, we can enable our AnyConnect and clientless SSL VPN users to select a connection profile in their client software or from the portal login page using the following steps:

- **AnyConnect Users:** Navigate to **Configuration > Remote Access VPN > Network (Client) Access > AnyConnect Connection Profiles.** In the Login Page Setting section of the window, select **Allow User to Select Connection Profile, Identified by Its Alias.**

- **Clientless SSL VPN Users:** Navigate to **Configuration > Remote Access VPN > Clientless SSL VPN Access > Connection Profiles.** In the Login Page Setting section of the window, select **Allow User to Select Connection Profile, Identified by Its Alias.**

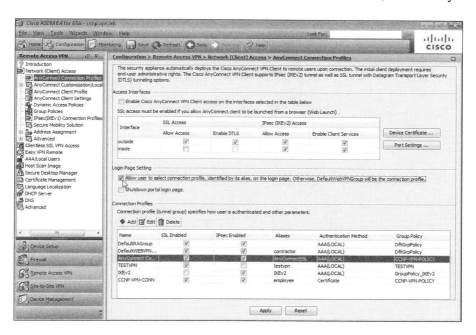

**Figure 2-3**   *Connection Profile Pane: Allow Group Alias Selection*

## Certificate to Connection Profile Mapping

If you have chosen to use digital certificate authentication for your connection profiles, the distinguished name (DN) values in a remote user's certificate can be used to select the appropriate connection profile. For example, if the remote user initiating a connection is a member of the Accounts team, his certificate DN value may equal OU=Accounts. Using certificate-to-connection profile maps, the ASA can be configured to match any connecting users with the value of OU=Accounts to a custom connection profile created for Accounts department personnel. You can apply the same actions to any DN values held in your user certificates (as discussed in Chapter 9 and Chapter 4, "Advanced Authentication and Authorization of AnyConnect VPNs").

## Per-User Connection Profile Lock

We can also assign a connection profile directly to remote users on an individual basis. For example, we might have a specific connection profile for our VPs and want to make the process of connecting as seamless as possible for them without their having to first enter or select a connection profile.

The process of assigning a connection profile directly to a user can be achieved in the properties menu of the user's account, as shown in Figure 2-4.

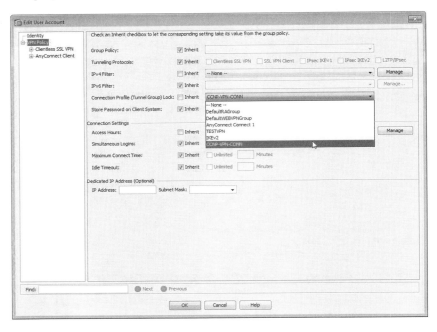

**Figure 2-4**   *Configuring Per-User Connection Profile Lock*

We begin by selecting the user account to edit from **Configuration > Device Management > Users/AAA > User Accounts**, and then click **Edit**. In the Edit User Account window, select **VPN Policy** from the menu on the left, and in the pane on the right side, uncheck the **Connection Profile (Tunnel Group) Lock Inherit** check box. Using the drop-down list, select the appropriate connection profile to be assigned to this user.

We see a great deal more of connection profiles and their use in the chapters that follow. It is important to note at this stage that we can only allow clientless SSL VPN and client-based (AnyConnect) VPN remote users the option to select a connection profile. As discussed in Chapter 15, "Deploying and Managing the Cisco VPN Client," when we work with IPsec remote-access VPNs, the connection profile name is configured in the client software as the group name and must match before a successful connection can occur.

## Default Connection Profiles

Besides our own custom connection profiles, default connection profiles are applied to a user's session if the various connection parameters in manually configured connection profiles are not satisfied and the user is not allowed to select the connection profile before login.

Three default connection profiles are configured on the ASA, as listed here. These cannot be removed, but they can be modified, allowing us to change the settings to match our environment:

- **DefaultRAGroup:** Used for client-based (AnyConnect) SSL VPNs and IPsec remote-access VPNs.

Key Topic

- **DefaultWEBVPNGroup:** Used for clientless SSL VPNs.

- **DefaultL2LGroup:** Used for IPsec LAN-to-LAN connections.

The default connection profiles, as mentioned earlier, are used mainly for global property assignment or a catchall mechanism for users that may only require a basic VPN portal (webmail and so on) and are not able to or allowed to select a connection profile. It is recommended that your own custom connection profiles be created for your specific VPN deployments, instead of relying on the default connection profiles for remote user connection establishment.

By default, when using plain old username and password-based authentication for remote user authentication, users are automatically connected to the appropriate default connection profile based on their connection method (that is, clientless SSL, IPsec, and so on). We can overcome this problem by providing our remote users with the means to select a connection profile before authenticating (either from a drop-down list in the clientless SSL portal or the AnyConnect client). If we have deployed username and password-based authentication (no certificates) for our clientless SSL and AnyConnect VPNs, however, and we have configured our ASA to provide our remote users with the ability to select a connection profile, users must select an available connection profile from the list in order to continue. If they do not select a connection profile, they are mapped to their default connection profile.

When using certificate-based authentication the game changes, and the default connection profile is used only if predefined fields within a user's certificate do not match the values we configure in Certificate to Connection Profile Mapping Rules for automatic connection profile assignment.

The process that occurs when using the Cisco IPsec VPN client is different from that just described for both clientless and full-tunnel connections, again depending on the type of authentication method in use. As you will see later in Chapter 15, "Deploying and Managing the Cisco VPN Client," when deploying IPsec remote-access connections using pre-shared key authentication, the connection profile name must be entered exactly into the client software (in the Group Name field). If the connection process fails, the client is not assigned to the default connection profile for the specific method of connection (DefaultRAGroup). Instead, the connection fails.

If we are using certificate-based authentication with the Cisco IPsec VPN client, we are not given the option of selecting or entering a connection profile/group name. Instead, we must either configure our own certificate to connection profile mappings, or by default, the ASA attempts to match the OU field value of the certificate to an available connection profile with the same name. If one or both of these methods fail, unlike with the pre-shared key method, the remote user is mapped to the DefaultRAGroup connection profile instead of being disconnected.

The DefaultL2LGroup acts as a catchall for any LAN-to-LAN IPsec VPN sessions that do not match on a manually administrator-configured connection profile, regardless of its authentication type, pre-shared-key, or if it is certificate based.

Note that, by default, neither DefaultWEBVPNGroup nor DefaultRAGroup allows for AnyConnect sessions, because these connection profiles have the DfltGrpPolicy group policy attached, which only permits clientless SSL VPN, IPsec VPN, and L2TP/IPsec sessions. These settings can, of course, be modified.

As you move through the rest of the book, you will many more uses of connection profiles with all available types of connectivity offered by the ASA device, in addition to many advanced features that are available within a connection profile.

Connection profiles are created by first navigating to **Configuration > Remote Access VPN** or **Site-to-Site VPN**. Depending on the chosen method of connectivity (whether this be clientless SSL, IKEv1, IKEv2, or so forth), select one of the following options in the Remote Access VPN or Site-to-Site VPN areas to continue:

**Remote Access VPN:**

- **Network (Client) Access:** Use for AnyConnect (full tunnel) SSL and IKEv2, Cisco IPsec VPN client, and IKEv1 connections.

- **Clientless SSL VPN:** Use for browser-based clientless SSL VPN connections.

**Site-to-Site VPN:**

- **Connection Profiles:** Use for all site-to-site connection profiles.

After navigating to the appropriate area, create a connection profile by selecting **Add** on the right side of the window. The Add Connection Profile window appears, as shown in Figure 2-5.

In this window, the connection profile is given a name, the authentication method selected, and custom attributes assigned (such as IP address pools, Dynamic Host Configuration Protocol (DHCP) servers, group policies, and so on). These settings are described in detail in later chapters.

## Understanding Group Policies

As you saw earlier, a group policy object is a container for the various attributes and post-login parameters that can be assigned to VPN users, and to endpoints such as IPv4 and IPv6 ACLs, DHCP servers, address pools, and so on.

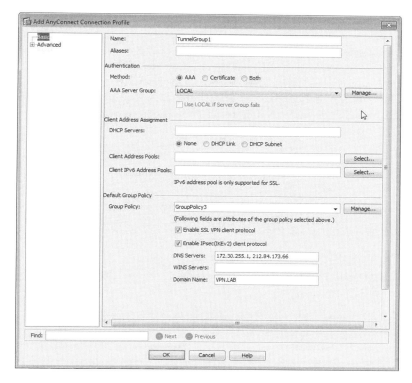

**Figure 2-5**    *Connection Profile Creation*

Group policies can simplify the configuration required by allowing for their assignment to multiple users or connection profiles. This provides a greater level of scale, flexibility, and management when working with multiple connection methods and remote users.

Group policies may be internal (local) or external (remote). Both internal and external group policies are configured on the ASA. However, unlike internal policies, which hold their configured attributes and parameters locally on the ASA, external group policy attributes and parameters are configured and stored on external AAA servers. During a login attempt, the configured AAA authorization servers are contacted and send back the relevant policy attributes and parameters, based on the connecting user's policy assignment.

For more information about external group policy objects, see Chapter 4, "Advanced Authentication and Authorization of AnyConnect VPNs." For the remainder of this section, we focus only on the deployment and configuration of local group policies.

Group policies, as previously mentioned, are applied to either a connection profile or a user account directly. They do not provide any function while they are unassigned.

Although we can select the connection method that a group policy can apply to (for example, IKEv1, IKEv2, or AnyConnect SSL), unlike connection profiles, group policy objects are not locally specific to a connection profile type. If we create a group policy in the Network (Client) Access area of the ASDM for our AnyConnect or IPsec remote-access clients, the same group policy is globally available among the other connection types, and we can select, edit, or delete it within the Group Policies section of the Site-to-Site or Clientless SSL VPN areas of the ASDM. This enables us to reuse our group policy objects, not just by multiple connection profiles of the same type, but by all connection profile types and remote users regardless of their connection method (depending on the configured protocols in the group policy itself). However, not all configuration areas or items may be available, depending on the configuration area you are using to add or edit your group policy object. For example, when configuring a site-to-site group policy object, there is no need for us to be able to see all the remote user-specific attributes and parameters that might be assigned, because they are unavailable for use in the connection type being configured.

Group policy objects are configured in any one of these three areas:

- **Configuration > Remote Access VPN > Network (client) Access > Group Policies**

- **Configuration > Remote Access VPN > Clientless SSL VPN > Group Policies**

- **Configuration > Site-to-Site VPN > Group Policies**

Select **Add > Internal Group Policy**, and the window shown in Figure 2-6 appears.

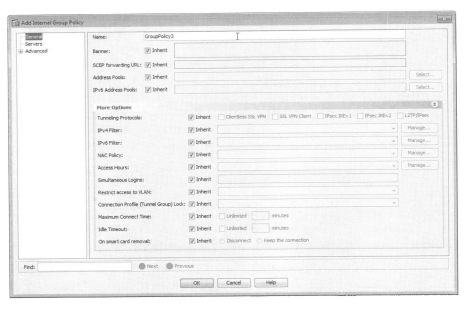

**Figure 2-6**   *Internal Group Policy Creation*

We begin by giving our group policy object a name, a banner, and address pools. If we expand the **More Options** section of the window, we are presented with a greater list of parameters that may be configured to further tailor the experience our remote users have when connecting to our VPN deployment. All these options are covered in later chapters. For now, it is just important to at least know they exist and how to get to them.

You might have noticed also in Figure 2-6 that all the fields in the Add Internal Group Policy window have the Inherit option in front of them. Similar to connection profiles, the ASA also has a default group policy object DfltGrpPolicy that cannot be deleted. However, its properties can be modified and indirectly applied to our configured group policies, as they all by default inherit the settings configured in DfltGrpPolicy.

## Configure User Attributes

We have several choices of which users to use. We can use local users or remote users that have been created specifically for our deployment on RADIUS, TACACS+, or other remote AAA servers. We can also use an existing database of users. For example, a company might want to use their existing Microsoft Windows Active Directory deployment for the management of new users and allow their internal users to connect into their environment remotely.

Many of the examples in this book use the internal user database (local users) available on the ASA. The policies and parameters we can assign to either local or remote users are the same by using either connection profiles or group policy objects. However, in a locally configured user, we can also assign attributes and policy objects directly to their user account using the various properties available. (For example, in the preceding sections we discussed the assignment of group policies and connection profiles to a user account directly.)

Local user accounts are configured on the ASA device in the **Device Management > Users/AAA > User Accounts** area of the ASDM. Begin by creating a new user account, shown in Figure 2-7, by selecting **Add**.

We enter a username, password, and the type of management access our user will have to the ASA device (for example, telnet, Secure Shell [SSH], ASDM). Depending on the type of user account we are creating (VPN User, Management Only, VPN User with Management Functions), select the appropriate level of management access to the ASA to grant the user. By default, any new user accounts created are given the option of Full Access to the ASA. However, if our users are only created for the purposes of connecting to our VPNs, there is no requirement for them to have management access to the ASA, and this option should be changed to **No ASDM, SSH, Telnet, or Console Access** instead.

We can further customize the user experience during their VPN connection by assigning the various options available, either when connecting through a clientless SSL VPN session or AnyConnect full-tunnel session (for example, bookmark lists, Smart Tunnel applications and access, manual or automatic download of the AnyConnect client). However, it is recommended if you have multiple users in your VPN deployment that all have similar parameters and settings attached to their account. Assignment of these attributes should be carried out using group policy objects or connection profiles for ease of management.

As you continue through this book, you will see the creation of local user accounts in detail, along with the advanced attributes that are available to them and the results that occur after their assignment.

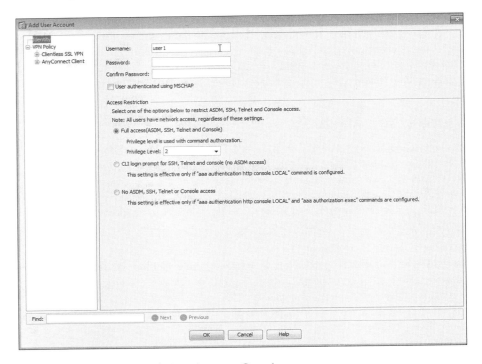

**Figure 2-7**   *ASDM Local User Account Creation*

# Using External Servers for AAA and Policies

As briefly discussed earlier, not only can we use remote AAA servers for the purposes of user creation and management, we can also use them for the purposes of policy assignment using external group policies.

The use of an external AAA server for the purposes of policy assignment is recommended. This provides centralized policy storage and management where a VPN deployment might have more than one ASA device available (for example, when using two or more ASA devices in a VPN cluster).

The ASA device supports the following external AAA server types and protocols for authorization purposes:

- RADIUS

- TACACS+

- LDAP

- NT Domain

- SDI

- Kerberos

- HTTP Form

Only two of the protocols are available for use with external group policy assignment: RADIUS and Lightweight Directory Access Protocol (LDAP). In earlier ASA releases, TACACS+ was also available for external policy assignment. However, because of the lack of support offered by the protocol for the purposes of policy assignment compared to the parameters offered by RADIUS and LDAP, TACACS+ has been removed for this purpose. (TACACS+ support has been removed for use with external group policy assignment only; the protocol still exists for use as an AAA server for user authentication purposes.)

To create a new external group policy object whose name will exist on the ASA device (although all attributes that are stored in the group policy exist only on the configured RADIUS or LDAP server), navigate to one of the following locations:

■ **Configuration > Remote Access VPN > Network (client) Access > Group Policies**

■ **Configuration > Remote Access VPN > Clientless SSL VPN > Group Policies**

■ **Configuration > Site-to-Site VPN > Group Policies**

Select **Add > External Group Policy** to begin the configuration process, shown in Figure 2-8.

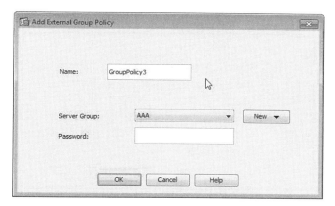

**Figure 2-8**   *ASDM Local User Account Creation*

The ASA asks for very few parameters in comparison to when creating an internal group policy, because we are only creating the container or name for the group policy on the ASA and specifying the AAA server that will store the policy attributes along with the password the ASA uses to authenticate against it.

Table 2-2 lists the available RADIUS attributes, attribute number, type, and values, respectively, which you may configure on an external RADIUS or LDAP server for the purposes of user policy assignment.

**Table 2-2**  *Supported RADIUS Attributes and Values*

| Attribute Name | Attribute Number | Type | Value |
| --- | --- | --- | --- |
| Access-Hours | 1 | String | Name of the time range (for example, Work Time) |
| Simultaneous-Logins | 2 | Integer | A number between 0 and 2,147,483,647 |
| Primary-DNS | 5 | String | IP address |
| Secondary-DNS | 6 | String | IP address |
| Primary-WINS | 7 | String | IP address |
| Secondary-WINS | 8 | String | IP address |
| SEP-Card-Assignment | 9 | Integer | Not used |
| Tunneling-Protocols | 11 | Integer | 1 = PPTP<br>2 = L2TP<br>4 = IPsec<br>8 = LT2P/IPsec<br>16 = WebVPN<br>4 and 8, mutually exclusive<br>0–11 and 16–27, legal values |
| IPsec-Sec-Association | 12 | String | Name of SA |
| IPsec-Authentication | 13 | Integer | 0 = None<br>1 = RADIUS<br>2 = LDAP (auth only)<br>3 = NT Domain<br>4 = SDI<br>5 = Internal<br>6 = RADIUS with expiry<br>7 = Kerberos/AD |
| Banner1 | 15 | String | Banner string |
| IPsec-Allow-Passwd-Store | 16 | Boolean | 0 = Disabled<br>1 = Enabled |
| Use-Client-Address | 17 | Boolean | 0 = Disabled<br>1 = Enabled |

**Table 2-2**  *Supported RADIUS Attributes and Values*

| Attribute Name | Attribute Number | Type | Value |
|---|---|---|---|
| PPTP-Encryption | 20 | Integer | Bitmap: |
| | | | 1 = Encryption required |
| | | | 2 = 40 bits |
| | | | 4 = 128 bits |
| | | | 8 = Stateless-Required |
| | | | 15 = 40/128-Encr/Stateless-Req |
| L2TP-Encryption | 21 | Integer | Bitmap: |
| | | | 1 = Encryption required |
| | | | 2 = 40 bits |
| | | | 4 = 128 bits |
| | | | 8 = Stateless-required |
| | | | 15 = 40/128-Encr/Stateless-Req |
| Group-Policy<br>Pre 8.2 use IETF-RADIUS-Class | 25 | String | Use one of the following formats<br><group policy name><br>OU=<group policy name> |
| IPsec-Split-Tunnel-List | 27 | String | Name of the ACL used for split tunneling |
| IPsec-Default-Domain | 28 | String | Client default domain name. Enter 1–255 characters. |
| IPsec-Split-DNS-Names | 29 | String | Client secondary default domain name. Enter 1–255 characters. |
| IPsec-Tunnel-Type | 30 | Integer | 1 = LAN-to-LAN<br>2 = Remote access |
| IPsec-Mode-Config | 31 | Boolean | 0 = Disabled<br>1 = Enabled |
| IPsec-User-Group-Lock | 33 | Boolean | 0 = Disabled<br>1 = Enabled |
| IPsec-Over-UDP | 34 | Integer | 0 = Disabled<br>1 = Enabled |
| IPsec-Over-UDP-Port | 35 | Integer | 4001–49151<br>Default = 10000 |
| Banner2 | 36 | String | If configured banner string is concatenated to banner1 |

**Table 2-2**   *Supported RADIUS Attributes and Values*

| Attribute Name | Attribute Number | Type | Value |
|---|---|---|---|
| PPTP-MPPC-Compression | 37 | Integer | 0 = Disabled<br>1 = Enabled |
| L2TP-MPPC-Compression | 38 | Integer | 0 = Disabled<br>1 = Enabled |
| IPsec-IP-Compression | 39 | Integer | 0 = Disabled<br>1 = Enabled |
| IPsec-IKE-Peer-ID-Check | 40 | Integer | 1 = Required<br>2 = If supported by peer certificate<br>3 = Do not check |
| IKE-Keep-Alive | 41 | Boolean | 0 = Disabled<br>1 = Enabled |
| IPsec-Auth-On-Rekey | 42 | Boolean | 0 = Disabled<br>1 = Enabled |
| Required-Client-Firewall-Vendor-Code | 45 | Integer | 1 = Cisco Systems (with Cisco integrated client)<br>2 = Zone Labs<br>3 = NetworkICE<br>4 = Sygate<br>5 = Cisco Systems (with Cisco IPS agent) |
| Required-Client-Firewall-Product-Code | 46 | Integer | Cisco Systems Products:<br>1 = Cisco IPS Agent or CIC<br>Zone Labs Products:<br>1 = Zone Alarm<br>2 = Zone AlarmPro<br>3 = Zone Labs Integrity<br>NetworkICE Product:<br>1 = BlackICE Defender/Agent<br>Sygate Products:<br>1 = Personal Firewall<br>2 = Personal Firewall Pro<br>3 = Security Agent |
| Required-Client-Firewall-Description | 47 | String | Enter a description |

**Table 2-2** *Supported RADIUS Attributes and Values*

| Attribute Name | Attribute Number | Type | Value |
|---|---|---|---|
| Require-HW-Client-Auth | 48 | Boolean | 0 = Disabled<br>1 = Enabled |
| Required-Individual-User-Auth | 49 | Integer | 0 = Disabled<br>1 = Enabled |
| Authenticated-User-Idle-Timeout | 50 | Integer | 1–35,791,394 minutes |
| Cisco-IP-Phone-Bypass | 51 | Integer | 0 = Disabled<br>1 = Enabled |
| IPsec-Split-Tunneling-Policy | 55 | Integer | 0 = No split tunneling<br>1 = Split tunneling<br>3 = Local LAN permitted |
| IPsec-Required-Client-Firewall-Capability | 56 | Integer | 0 = None<br>1 = Policy defined by remote FW Are-You-There (AYT)<br>2 = Policy pushed CPP<br>4 = Policy from server |
| IPsec-Client-Firewall-Filter-Name | 57 | String | Enter the name of the firewall policy filter |
| IPsec-Client-Firewall-Filter-Optional | 58 | Integer | 0 = Required<br>1 = Optional |
| IPsec-Backup-Servers | 59 | String | 1 = Use client-configured list<br>2 = Disable and clear client list<br>3 = Use backup server list |
| IPsec-Backup-Server-List | 60 | String | Server addresses (space, delimited) |
| DHCP-Network-Scope | 61 | String | IP address |
| Intercept-DHCP-Configure-Msg | 62 | Boolean | 0 = Disabled<br>1 = Enabled |
| MS-Client-Subnet-Mask | 63 | Boolean | IP address |
| Allow-Network-Extension-Mode | 64 | Boolean | 0 = Disabled<br>1 = Enabled |

**Table 2-2**  *Supported RADIUS Attributes and Values*

| Attribute Name | Attribute Number | Type | Value |
|---|---|---|---|
| Authorization-Type | 65 | Integer | 0 = None |
| | | | 1 = RADIUS |
| | | | 2 = LDAP |
| Authorization-Required | 66 | Integer | 0 = No |
| | | | 1 = Yes |
| Authorization-DN-Field | 67 | String | Possible values: UID, OU, O, CN, L, SP, C, EA, T, N, SN, I, GENQ, DNQ, SER, use-entire-name |
| IKE-Keepalive-Confidence-Interval | 68 | Integer | 10–300 seconds |
| WebVPN-Content-Filter-Parameters | 69 | Integer | 1 = JAVA ActiveX |
| | | | 2 = JavaScript |
| | | | 3 = Image |
| | | | 4 = Cookies in images |
| WebVPN-URL-List | 71 | String | Url-list-name |
| WebVPN-Port-Forward-List | 72 | String | Port-forward list name |
| WebVPN-Access-List | 73 | String | Access list name |
| Cisco-LEAP-Bypass | 75 | Integer | 0 = Disabled |
| | | | 1 = Enabled |
| WebVPN-Homepage | 76 | String | Enter the URL of the home page |
| Client-Type-Version-Limiting | 77 | String | IPsec VPN version number string |
| WebVPN-Port-Forwarding-Name | 79 | String | Example: "Company Apps" replaces the Application Access string on the clientless SSL VPN portal page |
| IE-Proxy-Server | 80 | String | IP address |
| IE-Proxy-Server-Policy | 81 | Integer | 0 = No Modify |
| | | | 1 = No Proxy |
| | | | 2 = Auto Detect |
| | | | 3 = Use Concentrator Setting |
| IE-Proxy-Exception-List | 82 | String | Newline (\n) separated list of DNS domains |

**Table 2-2**   *Supported RADIUS Attributes and Values*

| Attribute Name | Attribute Number | Type | Value |
|---|---|---|---|
| IE-Proxy-Bypass-Local | 83 | Integer | 0 = None<br>1 = Local |
| IKE-Keepalive-Retry-Interval | 84 | Integer | 2–10 seconds |
| Tunnel-Group-Lock | 85 | String | Name of the tunnel group or None |
| Access-list-inbound | 86 | String | Access list ID |
| Access-list Outbound | 87 | String | Access list ID |
| Perfect-Forward-Secret-Enable | 88 | Boolean | 0 = No<br>1 = Yes |
| NAC-Enable | 89 | Integer | 0 = No<br>1 = Yes |
| NAC-Status-Query-Timer | 90 | Integer | 30–1,800 seconds |
| NAC-Revalidation-Timer | 91 | Integer | 300–86,400 seconds |
| NAC-Default-ACL | 92 | String | Access-list |
| WebVPN-URL-Entry-Enable | 93 | Integer | 0 = Disabled<br>1 = Enabled |
| WebVPN-File-Access-Enable | 94 | Integer | 0 = Disabled<br>1 = Enabled |
| WebVPN-File-Server-Entry-Enable | 95 | Integer | 0 = Disabled<br>1 = Enabled |
| WebVPN-File-Server-Browsing-Enable | 96 | Integer | 0 = Disabled<br>1 = Enabled |
| WebVPN-Port-Forwarding-Enable | 97 | Integer | 0 = Disabled<br>1 = Enabled |
| WebVPN-Outlook-Exchange-Proxy-Enable | 98 | Integer | 0 = Disabled<br>1 = Enabled |
| WebVPN-Port-Forwarding-HTTP-Proxy | 99 | Integer | 0 = Disabled<br>1 = Enabled |

**Table 2-2**  *Supported RADIUS Attributes and Values*

| Attribute Name | Attribute Number | Type | Value |
|---|---|---|---|
| WebVPN-Auto-Applet-Download-Enable | 100 | Integer | 0 = Disabled<br>1 = Enabled |
| WebVPN-Citrix-Metaframe-Enable | 101 | Integer | 0 = Disabled<br>1 = Enabled |
| WebVPN-Apply ACL | 102 | Integer | 0 = Disabled<br>1 = Enabled |
| WebVPN-SSL-VPN-Client-Enable | 103 | Integer | 0 = Disabled<br>1 = Enabled |
| WebVPN-SSL-VPN-Client-Required | 104 | Integer | 0 = Disabled<br>1 = Enabled |
| WebVPN-SSL-Client-Keep-Installation | 105 | Integer | 0 = Disabled<br>1 = Enabled |
| SVC-Keepalive | 107 | Integer | 0 = Off<br>15–600 seconds |
| SVC-DPD-Interval-Client | 108 | Integer | 0 = Off<br>5–3600 seconds |
| SVC-DPD-Interval-Gateway | 109 | Integer | 0 = Off<br>5–3600 seconds |
| SVC-Rekey-Time | 110 | Integer | 0 = Disabled<br>1–10,080 minutes |
| WebVPN-Deny-Message | 116 | String | Valid string (up to 500 characters) |
| Extended-Authentication-On-Rekey | 122 | Integer | 0 = Disabled<br>1 = Enabled |
| SVC-DTLS | 123 | Integer | 0 = False<br>1 = True |
| SVC-MTU | 125 | Integer | MTU value<br>256–1,406 in bytes |
| SVC-Modules | 127 | String | String (name of module) |
| SVC-Profiles | 128 | String | String (name of profile) |

**Table 2-2**   *Supported RADIUS Attributes and Values*

| Attribute Name | Attribute Number | Type | Value |
|---|---|---|---|
| SVC-Ask | 131 | String | 0 = Disabled<br>1 = Enabled<br>3 = Enabled default service<br>5 = Enable default clientless |
| SVC-Ask-Timeout | 132 | Integer | 5–120 seconds |
| IE-Proxy-PAC-URL | 133 | String | PAC address |
| Strip-Realm | 135 | Boolean | 0 = Disabled<br>1 = Enabled |
| Smart-Tunnel | 136 | String | Name of Smart Tunnel |
| WebVPN-ActiveX-Relay | 137 | Integer | 0 = Disabled<br>Otherwise = Enabled |
| Smart-Tunnel-Auto | 138 | Integer | 0 = Disabled<br>1 = Enabled<br>2 = AutoStart |
| Smart-Tunnel-Auto-Signon-Enable | 139 | String | Name of Smart Tunnel auto sign-on list appended by domain name |
| VLAN | 140 | Integer | 0–4094 |
| NAC-Settings | 141 | String | Name of NAC policy |
| Member-Of | 145 | String | Comma-separated string (for example, Engineering, Sales) |
| Address-Pool | 217 | String | Name of IP local pool |
| IPv6-Address-Pool | 218 | String | Name of IP local pool |
| IPV6-VPN-Filter | 219 | String | ACL name |
| Privilege-level | 220 | Integer | Enter between 0 and 15 |
| WebVPN-Macro-Value1 | 223 | String | Unbounded. See the SSL VPN Deployment Guide at Cisco.com for examples. |
| WebVPN-Macro-Value-2 | 224 | String | Unbounded. See the SSL VPN Deployment Guide at Cisco.com for examples. |

# Exam Preparation Tasks

As mentioned in the section "How to Use This Book" in the Introduction, you have a couple of choices for exam preparation: the memory tables in Appendix C, Chapter 23, "Final Exam Preparation," and the exam simulation questions on the CD-ROM.

## Review All Key Topics

Review the most important topics in the chapter, noted with the key topics icon in the outer margin of the page. Table 2-3 lists a reference of these key topics and the page numbers on which each is found.

**Table 2-3**  *Key Topics*

| Key Topic Element | Description | Page |
|---|---|---|
| Bulleted List | The benefits of the modular policy assignment of the ASA | 49 |
| List | ASA policy inheritance | 50 |
| Bulleted List | Available connection profile selection and assignment methods | 52 |
| Bulleted List | Default connection profiles | 55 |
| Topic | Understanding group policies | 56 |
| Bulleted List | Available AAA server types and protocols | 60 |

## Complete Tables and Lists from Memory

Print a copy of Appendix C, "Memory Tables" (found on the CD), or at least the section for this chapter, and complete the tables and lists from memory. Appendix D, "Memory Tables Answer Key," also on the CD, includes completed tables and lists to check your work.

## Define Key Terms

Define the following key terms from this chapter and check your answers in the glossary:

connection profile, internal group policy, external group policy

This chapter covers the following subjects:

- **Full-Tunnel VPN Technology Overview:** In this section, we review the operation of full-tunnel VPN technology and the operation of SSL/TLS and DTLS. We also introduce IKEv2 operation.

- **Configuration Procedures, Deployment Strategies, and Information Gathering:** In this section, we discuss the common implementation criteria for a full-tunnel SSL VPN and some of the important questions and information required before you continue with your deployment. We also take a brief look at the available installation options with the AnyConnect client software in preparation for an in-depth look in later chapters.

- **Deploying Your First Full-Tunnel AnyConnect SSL VPN Solution:** In this section, we take a look at the steps required to enable a full SSL VPN tunnel using the AnyConnect client.

- **Deploying Your First AnyConnect IKEv2 VPN Solution:** In this section, we briefly cover the configuration steps required to enable an IKEv2 for use with the AnyConnect client.

- **Client IP Address Allocation:** In this section, we discuss the address-allocation methods that are available for assigning an IP address to our remote users.

- **Advanced Controls for Your Environment:** In this section, we discuss the advanced methods of controlling our remote user's access to internal resources through the VPN tunnel using ACLs, downloadable ACLs, split tunneling, and so on.

- **Troubleshooting the AnyConnect Client:** In this section, we review the available troubleshooting methods included with the AnyConnect client using DART, logging, and statistical views.

## CHAPTER 3

# Deploying an AnyConnect Remote-Access VPN Solution

As we evaluate the application access required for remote use by our users and their various requirements and expectations (which can be in a constant state of flux and growth), we may begin to realize that a clientless Secure Sockets Layer virtual private network (SSL VPN) solution just cannot cut it for the type of environment demanded. We also discover that a remote-access solution is required that will enable remote users to quickly and effortlessly connect into their corporate headquarters with the minimal amount of fuss and time. So, there goes the Cisco IPsec VPN client, too, because there is no easy way of distributing the software to our users, automatically installing it, and deploying new client profiles on-the-fly should they require new features, modules, and so on. What we need is a full-tunnel VPN solution that we can deploy to our users wherever they are, install and connect automatically, detect when the user is in the office or not, and download and install policy updates automatically. What we need is AnyConnect.

## "Do I Know This Already?" Quiz

The "Do I Know This Already?" quiz helps you determine your level of knowledge on this chapter's topics before you begin. Table 3-1 details the major topics discussed in this chapter and their corresponding quiz sections.

**Table 3-1** *"Do I Know This Already?" Section-to-Question Mapping*

| Foundation Topics Section | Questions |
|---|---|
| Full Tunnel VPN Technology Overview | 1, 2, 3, 8, 9, 10 |
| Deploying Your First Full-Tunnel AnyConnect SSL VPN Solution | 4 |
| Client IP Address Allocation | 5, 7 |
| Advanced Controls for Your Environment | 6 |
| Troubleshooting the AnyConnect Client | 11, 12 |

1. Which of the following are available methods of connection using the AnyConnect Secure Mobility Client? (Choose all that apply.)

   a. IKEv1

   b. IKEv2

   c. SSL

   d. PPTP

2. When preparing to deploy a full-tunnel VPN connection that will provide for users running delay-sensitive voice and video applications, which protocol should you consider using?

   a. SSL

   b. IKEv2

   c. DTLS

   d. IKEv1

3. By default, how many message pairs are exchanged in a typical IKEv2 connection?

   a. 2

   b. 4

   c. 5

   d. 6

4. When preparing to deploy a full-tunnel SSL VPN connection, which of the following are not typical configuration steps required? (Choose all that apply.)

   a. Configure ASA interface IP address

   b. Configure split tunneling

   c. Configure connection profiles

   d. Configure SSL/DTLS on the ASA interfaces

5. Which of the following are available methods for remote user IP address assignment? (Choose all that apply.)

   a. DHCP

   b. Local address pools

   c. Authentication servers

   d. BOOTP

6. Which method can be used to prevent user web traffic from traveling through the VPN tunnel?

   a. ACLs

   b. DAPs

   c. Split tunneling

   d. Group policies

7. When configuring IP address-allocation methods for your remote users, which of the following objects can they be bound to? (Choose all that apply.)

   a. User direct assignment

   b. Group policies

   c. Connection profiles

   d. DAPs

8. Which message during the SSL connection-establishment phase contains the cipher suites available on the remote client?

   a. ServerHello

   b. ClientHello

   c. Certificate

   d. ChangeCipherSpec

9. How many IKE message-exchange phases are involved during an IKEv2 connection establishment?

   a. 1

   b. 2

   c. 4

   d. 6

10. During which IKEv2 exchange is the first CHILD_SA created?

    a. IKE_SA_INIT

    b. IKE_AUTH

11. When troubleshooting an error during AnyConnect client VPN establishment, which tab in the AnyConnect client can provide you with a step-by-step explanation of the connection process?

    a. Preferences

    b. Statistics

    c. Message History

    d. Routes

12. When troubleshooting an error with your AnyConnect client installation with the assistance of a TAC engineer, which module can you use to provide them with all client, system, and module information available?

    a. NAM

    b. DART

    c. Telemetry

    d. SBL

## Foundation Topics

# Full SSL VPN Technology Overview

There is no doubt about it: The AnyConnect Secure Mobility Client is the future of Cisco's remote client VPN strategy and is worth keeping an eye on, as more features are added to it with each release of code for the Adaptive Security Appliance (ASA). With the addition of Internet Key Exchange Version 2 (IKEv2; RFC 4306), support in ASA Version 8.4(1), and the AnyConnect Secure Mobility Client 3.0.1, we can provide our remote users with not only a flexible and scalable remote-access VPN deployment but also a future-proof and highly secure one.

The AnyConnect client operates by building a Secure Sockets Layer/Transport Layer Security (SSL/TLS), Datagram Transport Layer Security (DTLS), or IKEv2 connection and tunneling remote user application traffic through the established session, as shown in Figure 3-1.

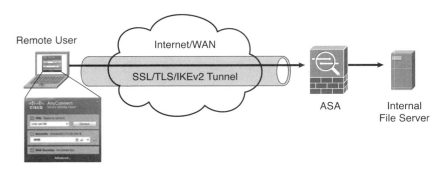

**Figure 3-1**    *Full-Tunnel VPN Connection*

The advantage of a full-tunnel connection is the ability to natively support applications that would otherwise require access either using plug-ins, smart tunnels, or port forwarding when operating through a clientless SSL VPN connection (for example, Remote Desktop Plug-in [RDP], Telnet). Another advantage of the AnyConnect client is the ability of the ASA administrator to configure either the automatic installation/update and removal of the client software during and after a connection attempt or to keep the AnyConnect client installed on the user's device for further use at another time. As a result, the AnyConnect client is becoming the preferred method of full-tunnel VPN connections over the older IPsec VPN client software.

> **Key Topic**

### SSL/TLS

The AnyConnect client was first released with SSL/TLS support to replace the older SVC (SSL VPN client), which had been released with ASA code Version 7.1 to complement the first release of WebVPN support on the ASA devices—or as we know it now, clientless SSL VPN.

SSL/TLS protocols have the advantage of being mature and widely adopted by clients, servers, and the Internet community as a whole. We encounter SSL/TLS on a daily basis when browsing and shopping on the web, because these protocols allow online merchants and site owners to secure the traffic between their servers and a visitor's browser, providing for data confidentiality and integrity. In addition, SSL/TLS is often deployed alongside Public Key Infrastructure (PKI) to provide a visitor to a site the advantage of authenticating the device they are connecting to with the help of a third-party certificate authority (CA). This section provides a brief review of SSL/TLS and the connection process that is carried out between a client and server. For an in-depth discussion of the SSL/TLS protocols, take a look at Chapter 9, "Deploying a Clientless SSL VPN Solution."

Three versions of the SSL protocol are available, as are two versions of the TLS protocol:

■   SSL 1.0 (deprecated)

■   SSL 2.0 (not recommended for use in production environments)

■   SSL 3.0

■   TLS 1.1 (SSL 3.1)

■   TLS 1.2

SSL is a proprietary protocol developed by Netscape in 1994. Because of the heavy use of the protocol in its own browser and Microsoft adopting the protocol, SSL saw widespread use among the Internet community. In 1999, the IETF published the TLS 1.1 standard, which has been unofficially labeled SSL 3.1 because of its similarities to the SSL 3.0 protocol. However, significant differences exist between SSL and TLS that prohibit their interoperation. TLS 1.2 is the latest version of TLS to be developed by the IETF. As we all prefer the open standards here, we continue our discussion by using *TLS* to refer to both the SSL and TLS protocols.

Because of the inherent weaknesses in the older versions of SSL, SSL 1.0 and SSL 2.0 are no longer supported in many operating systems and Internet browsers.

The TLS negotiations between client and server involve the negotiation of the protocol supported between them. The client sends the protocols supported in order of priority from latest version to earliest (TLS1.2, TLS1.1, SSL 3.0). The receiving server looks through its own supported protocols and chooses the latest protocol version it has that matches the client's version.

The TLS protocol is situated between the session and transport layers of the Open Systems Interconnection (OSI) model, as shown in Figure 3-2. TLS does not include any mechanism for reliable packet delivery or reordering. Instead, the protocol relies on other higher-layer protocols in the OSI model for ordered and guaranteed delivery of packets. TCP is the transport layer of choice for this situation with its sequencing, reordering, and reliable delivery functionality.

TLS transports information between clients and servers in messages called records. Records provide a common framework for the packaging of transported data and therefore do not require any changes to be made to application layer data before it is sent and received through the tunnel. (For further information about the record packet format, see

Chapter 9.) However, before application data can be transported securely between clients and servers, a TLS tunnel must be created.

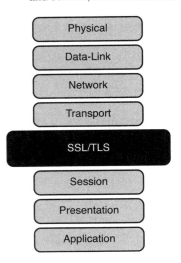

**Figure 3-2**   *SSL/TLS Protocol Implementation in the OSI Layer*

A TLS tunnel is created by using a handshake mechanism between client and server, during which all authentication, privacy, and integrity protocols are negotiated, and random numbers (nonces) are exchanged for the purposes of encryption key creation. We will review each step of the handshake process, illustrated in Figure 3-3, in further detail.

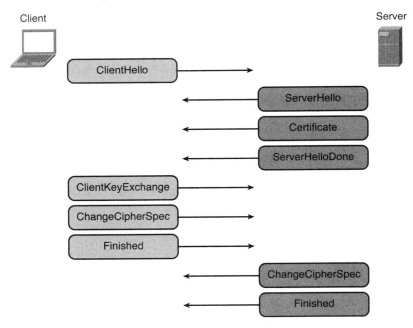

**Figure 3-3**   *TLS Handshake Process*

The process begins with the client sending a ClientHello to the server. In the ClientHello packet, the client includes a list of supported cipher suites that include the supported encryption, authentication, and integrity protocols in a form similar to TLS_RSA_WITH_DES_CBC_SHA. In addition, the client includes the following:

- **A session ID:** If the client is resuming an already established session, the session ID is the same as the original session ID. However, if this is a new session, the session ID is Null.

- **Compression schemes** supported by the client.

- **The latest SSL/TLS protocol version supported:** For example, 3.1: TLS 1.1, 3.0: SSL 3.0.

- **A random number** used by both the client and server for the purposes of generating a master encryption key (secret). The random number is a combination of the client's or server's date and time and a 28-byte pseudo-random number.

After receiving the ClientHello packet, the server responds with its own ServerHello packet, which includes the chosen compression schemes (if any were included in the received ClientHello), its latest SSL/TLS protocol version, a cipher suite that matches the protocols and versions included in the ClientHello packet, and its own random number. At this point in the conversation, the client and server have successfully negotiated the necessary encryption, authentication, and integrity protocols.

Shortly after, the server sends the client the certificate packet that includes a copy of its digital certificate. Upon receipt, the client checks the validity of the certificate by first making sure it has a certificate for the CA that issued the server's certificate among the list of trusted root CA certificates. If a trusted CA certificate exists, the client can use the CA's public key stored in the certificate against the key that signed the server's certificate. If all is still okay, the client then validates the fields in the server's certificate by making sure the validity period (issued from and to) is in the current date and time configured on its system, the server's hostname matches the name in the certificate file, and the certificate serial number is not present on any current certificate revocation lists (CRL).

After sending its certificate, the server sends the ServerHelloDone packet to the client, indicating it has no more information to send.

The client sends a ClientKeyExchange message to the server, which includes the protocol version number originally sent in the ClientHello message, to prevent replay attacks, and a pre_master secret. The pre_master secret is used by both the client and server to generate the master secret. The pre_master secret can vary in length and the information carried within it depending on the cipher suite negotiated in earlier messages. Before being sent, it is encrypted using the server's public key obtained from its certificate.

The server decrypts the received ClientKeyExchange message using its private key matching the public key from its certificate. The client and server now use the pre_master secret, along with both random numbers exchanged in each of the hello messages and a pseudo random function to generate the master encryption key. This key is then divided equally to create the keys used for message encryption, encryption algorithm initialization vectors and integrity-checking purposes.

The client sends a ChangeCipherSpec message to the server as a sign that everything sent from now on will be encrypted using the keys and protocols as established in the earlier messages, followed by a Finish message.

The server sends the client a ChangeCipherSpec message to indicate that everything sent from now on will also be encrypted, followed by a Finish message.

What might seem like a lengthy process occurs in seconds without any user interaction (unless a certificate or protocol error is encountered). After the tunnel has established successfully, it can be used to transport application data between the server and client.

## DTLS

> **Key Topic**

Recall that TCP is used by SSL/TLS because of the need for support for message reordering, retransmission, and reliable delivery purposes. However, for many delay-sensitive protocols (for example, voice and video), the benefits of TCP are often sacrificed to make way for faster transmission of data using User Datagram Protocol (UDP), so a problem surfaced when network designers and engineers needed to send delay-sensitive applications through an SSL/TLS tunnel. For this reason, DTLS (RFC 4347) was born. DTLS is based on the original implementation of TLS, but instead operates using the UDP transport protocol for faster packet delivery. Additional parameters, fields, and functions allow it to provide reliable message delivery, message reordering, fragmentation, and anti-replay natively.

To provide the functions of message reordering and reliable delivery, the DTLS protocol has added two new fields to the TLS record layer format: the Sequence Number and the Epoch. The sequence number increments for each packet sent between the client and server. DTLS also uses a windowing system for anti-replay purposes, providing the protocol to be able to distinguish between packets that are yet to be received and should be processed further and packets that have already been received. (Any packets containing sequence numbers in this range should be dropped.)

Unlike the implicit sequence number used by TCP, the sequence number in DTLS is defined explicitly. Therefore, there is a potential for a client or server taking part in many DTLS conversations and encountering DTLS packets from different conversations using the same sequence number. For this reason, the Epoch field is used to distinguish the different conversations that may be occurring at the same time. The Epoch field begins at zero during the handshake process and increments each time a ChangeCipherSpec packet is sent. Although the Epoch is reset to zero each time the handshake occurs between client and server, it is suggested that because of the minimal number of conversations that will require a "re-handshake," this should not pose much of an overlapping-conversations problem.

In addition to the changes DTLS makes to the TLS protocol, as described previously, the protocol can also prevent potential denial-of-service (DoS) attacks by using an optional authentication cookie mechanism that is inserted into the handshake phase. Using an authentication cookie allows the server to validate the identity of the client by replying to the client with a HelloVerifyRequest message after receiving a ClientHello message. The HelloVerifyRequest message contains the authentication cookie generated by the server. Upon receipt of the HelloVerifyRequest packet, the client sends the server another ClientHello that this time contains the received authentication cookie using a new "cookie" field created explicitly by DTLS in the ClientHello packet for carrying the authentication cookie. The server can now confirm the identity of the client on receiving and validating the authentication cookie, as shown in Figure 3-4.

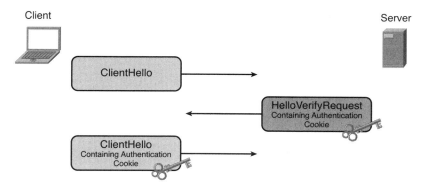

**Figure 3-4**  *DTLS Authentication Cookie Client Identity Verification Process (DoS Mitigation)*

Although this process describes the use of the HelloVerifyRequest packet sent by the server for sending the authentication cookie, this packet has also been added to the existing TLS handshake phase for providing state information. For example, DTLS prevents against packet loss using timers on the client and server. After the client has started a new handshake by sending the ClientHello packet to a server, it starts a timer (based loosely on the TCP RTT). Upon receipt of the ClientHello, the server replies to the client with a HelloVerifyRequest packet, and the client resets the timer. If the original ClientHello message had been dropped because of congestion in the path between the client and server, the server does not receive a packet and therefore does not respond to the client. The client's timer will expire, resulting in the client sending a new ClientHello message to the server.

So, you can see that in addition to using UDP to overcome the speed limitations that can be imposed on delay-sensitive applications with TCP, DTLS has extended TLS to provide for similar functions carried out by TCP but still allows delay-sensitive applications to enjoy the faster transmission offered by using UDP without additional overhead.

The AnyConnect client supports the use of DTLS with the addition of a native TLS tunnel. If at any point during communications the DTLS tunnel is torn down between the client and server, the AnyConnect client can fall back to the established TLS tunnel for data transmission.

## IKEv2

The original IKEv1 protocol has been around for many years and enjoys widespread deployment in site-to-site VPN tunnels and remote-access VPNs. The Cisco IPsec VPN client supports the IKEv1 protocol for the purposes of establishing an IPsec remote-access connection. However, difficulties were encountered with the complexity of IKEv1 and its implementation. In addition, the protocol lacked initial support for the extended capabilities required by remote clients (for example, NAT-Traversal), which ultimately led to many vendors implementing their own versions of required features, even though additional standards had later been created to provide for a standardized application of NAT-T, legacy authentication, and remote-address acquisition.

Both IKEv1 and IKEv2 use UDP for the encapsulation and transmission of information between peers. Although the header format used by both protocol implementations is similar enough to allow them to simultaneously use the same UDP port (500), the two protocols cannot interoperate with each other.

IKEv2 (RFC 4306) was created to simplify and streamline the processes and architecture of IKEv1. So, IKEv2 (RFC 4306) combines the contents of the ISAKMP (RFC 2048), IKE (RFC 2409), Internet Domain of Interpretation (RFC 2407), NAT-Traversal, legacy authentication, and remote-address acquisition, which had previously been documented separately.

IKEv2 has streamlined the original IKEv1 packet exchanges during Phase 1 and Phase 2 operation (Main mode, Aggressive mode, and Quick mode) used to create IKE and IPsec security associations (SA) for a secure communications tunnel. IKEv1 uses either nine messages (Main mode = 6 + Quick mode = 3) or six messages (Aggressive mode = 3 + Quick mode = 3) for successful operation. However, IKEv2 introduces a new packet-exchange process using just four messages. A successful message exchange involves a pair of messages. IKEv2 uses the following new exchange types (which are used either for Phase 1 or Phase 2 operation) to replace the IKEv1 Main mode, Aggressive mode, and Quick modes:

- IKE_SA_INIT (Phase 1)

- IKE_AUTH (Phase 1 and 2)

The first exchange, IKE_SA_INIT, is used to negotiate the security parameters by sending IKEv2 proposals, including the configured encryption and integrity protocols, Diffie-Hellman values, and nonces (random) numbers. At this point, the two peers generate SKEYSEED (a seed security key value) from which all future IKE keys are generated. The messages that follow in later exchanges are encrypted and authenticated using keys also generated from the SKEYSEED value.

The second exchange, IKE_AUTH, operates over the IKE_SA created by the IKE_SA_INIT exchanges and is used to validate the identity of the peers and negotiate the various encryption, authentication, and integrity protocols to establish the first CHILD_SA for use by Encapsulating Security Payload (ESP) or Authentication Header (AH) in which IPsec communication occurs. Peers are validated using pre-shared keys, certificates, or Extensible Authentication Protocol (EAP) (allowing for legacy authentication methods between peers). These two exchanges are shown in Figure 3-5.

The first CHILD_SA created in the second exchange is commonly the only SA created for IPsec communication. However, if an application or peer requires the use of additional SAs to secure traffic through an encrypted tunnel, IKEv2 uses the CREATE_CHILD_SA exchange. During the CREATE_CHILD_SA exchange, new Diffie-Hellman values may be generated and cryptographic protocols used. (That is, there is no requirement for later SAs to use the same key material created during the initial IKE_SA_INIT exchange.) This behavior is similar in function to the use of Perfect Forwarding Secrecy (PFS), whereby during an IKEv1 Quick mode exchange, new Diffie-Hellman values may be used to prevent the reuse of key material created in the previous Phase 1 exchanges. You'll usually have multiple CREATE_CHILD_SA exchanges to create multiple SAs for securing data traffic, if you do not want to multiplex multiple source/destination traffic pairs over the same SA.

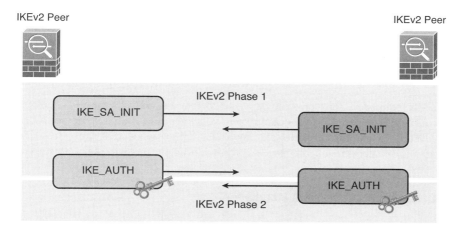

**Figure 3-5** *IKEv2 Message Exchange and Tunnel Creation Between Peers*

IKEv2 also implements a fourth exchange type: INFORMATIONAL. This message type is used to exchange error and management information between peers.

As mentioned earlier, IKEv2 was created to combine many of the existing standards used by IKEv1. For example, NAT-T is now a part of the IKEv2 standard and is a "built-in" function of the protocol, as is a keepalive function between peers allowing for an IKEv2 peer to recognize when a tunnel is down and facilitate the regeneration of the tunnel.

IKEv2 can also reduce the overhead experienced by VPN peers. For example, multiple subnets and networks may be included into an exchange and an SA created for all of them, whereas IKEv1 requires a separate SA for each subnet/network source and destination pair.

## Configuration Procedures, Deployment Strategies, and Information Gathering

As previously discussed, the AnyConnect client can support either SSL or IPsec with the introduction of IKEv2. AnyConnect exhibits the same behavior independent of the protocol in use, which allows the same policies, modules, and user mobility functions. Your choice of either protocol will come down to the security level imposed by your organization. For example, if your organization requires a very high level of protection for data incoming from a remote client, you might choose to deploy an IPsec connection using IKEv2.

We must also take into consideration the use of any current or future use of delay-sensitive applications that might require frequent use by our remote users. If so, we can implement DTLS, which requires the use of SSL/TLS rather than IKEv2 (because DTLS cannot operate over IKEv2 connections).

If the remote user base requires a mix of DTLS/TLS and IPsec connections using IKEv2, we can deploy multiple connection profiles and allow users to select a connection profile either manually in the AnyConnect client or automatically if using certificate-based authentication. The use of connection profile aliases and selection is described in detail in Chapter 2, "Configuring Policies, Inheritance, and Attributes."

Until we know and understand the *who*, *what*, *when*, and *why* of it all, we cannot accurately prepare for our deployment. An audit of the remote user base can reveal the environment a VPN deployment will cater for. The key is to understand to whom the VPN solution is being deployed, the resources they require, and the security implications (if any) that might be included with such access. This may involve talking to existing security personnel and management teams to accurately gauge the current level of internal access and the access required by the teams and departments that will be using the VPN deployment. (As you speak to people in the organization, you will notice these two do not often go hand in hand.) To gain further understanding of the current connectivity situation, any pitfalls, and improvements that can be made, it is often prudent to talk to the remote users themselves.

## AnyConnect Secure Mobility Client Installation

When installing the AnyConnect client software for use by remote users, we have two installation options:

- Web deployment

- Manual predeployment

The web deployment method enables us to publish the AnyConnect client software to our remote users through a direct URL to the ASA device. After users have browsed to the URL, the AnyConnect software can either be downloaded manually via a prompt or installed automatically. With this installation method, we can control the automatic uninstall of the client software after the remote user's VPN connection has disconnected (either because of user interaction or a timeout).

The manual predeployment method allows for the installation to be carried out interactively (manually) by either the remote users themselves or a support representative. However, we can also use the files available for use with the predeployment method (distinguished by the *predeploy* in their filename) for the automatic distribution and installation by another means other than web deployment (for example, using Microsoft group policies).

The choice ultimately depends on the environment the AnyConnect remote-access VPN will be deployed to. For example, if users are seldom in the corporate office environment and spend the majority of their time on the road, the web deployment method of installation may suit their needs because it allows for an easy automatic installation upon opening a URL to the SSL VPN service, which allows for the automatic download and installation of the client software.

For further information about each deployment method, the available files, types, and the configuration/installation on the ASA and remote user devices, see Chapter 5, "Advanced Deployment and Management of the AnyConnect Client."

# Deploying Your First Full-Tunnel AnyConnect SSL VPN Solution

When preparing to deploy your first full-tunnel AnyConnect SSL VPN on an ASA device, a number of steps must be completed before remote users can connect to the device and begin using the connection for access to internal resources:

■ **IP addressing:** The ASA device requires an IP address for the external- and internal-facing interfaces (and any demilitarized zone [DMZ] or other internal networks that may be required). Therefore, you must have the appropriate knowledge of your organization's IP addressing policy to complete this step and assign the device-required addresses.

■ **Hostname, domain name, and Domain Name System (DNS):** SSL requires the ASA to have a hostname and domain name combination configured before an RSA key pair can be generated to secure packets between the ASA and remote clients. Give your ASA a hostname and configure a domain name. In addition, configure the addresses of your organization's internal DNS servers to allow users access by fully qualified domain name (FQDN) to any internal or external resources they require through the SSL VPN tunnel after it has successfully established.

■ **Enroll with a CA and become a member of a PKI:** The use of SSL on your ASA device also requires the ASA to have an identity certificate installed, which allows for the successful authentication of the ASA.

■ **Enable the relevant interfaces for SSL/DTLS and AnyConnect client access:** Before SSL, DTLS, and AnyConnect client access can occur, you need to specify which interface the services will be available on.

■ **Create a connection profile:** In this step, create a new connection profile and enable it for use with SSL VPN connections. A connection profile provides your AnyConnect users with prelogin settings like the authentication and authorization methods, DNS servers and domain name, IP address pool, and so on.

## IP Addressing

Before your remote users and internal resources can contact each other through the ASA device, you must first assign IP addresses to the relevant interfaces of the ASA device. To assign the correct addresses to the correct interfaces, you must know the internal IP address allocation plan. Carry out this task in **Configuration > Device Setup > Interfaces**.

As shown in Figure 3-6, select the relevant interfaces from in the Interfaces window and click **Edit**. In the Edit Interface window, enter the interface name (Outside, Inside, DMZ), and assign a security level and an IP address.

## Hostname, Domain Name, and DNS

Before you can generate a certificate-signing request (CSR) to send to a CA for creation of your ASA's digital certificate, the ASA must have a hostname and domain name configured. Enter this information in the Device Name/Password pane, located via **Configuration > Device Setup > Device Name/Password**.

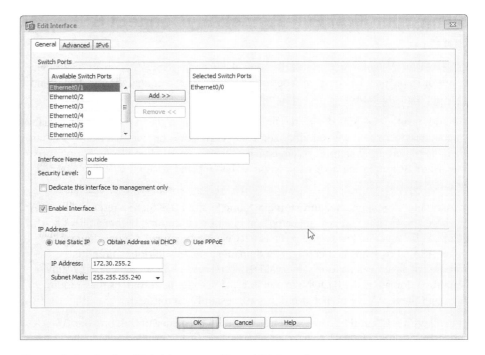

**Figure 3-6** *Assign IP Addresses to Your ASA Interfaces*

Before AnyConnect users can connect to internal resources by name or connect to the Internet through their SSL VPN tunnel, the ASA device must be configured with internal DNS server addresses. Enter the addresses in the **Configuration > Device Management > DNS > DNS Client** area of the ASDM. Optionally, you can also choose to configure a global DNS server group that applies to all DNS queries regardless of domain, or choose to configure multiple DNS server groups with up to six DNS servers in each group, with each DNS server group responsible for one domain. In addition, you can specify the time-out and retry values for each group.

### Enroll with a CA and Become a Member of a PKI

By default, the ASA device creates a self-signed certificate for SSL authentication purposes. However, to allow access to remote users outside of your organization, it is best practice to purchase a valid certificate from a trusted CA, which will prevent any certificate validation errors.

Cisco ASA customers can purchase a digital certificate at a discounted price from Entrust or can apply for a 3-month trial certificate from them. You can access more information about this offer in the ASDM by navigating to **Configuration > Remote Access VPN > Certificate Management > Identity Certificates > Enroll with Entrust** or by visiting http://www.entrust.net/cisco.

Two tasks must be completed for the successful installation and authorization of an identity certificate for your ASA:

■   Add an identity certificate

■   Add the signing root CA certificate

## Add an Identity Certificate

Unless you are generating a self-signed certificate, a CSR must be created for the purposes of sending to a CA for signing. The procedure used here to create a CSR is the same for any CA and is not specific to Entrust.

Begin by navigating to **Configuration > Remote Access VPN > Certificate Management > Identity Certificates**. In the Identity Certificates pane, click **Add** on the right side. The Add Identity Certificates window opens. This process will also create a trustpoint that will serve as a container for the configuration associated with your identity certificate for further use in the ASA. Enter a name for the trustpoint, and now you have two options:

■   **Import the identity certificate from a file:** If you are importing an identity certificate you have already purchased offline, select this option. Enter the path to the certificate file on your local device and optionally the passphrase required for access to the certificate

■   **Add a new identity certificate:** Because for this example we are creating a new CSR to send to a CA for the purposes of generating a new certificate for us, we select this option.

To continue select **New** next to the Key Pair field to create a new key pair for use with your certificate. In the Add Key Pair window, select **Enter New Key Pair Name** and enter a name for the key pair, and then select a size for the keys (512, 768, 1024, or 2048). For this example, we selected 2048 and left the Usage for the key pair as **General Purpose**. Finally, click **Generate Now**. Back in the Add Identity Certificate window, you can optionally enter values for your certificate's subject DN (for example, the FQDN of your ASA device or your company address or such). If you are creating a CSR for the purpose of sending to a public CA, the CSR generally requires the inclusion of the company name, the device FQDN, company address, country, and administrative contact details in the certificate before the certificate will be issued.

After entering the necessary information into the window as shown in Figure 3-7, click **Add Certificate**, and in the Identity Certificate Request window, save the generated CSR to your local device. You can now send the CSR to a CA for generation and retrieval of your ASA's digital certificate.

After you have received the certificate file back from the issuing CA, you can install it by selecting the generated trustpoint from the list of those shown in the Identity Certificates window and clicking **Import**. In the Import Identity Certificate window, you can either select the received file from a local path on your device or paste the contents of the received file into the window.

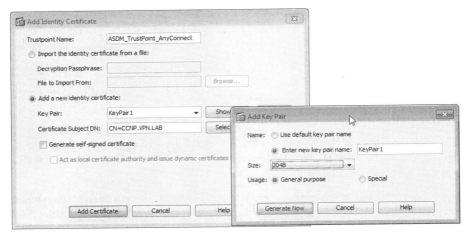

**Figure 3-7**   *Adding an Identity Certificate: CSR Generation for Your ASA*

### Add the Signing Root CA Certificate

By default, the ASA has no CA root certificates installed. So before your installed identity certificate can be validated for its authenticity by remote users, the ASA requires the certificate of the CA and intermediate CAs responsible for signing and creating the certificate installed on your device. When the CA issues an identity certificate, it usually also sends the certificates of their root CA to add. However, if you do not have a copy, it is possible to download one from the issuing CA's website. A few common locations for downloading the root CA certificates of popular public certificate authorities are as follows:

■   https://www.entrust.net/downloads/root_index.cfm

■   http://www.globalsign.com/support/intermediate-root-install.html

■   http://www.verisign.com/support/roots.html

Install the root CA certificate in **Configuration > Remote Access VPN > Certificate Management > CA Certificates.** In the CA Certificates pane, click **Add** on the right side, and the Install Certificate window opens, as shown in Figure 3-8.

In this window, enter a new trustpoint name that contains the configuration for this CA certificate. You can then install the certificate from a file on your local device, paste the certificate file contents into the window, or retrieve the certificate automatically using Secure Certificate Enrollment Protocol (SCEP). (Details about SCEP and the protocol's function with certificate retrieval are covered in Chapter 4, "Advanced Authentication and Authorization of AnyConnect VPNs.") After selecting the appropriate installation method, click **Install Certificate**, and the CA certificate will be displayed in the CA Certificates window.

### Enable the Interfaces for SSL/DTLS and AnyConnect Client Connections

Now you can enable SSL on the outside interface and optionally DTLS (DTLS is automatically enabled when SSL is selected) in the AnyConnect Connection Profiles window

(**Configuration > Remote Access VPN > Network (Client) Access > AnyConnect Connection Profiles**), shown in Figure 3-9.

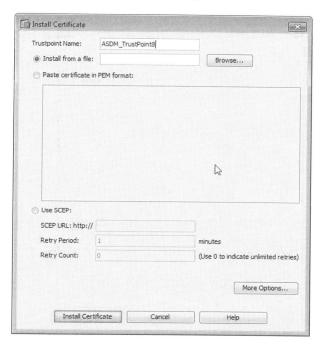

**Figure 3-8**  *Add CA Certificate Window*

SSL and DTLS can be enabled on the external interface by checking the **Allow Access** check box next to the outside interface under the SSL heading. You must also select **Enable Cisco AnyConnect VPN Client Access** on the interfaces selected in the table below before your ASA will accept connections from AnyConnect clients.

## Create a Connection Profile

After enabling SSL and incoming AnyConnect connections on the ASA, you can create a connection profile to allow remote users to connect into your environment.

In the Connections Profile section of the window, click **Add**, and the Add AnyConnect Connection Profile window opens, as shown in Figure 3-10.

For this example, we enter the following details in the connection profile, which will enable the correct VPN operation for our remote users:

■ **Name:** For the connection profile, we have entered the name AnyConnect Connection1.

■ **Authentication Method:** LOCAL. By selecting this option, remote users with an account configured in the ASA's local authentication database can be authenticated successfully.

For the purposes of this example, we have created a test user called **EzUser1** with a password of **security** in the local authentication database of the ASA.

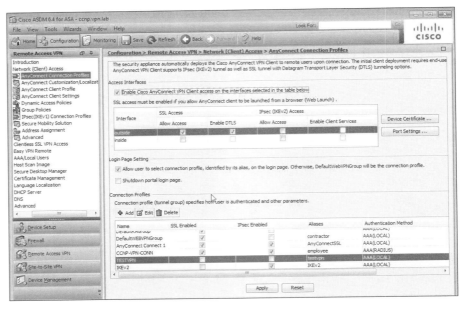

**Figure 3-9**   *Enabling AnyConnect Connections and SSL/DTLS on the ASA*

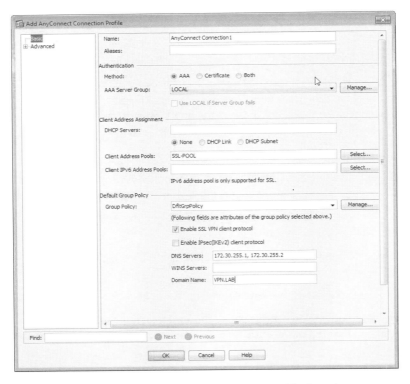

**Figure 3-10**   *Basic AnyConnect Connection Profile Creation*

As shown in Figure 3-11, we have also selected the option of **No ASDM, SSH, Telnet or Console Access,** because our test user will only require access to our SSL VPN and not have management access to the ASA.

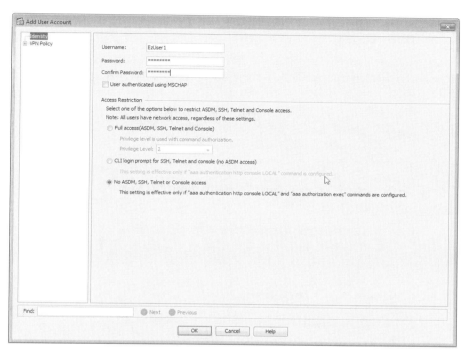

**Figure 3-11**  *Creation of Our Test Remote User EzUser1*

In this window, we also make the following choices:

- **Client Address Pool:** SSL-POOL. We have created an IP address pool that includes the address range 192.168.2.0: 192.168.2.254. We can optionally assign an IPv6 address pool to our clients only for use with the SSL full-tunnel VPN.

- **Group Policy:** We are using the default group policy (DfltGrpPolicy) object for our connection profile. However, if we had chosen to create our own group policy for the purposes of advanced or custom policy attribute assignment, we could have selected **Manage,** which would allow us to select, edit, or delete our current group policy objects or create a new one.

- **Enable SSL VPN Client Protocol:** We select this option to enable our connection profile for the SSL VPN protocol.

- **DNS Servers and Domain Name:** We enter two DNS servers for use by our AnyConnect remote users for name resolution through the SSL VPN tunnel.

Next, you create an alias and group URL for your connection profile. This will allow the remote users that may already have the AnyConnect client installed to select the connection profile from a drop-down list of available profiles in the software. (This requires users to be allowed to select a connection profile under Login Page Settings, as shown in Figure 3-9.) For remote users without the AnyConnect client installed, you must allow them to navigate to your connection profile directly in their browser by accessing a specific URL. In later chapters, we cover the advanced options available when deploying the AnyConnect client and the configuration of automatic installation when remote users open our connection profiles group URL in their browser.

For this example, we have entered an alias of AnyConnectSSL1 and a group URL of https://ccnp.vpn.lab/AnyConnectSSL1, as shown in Figure 3-12.

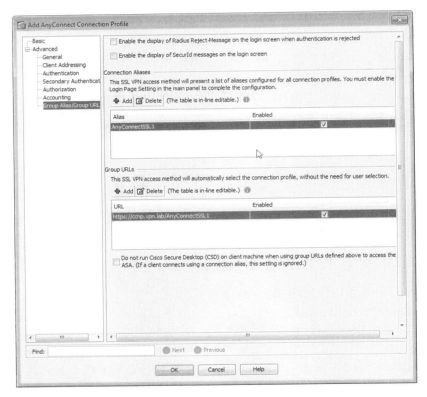

**Figure 3-12** *AnyConnect Connection Profile Alias and Group URL Configuration*

## Deploying Your First AnyConnect IKEv2 VPN Solution

The process of creating an IKEv2 AnyConnect connection is similar to those for SSL connectivity. The following steps are required for the successful deployment of an IKEv2 connection:

**Step 1.** Configure ASA interface IP addresses.

**Step 2.** Enter the hostname and domain name.

**Step 3.**   Enroll with a CA and become a member of a PKI (only if certificate-based authentication is required).

**Step 4.**   Enable the relevant interfaces for IKEv2 and AnyConnect client access. Before IKEv2 and AnyConnect client access can occur, we need to specify which interface the services will be available on.

**Step 5.**   Create a connection profile. In this step, we create a new connection profile and enable it for IKEv2 connectivity.

This section reviews only Step 4 and Step 5. Refer to the earlier SSL connectivity section for information about completing Steps 1, 2, and 3 (IP addressing, DNS, PKI, and so on).

## Enable the Relevant Interfaces for IKEv2 and AnyConnect Client Access

Begin by navigating to **Configuration > Remote Access VPN > Network (Client) Access > AnyConnect Connection Profiles** in the ASA.

As shown in Figure 3-13, you must enable IKEv2 access on the interface. When you select IKEv2, the Enable Client Services check box becomes checked automatically, which allows for profile downloads, AnyConnect client software updates, and SCEP certificate enrollment to occur.

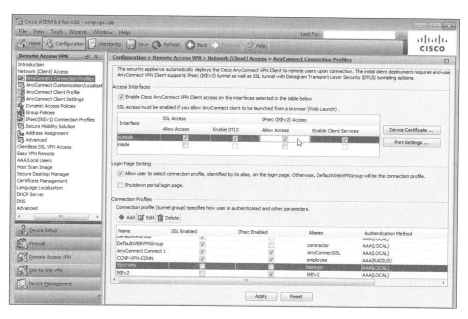

**Figure 3-13**   *Enable Incoming AnyConnect and IKEv2 Connections*

As discussed earlier, you must also select the Enable Cisco AnyConnect VPN Client Access on the interfaces selected in the table below the check box before the ASA can accept incoming AnyConnect client connections.

### Create a Connection Profile

After you have enabled IKEv2 and incoming AnyConnect connections on the ASA, you can create a connection profile to allow remote users to connect into your environment using the configured protocol.

Click **Add** in the AnyConnect Connection Profiles section of the window, and the Add AnyConnect Connection Profile window opens, as shown in Figure 3-14.

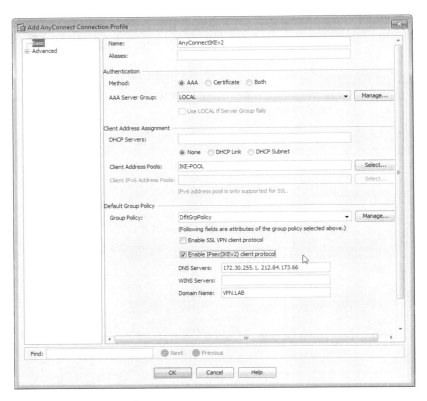

**Figure 3-14**   *Basic AnyConnect Connection Profile Creation*

In this window, we entered the name **AnyConnectIKEv2** so that our users can easily identify our connection profile. We also entered the following configuration parameters for our profile:

■   **Authentication Method:** LOCAL.

■   **Client Address Pool:** We selected a predefined IP address pool named IKE-Pool for the purposes of address assignment to our AnyConnect users.

■   **Group Policy:** We kept the default group policy (DfltGrpPolicy) object for our connection profile. However, we need to add a custom client profile object to the Dflt-GrpPolicy object for client IKEv2 authentication.

- **Enable IPsec (IKEv2) Client Protocol:** Checked.

- **DNS Servers and Domain Name:** We entered our two internal DNS servers (172.30.255.1 and 172.30.255.2), including the domain name VPN.LAB for the correct operation of name-to-IP address mappings for internal or external resources requested by our AnyConnect users.

We also entered a group URL and connection alias in the **Advanced > Group URL/Group Alias** section of the Edit Connection Profile window. This allows our users with or without the AnyConnect client to choose our new connection profile from either a drop-down list or by entering a direct URL in their browser.

In addition to the IKEv2 configuration required in our connection profile, we need to enable IKEv2 and optional authentication parameters that will be downloaded to our AnyConnect clients during their connection attempt.

We enable IKEv2 by first creating an AnyConnect client profile in the AnyConnect Client Profile window (**Configuration > Remote Access VPN > Network (Client) Access > AnyConnect Client Profile**) and then clicking **Add** to open the Add AnyConnect Client Profile window, as shown in Figure 3-15.

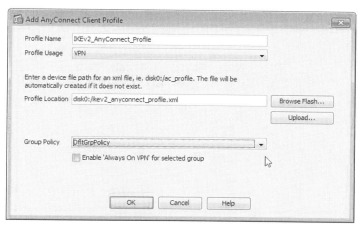

**Figure 3-15**  *AnyConnect Client Profile Creation*

We enter a name for our client profile of **IKEv2_AnyConnect_Profile**, because we are creating our profile for use by the core AnyConnect client software (not the optional modules NAM, Telemetry, and so on). We keep the default profile usage selection as VPN, and (optionally) select the location where our profile XML file will be kept, using the Profile Location field. (Unless we have a specific location where we require our client profiles to be kept on our ASA device, it is recommended to keep the default value.)

Finally, we select the default group policy object (**DfltGrpPolicy**) that our policy will be applied to (as we selected earlier). This allows for the profile to be downloaded by users of our connection profile.

**Note:**   For the purposes of this example, we are not causing any security risks by allowing IKEv2 access using the default group policy object that, if you recall, is applied to all users by default if a connection profile is not chosen before login. In a production network, it is recommended to use a custom group policy object that meets the specific security requirements of your organization. You can read about additional uses for group policies in Chapter 4.

After entering the necessary configuration information described, we click **OK** to create the new profile. We can now select our profile from the list in the AnyConnect client profile window and click **Edit** to enter our IKEv2 specific configuration.

Using the AnyConnect Client Profile Editor, we need to specify the use of IKEv2 with our ASA. Navigate to **VPN > Server List** and click **Add** to open the Server List Entry window, shown in Figure 3-16.

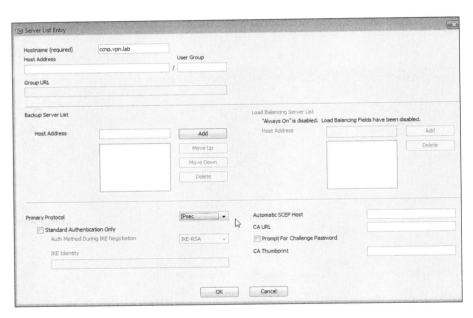

**Figure 3-16**   *AnyConnect Client Profile IKEv2 Configuration*

In the Primary Protocol section of the window, we change the protocol value in the dropdown list from SSL to IPsec. We can optionally enable IKE-RSA, EAP-MD5, EAP-MSCHAPV2, or EAP-GTC. In addition, we can enter an IKE identity used for client authentication by checking the **Standard Authentication Only** box. By default, the ASA authenticates the client using a proprietary EAP method used only with the AnyConnect client. Enabling standard authentication limits dynamic download features of the client and disables the ASA's ability to configure settings such as session timeout, idle timeout, split tunneling, split DNS, and Microsoft Internet Explorer (MSIE) proxy configurations.

IKE identity can be configured only if standard-based authentication is used along with standard EAP methods. We complete our configuration by clicking **OK** in the Server List Entry window and again in the AnyConnect Client Profile Editor to save our profile.

# Client IP Address Allocation

So far, our examples all use an IP address pool that we locally defined on the ASA device for the purposes of address assignment to our AnyConnect users.

However, there are a few methods for address allocation to choose from, depending on your internal address-assignment policy. For example, if you are using external authentication, authorization, and accounting (AAA) servers for authentication and authorization purposes, or if you have an existing internal Dynamic Host Control Protocol (DHCP) server you want to extend to your remote users, the address-allocation methods available for configuration are as follows:

- Authentication server

- DHCP

- Internal address pools

- Direct user assignment

**Key Topic**

These four methods (except direct user assignment) are tried in order until an address can be found for both AnyConnect and IPsec remote-access clients. If direct user assignment is configured, none of the remaining methods are tried.

By default, the ASA uses the authentication server and internal address pools for client address-assignment purposes based on the default address-assignment policy shown in Figure 3-17.

As shown in Figure 3-17, you can access the ASA's address-assignment policy in **Configuration > Remote Access VPN > Network (Client) Access > Address Assignment > Assignment Policy**. In this window, add DHCP by checking the **Use DHCP** option. You can remove the options of authentication servers or internal address pools by unchecking the respective boxes for each method.

In the Assignment Policy window, you can also specify the period in minutes (default 5) between the release of an IP address from an internal address pool and the subsequent assignment/reuse of the same address.

After you have specified the options required for your address-assignment policy, you can configure the specific address-assignment methods for remote AnyConnect users. Configure the address-assignment methods using the available policy attributes in the following three areas:

- Connection profile address assignment

- Group policy address assignment

- Direct user address assignment

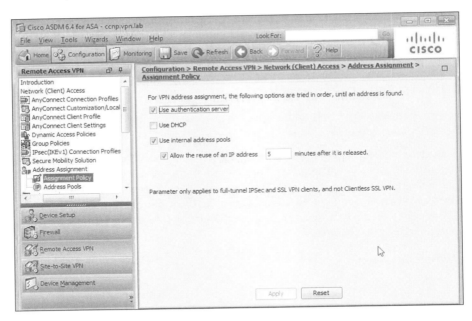

**Figure 3-17**   *ASA IP Address-Assignment Policy*

## Connection Profile Address Assignment

As you have seen in earlier configuration examples, you can add address-assignment methods to the General pane of your connection profiles. Begin by opening the relevant connection profile in **Configuration > Remote Access VPN > Network (Client) Access > AnyConnect Connection Profiles**, as shown in Figure 3-18.

In this window, the following options are available address-assignment methods to choose from:

- **DHCP Servers:** Enter the IP addresses of the available DHCP servers on the network in comma-separated form. You can enter up to 10 servers into the field, and each will be used in turn until a response is received. Your DHCP servers can either be situated on your internal, DMZ network or in an external network. By default, no DHCP options are in use (as noted by the selection of None beneath the DHCP Servers IP address field). However, DHCP servers operate by assigning IP addresses to clients based on either the IP address held in the giaddr field of a DHCP message set by the DHCP relay agent (in this case, the giaddr will be that of the ASA's address assigned to the interface facing the DHCP server, which will restrict address allocation only to one subnet, directly connected to the firewall) or the subnet on which the request had been received if the giaddr field is zero. However, youmay require the server to assign your remote clients an IP address from an internal address pool containing a subnet that is not in use anywhere else in your network. Therefore, based on the default behavior of DHCP, the server may assign your remote users an address from either an incorrect address pool or not at all. You could enable DHCP Link (RFC3527), which allows the ASA to modify the giaddr field contents to include the IP address of the interface the remote user had connected to the ASA on, in addition to using a new

Link Selection suboption to determine the subnet from which to assign IP addresses. This option is typically enabled if you require your DHCP server to allocate IP addresses to your remote users using configured scopes that contain addresses from a different subnet/network than that configured on the ASA's internal (DHCP server facing) interface.

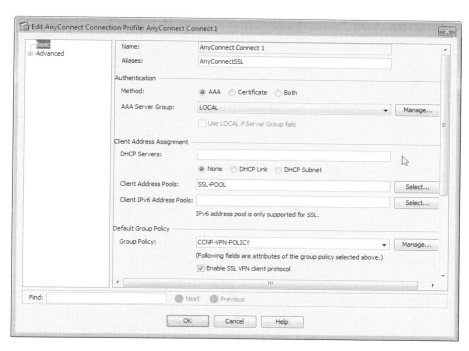

**Figure 3-18**   *Connection Profile Client Address-Assignment Methods/Properties*

- **Client Address Pools:** You have seen these in earlier configuration examples. You can either select an existing address pool by clicking **Select** and choosing one you have already configured from the list that appears in the Select Address Pool window, or select or enter (comma-separated) up to six address pools in the connection profile that will be tried (in order from left to right). If you have not yet created any address pools, you can create a new one by clicking **Add** in the Select Address Pool window.

  You can also choose to preconfigure address pools before entering the configuration mode for the connection profile/user account. You can achieve this task in the Address Pools window of the ASDM (**Configuration > Remote Access VPN > Network (Client) Access > Address Assignment > Address Pools**). In this window, you can add, edit, or delete address pools. When adding a new address pool in the Add IP Pool window, enter the following required information:

  - **Name:** Begin by entering a name for the pool that will help distinguish between other pools that may exist on the device.

  - **Starting IP Address:** Enter the starting IPv4 address of the range or subnet we are adding.

- **Ending IP Address:** Enter the last IPv4 address of the range or subnet.

- **Subnet Mask:** Either enter the subnet mask we are using with the IP address range or subnet added previously, or choose a subnet mask from the drop-down list.

■ **Client IPv6 Address Pools:** These are created using the same address pool options mentioned in the previous point, and their configurations are also stored in the Address Pools window (**Configuration > Remote Access VPN > Network (Client) Access > Address Assignment > Address Pools**). After clicking **Add** in the Address Pools window (or in the Select Address Pools window directly in the configuration of a connection profile or user account), enter a name for the pool and the start address of the pool. As soon as the ASDM notices that an IPv6 address is being entered (by the existence of a double colon (::) or colon followed by a number 1 to 9 or letter A to F (:1–9/A–F), the available fields will change from those shown in the previous point to these:

  - **Name:** Enter a name for the IPv6 address pool you are creating.

  - **Starting IP Address:** Enter the IPv6 address for the beginning of your range or subnet you are configuring for allocation to users.

  - **Prefix Length:** Enter the decimal prefix length for example /64, /48, and so on.

  - **Number of Addresses:** Enter the number of addresses used in your pool.

■ Similar to our IPv4 address pools, you can select or enter (comma-separated) up to six IPv6 address pools in a connection profile that will be tried (in order from left to right).

**Note:** It is important to note that after you have created an address pool, you cannot change the name of the pool. Therefore, if you make a mistake or require the name to be changed for any reason, you must first remove the address pool and then re-create it.

Also, you cannot create multiple address pools that contain the same addresses. Therefore, you might find it easier in the future to use a naming convention that is not connection protocol/type specific when assigning a name to your address pools, especially if you plan to assign them to many connection profiles/users accounts of differing connection methods.

### Group Policy Address Assignment

You can also select IPv4 or IPv6 address pools in the General pane of the group policy settings. Navigate to **Configuration > Remote Access VPN > Network (Client) Access > Group Policies**, select the appropriate group policy object to edit, and click **Edit**.

As shown in Figure 3-19, we begin by unchecking the **Inherit** option next to either the Address Pools or IPv6 Address Pools field or both, depending on which address-assignment method we want to deploy to our remote users. Also similar to our connection profile address pool usage, we can enter up to six address pools in a comma-separated list for use in order from right to left until all available addresses are used.

We also have the option of entering a DHCP scope with the Servers window of our group policy settings, by selecting **Servers** from the menu, also shown in the left of Figure 3-19.

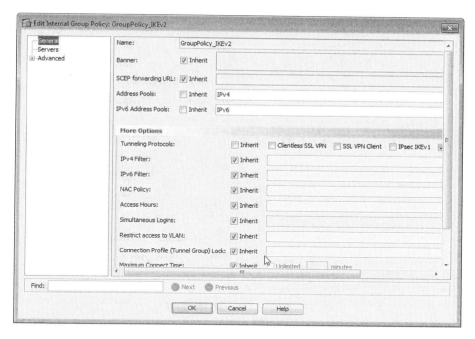

**Figure 3-19**  *Group Policy Address Pool Assignment*

In the Servers window of our group policy configuration, expand the **More Options** section to allow the DHCP Scope field to become available.

By unchecking the **Inherit** option, you can enter the IP subnet address that will be used by the ASA's internal server or an external DHCP server to choose the appropriate scope and assign an IP address. As shown in Figure 3-20, we have configured the address 192.168.1.0. During a connection attempt by a remote user, this value is used by the ASA's DHCP server to locate an available IP address from the 192.168.1.0 scope (if configured). If the DHCP server is not configured on the ASA but on a remote server, the DHCP scope configured value is set as the giaddr field by the ASA relay agent function. This makes the DHCP server also reply with a DHCP packet to the giaddr address. Therefore, you need to make sure that the value you set here is routable toward the ASA in your internal network. Otherwise, DHCP server replies will never reach the ASA.

You can configure the local DHCP server of the ASA in the following areas of the ASDM:

■ **Configuration > Device Management > DHCP > DHCP Server**

■ **Configuration > Remote Access VPN > DHCP Server**

Start by selecting an available interface from the list shown in the window and clicking **Add** to create a new DHCP scope for that interface, or click **Edit** to edit an existing one, as shown in Figure 3-21.

Table 3-2 lists the fields available when entering or editing a scope for use with the ASA's local DHCP server.

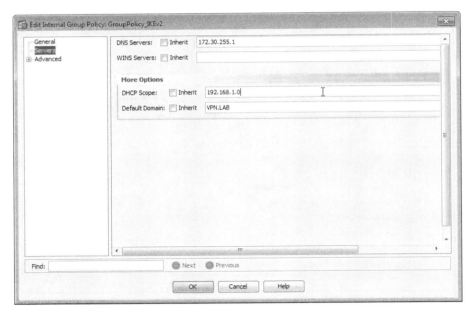

**Figure 3-20**   *DHCP Server Scope Group Policy Configuration*

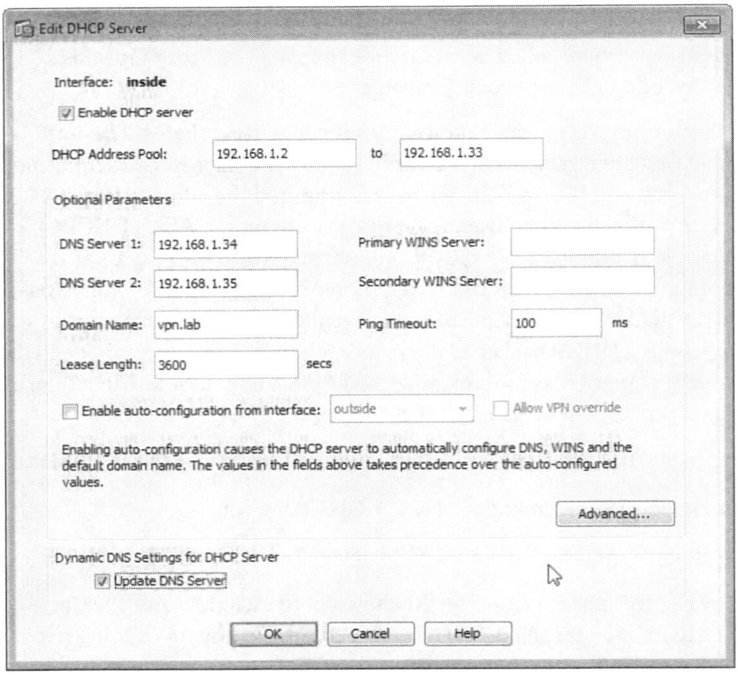

**Figure 3-21**   *ASA Local DHCP Server Configuration*

**Table 3-2**  *ASA Local DHCP Server Configuration Fields*

| Field | Description |
|---|---|
| DHCP Enabled | Select this option to enable the DHCP server for the specific interface you have chosen to configure your scope for. |
| DHCP Address Pool | Enter the start and end IP addresses of the subnet or range you want to use for the purposes of address assignment to your remote users. |
| DNS Server 1 | Enter the IP address of a DNS server in use in the network of the interface you are using or that is available to the IP addresses in the scope you are configuring. |
| DNS Server 2 | Enter the IP address of a secondary DNS server if you have one available. |
| Primary WINS Server | Enter the IP address of any WINS servers that may be available to remote Windows users assigned an IP address in this scope. |
| Secondary WINS Server | Enter the IP address of a secondary WINS servers if available. |
| Domain Name | Enter the default domain name that will be used by your remote users to prefix against any devices they might attempt to access by name. |
| Lease Length | Enter the amount of time in seconds that an IP address lease will last before the DHCP server can reclaim it back if there is no further communication with the client. Normally, after half of the lease time, the client should try to increase the lease time again to its maximum value. This is a proactive way for the client to try to keep its IP address assigned. |
| Ping Timeout | Enter an amount of time in milliseconds that the DHCP server should wait for a response before assuming the IP address it is attempting to offer to a remote user is available (not already assigned). |
| Enable Auto-Configuration from Interface | Enable this option if you are retrieving all the information in the previous fields (that is, DNS, WINS, domain name, and so on) dynamically from a source on the interface selected. This will allow you to use the dynamically learned information and give this to remote users to use. However, if you have configured any addresses explicitly using the fields mentioned earlier, this will be preferred over any dynamically learned information. |
| Update DNS Server | Select this option if you want to enable dynamic DNS updates. Any remote users assigned an IP address from your DHCP scope will also have their corresponding DNS entry information updated. |

The benefit of assigning your address pools to group policies instead of in your connection profiles is the automatic assignment of the same address pool to multiple connection profiles if they have the same group policy object applied. If you have many connection profiles configured on your device, this can save you a great deal of configuration time.

### Direct User Address Assignment

This option enables you to assign a specific IP address to remote users if, for example, you are tracking their use, have enabled specific access rules/lists in your environment for the address you are assigning them, and so forth.

Enter the specific IP address in a remote user's local account properties by first selecting the appropriate user account in **Configuration > Remote Access VPN > AAA/Local Users > Local Users**, and then clicking **Edit**.

In the Edit User Account window, shown in Figure 3-22, choose the **VPN Policy** item from the menu on the left, and then in the VPN Policy window, locate the Dedicated IP address (Optional) section and enter the IP address and the subnet mask.

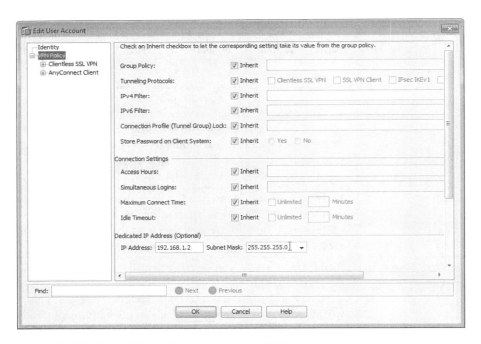

**Figure 3-22**   *Enter Direct User Assignment IP Address*

## Advanced Controls for Your Environment

Now that we have provided our remote users with connectivity into our environment and allocated them an IP address for communication with our internal resources, we need to control the access they have to our corporate environment and internal resources or allow them access to the resources on their local network (for example, a network-attached

printer) while at the same time remaining connected to the VPN and able to access resources through it. Furthermore, we can restrict the time of day they are able to connect
into our environment using the VPN. For example, we might want to allow users access to
our internal resources only during working hours (for example, 9 a.m. until 6 p.m.).

Carry out these tasks by using one of the following methods:

- Access control lists (ACL) and downloadable ACLs

- Split tunneling

- Access hours/time range

## ACLs and Downloadable ACLs

Access control lists can be applied to remote users through the use of a group policy,
DAPs (Dynamic Access Policies), or directly to their local user account configured on the
ASA. You can configure standard ACLs to either permit or deny access from a remote user
to an internal subnet or specific destination, or you can configure an extended ACL to either permit or deny a remote user access to an internal resource based on the source/desti-
nation/protocol/port parameters (depending on the level of granularity you require for
your rules).

You configure global ACLs in **Configuration > Firewall > Advanced > ACL Manager**,
shown in Figure 3-23.

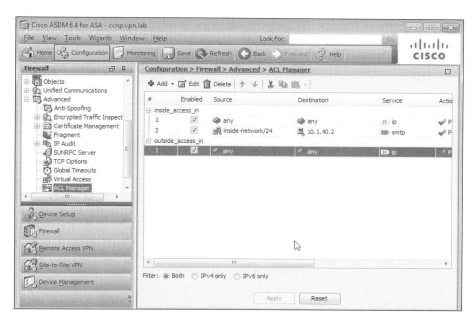

**Figure 3-23**  *ASDM ACL Manager Window*

Begin your ACL configuration by creating a new ACL and then creating the associated
access control entries (ACE). The ACL performs the role of a container, and the ACEs

contained in the ACL each hold the specific rule information you configure. For our example, we create a new ACL to limit Secure Shell (SSH) access from the remote user IP address 192.168.2.111 to the internal server address 172.16.30.13 on port 22. All other traffic will be blocked by the default implicit **deny any any rule** at the end of the ACL. We begin by clicking **Add > Add ACL** in the ACL Manager window. When prompted, we give our ACL the name **Server_SSH_ACCESS**. Next, we select our new ACL from the list shown in the ACL Manager window and click **Add > Add ACE**.

As shown in Figure 3-24, we configure our ACE with the following details:

- **Action:** Permit

- **Source:** 192.168.2.111

- **Destination:** 172.16.30.13

- **Service:** SSH

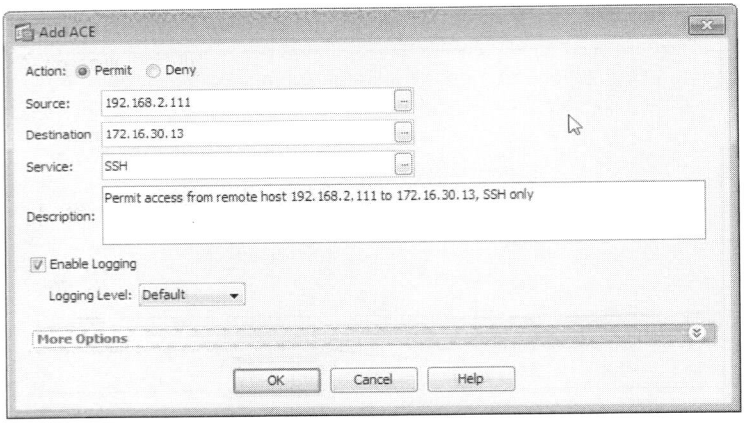

**Figure 3-24** *ASDM ACE Configuration*

We have also entered a description for us and other firewall administrators to easily identify the rule in the future. In addition, we have left the default Enable Logging checked, which creates a log of all packets dropped as a cause of this rule (if the action had been deny).

After we have created our new ACL and associated ACE entry, we can assign them to a group policy or local user account on the ASA. For this example, we are assigning our ACL to a group policy object.

As shown in Figure 3-25, we select our group policy object in the group policy pane located at **Configuration > Remote Access VPN > Network (Client) Access > Group Policies** and click **Edit**. In the Edit Internal Group Policy <policy name> window, we uncheck the **Inherit** option next to IPv4Filter or IPv6Filter (depending on the IP protocol in use and for which the ACL has been configured). In this example, we choose IPv4 and use the drop-down list that appears to select our newly created ACL.

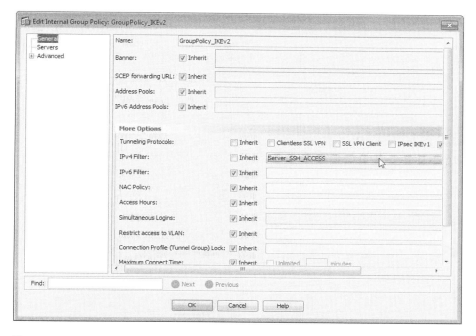

**Figure 3-25**  *Group Policy ACL Assignment*

Downloadable ACLs are configured on a remote AAA server for direct assignment to users during a successful authentication attempt. The downloaded ACLs are merged with any locally configured ACLs by adding the specific rules/ACEs to the end of the configured list. Downloadable ACL configuration is beyond the scope of this book. For future reference, however, it is important to know it exists.

## Split Tunneling

Split tunneling provides a way to control access through a VPN connection by specifying the destination networks, subnets, or hosts a remote user must use the VPN tunnel for to access, Access to all remaining (unspecified) destinations is sent to the destination directly and not through the VPN tunnel.

By default, all remote user packets are sent through the VPN tunnel toward the ASA. For this reason, there are two common scenarios for the deployment of split tunneling:

■   Allowing users access to devices on their local LAN connection (for example, a network printer).

■   Preventing remote user Internet traffic from traversing the VPN tunnel and causing unnecessary overhead on the ASA device and consumption of available bandwidth.

Many corporations in the past have preferred for remote user web traffic to travel through the VPN tunnel for the purposes of web filtering. For example, they may have a centralized web-filtering device in their network that denies, allows, or logs user access to specific websites. However, with the use of the optional Web Security module for the AnyConnect client, organizations can now use a decentralized cloud-based web security deployment through the use of Cisco IronPort devices, removing the requirement for all web traffic to traverse the VPN tunnel.

For the correct split-tunneling operation, you must configure both split tunneling in the group policy applied to remote users through a connection profile or user account directly and in the AnyConnect client software. The AnyConnect client configuration can be achieved either through a client profile or the users enabling the option manually.

The first step in configuring split tunneling is to assign the policy behavior (which networks will be tunneled through the VPN) and optionally a network list (only standard ACLs are supported) that will be used, along with the policy, to identify the network addresses that will or will not be tunneled. Select the group policy object from **Configuration > Remote Access VPN > Network (Client) Access > Group Policies**, click **Edit**, and in the Edit Internal Group Policy <policy name> window, navigate to the **Advanced > Split Tunneling** pane using the menu on the left, shown in Figure 3-26.

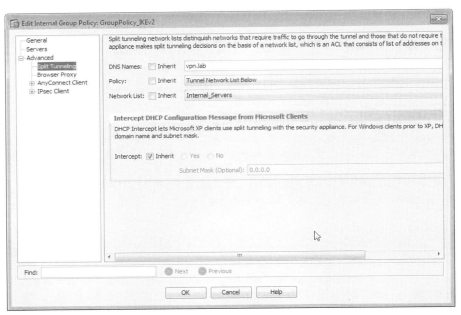

**Figure 3-26**   *Group Policy Split-Tunneling Configuration*

For this example, we have configured our split-tunneling policy to only Tunnel Network List Below and have identified the networks/subnets to be tunneled by using the standard ACL Internal_Servers that we have configured to contain our internal subnet (192.168.1.0). The resulting behavior is all traffic to the subnet 192.168.1.0 travels through the established VPN connection, and all remaining traffic (Internet, local LAN, and so on) travels directly to the destination from the remote user's device without first traveling through the tunnel. We have two other options when choosing a policy behavior: Tunnel All Networks (default) and Exclude Network List Below. The latter also requires the use of an ACL for network/subnet identification. We can also optionally enable DHCP intercept for use with Windows XP machines. By configuring this option, the ASA can intercept DHCP inform messages sent by Windows XP machines and reply back with the domain name, subnet mask, and a list of internal routes to networks/subnets through the VPN tunnel. We can also optionally configure a subnet mask that will be provided to users' Windows XP devices.

After completing the group policy configuration, you can configure your remote user settings. As mentioned earlier, you can do so either manually by the remote user in the Any-Connect client or by the configuration of a client profile on the ASA, which will be downloaded by AnyConnect clients during their connection attempt and optionally remove the ability of remote users to manually disable or enable our configuration.

Figure 3-27 shows the Enable Local LAN Access option that can be configured manually by a remote user in the AnyConnect client settings. This option is available by clicking the **Advanced** link in the AnyConnect client software and, in the AnyConnect Secure Mobility Client window that opens, selecting **VPN, Preferences**. By default, the Enable Local LAN Access option is unchecked, meaning split tunneling is not in effect even if configured on the ASA.

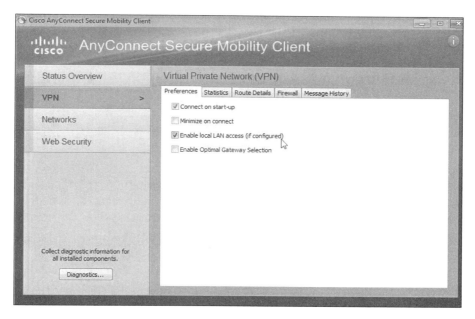

**Figure 3-27**    *AnyConnect Enable Local LAN Access (Split Tunneling)*

You can also configure the local LAN access setting in an AnyConnect client profile that will be automatically downloaded and implemented by the AnyConnect client during the remote user's connection attempt, as shown in Figure 3-28.

You can edit or create new AnyConnect client profiles in **Configuration > Remote Access VPN > Network (Client) Access > AnyConnect Client Profile**. In the AnyConnect client profile, we select the **Preferences (Part 1)** option from the menu on the left and select **Local LAN Access**. Optionally, you can remove the Enable Local LAN Access option from our remote user's AnyConnect client software to prevent them from removing the setting we have configured by unchecking the **User Controllable** check box next to Local LAN Access. As we progress through the advanced AnyConnect chapters that follow, you will see the use of AnyConnect client profiles in detail.

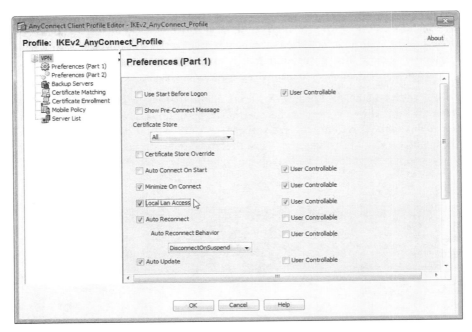

**Figure 3-28**   *AnyConnect Client Profile Local LAN Access Setting*

## Access Hours/Time Range

In addition to controlling remote user access in your environment by using ACLs and split tunneling, you can control when they can or cannot connect during a specific day or week (for example, Monday to Friday, 9 a.m. to 6 p.m.).

You can configure the access hours your VPN will be available by using a global time range that can be applied either to our ASA's local users directly or in your group policies.

A time range is configured by navigating to **Configuration > Firewall > Objects > Time Ranges** and clicking **Add**.

In the Add Time Range window, assign a name to the new time range, and then choose the start and end times. By default, the time range starts immediately and continues to run. However, you can specify a date and time in the future for when the time range will start and, optionally, when it will end. You can configure a recurring time range to specify the days and hours that your time range will take effect by clicking **Add** in the Recurring Time Ranges section of the window.

As shown in Figure 3-29, in the Add Recurring Time Range window, you can select the days of the week that our time range will be in effect (for example, weekdays, weekends, individual days, and so on) and, optionally, the times during these days thaty our time range will be in effect. Optionally, you can specify a weekly interval that your time range will run for (for example, from Monday at 0900 until Friday at 1800).

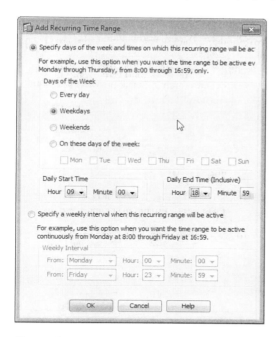

**Figure 3-29**  *ASA Time Range Configuration*

After you have created your time range, you can assign it to a local user account config-ured on the ASA by selecting the appropriate user account from the list available in **Configuration > Remote Access VPN > Network (Client) Access > AAA/Local Users > User Accounts** and clicking **Edit** to open the user account properties. In the Edit User Ac-count window, uncheck the **Inherit** check box, and then select the time range using the drop-down list that appears.

You can also assign a time range to a group policy, as shown in Figure 3-30. We begin by selecting our group policy object in **Configuration > Remote Access VPN > Network (Client) Access > Group Policies** and clicking **Edit**. In the Edit Internal Group Policy <pol-icy name> window, we expand the **More Options** section of the General pane, uncheck the **Inherit** check box, and select the time range from the drop-down list that appears.

## Troubleshooting the AnyConnect Secure Mobility Client

You can troubleshoot the AnyConnect client and any connectivity errors that may be oc-curring by using the tools and statistics/information that are available either in the Any-Connect client or with the installation of the optional DART (Diagnostic and Reporting Tool) module.

The AnyConnect Client Statistics tab, available in the **Advanced > VPN > Statistics** sec-tion of the client software, can provide you with a great deal of important information about the user's current connection state, the amount of information sent and received through the tunnel, the current protocols in use, IP addresses, and policies. For example, the Statistics window in Figure 3-31 shows an established connection. We can see the client is connected, has an IP address of 192.168.2.12 assigned, and is using the RSA_AES_128_SHA_1 cipher suite. We can also see that split tunneling is enabled on the user's connection, indicated by Mode: Split Include Line. In addition to Mode: Split Include being present within the Statistics tab, we can see which specific networks are tunneled with addition of routes on the Route Details tab. By default, the only route configured is 0.0.0.0, meaning tunnel all traffic.

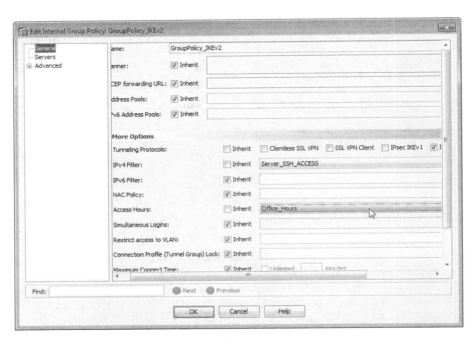

**Figure 3-30**   *Assign a Time Range to Your Group Policy Object*

On the Message History tab, you can also view the step-by-step approach the client software has taken when trying to establish a connection. This tab, shown in Figure 3-32, provides an invaluable source of information when troubleshooting client connectivity or possible software incompatibilities, because you can see the last step that was taken by the client software before a connection attempt failed or succeeded, in addition to any errors that might have occurred.

Figure 3-32 shows an example of the information that is available on the Message History tab. The information shown walks you through a successful connection attempt:

■   HostScan performs posture assessment and checks for installed firewall and antivirus products.

■   HostScan checks the results of the posture assessment obtained against the actions configured inside the applied DAP.

■   AnyConnect checks for client profile updates.

■   AnyConnect checks for available client software updates.

- AnyConnect checks for customization updates.
- AnyConnect performs any updates required based on the results of the last three actions.
- The AnyConnect client proceeds to activate the VPN adapter on the local VPN device and establishes a VPN tunnel to the ASA.

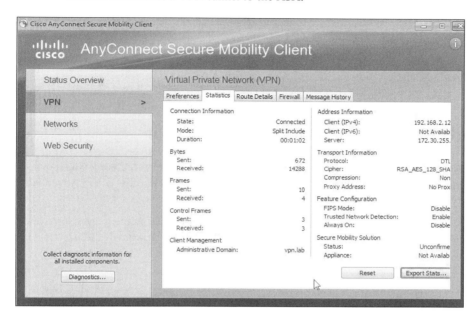

**Figure 3-31**   *AnyConnect Secure Mobility Client Connection Statistics Window*

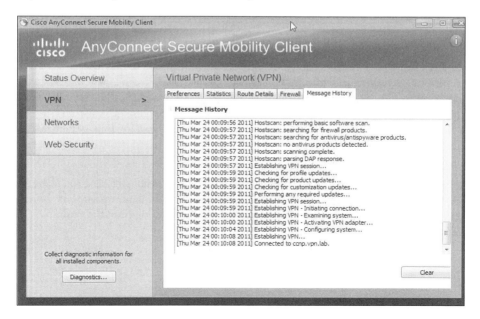

**Figure 3-32**   *AnyConnect Secure Mobility Client Connection Message History Window*

DART can be used to obtain a large amount of in-depth logging and local system information for the client software, installed modules, and user's device. This information is usually sent to a support representative or TAC engineer when troubleshooting an error with the AnyConnect client software or remote user's connection to the ASA. DART can run on Windows XP, Window Vista, Windows 7, Mac OS 10.5, Mac OS 10.6, and Linux Red Hat (32-bit versions only).

DART is an optional module and by default is not installed with the AnyConnect client software. The DART module can either be installed manually during the predeploy package installation or as a separate installation file, or you can configure the automatic download and installation of the module during the remote user's connection. To configure the automatic download and installation of the DART module, you need to upload an Any-Connect client web-deploy package that contains the DART module to our ASA. You can download these from Cisco.com (and recognize them based on the use of *dart* in the filename). You can then carry out the configuration in the group policy assigned to a remote user or connection profile. Start by opening the appropriate group policy object from **Configuration > Remote Access VPN > Network (Client) Access > Group Policies** and clicking **Edit**. In the Edit Internal Group Policy <policy name> window, select **Advanced > AnyConnect Client** from the menu on the left.

In the AnyConnect Client pane of the Edit Internal Group Policy <policy name>, uncheck the **Inherit** check box next to the Optional Client Modules to Download and use the drop-down box to select the **AnyConnect DART** module from the list, as shown in Figure 3-33.

The next time AnyConnect users connect to your VPN connection, the DART module automatically downloads and installs. When required, the DART module can be used by clicking the Diagnostics link in the Advanced options of the AnyConnect client.

After clicking the Diagnostics link in the AnyConnect client software, the user is presented with the screen shown in Figure 3-34, introducing us to DART and its purpose.

After clicking **Next** on the first screen of the DART Wizard, they are presented with the Bundle Creation Option screen, shown in Figure 3-35. In this screen, they can go with the default option of gathering all information available (client software log information, system information, module logging and information, and so on), which will be saved to their desktop in the zipped file DARTBundle.zip. Alternatively, they can select **Custom** and click **Next**. In that case, they are presented with the list of available logging, system, and module options we can either leave selected or deselect to remove them from the information-gathering process.

For this example, we use the Default option of collecting all possible information using DART. When we click Next, the DART module begins to gather all information, as shown in Figure 3-36. When DART finishes, the information is saved to our desktop in the DARTBundle.zip file.

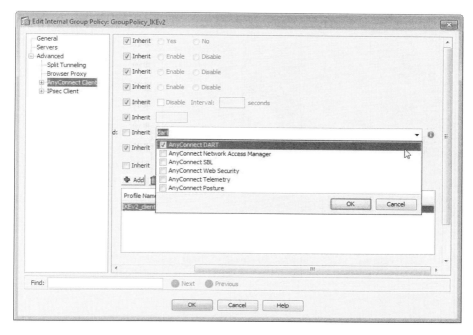

**Figure 3-33**  *Enable AnyConnect DART Module Automatic Installation*

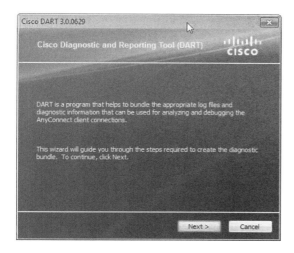

**Figure 3-34**  *AnyConnect DART First Screen*

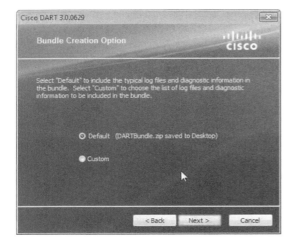

**Figure 3-35**    *AnyConnect DART: Choose Bundle Creation Type*

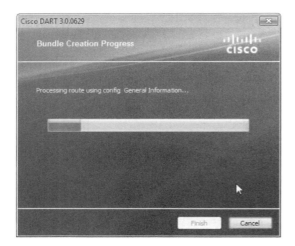

**Figure 3-36**    *AnyConnect DART: Bundle Creation Process*

# Exam Preparation Tasks

As mentioned in the section "How to Use This Book" in the Introduction, you have a couple of choices for exam preparation: the memory tables in Appendix C, Chapter 23, "Final Exam Preparation," and the exam simulation questions on the CD-ROM.

## Review All Key Topics

Review the most important topics in the chapter, noted with the Key Topic icon in the outer margin of the page. Table 3-3 lists a reference of these key topics and the page numbers on which each is found.

**Table 3-3**    *Key Topics*

| Key Topic Element | Description | Page |
| --- | --- | --- |
| Topic | SSL/TLS protocol overview | 76 |
| Topic | DTLS protocol overview | 80 |
| Topic | IKEv2 protocol overview | 81 |
| Bulleted List | SSL VPN connection configuration | 85 |
| Bulleted List | IKEv2 VPN connection configuration | 92 |
| Bulleted List | IP address-assignment methods | 97 |
| Topic | Controlling network access with ACLs | 105 |
| Topic | Configuring split tunneling | 107 |

## Complete Tables and Lists from Memory

Print a copy of Appendix C, "Memory Tables" (found on the CD), or at least the section for this chapter, and complete the tables and lists from memory. Appendix D, "Memory Tables Answer Key," also on the CD, includes completed tables and lists to check your work.

## Define Key Terms

Define the following key terms from this chapter, and check your answers in the glossary:

DART, split tunneling

This chapter covers the following subjects:

- **Authentication Options and Strategies:** In this section, we discuss the available options when choosing an advanced authentication scheme and cover certificate-mapping and certificate-validation procedures. We also review the deployment of an internal and external PKI scheme.

- **Provisioning Certificates as a Local CA:** In this section, we discuss the steps required to enable the ASA's local CA server and the provisioning of digital certificates to our users.

- **Configuring Certificate Mappings:** In this section, we look closer at certificate mappings and discuss the various options available for their use.

- **Provisioning Certificates from a Third-Party CA:** In this section, we walk through the steps required to generate a CRL for our ASA device and the import of the received certificate in return from a public CA.

- **Advanced PKI Deployment Strategies:** In this section, we discuss the additional revocation list retrieval methods available when deploying PKI authentication.

- **Doubling Up on Client Authentication:** In this section, we cover how to implement digital certificates and examine the use of user passwords and additional security measures.

- **Troubleshooting Your Advanced Configuration:** In this section, we review the tools you can use to troubleshoot an AnyConnect client deployment.

# CHAPTER 4

# Advanced Authentication and Authorization of AnyConnect VPNs

Now that you have covered a basic deployment of the AnyConnect VPN Client, using local username and password information configured on the Adaptive Security Appliance (ASA) device, we can explore the advanced methods available to authenticate and authorize remote users.

This chapter builds on Chapter 3, "AnyConnect Remote-Access VPN Solution." We explore the advanced authentication that can be employed by using third-party servers, digital certificates, or a combination of both. With regard to digital certificates, we then cover the configuration of the ASA's local certificate authority (CA) server and the deployment of user certificates through it. Finally, we examine the assignment of connection profiles and associated policies using various certificate-mapping criteria.

## "Do I Know This Already?" Quiz

The "Do I Know This Already?" quiz helps you determine your level of knowledge on this chapter's topics before you begin. Table 4-1 details the major topics discussed in this chapter and their corresponding quiz sections.

**Table 4-1** *"Do I Know This Already?" Section-to-Question Mapping*

| Foundation Topics Section | Questions |
| --- | --- |
| Provisioning Certificates as a Local CA | 2 |
| Configuring Certificate Mappings | 3 |
| Advanced PKI Deployment Strategies | 1, 7 |
| Provisioning Certificates from a Third-Party CA | 4, 5, 6 |

1. When configuring certificate revocation, which two of the following are available legitimate options?

   a. SCEP

   b. OCSP

   c. CRL

   d. CSR

2. After configuring the ASA local CA server and before you can make any changes to the configuration, what must be done?

   a. The local CA must be deleted.

   b. The local CA must be disabled.

   c. The local CA must be enabled.

   d. The local CA must be created.

3. When configuring certificate mapping, which of the following are valid DN fields that can be matched on? (Choose all that apply.)

   a. CN

   b. PWL

   c. OU

   d. S

4. Which of the following are available automatic certificate-retrieval methods using the AnyConnect client?

   a. Inside an SSL VPN tunnel

   b. Outside an SSL VPN tunnel

   c. Both of the above

5. An AnyConnect client uses which protocol through a VPN tunnel for automatic certificate retrieval?

   a. SCEP

   b. HTTP

   c. FTP

   d. LDAP

6. When configuring the automatic retrieval of a certificate in a VPN tunnel using the AnyConnect client, where must the issuing server URL be added?

   a. AnyConnect connection profile

   b. AnyConnect client profile

   c. Group policy object

   d. User attribute

7. When configuring certificate revocation, which is the recommended method?

   a. OCSP

   b. CRL

# Foundation Topics

## Authentication Options and Strategies

As you saw earlier, the process of deploying a basic SSL VPN is straightforward. However, when considering a large-scale or real-life deployment, you might want to use a more advanced method of authentication. The three methods available are as follows:

■ **Centralized AAA authentication:** Authentication, authorization, and accounting (AAA) server groups can be configured on the ASA. This allows the authentication of remote users to take place against a server in your environment (for example, RADIUS, TACACS+, Lightweight Directory Access Protocol [LDAP], Active Directory, or RSA server).

■ **Digital certificates:** Remote users/clients are provided with their own digital certificate for the purposes of authentication. The ASA device can then check the validity of their certificate file by the digital signature of the CA that the ASA is configured to trust.

■ **Double/triple authentication:** A combination of digital certificates and two or more centralized AAA authentication servers can be used for remote user authentication.

The available authentication server types that can be configured directly in a AAA server group are listed here and illustrated in Figure 4-1:

■ RADIUS

■ TACACS+

■ Kerberos

■ Windows Active Directory

■ LDAP

■ RSA server

If a remote user's credentials are not found on configured RADIUS and TACACS+ servers, these servers can be configured to check a remote user's credentials against a back-end database on one of the following server types:

■ Windows Active Directory

■ LDAP

■ RSA server

■ Open Database Connectivity (ODBC)

When combining authentication methods with digital certificates, the ASA begins the authentication process by sending its certificate to the remote user during the Secure Sockets Layer (SSL) handshake process. The remote user then checks the validity of the ASA's certificate using the CA root's certificate and public key, stored in its trusted root certificate store.

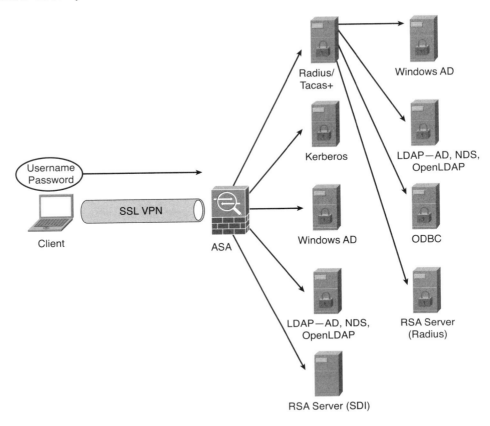

**Figure 4-1**  *Available Centralized AAA Authentication Servers*

Upon successfully authenticating the ASA's certificate, the remote user (on being prompted for one) then sends the ASA a copy of its own digital certificate. The ASA performs the same operation against the remote user's certificate for authentication purposes. If successful, the ASA continues by prompting the remote user for his username and password credentials, which allows for the subsequent authentication attempts against a centralized AAA server.

The process briefly described here occurs during the SSL handshake phase that we have discussed earlier. If you recall, after the ServerHello and ClientHello packets are sent and received, the server sends its certificate and optionally can prompt for a user certificate by sending the CertificateRequest message followed by the ServerHelloDone message. The client responds to the CertificateRequest with its own Certificate message containing its digital certificate, and optionally the certificate chain that includes the list of CAs responsible for issuing the certificate.

After sending the server a copy of its certificate, the client then sends another new message, this time of the type CertificateVerify. This message (which is encrypted using its private key) contains the signature/hash, which is then computed over all the messages sent up to this point. The server receives the CertificateVerify message, and with the corresponding public key (which was sent with the client's certificate file) decrypts the information. Successful decryption verifies that the certificate belongs to the client.

The handshake process then continues. The client and server each use the parameters received in earlier messages to generate the master secret. Figure 4-2 shows the SSL handshake process, including the messages that are used when client authentication is in operation.

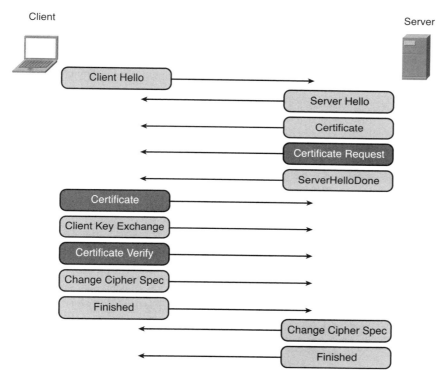

**Figure 4-2**   *SSL Handshake Process with Client Authentication*

**Note:**   It is recommended when deploying a double or triple authentication scheme that the RSA server be at the top of the authentication servers that are tried after a user is first successfully authenticated using digital certificates. This is because the RSA one-time password scheme provides a highly secure authentication process.

The following is a brief list of considerations when reviewing the available authentication methods:

■   **The level of scale and scope for growth available:** Will the proposed method allow for a rapid rollout of multiple users or the removal of many?

■   **The manageability:** Will you be able to modify the attributes of many users simultaneously? Do you have any granularity when dealing with departments of multiple users and specific policies for one user?

■ **Existing security policy:** Will the proposed authentication method be able to deliver the parameters you require for your policy. For example, will you be able to control the amount of time between password resets? Will parameters be sent in plain text or encrypted?

■ **Existing infrastructure:** Will your current infrastructure be able to cope with the introduction of a new authentication method? Are you required to work with third-party vendors when, for example, you are implementing an external Public Key Infrastructure (PKI) solution?

Although not by any means exhaustive, this list provides a good starting point for the type of questions you should be asking yourself (or the relevant security and administrative personnel in your organization) before proposing an authentication scheme for use in an environment.

In addition to the use of digital certificates for authentication purposes, you can use the information stored in them (attributes) for role and connection mapping. This allows you to tailor the remote user's current connection based on their location, department, country, and so on. Figure 4-3 shows an example of certificate mapping in action.

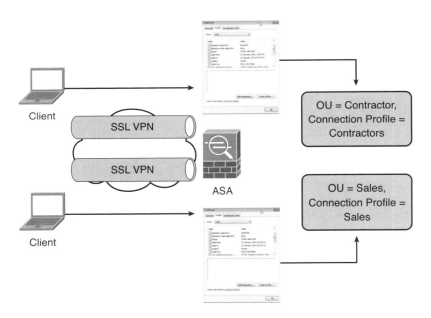

**Figure 4-3**  *Certificate Mapping*

Certificate mapping can be used to select specific attributes in a user's digital certificate and direct the user to the appropriate connection profile. As shown in Figure 4-3, two users are attempting to connect into our environment and have presented our ASA with their certificates for authentication purposes. A certificate-to-connection profile mapping has been created, whereby we examine the organizational unit (OU) of the certificate. Based on the users' departments, they are directed to use the appropriate connection profile. We take a closer look at certificate-to-connection profile mapping later in this chapter and review the configuration required to implement one.

The overall operation of PKI can either be deployed in your environment using your own servers for CA root operations (such as the generation and revocation of certificates) or by using an external/commercial PKI provider. Ultimately, the choice you make will likely be based on cost, scalability, and the manageability of the solution.

If you are considering the use of a third-party CA, ask these questions: Are they able to provide your clients with a certificate file automatically, on demand? Will they require administrative functions to be carried out by members of your organization or the third party, which might slow down your overall deployment?

When considering deploying your own CA for client certificate generation, it is important to consider the method of deployment you will offer to users: Are they required to fill in a web or paper-based form? Do you have the necessary resources in-house to handle the certificate-generation and -revocation process? You also need to make sure that your internal CA's signature has been deployed to clients and imported into their devices' trusted root certificate stores. Otherwise, they will receive an error when establishing a connection to your ASA device and be presented with a certificate file they do not trust.

Regardless of the PKI method you choose (internal or external), the process of configuring your connection to use digital certificates on the client and the ASA is the same. In other words, the devices do not care where the certificate has come from, as long as they trust it and the person who issued it, that the person providing them with the certificate is who he says he is, and the information in the certificate (validity period, common name, and so on) is valid.

In addition to running your own internal CA, an important requirement for the successful deployment and validation of your certificates is to have the correct date and time set on your CA. In the next section, we review the steps required to configure the local CA server available on the ASA. To aid you in determining whether the updated and correct time and date is set on your ASA device, you can configure the Network Time Protocol (NTP) client function to query and synchronize with a public time server.

You can configure an NTP server in the system time settings of the Adaptive Security Device Manager (ASDM) by navigating to **Configuration > Device Setup > System Time > NTP**. By default, the ASA does not use any NTP servers and relies on you to enter the correct date and time when first using the device. To enter your device's first NTP server, in the NTP pane, click **Add**.

Table 4-2 lists the available fields and respective values in the Add NTP Server Configuration window.

**Table 4-2**  *Add NTP Server Configuration Window Fields and Values*

| Field | Value |
| --- | --- |
| IP Address | Enter the IP address of the NTP server you want to add. |
| Interface | Select the interface that is used to reach the configured server from the drop-down list of available interfaces. |

**Table 4-2**   *Add NTP Server Configuration Window Fields and Values*

| Field | Value |
|-------|-------|
| Authentication Key | Enter a number for the authentication key used between the ASA device and the NTP server. |
| Trusted | Select this option to confirm that this authentication key is trusted. For authentication to function correctly, this box must be checked. |
| Key Value | Enter the authentication key. |
| Re-Enter Key Value | Reenter the authentication key to confirm the entry is correct. |

Figure 4-4 shows the Add NTP Server Configuration dialog with the values we are using for this example.

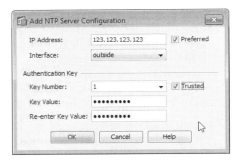

**Figure 4-4**   *ASA Add NTP Server Configuration*

## Provisioning Certificates as a Local CA

By default, the local CA server is disabled and must be created before you can enable it for use in your environment. After selecting the option to create the CA server (as you will see in a moment), the ASA generates the necessary certificate and user. The ASA then creates a new key pair and its own CA certificate that can later be downloaded by users and imported into their trusted root certificate stores, to be used during the certificate-validation process.

You create and enable the ASA CA server by navigating to **Configuration > Remote Access VPN > Certificate Management > Local Certificate Authority > CA Server.**

In the CA Server pane, first check the **Create the Certificate Authority Server** check box, and then click the radio button to enable it. Table 4-3 lists the available fields and the values that may be entered to successfully configure the local CA server.

**Table 4-3**  *ASA Local CA Server Configuration*

| Field | Value |
| --- | --- |
| Passphrase | Enter a passphrase with a minimum of seven alphanumeric characters for use in securing the CA server enabling/disabling, key pair, and CA certificate archives. |
| Issuer Name | Enter the hostname that will be used as the issuer name in your certificates deployed to remote users. After enabling the server, this value cannot be changed. |
| CA Server Key Size | Enter the size of the modulus used to generate the server public/private key pair. This value cannot be changed after enabling the CA server. Choose from 512, 768, 1024, or 2048 bits (default 1024). |
| Client Key Size | Enter the size of the key pair generated for client certificates. Choose from 512, 768, 1024, and 2048 bits (default 1024). |
| CA Certificate Lifetime | Enter the lifetime of the CA certificate that is generated for the ASA device as a number of days. Default is 3650 (10 years). |
| Client Certificate Lifetime | Enter the lifetime of any client certificates that are generated as a number of days. Default is 365 (1 year). |
| SMTP Server, Server Name/IP address | Enter the hostname or IP address of the mail server the ASA device can use to relay enrollment emails to users. |
| SMTP Server, From Address | Enter the email address you want your enrollment emails to appear from (for example, enrollment@company.com). |
| SMTP Server, Subject | Enter the text that will be used for the subject of enrollment emails sent to users. |
| CRL Distribution Point URL | Enter the URL accessible on the ASA device that users will access to retrieve the CRL (certificate revocation list) from. Default is http://hostname/+CSCOCA+/asa_ca.crl. |
| Publish-CRL Interface and Port | Select the interface where the CRL will be made available to users from the drop-down list of available interfaces and optionally specify a port (default 80). |
| CRL Lifetime | Enter the lifetime of the CRL in hours (default 6). |
| Database Storage Location | Select a location for the CA Server database to be held. This can either be on the local flash (default) or on a removable disk. |

**Table 4-3**  *ASA Local CA Server Configuration*

| Field | Value |
|---|---|
| Default Subject Name | Enter the subject name that will appended to a user's username in his or her generated certificate. The DN attributes that can be entered are as follows:<br><br>CN (Common Name)<br><br>SN (Surname)<br><br>O (Organization Name)<br><br>L (Locality)<br><br>C (Country)<br><br>OU (Organization Unit)<br><br>EA (Email Address)<br><br>ST (State/Province)<br><br>T (Title) |
| Enrollment Period | Enter the amount of time in hours users have available to fulfill their enrollment and download their certificate after being created in the local CA user database (default 24 hours). |
| One-Time Password Expiration | Enter the amount of time in hours that a one-time password emailed to the user in the enrollment request is valid before a new one must be generated (default 72 hours). |
| Certificate Expiration Reminder | Enter the amount of days before users are emailed a reminder of their upcoming certificate expiration by the local CA server (default 14 days). |

Figure 4-5 shows the local CA Server window with our configuration items entered into the necessary fields. We have also chosen to keep the default lifetime and expiration values for the purposes of this example.

After enabling the server and applying your configuration to the ASA, the local CA configuration fields are dimmed and cannot be edited. Therefore, before you can make any changes to the local CA configuration, you must first disable the server. If you are running the server in a production environment, I advise against carrying out this action during regular business hours, because all associated CRLs, enrollment actions, and user databases will become unavailable.

Now that you have enabled the local CA server, the user database becomes available, and you can proceed with entering accounts for your users who require certificates and allow them to enroll and download their certificate file from the ASA.

The Manage User Database pane is accessed by navigating to **Configuration > Remote Access VPN > Certificate Management > Local Certificate Authority > Manage User Database**. In this window, you can view the users currently in the database, view each user's email address, the subject name (configured when creating the local CA server), enrollment status, and whether they hold a certificate. You can also allow users to enroll and download their certificate file, by selecting a user from the list and clicking **Allow Enrollment**. You can view the current OTP (one-time password) generated for users to access the enrollment URL and download their certificate, or generate a new OTP if you believe the existing one may have become compromised and email or resend the OTP to users.

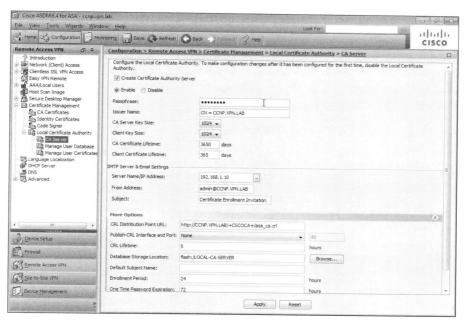

**Figure 4-5**  *ASA Local CA Server Configuration Window*

By default, no user accounts are configured. So, to enter the parameters required for your first user account, click **Add** and enter the details required into the dialog box, as shown in Figure 4-6. You must make sure when entering the user's details that you have the correct values, because after creating a user account, you cannot edit the username. Therefore, if you have entered the incorrect username, you must remove and re-create the user account.

**Figure 4-6**  *Local CA Server Add User Account*

You can enter the following information into the Add User dialog box:

■   Username

■   Email ID

- Subject (DN String)

- Allow Enrollment

If you do not want the user to be able to enroll for and download a new certificate, uncheck **Allow Enrollment**. Otherwise, after clicking **Add User**, the account is created in the database, and an enrollment email is sent to the user's address (entered in the Email ID field). Example 4-1 shows the contents of the enrollment email our user will receive after having been added into the user database. Users are given their username, OTP, and the URL they can use to access and download their certificate file. The enrollment period is also contained in the email, allowing users to see the length of time they have left before their enrollment period expires (entered during the creation of the local CA server).

**Example 4-1**   *ASA Local CA User Enrollment Email*

```
You have been granted access to enroll for a certificate.


The credentials below can be used to obtain your certificate.
 Username: employee1
 One-time Password: B3DC9569C6572F1A
 Enrollment is allowed until: 07:50:36 UTC Mon Nov 22 2010

NOTE: The one-time password is also used as the passphrase to unlock the
certificate file.

Please visit the following site to obtain your certificate:

https://<asa hostname>/+CSCOCA+/enroll.html
You may be asked to verify the fingerprint/thumbprint of the CA certificate
during installation of the certificates. The fingerprint/thumbprint
should be:
 MD5: F39470FE 493EC3C1 210416D2 42F4B0CB
 SHA1: A8BC57F3 CBE92751 961DEFF6 2A09AA5F 58E72A80
```

Now your users can select the link included in the email and visit it to download their certificate. To confirm their identification, they must first enter their username and the OTP received in the email, as shown in Figure 4-7.

After the user enters their credentials, they click the **Submit** button and are automatically asked if they want to save or open the certificate file. They choose **Save** and finish downloading. If your users are on a device running a Microsoft Windows OS, they can double-click the certificate file to start the Certificate Import Wizard and follow the wizard through each step until the certificate has been imported successfully.

After your users have successfully carried out enrollment and downloaded the certificate file, you can manage their certificate in the Manage User Certificates window by navigating to **Configuration > Remote Access VPN > Certificate Management > Local Certificate Authority > Manage User Certificates.** Figure 4-8 shows the Manage User Certificates window with our user listed, along with his certificate's serial number and the current status (Revoked or Not Revoked).

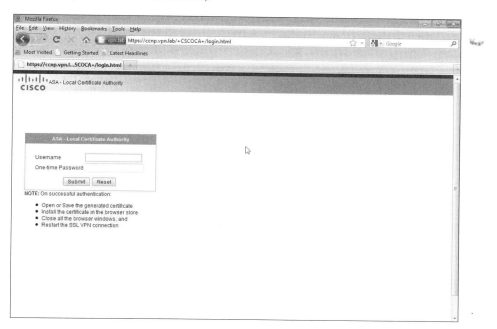

**Figure 4-7**    *Local CA Certificate Download Portal*

In this window, you can revoke the user certificate if the user has left the company or the certificate data becomes invalid (for example, the department or name changes and the user requires a new certificate). You can also unrevoke the certificate, allowing the user to use it for authentication procedures again (for example, after security breaches have been investigated or the user's vacation has ended).

Now that you have successfully enabled the ASA's local CA server and entered your remote user's account into the user database, you need to enable certificate-based authentication in an AnyConnect connection profile (tunnel group). You do so by first navigating to **Configuration > Remote Access VPN > Network (Client) Access > AnyConnect Connection Profiles.** Select the connection profile from the list of those available and click **Edit** to open a configuration window. Now select **Certificate** as the authentication method, as shown in Figure 4-9.

Optionally, you can specify the components of the certificate used by the ASA to select the username for authentication purposes in the **Advanced > Authentication** pane. By default, the common name (CN) is used as the primary component and the organizational unit (OU) as the secondary. However, you may choose any component available in the drop-down lists. The option to select the username from the various certificate fields is used when both certificate and user/password authentication methods are deployed together, allowing the Username field to be populated automatically for login purposes. This requires you to select Both as authentication method rather than Certificate or AAA.

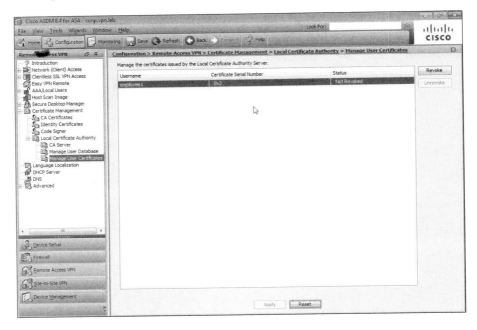

**Figure 4-8** *Local CA Manage User Certificates Window*

You also have the option to use the entire DN string as the username, or a script that has previously been written and uploaded to the ASA's flash to carry out the task. (Note that the script is supported only in Lua language.)

Instead of using the web enrollment example provided by the ASA's enrollment website, the AnyConnect client can carry out the task of auto-enrollment with a CA server. For example, if a user opens the AnyConnect client and attempts to connect to your newly created certificate-based Secure Sockets Layer virtual private network (SSL VPN), their attempt fails, and the AnyConnect client shows a message alerting them to the fact that a certificate is required to successfully connect. This also implies that Certificate was used as the authentication method in the connection profile and you have configured it successfully.

After this has occurred, the Get Certificate button becomes available in the AnyConnect client, allowing users to start the enrollment process, as shown in Figure 4-10.

When users click **Get Certificate**, they are presented with a Username and Password box along with the instructions for entering the username and OTP they received in the email generated after creating their account in the ASA's CA database.

At this point in the process, users enter their username and OTP as requested and click **Connect**. The AnyConnect client now sends the enrollment request to the ASA's local CA server, and if the details users enter are correct, they receive their certificate file, and the AnyConnect client successfully connects to the VPN.

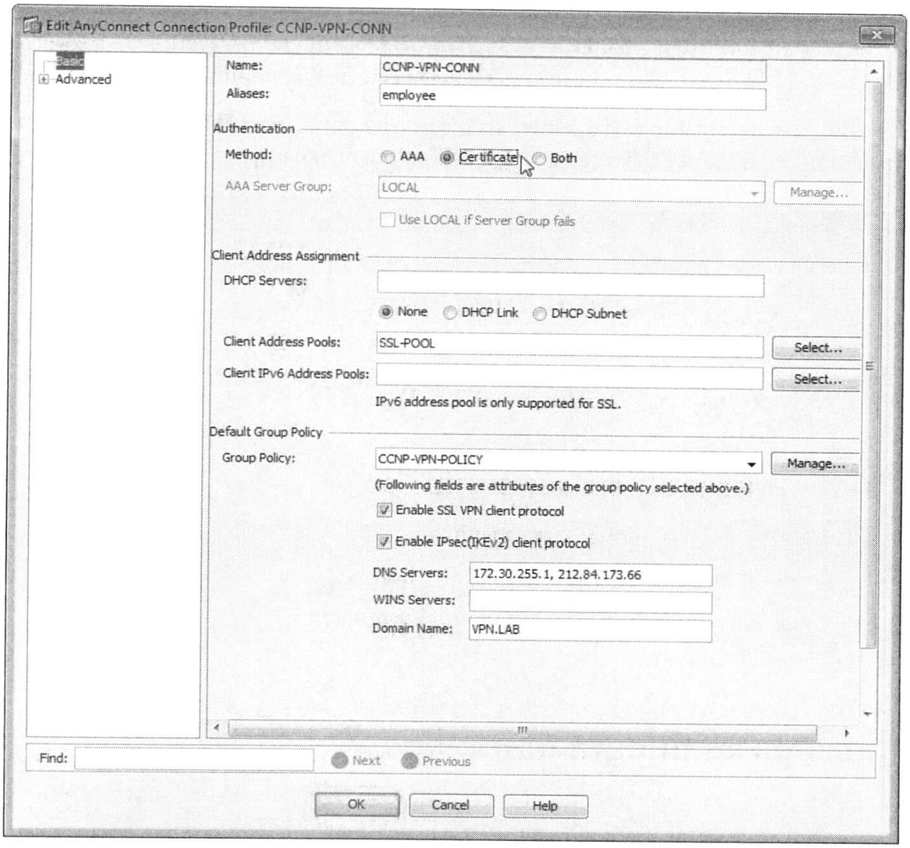

**Figure 4-9** *AnyConnect Connection Profile Certificate-Based Authentication Configuration*

**Figure 4-10** *Cisco AnyConnect Client Automatic Enrollment*

During the process of enrollment, users may be prompted to install a number of CA and intermediate CA certificates to confirm they are trusted hosts and the certificate information is correct before they are imported into the device's certificate store.

Figure 4-11 shows an example of a remote user carrying out the enrollment process by entering their username and OTP received in their enrollment email.

**Figure 4-11**   *Cisco AnyConnect Client Automatic Enrollment*

## Configuring Certificate Mappings

You can also control the user's environment based on the DN information that is held in the user's certificate file (for example, the user's OU, ST, and C).

After you have gathered the required information from a user's certificate file, you can assign the user to the appropriate connection profile, allowing you to specify particular group policies, authentication servers, Domain Name System (DNS) servers, and so on.

You can achieve these actions through certificate-to-connection profile maps. If you have deployed digital certificates to your users for the purposes of authentication and have a wide and diverse user base, this tool can provide a great benefit both to your users and your management of them. Begin the configuration by creating a map and specifying the connection profile associated with it. In your new map, create one or more rules configured to search for the DN parameters and values that you specify. For example, you may have one global map set up for remote users in the United States (C) that maps to a global connection profile, and a second map that matches certificates for users who come from both the United States (C) and work in the Sales department (OU).

Certificate-to-connection profile maps are created by first navigating to **Configuration > Remote Access VPN > Advanced > Certificate to SSL VPN Connection Profile Maps.** This window contains two sections:

■   Certificate-to-Connection Profile Maps

■   Mapping Criteria

The Mapping Criteria section is where the rules for your connection maps are defined. (For example, the contents of the certificate being analyzed contain the specific DN value you are looking for.) However, before you can create any mapping criteria, you must first create a connection mapping in the Certificate-to-Connection Profile Maps section.

## Certificate-to-Connection Profile Maps

As shown in Figure 4-12, you can create connection maps by entering a name or selecting an existing map from the drop-down list.

**Figure 4-12**    *Certificate-to-Connection Profile Maps*

Give the map a priority between 1 and 65535. Connection maps are analyzed in priority order from lowest number to highest until a match occurs in the associated mapping criteria. The final task for configuration in this window is to select the connection profile (tunnel group) that will be applied to the connecting user (the owner of the certificate) if all the associated mapping rules match the values in the certificate. In this step, you can create both multiple certificate-to-connection profile maps and one or more entries in the same map.

When encountering multiple certificate-to-connection profile maps, the ASA may take other configuration items into consideration in addition to the configured priority when deciding on the order in which they are processed.

When evaluating the certificate-to-profile maps, the ASA decides as follows:

1. Top-down, from lowest priority to highest priority.
2. If multiple maps exist with the same priority number, these are ordered top-down in alphabetic order.

However, if you look at the command-line interface (CLI) side and how these are ordered and will finally be processed, the rules differ slightly:

1. Top-down, from lowest priority to highest priority.
2. If multiple maps exist with the same priority number, these are ordered top-down based on the order of their configuration.

Consider, for example, the configuration of the following certificate-to-connection profile maps using the ASDM:

1. Create a map called UK and assign this entry a priority 10.
2. Create a map called US and assign this entry a priority of 10.
3. Create a map called Romania and assign this entry a priority of 10.

The end result of this configuration is shown in the following list. Because each certificate-to-connection profile map has the same priority, these maps are processed in alphabetic order to determine the connection profile to be assigned to an SSL VPN session:

1. Romania map with entry of priority 10.
2. UK map with entry of priority 10.
3. US map with entry of priority 10.

The following list describes the events that occur based on a match occurring (or not) between configured certificate-to-connection profile maps and a remote user's certificate file. Also notice how the end result changes based on whether you have provided remote users with the ability to select a connection profile before login:

1. If there is no match against configured rules, and clients are restricted from selecting the connection profile at the login step, the session is assigned to the DefaultWEB-VPNGroup connection profile.
2. If there is no match against configured rules, but clients are allowed to select the connection profile at the login step, the session is assigned to the selected connection profile.
3. If there is a match against configured rules, and clients are restricted from selecting the connection profile at the login step, the session is assigned to the connection profile from the matched certificate-to-connection profile map.
4. If there is a match against configured rules, and clients are allowed to select the connection profile at the login step, the user can select only the connection profile from the matched certificate-to-connection profile map.

## Mapping Criteria

After creating a certificate-to-connection profile map, you can create and assign rules that will match the criteria you require to be present in users' certificate files for them to be assigned to the connection profile you have chosen.

As mentioned earlier, the rules created are set up to look for DN attributes and values that may have been entered into the user's certificate file, allowing you to identify information (such as connecting country, state, department, office, username, and so on). To create your mapping criteria, first select the map created earlier and click **Add** in the Mapping Criteria section.

In the Add Certificate Matching Rule Criterion window, select the fields you are looking for in the certificate. These fields might be Subject or Alternative Subject, or a component of the field (for example, C or OU). Then choose the Operator value: Equals, Contains,

Does Not Equal, Does Not Contain (and the value). This enables you to make an accurate match. If for example you want to match a user certificate based on the user's being in the Support department, the rule would contain the following configuration:

- **Field:** Subject

- **Component:** Organizational Unit (OU)

- **Operator:** Equals

- **Value:** Support

Figure 4-13 shows an example of the configuration that may be entered if you want to assign a user to a connection profile based on his certificate having the country component value of US.

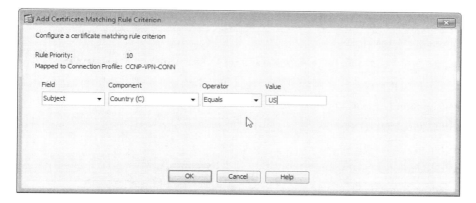

**Figure 4-13** *Certificate-to-Connection Profile Mapping Criteria Configuration*

The following is a list of the current DN criteria of which the stored values can be used to match against in a user's certificate. You can have as many rules configured in a connection profile map as required. However, all rules in a connection profile map must match before the chosen connection profile is applied:

- Subject
  - Country (C)
  - Common Name (CN)
  - DN Qualifier (DNQ)
  - Email Address (EA)
  - Generational Qualifier (GENQ)
  - Given Name (GN)
  - Initials (I)

- Locality (L)
- Name (N)
- Organization (O)
- Organization Unit (OU)
- Serial Number (SER)
- Surname (SN)
- State/Province (SP)
- Title (T)
- User ID (UID)
- Unstructured Name (UNAME)
- IP Address (IP)
- Domain Component (DC)
- Alternative Subject
- Issuer
  - Country (C)
  - Common Name (CN)
  - DN Qualifier (DNQ)
  - Email Address (EA)
  - Generational Qualifier (GENQ)
  - Given Name (GN)
  - Initials (I)
  - Locality (L)
  - Name (N)
  - Organization (O)
  - Organization Unit (OU)
  - Serial Number (SER)
  - Surname (SN)
  - State/Province (SP)
  - Title (T)
  - User ID (UID)
  - Unstructured Name (UNAME)
  - IP Address (IP)
  - Domain Component (DC)
- Extended Key Usage

# Provisioning Certificates from a Third-Party CA

As discussed earlier in this chapter, you have the option to use either a local/internal CA server or a public/commercial CA. When deciding on an enrollment and deployment method for your user certificates, you can choose from Manual or Automatic.

An example of a manual enrollment and deployment method is a remote user having to enter her details into a web- or paper-based form, an administrator or third-party manually approving the request, or the user receiving the certificate in an email and installing the certificate in her device's local certificate store.

The AnyConnect client can use certificates in a device's personal certificate store for the purposes of authentication. However, when deploying certificates in a large or enterprise environment, an automatic method of enrollment and deployment is usually preferred because it is much more efficient when user input is not required.

There are two automatic methods of certificate enrollment and deployment with the AnyConnect client, one of which you have already seen in the earlier example in the "Provisioning Certificates as a Local CA" section:

**Key Topic**

■ **Enrollment inside an SSL VPN tunnel:** This method requires two connection profiles, one configured with certificate-based authentication and the second without. The connection profile without certificate-based authentication is used for the purposes of enrollment and will allow access only to the CA. Upon connecting, the AnyConnect client receives a profile that includes the Simple Certificate Enrollment Protocol (SCEP) parameters. The AnyConnect client then sends an enrollment request to the server through the SSL VPN tunnel. The server replies with the certificate file (and those of any root CA servers). The AnyConnect client receives the certificate, installs it, and disconnects from the SSL VPN, allowing the user to now connect to the connection profile using certificate-based authentication for network access.

SCEP is an automatic method of certificate request, renewal, and revocation from a CA, created by Cisco. At the time of this writing, SCEP is currently in the Internet-draft status of the RFC process. However, many CA servers that are distributed allow for either the direct configuration of the SCEP protocol or an optional add-in that may be installed. (For example, the CA server that runs on top of Windows Server 2003 can enable SCEP with the installation of an add-in.) SCEP uses HTTP for communication, and messages are transmitted between the requestor (client) and the CA to enable the successful retrieval of a certificate.

SCEP can operate in either one of two modes when authenticating a client:

■ Manual mode
■ Pre-Shared Key mode

In Manual mode, the client is authenticated using a message digest/fingerprint over the certificate request message, which uses either Secure Hash 1 (SHA-1) or message digest 5 (MD5). It is typically used if a pre-shared key is unavailable. The message digest is sent to the CA by the client using an out-of-band method. Upon receiving the digest, the CA calculates one of its own, using the received message from the client. If the two digests match, the requestor/client has been authenticated.

In Pre-Shared Key mode, the CA prompts clients for a shared secret that has been given to them before attempting the request. The client enters the secret when prompted, and if the value matches that of the CA's version, the client is authenticated and communication between the two can resume.

■ **Enrollment outside an SSL VPN tunnel:** You have already seen an example of this deployment during our discussion about the local CA server. The AnyConnect client prompts the user to click the **Get Certificate** button to start the enrollment process. The user then enters her username and OTP received from the CA server, and the AnyConnect client sends the enrollment request to the CA outside of any SSL VPN tunnel. Upon receiving the issued certificate, the AnyConnect client installs it, and the user can now proceed to connect to the SSL VPN.

Because you have already seen an example of the enrollment outside an SSL VPN tunnel process, there is no need for us to cover old ground here. So, this section focuses on the enrollment inside an SSL VPN tunnel process.

Figure 4-14 shows, on a high level, the environment that must set up between remote users and the ASA device for successful certificate enrollment within an SSL VPN tunnel.

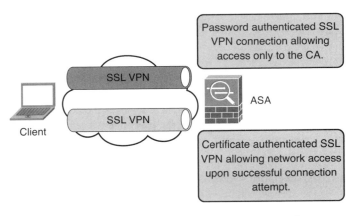

**Figure 4-14** *Enrollment Inside an SSL VPN Tunnel*

For users to be able to successfully connect, enroll for a certificate, disconnect, and connect to the certificate-based VPN connection, the following steps must be completed:

**Step 1.** Configure an Extensible Markup Language (XML) profile for use by the AnyConnect client containing the SCEP parameters required for communication with the CA.

**Step 2.** Configure a dedicated connection profile with password-based authentication used by clients for the purposes of enrollment. Communication only to the CA must be allowed through this connection.

**Step 3.** Enroll the AnyConnect client into a PKI.

**Step 4.** Optionally, configure client certificate selection.

**Step 5.**    Import the issuing CA's certificate into the ASA's certificate store, allowing the ASA to verify the connecting clients.

**Step 6.**    Configure a connection profile used by clients for network access using certificate-based authentication.

The following sections discuss the configuration and information required for to complete these tasks.

## Configure an XML Profile for Use by the AnyConnect Client

In this step, you configure an XML profile that stores the SCEP settings entered for successful communication with the CA to occur. This profile is downloaded by the AnyConnect client during the connection process. XML profiles are discussed in more detail in Chapter 5, "Advanced Deployment and Management of the AnyConnect Client."

By default, no profiles on the ASA are sent to clients during their connection attempt, so you need to create a new one before you can go any further. Carry out this task by navigating to **Configuration > Remote Access VPN > Network (Client) Access > AnyConnect Client Profile**. In this window, click **Add** and enter the details for the profile in the fields that appear. An example configuration for this task is as follows:

- **Profile Name:** enrollment.

- **Profile Location:** disk0:/enrollment.xml (This field autopopulates when we enter the name.)

- **Group Policy:** Unassigned (The default of Unassigned is left here because we are just creating a basic profile at the moment.)

After entering this information shown, we click **OK** and are taken back to the Client Profile window, where we can see our new profile is now listed.

To begin editing the profile settings and entering the required SCEP information, select the client profile from the list and click **Edit**. The AnyConnect Client Profile Editor window opens, as shown in Figure 4-15. This is the exact same graphical user interface (GUI) you receive if you choose to use the PC version of the AnyConnect Client Profile Editor. In that version, you create a profile and then import it onto the ASA by clicking the **Import** button rather than the **Edit** button.

In the AnyConnect Client Profile Editor window, choose the **Certificate Enrollment** menu item from the list and enter the SCEP information. As shown in Figure 4-15, there are a number of fields and options available (described in Table 4-4). For this example, we have entered the information shown both in the figure and in the table.

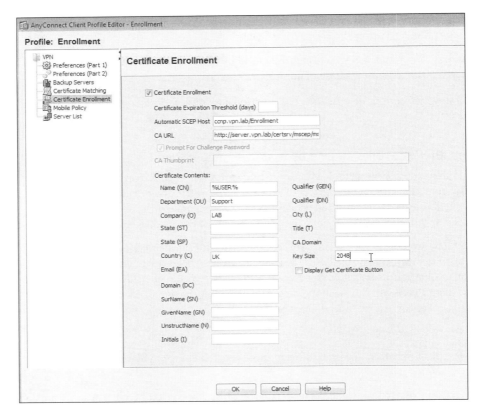

**Figure 4-15**  *Cisco AnyConnect Profile Editor*

**Table 4-4**  *Cisco AnyConnect Profile Editor Certificate Enrollment Fields and Values*

| Field | Value |
| --- | --- |
| Certificate Enrollment | Checked = enabled. |
| | Unchecked = disabled. (For our example, this option is se-lected.) |
| Certificate Expiration Threshold | Enter the number of days from 0 to 180 before a user certificate expires when the AnyConnect client begins to warn users of their expiration and enable the renewal using the Get Certificate button (if available). |
| Automatic SCEP Host | Enter the FQDN of the ASA, followed by the name of the connection profile set up only for enrollment. The two values should be separated by a slash. (In our configuration for this task, we have entered ccnp.vpn.lab/enrollment.) When the AnyConnect client sees a connection attempt to this host and connection profile, the SCEP process begins. |

**Table 4-4**  *Cisco AnyConnect Profile Editor Certificate Enrollment Fields and Values*

| Field | Value |
| --- | --- |
| CA URL | Enter the full path to the CA or registration authority (RA) server that is responsible for the issuing of your client certificates and that can fulfill the SCEP process. For our example, we have entered http://server.vpn.lab/certsrv/mscep/mscep.dll. |
| Prompt for Challenge Password | As you saw earlier, SCEP has two modes available for client authentication. Check this box if you are using pre-shared key authentication and want your clients to enter a password when prompted during the certificate request phase. |
| Thumbprint | If you have chosen to use message digest authentication (Manual mode) rather than pre-shared keys, you can enter the thumbprint generated by the client here. (For our example, we have chosen pre-shared key authentication, so this field is left blank [default].) |
| Certificate Contents - Name (CN) | In this field, type in the variable name %USER% as we have for our example, and the certificate CN will be populated with the connected user's username. |
| Certificate Contents - Department (OU) | Enter the department of the connecting user for entry into the certificate. For our example, we entered Support. |
| Certificate Contents - Company (O) | Enter the company of the user for entry into the certificate. For our example, we entered LAB. |
| Certificate Contents - State (ST) | Enter the state of the user for entry into the certificate. |
| Certificate Contents - Country (UK) | Enter the country of the user for entry into the certificate. For our example, we entered UK. |
| Certificate Contents - Email (EA) | Enter the user's email address for entry into the certificate. |
| Certificate Contents - Domain (DC) | Enter the name of the domain for which a user is a member for entry into the certificate. |
| Certificate Contents - Surname (SN) | Enter the user's surname for entry into the certificate. |
| Certificate Contents - GivenName (GN) | Enter the user's first name for entry into the certificate. |
| Certificate Contents - UnstructName (N) | Use this field to enter any other name the user may be known by (for example, a nickname) for entry into the certificate. |
| Certificate Contents - Initials (I) | Enter the user's initials for entry into the certificate. |

**Table 4-4**  *Cisco AnyConnect Profile Editor Certificate Enrollment Fields and Values*

| Field | Value |
| --- | --- |
| Certificate Contents - Qualifier (GEN) | Use this field to enter the generation of the user (for example, Jr.) for entry into the certificate. |
| Certificate Contents - Qualifier (DN) | Enter a qualifier (version) for the entire DN string for entry into the certificate. |
| Certificate Contents - City (L) | Enter the city where the user resides for entry into the certificate. |
| Certificate Contents - Title (T) | Enter the user's title (for example, Mr, Mrs, Miss, Dr) for entry into the certificate. |
| Certificate Contents - CA Domain | Use this field to enter the domain of the CA server. (For example, our entry would be vpn.lab.) |
| Certificate Contents - Key Size | Select the key size you require to be used for client key generation used with the certificate file (for example, 512, 1024, 2048). |
| Display Get Certificate Button | Check this box to enable the display of the Get Certificate button to users if you want to enable them to manually request a certificate. However, if using an automatic process with a dedicated VPN tunnel, it is generally recommended not to enable this function because the Get Certificate button will become available to users as their certificate approaches its validity date or becomes valid, allowing them to request a certificate directly outside of a VPN tunnel. |

### Configure a Dedicated Connection Profile for Enrollment

After creating a policy for use by AnyConnect clients, you can create a dedicated connection profile, which will be used only for enrollment and subsequently only allow access to the CA server.

Create the connection profile (tunnel groups) for use with the AnyConnect client by navigating to **Configuration > Remote Access VPN > Network (Client) Access > AnyConnect Connection Profiles.**

To create a new connection profile for the enrollment process, click **Add** in the Connection Profiles section, and in the Add SSL VPN Connection Profile window, enter the following details for the profile:

■   **Name:** Enrollment

■   **Alias:** Enrollment (This must match the value entered in the Automatic SCEP Host field mentioned earlier when we were creating an AnyConnect connection profile.)

■   **Authentication:** LOCAL

All other settings used will be set up in a custom group policy. For you to create this policy, select **Manage** next to the group policy drop-down list, which allows you to select from the available group policies. In the Manage Group Policies window that opens, click **Add** to create a new group policy and give the policy a name. For our example, we have used Enrollment-Policy. We have also assigned a pool of IPv4 addresses that we had configured earlier for assignment to our clients.

To restrict our client's access only to the address of the CA server, we have used a combination of split tunneling and access control lists (ACL). We set this up by navigating to **Advanced > Split Tunneling**. In the Split Tunneling pane, we select the following options:

- **Policy:** Uncheck the **Inherit** option (default) and check **Tunnel Only the Network List Below**.

- **Network List:** Uncheck the **Inherit** option (default) and select a predefined ACL, or click **Manage** to allow the existing ACLs to be edited (or a new one to be created). For our example, we have used a predefined ACL that includes only a **permit** statement to the CA server's IP address that we are using. Note that only standard ACLs are supported for split tunneling.

**Note:**  Split tunneling and ACLs are covered in greater detail in Chapter 3, "Deploying an AnyConnect Remote-Access VPN Solution."

Now you can assign the AnyConnect client's XML profile (created earlier) to the connection profile using the group policy. Navigate to **Advanced > SSL VPN Client**, uncheck the **Inherit** option next to Client Profiles to Download, and click **Add**. In the Select AnyConnect Client Profiles window, select the newly created profile from the drop-down list and click **OK** to return to the Group Policy Settings window. Now you have entered enough information required for a basic configuration, so click **OK** to save the group policy. If it is not already, select the group policy you have just created in the Edit Group Policies window and click **OK** to be returned to the Connection Profile window, and finally click **OK** to save the new connection profile.

Figure 4-16 shows our configuration for the connection profile we have just created and the Edit Group Policy window and the Select AnyConnect Client Profiles window used for this example.

## Enroll the AnyConnect Client into a PKI

At this point you have now configured enough on the ASA device for a remote user to be able to connect to a connection profile (used for enrollment only) and request a certificate from the CA server, which is accomplished by enrolling the AnyConnect client into a PKI.

The remote user carries out this task by opening the AnyConnect client software and selecting from the drop-down list of available groups the connection profile using the alias created (Enrollment). They also need to enter a username and password because, if you recall during the earlier task, LOCAL authentication had been configured for clients to authenticate to the ASA device. (This is fine for an example. However, if you are deploying this connection for a production network, I recommend a RADIUS/third-party authentication server.)

After they enter their details and click **Connect**, the AnyConnect client establishes the connection to the ASA. During the connection stage, the XML profile created earlier is

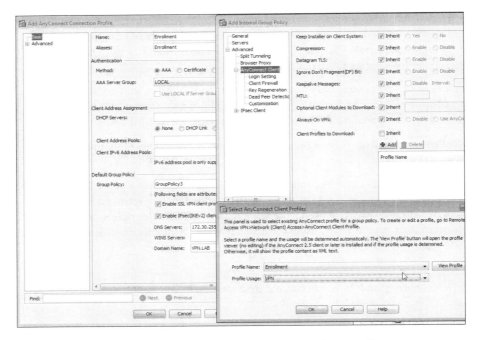

**Figure 4-16**    *Creating a Dedicated Connection Profile for Enrollment*

downloaded by the client, and a certificate request is sent to the CA using the SCEP URL, according to the settings in the XML profile.

As you can see in Figure 4-17, the client is prompted to authenticate the CA server using the thumbprint (message digest) that should have already been exchanged using an

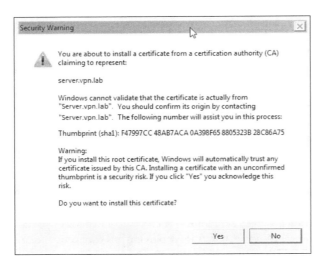

**Figure 4-17**    *Requesting a Client Certificate Using SCEP*

out-of-band method. After validating the CA server's identity by comparing the hash value to that presented by the CA server, they click **OK**, and the requested certificates are successfully installed in their local certificate store.

## Optionally, Configure Client Certificate Selection

In this optional task, you can use a new XML client connection profile to specify which installed client certificate will be presented to the ASA device during a connection attempt. For this example, we created a new client profile in **Configuration > Remote Access VPN > Network (Client) Access > AnyConnect Client Profile** and called it **Certificate-Mapping**.

You have two options when controlling client certificates for authentication purposes: allowing the user to select the appropriate certificate from a list; or setting up automatic certificate selection, whereby the AnyConnect client presents a certificate to the ASA based on the connection profile in use and the mapping you have configured.

By default, the AnyConnect client tries to use the automatic process of selecting a certificate, and the user will not be able to select one. However, because there are no default certificate-mapping rules created, the AnyConnect client tries to use the first certificate available in the device's store.

As shown in Figure 4-18, you can disable the use of automatic certificate selection by unchecking **Disable Certificate Selection** in **AnyConnect Client Profile Editor > Preferences (Part 2)**. To enable it again, simply check the box.

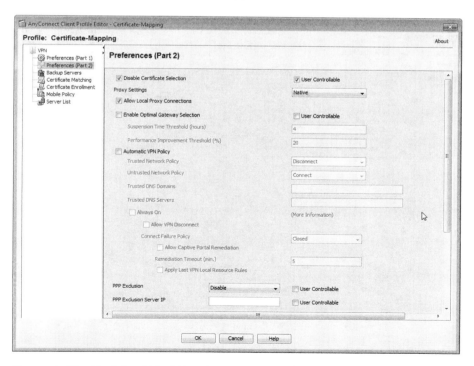

**Figure 4-18**  *Enabling/Disabling Automatic Certificate Selection*

If you choose to leave the default of Automatic Certificate Selection enabled, you can set up certificate matching to select the appropriate certificate, based on the DN attributes and values you specify.

For this example, we have chosen to select the client certificate based on the issuing CA servers CN value (server name). This will be the same value as the hostname you saw in the previous section, when the remote user had been prompted to validate the CA's identity (refer to Figure 4-17).

As shown in Figure 4-19, in the **Client Profile Editor > Certificate Matching** window under the Distinguished name section, we have clicked **Add** and from the list of available DN fields have selected **ISSUER-CN** and entered the value **SERVER.VPN.LAB**. As mentioned, this will match the issuer's name in the previously downloaded and installed certificate.

Before the AnyConnect client can use the profile, you must map it to the connection profile you require the specified certificate to be presented for during authentication. You can accomplish this by enabling the profile download in the group policy associated with the connection profile.

You've already seen the same task in the "configure a dedicated connection profile for enrollment" step by navigating to **Configuration > Remote Access VPN > Network (Client) Access > Group Policies.**

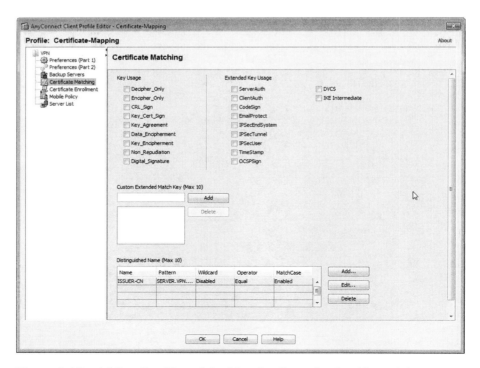

**Figure 4-19** *Adding Certificate-Matching Attributes for Certificate Selection*

Select the appropriate group policy object from the list of those available and click **Edit** to open the Group Policies Properties window. Then navigate to **Advanced > AnyConnect Client** in the Properties window. In the Client Profiles to Download section, uncheck the **Inherit** option and click **Add**. In the Select AnyConnect Client Profiles window, select the new client policy created and click **OK**, then **OK** again to close the group policy settings. Note that the configured connection profile to which the group policy will be attached needs to use Certificate as the authentication method, as you will see later.

## Import the Issuing CA's Certificate into the ASA's

This step is required for the ASA device to successfully authenticate the certificates presented by remote users.

After receiving a client certificate, the ASA checks the validity (valid from and to date) and then checks the issuing CA's DN string against the DN of the CA certificate in its trusted root certificate store. If the DNs match, the ASA has confirmed the CA is indeed trusted. The ASA moves on to authenticate the digital signature of the received certificate using the CA's public key held with the certificate in its trusted root CA certificate store. If the signature is matched, the ASA can verify the correct public/private key pair has been used by the CA to sign the certificate, and the authentication process continues with the ASA checking for a valid hostname in the certificate.

If during this authentication process the ASA is unable to locate the certificate of the issuing CA in its trusted root store, the certificate is considered invalid, and the authentication process fails.

You have two choices when importing the CA certificate into the trusted CA store on the ASA, as shown in Figure 4-20. You can manually retrieve the certificate and upload/paste the contents and install to the ASA, or use SCEP for automatic retrieval and installation. For this example, we run through the process of configuring SCEP for our certificate retrieval and installation, because it makes sense for you to see both the configuration required for remote users and ASA device.

Configure the CA certificate retrieval using SCEP by first navigating to **Configuration > Remote Access VPN > Certificate Management > CA Certificates**.

Click **Add** on the right side, and in the Install Certificate window, then check the **Use SCEP** option in the lower section of the window. Enter the full SCEP URL to the CA (as you saw in the earlier section when creating an AnyConnect client profile), and then enter a value for the retry period in minutes (default 1) followed by the number of times the ASA should attempt to retrieve the certificate (default 0 - unlimited).

After entering the information, click **Install Certificate**, and the ASA displays a dialog box with the status of the request. If the request is successful, you receive a prompt similar to the one received in the "Enrolling the AnyConnect Client into a PKI" section, asking you to validate the CA's identity. However, if the request fails, the ASA continues to try again until reaching the attempts limit (unless the limit is 0), and the ASA continues to attempt the certificate until you click **Cancel**.

**Figure 4-20** *Adding CA Certificate to Trusted Store*

### Create a Connection Profile Using Certificate-Based Authentication

For the final step required for the deployment, you can now configure the connection pro-file that will be used by your connecting users for network access. This configuration uses certificate-based authentication to validate the certificates presented by remote users.

Begin by creating a new connection profile (as you have seen in previous tasks) by navi-gating to **Configuration > Remote Access VPN > Network (Client) Access > AnyCon-nect Connection Profiles** and clicking **Add**.

As shown in Figure 4-21, we created a basic connection profile for this task. We entered the name and alias as **Certificate-Based** for easy identification by our user. (Of course, if this were a production environment, a more appropriate name should be used.) We also se-lected the authentication method **Certificate**, assigned an IPv4 address pool, and assigned the default group policy to it. We could also have assigned the group policy created/ed-ited in the section "Optionally, Configure Client Certificate Selection" so that on connec-tion, the correct certificate would be automatically selected by AnyConnect and presented over to the ASA.

Our users can now open their AnyConnect client, select the new Certificate-Based con-nection profile, and authenticate using the certificates previously obtained using the En-rollment connection profile.

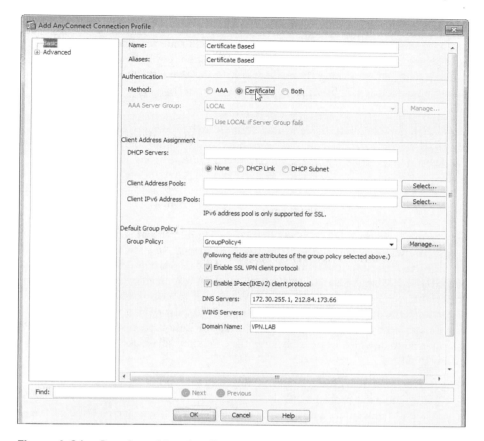

**Figure 4-21**    *Creating a New AnyConnect Connection Profile for Certificate-Based Auth*

## Advanced PKI Deployment Strategies

So far in this chapter, we have discussed the implementation of certificate-based authentication using either an internal or external PKI deployment, and have covered some common strategies and information that you need to prepare an appropriate deployment for your organization.

However, what happens when a user's private key has been compromised? How can you resolve the issue of a certificate going to an incorrect user or even an attacker posing as a genuine user?

Two methods enable you to control the status of certificates that have been issued:

- **CRLs:** Certificate revocation lists
- **OCSP:** Online Certificate Status Protocol

### CRLs

Certificate revocation lists, defined in RFCs 3280 and 5280, are the older method for the online checking of a certificate's status. The CRL contains a list of CNs, serial numbers, the date revoked, and the issuing CA name of certificates that have been revoked and should not be used. The CRL is made available to authenticating devices by a URL contained in the certificate of the device being authenticated.

CRLs are often published immediately after a certificate has been revoked and added to the list. However, they are also published periodically. The validity of the CA issuing the CRL is checked in the same way as the validity of a certificate: using a combination of a digital fingerprint and the server's public key.

### OCSP

Online Certificate Status Protocol (RFC 2560) is the alternative and preferred method, due to the bandwidth savings and faster transaction time. OCSP allows an authenticating device to send a request for the status of a certificate by its serial number to an OCSP responder, whose role can be carried out by either the CA responsible for issuing the certificate being authenticated or a subordinate CA/RA. The responder sends back to the requestor (authentication device) a status of Good, Revoked, or Unknown. If a revoked or unknown status is received by the requestor, the authentication process fails. With OCSP, there is no need to download a possibly large file containing all revoked certificates, as is the case with CRL.

OCSP messages are sent in clear text and are therefore susceptible to man-in-the-middle attacks. To overcome this problem, OCSP can be configured on the requestor to send a nonce (a randomly generated number) that must be included in sent and received messages for the purposes of message integrity checking.

Figure 4-22 shows a typical OCSP conversation that has been carried out between a web browser and a CA. In the fourth line, after the TCP connection has been built (using the three-way handshake), the user's web browser sends a request to the responder that includes the serial number of the certificate it is in the process of authenticating. In the sixth line (highlighted), the web browser receives a response of Good from the responder (as you can see in the highlighted field in the lower section of the figure), and the TCP connection is then gracefully closed.

OCSP is the preferred method for checking a certificate's status, and Cisco now recommend using CRL only if no other method is available.

The ASA can be configured to check for the existence of revoked certificates by either the CRL or OCSP methods by navigating to **Configuration > Remote Access VPN > Certificate Management > CA Certificates.**

In the CA Certificates window, highlight the CA certificate for which you want to set up a revocation list, and click **Edit** to enter the Edit Options for CA Certificate window, shown in Figure 4-23.

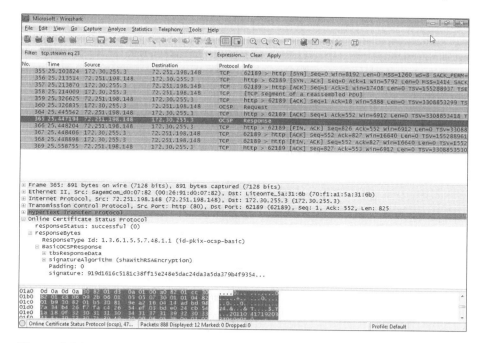

**Figure 4-22**   *OCSP Request/Response Example*

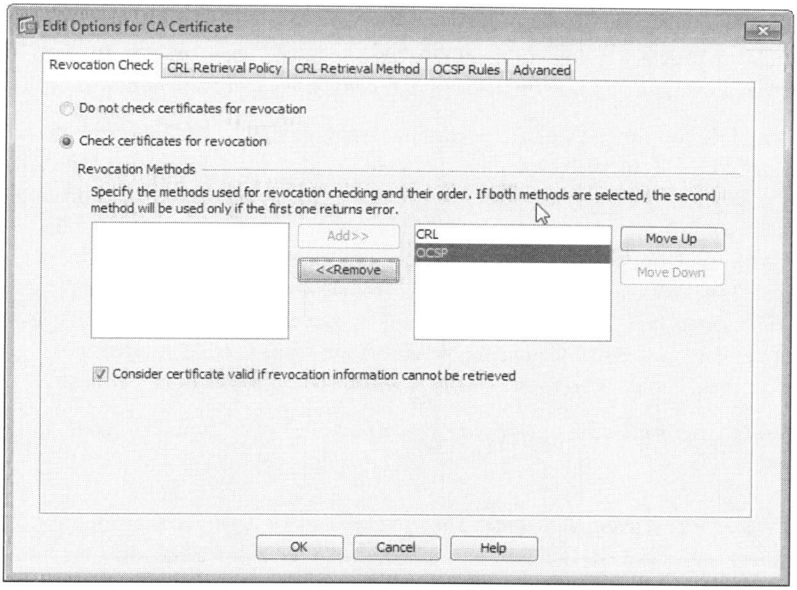

**Figure 4-23**   *Certificate Revocation List Configuration*

On the Revocation Check tab, select the preferred method for revocation checking. You can either select OCSP (recommended), CRL, or both. The order of the methods you choose is important. For example, if CRL is chosen first and remains at the top of the list after you choose OCSP, CRL is used unless the method of retrieval is unavailable, at which point OCSP is used. You can change the order of the revocation methods listed by selecting the one you want to move up or down and using the arrow buttons to move it. You can optionally configure the ASA to ignore any failures in obtaining a certificate's status and allow for the continuation of the authentication process regardless. However, it is at your discretion should you want to do so. (There, now you know where I stand on it.) Note that if the availability of the certificate cannot be verified, neither of configured methods (CRL or OCSP) is functional. And if the Consider Certificate Valid If Revocation Information Cannot Be Retrieved check box is not checked, the VPN session is not allowed to form.

On the next tab, CRL Retrieval Policy, you can specify the locations of the revocation list if you have chosen CRL as one of the revocation checking methods. You can either choose to leave the default option of using the CRL distribution point contained in the CA's certificate or enter static URLs, HTTP, or LDAP, which you might have retrieved from your public PKI provider's website. You can also use both, if the CDP in the certificate file becomes unavailable. The static URLs configured here are tightly related to the next section, where the protocol selected is used for CRL retrieval. LDAP URLs map to LDAP only, whereas HTTP URLs can map both to HTTP and SCEP.

On the CRL Retrieval Method tab, you can select the protocols that will be used when retrieving the CRL: LDAP, HTTP, SCEP, or a combination of the three. Only choose the protocols that you know have been configured by your CA for CRL purposes. Otherwise, you will be creating unnecessary overhead on the ASA and might introduce a delay during a user's authentication process. If you choose LDAP as one of the protocols for retrieval, you must also enter a username, password, server, and optionally a port (default 389).

On the OCSP Rules tab, you can use certificate-matching rules to match specific entries in the certificates that might be selected for revocation check. To create a new OCSP rule, click **Add**, and in the Add OCSP Rule window, select a preconfigured certificate map from the drop-down list, and select a CA from the drop-down list of available CA certificates installed. (Its public key is used for validating responses received from responders.) In the Index field, enter a priority for this rule (rules are checked in priority order from lowest number first to highest), and in the URL field, enter the URL to the OCSP responder that will be used to check the revocation status of any certificates matched using our certificate-mapping rule. (Certificate-mapping rules, discussed earlier, need to exist before you can configure any OCSP rules.)

On the Advanced tab, the following options are available that may be tuned for your specific environment:

- **CRL Cache Refresh Time (Minutes):** The range is 1 to 1440. Enter the amount of time in minutes the retrieved CRL will be cached until a request for the most recent copy is made. By default, this is set to 60 minutes (1 hour).

- **Enforce Next CRL Update:** Default Yes. Uncheck this option if you do not require CRLs to contain a "next update" value or one that is valid. However, by default, the CRL is required to contain a valid next update value.

- **OCSP URL:** Enter a global value used for the OCSP URL. By default, the ASA uses the configured OCSP URLs in the following order:
    - OCSP URL in a match certificate-override rule
    - OCSP URL configured on the Advanced tab (we are here)
    - AIA field of a remote user certificate

- **Disabled Nonce Extension:** By default, this option is unchecked, allowing for a nonce to be used for integrity checking of sent and received OCSP messages by the requestor.

- **Validation Policy:** Select the incoming client connections that can be validated using this CA. Choose from SSL, IPsec, or SSL and IPsec. By default, both SSL and IPsec are selected.

- **Accept Certificates Issued by This CA:** By default, this option is selected. However, if you suspect the CA might have become compromised, you can uncheck the option to render all certificates issued by the CA invalid.

- **Accept Certificates Issued by the Subordinate CAs of This CA:** By default, this option is selected. However, if you suspect a subordinate CA may have become compromised, you can uncheck the option to render all certificates issued by the subordinate CA invalid.

# Doubling Up on Client Authentication

You can increase the security of your SSL VPN deployment further by using the available authentication methods we discussed at the beginning of this chapter and thus requiring your users to authenticate twice or even three times.

To begin, clients typically authenticate using a certificate. When that authentication method succeeds, clients can then be authenticated using either one or two configured AAA servers. Double authentication is usually deployed when using OTPs or SecurID tokens. For example, before being allowed access, users are first authenticated using either a certificate or AAA server and then authenticated again using a PIN along with the current code displayed on their token.

The following are valid methods of double or triple authentication using the ASA:

- Certificate-based + AAA authentication

- Certificate-based + AAA authentication and username prefill from certificate

- Certificate-based + AAA authentication and username prefill and username hide

- Certificate-based + AAA authentication + AAA authentication, using optional username prefill or username hide

- AAA Authentication + AAA authentication, with optional username reuse for the second AAA authentication

In the example shown in Figure 4-24, we have configured double authentication using both certificates and an external AAA server by selecting **Both** as the authentication method in our AnyConnect connection profile (available at **Configuration > Remote Access VPN > Network (Client) Access > AnyConnect Connection Profiles**).

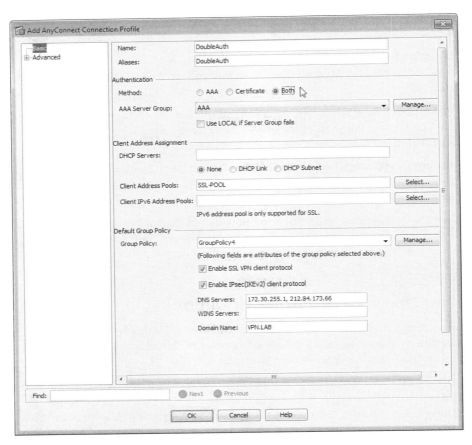

**Figure 4-24**    *Configuring Certificate-Based + AAA Authentication*

Now, when our remote users attempt to connect to our VPN using the selected connection profile, they are required to have a certificate installed, and they must enter a username and password into the AnyConnect client, as shown in Figure 4-25.

In our next example, we have enabled both the option to prefill the username retrieved from the user's certificate and the option to hide the username from the user. These options are configured in the **Advanced > Authentication** pane of the Edit Connection Profile window, as shown in Figure 4-26.

Now when remote users attempt to connect to our VPN connection, they are prompted for a password only after selecting the appropriate connection profile alias, as shown in Figure 4-27.

**Figure 4-25**  *AnyConnect Client Using Double Authentication*

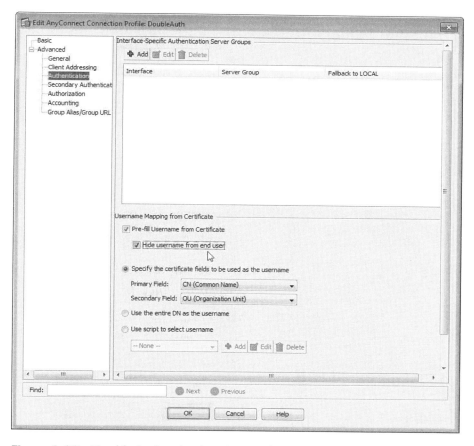

**Figure 4-26**  *Double Authentication, Optional Username Prefill, and Hide*

In our next example, shown in Figure 4-28, we configure triple authentication. Using the combination of certificate authentication + AAA authentication + AAA authentication, we can authenticate our users in three ways.

**Figure 4-27**   *AnyConnect Client Using Double Authentication, Username Prefill, and Hide*

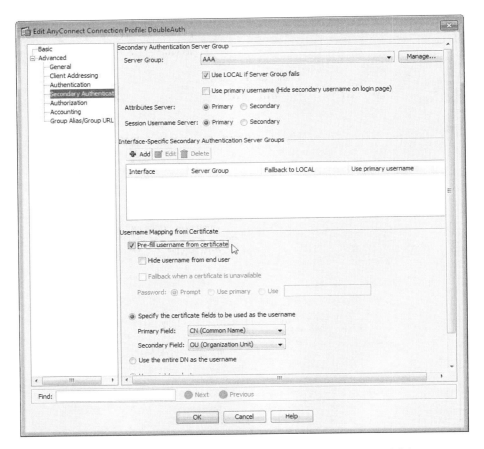

**Figure 4-28**   *Triple Authentication Example: Certificate + AAA + AAA*

We have kept our initial configuration from the earlier double authentication examples and have added an additional AAA server by selecting AAA as the server group in the **Advanced > Secondary Authentication** pane of the Connection Profiles window. We have also chosen the option to fall back to using LOCAL authentication should the authentication server fail for the second AAA authentication process. We have kept the option of username prefill from the certificate for the first AAA authentication process, as shown in our earlier double authentication examples, and have also enabled the username prefill to occur for the second AAA authentication process. Note that the username is no longer hidden.

Now, as shown in Figure 4-29, when our AnyConnect remote users attempt to connect to our SSL VPN, they are prompted for two passwords: one for authentication to the first AAA server and the second for authentication to the second AAA server. Notice also that usernames for both AAA processes have been prefilled using the Common Name (CN) field in the user's certificate.

**Figure 4-29**   *AnyConnect Client Using Triple Authentication, Username Prefill, and Hide*

As discussed at the beginning of this section, you can also set up double authentication using two AAA authentication servers without the use of certificates. This method of authentication can be used if an organization does not use a PKI deployment but has multiple authentication servers available (for example, an Active Directory server and an RSA SecurID server for use with OTPs).

To configure double authentication without using certificates, open the connection profile and in the Basic properties window, instead of selecting Both, select **AAA**, and then from the AAA Server Group drop-down box, choose your primary AAA server. In **Advanced > Secondary Authentication**, use the Server Group drop-down box to choose your secondary AAA server. You also have the option to pre-fill the username using the username that was with the primary AAA authentication server. Selecting this option also hides the secondary AAA Username box from the user.

As shown in Figure 4-30, we configured our connection profile for double AAA authentication by selecting AAA as the primary authentication method and AAA as the secondary authentication method in the **Advanced > Secondary Authentication** window (not shown).

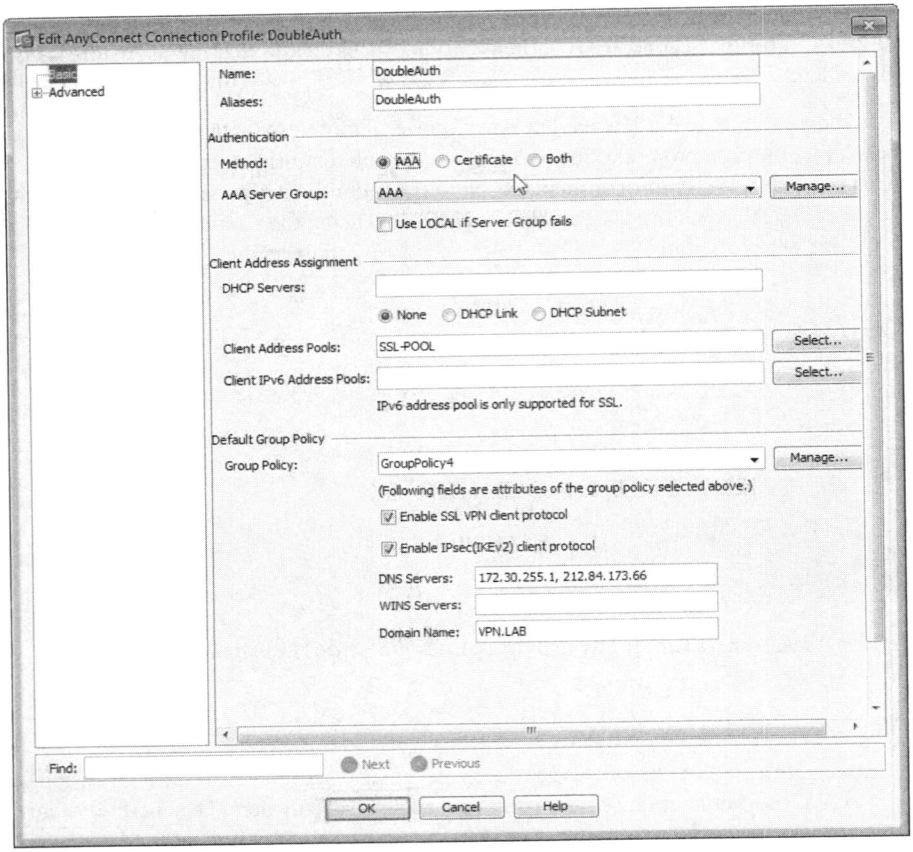

**Figure 4-30** *Double Authentication Using Two AAA Servers*

The resulting behavior, shown in Figure 4-31, is that our AnyConnect client is now prompted for a username and password for use with the primary AAA server and a username and password for use with the secondary AAA server.

**Figure 4-31** *AnyConnect Client Using Double AAA Authentication*

# Troubleshooting Your Advanced Configuration

When troubleshooting a connection, whether it is a basic or advanced method (for example, a simple username and password using the LOCAL ASA database or double authentication using certificates), the AnyConnect client can provide a vast amount of information to help to narrow down and ultimately resolve a problem.

The Message History tab can provide a detailed, step-by-step explanation of the current status and connection phase and any errors that may have occurred during the connection attempt. For example, in Figure 4-32, the Message History tab shows that our user encountered a failure when trying to connect to the ASA because the certificate required for authentication was not installed. After examining this output, we can request and install the client certificate either manually or using the Get Certificate button in the AnyConnect client. Note that in these examples, AnyConnect Secure Mobility Client Version 3.0 was used, which requires at least ASA 8.4.1.

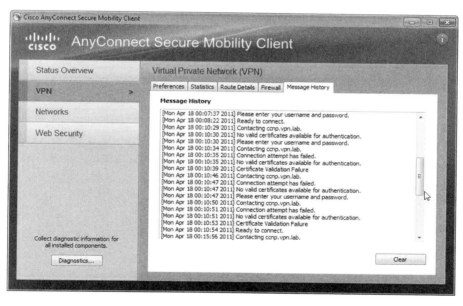

**Figure 4-32**  *AnyConnect Client Message History Tab*

An advanced way to gather the information you might need to troubleshoot is to use the Diagnostic AnyConnect Reporting Tool (DART). DART works independently of any installed AnyConnect client software or modules and is not version specific; so, we can install any version of DART with any version of the AnyConnect client.

DART works by compiling all current logging, software, module, and environment information into a compressed file ready for local examination or for sending to a TAC engineer.

DART can be installed manually by using a separate MSI file on a Windows device or automatically during the connection process.

You can enable the automatic installation of DART by first uploading an AnyConnect installation package that includes DART to the ASA's flash. (You can identify this by looking for *DART* in the filename.) In the group policy associated with the connection profile a user is connecting to, navigate to the **Advanced > AnyConnect Client** (navigate to **Advanced > SSL VPN Client** on pre-6.4 versions of ASDM), uncheck the **Inherit** option next to Optional Client Modules to Download, and from the drop-down list, choose **AnyConnect DART**, as shown in Figure 4-33.

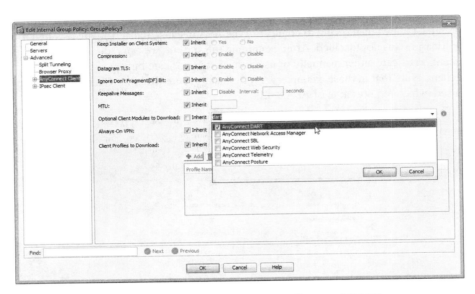

**Figure 4-33** *AnyConnect Enable Automatic Installation of DART*

Now when your clients next connect to our SSL VPN, they are automatically taken through the process of downloading and installing the DART module. After installation, they can run the module either from their Windows Programs menu or by clicking the **Diagnostics** button in the AnyConnect client.

# Exam Preparation Tasks

As mentioned in the section "How to Use This Book" in the Introduction, you have a couple of choices for exam preparation: the memory tables in Appendix C, Chapter 23, "Final Exam Preparation," and the exam simulation questions on the CD-ROM.

## Review All Key Topics

Review the most important topics in the chapter, noted with the Key Topic icon in the outer margin of the page. Table 4-5 lists a reference of these key topics and the page numbers on which each is found.

**Table 4-5**   *Key Topics*

| Key Topic Element | Description | Page |
|---|---|---|
| Bulleted List | Advanced authentication methods | 121 |
| Topic | Provisioning certificates as a local CA | 126 |
| Topic | AnyConnect automatic certificate enrollment | 132 |
| Bulleted List | Automatic enrollment methods | 139 |
| Bulleted List | Available authentication method combinations | 155 |

## Complete Tables and Lists from Memory

Print a copy of Appendix C, "Memory Tables" (found on the CD), or at least the section for this chapter, and complete the tables and lists from memory. Appendix D, "Memory Tables Answer Key," also on the CD, includes completed tables and lists to check your work.

## Define Key Terms

Define the following key terms from this chapter, and check your answers in the glossary:

DART, PKI

This chapter covers the following subjects:

- **Configuration Procedures, Deployment Strategies, and Information Gathering:** In this section, we discuss advanced deployment methods and the information we may require when deciding which method to deploy.

- **AnyConnect Installation Options:** In this section, we discuss the AnyConnect installation options available for an advanced deployment.

- **Managing AnyConnect Client Profiles:** In this section, we look closer at the preferences.xml file and discuss how to edit the profile on and offline and the options we have in an AnyConnect profile to customize the connecting user's experience.

- **Advanced Profile Features:** In this section, we review the advanced features through our profile deployment and discuss how to implement these.

- **Advanced AnyConnect Customization and Management:** In this section, we review the customization options for the AnyConnect client, such as uploading our own company logo. We also review the use of AnyConnect scripting and upgrade procedures for greater management of the client software.

## CHAPTER 5

# Advanced Deployment and Management of the AnyConnect Client

When preparing to deploy an AnyConnect virtual private network (VPN) connection to your remote users, an important task can be customizing the software to match your corporate environment. For example, the addition of a company logo and color scheme not only provides an aesthetically pleasing environment for your users but also an easy way for them to identify yours as the company they are connecting to. Also, if you are deploying your connection to a geographically and internationally dispersed user base, you can customize the language of any informational text and messages displayed by the AnyConnect client to ease the connection experience.

In addition to customizing the overall look and feel of the AnyConnect client, another important task to consider is how you will distribute the AnyConnect software and connection settings to your users. As discussed in this chapter, you have several installation options.

## "Do I Know This Already?" Quiz

The "Do I Know This Already?" quiz helps you determine your level of knowledge on this chapter's topics before you begin. Table 5-1 details the major topics discussed in this chapter and their corresponding quiz sections.

**Table 5-1**  *"Do I Know This Already?" Section-to-Question Mapping*

| Foundation Topics Section | Questions |
| --- | --- |
| AnyConnect Installation Options | 1, 2 |
| Managing AnyConnect Client Profiles | 3, 4, 6 |
| Advanced Profile Features | 5 |

1. When deploying the AnyConnect Secure Mobility Client, which two methods are available?

   a. Predeploy

   b. Web deploy

   c. Post-deploy

   d. Windows Add/Remove Programs

**2.** Which operating systems allow for a web deployment of the AnyConnect client? (Choose all that apply.)

   **a.** Mac OS X

   **b.** Google Chrome

   **c.** Windows XP

   **d.** Linux 64 bit

**3.** When configuring AnyConnect client profiles, which two methods of configuration are recommended?

   **a.** ASDM AnyConnect Profile Editor

   **b.** Notepad

   **c.** Windows AnyConnect Client Profile Editor

   **d.** ASDM AnyConnect Client Profile Editor

**4.** Which of the following are valid client profile types? (Choose all that apply.)

   **a.** NAM

   **b.** VPN

   **c.** IPsec

   **d.** Telemetry

   **e.** Web Security

**5.** When configuring your Automatic VPN Policy deployment, which two of the following can be added for the AnyConnect client to recognize the trusted network? (Choose all that apply.)

   **a.** DNS domain name

   **b.** IP address

   **c.** Access list

   **d.** DNS servers

**6.** Which file does the AnyConnect client use to store local user-specific information?

   **a.** Settings.xml

   **b.** Preferences.xml

   **c.** Preferences_global.xml

   **d.** Settings_global.xml

# Foundation Topics

## Configuration Procedures, Deployment Strategies, and Information Gathering

When preparing to deploy an AnyConnect VPN to your remote users and customize the various objects and parameters available in the client, it can be a great advantage to first understand the environment for which you intend the deployment. For example:

■ Will the VPN be available to geographically dispersed users?

■ Will some users connect to the VPN from another country that uses another language?

■ Will the remote user base consist entirely of corporate employees who spend a lot of time in the corporate office or will they be remote workers based permanently at home or third-party contractors/companies?

The answers to these questions provide a great deal of information and a good starting point when preparing to customize the AnyConnect client environment and deployment for users.

If, as shown in Figure 5-1, the VPN connection will be made available to third parties and remote workers who are permanently based outside your corporate environment, choosing to predeploy the installation of AnyConnect and associated modules may introduce an unnecessary level of administrative and support overhead. We might instead choose the web deploy method of operation, whereby the AnyConnect client can automatically download and install during the user's connection. If the vast majority of our remote users will be corporate users, it might be beneficial both from an administrative and software management point of view to predeploy the AnyConnect client using, for example, a Windows group policy or other internal software deployment method.

If your deployment will involve users in other countries who may use a native language other than English, you can tailor the experience for them by enabling their language and allowing for the selection of a particular language from a list of those available. In addition, custom logos and button images and a corporate color scheme can be applied to your AnyConnect deployment, extending the environment of your office and web presence to remote users.

You also have to make the decision of whether the AnyConnect client remains on the remote user's machine after the user disconnects from the VPN session or if it uninstalls automatically. If the VPN connection will be deployed to third-party users, or remote users will be accessing the VPN from a publicly available device, for example, it is prudent to have the application uninstall itself upon disconnection. If the VPN connection is used heavily by corporate remote users on company-owned devices, however, it can save them time for the client to remain installed on their device (thus allowing them to easily reconnect by locally launching the client).

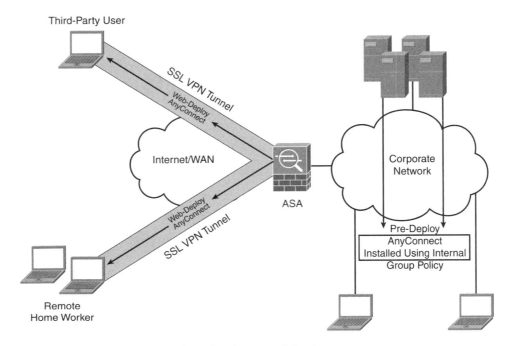

**Figure 5-1**  *AnyConnect Package Deployment Selection*

## AnyConnect Installation Options

You can deploy the AnyConnect VPN client software in either of two ways:

■ Manual predeployment

■ Automatic web deployment

As explained earlier, the choice of method is based on the environment and user base. For this example, both the manual and automatic deployment methods and their associated configuration are illustrated.

### Manual Predeployment

A predeployment install can be carried out by following the Install Wizard or, if you are deploying the software to an internal user group or department, for example, through a method such as Microsoft's Group Policy feature. Because the connection using an Any-Connect client depends on available licensing on your Adaptive Security Appliance (ASA) device, you might also choose the predeployment method based on an internal licensing or asset management program, which will help to track exactly who has the AnyConnect client software installed.

The manual installation process is pretty straightforward. Consider, for example, installing the client software onto a laptop for an internal user. You first obtain a copy of the latest AnyConnect client software predeployment package, which you can download from Cisco.com, provided you have a valid support agreement.

You can download the core client and module predeployment files either individually for Mac and Linux or as a packaged ISO file for Windows deployments. Table 5-2 lists the available predeployment packages and their relevant operating systems.

**Table 5-2**   *Available Cisco AnyConnect Predeployment Files*

| Filename | OS |
| --- | --- |
| Anyconnect-win-<version>-k9.iso | Windows ISO image |
| Anyconnect-macosx-i386-<version>-k9.dmg | Mac OS X DMG file |
| Anyconnect-linux-<version>-k9.tar.gz | Linux 32-bit TAR file |
| Anyconnect-Linux_64-<version>-k9.tar.gz | Linux 64-bit TAR file |

**Note:**  The current release of the Cisco AnyConnect client as of this writing is 3.0.0629. However, as new versions become available, the names of the files may change, and more modules/files may become available for download.

This example focuses only on the Windows installation process. After you have downloaded the required ISO file, you can extract its contents using a disk or unzip utility (such as WinRAR) to access the installation files. At this stage, you also gain access to the various module and core MSI files you can use for a corporate group policy deployment. Table 5-3 lists the files packaged in the ISO file and their purpose.

**Table 5-3**   *Cisco AnyConnect ISO Packaged Predeployment Files*

| File | Purpose |
| --- | --- |
| GUI.ico | The AnyConnect icon image |
| Setup.exe | Launches the Install utility (Setup.hta) |
| Anyconnect-dart-win-<version>-k9.msi | Diagnostic and Reporting Tool (DART) optional module |
| Anyconnect-gina-win-<version>-predeploy-k9.msi | Start Before Login (SBL) optional module |
| Anyconnect-nam-win-<version>.msi | Network Access Manager (NAM) optional module |
| Anyconnect-posture-win-<version>-predeploy-k9.msi | Posture optional module |
| Anyconnect-telemetry-win-<version>-predeploy-k9.msi | Telemetry optional module |
| Anyconnect-websecurity-win-<version>-predeploy-k9.msi | Web Security optional module |

**Table 5-3**   *Cisco AnyConnect ISO Packaged Predeployment Files*

| File | Purpose |
| --- | --- |
| Anyconnect-win-<version>-predeploy-k9.msi | AnyConnect core client |
| Autorun.inf | Autorun information file for Setup.exe |
| Cues_bg.jpg | A background image for the Install utility graphical user interface (GUI) |
| Setup.hta | Customizable Install utility HTML Application (HTA) |
| Update.txt | A text file containing the AnyConnect version number |

To begin the installation process, double-click the Setup.exe file. This, in turn, launches the Setup.hta HTML install utility, as shown in Figure 5-2.

**Figure 5-2**   *Cisco AnyConnect Client Setup.hta Web Install Utility*

After you launch the Setup.hta Install utility, the installation menu shows the installable modules. For example, if the core client software is already installed, you can install the optional modules. Without the AnyConnect client software installed, however, the only module that can be installed is DART. All remaining modules require the AnyConnect core client software to be installed first. The following are required to be installed in this order:

- AnyConnect core client software

- SBL, NAM, Posture, Web Security modules (in any order)

- Telemetry module (requires the installation of the Posture module)

When choosing to uninstall the core software and modules manually, the reverse operation of the preceding steps must be followed.

In addition, you can select whether to Lock Down Component Services during installation. If this option is selected, the Installer removes all user privileges from the installed AnyConnect services, preventing any of them from being stopped (even by an administrator). By installing the AnyConnect client module-by-module, this feature can be enabled or disabled per module. Note that this operation is one way only and cannot be removed unless the module is reinstalled.

The Setup.hta file is an HTML file containing VBScript and HTML code. If you are familiar with scripting languages, you can easily customize the installation options that are available to the user. As shown in Figure 5-3, we have kept the AnyConnect client Core installation option available and removed all optional modules apart from the SBL (Start Before Login) and DART (Diagnosis and Reporting Tool). We have also removed the Lock Down Component Services option.

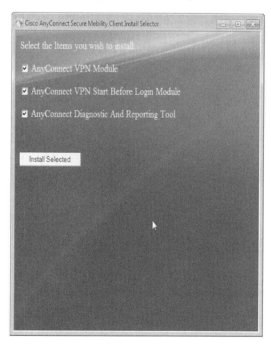

**Figure 5-3**  *Cisco AnyConnect Client Customized Setup.hta Web Install Utility*

To proceed with the manual installation of the selected files on a remote user's machine, click **Install Selected**. Doing so starts the installation procedures for the individual MSI files. When the "Installation Succeeded" message appears, the device must be restarted. The user is now ready to begin using the AnyConnect client.

## Automatic Web Deployment

When preparing to use the web deploy method to install AnyConnect, you must first retrieve the appropriate package file. These are either PKG or ZIP files and are available for download from Cisco.com (as long as you have a valid support contract).

Table 5-4 lists the available web deployment packages and their platform.

**Table 5-4**  *Cisco AnyConnect VPN Client Web Deploy Packages*

| Package | Platform |
| --- | --- |
| Anyconnect-win-<version>-k9.pkg | Windows |
| Anyconnect-macosx-i386-<version>-k9.pkg | MAC OS X |
| Anyconnect-linux-<version>-k9.pkg | Linux 32 bit |
| Anyconnect-linux-64-<version>-k9.pkg | Linux 64 bit |

After downloading the appropriate package, you must upload it to the flash of the ASA device. To do so, navigate to **Configuration > Remote Access VPN > Network (Client) Access> AnyConnect Client Settings** and click **Add**. You have a choice to browse the local flash for a package file you may have already uploaded, or to click **Upload** and select a downloaded file from your local machine. For this example, we selected the option to upload and used the **Browse Local Files** button to select our downloaded file, as shown in Figure 5-4. After selection, the Flash File System Path field is automatically populated with the name of the image and path where it will be saved on the local flash.

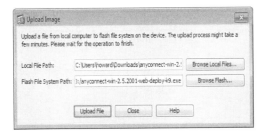

**Figure 5-4**  *ASA AnyConnect Client Package File Upload*

Key
Topic

After uploading the file, the connection profiles need to be configured to allow for the deployment of the AnyConnect client. You do so by navigating to **Configuration > Remote Access VPN > Network (Client) Access > AnyConnect Connect Profiles**.

For your AnyConnect deployment to succeed, Secure Sockets Layer (SSL) access and AnyConnect client access must both be enabled on the relevant interface. In the Access Interfaces section of the AnyConnect Connection Profiles window, shown in Figure 5-5, we enabled AnyConnect VPN Client Access on the selected interfaces and then selected the relevant interfaces for which we require the AnyConnect access to be available. Optionally, Datagram Transport Layer Security (DTLS) can be enabled on the same interfaces if DTLS operation is required for any latency-sensitive applications being used through the VPN tunnel.

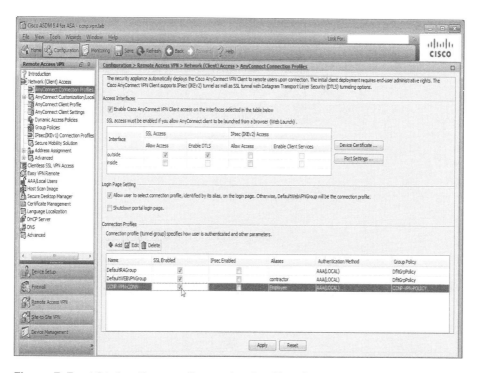

**Figure 5-5**    *ASA AnyConnect Connection Profile Edit*

Also shown in Figure 5-5, SSL must be enabled for the relevant connection profiles in the Connection Profiles section of the window. You can either select a preconfigured or default connection profile from the window and then check the **SSL Enabled** check box and optionally enable IPsec for the use of IKEv2 connections, or you can create a new connection profile by clicking **Add** in the section.

In this example, we chose the option to create a new connection profile. In the Add AnyConnect Connection Profile window, we gave our connection profile a name, chose the authentication type, and assigned an IP address pool and group policy. We then enabled SSL (and optionally IPsec [Internet Key Exchange Version 2, IKEv2]) for our connection profile, as shown in Figure 5-6.

**Figure 5-6** *ASA AnyConnect Connection Profile Creation*

After enabling AnyConnect for your connection profile, you can now edit the group policy settings that are applied to the connection profile to determine the behavior of the AnyConnect client installation method. For example, will you allow your users to choose whether the client will be used? Will it install automatically after a specific number of seconds, or will it automatically install as soon as users have logged in to the portal?

Configure your group policy settings by navigating to **Configuration > Remote Access VPN > Network (Client) Access > Group Policies**. Then choose the group policy assigned to the connection profile you selected or created earlier, and click **Edit** to open the Edit Internal Group Policy window.

In the Edit Internal Group Policy window, navigate to **Advanced > AnyConnect Client > Login Setting**. It is in here you are able to determine the behavior of the AnyConnect client installation during a remote user's login. Begin editing the settings by unchecking the **Inherit** option. Doing so prevents your group policy settings from relying on the default group policy settings that may or may not have been configured appropriately for your connection. Now in this window there are two sections, each containing its relevant login settings:

- **Post Login Setting:** Contains the options that may or may not be available to the remote user upon logging in to the web VPN portal.

- **Default Post Login Selection:** Contains the actions that will be applied if a selection is not made.

As shown in Figure 5-7, you can allow a remote user to choose during a set period of time (default is 20 seconds) whether the AnyConnect client software will be installed or if the AnyConnect client will continue to install automatically without any user input. If you allow a user to choose whether to install the client, after the time period has elapsed and the user has not made a choice, the default post-login selection action occurs. This either takes the user to the clientless SSL VPN portal page or proceeds to download and install the AnyConnect client. If you select the option to not prompt the user to choose, the configured default post login selection is applied anyway.

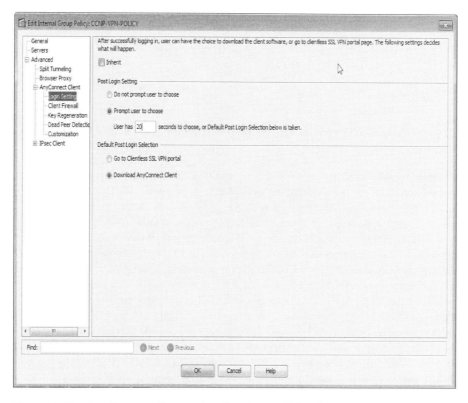

**Figure 5-7**  *AnyConnect Connection Post-Login Behavior*

To test the action, log in to your web VPN portal and choose your new AnyConnect connection profile from the list of profiles available. After 20 seconds of not making a choice, you are automatically presented with the AnyConnect web portal where the automatic download, installation, and connection of the VPN occurs, as shown in Figure 5-8.

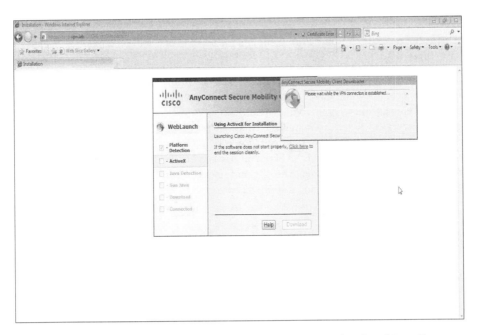

**Figure 5-8**    *AnyConnect Client Software Automatic Download and Install*

So, you have installed the AnyConnect on a remote user's machine automatically and the user is connected and getting on with his work, but what happens when he finishes and disconnects? Will you leave the AnyConnect client installed on his device for use at another time, or will you choose to remove the AnyConnect client if he no longer requires it? The behavior of whether the client software remains installed is selected in your group policy settings. You can choose to remove the software or leave it installed (default) by opening the group policy object in **Configuration > Remote Access VPN > Network (Client) Access > Group Policies**. Choose the appropriate group policy object from the list and click **Edit**. Then, in the Edit Internal Group Policy window, choose **Advanced > AnyConnect Client**. In the dialog that opens, the first option you have is Keep Installed on Client System. By default, this option leaves the client installed on the user's device. (This is true as long as no one has configured the default group policy to remove it. Remember that your group policy object is inheriting its settings from the default group policy object). However, if you want the AnyConnect client to remove itself upon disconnection, uncheck the **Inherit** option and click **No**.

The option to automatically remove the client software from the user's device applies only to the software that has been installed using the web deploy method. To remove the client software from a device that has had the software installed manually using the predeployment method, you can use **Add/Remove Programs** (on a Windows machine).

## Managing AnyConnect Client Profiles

You were introduced to AnyConnect client profiles briefly in Chapter 4, "Advanced Authentication and Authorization of AnyConnect VPNs," when creating a connection profile for certificate enrollment purposes. This section provides a more complete overview of the client profiles and the options they contain for an AnyConnect client.

AnyConnect client profiles store the administratively defined settings used by the various modules and core client settings for operation. For example, you can enable SBL (Start Before Login), minimize upon connection, split tunneling, module services, and so on. The client profiles are stored in the Extensible Markup Language (XML) file format on the ASA's flash device; and during a connection attempt, they are downloaded by the AnyConnect client.

At present, the client profiles that may be configured are as follows:

Key Topic

- **VPN:** Settings applied to the core AnyConnect client software

- **NAM:** Network Access Manager module settings for control of wireless and wired network device settings

- **Web Security:** The settings required for operation by the Web Security module (for example, which local ports to run on and which scanning hosts are available)

- **Telemetry:** The settings required for the Telemetry module operation (for example, service control and local device antivirus checking)

AnyConnect client profiles are assigned via group policies. However, because of the policy inheritance model, a client may be assigned more than one profile, if any client profiles have been deployed globally using the default group policy object.

Two methods are recommended to configure a client profile: using the AnyConnect Client Profile Editor available from the Adaptive Security Device Manager (ASDM) or using the Windows offline AnyConnect Client Profile Editor. Whereas one is offline and one is attached to the ASDM, the two editors allow for the same profile types and options to be configured (with the exception of the Telemetry module, which is editable on via the ASA's profile editor). All examples used throughout this book use the AnyConnect Client Profile Editor available from the ASDM.

In addition to the client profiles held on the ASA, the AnyConnect client holds settings in two files on the local device for use either before the user has logged in to the device locally or after. These settings are stored in Preference.xml files:

- **Preferences.xml:** Local user settings, name, last login, certificate data, ASA address, and so on

- **Preferences_global.xml:** Stores global AnyConnect settings that are used before a user logs on the local device (for example, start before login and default domain)

Example 5-1 shows the contents of a Preferences_global.xml file.

**Example 5-1**   *AnyConnect Preferences_global.xml file Contents*

```
<?xml version="1.0" encoding="UTF-8"?>
<AnyConnectPreferences>
<DefaultUser></DefaultUser>
<DefaultSecondUser></DefaultSecondUser>
<ClientCertificateThumbprint></ClientCertificateThumbprint>
<ServerCertificateThumbprint></ServerCertificateThumbprint>
<DefaultHost>172.30.255.2:443</DefaultHost>
<DefaultDomain>vpn.lab</DefaultDomain>
<DefaultGroup></DefaultGroup>
<ProxyHost></ProxyHost>
<ProxyPort></ProxyPort>
<SDITokenType>none</SDITokenType>
<ControllablePreferences>
<LocalLanAccess>false</LocalLanAccess>
<EnableAutomaticServerSelection>false</EnableAutomaticServerSelection>
  </ControllablePreferences>
</AnyConnectPreferences>
```

As you can see from the example, no user-specific settings are held in the Preferences_global.xml file (with the exception of the DefaultUser and DefaultSecondUser fields, which may be used during SBL operation).

The preferences files are stored in either a global location or a user-specific location. Table 5-5 lists the default locations for both files on Windows, Linux, and Mac OS X devices.

**Table 5-5**   *Default Preferences and Preferences_global XML File Locations per OS*

| OS | Type | File Path |
|---|---|---|
| Windows Vista/7 | User | C:\Users\username\AppData\Local\Cisco\Cisco AnyConnect VPN Client\preferences.xml |
| | Global | C:\ProgramData\Cisco\Cisco AnyConnect VPN Client\preferences_global.xml |
| Windows XP | User | C:\Documents and Settings\username\Local Settings\Application-Data\Cisco\Cisco AnyConnect VPNClient\preferences.xml |
| | Global | C:\Documents and Settings\AllUsers\Application Data\Cisco\Cisco AnyConnect VPNClient\preferences_global.xml |
| Linux | User | /home/username/.anyconnect |
| | Global | /opt/cisco/vpn/.anyconnect_global |
| Mac OS X | User | /Users/username/.anyconnect |
| | Global | /opt/cisco/vpn/.anyconnect_global |

To begin editing a client profile, you must first create one. By default, none are available. Navigate to **Configuration > Remote Access VPN > Network (Client) Access > Any-Connect Client Profile** and click **Add**. In the Add AnyConnect Client Profile window, give your profile a name and, from the drop-down list, select the type of profile or module that this profile will be applied to. As mentioned earlier, you have four types to choose from:

- VPN (core client software)

- NAM

- Web Security

- Telemetry

For this example, we choose VPN, because at this point we are interested in looking only at the available options for the core client software. The Profile Location field will have automatically populated itself based on the name of the profile. However, to store the profile in a different flash location on the ASA or give the file different name, it may be changed here. You can also select the group policy from a drop-down list. If a group policy is not selected in this window, you can later assign our profile to one in the main Any-Connect Client Profile window. Enter the required details, click **OK**, and are you are taken back to the main AnyConnect Client Profile window. To edit the settings for the newly created profile, select it from the window and click **Edit**. The AnyConnect Client Profile Editor then opens, as shown in Figure 5-9.

Table 5-6 describes the configurable settings in the Preferences (Part 1) window of the AnyConnect Client Profile Editor and their default values.

**Table 5-6**   *AnyConnect Client Profile Editor Preferences: Part 1*

| Setting | Description/Value |
| --- | --- |
| Use Start Before Login | Enable the use of the SBL module. By default, this is not checked. However, it is controllable by the connecting user in the AnyConnect client. |
| Show Preconnect Message | Check this option to allow for a custom message to be shown before the user connects to the VPN. |
| Certificate Store | Choose the default certificate store that will be used by the AnyConnect client during a connection attempt to a VPN that requires certificate-based authentication. Choose from All, Machine, User (default = All). On Linux and Mac devices, a certificate store can be created. |
| Certificate Store Override | Allow for the use of a certificate store even if the connecting user does not have administrative privileges (for example, the local machine store). |
| Auto Connect on Start | By default, this option is not checked and is user controllable. Check this option if you require the AnyConnect client to connect automatically when a user opens it. |

**Table 5-6**  *AnyConnect Client Profile Editor Preferences: Part 1*

| Setting | Description/Value |
|---|---|
| Minimize on Connect | By default, this option is checked and is user controllable. As soon as the AnyConnect has successfully connected to your VPN connection, the client will minimize. |
| Local LAN Access* | Check this option if the connecting user requires access to the local LAN at the same time as your VPN (for example, if the user requires access to a networked printer). By default, this option is not checked but is user controllable. |
| Auto Reconnect and Auto Reconnect Behavior | Use these options to determine what will happen during a user hibernating or placing his or her machine into a standby state. By default, the option to Auto Reconnect is checked with the behavior of DisconnectOnSuspend. However, this can be changed to ReconnectAfterResume if required. |
| Auto Update | Allow for the automatic update of the AnyConnect client software and modules if the administrator uploads newer versions of the AnyConnect client to the ASA device. By default, this option is checked but not user controllable. |
| RSA SecurID Integration | Choose the type of integration with RSA products that will be used (for example, a hardware token or software token). By default, Automatic is enabled. |
| Windows Logon Enforcement | Select to allow a VPN session to be established from a Remote Desktop (RDP) instance. (Split-tunneling configuration is required.) When the user who established the session logs out, the AnyConnect session is disconnected. There are two options: SingleLocalLogon and SingleLogon. SingleLocal-Logon allows only one local user to be logged on during the entire VPN session, and this user can establish the session while one or more remote users are logged on. SingleLogon allows only one user to be logged on during the entire VPN session, but no additional logons are allowed, locally or remotely. |
| Windows VPN Establishment | Either allow remote users (RDP) of the local machine to establish a VPN connection using the AnyConnect client by choosing the AllowRemoteUsers option or prevent the VPN connection initiated by a remote user connected to the local machine by choosing the LocalUsersOnly option. |
| Clear SmartCard PIN | Check this option to clear the PIN created by the users smartcard on connection to the VPN. |

*For the Local LAN Access feature to be functional (except being enabled in the AnyConnect XML profile, which is downloaded by the client), you also need to configure the necessary networks that will or will not be tunneled by the ASA within the relevant group policy. You will see more of split tunneling as we continue our discussion of the AnyConnect client, clientless SSL VPNs, and IPsec VPNs.

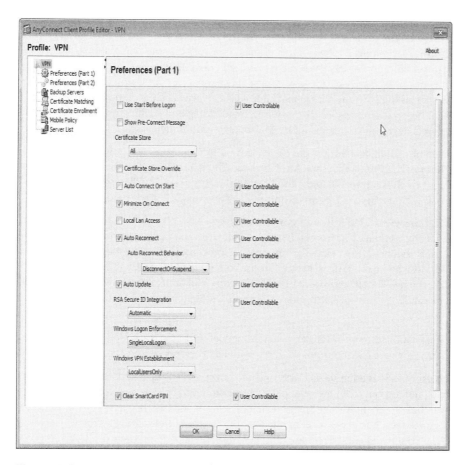

**Figure 5-9**   *ASDM AnyConnect Client Profile Editor*

# Advanced Profile Features

As you have seen, there are a number of settings and options to choose from when customizing the VPN environment for your connecting users. Some of these settings can be used to define the available prompts, buttons, and fields your user sees in the AnyConnect software. Other settings can provide users with an improved overall experience during their VPN connection by controlling the behavior of the AnyConnect client (for example, when a user logs out from his local machine or disconnects from his office network and reconnects using his home network later on).

This section covers two advanced features that you can enable to address the scenario just described:

- SBL (Start Before Login)

- Trusted Network Detection

### Start Before Login

SBL is a great feature to use if, for example, you run a Windows Active Directory network and your users are required to log in to a domain controller before being able to access their local machine. In this case, when enabling SBL, the AnyConnect client establishes a VPN connection to your ASA and sets up a secure tunnel to your corporate environment before users can log in to their local machine. This can also come in handy if your organization deploys prelogin policies that require downloading and running on the local machine before a user logs in (for example, Microsoft group policies).

You can enable SBL in a client profile by navigating to **Configuration > Remote Access VPN > Network (Client) Access > AnyConnect Client Profiles**. Choose the client profile from the list of those available and click **Edit**. In the AnyConnect Client Profile Editor, check the **Use Start Before Logon** option in the Preferences (Part 1) pane.

That's it! You have enabled SBL for your remote users. Now all you have to do is deploy the new setting to them. If it has not been done already, you need to apply your client profile to a user or connection using a group policy. You can do so in the AnyConnect Client Profile window by clicking the **Change Group Policy** button. The Change Group Policy for Profile <name> (in our example, VPN) dialog box will appear, as shown in Figure 5-10. This dialog includes a list of configured group policy objects to which you can apply your profile.

Before SBL is applied to your remote users, they need to log in to the VPN. After logging in, their AnyConnect client automatically downloads the updated profile.

After the user has logged in to the VPN and the new profile is updated, the user can then disconnect and log out from his machine. When coming to log back on to his machine, the user must click the **Switch User** button when running Windows. In the lower-right corner of the logon screen, the user can click the **Remote Login** button; doing so displays an icon for the AnyConnect client. After choosing the AnyConnect client, the user is presented with the familiar Username and Password box, as shown in Figure 5-11.

### Trusted Network Detection

Trusted Network Detection is typically used by remote users who spend time working from both a remote location and their corporate office using the same device. The AnyConnect client can be configured to look for certain parameters that enable it to recognize whether the network the local machine is currently using is a trusted (internal) network (for example, the corporate LAN) or if the network currently being used is untrusted (external) (for example, user's home or an Internet cafe).

Depending on the user's current location, you can configure the AnyConnect client to disconnect from its current VPN connection, pause a VPN connection, start a connection, or do nothing.

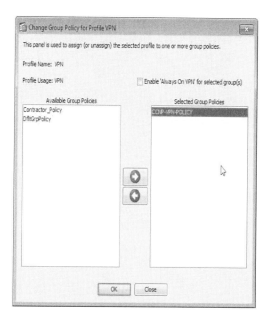

**Figure 5-10**    *Apply Your AnyConnect Client Profile to a Group Policy Object*

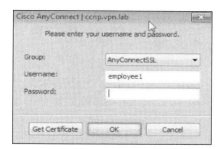

**Figure 5-11**    *Cisco AnyConnect SBL*

The settings required for a successful configuration of Trusted Network Detection are configured in the AnyConnect client profile, as you saw earlier. In the AnyConnect Client Profile Editor, navigate to Preferences (Part 2) and check **Automatic VPN Policy** to allow the trusted network detection settings to become available.

As shown in Figure 5-12, when you enable Automatic VPN Policy, the trusted and untrusted network policies are no longer dimmed.

Begin by selecting your Trusted Network Policy behavior (that is, what will happen when the local machine is on a trusted network). As you saw earlier, you can either choose to disconnect, pause, connect, or do nothing when the AnyConnect client finds out it is on a trusted network. For this example, we chose the default option **Disconnect**.

**Figure 5-12**  *AnyConnect Client Profile Editor: Enable Trusted Network Detection*

Next, choose what happens when the AnyConnect client finds out it is on an untrusted network. The default behavior is for the AnyConnect client to connect to the VPN. However, you can also set this to DoNothing if you prefer to allow users to manually start a connection when, for example, they are away from the office.

Next, define your trusted Domain Name System (DNS) domains/servers servers. The AnyConnect client uses this information to work out whether it is indeed on a trusted network or on an untrusted network. For example, if the local device receives the DNS suffix from a Dynamic Host Control Protocol (DHCP) server that matches the domain name configured in the AnyConnect profile, AnyConnect makes the determination that it is on a trusted network and carries out the action specified earlier. If you specify both domain name and DNS servers, both settings need to be matched for the network to be considered as trusted. When connected to a network, if the user is assigned multiple DNS servers, all these need to be specified in the Trusted DNS Servers section for the network to be considered as trusted. If you configure multiple domain names in the Trusted DNS Domains section, separated by commas, only one domain needs to be matched by the user network settings for the network to be considered as trusted.

Table 5-7 describes the configurable settings in the Preferences (Part 2) of the AnyConnect Client Profile Editor and their default values.

**Table 5-7**   *AnyConnect Client Profile Editor Preferences: Part 2*

| Setting | Description/Value |
| --- | --- |
| Disable Certificate Selection | Allow the user to select a certificate from a list of those available to use for authentication purposes, or only allow for the automatic selection of a certificate by the AnyConnect client based on certificate-matching rules created. By default, the option to allow the user to select a certificate is disabled. |
| Allow Local Proxy Connections | Check this option to allow for the use of the local proxy settings configured in IE or Safari for the AnyConnect session to be established. This, however, can be disabled if the proxy configuration can prevent the user from establishing a VPN connection when operating outside of the LAN. (For this, you need to select the IgnoreProxy option.) |
| Enable Optimal Gateway Selection | Select this option if you have multiple ASA devices available for connection and want the AnyConnect client to choose the appropriate ASA based on the optimal path (round-trip time, RTT) to each gateway. |
| Suspension Time Threshold | Enter the amount of time in hours that should elapse before the AnyConnect client attempts to connect to a different ASA gateway. If you find that your users are consistently swapping between gateways often, you can change this time to a higher amount. |
| Performance Improvement Threshold % | Enter the percentage value of the gain in performance the path to an ASA should have over your current ASA before the AnyConnect client attempts to switch the connection. By default, this value is 20%. |
| Automatic VPN Policy | Select this option if you want to enable the AnyConnect client to start or stop a VPN connection based on the local device's location (for example, moving from a trusted [LAN] connection to an untrusted [remote network] connection). |

**Table 5-7**   *AnyConnect Client Profile Editor Preferences: Part 2*

| Setting | Description/Value |
|---|---|
| Trusted Network Policy | Choose the behavior of the AnyConnect client based on the presence of the local machine in a trusted network (identified by domain name or DNS servers match). The available options are as follows:<br><br>**Disconnect:** Disconnects from the VPN.<br><br>**Connect:** Starts a new VPN connection.<br><br>**Do Nothing:** Maintains the current connection state.<br><br>**Pause:** Pauses the VPN connection without fully disconnecting, allowing for the AnyConnect client to quickly reconnect when detecting the local machines presence on a untrusted network. |
| Untrusted Network Policy | Choose the behavior of the AnyConnect client based on the presence of the local machine in an untrusted network. The available options are as follows:<br><br>**Connect:** Starts a new VPN connection.<br><br>**Do Nothing:** Maintains the current connection state. |
| Trusted DNS Domains | Enter the domain name of a trusted network. If the trusted network policy is enabled, the AnyConnect client attempts to use any received domain suffix to recognize the presence of the local machine on a trusted network. |
| Trusted DNS Servers | Enter the addresses of the DNS servers in use on a trusted network. The AnyConnect client attempts to use the DNS servers in use to recognize the presence of the local machine on a trusted network. |
| Always On | Allow for the AnyConnect client to initiate the VPN connection as soon as the user logs on to the local machine for security purposes. This option, however, may be disabled or enabled using the settings received in a group policy or Dynamic Access Policy (DAP). |
| Allow VPN Disconnect | When this is configured for Always On behavior, we can optionally remove the Disconnect button from the AnyConnect client to prevent the user from disconnecting. |
| Connect Failure Policy | Choose either Open or Closed to allow or restrict network access. For example, choose **Closed** if you require the user to have no local network access during a failure or disconnection of the VPN tunnel until the VPN is reestablished. |

**Table 5-7**   *AnyConnect Client Profile Editor Preferences: Part 2*

| Setting | Description/Value |
|---|---|
| Allow Captive Portal Remediation | Check this option if the Connect Failure Policy is set to close network access on a VPN disconnection. However, the user must connect to a Wi-Fi hotspot using a captive portal before an Internet connection is granted so that the AnyConnect session can be successfully established. |
| | Enter the remediation time in minutes (default 5) that AnyConnect can allow for captive portal registration before network access is restricted again. |
| Apply Last VPN Local Resource Rules | Check this option for the AnyConnect client to enforce the last firewall/VPN policy it had received from the ASA before disconnection if the VPN gateway is unreachable. For example, this policy may include up-to-date rules for local network access or restrictions. |
| PPP Exclusion | Allows for the exclusion of networks from the VPN policy to a PPP gateway if the presence of a PPP gateway has been determined. We have three options: |
| | **Automatic:** AnyConnect uses the PPP server IP address to exclude networks based on their next hop from VPN policies. |
| | **Disable:** Do not apply PPP exclusion. |
| | **Override:** Allows the user to configure PPP exclusion locally if the AnyConnect fails to automatically locate the PPP server IP address. |
| PPP Exclusion Server | Enter the IP address of the PPP server for exclusion, if the override option has been selected in the previous setting. |
| Enable Scripting | Check this option if you want to run scripts during a user connection and disconnection using the OnConnect and OnDisconnect functions. The scripts created must be uploaded to the ASA's flash using the respective OnConnect and OnDisconnect filenames. |
| Terminate Script on Next Event | Check this option if you want the AnyConnect client to terminate the OnConnect script if the VPN disconnects, or if the OnDisconnect script is still running while the user tries to establish a new VPN connection. |
| Enable Post SBL on Connect Script | Check this option if you want to enable to OnConnect script after a user has connected using SBL (only supported with Windows XP, Vista, or 7). |
| Retain VPN on Logoff | Check this option to keep the VPN connection enabled after the user has logged off from Windows. |

**Table 5-7**   *AnyConnect Client Profile Editor Preferences: Part 2*

| Setting | Description/Value |
| --- | --- |
| User Enforcement | Use in conjunction with the Retain VPN on Logoff setting. Choose to either allow AnyUser to connect using the VPN connection after logging on to Windows or only allow the previously logged-off user to connect using the already established connection. |
| Authentication Timeout (Seconds) | Enter the number of seconds between 10 and 120 (default 12) the AnyConnect client will wait for an authentication request from the ASA before prompting the user with an "Authentication Timed Out" message. |

# Advanced AnyConnect Customization and Management

When organizations deploy a VPN solution to remote users and third parties, an important aspect is customizing the software and extending the corporate environment beyond the office location.

You can customize the software using the available Customization/Localization menus in the ASDM by navigating to **Configuration > Remote Access VPN > Network (Client) Access > AnyConnect Customization/Localization**. In this menu, there are six panes to choose from that help achieve a basic level of customization by simply uploading logos or images (or a more advanced level of customization using scripts and transform sets). These panes are as follows:

■   Resources

■   Binary

■   Script

■   GUI Text and Messages

■   Customized Installer Transforms

■   Localized Installed Transforms

For basic customization, you can upload images in the Resources pane by clicking **Import**, giving the item a name (the name must match the image you are replacing exactly), selecting the platform (Windows, Linux, or Mac), and choosing the item from your local machine. This is illustrated in Figure 5-13.

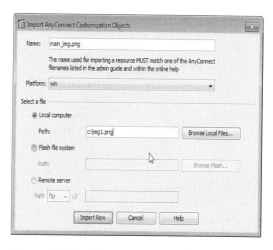

**Figure 5-13**  *Customization of the AnyConnect Client*

Table 5-8 lists the available images and their respective locations in the AnyConnect client, their image types, and their sizes.

**Table 5-8**  *Customizable AnyConnect Objects*

| Filename and AnyConnect Location | Size and Type |
|---|---|
| About.png | $24 \times 24$ |
| The About button in the upper-right corner of the Advanced dialog. | PNG |
| About_hover.png | $24 \times 24$ |
| The About button in the upper-right corner of the Advanced dialog. | PNG |
| ArrowDown.png | $16 \times 22$ |
| The button that enables the user to move networks down in the Networks list of the NAM Advanced window. | PNG |
| ArrowDownDisabled.png | $16 \times 22$ |
| The disabled button that enables the user to move networks down in the Networks list of the NAM Advanced window Configuration tab. | PNG |
| ArrowUp.png | $16 \times 22$ |
| The button that enables the user to move networks up in the Networks list of the NAM Advanced window Configuration tab. | PNG |
| ArrowUpDisabled.png | $16 \times 22$ |
| The disabled button that enables the user to move networks up in the Networks list of the NAM Advanced window Configuration tab. | PNG |

**Table 5-8** *Customizable AnyConnect Objects*

| Filename and AnyConnect Location | Size and Type |
|---|---|
| Company_logo.png<br><br>The company logo displayed in the upper-left corner of the tray flyout and Advanced dialog, and in the lower-right corner of the About dialog. | 97 × 58 (maximum)<br><br>PNG |
| Attention.ico<br><br>System tray icon alerting the user to a condition requiring attention or interaction (for example, a dialog about the user credentials). | 16 × 16<br><br>ICO |
| Error.ico<br><br>System tray icon alerting the user that something is critically wrong with one or more components. | 16 × 16<br><br>ICO |
| Neutral.ico<br><br>System tray icon indicating that client components are operating correctly. | 16 × 16<br><br>ICO |
| Vpn_connected.ico<br><br>System tray icon indicating that the VPN is connected. | 16 × 16<br><br>ICO |
| Cues_bg.jpg<br><br>The background image for the tray flyout, Advanced window, and About dialog. | 1260 × 1024<br><br>JPEG |
| Gradient.png<br><br>The gradient painted behind component titles in the Advanced window. | 1 × 38<br><br>PNG |
| GUI.tif<br><br>The application and system tray icon. | 16 × 16<br><br>TIF |
| Mftogglebtn.png<br><br>The background of the inactive menu option in the Advanced window. | 300 × 40<br><br>PNG |
| Mftogglebtn-down.png<br><br>The background of the Status Overview menu option (when active) in the Advanced window. | 300 × 40<br><br>PNG |
| Mftogglebtn-down-solid.png<br><br>The background used by Advanced window menu options, other than the Status Overview menu option, when the menu option is activated. | 300 × 40<br><br>PNG |
| Minimize.png<br><br>The minimize button for the tray flyout. | 16 × 16<br><br>PNG |
| Minimize-hover.png<br><br>The minimize button for the tray flyout when the user hovers over it. | 16 × 16<br><br>PNG |

**Table 5-8**  *Customizable AnyConnect Objects*

| Filename and AnyConnect Location | Size and Type |
|---|---|
| Pinned.png<br><br>The button in the NAM tray flyout tile that enables the user to automatically select a network. | 38 × 30<br><br>PNG |
| Pinned_button.png<br><br>The button in the NAM tray flyout tile that, when the user hovers on it, enables the user to automatically select a network. | 38 × 30<br><br>PNG |
| Pinned_button.png<br><br>The button in the NAM tray flyout tile that, when the user hovers on it, enables the user to automatically select a network. | 38 × 30<br><br>PNG |
| Status_ico_attention.png<br><br>Attention status icon used by each component in the tray flyout and Advanced window Status Overview pane, indicating that user attention is required. | 16 × 16<br><br>PNG |
| Status_ico_error.png<br><br>Error status icon used by each component in the tray flyout and Advanced window Status Overview pane indicating a serious error, such as the service being unreachable. | 16 × 16<br><br>PNG |
| Status_ico_good.png<br><br>Good status icon used by each component in the tray flyout and Advanced window Status Overview pane, indicating that each component is operating properly. | 16 × 16<br><br>PNG |
| Status_ico_neutral.png<br><br>Neutral status icon used by each component in the tray flyout and Advanced window Status Overview pane, indicating that the component is working but is not necessarily active. | 16 × 16<br><br>PNG |
| Status_ico_transition.png<br><br>Transition status icon used by each component in the tray flyout and Advanced window Status Overview pane, indicating that the component is between states, such as between connected and disconnected. | 16 × 16<br><br>PNG |
| Status_ico_trusted.png<br><br>Trusted status icon used by each component in the tray flyout and Advanced window Status Overview pane, indicating that the component is operating properly, but is disabled due to policy, such as set by the Trusted Network Detection (TND) feature. | 16 × 16<br><br>PNG |

**Table 5-8**  *Customizable AnyConnect Objects*

| Filename and AnyConnect Location | Size and Type |
|---|---|
| Transition_1.ico<br><br>System tray icon that shows along with transition_2.ico and transition_3.ico, indicating that one or more client components are in transition between states (for example, when the VPN is connecting or when NAM is connecting). The three icon files display in succession, appearing to be a single icon bouncing from left to right. | 16 × 16<br><br>PNG |
| Transition_2.ico<br><br>System tray icon that shows along with transition_1.ico and transition_3.ico, indicating that one or more client components are in transition between states (for example, when the VPN is connecting or when NAM is connecting). The three icon files display in succession, appearing to be a single icon bouncing from left to right. | 16 × 16<br><br>PNG |
| Transition_3.ico<br><br>System tray icon that shows along with transition_1.ico and transition_2.ico, indicating that one or more client components are in transition between states (for example, when the VPN is connecting or when NAM is connecting). The three icon files display in succession, appearing to be a single icon bouncing from left to right. | 16 × 16<br><br>PNG |
| Unpinned.png<br><br>The button in the NAM tray flyout tile that enables the user to connect exclusively to the current network.<br><br>The size is not adjustable. | 38 × 30<br><br>PNG |
| Unpinned_button.png<br><br>The button in the NAM tray flyout tile that appears when hovering over the unpinned.png button. When the user hovers over it, it enables the user to connect exclusively to the current network. | 38 × 30<br><br>PNG |

Advanced customizations can be achieved by uploading pre-created transform sets and executables using the Binary, Customized Installed Transforms, and Localized Installed transforms. Transforms are created for Windows platforms by using the Orca database editor made available in the windows installer software development kit (SDK). (Advanced customization using transforms and binary images is beyond the scope of this book.)

You can further customize your deployment by tailoring the available installation for users in multiple countries that use a native language other than English. You can enable additional languages for your deployment in the GUI Text and Messages window.

In the GUI Text and Messages window, click **Add**. In the Add Language Localization Entry window, select the language to add from the drop-down list of those available.

After selecting the appropriate language file, you can then proceed to edit the messages in the Translation pane within the Add Language Localization Entry window, as shown in Figure 5-14. In the pane, there are two main items: msgid and msgstr. The msgid is the original text that appears in each message displayed by the AnyConnect client. You can apply your own custom messages in the msgstr area beneath the msgid. It is important not to change the msgid contents, because this will affect all AnyConnect installations in your deployment.

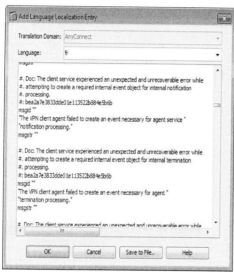

**Figure 5-14**  *AnyConnect Language and Message Customization*

You can also provide customization through the use of scripts that can be run either when a user connects or disconnects. Custom scripts must be created offline and uploaded to the ASA device before they can be used.

As shown in Figure 5-15, you upload custom scripts in the Scripts pane of the Customization/Localization area. Click **Import** to add a new script, and in the Import AnyConnect Customization Scripts window, enter a name for the script, choose the event when the script will run (either OnConnect or OnDisconnect), choose the platform from the drop-down list, and then browse to and select the script from your local machine.

**Figure 5-15**   *AnyConnect Script Upload*

# Exam Preparation Tasks

As mentioned in the section "How to Use This Book" in the Introduction, you have a couple of choices for exam preparation: the memory tables in Appendix C, Chapter 23, "Final Exam Preparation," and the exam simulation questions on the CD-ROM.

## Review All Key Topics

Review the most important topics in the chapter, noted with the Key Topic icon in the outer margin of the page. Table 5-9 lists a reference of these key topics and the page numbers on which each is found.

**Table 5-9**   *Key Topics*

| Key Topic Element | Description | Page |
|---|---|---|
| Topic | AnyConnect deployment methods | 168 |
| Topic | AnyConnect connection profile configuration | 172 |
| Bulleted List | AnyConnect client profile types | 177 |
| Topic | Advanced AnyConnect client profile settings | 182 |

## Complete Tables and Lists from Memory

Print a copy of Appendix C, "Memory Tables" (found on the CD), or at least the section for this chapter, and complete the tables and lists from memory. Appendix D, "Memory Tables Answer Key," also on the CD, includes completed tables and lists to check your work.

## Define Key Terms

Define the following key terms from this chapter, and check your answers in the glossary:

NAM, SBL

This chapter covers the following subjects:

■ **Configuration Procedures, Deployment Strategies, and Information Gathering:** In this section, we discuss the advanced methods available using AAA, group policies, and DAPs.

■ **Configuring Local and Remote Group Policies:** In this section, we review the role of the group policy object and the configuration required for the authorization and management of our remote users.

■ **Full SSL VPN Accountability:** In this section, we discuss the various accounting methods to manage our VPN operation.

■ **Authorization Through Dynamic Access Policies:** In this section, we review the operation and assignment of DAPs and how to configure items in a policy.

■ **Troubleshooting Advanced Authorization Settings:** In this section, we review the various troubleshooting tools and procedures available when facing problems with our advanced authorization deployment.

## CHAPTER 6

# Advanced Authorization Using AAA and DAPs

The examples so far in this book have shown how remote users can connect into our environment using a basic AnyConnect client virtual private network (VPN) deployment and access our resources through the established VPN tunnel. This chapter builds on what you have learned so far and introduces a number of the advanced authorization techniques that are available through the use of group policies, authentication, authorization, and accounting (AAA), and Dynamic Access Policy (DAP). In addition, this chapter covers the logging options that enable the tracking of our users and our VPN's overall operation.

## "Do I Know This Already?" Quiz

The "Do I Know This Already?" quiz helps you determine your level of knowledge on this chapter's topics before you begin. Table 6-1 details the major topics discussed in this chapter and their corresponding quiz sections.

**Table 6-1**  *"Do I Know This Already?" Section-to-Question Mapping*

| Foundation Topics Section | Questions |
| --- | --- |
| Configuring Local and Remote Group Policies | 2, 3, 6 |
| Full SSL VPN Accountability | 1 |
| Authorization Through Dynamic Access Policies | 4, 5 |

**1.** Which methods are valid methods used for logging purposes? (Choose all that apply.)

- **a.** Syslog
- **b.** NetFlow
- **c.** SFlow
- **d.** RADIUS accounting

**2.** When configuring external group policies, which of the following are valid server types to use? (Choose all that apply.)

   **a.** RADIUS

   **b.** TACACS+

   **c.** LDAP

   **d.** Windows domain controller

**3.** What is the primary difference between external and local group policies? (Choose all that apply.)

   **a.** External group policies are stored only on a remote server, and local group policies are stored only on the ASA.

   **b.** External group policy attributes are configured on a remote server.

   **c.** There are no differences apart from the name.

   **d.** Local and remote group policies are both configured on the ASA.

**4.** Select the valid policy types that are applied to a user in the policy inheritance model?

   **a.** DAP

   **b.** Connection profile group policy

   **c.** User group policy

   **d.** User attributes

   **e.** Default group policy

   **f.** All of the above

**5.** When evaluating your current policies against the policy inheritance model, which policy type is applied to the user first?

   **a.** DAP

   **b.** User attributes

   **c.** Default group policy

   **d.** Connection profile group policy

**6.** Which locations can an internal group policy be applied? (Choose two.)

   **a.** User account

   **b.** Connection profile

   **c.** DAP

   **d.** AAA server

## Foundation Topics

# Configuration Procedures, Deployment Strategies, and Information Gathering

With any VPN deployment, the task of authenticating and authorizing remote users so that they can access only the resources you make available to them is an important one. If we were to allow access to a third-party to our accounts database, for example, the outcome could be catastrophic for the company.

When planning the deployment of an authorization scheme to remote users to provide the resource access they should have or require for their successful day-to-day operation, you must first understand the overall network environment they will be accessing and any existing authorization or authentication schemes that might be in place to which you can build upon or extend. For example, do a large number of remote users require privileges that differ from each other, or can you manage and provide authorization to users based on their group membership and department in the company?

Also consider the method of deployment for user authorization against the available policy types on the ASA. For example, will users be authorized based on received parameters and policies from internal AAA servers, or will the task of authorization be based solely on the policies configured on the Adaptive Security Appliance (ASA) device, as shown in Figure 6-1?

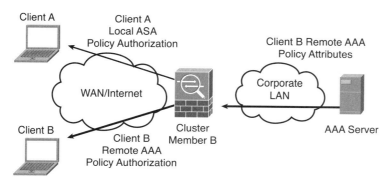

**Figure 6-1**  *Considering Your Authorization Deployment Options*

# Configuring Local and Remote Group Policies

You have seen group policy objects in earlier chapters provide basic authentication and authorization parameters. This section provides an advanced look at both local and remote group policies and their respective configurations.

Group policies enable you to assign attributes to users and groups based on their individual user account, group membership, or the connection profile. In group policy objects, you can define the number of simultaneous logins that can be made using the particular user account, restrict access to only the internal resources and subnets you allow using IPv4 and IPv6 access control lists (ACL), set up split tunneling, define the user's access hours (the time a user can and cannot log in), and much more, as you will see in a moment.

Two types of group policy objects can be configured. Which one is used is determined by the location of the policy attributes that are assigned to the user:

■ Local group policies

■ Remote group policies

Local group policies are group policy objects that have been configured along with their associated parameters on the ASA device. They are assigned either to users directly or via connection profiles. They can be merged with policies that are higher up in the hierarchical chain (for example, DAPs).

Remote group policies, however, are typically user or group specific, and their associated parameters are configured on an internal AAA server (for example, RADIUS or Lightweight Directory Access Protocol [LDAP]) in the form of A/V (attribute/value) pairs. During the establishment of a VPN connection, the ASA device can be configured to query available AAA servers for authorization parameters for the particular remote user. The server, if it has any, responds with the A/V pairs, and the ASA compiles the user's policy based on the received information.

External group policies are configured by navigating to **Configuration > Remote Access VPN > Network (Client) Access > Group Policies**. There, click **Add > External Group Policy**. The Add External Group Policy dialog opens, as shown in Figure 6-2.

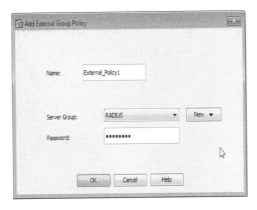

**Figure 6-2** *External Group Policy Configuration*

Enter a name for the group policy object, and then choose a server group and enter the appropriate password configured on the AAA server (if RADIUS server is selected). If no server groups have been created, click **New** and choose either **RADIUS** or **LDAP**, and click **OK** to save. Now you can add AAA servers to your newly created group by navigating to **Configuration > Device Management > Users/AAA > AAA Server Groups**.

Internal group policies are also created in the Group Policies window (**Configuration > Remote Access VPN > Network (Client) Access > Group Policies**), by clicking **Add > Internal Group Policy**. At that point, the Add Internal Group Policy dialog opens, as shown in Figure 6-3.

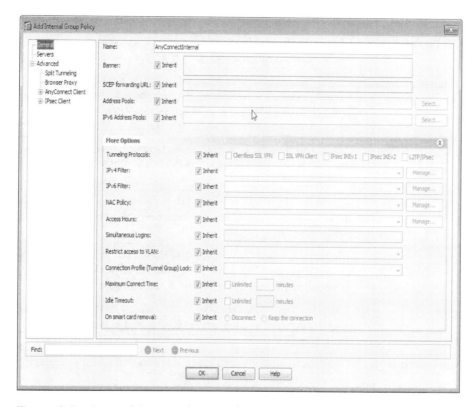

**Figure 6-3** *Internal Group Policy Configuration*

In this dialog, you can begin by giving the group policy object a name. Tables 6-2, 6-3, and 6-4 contain the available configuration options and values within the group policy General, Servers, and Browser Proxy (located in **Advanced > Browser Proxy**) group policy menu items, respectively.

**Table 6-2**   *Internal Group Policy, General Pane Configuration Items*

Key Topic

| Field | Value |
|---|---|
| Banner | Enter a banner that will be displayed to users during their connection attempt to the VPN. |
| SCEP Forwarding URL | Enter the URL that will be used by users of this group policy for the automatic request of digital certificates (if using certificate-based authentication). |

**Table 6-2** *Internal Group Policy, General Pane Configuration Items*

| Field | Value |
| --- | --- |
| Address Pools | Choose an IP address pool from the list or create a new one. An IP address will be assigned to users for use during their connection. |
| IPv6 Address Pools | Choose an IPv6 address pool from the list or create a new one. An IP address will be assigned to users for use during their connection. |
| Tunneling Protocols | Choose from the available tunneling protocols that this group policy object will apply to. Clientless SSL VPN, SSL VPN client, IPsec, and L2TP/IPsec are the available options. |
| IPv4 Filter | Choose an IPv4 ACL from the list or create a new one to restrict network access during users' connections only to the networks/hosts they require. |
| IPv6 Filter | Choose an IPv6 ACL from the list or create a new one to restrict network access during users' connections only to the networks/hosts they require. |
| NAC Policy | Choose a Network Access Control (NAC) policy from the list or create a new one. The NAC policy is used to perform posture assessment and validation for the connecting user. |
| Access Hours | Choose a time range from the list or create a new one (if, for example, you want to allow access to this connection only during work hours). |
| Simultaneous Logins | Enter the number of simultaneous logins that can appear for this user account (default 3). |
| Restrict Access to VLAN (5505 only) | Choose the only VLAN (Inside, Outside, DMZ) you will allow this connecting user to access. |
| Connection Profile (Tunnel Group) Lock | Choose the connection profile from the list. This group policy object is assigned to users only if they are connected using the selected connection profile. |
| Maximum Connect Time | Choose Unlimited or enter an amount of time in minutes the user is allowed to be connected for before being automatically disconnected (default Unlimited). |
| Idle Timeout | Choose Unlimited or enter an amount of time in minutes the user's connection can be idle before being automatically disconnected (default 30 minutes). |
| On Smart Card Removal | Choose the option to keep the user's connection connected or to disconnect the connection on the user removing his or her smartcard (default is to disconnect). |

**Table 6-3** *Internal Group Policy, Servers Pane Configuration Items*

| Field | Value |
| --- | --- |
| DNS Servers | Enter up to two Domain Name System (DNS) servers that may be used by your AnyConnect clients. |
| WINS Servers | Enter up to two WINS servers used by your AnyConnect clients for name-to-IP mapping purposes on a Windows network. |
| DHCP Scope | Enter the subnet address (that is, 192.168.1.0) of the scope that will be used to deploy IP addresses to your connecting AnyConnect clients from an internal/remote DHCP server. |
| Default Domain | Enter the default domain name that will be appended to requests generated by your AnyConnect clients for a hostname. For example, a ping to hostname ServerA would cause the configured domain name (for example, example.com) to be appended to the hostname, resulting in ServerA.example.com being the complete concatenation. |

**Table 6-4** *Internal Group Policy, Browser Proxy Pane Configuration Items*

| Field | Value |
| --- | --- |
| Proxy Server Policy | Choose from one of the following options to override the connecting users proxy settings (IE only):<br>■ Do Not Modify Client Proxy Settings<br>■ Do Not Use Proxy<br>■ Select Proxy Server Settings from the Following:<br>　■ Auto Detect Proxy<br>　■ Use Proxy Server Settings Given Below<br>　■ Use Proxy Auto Configuration (PAC) Given Below |
| Server Address and Port | Enter the proxy server address and port to be used by your connecting remote users (IE only). |
| Bypass Server for Local Addresses | Choose either Yes or No to allow direct access to devices on the local subnet without having to send the request via the proxy server (bypass). |
| Exceptions | Enter a comma-separated list of hostnames/domain names that will be accessed directly without first having to go via the proxy server. |
| PAC URL | Enter the URL to the PAC file that contains all the proxy-related configuration information to be downloaded and applied to your connecting users. (Enter this information only if you select Use Proxy Auto Configuration File (PAC) Given Below from the earlier fields.) |

**Table 6-4**   *Internal Group Policy, Browser Proxy Pane Configuration Items*

| Field | Value |
| --- | --- |
| Allow Proxy Lockdown for Client System | Choose either Yes or No to allow or deny, respectively, remote users to edit their local proxy settings. |

As you can gather from these tables, you have a great deal of flexibility when it comes to assigning the various parameters and authorization using ACLs. For this example, we have created a group policy object that will assign our AnyConnect users an IP address from the pool SSL-POOL containing the IP addresses 192.168.2.111 to 192.168.2.222 and only allow remote users access to the internal server on address 192.168.1.15 using the IPv4 ACL Client-Server. To accomplish this, we carried out the following actions:

■   Create a new internal group policy object and name it **AnyConnectUsers**.

■   Assign the IP address pool SSL-POOL by unchecking the **Inherit** option and clicking the **Select** button. In the Select IP Address Pools window that opens, click **Add**, and in the Add IP Pool dialog, enter the following details:

**Name:**   SSL-POOL

**Starting IP Address:**   192.168.2.111

**Ending IP Address:**   192.168.2.222

**Subnet Mask:**   255.255.255.0

■   Click **OK** to save the new IP address pool, and then choose it from the list, click the **Assign** button to add it to our group policies configuration, and click **OK** to return to our group policy window.

■   Expand **More Options** and uncheck the **Inherit** option next to the available tunneling protocols, and then select **SSL VPN Client** from the list.

■   Assign the IPv4 filter (ACL) by unchecking the **Inherit** option and clicking the **Manage** button on the right side of the field.

For this example, we created a new extended access list (we need to use extended because we are matching on both the source and destination of the communication) by clicking **Add > Add ACL**. In the Add ACL dialog that opens, enter the name **Client-Server** and click **OK**. Now create a rule permitting access only to the server 192.168.1.15. Click **Add > Add ACE** after first highlighting **Client-Server** ACL on the list, and then enter the details required to allow access from 192.168.2.0/24 to 192.168.1.15 using the protocol IP. Click **OK**, then **OK** again. At that point, we are returned to our original group policy configuration window. Note that in the ACL, the source addresses should match those that have been assigned to your remote users. Figure 6-4 shows the resulting group policy configuration. We can now assign this either to a user directly or to a connection profile that will apply to all of our connecting users (of the specific connection profile).

You can assign a group policy object directly to a local user by first navigating to his user account properties in **Configuration > Device Management > Users/AAA > User Accounts**. Select the individual user account to apply the group policy object to, and click **Edit**.

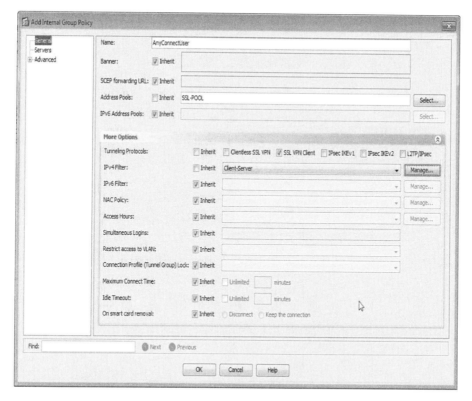

**Figure 6-4**   *Internal Group Policy Configuration*

In the Edit User Account window, choose the **VPN Policy** menu option from the left and uncheck **Inherit** next to the Group Policy drop-down list. You can now proceed to select your group policy object from the list of those available, as shown in Figure 6-5.

As mentioned earlier, a group policy can also be applied to a connection profile so as to apply to all users connecting into your organization using the particular connection profile.

Begin the assignment to a connection profile by navigating to **Configuration > Remote Access VPN > Network (Client) Access > AnyConnect Connection Profiles**. Here, select the connection profile from the list to which you would like the group policy applied, and then click **Edit**.

In the Edit AnyConnect Connection Profile dialog, navigate to the Default Group Policy section and, from the drop-down list, choose the group policy object to be applied, as shown in Figure 6-6.

In addition to the more general properties that can be assigned using a group policy object, you can assign advanced properties (for example, split tunneling exceptions and rules) and AnyConnect-specific properties.

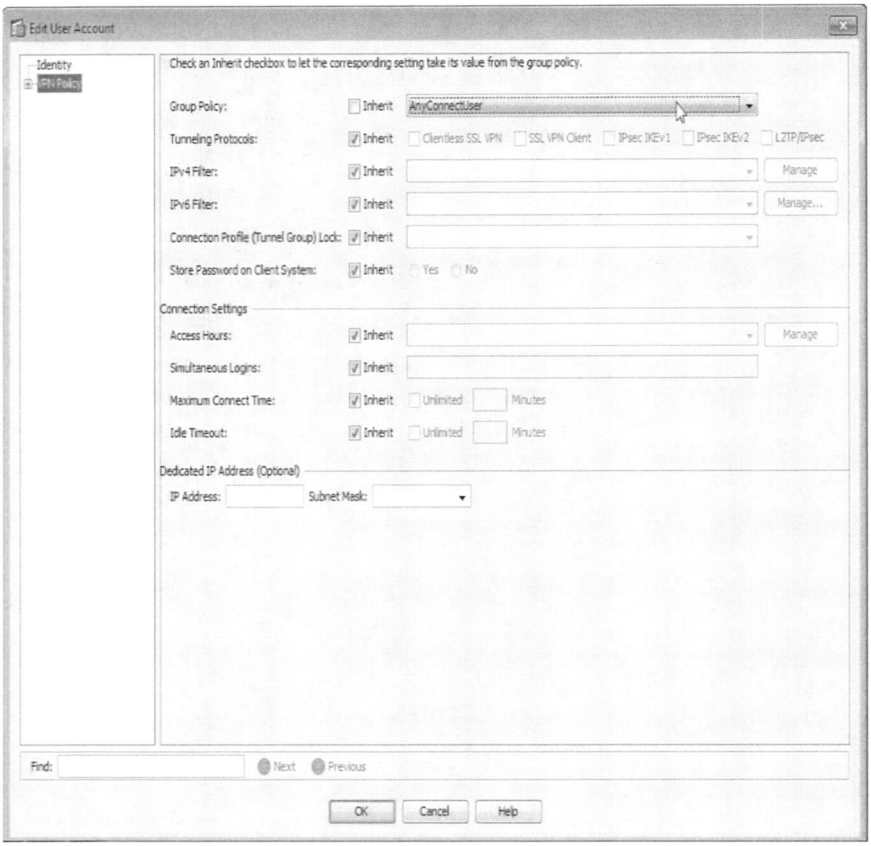

**Figure 6-5**   *Assigning a Group Policy Directly to a User*

The configuration in Figure 6-7 shows the split-tunneling properties in the **Advanced > Split Tunneling** location of the Edit Group Policy window.

For this example, we added the domain name vpn.lab as a DNS name, indicating to the AnyConnect client that any requests for DNS information for hosts in this domain should be tunneled (for example, fileserver.vpn.lab). In addition to our DNS names configuration, we selected the option to tunnel only networks on the list specified in the preconfigured ACL AnyConnect_Client_Local_Print by using the Policy and Network List fields. The configuration described will result in DNS requests for hosts/devices in the domain name vpn.lab or traffic matching that of the ACL AnyConnect_Client_Local_Print being sent by the AnyConnect client through the VPN tunnel to the destination. All other traffic (for example, local LAN or Internet) travels directly to its destination, effectively bypassing the VPN tunnel.

AnyConnect-specific properties can be configured in a group policy object by first navigating to **Advanced > AnyConnect Client**. (You have seen various properties in this group policy area in earlier chapters.) In the AnyConnect group policy specific property menus, you can assign permissions and properties such as keeping the AnyConnect client installed on the user's local device after disconnection, assignment of AnyConnect client profiles, and enabling dead peer detection (DPD). You can also configure whether the connecting user will be prompted to install the AnyConnect client, travel directly to the SSL portal bypassing AnyConnect installation, or if the AnyConnect client software should be installed automatically upon login.

**Figure 6-6**  *Assigning a Group Policy Object to a Connection Profile*

Figure 6-8 shows a basic use of the AnyConnect-specific properties in a group policy object. For this example, we enabled the AnyConnect client to stay installed on the connecting user's device after disconnecting from the VPN connection. We also enabled the use of Datagram Transport Layer Security (DTLS) to provide for latency-sensitive traffic the user may be transmitting and receiving through the VPN tunnel. The Always on VPN setting is taken from the properties configured in the available client profiles that are downloaded by the AnyConnect client, and we have also applied an AnyConnect client profile to the group policy using the Client Profile to Download section of the dialog.

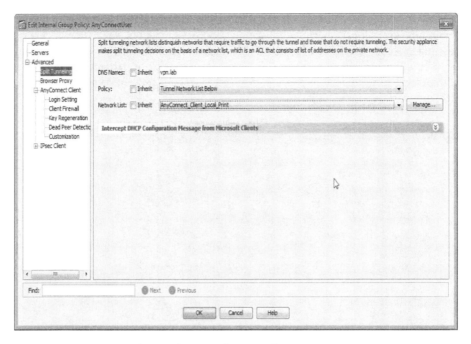

**Figure 6-7**    *Group Policy Split-Tunneling Configuration*

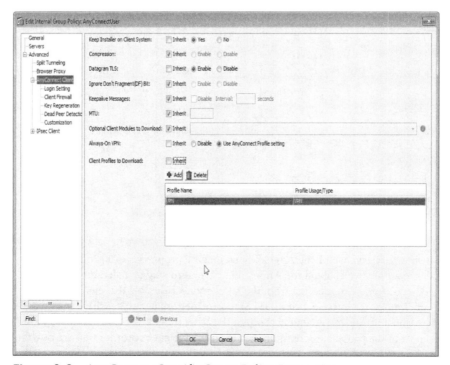

**Figure 6-8**    *AnyConnect-Specific Group Policy Properties*

# Full SSL VPN Accountability

When planning to use logging to monitor user activity, you have a few options, including syslog information, NetFlow, and RADIUS accounting. This section briefly introduces each of these methods and discusses how to configure them to keep track of the number of users connected to your VPN, the various encryption protocols that are used by connecting users, and so forth.

Syslog can provide a lot of information used for statistics-based analysis or information about the current ASA's health and the status of connecting users, along with any protocols they are using to connect to the environment.

In Figure 6-9, we enabled logging by navigating to **Configuration > Device Management > Logging > Logging Setup** and checking the **Enable Logging** box. We also specified that our logging information should be saved to the ASA's flash and kept the default values of 1024KB of flash to be used for logging information.

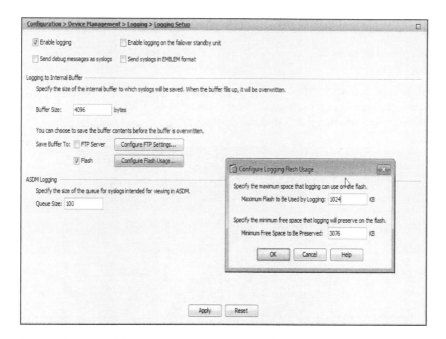

**Figure 6-9**   *Enable Logging in the ASDM and Specify Location*

You can specify the size of the logging buffer in this window (4096 bytes), which is displayed on the home page. If you use the command-line interface (CLI) **show logging** command, the log file will begin to roll over (when the logging information exceeds the 4096 bytes configured), and new information will overwrite the existing information.

You can also view logging information and statistics gathered by the ASA in the VPN Statistics window (**Monitoring > VPN > VPN Statistics**), from where you can choose to view the following:

- **Sessions:** The current session count and logged-in users

- **Crypto Statistics:** Number of encrypted packets, security association (SA) creations, and so on

- **Compression Statistics:** Current compressed data (bytes), resets, ratio, errors, and so forth

- **Encryption Statistics:** How many sessions (in number and percentage) that use a particular encryption algorithm

- **Global IKE/IPsec Statistics:** Active tunnels, packets in and out, and so on

- **NAC Session Summary:** Current NAC appliance sessions

- **Protocol Statistics:** The number and percentage of Internet Key Exchange Version 1 (IKEv1), IKEv2, Secure Sockets Layer (SSL), and Layer 2 Tunneling Protocol (L2TP) sessions established with the ASA device

- **VLAN Mapping Sessions:** The current VLAN mapping session count, VLANs, users, and so on

Figure 6-10 shows the current AnyConnect client session counts, the user who is currently connected, the connection profile and group policies used, the encryption/authentication algorithms used, and the user's IP address assignment.

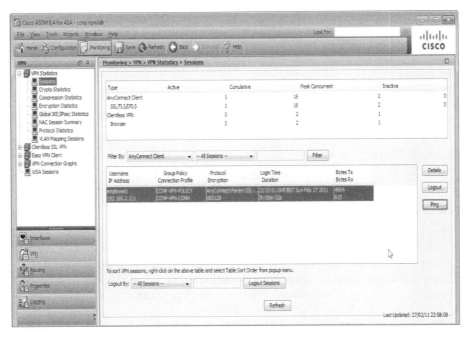

**Figure 6-10**   *Current AnyConnect Session Count and Active Users*

As shown in Figure 6-11, you can also view the current syslog information by using the real-time log viewer available in the ASDM location **Monitoring > Logging > Real-Time Log Viewer.** The figure displays a user that has successfully logged in and has been assigned an IP address and group policy.

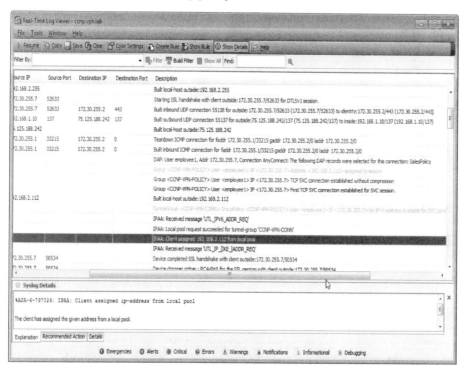

**Figure 6-11**   *ASDM Real-Time Log Viewer*

NetFlow logging can allow you to view information on a flow-by-flow basis, based on Layer 3 and Layer 4 information of a conversation. The NetFlow information is sent by the ASA to a server running a NetFlow collection service. Examples of popular NetFlow collectors are those created by Cisco (LAN Management Solution [LMS]), ManageEngine, and SolarWinds, among others.

NetFlow logging is set up by navigating to **Configuration > Device Management > Logging > NetFlow.**

The example in Figure 6-12 shows the addition of a server on our inside network running the collector software. The ASA sends its NetFlow information to this server using the IP address and port. The server, in turn, formats the information to display to us either through a web-enabled control panel or the software installed on the server.

RADIUS accounting information can be enabled so that administrators and support representatives can see whether a connection has succeeded or failed (and if failed, for what reason) by interrogating the RADIUS logging information.

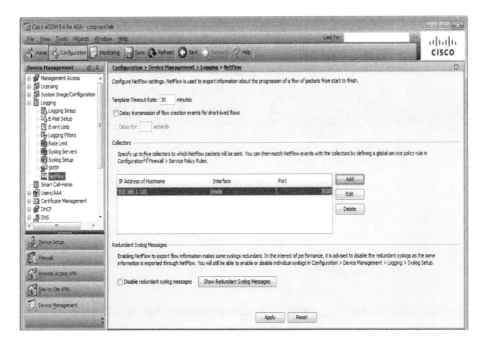

**Figure 6-12**  *ASA NetFlow Service Configuration*

Enable RADIUS accounting in the user's connection profile by navigating to **Configuration > Remote Access VPN > Network (Client) Access > AnyConnect Connection Profiles** and choosing the user's connection profile from the list of those available and clicking **Edit.** In the Edit AnyConnect Connect Profile window, choose **Advanced > Accounting,** and in the Accounting window, from the drop-down list, choose the RADIUS server group that contains the RADIUS servers to which the ASA will be sending its accounting information. You can, of course, create a new RADIUS or TACACS+ server group by clicking the **Manage** button if you do not have any groups currently available. Note that only RADIUS or TACACS+ can be used for VPN accounting purposes.

Figure 6-13 shows the configuration required to set up RADIUS accounting in a connection profile's Advanced settings.

After configuring RADIUS accounting servers, you can inspect the RADIUS accounting information on your RADIUS server implementation using the various logging options that are available. For example, you can search for a user or check top-ten user authentications, as shown in Figure 6-14, from an ACS Version 5.x graphical user interface (GUI). ACS (Access Control Server), a Cisco product providing an all-in-one AAA server implementation, enables us to deploy a centralized RADIUS, TACACS+, and so on server for the purposes of user AAA. There are two ACS deployment types available: Version 4.x, which runs on a Windows or Solaris server; and Version 5.x, which is available only on a rack-mountable device purchased from Cisco.

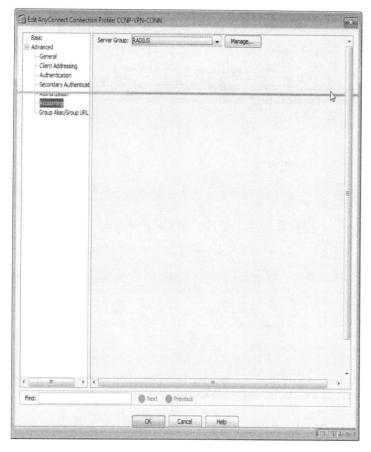

**Figure 6-13**  *AnyConnect Connection Profile RADIUS Accounting Configuration*

## Authorization Through Dynamic Access Policies

Based on the policy inheritance model covered in earlier chapters, DAPs take precedence over any group policy or user attributes that have been configured. For example, the current policy inheritance model is as follows:

- DAP (top of the hierarchy, applied first)

- User attributes

- Group policy

- Connection profile group policy

- Default group policy (bottom of the hierarchy, applied last)

Dynamic Access Records hold the configuration items required for user attribute assignment and are compiled to create a DAP.

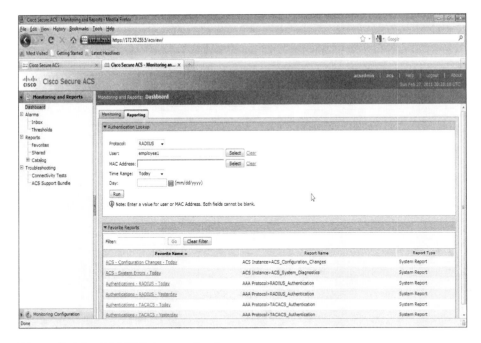

**Figure 6-14**  *RADIUS Accounting Server*

Dynamic Access Records are configured with a priority between 0 and 2147483647 (with 0 being the lower priority) and a collection of attributes for user assignment based on one or both of the following criteria:

■  User AAA attributes

■  Endpoint attributes (posture evaluation)

Multiple user AAA attributes can be configured from one of the following three AAA attribute types:

■  Cisco

■  LDAP

■  RADIUS

The action can be that of either match any, all, or none of the attributes configured.

A default policy of DfltAccessPolicy exists in the DAP list with a priority of 0. The attributes assigned can be edited in this policy. However, because this policy has been created to serve as the default, you cannot add or edit user AAA of endpoint attributes for matching purposes. The default policy acts as a catchall, and its settings apply to any session that did not match at least one administrator-created DAP record. DAP policies are explained in detail in Chapter 12, "Advanced Authorization Using Dynamic Access Policies."

DAP attributes are stored in an Extensible Markup Language (XML) file on the ASA's flash. The XML file can be downloaded from the ASA, modified offline using Notepad or another offline editor, and re-uploaded. However, the recommended configuration method is through the ASDM. Example 6-1 shows basic DAP XML file content.

**Example 6-1**   *Sample Dap.xml file Content*

```
<?xml version="1.0" encoding="UTF-8" standalone="yes"?>
<dapRecordList>
<dapRecord>
<dapName>
<value>DAP1</value>
</dapName>
<dapBasicView>
<dapSelection>
<dapPolicy>
<value>match-any</value>
</dapPolicy>
<attr>
<name>aaa.ldap.memberOf</name>
<value>sales</value>
<operation>EQ</operation>
<type>caseless</type>
</attr>
</dapSelection>
</dapBasicView>
</dapRecord>
</dapRecordList>
```

To create a DAP, navigate to **Configuration > Remote Access VPN > Network (Client) Access > Dynamic Access Policies** and click **Add** to bring up the Add Dynamic Access Policy dialog, shown in Figure 6-15.

As mentioned earlier and shown in Figure 6-11, DAPs can be configured to match a user based on a number of AAA/endpoint attributes (posture evaluation). After entering the items required for a DAP record to match a connecting user, you can choose the desired actions from in the Access/Authorization Policy attributes. These attributes include applying an ACL, terminating the user's connection, Always On settings, and so on. The advantage of using DAPs over group policies for policy application purposes is flexibility and granularity. You can match specific user accounts or groups rather than make a match based solely on a connection profile or the direct assignment to users. For example, if a user had been promoted, a configured DAP record may automatically be applied based on the user's group membership or AAA attributes instead of having to reconfigure the user's connection profile settings or user account attributes directly.

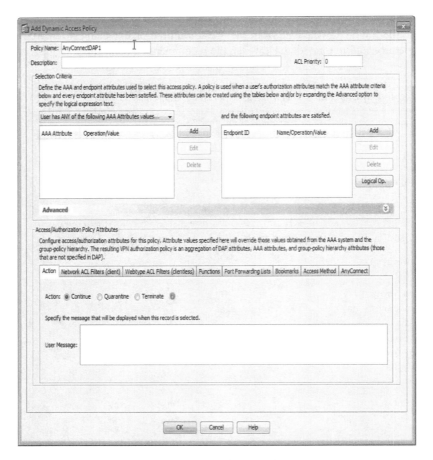

**Figure 6-15**  *Add Dynamic Access Policy Dialog*

# Troubleshooting Advanced Authorization Settings

We now take a look at some tools to help you troubleshoot an advanced authorization deployment. Ultimately, the task of troubleshooting can be made a lot easier by fully understanding your current environment. Documentation is always an important part of any network or security engineer's job, and without it, troubleshooting can be more difficult and more complex than first estimated.

As discussed earlier, you have access to a large amount of logging and monitoring information that can help a great deal when troubleshooting a connection.

It is also important to understand the role of your configured policy types and how they are applied to remote users using the hierarchical policy model. The current policy hierarchy is listed from top (preferred) to bottom (least preferred):

- DAP (top of the hierarchy, applied first)

- User attributes

- Group policy

- Connection profile group policy

- Default group policy (bottom of the hierarchy, applied last)

In the example shown in Figure 6-16, a DAP record is being applied to your user and overriding any settings you expect to see or receive in a configured group policy object. An incorrectly applied DAP has overridden the desired behavior of allowing the user to connect and be granted access to the network. Instead, the DAP has placed the user into a quarantine area, and the user has received a "Remediation Required" message and, for this example, our own custom "You Have Been Placed into Quarantine" message. If we had not configured our own message in a production environment, this might have been difficult to troubleshoot, because the user would have to explain to the support operative that he cannot do anything and is receiving a "Remediation Required" message. Along with a custom message, you can use the real-time log viewer at **Monitoring > Logging > Real-Time Log Viewer** and can see from the information available that employee1 user has been assigned a DAP.

**Figure 6-16**   *User DAP Assignment Troubleshooting*

From here, you can continue to troubleshoot by finding the DAP in your configuration and inspecting why this has happened. This example uses the Test Dynamic Access Policies in **Configuration > Remote Access VPN > Network (Client) Access > Dynamic Access Policies > Test Dynamic Access Policies**, shown in Figure 6-17.

We entered our user's username as an AAA attribute into the Test Dynamic Access Policies window and chose **Test Policy**. From the results shown in the lower section of the window in Figure 6-17, we can see that our user has been incorrectly assigned the DAP SalesPolicy when in fact this user is an engineer.

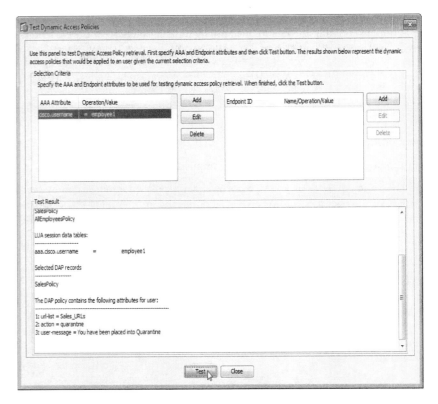

**Figure 6-17**   *Test Your DAPs*

## Exam Preparation Tasks

As mentioned in the section "How to Use This Book" in the Introduction, you have a couple of choices for exam preparation: the memory tables in Appendix C, Chapter 23, "Final Exam Preparation," and the exam simulation questions on the CD-ROM.

## Review All Key Topics

Review the most important topics in the chapter, noted with the Key Topic icon in the outer margin of the page. Table 6-5 lists a reference of these key topics and the page numbers on which each is found.

**Table 6-5**   *Key Topics*

| Key Topic Element | Description | Page |
|---|---|---|
| Bulleted List | Available group policy types | 200 |
| Table | Internal group policy general configuration items | 201 |
| Bulleted List | Available logging statistical and user information windows | 210 |
| Bulleted List | Policy inheritance model | 213 |

## Complete Tables and Lists from Memory

Print a copy of Appendix C, "Memory Tables" (found on the CD), or at least the section for this chapter, and complete the tables and lists from memory. Appendix D, "Memory Tables Answer Key," also on the CD, includes completed tables and lists to check your work.

## Define Key Terms

Define the following key terms from this chapter, and check your answers in the glossary:

DAP, external group policy, NetFlow

This chapter covers the following subjects:

■ **CSD Overview and Configuration:** In this section, we discuss the Cisco Secure Desktop (Vault) and the Cache Cleaner and other associated modules (for example, Keystroke Logger Detection) in addition to the operation and implementation.

■ **AnyConnect Posture Assessment and Host Scan:** In this section, we review the Basic and Advanced Endpoint Assessment Host Scan features, along with the licensing requirements and scan features made available upon activation.

■ **Configuring Prelogin Policies:** In this section, we review the operation of the flow-based environment available for prelogin attribute assessment and sample configurations.

■ **AnyConnect Network Access, Web Security, and Telemetry Modules:** In this section, we review the role of the NAM, Web Security, and Telemetry modules, in addition to their deployment and basic configuration.

# CHAPTER 7

# AnyConnect Integration with Cisco Secure Desktop and Optional Modules

In our exploration of the AnyConnect Secure Mobility Client so far, you have learned how to configure and allow remote users to access internal networks and resources. However, what happens if remote users connect into your environment using noncorporate or publicly accessible devices, such as a PC at an Internet cafe? Do you still want to allow them access to the same corporate resources and potentially leave important password, cached, or corporate information behind after they have finished their session?

Because of the ubiquitous access provided by an AnyConnect virtual private network (VPN) connection, your remote users can connect from any number of different environments and devices. Therefore, you need a way to know when your remote user is connected to a corporate-owned device (laptop, handheld device, and so on), and if the user is not, you need a method that allows for the successful deployment and creation of a secure and private environment for remote users during their connection that also cleans up after they leave.

In addition to the enhanced security offered by the various Host Scan, Cisco Secure Desktop (CSD), and Cache Cleaner modules, you can extend the security of your users' AnyConnect client configuration with the addition of separate modules for network access and configuration, web security, and filtering purposes.

This chapter reviews the CSD and associated modules (Cache Cleaner, Keystroke Logger Detection, and so on). For an in-depth discussion of the CSD, supported operating systems, and integration with Dynamic Access Protocol (DAP), see Chapter 13, "Clientless SSL VPN with Cisco Secure Desktop."

## "Do I Know This Already?" Quiz

The "Do I Know This Already?" quiz helps you determine your level of knowledge on this chapter's topics before you begin. Table 7-1 details the major topics discussed in this chapter and their corresponding quiz sections.

**Table 7-1** *"Do I Know This Already?" Section-to-Question Mapping*

| Foundation Topics Section | Questions |
| --- | --- |
| AnyConnect Posture Assessment and Host Scan | 1, 3, 6 |
| Configuring Prelogin Policies | 8 |
| AnyConnect Network Access, Web Security, and Telemetry Modules | 2, 4, 5, 7 |

**1.** Which of the following contain or are valid Host Scan images that you can upload and install on ASA 8.4? (Choose all that apply.)

   **a.**   AnyConnect client package

   **b.**   Cisco Secure Desktop package

   **c.**   Individual Host Scan package

   **d.**   ASA OS 8.4

**2.** Which of the following enables you to send viral activity and origin information to a WSA appliance?

   **a.**   AnyConnect core client

   **b.**   Posture Assessment module

   **c.**   Telemetry module

   **d.**   NAM module

**3.** When configuring Host Scan to perform remediation, which of the following must you enable on your ASA?

   **a.**   Host Scan

   **b.**   Endpoint Assessment

   **c.**   Cisco Secure Desktop

   **d.**   Advanced Endpoint Assessment

**4.** Which of the following AnyConnect modules can you use to manage remote user wired and wireless network connections?

   **a.**   Telemetry module

   **b.**   Web Security module

   **c.**   NAM module

   **d.**   AnyConnect core client

   **e.**   SBL module

**5.** Which of the following are used to configure the NAM, Telemetry, and Web Security module settings?

   **a.**   Group policies

   **b.**   Client profiles

   **c.**   DAPs

   **d.**   Connection profiles

**6.** Which of the following can AnyConnect client use to perform posture assessment of a remote users device? (Choose all that apply.)

   **a.** Host Scan

   **b.** NAM module

   **c.** Posture Assessment module

   **d.** Telemetry module

**7.** Which of the following can you use to send threat information to the Cisco Threat Awareness Center?

   **a.** Telemetry module

   **b.** NAM module

   **c.** Posture Assessment module

   **d.** Web Security module

**8.** Which of the following can you use in a prelogin policy for sequence criteria? (Choose all that apply.)

   **a.** IP address

   **b.** Digital certificate information

   **c.** Registry keys

   **d.** Local files

## Foundation Topics

# Cisco Secure Desktop Overview and Configuration

As with so many things in the world, we have to accept the bad with the good. It is good that remote users can receive a secure, mobile, and feature-rich experience when working through an AnyConnect VPN connection. However, with the potential for "anything-anywhere" access comes the threat of exposure to internal and corporate resources from unsecured end devices and potential attackers.

CSD can help mitigate the potential threats that exist with a remote user connecting from an unsecured device or network. The CSD first assesses the remote user's current environment, taking any remedial action that might be necessary to prepare the environment for a connection to the Adaptive Security Appliance (ASA). The CSD then secures the environment for users during their VPN session. Ultimately, then, the CSD removes all traces of the remote user having even used the device to connect to you.

When people first hear the term *Cisco Secure Desktop*, they usually first think of Vault, a secure encrypted partition created on a remote user's device for the temporary storage of files and settings during remote user VPN connections. After the remote user has disconnected from the VPN, the Vault removes the partition and any associated information that might have been cached on the local device (and optionally removes the Secure Desktop software itself). However, many pieces of the CSD puzzle either work together to provide each other with the information necessary to create the overall secure connectivity experience or independently scan the remote user's device and take any associated actions that might be configured for the results they gather.

Collectively, the following modules comprise the CSD. As discussed later in this chapter, they can work independently or in concert (as mentioned in the preceding paragraph):

- Host Scan
- Prelogin Assessment
- Secure Desktop (Vault)
- Cache Cleaner
- Keystroke Logger Detection
- Integration with DAP
- Host Emulation Detection
- Windows Mobile Device Management
- Standalone installation packages
- CSD Manual Launch

## Host Scan

Three types of Host Scan are available. Which one you choose depends on the attributes or software you want to search for on a remote user's device and the actions (if any) you want to take based on the results collected. You can choose from the following:

- Basic Host Scan

- Endpoint Assessment

- Advanced Endpoint Assessment

The ASA uses Host Scan to make policy decisions based on the remote user's OS, patch level, Registry keys (Windows only), local files, IP address, and digital certificates. In addition, Host Scan can detect keystroke loggers and host emulation. Beginning with AnyConnect Secure Mobility Client version 3.0.0 and ASA Version 8.4, the Host Scan module is available separately or as part of the AnyConnect software bundle. In earlier AnyConnect and ASA versions, the Host Scan module was available only as part of the CSD software.

The introduction of Host Scan as an independent module allows for updates to be deployed and installed more frequently than in earlier releases—that is, it is faster to release a new version of Host Scan and its list of supported software (antivirus, antispyware, and so on) than the full CSD package each time. AnyConnect client versions pre-3.0.0 can work with the up-to-date and future versions of the Host Scan module that are deployed independently. However, it is not possible to run AnyConnect 3.0.0 and later with earlier versions of the Host Scan module. For example, if an AnyConnect client using Version 3.0.1 attempts to connect to an ASA using the Host Scan version bundled with the CSD 2.2, the Prelogin Assessment will fail, and the connection attempt will be denied.

Endpoint Assessment extensions can be enabled to check the user's device for installed antivirus, antispyware, and firewall software, in addition to installed definition files or patches and standard Host Scan parameters mentioned earlier.

You can also purchase an additional license to enable Advanced Endpoint Assessment extensions that enable checking for locally installed antivirus, antispyware, firewall software, definitions, and patches, and also allows remediation to occur. For example, if the antivirus software you are checking for is an earlier version than that specified in your policy, you can automatically perform the actions to update it.

## Prelogin Assessment

The Prelogin Assessment enables you to check the user's device for OS version, Registry keys (Windows only), local filenames, digital certificates, and IP address before the user logs in to the AnyConnect VPN. The Prelogin Assessment feature is part of the CSD bundle and is configured at **Configuration > Remote Access VPN > Secure Desktop Manager > Prelogin Policy.**

In the Prelogin Policy window, you can create a step-by-step flow of events that take place against the user's device, based on the information retrieved by Host Scan. Each policy begins with a start node and is then configured with one or more sequences and subsequences that determine the action taken. Figure 7-1 displays a basic Prelogin Assessment policy deployment.

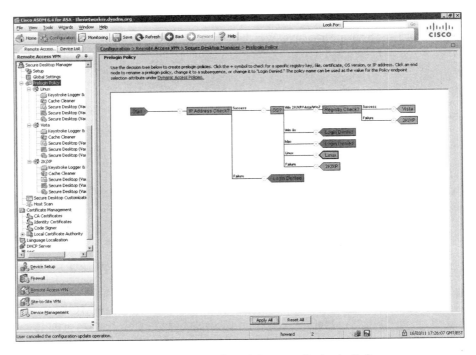

**Figure 7-1**   *ASDM Cisco Secure Desktop Manager, Prelogin Policy*

As shown in Figure 7-1, a prelogin policy has been configured with the initial sequence and subsequences that are followed depending on the information retrieved by Host Scan. The branches of each sequence or subsequence can lead to another subsequence, a deny action (the user is disconnected), or a policy that contains your CSD, Cache Cleaner, Keystroke Logger Detection, and Host Emulation Detection settings.

Figure 7-2 displays the questions that are asked in the initial IP address check. These two subsequences are based on the connecting user's OS and the policy or login denied actions that result in our sample prelogin policy.

## Secure Desktop (Vault)

The Vault is a secure partition on the remote user's device that is created during CSD installation and before the user's login. This provides a Secure Desktop area through which a user accesses the VPN connection.

In addition to creating a secure partition, you can control the user experience by allowing or denying access to locally installed programs, file systems, and the local desktop.

The CSD environment can be fully customized, allowing for the use of a corporate logo for a desktop background image, custom button images, and so on. You can also provide remote users with the option to save their files and settings accessed during a VPN session within the CSD. However, CSD reuse can occur only when a remote user attempts to establish a VPN connection from the same device.

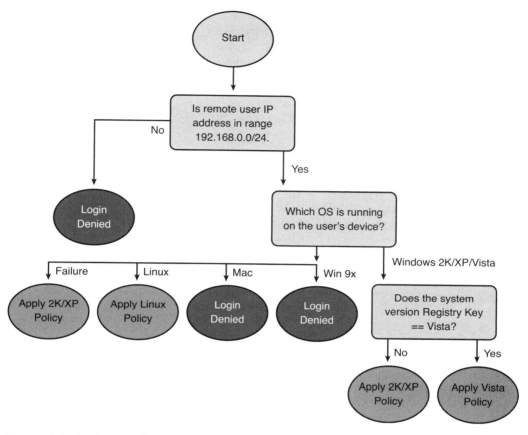

**Figure 7-2**   *Prelogin Policy Sequences, Subsequences, and Actions*

## Cache Cleaner

Cache Cleaner is an alternative to Secure Desktop that is typically used on a device that cannot run Secure Desktop (for example, a Mac, Linux, or Windows 7 device) and is normally used as backup to Secure Vault. After the user has finished the session, logs out, and closes the browser windows, the Cache Cleaner attempts to remove all history, cookies, autocompleted text, files cached by the browser, and saved passwords. This allows other people to use the device in the future without the risk of recovering any of the previous user's data. One of the main downsides with the Cache Cleaner program is that it monitors only the first browser window a user opens. Therefore, it is important to inform users that any subsequent browser windows that they open are not secure. For example, if they use IE to establish the Secure Sockets Layer virtual private network (SSL VPN) session but Mozilla to browse the Internet, upon SSL VPN session termination, cookies and so on from Mozilla are not inspected by Cache Cleaner.

The Cache Cleaner can operate in one of two modes, and the amount of cache information removed depends on the mode configured:

■  Clear the Whole Cache (IE only)

■  Clear the Current Session Cache

When configured to clear only the current session cache a minute after the user initially logs in to the VPN, Cache Cleaner takes a snapshot of the current browser cache. Later, when the VPN is disconnected, the Cache Cleaner removes all browser cache information and attempts to restore the snapshot taken at the beginning of the session. When configured to clear the whole cache (IE only), it makes no snapshot and removes the browser's entire cache.

### Keystroke Logger Detection

Keystroke Logger Detection, when enabled, downloads to the user's device (Windows 32 bit only) and scans for any known keylogging software installed. You can configure the Keystroke Logger Detection module with a list of known applications that may or may not have been approved by the administrator. If any unapproved software is located, the user can be prompted with a list of the application names that have been located and asked to approve them, or the VPN can be configured to terminate. The Keystroke Logger Detection module can detect both User and Kernel mode software keyloggers. However, it cannot detect the presence of hardware keyloggers.

### Integration with DAPs

Host Scan and CSD are heavily integrated with DAPs, in that they provide the criteria upon which DAPs base their policy selection and assignment. In addition to supporting the criteria supplied by Host Scan, DAPs can base their policy decisions on the results gathered by both the Endpoint Assessment and Advanced Endpoint Assessment modules.

### Host Emulation Detection

CSD can detect whether your remote user's SSL VPN session has originated from within a virtual machine environment, and it allows you to base your policy decision on the results received. For example, you might want to restrict access to remote users who are connecting into your organization using an OS within a virtual machine.

### Windows Mobile Device Management

When deploying the AnyConnect client to remote devices, the Host Scan module that is specific to mobile devices can perform additional posture checks.

### Standalone Installation Packages

As well as being able to automatically deploy the CSD package to remote users during a login attempt, it is possible to download standalone versions of the various CSD packages (OS specific) for manual or companywide automatic installation. However, any manually installed CSD packages cannot be automatically uninstalled from the user's machine if the ASA is configured to do so.

### CSD Manual Launch

Once CSD is installed locally on the user's device, it is possible for the user to open the CSD software and automatically start a clientless SSL VPN session without the need for Java or ActiveX controls.

During the prelogin stage to the end of a user's VPN session, the following steps are taken:

1. The user enters the SSL VPN URL or starts the AnyConnect client to access the SSL VPN.

2. The OS Detection module is downloaded, runs, and reports back the device's OS and patch level to the ASA.

3. The Host Scan module is downloaded and runs on the client device for additional policy-matching criteria (for example, Registry keys and local file systems).

4. Based on the OS Detection and Host Scan module information, the prelogin policy is matched and applied to the user or the connection is denied.

5. If the connection is allowed, the remote machine is checked for keyloggers and host emulation.

6. Depending on the prelogin policy applied, the Vault or Cache Cleaner downloads and installs on the user's device.

7. The user enters his VPN credentials and is authenticated using the configured authentication methods for the connection profile he is connecting to.

8. After successful authentication, any matching DAP records, group policies, and user attributes are applied in accordance with the ASA's hierarchal policy assignment model.

9. The SSL VPN session is established.

10. The user has finished with the SSL VPN session and logs out, or either the inactivity or idle timer expires.

11. The VPN session termination phase settings are applied. For example, cache data is removed, files are deleted, and Vault or Cache Cleaner is uninstalled.

As discussed in earlier chapters, a user connection consists of three stages. During each stage, the relevant CSD modules gather the required information (to review) for the correct policy attributes and actions to be applied before, during, and after the user connection. The three connection stages are as follows:

- Prelogin

- Post-login

- VPN session termination

The following sections examine the policy actions that take place during each of the connection stages.

## Prelogin Policies

During this stage, the user's current environment is scanned for key variables such as the OS, patch level, processes, files, Registry settings (Windows only), and digital certificates. In addition, you can check for the presence of installed antivirus, antispyware, or firewall software.

After remote users have navigated to the SSL VPN URL (unless connecting with AnyConnect), they are presented with the Cisco Secure Desktop WebLaunch page, as shown in Figure 7-3.

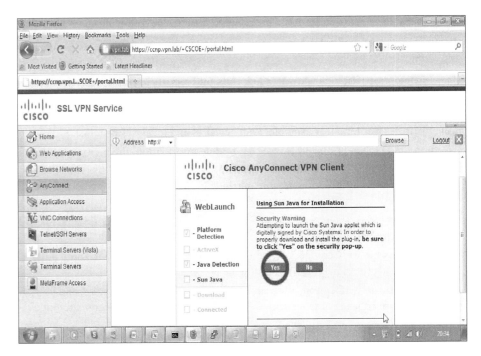

**Figure 7-3**  *Cisco Secure Desktop WebLaunch*

During the WebLaunch process, the following two stages occur:

■   The OS Detection module is launched for detection of the remote devices OS.

■   The Host Scan module is downloaded and installed.

The installation and running of these modules takes care of the Prelogin Assessment phase. These modules gather the information required for your prelogin policy assignment (for example, which OS is installed on our remote user's device, or whether the user's antivirus is running with the most up-to-date definitions installed). These settings are all determined by the Host Scan parameters you have defined, along with the prelogin policy you have configured (as explained in detail in the next section).

After the initial Prelogin Assessment, the ASA determines whether login is denied or allowed, matches the CSD policy applied to the user, and determine if the user will be using the Vault (Secure Desktop) or Cache Cleaner.

## Post-Login Policies

Depending on the policy that has been applied to the user at this stage, you can check whether the connecting user is doing so from a virtual machine and for any keylogging software that might have been intentionally or inadvertently installed on the remote device.

After the host emulation and keylogging software checks have been performed and passed, the Vault (Secure Desktop) or Cache Cleaner applications download and install on the remote device.

## VPN Session Termination

This stage is particularly important if your remote users are connecting from publicly accessible devices, such as an Internet cafe. You need to be able to remove all user settings, stored passwords, and cached credentials from the device to prevent user identity theft or session-replay attacks. You also need to decide whether the Secure Desktop (Vault) software and required modules should be removed upon the session terminating or remain on the user's device for future connections to the VPN.

As you can see, during each stage, the user's device is scanned for specific attributes that are used to determine the actions taken and behavior applied during the subsequent stages. The sections that follow describe the modules individually that are used for device information gathering, device security, remediation, and policy assignment during the three remote user connection stages.

# AnyConnect Posture Assessment and Host Scan

Key
Topic

As you saw in the review of the Host Scan module, with the release of the AnyConnect 3.0.0 and ASA 8.4, the Host Scan module is now independent of CSD and can either be uploaded to the ASA separately or bundled with the AnyConnect client installation file.

AnyConnect can perform the posture assessment of a remote user's device by using either the AnyConnect Posture Assessment module or Host Scan.

## AnyConnect Posture Assessment Module

The Posture Assessment module contains Host Scan in addition to the Keystroke Logger Detection, Host Emulation Detection, and Cache Cleaner applications. The module allows the AnyConnect client to perform posture assessment, search for installed or approved keylogging software, determine whether the remote user's environment is a virtual machine, and install the Cache Cleaner application for the monitoring and removal of user and cache information when remote users disconnect from their VPN session.

The Posture Assessment module can either be pushed down to remote users during their connection attempt by using a group policy object or installed along with any other required modules and the AnyConnect core client software using a predeployment package.

To modify the available modules for installation by remote users, open the group policy object that applies to the connection profile in use (**Configuration > Remote Access VPN > Network (Client) Access > Group Policy**). Then choose the group policy from the list and click **Edit**. In the Edit Internal Group Policy <name> window, choose **Advanced > AnyConnect Client** from the menu on the left, scroll down to the Optional Client Modules to Download section, and uncheck the **Inherit** option. Then, using the drop-down list, choose the **AnyConnect Posture** entry in addition to any other modules you require.

Figure 7-4 shows the selection of the AnyConnect Posture Assessment module in a group policy object. Upon initiating a new connection, the module is downloaded to your remote users and installed automatically.

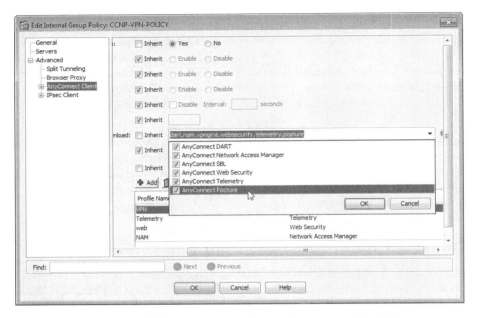

**Figure 7-4**    *Selection of the AnyConnect Posture Assessment Module*

## Host Scan

Starting from ASA 8.4, we can now upload a separate Host Scan image (included with the image are the support tables holding information for supported antivirus, antispyware, and firewall software). Uploading the separate image removes the requirement to rely on the version of Host Scan bundled with the CSD. This new method allows for the faster update and deployment of future Host Scan releases, because of newly supported antivirus, antispyware, and firewall software and Host Scan application core updates.

As shown in Figure 7-5, you can now use the new location in the Adaptive Security Device Manager (ASDM) to either upload a separate Host Scan image or specify an AnyConnect or CSD package that includes a Host Scan image. You can navigate to **Configuration > Remote Access VPN > Host Scan Image**, upload your Host Scan image, and check the **Enable Host Scan/CSD** check box to enable its use.

Custom Host Scan operations can be achieved by entering your own criteria for use when performing posture assessment against a remote user's device, in addition to the normal OS detection and so forth. After you have entered your custom Host Scan criteria (for example, the name of a file on the remote user device's file system), DAPs and your prelogin policies can use the information collected by Host Scan (whether the file exists, for example) to decide their policy assignment behavior. You enter custom criteria for Host Scan to search for in the Host Scan window (**Configuration > Remote Access VPN > Secure Desktop Manager > Host Scan**).

As shown in Figure 7-6, you can specify your own criteria for the Host Scan image to search for when conducting its posture assessment in the Host Scan window of the ASDM. You can also select the use of the Endpoint Assessment module (indicated by the checked box toward the bottom of the figure). For this example, we created a new Host Scan entry by specifying a filename (test.txt) that should be located in the root of the remote user's C:\ drive (Windows only). When performing posture assessment against a remote user's device, the Host Scan module searches for this file and records the results (found or not found) for later use by any DAPs you might have configured. You can then base your policy decision (for example, will the user connected be allowed or terminated) on the results offered by the Host Scan module.

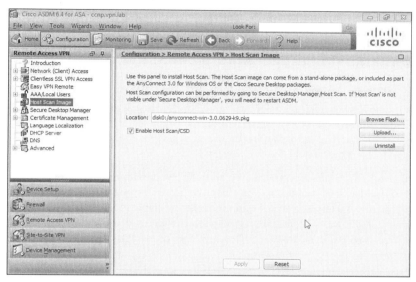

**Figure 7-5**  *ASA Host Scan Image Upload and Enable*

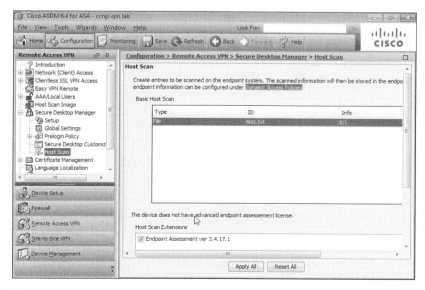

**Figure 7-6**  *Host Scan Custom Criteria Entry*

You are not just restricted to a scan for files on the remote user's file system. You can also use one of the following scan types to specify your Host Scan criteria:

- **Registry Scan:** Check for a particular Registry key and value on the local machine.

- **File Scan:** Check for a local file by name.

- **Process Scan:** Check for a running process name on the local machine (for example, winword.exe).

As mentioned previously, three different types of Host Scan are available:

- Basic Host Scan

- Host Scan Endpoint Assessment extensions

- Advanced Endpoint Assessment

Host Scan Endpoint Assessment extensions make use of the Host Scan support tables that are included with the Host Scan image. The Endpoint Assessment extensions can search for any known antivirus, antispyware, and firewall software in the support tables and feed the results back to the ASA for later use by DAPs.

The Advanced Endpoint Assessment is available through the purchase of an additional license from Cisco, and as soon as you have installed the license through **Configuration > Device Management > Licenses,** the extension becomes available to select in the Host Scan Extensions panel. When selected, this option allows for remediation and scanning for installed antivirus software that we are able to upgrade or install automatically with the Advanced Endpoint Assessment module.

As well as remediation, the Advanced Endpoint Assessment enables you to enforce rules or exceptions in personal firewall and antispyware programs. Based on the success or failure of the remediation attempts, you can allow or deny the user connection. This feature can be compared to a lightweight implementation of Network Access Control (NAC), which is used to perform posture assessment against a user's device and optionally perform remediation before granting network access.

## Configure Prelogin Policies

We can now look closer at the options and configuration tasks related to prelogin policies. A Prelogin policy uses the results obtained from either the Posture Assessment module or Host Scan modules to base its policy criteria upon (OS, file system, Registry, and so on).

Your user's experience is determined by the prelogin policy configuration and the matches that follow, and that is based on the information gathered by Host Scan and the policies attributes/settings (Cache Cleaner or Vault, Keylogger, and so forth).

As mentioned earlier, you can map the results gathered during the posture assessment phase against the policy actions configured in our prelogin policy using the flow-based graphical user interface (GUI) of the Prelogin Policy window (**Configuration > Remote Access VPN > Secure Desktop Manager > Prelogin Policy**).

By default, only one prelogin policy exists (named default) on the ASA. However, you can add more as you go or as your circumstances require. Figure 7-7 shows the default Prelogin Policy window.

Based on the current actions defined in the prelogin policy shown in Figure 7-7, CSD will install on all AnyConnect users.

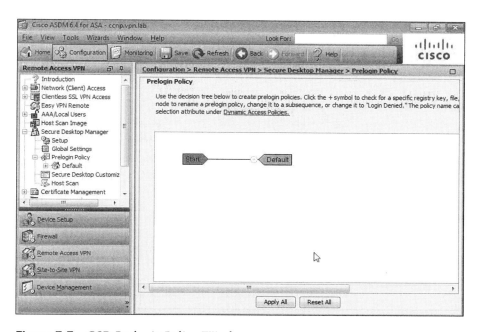

**Figure 7-7**   *CSD Prelogin Policy Window*

However, depending on the remote user environment, you can change the behavior that occurs based on the information gathered by the Host Scan application. For example, it is recommended practice to deploy CSD/Vault access to remote users connecting from public machines or devices that are not corporate owned (home PCs and such). However, for guests and remote users connecting from devices that are not running Microsoft Windows or are running unsupported CSD platforms, Cache Cleaner should be used instead.

In the prelogin policy, you can use the following criteria to determine whether a remote user is connecting from a corporate-owned device or other device:

■ **IP Address Check:** You can check for a specific IP address or subnet that a remote user is connecting from.

■ **Registry Check:** You can check for a specific key in the Windows Registry.

■ **File Check:** You can check for the existence of a particular local file on the user's device.

- **Certificate Check:** If your organization takes advantage of an internal or external Public Key Infrastructure (PKI), you can check for certain fields and values within certificates that might have been deployed to remote users or devices.

- **OS Check:** You can check for a particular OS running on a user's device.

For our example, we build upon the prelogin policy created in the previous section by first dividing our users based on their IP address. Doing so creates two new branches that can each have its own subsequence, a login denied action, or map to a policy.

We create a new subsequence that is attached to the Success branch of the IP Address Check? sequence. Our new subsequence will divide our remote users based on the OS they are using on their device.

Create the new subsequence by clicking the plus symbol (+) on the Success branch of the IP Address Check? sequence. You are then presented with the list of criteria we can select (Registry Check, IP Address, and so on). Choose **OS Check**, and then click **Add**.

Our sample prelogin policy is shown in Figure 7-8. Also shown are three new OS-specific policies we created and applied to the respective branches of the OS? subsequence.

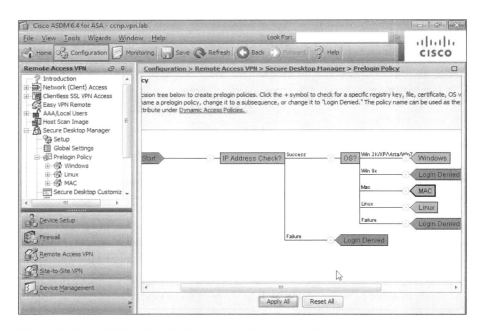

**Figure 7-8**  *Add New Match Criteria to a Prelogin Policy*

You can create new policies by selecting the action at the end of the subsequence branch you want to edit. For example, to change the Login Denied action associated with the Failure branch of our IP Address Check? sequence, choose **Login Denied.** You can then choose one of the three following actions:

- Login Denied

- Policy (Enter the name of an existing policy or a new one.)

- Subsequence

After entering the name of your new policies (for example, Linux), if the policy does not already exist, a new one is created. Each policy contains its own settings and attributes that are specific to Vault, Cache Cleaner, Keystroke Logger Detection, and so on. For example, you can create a policy named Windows that specifies the Vault will be used by the remote users this policy applies to. You then create a second policy named Linux and specify that the Cache Cleaner will be used by remote users of this policy. Also shown in Figure 7-8, you can see that our new policies have been created in the Prelogin Policy menu shown on the left side.

Figure 7-9 shows the menu on the left side of the ASDM. Each policy has its own Vault, Cache Cleaner, Keystroke Logger, and Host Emulation Detection submenus, enabling you to enter the settings/attributes you want applied to the remote users who are subject to the specific policy you configure. If you select the name of the policy in the left menu (for example, Windows, Linux, or Mac), you can choose whether the Vault or Cache Cleaner will be applied to remote users of this policy. Depending on your choice, you then use the appropriate submenus of the policy to set the specific settings/attributes of the program you have chosen (for example, Cache Cleaner cache or stored password settings, or Vault-allowed programs and switching between the local and Secure Desktop).

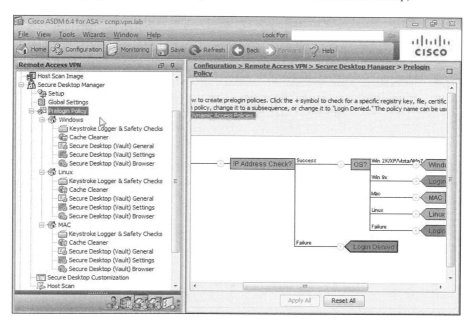

**Figure 7-9**   *Prelogin Policy Creation and Settings/Attributes Available*

For further information about prelogin policies and their settings, see Chapter 13, "Client-less SSL VPN with Cisco Secure Desktop."

# AnyConnect Network Access, Web Security, and Telemetry Modules

You have already seen some of the important updates that occurred with the release of AnyConnect 3.0.0 and ASA 8.4 (namely the introduction of Internet Key Exchange Version 2 [IKEv2] and the separation of Host Scan from CSD). However, there are more exciting updates we have yet to explore. In this final section, we take a closer look at them and the features they offer.

The following modules are available with AnyConnect 3.0.1 and later:

■ NAM (Network Access Manager)

■ Posture (Posture Assessment module)

■ SBL (Start Before Logon module)

■ DART (Diagnosis and Reporting Tool)

■ Web Security

■ Telemetry

We have already discussed some of these modules (for example, the DART and Posture Assessment modules). The SBL module is covered in greater depth in Chapter 5, "Advanced Deployment and Management of the AnyConnect Client." In this section, we review the operation of the NAM, Web Security, and Telemetry modules.

## NAM Module

The NAM module allows ASA administrators in a centralized location to manage both wired and wireless connectivity. The NAM settings are controlled through the use of AnyConnect client profiles applied to group policies that are downloaded to the AnyConnect client during the client's first log in to the ASA. NAM is a replacement for Cisco Secure Services Client, which was included in earlier versions of AnyConnect and prevents users from making network connections not compliant with enterprise-wide security policies.

NAM requires the AnyConnect core client to be installed on the remote user's device. In addition to ASDM 6.4 and ASA 8.4, the following operating systems are supported by the NAM module:

■ Windows 7 x86 (32 bit) and x64 (64 bit)

■ Windows Vista SP2 x86 (32 bit) and x64 (64 bit)

■ Windows XP x86 SP3 (32 bit)

■ Windows Server 2003 SP2 x86 (32 bit)

Through the NAM, you can group networks together based on their type and location. For example, you can create an OFFICE group that contains all wired and wireless networks that the user might be able to connect to when working in the office. Within your groups, you can then configure the settings that will apply to the available networks. As in our earlier example, we can create an OFFICE group that contains a connection profile for a wireless connection available in the user's office, and then create or add the wireless connection, entering security, pre-shared key information, and so on. The same can also apply for wired connections, allowing you to specify in NAM any dot1x or Cisco trustsec authentication or encryption to apply to the specific connection type.

In addition to any connections, security protocols, and parameters you can configure using NAM, you can specify whether the connections available to your users will become available before or after they have logged in to the network. For example, your user may be connecting to your corporate environment using a wired Ethernet connection. If you are running a Windows Active Directory (AD) network internally, you can tell NAM to allow the wired connection to operate before the user has logged in to his device. This would allow for any Windows group policy objects (GPO) that have machine-specific settings, and require (to function correctly) the policy to be downloaded and applied before the user has logged in.

To create an AnyConnect NAM client profile, navigate to **Configuration > Remote Access VPN > Network (Client) Access > AnyConnect Client Profiles**, click **Add** to open the Add AnyConnect Client Profile window, and enter a name for the NAM profile in the Profile Name section. Using the drop-down box next to the Profile Usage field, choose **NAM**. You can optionally select a group policy that your profile will apply to now, and also change the location on the ASA where the profiles will be stored (default is disk0:/).

After creating your NAM client profile, you can edit the various settings and add connection-specific groups. To do so, just choose the profile from the list of those shown in the AnyConnect Client Profile window and click **Edit**.

The AnyConnect Client Profile editor will open, as shown in Figure 7-10, where you configure the settings. After completing the configuration, you can assign the profile to a GPO that you will apply to your remote users.

As shown in Figure 7-11, you can apply a group policy to your client profile by first choosing the profile in the list and then clicking the **Change Group Policy** button. In the Change Group Policy for Profile NAM window, you choose the group policy from the list on the left and use the arrow buttons to move it to the right.

A NAM-specific window is also available (depending on client profile settings) in the AnyConnect client software. To access the NAM settings/logging information, choose **Advanced** in the AnyConnect client and in the AnyConnect Secure Mobility Client window, open the **Networks** tab on the left side.

In this window, you can (depending on client profile settings) enable or disable the NAM process, enable Wi-Fi, and view the networks that are available and those to which you are currently connected. On the Statistics tab, you can view the current wired and wireless connectivity settings (for example, the encryption and authentication methods, transmitted and received packets, MAC addresses, and SSID). Finally, on the History tab, you can view a list of status messages that can help when troubleshooting a problem with the NAM service or a connection on the user's device.

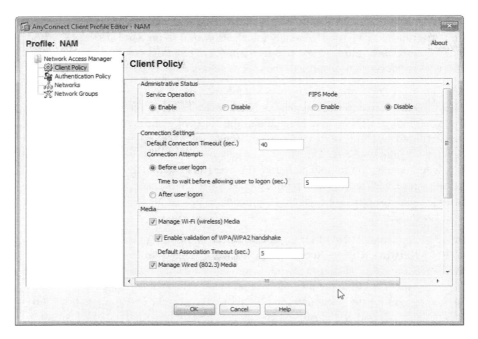

**Figure 7-10** *AnyConnect Client Profile Editor, Editing NAM-Specific Settings*

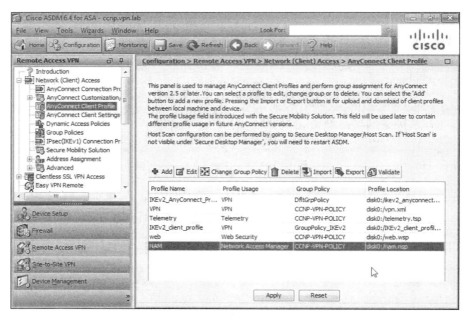

**Figure 7-11** *Applying a NAM Client Profile to a Group Policy*

Figure 7-12 shows an example of the NAM window available in the AnyConnect client. In this example, the name of the network or group is displayed in the Saved Networks window in addition to the SSID (if applicable), security offered by the connection, the type of connection (Wired/Wi-Fi), and privileges associated with the connection.

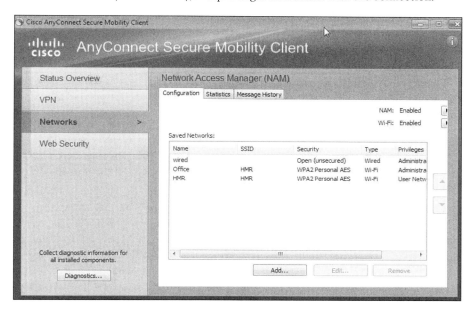

**Figure 7-12**   *Cisco AnyConnect NAM Window*

## Web Security Module

The Web Security module allows HTTP traffic to be directed to an external ScanSafe server for web-filtering purposes.

There are ScanSafe filtering servers spread throughout the Internet at different global locations, allowing remote users to always receive the best response (that is, lowest latency) by using a server that is in the same country or even state, instead of using a centralized server housed within your organization. A centralized server may lead to potential bottlenecks because all remote user Internet traffic has to traverse the established VPN tunnel and each remote user uses the same filtering server.

Optional beacon servers can be configured in your corporate LAN to allow the Web Security module to detect when a remote user is working in your office and should no longer use the remote ScanSafe servers. Security between the Web Security module and the beacon servers is confirmed by using a private/public key pair.

The Web Security module can be installed and operate without an ASA device (and thus allow users to take advantage of the ScanSafe filtering services). However, if you deploy the Web Security module in addition to an ASA device, the minimum requirement is to run ASDM 6.4 and ASA 8.4.

The Web Security module supports the following operating systems:

■   Windows XP SP3: x86 (32 bit) and x64 (64 bit)

■   Windows Vista SP2: x86 (32 bit) and x64 (64 bit)

■   Windows 7: x86 (32 bit) and x64 (64 bit)

If you plan to deploy one or more beacon servers within your organization for the purposes of deactivating the ScanSafe filtering requirement, depending on the location of your remote users, the Web Security module beacon server application supports the following operating systems:

■   Windows Server 2003, x86 (32 bit)

■   Windows Server 2008, x86 (32 bit)

There are no licensing requirements on the ASA to enable the Web Security module. However, to be able to take advantage of the ScanSafe filtering services, you must have a Secure Mobility for ScanSafe license in addition to a ScanSafe Web Filtering or ScanSafe Malware Scanning license.

To configure the various settings and options for the Web Security module using AnyConnect client profiles and apply these to the GPOs that will apply to remote users, navigate to **Configuration > Remote Access VPN > Network (Client) Access > AnyConnect Client Profiles** and click **Add**. In the Add AnyConnect Client Profile window, give your profile a name. Using the drop-down list next to the Profile Usage heading, choose **Web Security**. Optionally, you can choose the group policy you want your profile to apply to in addition to selecting a location where you can save the Web Security module file on the ASA (default is disk0:/).

After creating a new client profile for the purposes of assigning Web Security module settings, you can choose it from the list in the AnyConnect Client Profiles window of the ASDM and click **Edit**. The AnyConnect Client Profile Editor - <name> window will open, as shown in Figure 7-13.

In the Client Profile Editor, you can view a list of the current ScanSafe servers that are available to your Web Security users. You can choose the default filtering server based on our remote user's default geographic location (for example, US or UK). You can also specify the ports that the Web Security module will listen on for remote user web traffic for redirection to the ScanSafe server.

**Note:**   Although you can view a list of the available ScanSafe filtering servers, you cannot edit, remove, or add entries from the list. The Scanning Proxy list is automatically updated by ScanSafe every 24 hours. You can, however, choose entries from the list that will be hidden from your remote users, and choose the option to manually update the list now by contacting the ScanSafe servers.

Also within your client policy, in the Exceptions menu you can add exceptions that will bypass the filtering services option. In this menu, you can specify the following:

■   **Host Exceptions:** IP subnets, networks, or external website addresses

■   **Proxy Exceptions:** The addresses of any internal or external proxy servers

■   **Static Exceptions:** The IP addresses of any internal or external devices (for example, the ASA IP addresses and so on)

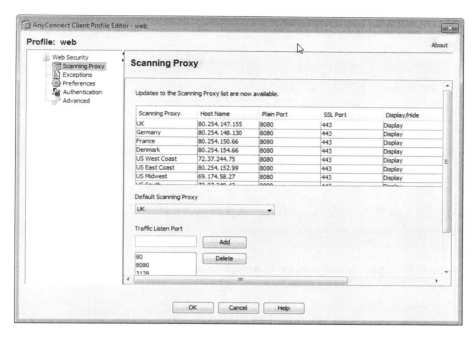

**Figure 7-13**   *AnyConnect Web Security Module Client Profile Configuration*

In the remaining menu options, you can enter the license key information for your ScanSafe filtering services, the beacon addresses and public key files, whether the Web Security module is user controllable by the AnyConnect client software, Domain Name System (DNS) timeouts, and debugging options.

You can also view the Web Security module installation in the AnyConnect client software by navigating to **Advanced > Web Security**. In this window, you can view the current scanning proxy/filtering server location, the license key information, and important statistics and debugging messages.

## Telemetry Module

The Telemetry module is used in addition to an installed Host Scan-supported antivirus on the remote user's device and an IronPort WSA (Web Security Appliance). In the event of viral or malicious activity occurring on the remote user's device, the actions carried out by the installed antivirus prompt the Telemetry module to send the WSA the information required to track the program/virus responsible all the way to the origin of the file. The WSA also sends the received information to the Cisco Threat Operations Center for further investigation.

For example, if a remote user has downloaded from a website a zipped file that contains a virus and later opens the file, unleashing the virus and causing havoc on the remote user's device, the remote user's installed antivirus will prompt or log the viral activity. This causes the Telemetry module to work backward through its collected logs of user/system activity to locate the origin of the virus. It sends this information to the WSA, enabling the WSA administrator and Cisco to trace the event of the viral activity back to the zipped file it had been extracted from, all the way to the website from which the file was downloaded.

The Telemetry module supports the following operating systems:

- Windows 7 (x86 [32 bit] and x64 [64 bit])

- Windows Vista with SP2 (x86 [32 bit] and x64 [64 bit])

- Windows XP SP3 (x86 [32 bit])

And it supports the following browsers:

- Internet Explorer 7 and 8

**Note:**   You can use other browsers, too, but doing so restricts the Telemetry module's URL origin-tracing capability, thus making it useless.

The Telemetry module also requires the following AnyConnect software to be installed on the remote user's device, loaded in order:

- AnyConnect client software

- Posture Assessment module

- Telemetry module

The Posture Assessment module contains the Host Scan image required by the Telemetry module for supported antivirus information. However, the Telemetry module also checks the ASA for any updated Host Scan images every 24 hours. In the event that a new image is found, it is automatically downloaded and installed.

Upon installation, the Telemetry module intercepts system, user, and application programming interface (API) function calls (before explorer.exe file activity is able to be tracked the remote user is required to log out and log in again) to track the origin activity of any downloaded files, URLs, copied files from removable devices, and so on, and works alongside the Host Scan-supported installed antivirus on the user's system. The Telemetry module stores all logged data in the following local directory on the remote user's device:

%ALLUSERSPROFILE%\Application Data\Cisco\Cisco AnyConnect Secure Mobility Client\Telemetry\data\

The Telemetry module is configured using AnyConnect client profiles, available for configuration at **Configuration > Remote Access VPN > Network (Client) Access > AnyConnect Client Profiles**. Follow the steps outlined earlier to create a new client profile. However, for correct operation, you must choose **Telemetry** from the Profile Usage dropdown list.

Figure 7-14 shows a Telemetry module configuration in the client profile settings. In this window, you can enable or disable the Telemetry service, enter the amount of information that can be stored in the history log (MB or days), modify the frequency (seconds) with which the locally installed antivirus is checked for information, and specify the number of retry attempts as the Telemetry module tries to send the logged information to the WSA appliance. In addition, you can enter exceptions for programs installed on the remote user's device that will not have their activity tracked.

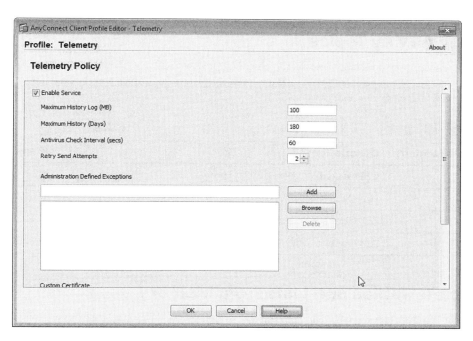

**Figure 7-14**   *AnyConnect Client Profile, Telemetry Module Configuration*

# Exam Preparation Tasks

As mentioned in the section "How to Use This Book" in the Introduction, you have a couple of choices for exam preparation: the memory tables in Appendix C, Chapter 23, "Final Exam Preparation," and the exam simulation questions on the CD-ROM.

## Review All Key Topics

Review the most important topics in the chapter, noted with the Key Topic icon in the outer margin of the page. Table 7-2 lists a reference of these key topics and the page numbers on which each is found.

**Table 7-2** *Key Topics*

| Key Topic Element | Description | Page |
|---|---|---|
| Bulleted List | CSD available modules | 224 |
| Bulleted List | Host Scan overview | 225 |
| Topic | AnyConnect Posture Assessment module and Host Scan | 231 |
| Topic | AnyConnect optional modules | 238 |

## Complete Tables and Lists from Memory

Print a copy of Appendix C, "Memory Tables" (found on the CD), or at least the section for this chapter, and complete the tables and lists from memory. Appendix D, "Memory Tables Answer Key," also on the CD, includes completed tables and lists to check your work.

## Define Key Terms

Define the following key terms from this chapter, and check your answers in the glossary:

Cache Cleaner, Host Scan, NAM (Network Access Manager), Posture Assignment module, Telemetry module, Vault, Web Security module

This chapter covers the following subjects:

- **Overview of HA and Redundancy Methods:** In this section, we discuss why and how to deploy HA and redundancy.

- **Deploying DTLS:** In this section, we review the operation of DTLS and its importance to delay- and drop-sensitive applications.

- **Performance Assurance with QoS:** In this section, we review the operation of QoS and various ASA QoS technologies.

- **AnyConnect Redundant Peering:** In this section, we discuss the procedure to enable redundant peering in the AnyConnect client for the purposes of automatic failover.

- **Hardware-Based Failover with VPNs:** In this section, we review the hardware failover method available on the ASA device.

- **Redundancy in the VPN Core:** In this section, we review the alternative methods of HA and redundancy available with the ASA (for example, VPN clustering and server load balancing with an external load balancer).

# CHAPTER 8

# AnyConnect High Availability and Performance

When approaching the task of designing and installing a network configuration, redundancy and high availability (HA) should be two considerations at the top of your list. The same applies when preparing to deploy a virtual private network (VPN) solution to your remote users. In addition to having the same level of access and workability they would normally have when working in the office, they expect to have the same level of redundancy and uptime that comes with a "wired-in" connection.

For a VPN offering, HA and redundancy seldom go hand in hand because of the limitation of being unable to provide a VPN deployment in an active/active configuration. However, as discussed throughout this chapter, you can reduce the amount downtime or loss of service remote users experience during a failover in a number of ways, including stateful failover, VPN clustering, and redundant peering.

In addition to the various HA and failover methods available, we need to consider the role of delay- and drop-sensitive applications users might be operating. This is highlighted further when we explore the various quality-of-service (QoS) mechanisms available on the Adaptive Security Appliance (ASA) device and the implementation of Datagram Transport Layer Security (DTLS).

## "Do I Know This Already?" Quiz

The "Do I Know This Already?" quiz helps you determine your level of knowledge on this chapter's topics before you begin. Table 8-1 details the major topics discussed in this chapter and their corresponding quiz sections.

Table 8-1   *"Do I Know This Already?" Section-to-Question Mapping*

| Foundation Topics Section | Questions |
| --- | --- |
| Overview of HA and Redundancy Methods | 1, 2, 3 |
| Deploying DTLS | 4 |
| AnyConnect Redundant Peering | 5 |
| Redundancy in the VPN Core | 6 |

1. Which of the following can provide for stateful HA between ASA devices during a failover?

    a. VPN load balancing

    b. Active/standby failover

    c. External load balancer

    d. AnyConnect redundant peering

2. Which of the following is not an available method of HA for use with VPN connectivity?

    a. Active/standby failover

    b. Active/active failover

    c. VPN load balancing

    d. External load balancer

3. When preparing to deploy HA methods for failover purposes, which of the following require configuration to the AnyConnect client software?

    a. VPN load balancing

    b. Active/standby failover

    c. External load balancer

    d. AnyConnect redundant peering

4. Your remote users are complaining of loss of quality during their voice calls when connected to the VPN. Which of the following protocols can you use to improve the performance of their applications?

    a. TCP

    b. TLS

    c. DTLS

    d. UDP

    e. DPD

5. Which of the following is used to provide for the AnyConnect client to automatically detect an unresponsive ASA device?

    a. TCP

    b. DTLS

    c. DPD

    d. SCEP

6. What is the name of the role performed by the ASA responsible of distributing Any-Connect client sessions and packets between available ASAs in a VPN load-balancing (clustering) configuration?

    a. Active

    b. Standby

    c. Forwarder

    d. Master

# Foundation Topics

# Overview of High Availability and Redundancy Methods

The following sections cover the current HA and redundancy methods available for use when running multiple ASA devices. After studying the details of the available methods, you can then make an informed decision about which method to implement based on your individual environment and requirements.

## Hardware-Based Failover

The hardware-based failover, configurable between two ASA devices that are identical in both hardware configuration and software version (major release.minor release(maintenance release) e.g. 8.1(1)), has been available since the time of the PIX firewall (the ASA device's firewall predecessor). However, unlike the PIX firewall and ASA pre-8.3(1) release that both required identical licenses to be installed on both appliances in ASA Version 8.3(1) and later, the requirement has been removed.

The two devices configured in a failover pair now negotiate their current session limits and so on based on the combination of the licenses installed on each of them up to the platform limit. Consider, for example, if one ASA device has an AnyConnect Premium license for 250 users installed, and the second ASA device has an AnyConnect Premium license for 100 users installed. The resulting configuration is that the failover pair supports up to 350 AnyConnect sessions so long as this number (350) of AnyConnect sessions does not exceed the current platform limits. The only exceptions to this rule are the ASA 5505 and ASA 5510 devices, which each require an installed Security Plus license before the failover configuration becomes available.

To facilitate a zero-downtime upgrade of a failover pair, the software restrictions were eased, in that for two units to remain in failover configuration, you do not need to run the same major (first number), minor (second number), and maintenance (third number) release software version on both units. For example, you can run 7.0(1) on one unit and 7.0(4) on a second unit and still maintain failover. However, restrictions still apply based on the level of major or minor releases to which you can upgrade. The following list explains the current upgrade options and their restrictions per release type (maintenance, minor, and major):

- **Maintenance release:** You can upgrade to any maintenance release within the same minor release. For example, you can upgrade from 8.0(1) to 8.0(5).

- **Minor release:** You can upgrade from your current minor release to the next available minor release, but you cannot skip one. For example, you can upgrade from 8.0 to 8.1 but not from 8.0 directly to 8.2.

- **Major release:** You can upgrade to the next available major release from the highest available minor release. For example, you can upgrade from 7.9 to 8.0 (assuming 7.9 is the last 7.x minor release available for the 7.x major release) but cannot upgrade from 7.1 to 8.0.

Regardless of the upgrade path you are undertaking, it is recommended that software version mismatches between your ASA devices be limited to short periods during upgrade windows.

Two types of hardware-based failover configuration are available: active/active and active/standby. However, only active/standby can be used for VPN purposes.

In active/standby configuration, one ASA device is active, forwarding and inspecting traffic, while the other is in standby mode, monitoring the state of the other until the time comes when it must take the active role (that is, when the current active device is restarted, becomes unavailable, or a monitored interface moves to a state other than up).

In addition to the device behavior during failover configuration (being either active or standby), active/standby configuration supports the following modes, which allow (or disallow) for session continuation during a failover:

■ **Stateful mode:** Stateful mode allows remote user sessions and connections to remain open and working after a failover has occurred between the two devices. (For example, the standby device has become the active device.) Remote users are unaware that a failover has occurred and can continue working without interruption. Stateful mode operates when the current active device shares its current state tables (xlate, uauth, and so on) with the standby device over a dedicated connection used for stateful synchronization, the existing failover interface, or an existing interface used for data transmission.

    The following features are unsupported during stateful mode operation:

    ■ Smart tunnels

    ■ Port forwarding

    ■ Plug-ins

    ■ Java applets

    ■ IPv6 clientless or AnyConnect sessions

    ■ Citrix authentication

    Should a failover occur, these states would not be synchronized between the active and standby devices, meaning the remote user would have to create a new session.

■ **Stateless mode:** Stateless mode is, well, stateless. This mode provides for no synchronization of state tables between the active and standby devices. Therefore, in the event of a failover occurring and the previous standby device becoming the active device, all user sessions and connections must be re-created for their operation to continue.

## VPN Clustering (VPN Load Balancing)

VPN clustering provides a method of redundancy to AnyConnect users by sharing the incoming connections (and thus the overall load between devices in the cluster). One device in the cluster is configured to perform the role of the master. The master device is responsible for handling incoming remote user connections and distributing them to the least loaded cluster member for further processing and synchronizing configuration between devices. This method does not require the ASA devices to be running identical hardware of software. However, because the limitations that can be imposed by unsupported commands/configurations on just one of your devices can affect all devices in the cluster, it is recommended that the ASA in a cluster operate using identical software.

## Redundant VPN Peering

Both the IPsec VPN client and AnyConnect client allow multiple ASA addresses to be configured as VPN servers. In the event of the primary ASA failing and becoming unavailable either before the client attempts to establish a new connection or during an established connection between the client and ASA, the AnyConnect client tries to connect to the next available address in their list of configured addresses. In the latter case, when the primary device becomes unavailable after a connection has already been successfully established between the AnyConnect client and the ASA, the AnyConnect client can detect the loss of communication between itself and the ASA using dead peer detection (DPD), which is discussed in detail in a moment. This method of redundancy is client-specific (configured in the AnyConnect client). Therefore, there are no requirements for your ASA devices to have identical hardware or software.

## External Load Balancing

In addition to the available hardware and software HA and redundancy methods discussed earlier, we can provide for redundancy between our devices in the way of load balancing using an external device. This method requires a load balancer (for example, an ACE 4710 appliance or module in a 6500/7600 switch/router). The Application Control Engine (ACE) is configured with a public-facing IP address known as a virtual IP address (VIP), which is used by remote users/AnyConnect clients as their VPN termination device address. Several ASAs can be made available behind the ACE and configured as real servers. The ACE, on receiving a request for the VIP, forwards it to one of the real servers (ASAs) it has configured.

From what you have learned so far in this chapter, you should now be able to decide which method is most appropriate for the specific environments you might be asked to configure. For example, if you require application access and user sessions to remain up even after a failover has occurred between the devices, and you have two ASA devices that have identical hardware and software configurations, active/standby in Stateful mode is for you. However, if you have no requirement to share session and application state between your devices and have a pair of ASAs that have identical hardware and software configurations, you can configure active/standby in Stateless mode.

In the second scenario, we could have also suggested VPN clustering. This would allow for the load to be shared between your ASA devices and allow for the support of more than two ASA devices. However, with this configuration, it is important to consider the effects of multiple ASA devices becoming unavailable and the potential load that had previously been supported by three ASA devices now has to be supported by just one. Because of this, many people prefer to use the active/standby hardware failover method in Stateful or Stateless mode, because this method can provide for a more deterministic approach during a failover situation (that is, if your active ASA becomes unavailable and all traffic is dealt with by the standby ASA). It is easy, considering you might have to trou-bleshoot only one device rather than several if operating a cluster of ASAs.

In addition to the methods described earlier, remember the role of redundant peering for your organization, which can help keep the configuration of ASAs simple. After all, you just configure the necessary firewall and VPN on them. However, with this deployment, you must consider the potential for an increase in management overhead that might result from device configurations having to be synchronized manually between your ASAs. Oth-erwise, this might lead to your remote users being unable to perform the operations they once did, if your primary ASA is unavailable and your users must now connect to an ASA with an older configuration.

Table 8-2 identifies the available HA and redundancy methods you have read about here and summarizes their respective advantages and disadvantages.

**Table 8-2**   *Advantages and Limitations of Various HA Methods*

| Method | Advantages | Disadvantages |
|---|---|---|
| Active/standby failover | Can provide stateful or stateless methods. Stateful operation is re-quired to prevent session reestab-lishment during or after a failover. | No load sharing or balancing occurs between devices. Only one device is active at a time. Lack of stateful failover support for clientless SSL VPN applications. |
| VPN load balanc-ing (clustering) | Allows for the load between devices to be shared among them based on the "least used" device receiving the latest connection attempt.<br><br>Differing hardware and software re-visions can be used.<br><br>Native, built-in ASA feature. | Cannot provide stateful failover, nondeterministic. |
| Redundant VPN servers | Allows for connections to be shared among available devices based on clients using different VPN server addresses.<br><br>Differing hardware and software re-visions can be used. | No active failover detection; clients must use DPD for peer detection.<br><br>Connections are not stateful.<br><br>Clientless SSL VPN cannot use this method for automatic reconnection. |
| Load balancing using an external load balancer | Allows for the load between devices to be shared among them. We have greater flexibility in choosing load-balancing algorithms than cluster-ing.<br><br>Differing hardware and software re-visions can be used. | Cannot provide stateful failover.<br><br>No active failover between devices. Clients must reconnect to the next available device after being discon-nected. |

# Deploying DTLS

As discussed in Chapter 3, "Deploying an AnyConnect Remote-Access VPN Solution," Datagram Transport Layer Security is commonly used for delay-sensitive applications (voice and video). Instead of completely rewriting the Transport Layer Security (TLS) standard, DTLS provides for enhancements of the TLS standard with the introduction of windowing and support for packet sequencing and reordering, lost/dropped packets, and so on. The greatest benefit that DTLS can provide for standard TLS when operating delay-sensitive applications is the use of User Datagram Protocol (UDP), which allows for faster transmission of application data without the additional overhead of TCP.

DTLS is only capable of running in an AnyConnect Secure Sockets Layer (SSL) VPN (not Internet Key Exchange Version 2 [IKEv2]). By default, DTLS is enabled when an interface is first enabled for SSL termination. However, if DTLS has been disabled, you might need to reenable it on an interface for successful delay-sensitive operation.

You begin by navigating in the Adaptive Security Device Manager (ASDM) to the Connection Profiles window (**Configuration > Remote Access VPN > Network (Client) Access > AnyConnect Connection Profiles**). There, you can enable or disable DTLS on a per-interface basis by checking the **Enable DTLS** check box next to the relevant interface in the Access Interfaces section of the window, as shown in Figure 8-1.

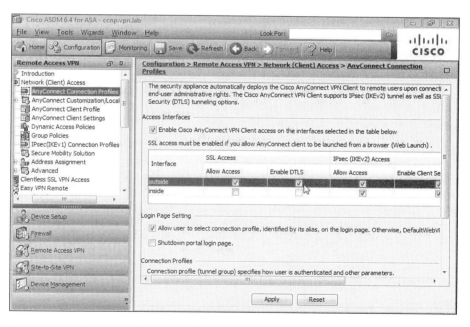

**Figure 8-1**   *Enable or Disable DTLS on a Per-Interface Basis*

In addition to configuring DTLS on an interface-by interface-basis, you can selectively enable DTLS in a group policy or directly in a local user account properties dialog (if the local user has an account configured directly on the ASA). You can configure DTLS in both a group policy and local user account in the following locations:

- **Group Policy Configuration: Configuration > Remote Access VPN > Network (Client) Access > Group Policies.** Choose the group policy object and click **Edit**. Then, in the Edit Internal Group Policy: <name> window, expand **Advanced > AnyConnect Client.**

- **User Properties: Configuration > Remote Access VPN > Network (Client) Access > AAA/Local Users > User Accounts.** Choose the user account from the list and click **Edit**. Then, in the Edit User Account window, expand **VPN Policy > AnyConnect Client.**

In both locations, uncheck the **Inherit** check box next to Datagram TLS, and then check the **Enable** check box (default).

You also need to enable DPD for correct fallback behavior so that in the event a communication error occurs between the AnyConnect client and the ASA, the AnyConnect client will attempt to fall back to using TLS rather than DTLS to solve any communication problems that might exist. DPD (enabling it and its operation) is discussed in more detail later in this chapter.

## Performance Assurance with QOS

In addition to performance improvements that can be made available to delay-sensitive application traffic, we can provide for QoS on the ASA through packet differentiation, shaping, and policing.

QoS allows us to differentiate between multiple traffic flows traveling through our VPN tunnel and provide them with a different level of service based on their endpoint information, packet markings, application type, and so forth.

When configuring QoS using the command-line interface (CLI) on the ASA, we use Modular Policy Framework (MPF) terminology, which is similar in functionality with Modular QoS CLI (MQC) from Cisco routers, which provide us with class maps, policy maps, and service policies that work in combination. This allows us to match packets/services (class maps) and apply either policing, shaping, or prioritization to the packets/services we match (policy maps). In addition, we can apply the policing, shaping, or prioritization rules that have previously been applied to our matched packets/services either on an interface or globally (service policy).

The following QoS actions can be applied to traffic traveling through a VPN on the ASA:

- **Policing:** You can apply policing to incoming or outgoing traffic, globally or per interface. Policing can enable you to rate limit the amount of traffic sent and received through an interface (for example, if you are connected using a 10-Mb interface but all traffic must not exceed 2 Mb). Traffic that exceeds the limit imposed using policing may either be dropped or transmitted, depending on your overall QoS strategy. In the VPN context, policing is available only for IPsec site-to-site and remote-access tunnels, and not for SSL VPN, be it client based (AnyConnect) or clientless.

- **Shaping:** You can apply shaping to outgoing traffic using the class-default class only, because the ASA requires all traffic to be matched for traffic shaping. This makes traffic shaping unavailable for VPN tunnels because (as discussed later) to apply QoS to VPN tunnels you need a specific command inside a class map, which is **match tunnel-group**, and this is not supported in class-default.

  Shaping, similar to policing, can enable you to rate limit the amount of traffic sent through an interface. However, unlike policing, the shaper places the packets into a buffer to achieve smoothing of a traffic flow to match the limit imposed, instead of dropping out of profile traffic (exceeding the bandwidth limit you have set). Note that traffic shaping is not supported on the ASA 5580.

- **Low-latency queuing (LLQ):** LLQ enables you to prioritize some packets/flows over others. For example, if you have voice and email traffic using the same connection, you can tell the ASA to always send the voice traffic ahead of the email (give it priority). LLQ is available for both IPsec and SSL VPN tunnels.

By default, all traffic sent and received through the ASA regardless of the application type is classed as best effort. However, this can cause problems when delay-sensitive applications (for example, voice and video applications, which typically send small packets at a constant rate) have to wait for other application data (for example, email or FTP, which typically send larger packet sizes of periodically burst large amounts of data at a time) to be sent during periods of congestion.

You can overcome this problem by implementing LLQ in your environment and assigning delay-sensitive (voice) packets to a priority queue. Any voice packets traveling through the interface your QoS policy is applied to will then be prioritized and sent before other applications, resulting in a smooth flow of packets.

LLQ is a combination of the older priority queuing (PQ) method and class-based weighted fair queuing (CBWFQ), which you would usually see configured on a router used in a QoS deployment. The older PQ method may result in queue-starvation occurrences (in which each matching packet is given priority and sent before any others). If you have voice and other application packets using the same link but you had assigned your voice packets to a priority queue using the older PQ, voice packets sent at a constant rate would mean your other application traffic would never be sent. LLQ resolves this problem by giving priority to selected traffic but at a policed rate (that is, I will prioritize your packets and send them first but only up to a certain rate).

When configuring QoS using the MPF on the CLI, you generally implement things in the following order:

- **Class map configuration:** Select the traffic to which you want to apply your QoS actions.

- **Policy map configuration:** Apply your chosen QoS actions to the traffic selected in the class map defined earlier.

- **Service policy configuration:** Apply your QoS matching and associated actions to an interface or globally.

However, when configuring QoS using the ASDM, although you still achieve the same results, the order of configuration is changed, as follows:

■   Service policy configuration

■   Class map configuration

■   Policy map configuration

### Basic ASDM QoS Configuration

For our configuration, the following requirements have been set:

■   Voice packets in AnyConnect sessions must be prioritized over all other packets.

■   All traffic must be policed to 2 Mb.

By default, on the ASA, no QoS policies are applied. Therefore, we must start with a blank configuration to create our service policies, class maps, and policy maps as discussed earlier. We begin the configuration by navigating to **Configuration > Firewall > Service Policy Rules**. Then, in the Service Policy Rules window, we click **Add > Add Service Policy Rule**.

Figure 8-2 shows the Add Service Policy Rule Wizard - Service Policy window. During this stage, we need to select an interface to which our service policy will apply.

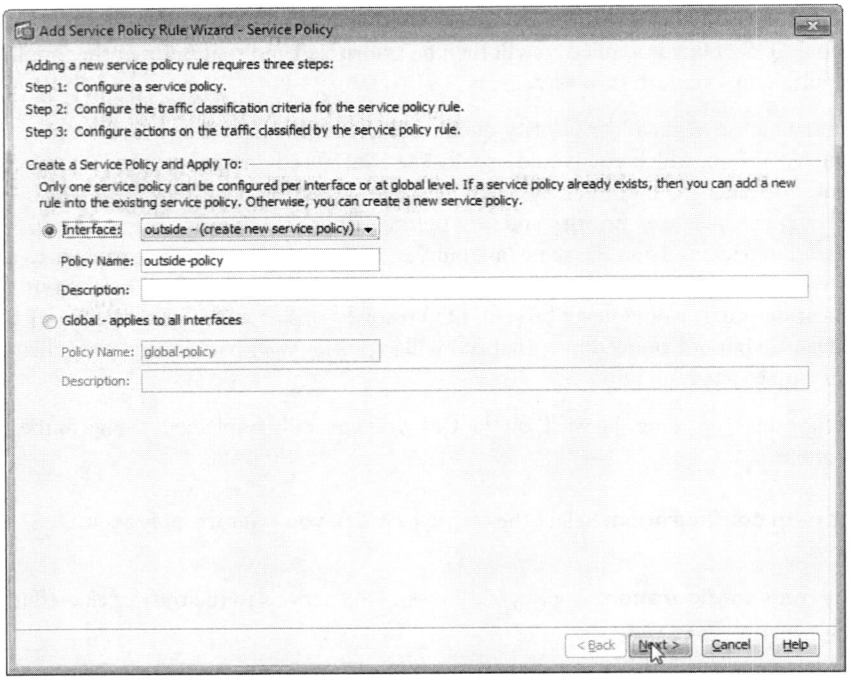

**Figure 8-2**   *ASA QoS Service Policy Configuration*

You can only have one service policy per interface or one assigned globally on the ASA. If we were to select an interface that already had a service policy applied, we would be allowed to either remove the existing policy and create a new one or add a new rule to the existing policy. As it stands, we have no policies configured on any of our interfaces (with the exception of the default policy that is applied globally), so we choose the outside interface. (Make sure the selected interface is the one terminating VPN tunnels if you want QoS policies apply to VPN traffic.) We are also required to give our service policy a name. For our example, we accept the default name of outside-policy that is created after we chose the interface. However, in a production environment, you might want to use your own naming scheme to allow you to easily and quickly identify the policy from others you might have created in the configuration. We then click **Next** to open the Traffic Classification Criteria window, shown in Figure 8-3.

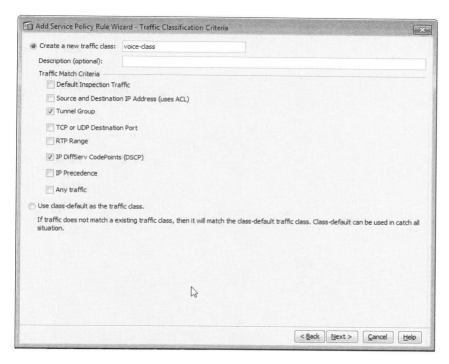

**Figure 8-3**   *ASA QoS Service Policy Configuration: Class Map/Traffic Selection*

In this window, we are given the opportunity to select the traffic that our QoS policy will apply to or match. This configuration step is known as creating the class map. For our example, we chose **Tunnel Group** because the traffic we will be matching will travel through our VPN tunnel and IP DSCP (differentiated services codepoint), which allows us to match the DSCP that has been preassigned to our voice packets by other devices in the network path. We can also optionally assign a name to our class map using this screen. For our example, we entered the name **voice-class**. Under normal operation, the ASA restricts use to only one **match** command per class map. However, for the purposes of applying QoS policies to VPN tunnels, we can use two **match** commands inside one class map, the restriction being that the **match tunnel-group** must be one of them (and the first to be configured). The second **match** command can only be one of **match dscp**, **match flow ip destination-address**, **match precedence**, **match rtp**, or **match port**.

In the next step, because we chose Tunnel Group as part of our match criteria in the previous window, we now have to select the VPN connection (connection profile) for the selected tunnel group or create a new one. After selecting or creating the appropriate connection profile, we click **Next**. Because we already have two **match** commands in our class map, we are not allowed to check the Match Flow Destination IP Address check box shown in Figure 8-4—the criteria used to define a flow is the destination IP address, and all traffic going to a unique destination IP address is considered a new flow.

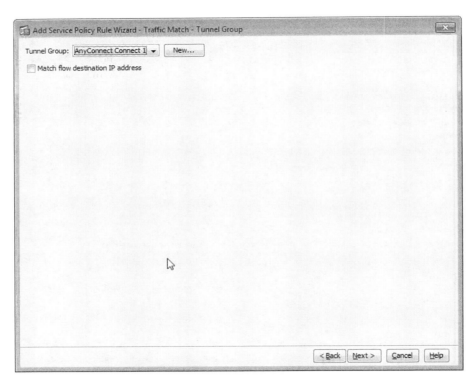

**Figure 8-4**  *ASA QoS Service Policy Configuration: Tunnel/VPN Selection*

After we have chosen our tunnel group, the traffic traveling through our VPN tunnel is matched by our class map. However, we also chose IP DSCP, so on the next screen, we must choose the appropriate IP DSCP value used to match our voice packets.

By default, voice traffic is applied the Expedited Forwarding (EF) (46) DSCP value, so we have chosen this from the list of available values on the left and used the buttons in the window to move it into the pane on the right to indicate our choice, as shown in Figure 8-5.

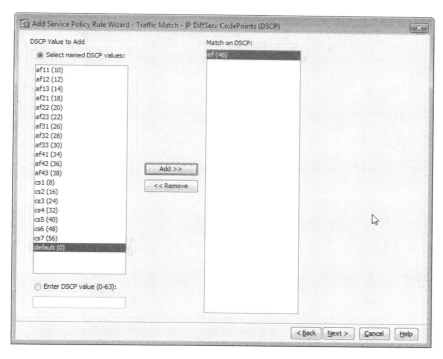

**Figure 8-5**   *ASA QoS Service Policy Configuration: IP DSCP Selection*

In the Add Service Policy Rule Wizard - Rule Actions window shown in Figure 8-6, we choose QoS actions that will be applied to the packets matched by our class map we have created. This configuration step is also known as creating the policy map. To apply our desired QoS actions for the prioritization of the matched voice traffic, we open the **QoS** tab and check **Enable Priority for This Flow**, which enables LLQ. Then we click **Finish**.

As shown in Figure 8-7, our new QoS policy has been applied to the outside interface. We can also view the traffic-match criteria in the Service Policy Rules window.

Next, we need to complete the results required in our example by policing all traffic to 2 Mb. We begin by clicking **Add > Add Service Policy Rule** again from the top menu of the Service Policy Rules window. In the Add Service Policy Rule Wizard - Service Policy window, we choose the outside interface we chose in our earlier configuration and click **Next**.

In the Add Service Policy Rule Wizard - Traffic Classification Criteria window, we check the **Use Class-Default as the Traffic Class** check box. This causes the actions defined in the policy map we create next to be applied to all remaining packets that are not matched using our previously defined voice-class class map. Figure 8-8 shows the configuration completed in this step.

Now within the Add Service Policy Rule Wizard - Rule Actions window, we open the **QoS** tab and check the **Enable Policing** and **Output Policing** check boxes. For this example, we are policing all remaining traffic to 2-Mb output.

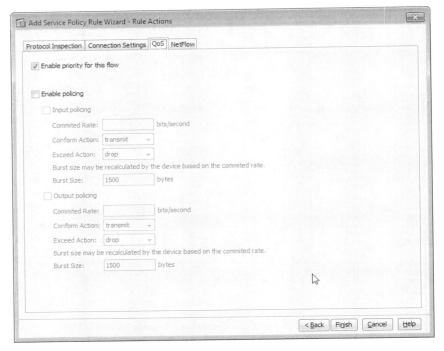

**Figure 8-6**   *ASA QoS Service Policy Configuration: Traffic Prioritization*

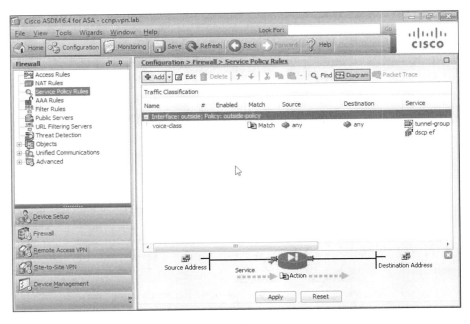

**Figure 8-7**   *ASA QoS Service Policy Configuration Review*

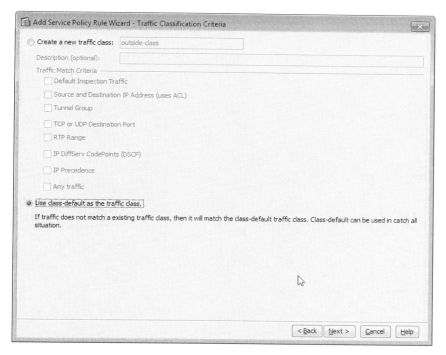

**Figure 8-8**  *ASA QoS Service Policy Configuration: Traffic Classification*

We enter the following details for our configuration, as shown in Figure 8-9:

- **Committed Rate (bps):** 2000000

- **Conform Action:** Transmit

- **Exceed Action:** Drop

- **Burst Size:** 1500 (default, left alone)

Our QoS configuration is complete. We have successfully enabled the prioritization for voice traffic traveling through our VPN tunnel and policed all remaining traffic to 2 Mb using the class-default class. Any traffic in the 2-Mb limit will be sent. Any out-of-profile traffic that exceeds the 2 Mb will be dropped.

The direction and match criteria of our QoS policies can be viewed in the Service Policy Rules window. To further guide your understanding, click **Diagram** in this window to see a visual representation of the configuration, as shown in Figure 8-10.

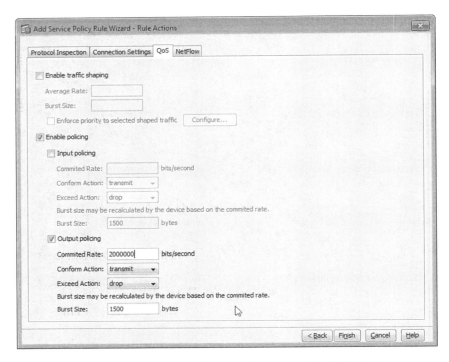

**Figure 8-9**    *ASA QoS Service Policy Configuration: Traffic Policing*

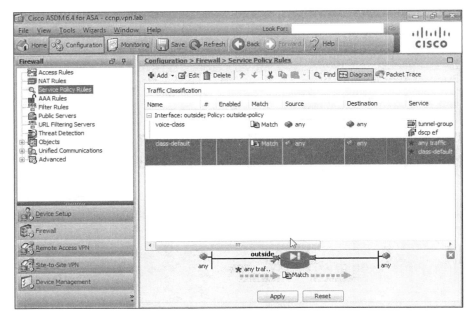

**Figure 8-10**    *ASA QoS Service Policy Configuration: Service Policy Verification*

# AnyConnect Redundant Peering and Failover

The AnyConnect client can be configured with up to ten backup servers (ASA devices) so that in the event of a failure occurring on the current ASA device, AnyConnect will attempt a connection to the next available ASA in the order they are configured.

In addition to trying one of the configured backup servers if the primary ASA is unavailable when establishing a new VPN session, the AnyConnect client uses dead peer detection (DPD) to detect when an ASA becomes unavailable during an established VPN connection. DPD is a keepalive mechanism that sends DPD_R_U_THERE packets to the ASA after a defined period of inactivity (default 30 seconds). After the AnyConnect client sends its first DPD_R_U_THERE packet, it expects a DPD_R_U_THERE_ACK back from the ASA. If the AnyConnect client does not receive an ACK from the ASA, it continues to send DPD_R_U_THERE packets until three have been sent. If at this point the AnyConnect client still has not received a response from the ASA, it tears down the connection and attempts to open a connection to the next available server configured in the Backup Servers list.

**Note:**   Recall from our earlier discussions about DTLS that for DTLS to fall back to TLS during a failure of the DTLS session, DPD needs to be enabled.

Without DPD, if the DTLS session experiences problems, the VPN session is terminated.

In addition, the frequency of keepalive messages can be adjusted from the default of 20 seconds. These are scoped to ensure that the SSL session through a proxy, firewall, or Network Address Translation (NAT) device remains active, even if the network devices in the path limit the time that the connection can stay idle. It also ensures that the connection idle timer on the VPN endpoint does not expire, by periodically sending keepalive messages. Whereas DPD makes sure there is connectivity with the VPN endpoint, keepalives maintain the session up and running.

Keepalives are configured in a group policies configuration or directly in a user's local user account properties (if the user has a local account configured on the ASA). The configuration areas and requirements in each area for the successful configuration of DPD are as follows:

- **Group policy configuration:** Configuration > Remote Access VPN > Network (Client) Access > Group Policies. Choose the group policy object and click **Edit**. Then, in the Edit Internal Group Policy: <name> window, expand **Advanced > AnyConnect Client**.

- **User properties:** Configuration, Remote Access VPN, Network (Client) Access > AAA/Local Users > User Accounts. Choose the user account from the list and click **Edit**. Then in the Edit User Account window, expand **VPN Policy > AnyConnect Client**.

In both of these locations, uncheck the **Inherit** option next to Keepalive Messages, and then optionally enter a timeout value (default 20 seconds). Keepalives can optionally be disabled in these windows by checking the **Disable** check box, although it is not recommended because the periodic keepalives are used to maintain the state of your VPN session. Without them, the ASA cannot know whether the session is up or down without manual intervention (you disconnect).

Figure 8-11 shows the configuration of keepalives in a group policy object. In this example, we kept the default timeout of 20 seconds.

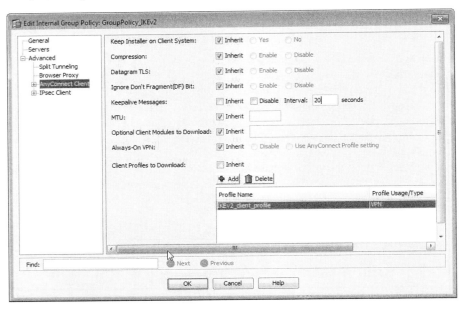

**Figure 8-11**   *Group Policy Keepalive (DPD) Configuration*

DPD is configured in a group policy or directly in a user's local user account properties (if the user has a local account configured on the ASA). The configuration areas and requirements in each area for the successful configuration of DPD are as follows:

■ **Group policy configuration:** Configuration > Remote Access VPN > Network (Client) Access > Group Policies. Choose the group policy object and click **Edit**. Then, in the Edit Internal Group Policy - <name> window, expand **Advanced > Any-Connect Client > Dead Peer Detection**.

■ **User properties:** Configuration > Remote Access VPN > Network (Client) Access > AAA/Local Users > User Accounts. Choose the user account from the list and click **Edit**. Then, in the Edit User Account window, expand **VPN Policy > AnyConnect Client, > Dead Peer Detection**.

In both of these locations, uncheck the **Inherit** option next to Gateway Side Detection or Client Side Detection, and then optionally enter a timeout value (default is 30 seconds). Figure 8-12 illustrates the DPD configuration within the group policy window. DPD can optionally be disabled in these windows by checking the **Disable** check box. For our example, we are more interested in the client-side detection, for us to be able to fall back to another VPN peer in case the current one becomes unavailable. The gateway-side detection mainly helps to free a hanged VPN session, thus freeing resources and allowing for other incoming VPN sessions, so you do not run out of available sessions because of a small number of licenses.

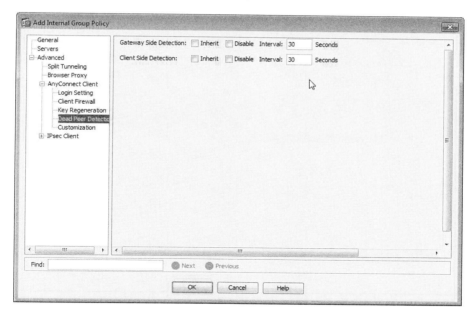

**Figure 8-12** *Group Policy DPD Configuration*

In addition to the keepalives and DPD configuration, the backup servers used by the Any-Connect client during a failover must also be configured in an AnyConnect client profile. The client profile is downloaded and installed automatically by AnyConnect clients during their next connection attempt.

Begin the configuration of an AnyConnect VPN client profile by navigating to **Configuration > Remote Access VPN > Network (Client) Access > AnyConnect Client Profile**. Then, choose an AnyConnect client profile from the list and click **Edit**.

In the AnyConnect Client Profile Editor - <name> window, choose the **Backup Servers** option from the menu on the left, and using the pane that appears, shown in Figure 8-13, on the right side, enter the IP addresses of the available ASA devices in the list. If you recall, the ASA devices entered are tried in order from top to bottom. it is possible to reorder the list by choosing the appropriate IP addresses shown and using the Move Up and Move Down buttons.

# Hardware-Based Failover with VPNs

As discussed earlier, active/standby failover can be deployed in either Stateful or Stateless modes to allow remote user's application and connection sessions to either remain open or drop during a failover. Which method you choose to deploy will depend on your environment and requirements. However, the only main difference between the two during configuration is the assignment of an additional interface (unused failover or existing data interface) for stateful operation, as shown in Figure 8-14.

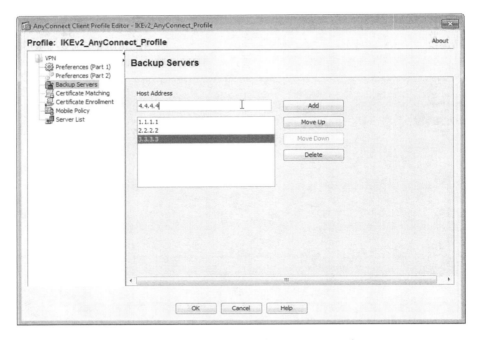

**Figure 8-13**   *AnyConnect Client Profile Backup Server Configuration*

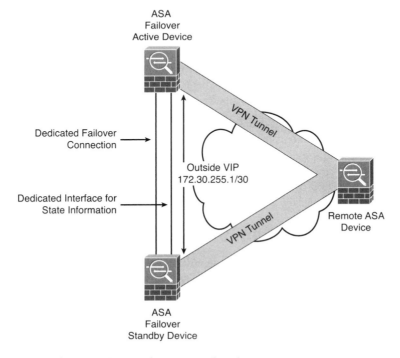

**Figure 8-14**   *ASA Hardware-Based Failover*

Three steps are required to configure hardware-based failover (and one optional step is available), as follows:

**Step 1.**   Configure LAN failover interfaces.

**Step 2.**   Configure standby addresses on interfaces used for traffic forwarding.

**Step 3.**   Define failover criteria.

**Optional**   Configure nondefault MAC addresses.

## Configure LAN Failover Interfaces

In this step, select the interfaces that will be used for failover deployment and optionally the stateful connection. You can select the same interface for both roles. However, it is recommended to use separate physical interfaces because of the large amount of information that may be sent across the stateful link. During this step, enter the active and standby IP addresses that will be configured on each of the devices based on their role (active or standby). You can also configure IP addresses for the two devices on both the failover and optional stateful link, and configure the role (primary or secondary) of the device (active or standby, respectively, under normal operating conditions).

You begin the configuration of an ASA failover pair by navigating to **Configuration > Device Management > High Availability > Failover**.

Figure 8-15 shows an example configuration and details entered to enable active/standby failover in addition to stateful operation. In this window, you can optionally enter a 32-character hexadecimal key used to encrypt the data sent between devices across the failover link. Without this optional step, all data transmitted across the failover link is sent in clear text.

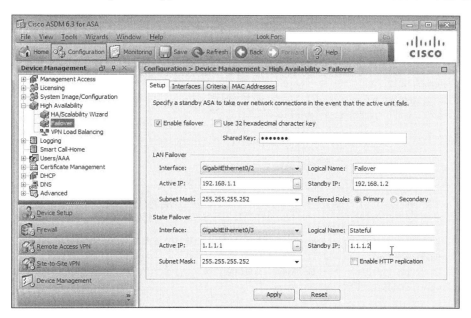

**Figure 8-15**   *ASA ASDM Failover Pair Configuration*

## Configure Standby Addresses on Interfaces Used for Traffic Forwarding

Next, the Interfaces tab of the Failover window is used to configure the standby IP addresses that will be used by the peer ASA device, as shown in Figure 8-16.

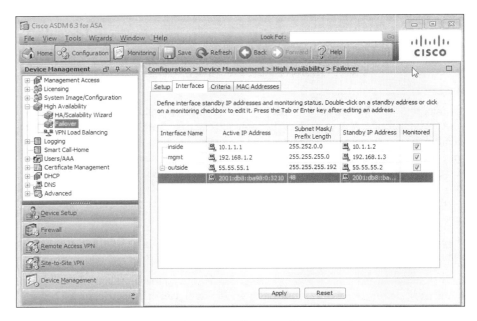

**Figure 8-16**   *ASA ASDM Failover Standby IP Address Configuration*

## Define Failover Criteria

During this step, criteria that will cause the ASA devices to fail over between active and standby roles can be specified. A failover can occur based on a number of interfaces being in a down or unknown state. By default, a failover occurs if only one interface is in any state other than up. However, this can be changed to either a number between 1 and 250 or a percentage of overall monitored interfaces.

Figure 8-17 displays the default values for failover criteria configuration.

## Configure Nondefault MAC Addresses

Now that you have seen the three mandatory steps required for a basic failover configuration, it is possible to optionally configure virtual interface MAC addresses that will be used to represent the ASA's Inside, Outside, DMZ, etc. interfaces.

Although optional, this step is recommended because of the potential downtime that may be caused if a standby/secondary device were ever to become available (up and running) before the primary/active. This behavior is detailed in Chapter 19, "High Availability and Performance for Easy VPN."

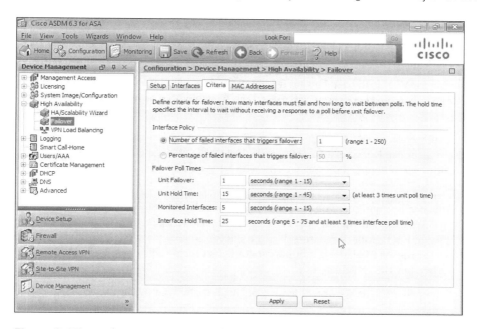

**Figure 8-17**  *Failover Criteria: Interfaces and Timeouts*

Virtual MAC (VMAC) addresses can be configured using the MAC Addresses tab of the Failover window. Start by clicking **Add**. (By default, none are configured.) In the Edit Interface MAC Addresses window, choose each of the interfaces responsible for forwarding and enter both the active interface MAC address and the interface MAC address of the standby device, as shown in Figure 8-18. Continue this operation for each interface responsible for traffic forwarding.

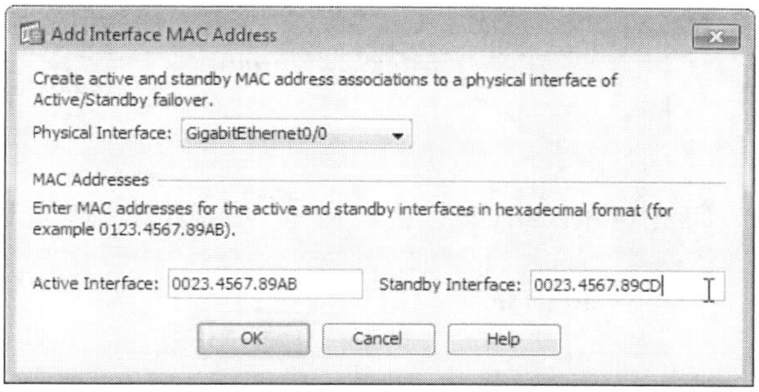

**Figure 8-18**  *Failover VMAC Configuration*

# Redundancy in the VPN Core

This section introduces the alternative methods available for HA that are achieved using additional features available within the ASA software or external equipment; for example, a Load Balancer. The information in this section will prove to be useful when it isn't possible to use the hardware failover feature of the ASA due to a hardware or software mismatch.

## VPN Clustering

An alternative way to implement a stateless HA scheme is to use the ASA's VPN load-balancing feature.

Clustering (or VPN load balancing, as it is more commonly known) can be used to divide AnyConnect remote client sessions between the available ASA devices without the need for identical hardware and software.

After a failover on one ASA occurs, any AnyConnect client sessions that the failed ASA had been responsible for must be re-created on the newly delegated ASA (by the master ASA). However, if connected using a client with DPD enabled, the client can automatically reconnect to the virtual cluster address (VIP) for session reestablishment.

Clustering can be configured on an ASA 5510 only with an installed Security Plus license, or on an ASA 5520 and later device. The devices are also required to have an installed Triple Digital Encryption Standard/Advanced Encryption Standard (3DES/AES) license for operation. If the load-balancing module cannot detect the presence of a 3DES/AES license, it becomes unavailable.

As shown in Figure 8-19, the task of load balancing is carried out by the master ASA device.

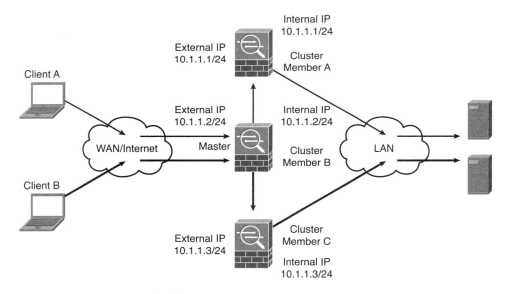

**Figure 8-19**   *VPN Load-Balancing Operation*

The master device is the first to start up and automatically assumes the role. However, if multiple devices are configured for the same cluster and restarted at the same time, the device with the higher priority wins the election and becomes the master instead.

If at any point during operation the master device becomes unavailable or fails, the cluster member with the highest priority becomes the active master in its place. There is no pre-empting once the active master has been elected. For example, if an active master already exists for a cluster and a new cluster member with a higher priority is introduced during operation, it cannot take over the role from the active master while it is still available.

The configuration required to create a cluster and add members is straightforward. All members of the same cluster must have an identical virtual cluster IP address, UDP port, and IPsec encryption key (used to encrypt messages between active members). In addition, each device's public and private interfaces must be on the same network.

Figure 8-20 shows the load balancing (VPN cluster) configuration window available in the ASDM at **Configuration > Remote Access VPN > Load Balancing**.

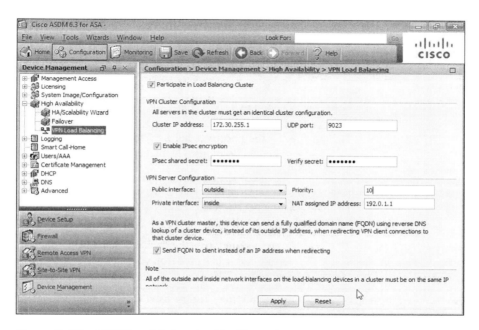

**Figure 8-20**   *VPN Load-Balancing Configuration*

Table 8-3 describes the configurable fields.

**Table 8-3**   *VPN Load-Balancing Editable Fields and Values*

| Field | Value |
| --- | --- |
| Participate in Load Balancing Cluster* | Disabled by default. Before this device can join an active cluster or become the master of a new one, you must check this option. |
| Cluster IP Address* | Enter the virtual cluster IP address to be used by this cluster. All members of the cluster must have the same address configured. |

**Table 8-3**  *VPN Load-Balancing Editable Fields and Values*

| Field | Value |
|---|---|
| UDP Port* | Enter the UDP port used for cluster member communication. This port must be unused on the network (default is 9023). |
| Enable IPsec Encryption* | For messages between cluster members to be encrypted instead of sent in plain text, check this option. |
| IPsec Shared Secret* | Enter the shared secret that will be used by each cluster member to encrypt the messages between them. |
| Verify Secret* | Enter the secret from the preceding step again to confirm your entry. |
| Public Interface | Choose from the drop-down list your public/external-facing interface. Cluster member interfaces must be on the same network. |
| Priority | Enter the priority value 1–10 for this device used for master negotiations. The higher value wins (default is 10). |
| Private Interface | Choose from the drop-down list your private/internal-facing interface. Cluster member interfaces must be on the same network. |
| NAT Assigned IP Address | Enter the IP address the device is being NAT'ed to. If you are not using a NAT on your network, leave this field blank. |
| Send FQDN to Client Instead of an IP Address When Redirecting | By default, the cluster master sends the IP address of a cluster member to a connecting user/client when redirecting. However, if using certificates, the master can be configured to send the FQDN after performing a reverse DNS lookup of the cluster member it is redirecting to. |

**Note:**  *These values must match on each cluster member before successful operation can commence.

## Load Balancing Using an External Load Balancer

A similar behavior to that of VPN load balancing available on the ASA can be achieved with the implementation of an external load balancer (for example, an ACE 4710 appliance or module in a 6500/7600 switch/router). This design would typically be implemented, illustrated in Figure 8-21, when ASA devices are running different hardware or software. In addition, the active/standby failover features of the ASA would be unavailable.

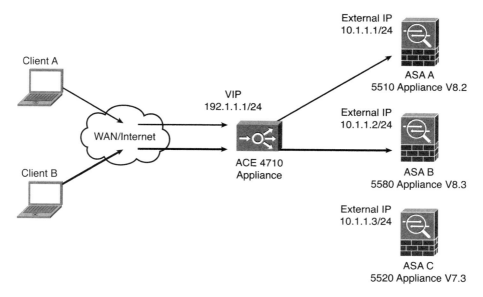

**Figure 8-21**   *AnyConnect Client Load Balancing Using an External Load Balancer*

In this configuration, the ACE appliance will have a VIP configured, which will usually be a publicly available IP address that your AnyConnect users will connect to.

Several ASAs can be configured as real servers on the internal network of the ACE appliance. Upon receiving a request for the VIP address, the ACE forwards it to one of the configured real servers (ASAs). Which ASA receives the request depends on the type of load-balancing algorithm configured on the ACE. By default, the behavior is round-robin, meaning if there are three ASAs connected to the ACE and three AnyConnect clients, each sends a request to the ACE VIP address, the ACE sends client request one to ASA-A, client request two to ASA-B, and client request three to ASA-C.

Because there is no session awareness (Stateless mode) between the ASA devices in this scenario, the ACE appliance would typically be configured to forward any future or ongoing requests to the same ASA device it had already connected to. This is known as sticky behavior because the client session "sticks" to the same ASA device instead of being distributed to the other available devices.

# Exam Preparation Tasks

As mentioned in the section "How to Use This Book" in the Introduction, you have a couple of choices for exam preparation: the memory tables in Appendix C, Chapter 23, "Final Exam Preparation," and the exam simulation questions on the CD-ROM.

## Review All Key Topics

Review the most important topics in the chapter, noted with the Key Topic icon in the outer margin of the page. Table 8-4 lists a reference of these key topics and the page numbers on which each is found.

**Table 8-4**  *Key Topics*

| Key Topic Element | Description | Page |
|---|---|---|
| Table | Advantages and limitations of available HA methods | 254 |
| Topic | Deploying DTLS | 255 |
| Subtopic | DPD operation and configuration | 265 |
| Subtopic | Configuring VMACs for hardware failover operation | 270 |
| Subtopic | VPN load balancing/clustering | 272 |

## Complete Tables and Lists from Memory

Print a copy of Appendix C, "Memory Tables" (found on the CD), or at least the section for this chapter, and complete the tables and lists from memory. Appendix D, "Memory Tables Answer Key," also on the CD, includes completed tables and lists to check your work.

## Define Key Terms

Define the following key terms from this chapter, and check your answers in the glossary:

clustering, DPD (dead peer detection), DTLS (Datagram Transport Layer Security), LLQ (low-latency queuing), VMAC

This chapter covers the following subjects:

- **Clientless SSL VPN Overview:** This section introduces you to the clientless SSL VPN available on all Cisco ASA devices. We discuss scenarios that may lead to the implementation and use of a clientless SSL VPN and the common building blocks used to create one.

- **Deployment Procedures and Strategies:** This section briefly discusses the design recommendations that can be followed and steps to help you prepare for an SSL VPN deployment.

- **Deploying Your First Clientless SSL VPN Solution:** This section presents a configuration example of a basic clientless SSL VPN solution that allows users to log in using accounts created for them in the local user database.

- **Basic Access Control:** This section discusses the use of basic access control to allow user access to resources such as URLs, bookmarks, and file shares within the clientless SSL VPN portal. This section also briefly examines group policies that you can use to achieve a greater level of granularity when controlling user access to resources.

- **Content Transformation:** This section discusses the ASA's role during content rewriting and how to include or exempt specific resources from being rewritten. The section also covers the use of Java applet signing and the Application Helper feature.

- **Troubleshooting a Basic Clientless SSL VPN:** This section explains how to troubleshoot a clientless SSL VPN.

## CHAPTER 9

# Deploying a Clientless SSL VPN Solution

When you take the CCNP Security VPN exam, you are expected to be able to configure and verify a clientless Secure Sockets Layer virtual private network (SSL VPN) while meeting the security policy requirements that are given to you at the time. By reviewing and understanding the information within this chapter and those that follow, you should be well equipped with the knowledge required for such a task.

This chapter starts by building on your existing understanding of the technology behind an SSL VPN and the building blocks associated with creating one. Armed with this information, we then explore the steps required to create a basic clientless SSL VPN and test your ability to log in using local user accounts configured on the ASA.

After being able to log in and view the portal page, you also need to make sure that remote users have access only to the resources they should have and cannot browse to anything you have not defined for them. As one way to achieve this, we review the group policy configuration tasks using the Adaptive Security Device Manager (ASDM). And finally, we take a look at a few of the added extras you can configure for users of your SSL VPN, such as content rewriting and Java signing, and the important steps you need for troubleshooting common failures you may encounter.

## "Do I Know This Already?" Quiz

The "Do I Know This Already?" quiz helps you determine your level of knowledge on this chapter's topics before you begin. Table 9-1 details the major topics discussed in this chapter and their corresponding quiz sections.

**Table 9-1** *"Do I Know This Already?" Section-to-Question Mapping*

| Foundation Topics Section | Questions |
| --- | --- |
| Deploying Your First Clientless SSL VPN Solution | 1, 3, 4, 6–10 |
| Troubleshooting a Basic Clientless SSL VPN Solution | 5 |
| Content Transformation | 2 |

**1.** Which two of the following are required when creating a CSR for an identity certificate?

    **a.** DNS

    **b.** Hostname

    **c.** NTP server

    **d.** Domain name

**2.** What file is required for the operation of the ASA Application Helper?

    **a.** XML

    **b.** HTML

    **c.** APCF

    **d.** OCSP

**3.** Which ASDM location is used to import an identity certificate?

    **a.** Configure > Remote Access VPN > Clientless SSL VPN Access > Portal

    **b.** Monitoring > Interfaces

    **c.** Home > Certificates

    **d.** Configuration > Device Management > Certificates > CA Certificates

    **e.** Configuration > Device Management > Certificates > Identity Certificates

**4.** When creating a new DNS group, what is the maximum number of DNS servers that you can add?

    **a.** 2

    **b.** 3

    **c.** 4

    **d.** 6

    **e.** 100

**5.** When troubleshooting an SSL tunnel establishment attempt, which two ASDM locations can you use to view syslog debugging information?

    **a.** Home

    **b.** Monitoring > Interfaces > ARP Table

    **c.** Monitoring > Logging >Real-Time Log Viewer

    **d.** Monitoring > VPN > Sessions

    **e.** Show Logging

**6.** Which configuration command is used in the CLI to create a new RSA key pair?

    **a.** crypto ca trustpoint TrustPoint0

    **b.** crypto key zeroize rsa noconfirm

    **c.** do show run

    **d.** crypto key generate rsa modulus 2048

    **e.** crypto key generate rsa modulus 4096

**7.** When configuring RSA key pairs, which modulus values are available on the ASA device? (Choose all that apply.)

   **a.** 1024

   **b.** 16384

   **c.** 768

   **d.** 512

   **e.** 2048

**8.** Which is the default authentication scheme used by the DefaultWEBVPNGroup connection profile?

   **a.** AAA(RADIUS)

   **b.** AAA(TACACS+)

   **c.** AAA(LOCAL)

   **d.** AAA(LDAP)

   **e.** None

**9.** When configuring the CA CRL revocation-retrieval policy, which methods are available? (Choose all that apply.)

   **a.** FTP

   **b.** HTTPS

   **c.** HTTP

   **d.** TFTP

   **e.** LDAP

   **f.** SCEP

**10.** A user is complaining of being unable to open external or internal URLs directly or from the bookmark list. What could be the problem?

   **a.** The user is not really connected to the SSL VPN.

   **b.** The user is connected to somebody else's SSL VPN.

   **c.** The user has not been given an IP address by the ASA.

   **d.** The administrator has not configured a DNS server group.

   **e.** The ASA device has experienced a blue screen error.

   **f.** The administrator has not configured a hostname.

## Foundation Topics

## Clientless SSL VPN Overview

Your manager is out of the office for the week attending a technical conference for the release of the latest and greatest gadget, so you are taking things easy this morning and sipping your coffee while clicking through your latest emails, although you are unaware that at this very moment he is trying to connect from his hotel room to your corporate headquarters to upload his notes from the previous day. After a few failed attempts to get the VPN client installed on his laptop to connect, he asks the hotel staff whether there are any restrictions on their wireless network. Your manager—now equipped with the information and frustration that everything out to the Internet is blocked except for HTTP and HTTPS—calls you, the company's resident security guru, to ask how he can continue to work.

Sound familiar? With the number of remote and home workers ever increasing, and the daily emergence of new security threats businesses face from the Internet, this scenario is becoming more common. The need for a new technology that would allow authorized users to quickly and easily connect to their workplace from anywhere using almost any device had arisen. The answer: the clientless SSL VPN.

One key element behind the popularity and growth of the SSL VPN is in the name *Secure Socket Layer*. SSL, or Hypertext Transfer Protocol Secure (HTTPS), as it is more commonly referred to, has been around since the early 1990s, and it is rare to see HTTP access allowed in an environment without its partner HTTPS. The initial support work involved with a new VPN client deployment has been substantially reduced, due to no longer needing additional ports or protocols to be enabled or allowed and new software having to be installed.

The SSL VPN has allowed companies large and small to deploy ubiquitous access to visitor and staff resources quickly and easily while maintaining their corporate security policies and effectively removing the support burden that once might have occurred with third-party VPN client software and incompatible operating systems or hardware.

SSL VPNs are often deployed to allow access to a company intranet, Microsoft Share-Point, or web mail. The SSL VPN enables users to connect from a handheld device (smartphone or PDA), a public Internet café, or a corporate laptop. Users within these environments usually are just opening a calendar, editing a document, or reading email within a web page. So, the need for an installed VPN client can almost be construed as overkill in this situation.

Consider, for example, the following situation: John, a salesman from your company, has collected his new laptop this morning on the way to a customer site but needs access to an important quotation saved on the corporate file server. After reassuring the customer with "Don't worry, we have a VPN," he inserts the CD the support desk gave him containing the VPN client software into his laptop and follows the prompts to install it. Installation complete, he now restarts his machine as instructed and checks with the customer's support team to make sure the necessary protocols and ports are allowed through their firewall. With the laptop now running, he opens the software, chooses to create a new connection, and diligently enters the group name, shared secret, and hostname from the piece of paper he pulls from his pocket. He clicks Connect, enters his username and password when prompted, and then double-clicks a familiar shared drive on his computer. Prompted again, he enters a username and password and searches for the file. Sounds like a lot of work, doesn't it?

If the company John works for had invested in the deployment of an SSL VPN solution, he could have easily accessed the portal URL using his default installed browser, because SSL and Transport Layer Security (TLS) are already enabled in all popular browser applications today. In that case, he would not have had to turn on anything or install anything new (with maybe the exception of having to click Allow on an installed pop-up blocker). He would be presented with an aesthetically pleasing customized portal, where he would enter his corporate username and password and click the Login button to gain access to the resources he needs, in the form of hyperlinks and menu bars listed neatly on the page.

Single Sign-On (SSO) is another feature of the SSL VPN that is explored in greater detail later. However, in reference to this example, it is worth a brief mention here. You might have noticed earlier that John was prompted twice for a username and password: once during the initial connection phase and again when opening the corporate shared drive. SSO can be implemented within a clientless SSL VPN to prevent users from being prompted for their credentials multiple times when trying to access certain resources. Adaptive Security Appliance (ASA) achieves this by caching the credentials or storing them within predefined variables during the initial user login and effectively becomes an authentication proxy between the user and resource. If configured, this could have removed another step from this scenario and made John's life even easier.

# SSL VPN Building Blocks

Key Topic

As discussed in the preceding section, the SSL protocol's existing widespread support and implementation is the main reason for the surge in popularity and deployment of SSL VPN solutions. This section provides a recap of the SSL/TLS tunnel-establishment phase, which leads to the subsequent transfer of data.

## SSL/TLS Recap

Originally developed by Netscape in 1994, the SSL protocol quickly became dominant for use in applications and servers when transferring secured data across the Internet. Back then, during the consumer infancy of the Internet, the World Wide Web Consortium decided that a secure way to transfer web traffic across the Internet was needed to encourage e-commerce providers onto the Internet. Initially, the consortium voted in favor of using S-HTTP (Secure Hypertext Transfer Protocol), a protocol that had also been developed for secure Internet communication during the mid-1990s. However, because Netscape was already using its own secure implementation (SSL) in their browser and Microsoft had adopted the use of the SSL protocol within its operating systems, the decision was made to use HTTPS, a combination of the SSL and HTTP protocols. The standard was later created for HTTPS and is defined in RFC 2818.

There are three versions of SSL, aptly named SSL 1.0, SSL 2.0, and SSL 3.0. Although SSL Version 1.0 was never released, the Internet community quickly adopted the use of SSL 2.0.

TLS is a standards-based implementation of SSL 3.0 (known as SSL 3.1). Because SSL is a proprietary protocol, the Internet Engineering Task Force (IETF) published the standard in 1999, details of which you can find in RFC 2246. (The most recent version of the standard is RFC 5246 TLS 1.2.) Although SSL and TLS are similar, significant differences exist so that the protocols do not interoperate.

SSL provides message authentication, confidentiality, and integrity through the combination of the underlying cryptographic protocols (reviewed later in this chapter). SSL sits between the application and transport layers of the Open Systems Interconnection (OSI) model, as shown in Figure 9-1, and includes no mechanism for reliable packet delivery. Therefore, the protocol relies on other higher-layer protocols within the OSI model and the VPN termination device for ordered and guaranteed delivery of packets. For these reasons, TCP is the transport layer of choice for this situation, with its sequencing, reordering, and reliable delivery functionality. (See Chapter 3, "Deploying an AnyConnect Remote Access VPN Solution," for further coverage of using User Datagram Protocol [UDP] and SSL with Datagram Transport Layer Security [DTLS].)

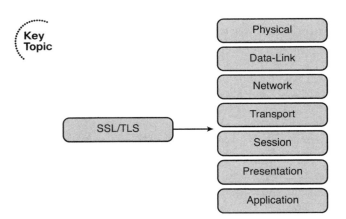

**Figure 9-1** *SSL's OSI Layer Position*

Within an SSL packet is the Record protocol responsible for packaging the lower-level messages to be transmitted. For example, the Record protocol fragments, assembles, applies, and removes MAC hashing and compression schemes and encrypts or decrypts the messages encapsulated within it. The overall hash, encryption algorithms, and compression schemes are negotiated by the lower-level protocols it encapsulates, as you will see in a moment.

Figure 9-2 shows the format of a Record protocol message.

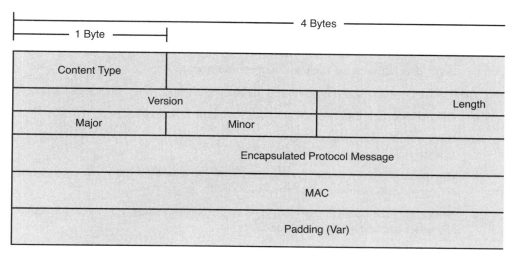

**Figure 9-2**  *SSL Record Protocol Format*

- **Content Type:** Indicates the message encapsulated in this record. The message could be one of four values:
  - **Handshake:** 22
  - **ChangeCipherSpec:** 20
  - **Application:** 23
  - **Alert:** 21

- **Version:** Indicates the version of the protocol. For example:
  - **SSL 2.0:** Major 2, Minor 0
  - **SSL 3.0:** Major 3, Minor 0
  - **TLS 1.0:** Major 3, Minor 1 (known as SSL 3.1)

- **Length:** The length of this record.

- **Encapsulated Protocol Message:** Carries the messages or application data sent between client and server during a conversation. After the authentication, encryption, and hash parameters have been negotiated, this field may be encrypted.

- **MAC:** The MAC calculated for the application data held in the encapsulated protocol message. The protocol used for the MAC is negotiated between client and server using the ClientHello and ServerHello messages.

- **Padding:** Used alongside MAC protocols that operate as block ciphers to pad the message length to an even block size. This field is not required with stream ciphers.

## SSL Tunnel Negotiation

SSL establishes a connection between both the client (typically the user's web browser) and server by sending a number of messages encapsulated within the Record protocol described in the preceding section. This section walks you through the SSL tunnel negotiation process, the messages involved, and their parameters and use, which all occur during a phase called the handshake. The handshake is one of two phases involved in the building blocks of an SSL tunnel, the second being the application phase, during which the transmission of data between the client and server takes place.

The following messages are sent between the client and server within the handshake phase:

- **ClientHello:** Sent from the client to the server, the first message to be sent

- **ServerHello:** Sent from the server to the client as the server's response to the ClientHello

- **Certificate:** Sent from the server to the client, and used by the client to authenticate the server and obtain a copy of the server's public key

- **ServerHelloDone:** Sent from the server to the client to indicate that all information the server has or expects to send has been

- **ClientKeyExchange:** Sent from the client to the server containing information used to create a master key

- **ChangeCipherSpec:** Sent by the client after successful negotiation of all parameters have completed to indicate all messages from this point onward will be encrypted

- **Finish:** Sent by the client to indicate the completion of its part in the tunnel-establishment phase

- **ChangeCipherSpec:** Sent by the server after successful negotiation of all parameters have completed to indicate all messages from this point onward will be encrypted

- **Finish:** Sent by the server to indicate the completion of its part in the tunnel-establishment phase

## Handshake

During the handshake stage, various parameters are negotiated between the client and server. The client starts the conversation by sending a ClientHello packet to the server, which takes the form shown in Figure 9-3.

The following list describes the data included within the Handshake Message Data field of the ClientHello packet:

- **The cipher suite** lists the available protocols for encryption and their key lengths. Protocols used for message hashing and integrity checks (for example, an available cipher) are listed in the form of TLS_RSA_WITH_DES_CBC_SHA.

- **A random number** is used to construct the master key. The random number is a 4-byte field created with a combination of the client's configured date and time and a 28-byte pseudorandom number.

- **The protocol version:** The higher value is preferred. For example, if TLS is available, it is the preferred protocol, then SSL 3.0, then SSL 2.0. (A few vendors have already removed SSL 2.0 support from their browsers.) Common version numbers include the following:

  - **3.1:** TLS
  - **3:** SSL 3.0
  - **2:** SSL 2.0

- **Any compression schemes** supported by the client are included.

- **A session ID:** If this is a new conversation, the session ID is null. If the client is trying to reconnect to an existing session, the ID is placed into the session ID during this stage.

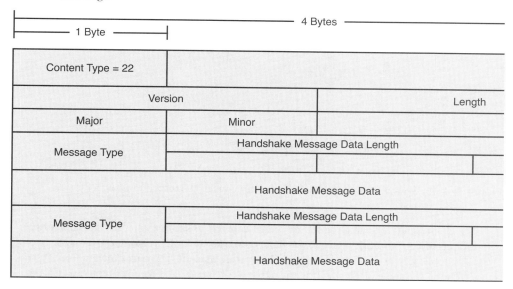

**Figure 9-3**    *SSL/TLS ClientHello/ServerHello Packet Format*

After the server has received the ClientHello message, it responds with its own Server-Hello message. This packet is similar in construction to the original ClientHello message. However, the server generates and includes its own random number for creation of the master key and chooses a compression scheme from the list of supported schemes it receives from the client.

Instead of the server sending the client a list of the cipher suites it supports, the server chooses from the highest supported version of protocols it has, based on the list it received from the client. For example, if the client had sent a cipher suite including Advanced Encryption Standard 256 (AES-256) and Secure Hash 1 (SHA-1), and the server could not find an entry for any protocol version higher (more secure) but had these protocols installed, it would choose to use these and send the name of the cipher back to the client to confirm its choice. As mentioned earlier, the client also sends the server a session ID in its ClientHello message. If the session ID is null, the server generates a new session ID and includes this in its ServerHello to the client. If the session ID received from the client is not null and that of an existing session, however, the server restarts the existing session where possible.

At this stage, after the ClientHello and ServerHello messages have been sent and received, and the protocol, encryption, hash, and authentication algorithms have been negotiated, the server sends its certificate to the client, which contains a copy of the server's public key, as shown in Figure 9-4.

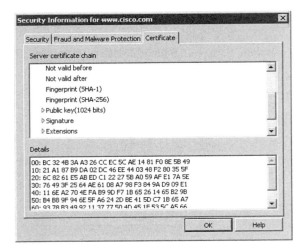

**Figure 9-4**   *A Server Certificate Displaying the Server's Attached Public Key*

The client, upon receiving the server's certificate, checks to see whether the name of the root certificate authority (CA) exists in its own trusted root CA store, retrieves the root CA's public key, and validates the digital signature using it. The client then moves on to validating the server by inspecting the name of the server it is connecting to against the name held in the certificate file, the current date and time against the certificates valid from-to values, and the certificate revocation list (CRL).

At this point in the tunnel negotiation, the server sends the client the ServerHelloDone message, indicating to the client that the server has finished sending the information it has.

The client now sends a ClientKeyExchange message to the server, which includes the protocol version number originally sent in the ClientHello message and a pre_master secret used by both the server and client, to generate the master secret for encryption. Depending on the cipher suite negotiated in earlier messages, the pre_master secret can vary in length and the information carried within it. The pre_master secret is typically composed of the client's SSL/TLS version number and a string of random bytes, and before being transmitted it is encrypted using the server's public key. The client sends the protocol version again to prevent a rollback attack (attacks that attempt to fool the server and client into using a lower version of the protocol).

The server then decrypts the pre_master secret using its private key matching the public key from its certificate. Both client and server now use the pre_master secret along with both random numbers to generate the master key, which is then used to create the symmetric keys used for message encryption, key seed identification and integrity-checking purposes.

The client now sends a ChangeCipherSpec (CCS) message to the server as a sign that everything sent from now on will be encrypted using the keys and protocols as established in the earlier messages, followed by a Finish message. The server also sends the client a CCS message to indicate the same state, followed by a Finish message. The diagram in Figure 9-5 illustrates the packet format of the CCS message. The CCS protocol type is currently set to 1 because it is the only available protocol type in a CCS message.

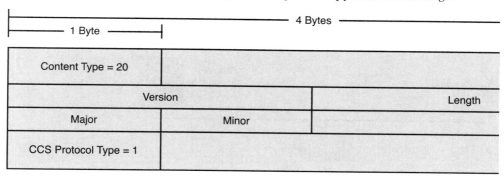

**Figure 9-5**  *ChangeCipherSpec Packet Format*

# Deployment Procedures and Strategies

Now that you have a good understanding of the overall SSL/TLS negotiation and the accompanying protocols that work behind the scenes to provide for secure and authenticated access, we can move on to a discussion of the items and tasks that are generally considered when designing an SSL VPN deployment.

## Physical Topology

Three common design methodologies are recommended and used when implementing an SSL VPN device into your existing network:

- In parallel with your firewall device, as shown in Figure 9-6.

- Inline with your firewall device, as shown in Figure 9-7.

- Placed inside a demilitarized zone (DMZ) for greater segregation from your network, as shown in Figure 9-8.

The most popular design is placing the SSL VPN appliance into its own DMZ, allowing for greater scale and ease of management. Unlike the parallel design, this removes the threat of attackers from the Internet being able to have direct public access to your device without first having to pass through a firewall. It also removes the possibility of inbound traffic being checked by the firewall twice, which can happen when using the inline design.

It is also important to remember that ASA 5500 devices are also firewall devices. If you are designing the topology for a small to medium business (SMB) network, you also have the possibility of "collapsing" the two roles (SSL VPN termination and firewall) into the same physical device to minimize the overall cost of deployment.

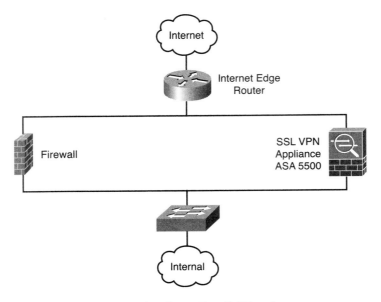

**Figure 9-6**   *SSL VPN Appliance Parallel Topology*

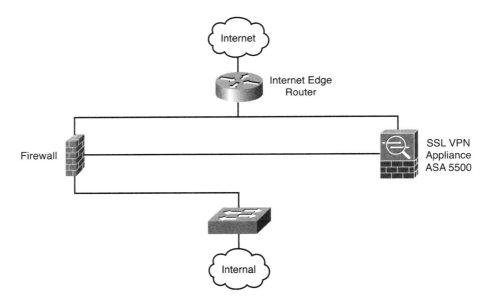

**Figure 9-7**   *SSL VPN Appliance Inline Topology*

The relevant traffic needs to be allowed through your existing security infrastructure (firewall) to your appliance for successful VPN deployment. However, this is just a case of allowing HTTPS to the address of your VPN appliance. (You might also choose to allow through the necessary ports/protocols for IPsec VPNs, depending on your individual deployment.)

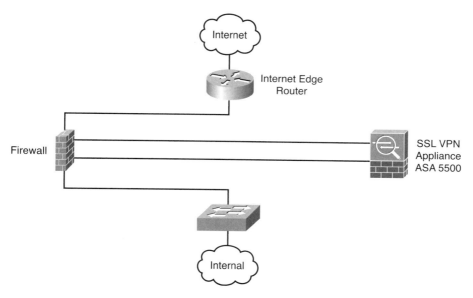

**Figure 9-8**  *SSL VPN Appliance DMZ Topology*

An important consideration when designing your SSL VPN is the resource access required by your users and the type of SSL VPN deployment you require. What sets an SSL VPN apart from an IPsec VPN is being able to offer users a completely different experience based on their location, connection method, or access privileges.

You can configure five options to provide that experience:

- **Reverse proxy:** Also known as the clientless SSL VPN, the reverse-proxy method of connection provides the benefits of ubiquitous connectivity (anywhere, anytime, from anything connectivity—within reason, of course). This particular connection method is commonly deployed for user access to internal web-enabled resources (Microsoft SharePoint or web mail, for example). This method of connectivity allows for a greater level of granularity when configuring user access to resources. However, resource access is typically limited to only those who are "web enabled."

- **Port forwarding:** This connection method does not require the use of a full-featured software client for applications' access to the internal network, but instead allows users to use familiar installed applications by the use of port forwarding using a downloadable Java applet. Typically, the use of this connection method is for users accessing a Telnet application. The program's connection/server settings must be changed from the default server addresses to the local loopback address where port 23 is listening and forwarded to the VPN appliance.

Port forwarding has a few downsides from the user's point of view. Users require local administrator access for installation and changes to installed application settings, because the application used for port-forwarding purposes must be installed on the local PC. Only TCP applications using static port assignments can be used, and client certificates cannot be used because the Java Runtime Environment (JRE) cannot access the local certificate store. Because of these reasons and others, port forwarding is now considered a legacy application, and Cisco recommends the use of plug-ins or smart tunnels.

■ **Client/server plug-ins:** Plug-ins enable users to access their familiar applications from within the browser window. This feature continues the ubiquitous ideal of SSL VPNs, where unlike port forwarding, the client can connect to the VPN and use the application from a public computer without any need for the application to be locally installed. Available plug-ins include Remote Desktop (RDP), Ubuntu's remote desktop (VNC), Secure Shell (SSH), Telnet, and Citrix.

■ **Smart tunnels:** Smart tunnels enable users to access familiar applications from outside the browser window (email, SSH, Telnet, and RDP, for example). The smart tunnel client requires the exact executable name of the local PC's application process, including the extension (such as .exe), to be configured on the ASA, and it redirects any requests from the process to the ASA device through the SSL tunnel. Unlike with the plug-ins feature, the applications used by the client need to be installed locally on the PC in use. However, this feature can allow clients to use their existing application without the need to change any settings, and therefore the need for local administrator rights is removed as a requirement. Access using smart tunnels is usually granted for users accessing resources from a company-owned computer/laptop, due to the need for installed and configured applications.

■ **Full tunnel with AnyConnect:** Similar to the IPsec client implementation, this method of access enables users to tunnel into the internal network and access network resources from their machines without having to choose a URL or change their local application settings. The experience offered to users is similar to that of being at their desk in the office. For further information about the AnyConnect VPN, see Chapters 3 through 6.

As mentioned earlier, when using a clientless SSL VPN, resource access is presented to users in the form of URLs or hyperlinks listed within the portal that loads after a successful login attempt.

One of the most effective ways to control user access is through the use of login URLs. Each VPN connection profile (also known as a tunnel group) defined on the ASA can be configured to use a separate login page or choose from a list of defined groups at a central login page. This would, for example, allow a user from the Sales department to browse to https://your.device.com/sales and guests to browse to https://your.device.com/visitor. Each URL or login page has its own unique set of security policies and authentication parameters, allowing for greater flexibility when managing separate groups of users, login and connection type, and the resources users can access.

Depending on the attributes and parameters your security policies take into account when evaluating a user's access requirements, you can choose to allow or deny the user access to certain resources through the use of group policies and Dynamic Access Policies (DAP) and to check for attributes such as operating system, Windows group membership, RADIUS attributes, Registry keys, antivirus, and so on.

# Deploying Your First Clientless SSL VPN Solution

Now that you have a good understanding of the tunnel-negotiation process that occurs during the creation of an SSL/TLS connection and have reviewed the various options to keep in mind when deploying an SSL VPN, we are ready to move on and configure a basic clientless SSL VPN.

When preparing to deploy a basic clientless SSL VPN for the first time, a few key items must be completed before you can test access and move on to providing for advanced access and features, as follows (in order):

**Step 1.** **IP addressing:** It is important to know the IP addressing plan for the site on which you are installing the ASA because you need an IP address for the external interface (the one closest to VPN clients and terminating SSL VPN sessions).

**Step 2.** **Configure a hostname, domain name, and Domain Name System (DNS):** Before publishing the relevant SSL VPN URLs to users, you configure your ASA with a hostname and a domain name,. You also enter the addresses of any internal and external DNS servers to allow user access to any bookmarks or external URLs they browse to using your SSL VPN.

**Step 3.** **Enroll with a CA and become a member of a PKI:** Because users will be accessing the device externally over an SSL connection, a device certificate is required for successful authentication of the ASA. Another option is to use a locally generated self-signed certificate.

**Step 4.** **Enable the relevant interfaces for SSL VPN access:** Before SSL VPN access can occur, you need to specify which interface the service will be available on.

**Step 5.** **Create LOCAL user accounts:** Because this is a basic SSL VPN, you use LOCAL authentication for user access. Doing so requires that you to create the user accounts on the ASA device.

**Step 6.** **Create a Connection Profile (optional but recommended so that the DefaultWEBVPNGroup is not used):** In this step, create a new connection profile and map it to users through group policies or user attributes. A connection profile is used for prelogin settings such as authentication method, DNS servers and domain name, and portal customization.

## IP Addressing

Before you can allow users access to your SSL VPN, you need to make sure the ASA device can be contacted from external locations. This requires the configuration of an IP address on your external interface. In an installation, you usually already have this or have the necessary knowledge of your IP addressing plan to be able to allocate an address to the device.

## Hostname, Domain Name, and DNS

Before you generate a certificate request to send to a CA for creation of a digital certificate, you need to give the ASA device a hostname and configure your local domain name. It can also be of benefit while troubleshooting a networking environment for devices to have a meaningful hostname. (That is, some providers use a networkwide naming convention of roomnumber_racknumber_racklocation_device, whereas others might prefer a more Star Wars- or Muppets-centric theme.) In any case, you can enter this information within the Device Name/Password pane located at **Configuration > Device Setup > Device Name/Password.**

As mentioned earlier, if you want your users connecting to the SSL VPN to be able to browse to websites, servers, or bookmarks using the hostname or fully qualified domain name (FQDN), you must enter your internal and external DNS servers. If you do not carry out this step, when users enter a domain name (www.cisco.com, for example) into the URL field and click Browse, they will be presented with an error indicating that the domain Cisco.com could not be found. To enter the external or internal DNS servers, browse to **Configuration > Device Management > DNS > DNS Client**, where you can either choose to configure a global DNS server group that applies to all queries regardless of domain or choose to configure multiple DNS server groups with up to six DNS servers in each group, which will allow you to specify the timeout and retry values and the domain name per group.

## Become a Member of a Public Key Infrastructure

By default, the ASA device creates a self-signed certificate for SSL authentication. This is fine for a test or lab environment. However, when you come to allowing access to remote users outside of your organization, you will usually purchase a valid certificate from a recognized CA to instill trust into the hearts and minds of your remote users (and to prevent them from receiving any browser warnings about your certificate being invalid).

At the time of this writing, Cisco ASA customers can purchase a digital certificate at a discounted price from Entrust, or they can apply for a three-month trial certificate from them. You can access more information about this offer in the Adaptive Security Device Manager (ASDM) by navigating to **Configuration > Device Management > Certificate Management > Identity Certificates > Enroll with Entrust**. Alternatively, you can visit the page directly at http://www.entrust.net/cisco.

In the section that follows, we walk through the steps for generating a certificate request and installing the received certificate. These instructions can be followed for any CA and are not specific to Entrust.

## Adding a CA Root Certificate

The process of adding a CA root certificate is straightforward and easy enough. In its out-of-the-box state, the ASA has no default CA root certificates installed. So, before you add an identity certificate for the ASA, you first need to add the certificate of the issuing CA from which you purchased your certificate. When the CA issues an identity certificate, it usually sends the certificates of their root CA to add, as well. If you do not have a copy, however, these are normally easy to locate and download from the CA's website. A few locations to download common root CA certificates are listed here:

- https://www.entrust.net/downloads/root_index.cfm

- http://www.globalsign.com/support/intermediate-root-install.html

- http://www.verisign.com/support/roots.html

Otherwise, if you have an in-house deployed CA, specific URLs exist and are publicly available, depending on the operating system vendor this is hosted on.

Now that you have your CA's root certificate, in the ASDM, navigate to **Configuration > Device Management > Certificate Management > CA Certificates** and click the **Add** button on the right side. The Install Certificate window will open, as shown in Figure 9-9.

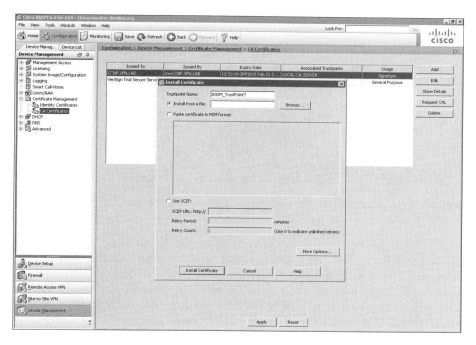

**Figure 9-9**   *Installing the CA Root Certificate*

Within the Install Certificate window, you have the option to enter a trustpoint name for the CA certificate you are importing. It is generally advisable to enter the name of the root CA, which will make life a bit easier for you when you come to install new certificates or troubleshoot existing ones. You have three options for how you want to install the certificate, depending on how you retrieved the root certificate (downloaded it from the CA's site in a zip file, copied a base64 output to your Clipboard, or used Simple Certificate Enrollment Protocol [SCEP] to retrieve the file). Your method dictates which option you choose. For this example, we copied the base64 output of the VeriSign root certificate from their website and chose the option to **Paste the Certificate in PEM Format** to add it.

### Certificate Revocation List

You now set the parameters your ASA will use to check and retrieve the CRL. To do so, click the **More Options** button. The Configuration Options for CA Certificate window will appear, as shown in Figure 9-10.

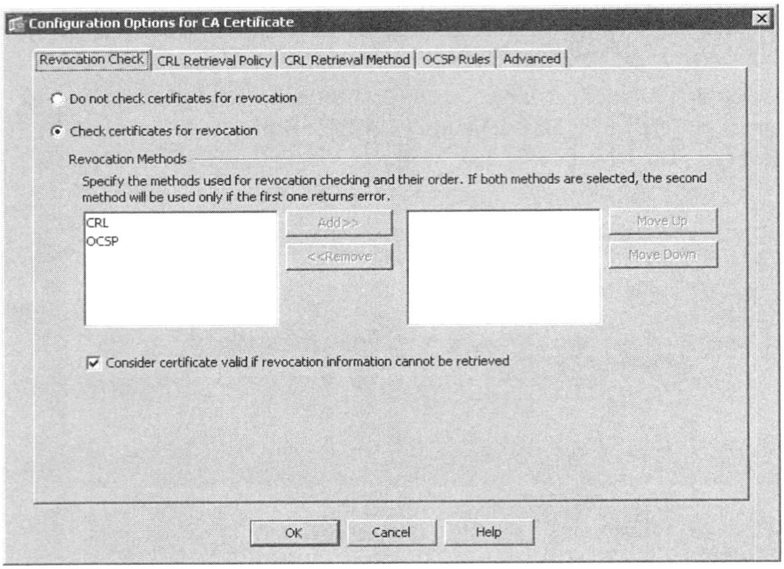

**Figure 9-10**   *CA Certificate CRL Options*

Within the Configuration Options for CA Certificate window, you can enter the method you use to check for the CRL, the protocol you use to retrieve the CRL, and the locations you retrieve it from. If you are using Online Certificate Status Protocol (OCSP), you can enter the certificate to rule mappings you want to use with this certificate. Finally, you can set advanced options, such as the type of VPN this certificate can be used for and the OCSP server URL. The Configuration Options for CA Certificate window, as shown in Figure 9-10, presents five tabs where you enter your settings:

- Revocation Check

- CRL Retrieval Policy

- CRL Retrieval Method

- OCSP Rules

- Advanced

### Revocation Check

On the Revocation Check tab, you have the option to turn off certificate revocation checking or leave it at the default of on. However, by default, no revocation-checking methods are chosen, and the check box to consider a certificate valid if the CRL cannot be retrieved is selected, meaning that all certificates, by default, are considered valid by the CA.

Depending on your own implementation, you choose CRL, OCSP, or both.

If you choose OCSP, you can optionally create OCSP rules that use preconfigured certificate mappings to control the OCSP actions applied to specific certificates on the OCSP

Rules tab, and on the Advanced tab, you can enter information such as the server URL and disabling the use of nonces. If you decide to choose both CRL and OCSP methods, note that the second option in the list is used only if the first returns an error. Therefore, if it is important to use OCSP as a primary means of checking the list and have CRL used only if there is an error with the OCSP server, make sure the OCSP method is at the top of the list. You can change the order of methods using the Move Up and Move Down buttons to the right of the window.

For this example, we chose to use CRL for our revocation check by choosing **CRL** from the available revocation methods and clicking **Add**. Then we unchecked the box to make sure the CRL is always checked. Therefore, if it is unavailable, the certificates will be marked as invalid.

### CRL Retrieval Policy

From here, you can choose whether you want to use the CRL location stored in the certificate or a specific URL to a known revocation list (this information may be published on your CA's website) or both. If you choose the option to enter the specific URLs, you are given the option of entering either an HTTP:// or LDAP:// URL, and the URLs you enter will be listed in an order of preference from top to bottom. After you have finished entering all the URLs, use the Move Up and Move Down buttons to the right of the window to set your order of preference.

### CRL Retrieval Method

Next, choose the retrieval methods that can be used to download the CRL: Lightweight Directory Access Protocol (LDAP), HTTP, SCEP, or all three. If you choose LDAP, you must enter a username and password and optionally specify the default server name or IP address. After you have entered the server name or IP, you have the option to change the LDAP port. However, if your CA has not listed a specific port, it is recommended to keep the default of 389.

Although by default all three options (LDAP, HTTP, and SCEP) are enabled, I have unchecked everything except for HTTP.

### OCSP Rules

On the OCSP Rules tab, you can allocate your predefined certificate mappings and rules to the certificates imported into your ASA. Although we had earlier selected only CRL as the revocation list method for this example (rather than OCSP), for the purposes of the exam, it is worth a mention here.

Certificate mappings can be used to map a certificate to a connection profile based on the criteria that was selected or configured explicitly in a certificate-matching rule. Certificate mappings and rules first need to be configured in **Configure > Remote Access VPN > Network (Client) Access > Advanced > IPsec > Certificate to Connection Profile Maps**. There are two sections to configure:

- Policy
- Rules

In the Policy window, you are presented with common criteria that can be selected to enable the certificate-to-connection profile mapping, based on a match. The ASA starts from the top of the list of options you select and works toward the bottom of the list until it finds a match (the top of the list having the higher priority).

Figure 9-11 shows the Policy window and the common criteria that you can choose. By default, all criteria are chosen, except for Use the Configured Rules to Match a Certificate to a Connection Profile.

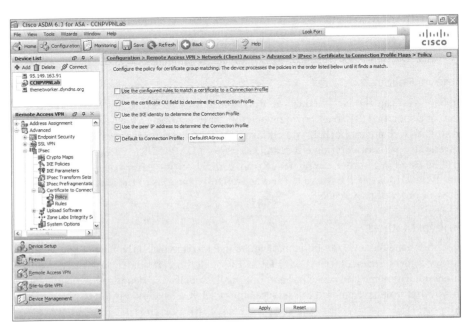

**Figure 9-11** *Certificate to Connection Profile Maps: Policy Configuration*

**Note:** If you do configure your own mapping rules within the Rules window, you need to check the Use Configured Rules to Match a Certificate box for your rules to be considered in the certificate-to-connection profile-mapping process.

Within the Rules window, you can take a more granular approach to certificate mapping, whereby you can select your own criteria or fields to match within the certificate. Start by configuring a certificate-to-connection profile map. You can either use an existing map or create a new one. Give your profile map a priority and associate it with a connection profile/tunnel group. The priority values must be between 1 and 65535, with the highest priority being the lowest value (that is, 1). By default, the DefaultCertificateMap is given a priority of 10. Although you cannot change the default priority, you can delete the map and re-create it or create your own custom default map and give it a priority value of 65535 so that it is always evaluated last. This is shown in Figure 9-12.

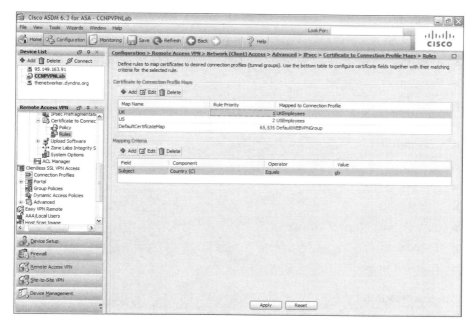

**Figure 9-12**  *Certificate to Connection Profile Maps: Rule Configuration*

For example, you may choose to present all U.S. employees a different certificate from that presented to U.K. employees who access your SSL VPN. As shown in Figure 9-12, we matched the country code GB in the certificate and mapped it to the UKEmployees connection profile.

Depending on the criteria you selected to match within the certificate, you can use one of the following operands per rule:

- Equals

- Contains

- Does Not Equal

- Does Not Contain

The criteria that can be matched against in a rule are as follows:

- **Subject**
    - Country (C)
    - Common Name (CN)
    - DN Qualifier (DNQ)
    - Email Address (EA)
    - Generational Qualifier (GENQ)
    - Given Name (GN)

- Initials (I)
- Locality (L)
- Name (N)
- Organization (O)
- Organization Unit (OU)
- Serial Number (SER)
- Surname (SN)
- State/Province (SP)
- Title (T)
- User ID (UID)
- Unstructured Name (UNAME)
- IP Address (IP)
- Domain Component (DC)

- **Alternative Subject**
- **Issuer**
  - Country (C)
  - Common Name (CN)
  - DN Qualifier (DNQ)
  - Email Address (EA)
  - Generational Qualifier (GENQ)
  - Given Name (GN)
  - Initials (I)
  - Locality (L)
  - Name (N)
  - Organization (O)
  - Organization Unit (OU)
  - Serial Number (SER)
  - Surname (SN)
  - State/Province (SP)
  - Title (T)
  - User ID (UID)
  - Unstructured Name (UNAME)
  - IP Address (IP)
  - Domain Component (DC)

- **Extended Key Usage**

Now back to the original configuration of the CA certificate. We have covered the OCSP Rules tab. The last tab available in the Edit Options for CA Certificate window is the Advanced tab.

### Advanced

On this tab, you can configure the CRL cache refresh time, which is set to a default of 60 minutes. You also can enter the OCSP server URL, choose to accept the certificates issued by the CA (or subordinate CA of the CA you are importing the certificate from), and more important, control whether this certificate will be used for SSL, IPsec, or both types of client connections. Unless you have chosen to use certificate-based authentication with both your IPsec and SSL connections and are using a separate CA certificate for each connection type, you can choose to leave this at the default value of SSL and IPsec.

As shown in Figure 9-13, after entering the information and clicking **OK**, the import operation was successful, and the CA is now listed in the window along with its certificate expiry date, issued by, issued to and usage values, and the trustpoint name entered.

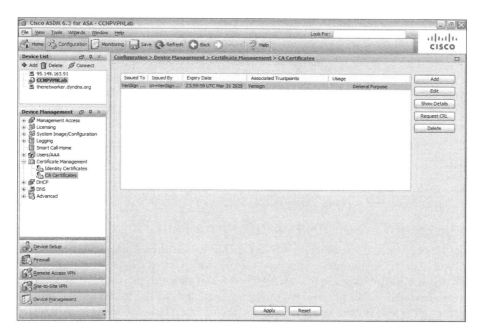

**Figure 9-13**   *CA Certificate Import Complete*

The majority of tasks you can carry out using the ASDM can also be performed via the command-line interface (CLI). The commands to configure the same trustpoint, CRL revocation, and retrieval methods are shown here. In the following section we take a look at the CLI process to manually import a CA certificate.

To create a trustpoint and configure it for manual enrollment, enter the following:

```
ciscoasa(config)# crypto ca trustpoint TrustPoint0
ciscoasa(config-ca-trustpoint)# enrollment terminal
```

Table 9-2 lists the commands available for the **enrollment** keyword.

**Table 9-2** *Certificate Enrollment/Import Type*

| Command | Command Options/Explanation |
|---|---|
| **Retry** (count \| period) | Command used to configure the number of times (count) 0–100 (0 = un-limited) and frequency (period) in minutes between those attempts (1–60). Used with SCEP retrieval. |
| **Self** | Generate a self-signed certificate. |
| **Terminal** | Use this command when cutting and pasting a certificate file into the configuration. |
| **Url** | Use this command to enter the server and full path to the file when using SCEP. |

After creating a trustpoint and setting the certificate-retrieval method, you can continue to configure the revocation methods. Start by entering the **revocation-check** command, followed by the **crl** keyword, because for this example we have chosen to use CRL for therevocation method. As shown in the earlier example using the ASDM, you can also enter OCSP or choose None:

```
ciscoasa(config-ca-trustpoint)# revocation-check crl
```

To enter multiple check methods, enter them in the order you would like them to be used following the **revocation-check** command, as follows:

```
ciscoasa(config-ca-trustpoint)# revocation-check crl ocsp
```

A number of commands are available within the config-ca-trustpoint mode. Many of them allow you to enter the information required for automatic certificate enrollment using SCEP. Because we are using the manual method for this example, they are not required at this time; however, for the purposes of the exam, it will benefit you to review the commands and their use. For this example, we continue to enter the commands required for CRL revocation checks. Table 9-3 lists the rest of the available commands.

Now we enter CRL configuration mode to set the retrieval options. The change of mode can be noted by the new prompt that appears after the command, as shown in line 2 of the following output. We then proceed to configure the cache timeout to 1440 minutes (remember, the default of 60 minutes) and tell the ASA to also consider the NextUpdate field in the received CRL from the CA with the use of the **enforcenextupdate** command.

The NextUpdate is sometimes added to the CRL and can be used by clients to dynamically set their cache timeouts. The existence of the NextUpdate field depends on the CA, because it is an optional field. However, if the ASA receives this field from the CA and also has a cache timeout set locally, it uses the lower of the two. For example, if the ASA had a default cache timeout of 60 minutes and the NextUpdate field in the received CRL has been set to 30 minutes, the received value of 30 is chosen as the timeout, and all entries within the CRL file for this certificate are then aged out after this time.

We then use the **protocol http** command to configure the protocol used for CRL retrieval as HTTP. This is similar to the ASDM configuration, and we are also presented with the option of using HTTP, LDAP, SCEP, or a combination of all three. Also similar to the ASDM configuration, we have the option of entering a URL for the CRL location using the **url** command, and we can enter up to five URLs, each with a separate priority of 1 to 5, where they will be tried in order of priority (highest to lowest, with 1 being the highest priority):

```
ciscoasa(config-ca-trustpoint)# crl configure
ciscoasa(config-ca-crl)# cache-time 1440
ciscoasa(config-ca-crl)# enforcenextupdate
ciscoasa(config-ca-crl)# protocol http
ciscoasa(config-ca-crl)# url 1 http://5.5.5.5/CertEnroll/CA.crl
```

We can now go back to the original trustpoint configuration mode by entering the **exit** command to take us out of the CRL configuration mode. From here, we specify the key pair name, whose public key will be used and signed by the CA, resulting in the identity certificate of the ASA. If RSA key pair is generated but not named/labeled, its default name is Default-RSA-Key and is used in the certificate-request process if no key pair name is configured in trustpoint configuration mode.

```
ciscoasa(config-ca-crl)# exit
ciscoasa(config-ca-trustpoint)# keypair KeyPair1
```

Next, we can generate the key pair. The following command is used to generate a new key pair using the name KeyPair1 and modulus of 2048:

```
ciscoasa(config)# crypto key generate rsa label KeyPair1 modulus 2048
INFO: The name for the keys will be: KeyPair1
Keypair generation process begin. Please wait...
```

You can also add the optional command **noconfirm** to the end of this command to prevent the ASA from prompting you for further information throughout the process.

No messages alert us when the key generation has completed. The CLI prompt simply returns to a new line awaiting a command. However, you can confirm the existence of your newly created key pair with the **show crypto key mypubkey rsa** command, as shown in Example 9-1.

**Example 9-1**  *Installed Crypto RSA Keys View*

```
ciscoasa# show crypto key mypubkey rsa
Key pair was generated at: 15:22:51 UTC Nov 7 2010
Key name: <Default-RSA-Key>
 Usage: General Purpose Key
 Modulus Size (bits): 1024
 Key Data:
  30819f30 0d06092a 864886f7 0d010101 05000381 8d003081 89028181 00b3080b
  4acdb040 cf4b8b74 7e2e55c4 b4450f95 839a4734 5a9ec955 6bc501c8 1fb07864
  19ffc4e3 e51d0e72 b78f2cc8 2ab6f3f5 a1678cce 4794cdf5 cfab8528 80a40806
  d452c333 d566b269 7d882afc 2606b231 fcd4b839 c40774d2 c78726fe ad40fdca
  1e6ba506 d84f20bf 37bea62a b8caf760 c0fa646f 29942457 1f2df6f6 6f020301 0001
Key pair was generated at: 16:11:19 UTC Nov 7 2010
Key name: KeyPair1

 Usage: General Purpose Key
 Modulus Size (bits): 2048
 Key Data:
  30820122 300d0609 2a864886 f70d0101 01050003 82010f00 3082010a 02820101
  00d2615d baf0f5d0 eaff599e 685561aa 574a3468 5a923858 6cbf43b5 0cc1e705
  c8715429 baf46052 49805f6a b05eabf9 e9c5e09e 537fb233 751f3ae6 de238069
  4e7799da fa4cc112 fb596556 bd38168f 46b7b0ff 9fa6884a e3027889 afbba6f5
  f3e5ac6a fa1bad37 68c96ea9 1fec11e0 5512686e 19badd91 73b3a811 dbc4bfae
  75de4621 8f020d7f 8f42ce84 39597384 b5abec04 00f00a7b ede2211d 023dc1fb
  e4d51508 7589ebdb 86a0d1e0 45350384 9880fc67 e603f353 4ec9f0cc 4d0a0caa
  0d8657ba 434933bb 7768f567 8de878ac 1be848bc 29e205f6 e9dc719f 74c7e056
  4998fe1b 5d315576 3d4864af 9b89ff23 9181a6a8 a7e1157b 76555a3c d9fe7442
  59020301 0001
ciscoasa#
```

To manually enter the root CA certificate, enter the command **crypto ca authenticate TrustPoint0** (**TrustPoint0** should be replaced with the name of the trustpoint you've previously created) shown in Example 1-2, and we are given the option of entering the following subcommands with the **crypto ca authenticate** command:

- **FingerPrint:** We can enter an optional fingerprint (message digest 5 [MD5] signature) that may have been sent with the certificate file to authenticate the certificate contents, if the CA requires it.

- **Noninteractive:** This command is used only with the ASDM when entering a certificate using the manual method and should not be entered using the CLI.

After the command has been entered, we follow the prompt to paste the certificate output into the CLI and end with **quit** on a separate line. We are then asked to verify the fingerprint of the certificate against that sent to us by the CA. (You may or may not receive this depending on how you retrieved the original certificate.) Example 9-2 shows this output.

**Example 9-2**   *CA Certificate Import Process*

```
ciscoasa(config)# crypto ca authenticate TrustPoint0
Enter the base 64 encoded CA certificate.
End with the word "quit" on a line by itself
-----BEGIN CERTIFICATE-----
MIIEVzCCAz+gAwIBAgIQFoFkpCjKEt+rEvGfsbk1VDANBgkqhkiG9w0BAQUFADCB
jDELMAkGA1UEBhMCVVMxFzAVBgNVBAoTDlZlcmlTaWduLCBJbmMuMTAwLgYDVQQL
EydGb3IgVGVzdCBQdXJwb3NlcyBPbmx5LiAgTm8gYXNzdXJhbmN1cy4xMjAwBgNV
BAMTKVZlcmlTaWduIFRyaWFsIFNlY3VyZSBTZXJ2ZXIgUm9vdCBDQSAtIEcyMB4X
DTA5MDQwMTAwMDAwMFoXDTI5MDMzMTIzNTk1OVowgYwxCzAJBgNVBAYTAlVTMRcw
FQYDVQQKEw5WZXJpU2lnbiwgSW5jLjEwMC4GA1UECxMnRm9yIFRlc3QgUHVycG9z
ZXMgT25seS4gIE5vIGFzc3VyYW5jZXMuMTIwMAYDVQQDEylWZXJpU2lnbiBUcmlh
bCBTZWN1cmUgU2VydmVyIFJvb3QgQ0EgLSBHMjCCASIwDQYJKoZIhvcNAQEBBQAD
ggEPADCCAQoCggEBAMCJggWnSVAcIomnvCFhXlCdgafCKCDxVSNQY2jhYGZXcZsq
ToJmDQ7b9JO39VCPnXELOENP2+4FNCUQnzarLfghsJ8kQ9pxjRTfcMp0bsH+Gk/1
qLDgvf9WuiBa5SM/jXNvroEQZwPuMZg4r2E2k0412VTq9ColODYNDZw3ziiYdSjV
fY3VfbsLSXJIh2jaJC5kVRsUsx72s4/wgGXbb+P/XKr15nMIB0yH9A5tiCCXQ5nO
EV7/ddZqmL3zdeAtyGmijOxjwiy+GS6xr7KACfbPEJYZYaS/P0wctIOyQy6CkNKL
o5vDDkOZks0zjf6RAzNXZndvsXEJpQe5WO1avm8CAwEAAaOBsjCBrzAPBgNVHRMB
Af8EBTADAQH/MA4GA1UdDwEB/wQEAwIBBjBtBggrBgEFBQcBDARhMF+hXaBbMFkw
VzBVFglpbWFnZS9naWYwITAfMAcGBSsOAwIaBBSP5dMahqyNjmvDz4Bq1EgYLHsZ
LjAlFiNodHRwOi8vbG9nby52ZXJpc2lnbi5jb20vdnNsb2dvLmdpZjAdBgNVHQ4E
FgQUSBnnkm+SnTRjmcDwmcjWpYYMf2UwDQYJKoZIhvcNAQEFBQADggEBADuswa8C
0hunHp17KJQ0WwNRQCp8f/u4L8Hz/TiGfybnaMXgn0sKI8Xe79iGE91M7vrzh0Gt
ap0GLShkiqHGsHkIxBcVMFbEQ1VS63XhTeg36cWQ1EjOHmu+8tQe0oZuwFsYYdfs
n4EZcpspiep9LFc/hu4FE8SsY6MiasHR2Ay97UsC9A3S7ZaoHfdwyhtcINXCu2lX
W0Gpi3vzWRvwqgua6dm2WVKJfvPfmS1mAP0YmTcIwjdiNXiU6sSsJEoNlTR9zCoo
4oKQ8wVoWZpbuPZb5geszhS7YsABUPIAAfF1YQCiMULtpa6HFzzm7sdf72N3HfwE
aQNg95KnKGrrDUI=
-----END CERTIFICATE-----
quit

INFO: Certificate has the following attributes:
Fingerprint:     e019f5fc c09a130e 38b7bf0d 0240d3c2
Do you accept this certificate? [yes/no]: yes

Trustpoint CA certificate accepted.

% Certificate successfully imported
ciscoasa(config)#
```

Table 9-3 describes the automatic certificate enrollment commands. Note that this table also includes those commands not previously mentioned but available within the config-ca-trustpoint mode for automatic certificate enrollment or the creation of identity certificates.

**Table 9-3** *Automatic Certificate Enrollment Commands*

| Command | Command Options/Explanation |
|---------|------------------------------|
| email *<email address>* | Enter the email address of the technical/administrative contact for your organization. This included in the Subject Alternative Name field of the certificate. |
| fqdn *<cisco.com>* | Enter the fully qualified domain name to be used within the certificate. This will be sent to the CA and included in the Subject Alternative Name field. |
| ip-address *<ASA IP address>* | Use this command to tell the CA to include the IP address of the ASA within the certificate. |
| ocsp url *<url>* | Used to tell the ASA to check all certificates with the server entered instead of that found within the AIA extension of the certificate. |
| ocsp disable-nonce | Disables nonce extensions that are used to avoid replay attacks by cryptographically binding requests with responses. |
| password *<password>* | Enter a password for revocation requests to be authenticated by the server with. |
| subject-name *<name>* | Enter the name you want entered into the certificate DN field in X.509 format. To prevent errors within the command, enclose your name within quotes (that is, "**ciscocomcert**"). |
| serial-number | Tells the issuing CA to include this ASA's serial number in the certificate. |

After successfully importing a root certificate, it is time to generate a CSR (certificate request) for the ASA identity certificate. Within the ASDM, navigate to **Configuration > Device Management > Certificate Management > Identity Certificates** and click the **Add** button. The Add Identity Certificate window will open, as shown in Figure 9-14.

**Figure 9-14** *Add Identity Certificate: Generate CSR*

Within this window, you must enter a name for the trustpoint and can choose the default action of importing an existing certificate from a file, add a new identity certificate, or generate a self-signed certificate. The name of the trustpoint needs to be the same as the previously imported CA certificate, because you cannot enroll or request a certificate from a CA unless you have authenticated to it. To begin the process of creating a new CSR, start by clicking the **Add a New Identity Certificate** radio button, and then click the now-available **New** button to create a new key pair.

In the Add Key Pair window that opens, you are asked to enter a name for the key pair. Choose one that you can use to easily distinguish it from others that you may create later or have already created. Select the key modulus size (either 1024 or 2048) and the usage. The vast majority of CAs still accept a key size of 1024.

After clicking **Generate Now** and waiting a short time while the key pair is created, you are returned to the Add Identity Certificate window. From the drop-down list, choose the key pair you just created, and then click the **Select** button to the right of the Certificate Subject DN box.

As shown in Figure 9-15, the Certificate Subject DN will now open, and you use this window to enter Distinguished Name (DN) identity certificate attributes, such as Common Name (CN), Department (OU), and so on. At least one attribute needs to be configured for successful enrollment in most cases.

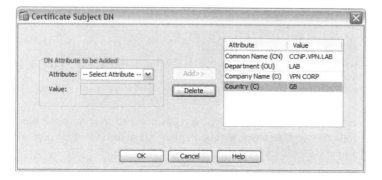

**Figure 9-15**   *Add Identity Certificate: Enter CSR Details*

As you can see in this figure, the values for CN, OU, O, and C have been entered by choosing them from the list of available attributes in the Attributes drop-down menu, entering the necessary information into the Value field, and clicking **Add**. Because for this example we are generating a CSR for a lab environment, we are okay with the details shown. However, when generating a CSR for a valid public certificate, the CA would require you to enter the information from all the attributes available in the drop-down menu for them to be able to check your authenticity. The attributes available are as follows:

■   Common Name (CN)

■   Department (OU) (also known as organization unit, hence the OU)

- Company Name (CN)

- Country (C)

- State (ST)

- Location (L)

- Email Address (EA)

When you have finished entering all the information required, click **OK**, and you are once again returned to the previous Add Identity Certificate window. You are now able to see that the details previously entered have been formatted as Attribute=Value in a continuous string ready to be processed in the CSR generation.

Next, click the **Add Certificate** button, and after the familiar "loading" window has flashed up and closed, you are presented with a new window asking you to enter a location for the CSR to be saved locally on your PC. As you can see in Figure 9-16, we entered the location C:\asa-csr.txt. Then, shortly after clicking the **OK** button, we received a message indicating that the file had been saved successfully.

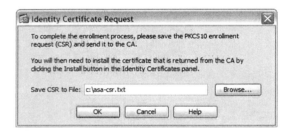

**Figure 9-16** *Add Identity Certificate: Save the CSR Locally to Your PC*

After generating a CSR and saving a copy on your PC, you can proceed to submit the file containing your CSR to your chosen CA, along with any other information they require in the way of personal or company identification (and, of course, their fee).

Depending on how fast your individual CA's turnaround time is, you might be sent your certificate within a matter of hour or days, or they may contact you if they require further information about your request. When you do receive the certificate, all that is left to do is finish the request process and import it into your ASA's configuration.

You can finish the import process by choosing **Install** from the right side of the Identity Certificates window. At this stage, the Install Identity Certificate window opens, and you will have the option to import the certificate from a file or to copy and paste the base64-encoded certificate into the window (see Figure 9-17). Depending on how your certificate was sent to you by the issuing CA, the certificate contents can be in a zip or text file attachment or included in the body of an email. Choose the appropriate option for your certificate installment and click **Install Certificate**.

After a few moments, you should receive a pop-up alerting you that the certificate has installed successfully. If you receive an error instead, especially if you are copying and pasting the certificate contents, make sure you have not added any unnecessary spaces or text to the encoding. The file or contents of the message may have also been corrupted due to spam or antivirus settings within your email. In this situation, your CA will have normally included a link in the email for you to be able to download the certificate instead. Once you have downloaded/retrieved the certificate from your CA, simply repeat the process to install your certificate.

**Figure 9-17**   *Installing an Identity Certificate*

When the install process completes, you are returned to the Identity Certificates window, and your new certificate should now be listed, displaying the issued to, issued by, validity date, the trustpoint name you entered earlier, and the certificate usage.

The process used to generate an identity certificate from the CLI is similar to that shown earlier and in Table 9-2.

In this next example, we have already created the trustpoint CLI-New and entered our email address, FQDN, password, and entered the **enrollment terminal** command to let the ASA know we be manually cutting and pasting our certificate into the CLI after receiving it from our issuing CA.

To complete the process, issue the **crypto ca enroll** *<trustpoint>* command to create and generate our CSR, as shown in Example 9-3.

**Note:**   It is not shown in Example 9-3, but as discussed earlier about these configuration steps, we entered the domain name and hostname of our ASA using the commands **domain-name** *<fqdn>* and **hostname** *<hostname>*. Without these commands, the ASA uses the default hostname and domain name to set the DN within your certificate request.

**Example 9-3**   *Generate Identity Certificate CSR*

```
CCNP(config)# crypto ca trustpoint CLI-New
CCNP(config-ca-trustpoint)# enrollment terminal
CCNP(config-ca-trustpoint)# crypto ca enroll CLI-New
% Start certificate enrollment ..

% The fully-qualified domain name in the certificate will be: CCNP.LAB.COM
```

```
% Include the device serial number in the subject name? [yes/no]: no

Display Certificate Request to terminal? [yes/no]: yes
Certificate Request follows:
-----BEGIN CERTIFICATE REQUEST-----
MIIBlzCCAQACAQAwHTEbMBkGCSqGSIb3DQEJAhYMQ0NOUC5MQUIuQ09NMIGfMA0G
CSqGSIb3DQEBAQUAA4GNADCBiQKBgQCzCAtKzbBAz0uLdH4uVcS0RQ+Vg5pHNFqe
yVVrxQHIH7B4ZBn/xOPlHQ5yt48syCq28/WhZ4zOR5TN9c+rhSiApAgG1FLDM9Vm
sml9iCr8JgayMfzUuDnEB3TSx4cm/q1A/coea6UG2E8gvze+piq4yvdgwPpkbymU
JFcfLfb2bwIDAQABoDow0AYJKoZIhvcNAQkOMSswKTAOBgNVHQ8BAf8EBAMCBaAw
FwYDVR0RBBAwDoIMQ0NOUC5MQUIuQ09NMA0GCSqGSIb3DQEBBQUAA4GADz2Q6A0
+PcIzbcWtyiHB0RwYd6l7Gq2OTVg3B5wuYEg5Raqer1H8BUZ1n6GSxjmOYafQgvZ
JdkD9YvInOB5zh3fBzPNxp3ldPhkDYCo+QVLvp8aI3nw7KJEICh526RnGy+VWvS9
328kC3QxK04NHuNg3J0W24fKrDKyhAeAPYrR
-----END CERTIFICATE REQUEST-----

Redisplay enrollment request? [yes/no]: no
CCNP(config)#
```

As shown in Example 9-3, the CSR is generated with the domain name and hostname combination of CCNP.LAB.COM and displayed to the terminal. You can now copy and paste this into a form or email it to a CA for certificate generation.

When you receive the certificate back from the issuing CA, you can use the command **crypto ca import CRL-New** <pkcs12|*certificate*> <*passphrase*> to complete the import process and paste the received certificate file into the terminal, as shown in Example 9-4.

**Example 9-4** *Import Identity Certificate*

```
CCNP(config)# crypto ca import CRL-New pkcs12 passphrase

Enter the base 64 encoded pkcs12.
End with the word "quit" on a line by itself:
-----BEGIN CERTIFICATE-----
MIIFvDCCBKSgAwIBAgIQPw6Lnube3lvIG0upxkE1oTANBgkqhkiG9w0BAQUFADCB
yzELMAkGA1UEBhMCVVMxFzAVBgNVBAoTD1Z1cm1TaWduLCBJbmMuMTAwLgYDVQQL
EydGb3IgVGVzdCBQdXJwb3NlcyBPbmx5LiAgTm8gYXNzdXJhbmNlcy4xQjBABgNV
BAsTOVRlcm1zIG9mIHVzZSBhdCBodHRwczovL3d3dy52ZXJpc2lnbi5jb20vY3Bz
L3Rlc3RjYSAoYykwOTEtMCsGA1UEAxMkVmVyaVNpZ24gVHJpYWwgU2VjdXJlIFNl
cnZlciBDQSAtIEcyMB4XDTEwMTEwNDAwMDAwMFoXDTEwMTExODIzNTk1OVowgZAx
```

```
CzAJBgNVBAYTAkdCMRIwEAYDVQQIEwlCRVJLU0hJUkUxDDAKBgNVBAoUA0xBQjjEM
MAoGA1UECxQDTEFCMTowOAYDVQQLFDFUZXJtcyBvZiB1c2UgYXQgd3d3LnZlcmlz
27ucHyy4Mds/helgCHeWKLQOQCQYgoiNzB41S0NwPw2s+K/oMsobVYJSBfOtzMti
cT/IGBWEECtVguh34q1hUQCmItEqtCneX+zoemmg/pM=
-----END CERTIFICATE-----
quit
INFO: Certificate successfully imported
CCNP(config)#
```

### Enable the Relevant Interfaces for SSL

After generating and importing the certificates, you can enable SSL VPN on the outside interface of your ASA. By default, none of the interfaces on the ASA are set up to allow for SSL VPN access, so you need to configure access on the interface from which users will be accessing the SSL VPN. In the majority of customer deployments, the outside interface is used for access. However, this might differ depending on the specific details of the implementation. For the purposes of this example and the exam, SSL access is configured on the external outside interface in the location **Configuration > Remote Access VPN > Clientless SSL VPN Access > Connection Profiles**, as shown in Figure 9-18.

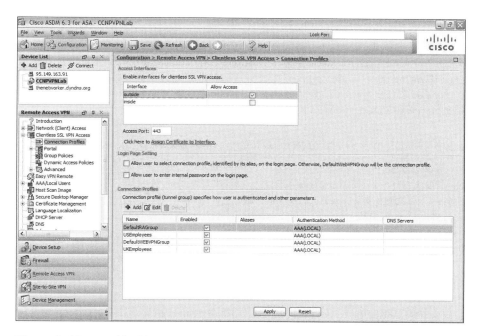

**Figure 9-18** *Enable SSL VPN Access on the External Interface*

Note that this enables both TLS and DTLS, although for clientless SSL VPN sessions, DTLS is not applicable. To enable only SSL/TLS tunneling from the CLI, enable it using command **enable outside tls-only** under WebVPN configuration mode.

You also need to assign the identity certificate imported earlier to the outside interface so that remote users will be presented with it. To assign the identify certificate, either click the **Assign Certificate to Interface** link or navigate to **Configuration > Remote Access VPN > Advanced > SSL Settings** to open the relevant pane.

By default, no certificates are assigned to the interfaces of the ASA, and it presents the user with a fallback or self-generated certificate during an SSL certificate establishment. However, because you might have paid for a certificate and imported it into the ASA configuration, you might as well use it. It is also poor practice to present a user with a self-generated certificate; doing so will cause the user's browsers to display a number of error messages warning them about an invalid certificate. As network engineers, we have a responsibility not only to provide as safe an environment for our users as possible but to also provide them with the reassurance that everything they are doing within their working environment is protected.

Figure 9-19 shows the SSL Settings window, where you can assign your identity certificate to the outside interface. Carry out this action by choosing the interface from the list shown within the Certificates window and clicking **Edit**, as shown in Figure 9-19. Within the new window, Select SSL Certificate, choose the installed identity certificate from the drop-down menu next to Primary Enrolled Certificate and click **OK** to complete the operation.

From the CLI, this is a relatively simple process, as demonstrated in Example 9-5. First, enter the command **webvpn** to enter into the SSL VPN mode, and then specify the interfaces on which you want to enable the service, using the command **enable** *<outside | inside>*. After configuring the outside interface for SSL VPN termination, you then map the trustpoint (defined earlier in the chapter) to the outside interface, which automatically maps the identity certificate associated with the trustpoint to the interface outside.

**Example 9-5**    *Enable WebVPN and Map the Identity Certificate to the Outside Interface*

```
CCNP(config)# webvpn
CCNP(config-webvpn)# enable outside
INFO: WebVPN and DTLS are enabled on 'outside'.
CCNP(config-webvpn)# exit
CCNP(config)# ssl trust-point CLI-New outside
CCNP(config)#
```

## Create Local User Accounts for Authentication

You are now in a position to create a couple of user accounts to test access to your basic SSL VPN.

By default, the DefaultWEBVPNGroup connection profile is configured to use LOCAL authentication, so there is no need to make any changes to this just yet. You are only aiming for your users to be able to log in to the VPN and view the portal page at this point.

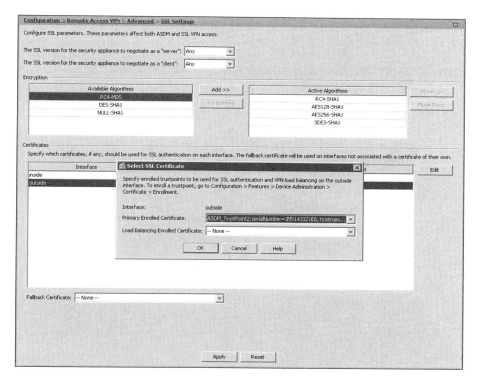

**Figure 9-19**    *Map Identity Certificate to Outside Interface*

Remember that any newly created connection profile will inherit its WebVPN settings from the DefaultWEBVPNGroup connection profile, which exists by default on the ASA.

For this example, we create two users, employee1 and contractor1, that will be used for our test. In the ASDM, navigate to **Configure > Remote Access VPN > AAA/Local Users > Local Users** and click **Add**. The **Add User Account** window will appear. We enter the name of our user, **employee1**, and enter and confirm the password **thisismypassword** for this account, as shown in Figure 9-20. We then repeat the procedure to create the contractor1 user.

Because the employee1 and contractor1 user accounts will be used only to test access to the SSL VPN for now, we also chose the option under Access Restriction for the account to have no ASDM, SSH, Telnet, or Console access. This effectively makes the user accounts VPN-only accounts. You may create a user account that will require access to the ASDM or CLI for troubleshooting purposes. This might be required, for example, for a member of the support team when working remotely, and there are two remaining options, as shown in Figure 9-20, from which you can choose.

The first is Full Access, which will allow the user access to the ASDM and CLI through the use of SSH, Telnet, and Console (where available) while keeping the VPN access functionality. If you are using authentication, authorization, and accounting (AAA) for command authorization purposes, you also have the option to set the user's privilege level, with 1 being the lowest and 15 the highest. This is explored later in Chapter 12, "Advanced Authorization Using Dynamic Access Policies."

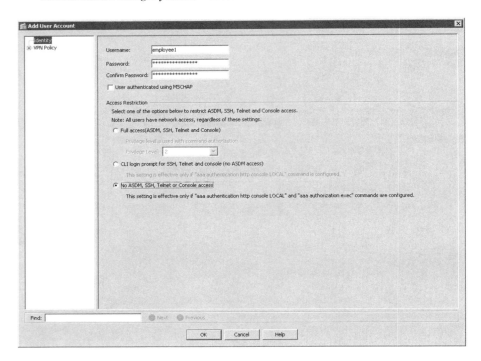

**Figure 9-20**   *ASDM: Add Local User Account*

The second option allows you to grant a user access to the CLI through either SSH, Telnet, or Console access (where available) but not the ASDM. You can also restrict VPN access.

**Note:**   It is important to note that when restricting user access rights to the ASDM, SSH, Telnet, and Console, this does not stop the user's ability to log in to the portal and gain network access. We cover user access with group policies, web ACLs, and DAP later in the chapter.

When you have finished entering the username and password and configuring access restrictions, click **OK** to complete the user account creation. Now repeat the steps previously outlined to create any remaining user accounts you require. Remember that the users are assigned to the DefaultWebVPNGroup, so there is no need at this time to configure user-specific attributes for these test accounts. Example 9-6 shows the command lines for creating the two local user accounts for this example configuration.

**Example 9-6**   *Create Local User Accounts*

```
CCNP(config)# username employee1 password thisismypassword encrypted
CCNP(config)# username contractor1 password thisismypassword encrypted
```

## Create a Connection Profile (Optional)

Creating a new connection profile is as an optional step. At this stage, you have configured enough information to allow a remote user to log in using the default connection profile (DefaultWEBVPNGroup). For the exam, however, it is important to know how to create a basic connection profile. All other necessary prelogin parameters have been configured, so this is the right stage to create a basic connection profile. We discuss advanced connection profile options and configurations in later chapters, as we progress further into customization.

To create a new connection profile, begin by navigating to **Configuration > Remote Access VPN > Clientless SSL VPN Access > Connection Profiles** within the ASDM. You should notice immediately at the bottom of the Connection Profiles window that two profiles have been created by default: the DefaultRAGroup and the DefaultWEBVPNGroup. Both of these connection profiles are configured to allow clientless SSL VPN access. However, in a moment, you will see how this can be restricted to deny clientless SSL VPN access through the connection profile options.

You encountered the Connection Profiles window earlier when you originally enabled the outside interface for clientless SSL VPN access, so this option should already be checked, and the access port should be set to 443. Figure 9-18 shows the window.

Beneath the Interfaces section, in the Login Page section, you can choose the option of allowing users to select their connection profile when at the login page for the SSL VPN. This is a typical choice if you have many departments or differing groups of users connecting to the same VPN appliance. In this case, the administrator (you) can configure a connection profile per user group with the profile alias set to the group name. (For example, the connection profile alias engineering would be configured for the user group engineering.) Remote users can then be given the option of choosing from a drop-down list the group they are a member of and logging in and are presented with the appropriate bookmarks, applications, and so on. The option to allow users to enter their internal password is discussed in greater detail later. However, this is typically used in an environment where the ASA and internal network have different authentication policies set up between them, and the user might use a different password to log in to the SSL VPN than the password used to access internal resources.

**Key Topic**

To create your new connection profile, click **Add** from the bottom of the window under the Connection Profiles heading. The Add Clientless SSL VPN Connection Profile window appears, and you are presented with two options on the left of the window:

- Basic
- Advanced

We start by first examining the Basic option area of the window because this is the main area where you enter the information when creating a new profile. In the fields described in Table 9-4, you can enter the basic information required to get your users connected.

**Table 9-4**  *Connection Profile Creation, Basic Settings*

| Field | Description |
|---|---|
| Name | Enter a unique name for the connection profile used internally on the ASA. |
| Aliases | Enter a name for this connection profile to be accessed by a remote user through the direct URL entry (for example, www.myasa.com/alias-name) or selection from a drop-down box. This field is typically the user's department or group name. |
| Method | Choose **AAA**, **Certificate**, or **Both** as authentication schemes. |
| AAA Server Group | Choose from a list of defined server groups or create a new one. The default group is set to **LOCAL**. We leave this as default for our profile. |
| DNS Server Group | Select from a predefined DNS server group or create a new one (as discussed earlier). |
| Servers | Upon selecting a server group, this field is prepopulated with the servers included in the group. Otherwise, you can enter specific DNS servers here. |
| Domain Name | Upon selecting a server group, this field is prepopulated with the domain name included in the group. Otherwise, you can enter a specific domain name here. |
| Group Policy | Select from a list of predefined group policy objects or create a new one. For this example of a basic SSL VPN, we use the default value of **DfltGrpPolicy**. |
| Enable Clientless SSL VPN protocol | By default, this option box is checked to enable all connection profiles for clientless SSL VPN. However, if you are creating an AnyConnect- or IPsec-only connection profile, uncheck this box. |

From this table, you can see you have the basic information required for your users to log in. At a bare minimum, the SSL VPN connection will require only these fields to be populated. You can then take a more granular approach and enter specific authentication, accounting, NetBIOS, and other settings. As we move on through the chapters of this book discussing advanced application access, portal customization, and AAA, we explore the advanced settings that are required for each topic and how you can use the connection profile to match your profiles/customizations.

The Advanced option from the menu on the left lists multiple configurable subsections, as follows:

■   General

■   Authentication

■   Secondary Authentication

- Authorization

- Accounting

- NetBIOS Servers

- Clientless SSL VPN

You have now completed enough of the information required for you to be able to log in and see your VPN portal for the first time.

Open a web browser, type in the full hostname of your ASA device (or the IP address if the FQDN is not DNS resolvable, but bear in mind you might receive a certificate error), and click **Go.**

If everything so far has gone to plan, you should be presented with a login page similar to that shown in Figure 9-21.

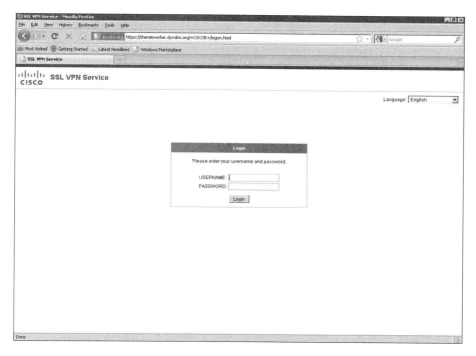

**Figure 9-21**    *Basic SSL VPN Login Page*

Enter the username and password for a user created in the earlier step, and click **Login** to be taken through to the default portal page shown in Figure 9-22.

Success! You can log in and access the portal. Although there is not a lot you can do from here because you do not have any bookmarks to click or network resources to access, you can, however, test the SSL rewrite function by entering an address in the address bar toward the top of the home page and clicking **Browse.** For example, I chose to browse to http://www.cisco.com. My request was sent to the ASA through the established SSL tunnel and proxied by the ASA device. Upon receiving the reply from server with the index page for Cisco.com, the ASA's rewrite function rewrote any links embedded within the page and delivered them back to my browser, as shown in Figure 9-23. If I were to click one of the links shown on the page in the figure, the request from my browser would be sent directly to the ASA (SSL server), and the ASA would forward the request details to Cisco.com on my behalf, forcing the traffic sent between me and the ASA through the encrypted SSL tunnel.

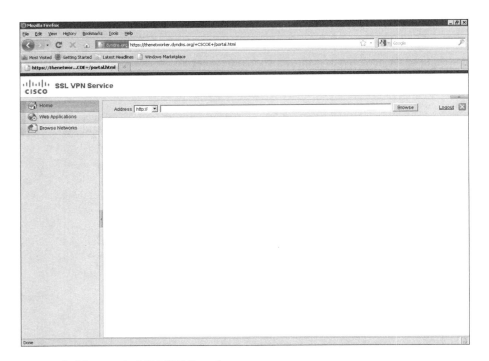

**Figure 9-22**  *Basic SSL VPN Portal*

Note that for traffic to come in and go out on the same interface, **same-security-traffic permit intra-interface** does not need to be enabled. This is required only for traffic where both source and destination are identifiable by IP addresses, as is the case for IPsec VPN or AnyConnect SSL VPN. For clientless SSL VPN, the ASA acts like a proxy and the rule does not apply.

Also notice that in the upper-right corner of the web page, the floating toolbar has appeared, which loaded after my request for the web page. Depending on your browser and version, this might open as a pop-up in a separate window. The toolbar allows me to enter a new URL to navigate through the SSL VPN, return to the portal home page, or log out from the clientless SSL VPN session.

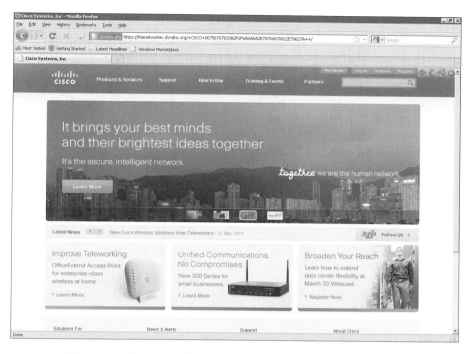

**Figure 9-23**  *Basic SSL Portal URL Request*

## Basic Access Control

As discussed in the previous section, the tasks to allow a user access to a basic SSL VPN portal are straightforward enough to be completed in a few easy steps. However, the example we have worked through is only a basic SSL VPN. As a result, all users are limited to what they can achieve when logged in.

Cisco provides many tools that enable you to customize, design, secure, and deploy various sections of our clientless SSL VPN, from access control through the use of separate login pages, bookmark assignment based on the users' windows Active Directory (AD) group membership, home folder and drive mapping with the use of session cookies, and resource and tunnel assignment based on LDAP or RADIUS attributes using DAP. The list, although not endless, at first glance can appear to be.

In later sections, we discuss providing your configured user with a separate URL for login purposes, which links us nicely to the first of many discussions we have that cover group policies on the ASA. During this discussion, we cover the use of group policies to publish or revoke bookmark, URL entry, and file access, depending on the logged-in user's group membership.

## Bookmarks

The resources you make available to a user are listed in the form of Bookmarks/Links on the page within the Portal area. Depending on the overall user access level being configured, four types of bookmarks can be created:

- HTTP

- HTTPS

- CIFS (Common Internet File System)

- FTP

## HTTP and HTTPS

HTTP or HTTPS bookmarks are generally used to grant a user access to an internal intranet portal (for example, SharePoint or web mail access) to a front-end exchange server. These bookmarks are entered in the same format as a URL you enter directly into your browser (for example, http://www.cisco.com), and the ASA then rewrites or mangles the individual bookmarks and sends them to the client browser. As a result of the rewrite, any requests for the bookmark travel to the ASA. For example, we create a new bookmark, Cisco, with the destination URL of http://www.cisco.com. Upon entering the URL, the ASA runs it through the internal rewrite engine, and the URL is presented to the client as the following JavaScript link:

```
parent.doURL('756767633A2F2F6A6A6A2E70766670622E70627A',null,'get',false,'no',
  false)
```

This might look like a bunch of gibberish because of the rewriting. However, when we click the Cisco bookmark, the request is interpreted by the client browser's JavaScript engine and passed back to the ASA. The ASA then rewrites the outgoing URL as http://www.cisco.com. The rewrite operation can also be carried out by the client using the browser's JavaScript engine and is the default behavior for user-entered URLs from the portal or a Java applet downloaded by the client. The main purpose of offloading the rewrite to the client is to help maximize the available resources of the ASA for other functions that might need to be completed, or for dynamic web content that might not be easily rewritten.

Whenever a user clicks an HTTPS bookmark, the ASA establishes a direct SSL session between itself and the web or mail server being accessed, and it performs the process of certificate validation on behalf of the client. The client never directly receives a copy of the server's certificate, and therefore the client cannot carry out its own verification/authentication of the server. Note, however, that the current implementation of SSL VPN on the ASA does not permit any communication with sites that present an invalid or expired certificate. It will also not carry out any CA certificate validation for SSL-enabled sites being accessed through the SSL VPN. It is up to you to decide whether to give users access to any web-enabled internal resources using SSL, or if there is no benefit to providing SSL VPN users with links to internal SSL resources and you will provide them with an HTTP link to the resource instead.

## CIFS

Common Internet File System bookmarks enable users to access common internal file shares. When clicking a CIFS link, the user may or may not be asked to log in (based on the permissions assigned to the file share and whether SSO has been implemented for the tunnel group), and then files and folders are presented to the user in the familiar Explorer format within the portal page. Because of the URL rewrite, users can access them by choosing the requested file or folder within the window. CIFS URLs are entered in the same format as that for HTTP, HTTPS, and FTP: cifs://file-server-name/share-name.

## FTP

When users access an FTP site through the portal, files and folders are displayed in the familiar Explorer format. An organization might choose to grant a user access to an FTP resource if, for example, they do not use any Windows file shares internally, or if the user is a contractor who needs access to a company web server.

Figure 9-24 shows the Add Bookmark List window that appears when you navigate to **Configuration > Remote Access VPN > Clientless SSL VPN Access > Portal > Bookmarks**, and click **Add**.

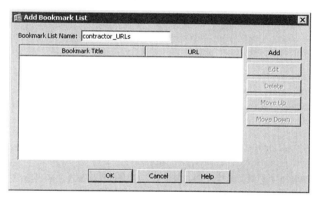

**Figure 9-24**  *Create Bookmark List*

As shown in Figure 9-24, you are asked to enter a name for the bookmark list. This name is used internally when you come to add/map the list to a group policy or later in a DAP, so it is normally best practice to enter a meaningful name (for example, Contractor_URLs).

After you have entered the URLs you are granting access to, the buttons Edit, Delete, Move Up, and Move Down become available. These buttons allow you to change settings for the selected bookmark, remove it, or move it to the desired location in the list. The order of the bookmarks in this window is the order in which they are presented to the user in the portal page.

**Note:**   After you have entered the name for your bookmark list and saved it, you are then unable to change the name. Any future name changes require the deletion and re-creation of the list. It is important to keep in mind now any naming convention you want to use to present resources to your users. You might kick yourself later if you have to re-create a list containing more than 50 bookmarks.

To add URLs to your bookmark list, click **Add** on the right of the window. The Add Bookmark window will open, with a number of fields into which you can enter the information required by your users. The only two required fields for creation of the bookmark are the bookmark title (the name presented to the user) and the URL, for which you will choose the type (HTTP, HTTPS, CIFS, or FTP) from the drop-down list.

Table 9-5 describes the other fields in the Add Bookmark window.

**Table 9-5**  *Add Bookmark Optional and Advanced Fields*

| Field | Description |
|---|---|
| Subtitle (Optional) | Enter a subtitle or informative description for this bookmark to present users with when viewing the bookmark list. |
| Thumbnail (Optional) | Enter a thumbnail image for the bookmark for users to easily distinguish with a visual aid and text. |
| Enable Smart Tunnel (Optional) | Enable the bookmark access over a smart tunnel. The use of smart tunnels is discussed later in this book. Enabling Smart Tunnel for URL may result in all browser traffic be tunneled through the SSL tunnel. |
| Allow the Users to Bookmark the Link (Optional) | By default, this option is selected to allow users to save a bookmark of the page offline. Exercise caution, however, when assigning this permission to users. If you can, try to allow only client-based users to carry out this action, because potential security threats exist if a user creates a bookmark on a public machine. |
| URL Method (Advanced) Get \| Post | By default, this option is set to GET, because we are not sending any information to the web server either through forms or session macros. We discuss the GET and POST options later in this book. |
| Post Parameters (Advanced) | This option is used only when the URL method has been changed to POST from the default of GET. We discuss the use of forms and macros in later chapters. |

When you finish entering all the information your users may require, you can repeat the process for each bookmark you want to publish.

When the bookmark list is complete, apply and save your changes to flash. Your bookmark list will then display within the Bookmarks pane using the name you assigned to it earlier. To assign your bookmark list to a user or group, choose it within User Attributes or a group policy object. However, because you have no defined group policy objects yet and by default the DefaultGrpPolicy does not contain any bookmark lists, you need to assign a list.

Editing the default group policies is generally frowned upon because these are mainly used as a catchall policy for global settings. Under typical circumstances, you aim to restrict access to as much of your internal information as possible and only grant a user limited access. The next section explains how to create a group policy to which you can apply a bookmark list.

## Group Policies

Group policies are used as a post-login access policy object to restrict user and connection profile access to only the resources you want them to be able to access. Group policies act as a container for other objects that can be defined and applied to a user or connection profile for a granular and scalable extension of your existing security policy (for example, bookmark lists or web ACLs).

It is within group policies that you can also define the portal customization available for the particular user or connection group and control file access, port forwarding, and smart tunnel behavior, login timeout settings, and SSO.

At this point, we do not cover every option available when configuring a group policy object, because this chapter serves as just an introduction to the SSL VPN and basic clientless SSL VPN configuration. We start by creating a new group policy object, which we apply to a user account created using the earlier steps. We then review the assignment of a bookmark list and explain the removal of the URL entry field from the portal to prevent users from accessing anything other than your defined bookmarks.

To begin the creation of a group policy object, navigate within the ASDM to **Configuration > Remote Access VPN > Clientless SSL VPN Access > Group Policies**. At the moment, note that only the one default group policy for DfltGrpPolicy exists (depending on your ASA's configuration, I am assuming a device from Factory Reset State in these examples). Because you are creating a new group policy, click **Add** at the top of the pane. You are immediately presented with the Add Internal Group Policy window.

The Add Internal Group Policy window contains the following links to enter further configuration information on the left side:

- General
- Portal
- More Options

Because we are aiming to keep things simple at this time, we stick to the General and Portal panes for entering configuration information and explore the More Options area in later chapters, when we configure advanced settings.

Table 9-6 describes the fields in the General pane.

**Table 9-6**   *Group Policy General Configuration*

| Field | Description |
|---|---|
| Name | Enter a name for this group policy object to be used later when assigning it to a user or connection profile. |
| Banner | Enter a welcome banner that users first see when logging in to the SSL VPN. If the Inherit option is checked, this policy inherits this option from the default group policy. |
| Tunneling Protocols | Choose the protocols this group policy will apply to (for example, clientless SSL VPN, IPsec). By default, this option inherits from the default policy. |
| Web ACL | Assign a web ACL to the group policy for purposes of preventing access to certain URLs or TCP services. Only one web ACL can be applied per group policy. (Web ACLs are discussed in greater detail in chapters that follow.) By default, this option inherits from the default policy. |
| Access Hours | Assign the time profile for this group policy (for example, if you want the VPN to be available only during office hours). By default, this option inherits from the default policy. |
| Simultaneous Logins | Enter the number of simultaneous user logins allowed per user (default 3). By default, this option inherits from the default policy. |
| Restrict Access to VLAN | Restrict user access over this SSL VPN to the following VLAN (affects only tunnel or client VPNs). By default, this option inherits from the default policy. |
| Connection Profile (Tunnel Group) Lock | Assign the users within this group policy to the following connection profile. This disallows the connection profile to change based on user location, attributes, and so on. By default, this option inherits from the default policy and is disabled. |
| Maximum Connect Time | Enter the maximum connection timeout per SSL VPN session for this group policy (default Unlimited). By default, this option inherits from the default policy. |
| Idle Timeout | Enter the idle timeout per SSL VPN session for this group policy (default 30 minutes). By default, this option inherits from the default policy. |

Begin by entering the group policy name, choose clientless SSL VPN, and leave all other protocols unchecked for the tunnel protocols using this VPN. All other options should be left at their default of Inherit, which will serve the purpose for this test.

Now you can move on to the Portal pane, where you can assign a bookmark list to this policy. You can also remove the users' ability to browse directly using the URL Entry field, which will restrict users' navigation to only your bookmark list, as you will see in a moment.

As with the General pane, the Portal pane contains additional options that are not required for this particular example. However, these configuration options are important to know because they provide granularity you may require for controlling user access within the SSL VPN portal. Table 9-7 describes these options.

**Table 9-7**   *Policy Configuration for Group Policies*

| Field | Description |
|---|---|
| Bookmark List | Use this field to select a predefined bookmark list. By default, this option inherits from the default policy. |
| URL Entry | The options available are Enable and Disable. When this option is disabled, users cannot enter direct HTTP or HTTPS URLs within the SSL portal. The opposite occurs when we choose Enable (default is Enable). By default, this option inherits from the default policy. |
| File Server Entry | The options available are Enable and Disable. When this option is disabled, users cannot enter direct CIFS URLS within the SSL portal. The opposite occurs when we choose Enable (default is Enable). By default, this option inherits from the default policy. |
| File Server Browsing | When enabled, this setting allows users to browse for available file servers on the network. By default, this option inherits from the default policy. |
| Hidden Share Access | Enables/disables access to hidden shares for CIFS files, which are identified by the dollar sign ($) at the end of the share name. |
| Port Forwarding List | Assign a defined port-forwarding list (or create a new list) to allow users access to TCP-based applications through the use of a Java applet. By default, this option inherits from the default policy. However, no default port-forwarding lists are defined. |
| Auto Applet Download | Enable/disable automatic download of the Java applet for port forwarding when a user logs in. By default, this option is unselected. |
| Applet Name | Enter a custom title you want to add to the Java applet. By default, this is set to Application Access. |
| Smart Tunnel Application | Choose from a list of predefined Winsock applications installed on the client for TCP application access (or create a new one). Check the **Auto Start** box to start smart tunnel access after the client has logged in. |

**Table 9-7**  *Policy Configuration for Group Policies*

| Field | Description |
|---|---|
| Auto Sign-On Server* | Choose from a predefined list of servers (or enter a new one) for SSO purposes when using smart tunnel connectivity. Optionally, enter the Windows domain name to pass with the user credentials to the server. |
| ActiveX Relay | Allow users to take advantage of the Microsoft Office ability to launch in a browser using an ActiveX object. Documents are uploaded and downloaded across the SSL tunnel. |
| HTTP Proxy | We are given three options with this field: Enabled, Disabled (default), and Auto-Start. When enabled, the ASA forwards a Java applet to the client for rewrite/proxy purposes. When Auto-Start is checked, the actions described are available from user login. |
| HTTP Compression | Enables HTTP compression over the SSL tunnel between client and server. Choose to either enable or disable this option. |

To apply a bookmark, URL or File Server list, uncheck the **Inherit** box for the Bookmark List, URL Entry, and File Server Entry fields, respectively, and select your list depending on the type of list you have created. You can also select the option to disable URL entry and file server entry. For example, if you have disabled only the URL entry, remote users would still be able to enter addresses into the field. However, they would have been able to select only the CIFS:// or FTP:// prefix for their URL. Depending on your own preferences, you might want to remove the field entirely from the page. To accomplish this, make sure to follow the example and disable the **URL Entry** and **File Server Entry** options.

Now that you have created a group policy object and entered the security parameters and bookmark list, you need to assign the policy to a user.

There are two ways to map a policy to a user account: through the use of a connection profile, or within the user account settings directly. Because you are only aiming to test user access and view a bookmark list at this time, you can assign the policy directly to a user account. (We discuss the creation of connection profiles in greater depth in later chapters.)

To assign the policy, navigate to **Configuration > Remote Access VPN > AAA/Local Users > Local Users**.

Select the user account and click **Edit** on the right side.

Under the VPN Policy tab, notice the VPN group policy is currently set to the default of Inherit Group Policy, which would end up with the user in your current configuration receiving the DfltGrpPolicy. However, if you had assigned a group policy to the connection profile for the user, this would have been applied to the user instead based on the policy inheritance model.

In the Edit User Account window, choose **VPN Policy** from the pane on the left. Under the Group Policy check box on the right, now uncheck the default option to inherit the group policy object. From the drop-down box that appears, select your new group policy, and click **OK**.

Now you can open a browser to your SSL VPN login page, enter the credentials for your configured user when prompted, and click **Login**. You are redirected to the portal, where you can see your bookmark list, as shown in Figure 9-25.

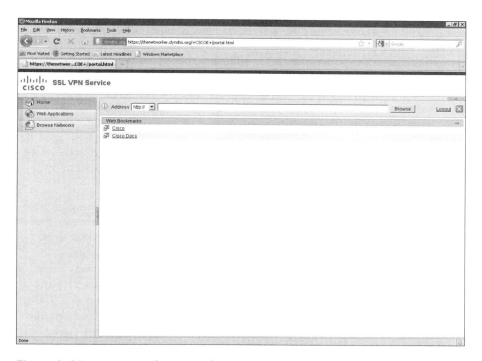

**Figure 9-25**   *User Portal with Bookmarks List and Basic Access Control*

# Content Transformation

This section explains the additional functions the ASA provides for gateway content rewriting, bypassing its rewrite engine if your users are experiencing problems with content access or if specific web resources are unable to function correctly through the SSL tunnel. We also take a look at the Application Helper configuration and sample APCF files for additional support of your web applications that might experience errors or are unsupported by the native ASA functions. Finally, we take a look at Java code signing: the ability to add code signatures to downloaded Java applets for application code integrity checks.

## Gateway Content Rewriting

As discussed in earlier chapters covering the establishment and use of an SSL VPN with the AnyConnect client, the ASA performs rewriting through the use of a rewriting engine or can offload the rewriting and mangling tasks to a client browser with the use of Java proxy applet. By default, all content traveling through (requested by and returning to the client) is rewritten. However, the ASA also allows the use of custom rewrite rules for us to be able to bypass the rewrite engine for specific URLs or a range of URLs that we define.

For example, you might want to bypass the rewrite rules for any Internet (HTTP or HTTPS) sites or websites on the user's local LAN. Bypassing the content-rewrite engine produces a similar behavior to that of split tunneling (used within a full-tunnel or IPsec client VPN), whereby we can prevent access to specific resources from traveling through the SSL tunnel and effectively save the available resources on our ASA for other, more important tasks we might require it to be doing at the time. Another good example for bypassing the content-rewrite engine is for user access to secure Internet banking websites. When a client accesses a website using HTTPS through the SSL tunnel, the ASA negotiates the SSL tunnel to the bank's website on behalf of the client and processes any certificates it receives for authentication purposes. However, the client is not presented with the bank's digital certificate when accessing the user's account details, and subsequently, many banks allow their customers to download software to install on their PCs that may warn them they are not accessing the bank's website as they should be. This can cause the most advanced of users to close their session in a fit of panic. Therefore, we can enter the necessary rules on the ASA device to tell it any specific banking websites need to be bypassed from the content-rewrite rules.

You can define your content-rewrite rules in the ASDM by navigating to **Configure > Remote Access VPN > Clientless SSL VPN Access > Advanced > Content Rewrite**. From here, you are presented with the Configure Content Rewriting window, with the default rewrite rule listed in the window. Each rule entered is configured with a priority/Rule number from 1 to 65535 and is assessed by the ASA using the order of highest priority/lowest rule number to lowest priority/highest rule number. The default rewrite rule is automatically given the priority 65535, and it cannot be edited or removed. Therefore, any rules that we add are configured with a lower priority and are preferred or take precedence over the default.

To add a rule to bypass the content-rewrite engine, click the **Add** button to create a new one. In the Add Content Rewrite Rule window, specify the information described in Table 9-8.

**Table 9-8**   *Content-Rewrite Configuration*

| Field | Description |
|---|---|
| Enable Content Rewrite | Checked by default. If left checked, this causes the ASA to enable to the rewrite engine function for the URL mask we enter. |
| Rule Number | Enter a value from 1 to 65534 (default 65535). The lower the number, the higher the priority. |
| Rule Name | Enter a name you want to use for this rule. |

**Table 9-8**  *Content-Rewrite Configuration*

| Field | Description |
|---|---|
| Resource Mask | The resource mask can take a string of up to 300 characters and has limited support of regular expression matching, as shown here. However, use of the expressions must be accompanied by one alphanumeric character:<br><br>* - Wildcard matches anything.<br><br>? - Matches any single character.<br><br>[!seq] - Matches any character not in sequence.<br><br>[seq] - Matches any character in sequence. |

Based on these fields and rules, if you were to enter a new content-rewrite rule with a resource mask of https://* and uncheck **Enable Content Rewrite**, all HTTPS sites would bypass the rewrite engine and not travel through our SSL tunnel. This would at least fix the problem with the previous user's attempt to access his Internet banking website. Likewise, if you were to enter the resource mask of http://[!www], any websites your users browse to without entering the www prefix would bypass the rewrite engine.

## Application Helper Profiles

The ASA's Application Helper allows for natively unsupported/nonstandard applications used through the SSL VPN to be displayed correctly based on the information held within the application code.

The Application Helper achieves this task through the use of an Extensible Markup Language (XML) APCF script that has been defined offline and loaded into the ASA's flash. It can also be linked to an external HTTP, HTTPS, or FTP server. The APCF file itself is formatted with stream editor (sed) syntax for string transformation.

When first examining the underlying code of an APCF file, you can determine the actions to be carried out and the particular section of the applications code (header, body, request, response) during the current operation of the application (pre, post) from the familiar XML output that you have seen many times with other applications. For example, if any of you have ever dabbled in the odd web development or worked with a Cisco VoIP installation, XML files should be familiar to you.

Example 9-7 lists the XML output of a sample APCF file.

**Example 9-7**  *APCF File Output*

```
<APCF>
<version>1.0</version>
<application>
  <id>Do not compress content from cisco.com</id>
  <apcf-entities>
      <process-request-header>
```

```
        <conditions>
          <server-fnmatch>*.cisco.com</server-fnmatch>
        </conditions>
          <action>
            <do><no-gzip/></do>
          </action>
      </process-request-header>
  </apcf-entities>
</application>
</APCF>
```

You can follow the syntax of the file shown in Example 9-7 for the familiar hierarchal XML syntax. The syntax of the file to pay particular attention to is enclosed in the opening **<apcf-entities>** and closing **</apcf-entities>** tags. The tag **<process-request-header>** indicates the APCF processing should occur at the header stage of the received file. Within the **<conditions></conditions>** tags, the ASA has been set to use regular expression matching any address from the domain Cisco.com. Beneath this, the actions specify that, based on a match of the condition field (for example, www.cisco.com or ftp.cisco.com), gzip compression should not be applied to the received information.

To load an Application Helper APCF file into the ASA's flash, navigate within the ASDM to **Configuration > Remote Access VPN > Clientless SSL VPN Access > Advanced > Application Helper** and click **Add**. The Add APCF Profile window will open, in which you can do one of the following actions:

■ Select an existing file from flash.

■ Upload an APCF file to flash.

■ Specify an HTTP, HTTPS, TFTP, or FTP path.

After you have chosen the option that meets your requirements (that is, your location to the APCF file), click the **OK** button. APCF files are listed in the order of entry into the ASA from top to bottom. When you upload a new APCF file, it is placed at the bottom of the list. Therefore, the oldest files are used first. If you require your most recent file to be used first, you can choose it from the list and use the Move Up and Move Down buttons to the right of the window to change processing order.

**Note:** Application Helper profiles (APCF files) are created by Cisco engineers to solve a specific application problem at the time. You can easily create adverse effects and actually slow down the performance of your ASA if you enter the wrong information into an APCF file. Therefore, it is recommended that you check with Cisco TAC the syntax of any APCF files you create manually.

## Java Code Signing

Upon creation of a Java applet or program at the end of the build process, a digital signature can be added to the application to provide the client with a way to verify that the application's underlying code has not been tampered with between the server sending it and the client receiving it. The ASA can be configured to add a digital signature to Java objects for code-verification processes on the receiving client, because the ASA's rewrite operation has the potential to modify any stored links within the file and render the current signature useless.

To add a digital signature for code-verification processes, navigate to **Configuration > Remote Access VPN > Clientless SSL VPN Access > Advanced > Java Code Signer.**

By default, no signature files are available for code signing on the ASA. To add them, go to **Configure > Remote Access VPN > Certificate Management > Code Signer** and follow the enroll and import process, similar to the certificate-import process described earlier in this chapter. You can purchase a digital signature for code signing from many public CAs or application vendors. For example, if you create Java applications that run on BlackBerry devices, you must apply for and purchase digital signature keys from RIM directly.

# Troubleshooting a Basic Clientless SSL VPN

When troubleshooting a basic clientless SSL VPN session, the most common causes of problems for users are as follows:

- Session establishment
- Certificate errors

## Troubleshooting Session Establishment

So, you are receiving calls from a remote user, John, saying he cannot access the SSL VPN from his location. Your first check should be whether this is happening for everyone, or is it only John who is affected? At times, the answer to this question can be simple: When you have worked in a network support environment for long enough, you get used to the fact that people contact you only when they are having problems, and depending on your environment, you might receive a large number or very few calls per day. However, one thing you can usually be sure of is if there is a problem occurring that is affecting all of your users' abilities to carry out their work, your phones will ring like they have never rung before. If you are in an environment where user location is widely dispersed geographically, and you may have the odd user login in the morning from the United Kingdom and several logins in the late afternoon from the United States, the chances of everybody calling you at the same time is minimal. So, instead of waiting for the majority of your users to try to connect and see whether they have a problem (by the way, I do not recommend this strategy), you have a few options:

- **Test the connection yourself:** This can be carried out from a remote location or public connection (for example, a backup ADSL or 3G Mobile).

- **Use the ASDM monitoring tool to obtain user session information:** By viewing the number of user sessions currently underway, you should be able to loosely determine whether a problem is occurring. For example, if your one user (John) cannot connect, but you see that another user (Patrick) has been connected and accessing resources for the majority of the day, it is likely that John's problem is local only to his account/access.

■ **Use syslog:** You can view the connection attempts through syslog, either viewing from the CLI by issuing the **show logging** command, or using the ASDM logging facility by navigating to **Monitoring > Logging**. (Leave the settings at their defaults of logging level debugging and buffer limit 1000 and click **View**.) The Real-Time Log Viewer window will appear, in which you can view and filter debugging messages being reported by the device.

You can access the ASDM user session monitoring tool from **Monitoring > VPN > VPN Statistics > Sessions**. You can use it to determine the number of VPN sessions currently established, the protocol used (clientless, IPsec, and so on), username, group policy and connection profile, IP addresses, protocol/encryption, and session duration. You can also filter the results currently displayed within the window to view only a particular VPN protocol type, username, IP address, and so forth.

When troubleshooting a client connection to the ASA, two of the most invaluable commands are **ping** and **traceroute**. These are installed by default on all client operating systems, so there should be no need to have to talk a user through their installation. The **ping** command can be used to check for basic Layer 3 connectivity to the ASA device IP address (if Internet Control Message Protocol [ICMP] echo is allowed on the SSL client-facing interface). If the command fails, it is worth checking the client's connection to the Internet to determine whether the user can contact any other public websites. The **traceroute** command can also be used to check the Layer 3 path between the client and the ASA device. If something is configured incorrectly or broken in between the client and ASA, this tool can be a valuable resource for locating the problem and identifying potential steps or locations for further troubleshooting.

If the client has confirmed Layer 3 connectivity to the ASA device IP address, the NSLookup (Windows) and dig (Linux/UNIX) tools can be used to confirm that the client's lookup of the ASA's FQDN is working correctly. These tools can be used to determine potential DNS faults and areas for further troubleshooting.

The following steps aid in the troubleshooting of SSL VPN establishment. Follow the steps to narrow down the problem you are experiencing:

**Step 1.**    Observe the SSL establishment phase for any incompatible protocol versions or cipher suites. If protocol errors have occurred, you can see these in the syslog real-time viewer within the ASDM or within the client browser. Some browsers, such as Mozilla, return messages that are easier to read and understand. Others, such as Internet Explorer, provide more generic error messages.

**Step 2.**    After confirming SSL establishment has completed successfully, check for user authentication errors within the ASDM real-time viewer. Authentication errors (for example, an incorrect password or username) also display to the client upon submission.

**Step 3.**    Check the user's associated connection profile/tunnel group and group policy objects for clientless SSL VPN being allowed under the Protocols section.

After the user session has established successfully and you have confirmed the user is logged in but cannot access resources from within the SSL portal or through the SSL tunnel, follow the troubleshooting steps here to locate the problem:

**Step 1.**   Verify whether the ASA device is allowing traffic through the SSL tunnel without denying it. If there are any errors, examine the ASDM syslog output to display them.

**Step 2.**   Check any content-rewrite rules configured to determine whether inside resources are incorrectly being sent by the user to the Internet directly (and thus bypassing the rewrite engine by mistake).

**Step 3.**   Verify the HTML content being passed back to the client by the ASA.

Packet-sniffing tools can be used locally on the PC to check for the content being returned by the ASA when a user clicks a link and so forth.

**Step 4.**   Verify the DNS server configuration on the ASA. If the ASA does not have any DNS servers or DNS server groups assigned, the client cannot browse resources internal or external by name through the SSL VPN portal.

## Troubleshooting Certificate Errors

This section describes the common causes of certificate errors. However, note that during the certificate-creation phase, clients should be given no reason to doubt the secure nature of their connectivity into your organization. Certificate errors should not happen.

- **Certificate expires:** One of the main and most common of all reasons for certificate errors is that certificate validity has expired, causing the client to receive an "Invalid certificate" error. Some browsers go to great lengths to prevent or warn users about accepting "Invalid certificate" errors, as they should. However, the responsibility still rests with the person whose job it is to manage the renewals each year.

- **Invalid hostname or hostname mismatch:** This can occur if a user browses to an older version of a URL (for example, a saved bookmark that has not been updated) or a DNS A-record that has been set up for access by a different user group without a matching certificate. A user also may have navigated to the server's hostname directly instead of the matching FQDN within the certificate file. This sometimes happens when the Canonical Name (CN) from the identity certificate is not identical to the address/hostname you've typed in the browser.

- **Invalid CA root certificate:** This can be generated for a number of reasons. The most common is when the root certificate is not included with the client's browser. This can be due to the issue of a new CA, where the browser's manufacturer might not have released the required update or the client might not have updated the browser in a while and so the certificate has not had a chance to install. This is also common with self-signed certificates or if the CA is an internal CA. If you are using an internal CA for your users, the necessary CA root certificates must be deployed to the clients. However, when allowing access to the public or guests, it is generally common practice to offer a self-signed certificate.

- **Revoked certificate:** You must make sure the certificate you've received and installed onto your devices is from a trusted CA and has not been compromised in any way during transmission.

- **Connection partially encrypted:** This error occurs when components that are used to construct the page being viewed are linked to or retrieving information from remote sources over an unsecured channel. This error should not occur when accessing the SSL VPN portal. If it does, check the content of the received page or contact Cisco TAC for further troubleshooting.

# Exam Preparation Tasks

As mentioned in the section "How to Use This Book" in the Introduction, you have a couple of choices for exam preparation: the memory tables in Appendix C, Chapter 23, "Final Exam Preparation," and the exam simulation questions on the CD-ROM.

## Review All Key Topics

Review the most important topics in the chapter, noted with the Key Topic icon in the outer margin of the page. Table 9-9 lists a reference of these key topics and the page numbers on which each is found.

**Table 9-9**   *Key Topics*

| Key Topic Element | Description | Page |
| --- | --- | --- |
| Topic | SSL VPN building blocks | 283 |
| Figure 9-1 | SSL OSI model location | 284 |
| Bulleted List | SSL VPN deployment strategies | 291 |
| Topic | Certificate revocation lists | 295 |
| Topic | Connection profile aliases | 315 |
| Table | Connection profile basic requirements | 316 |
| Topic | Bookmark lists | 320 |
| Table | Content rewrite | 328 |
| Topic | Application Helper | 329 |
| Step List | Troubleshooting steps | 332 |

## Complete Tables and Lists from Memory

Print a copy of Appendix C, "Memory Tables" (found on the CD), or at least the section for this chapter, and complete the tables and lists from memory. Appendix D, "Memory Tables Answer Key," also on the CD, includes completed tables and lists to check your work.

## Define Key Terms

Define the following key terms from this chapter, and check your answers in the glossary:

AAA(LOCAL), APCF, bookmark list, CIFS (Common Internet File System), Code Signing, content rewrite engine, CSR (Certificate Signing Request), digital signature, DNS (Domain Name System), group policy, LDAP (Lightweight Directory Access Protocol), Resource Mask, XML (Extensible Markup Language)

This chapter covers the following subjects:

- **Overview of Advanced Clientless SSL VPN Settings:** In this section, we discuss the various options you have for deploying application access through your SSL VPN tunnel to remote users and any advantages or disadvantages each option may have.

- **Application Access Through Port Forwarding:** In this section, we discuss the components involved and behavior of application access using the Port Forwarding applet, the applications supported using the Port Forwarding applet, and TCP support. We also review the reasons why this type of access is now regarded as legacy in comparison to other application access options.

- **Application Access Using Client-Server Plug-Ins:** In this section, we discuss the implementation of client-server plug-ins for your remote users through the SSL VPN portal. We also look at the plug-ins available, the process of downloading and installing them on your ASA device, how to add them to a bookmark list, and finally their operation and customization.

- **Application Access Through Smart Tunnels:** In this section, you discover the powerful application smart tunnels within your environment and learn how to enable their implementation for remote users through your SSL VPN portal. This section also covers the applications currently supported through them and their support on varying operating systems.

- **Configuring SSL/TLS Proxies:** In this section, we review the operation and implementation of email, HTTP, and HTTPS proxies and their use cases.

- **Troubleshooting Advanced Application Access:** In this section, we review the techniques and common questions you ask when troubleshooting application access through your SSL VPN.

## CHAPTER 10

# Advanced Clientless SSL VPN Settings

In previous chapters, we reviewed the various protocols involved when creating and maintaining a Secure Sockets Layer virtual private network (SSL VPN) tunnel and the steps involved in creating and deploying a basic SSL VPN. Now we can move on to another important topic you need to understand, not only for the exam but for the successful deployment of any SSL VPN you might come to install during your professional career: allowing application access to remote users.

With a basic clientless SSL VPN, you have given enough access to your users for them to access resources (for example, web mail, file servers, and intranet sites/portals) through bookmarks or direct URL input. However, to enhance the productivity of your remote users, you can deploy access to the familiar applications they use when in the office (for example, Remote Desktop [RDP], Citrix, Virtual Network Computing [VNC], and SSL/Telnet), allowing them to fulfill the vast majority of their normal work duties while maintaining the ubiquitous access provided by an SSL VPN.

## "Do I Know This Already?" Quiz

The "Do I Know This Already?" quiz helps you determine your level of knowledge on this chapter's topics before you begin. Table 10-1 details the major topics discussed in this chapter and their corresponding quiz sections.

**Table 10-1**  *"Do I Know This Already?" Section-to-Question Mapping*

| Foundation Topics Section | Questions |
| --- | --- |
| Application Access Through Smart Tunnels | 1, 4, 8, 9 |
| Application Access Through Client/Server Plug-Ins | 2 |
| Application Access Through Port Forwarding | 6, 10 |
| Configuring SSL/TLS Proxies | 3, 7 |
| Troubleshooting Advanced Application Access | 5 |

**1.** When creating a new smart tunnel entry with the ASDM, which operating systems are available for you to select? (Choose all that apply.)

  **a.** Windows

  **b.** Google

  **c.** Linux

  **d.** Mac

**2.** Which of the following are available client/server plug-ins from Cisco.com? (Choose all that apply.)

  **a.** RDP2

  **b.** RDP

  **c.** Limewire

  **d.** ICA

  **e.** VNC

  **f.** Internet Explorer 8

  **g.** SSH/Telnet

**3.** Which three of the following are available protocols when configuring the ASA email proxy?

  **a.** HTTPS

  **b.** POP3

  **c.** SMTPS

  **d.** SMTP

  **e.** POP3S

  **f.** IMAP4S

**4.** When assigning a new smart tunnel list, how many can you apply per group?

  **a.** 1

  **b.** 2

  **c.** 3

  **d.** 4

  **e.** 256

**5.** When troubleshooting application access through your SSL VPN, which three areas should be considered?

  **a.** Client

  **b.** Router

  **c.** Application server

  **d.** ASA

  **e.** CA

**6.** Which configuration command enables you to create a new port forwarding entry in List1?

   **a.** smart-tunnel list List1 mstsc.exe platform windows

   **b.** port forward List1 3001 192.168.1.2 telnet Telnet Server

   **c.** port forward List1 telnet Telnet Server

   **d.** port forward list List1 3001 192.168.1.2 telnet Telnet Server

**7.** Where in the ASDM do you go to configure the email proxy settings?

   **a.** Configuration > Remote Access VPN > Clientless SSL VPN Access > Advanced > Proxies

   **b.** Configuration > Remote Access VPN > Clientless SSL VPN Access > Portal > Bookmarks

   **c.** Configuration > Remote Access VPN > Advanced > SSL Settings

   **d.** Configuration > Remote Access VPN > Advanced > E-Mail Proxy

**8.** Which two locations can you use to enable the use of smart tunnels?

   **a.** Smart tunnel lists

   **b.** Port forwarding

   **c.** Bookmarks

   **d.** Secure Desktop Manager

**9.** You have recently deployed a new application using smart tunnels, but now users complain that their web browsing outside of the SSL VPN is slow. What could be the cause?

   **a.** You enabled port forwarding instead.

   **b.** There is a problem with the Java applet.

   **c.** You selected the Smart Tunnel option for a web bookmark.

   **d.** Your smart tunnel list has not been applied correctly.

**10.** Which two are required for port forwarding to work on a client device?

   **a.** The user must have local administrator rights.

   **b.** The user must be a power user.

   **c.** The user must have Internet Explorer installed.

   **d.** The application must be installed locally.

## Foundation Topics

## Overview of Advanced Clientless SSL VPN Settings

This chapter assumes you already have a working basic clientless SSL VPN set up on your Adaptive Security Appliance (ASA) device, and we build on the existing configuration. If you need to review the requirements for setting up a basic clientless SSL VPN, see Chapter 9, "Deploying a Clientless VPN Solution," for an in-depth discussion.

The ability of a remote user to access the information and programs he needs when connected to your SSL VPN is a basic requirement for anyone working away from his or her native environment. You have a few options available when allowing application access through your SSL VPN. Which one you decide to use will ultimately depend on the environment from which the user is connecting. For example, is the user on a company-owned device or connecting from an Internet cafe?

Before you begin the process of granting a user application access through the SSL VPN, you should review the potential solutions:

- **Port forwarding:** One of the first types of application access Cisco offered on the SSL VPN way back when version numbers used to begin with 7.x, the port forwarding solution is implemented by way of a Java applet that can be opened by clicking the appropriate link within the user's portal. The applet then listens on the local machine loopback address using specific and well-known application ports, as defined by the administrator (you) from within the Adaptive Security Device Manager (ASDM) or command-line interface (CLI). There are drawbacks with this solution, as discussed later in the chapter. For example, the client application must be installed on the remote user's machine, and the remote user also requires administrative access to the local machine.

- **Client-server plug-ins:** By far one of the most robust and convenient ways to allow application access to users is through the use of client-server plug-ins. These are available for download from Cisco.com and can be added to an existing or new bookmark list for a remote user to be able to click the link and have the application open in front of them. Because access is through a plug-in, the user does not need the full client (fat) version of the application. There is also no requirement for the remote user to have administrative functions on the local PC, meaning that the ubiquitous nature of an SSL VPN solution is maintained (that is, users can connect via almost any available location and method). The main drawback with the plug-in solution is the lack of supported plug-ins available. At the time of this writing, Cisco offers the following plug-ins for download:
  - RDP (Remote Desktop)
  - RDP2 (for use with newer Windows 2003, 2008, Vista, and 7 machines)
  - Citrix ICA Client
  - SSH/Telnet
  - VNC

- VPN AUTH and POST plug-ins to be used for SSO (Single Sign-On)

However, as more SSL VPN solutions are deployed and more applications are required, this will be one of the motivating factors for further plug-in development. We have also noticed a much greater number of thin client versions of popular and new programs being developed and released, so the requirement for plug-ins may even decrease as we move further into the future.

- **Smart tunnels:** Smart tunnel access is the next evolution of application access with regard to port forwarding and plug-ins. Through the implementation of smart tunnels, remote users can use their existing, locally installed applications. When the remote user requests application access or selects the appropriate bookmark, the smart tunnel causes a small Java applet to be downloaded to the client machine and run silently in the background. If at any time it encounters a request or other activity from one of the particular processes it has been set up to watch, any traffic originating from or traveling to the responsible application traverses the SSL VPN tunnel.

As you can guess, however, there are advantages and disadvantages to the operation of smart tunnels. Unlike using client-server plug-ins, the local application must be installed on the client PC. However, there is no requirement for the user to have local administrative rights on the client machine because the application settings can remain as they are for operation.

Table 10-2 summarizes the various options for application access and shows the advantages and disadvantages for each.

**Table 10-2** *Application Access Methods*

| Method | Advantages/Disadvantages |
|---|---|
| Port forwarding | Allows limited application access for remote users through the SSL VPN tunnel. |
| | Requires local administrator rights on client machine. |
| | Requires client applications to be locally installed. |
| | Limited to TCP applications using well-known static ports. |
| | Windows, Mac OS X, and limited Linux OS support. |
| Client-server plug-in | Allows application access for remote users through the SSL VPN tunnel. |
| | Does not require client application to be locally installed. |
| | Does not require local administrator access. |
| | Limited to plug-in range available from Cisco.com (RDP, RDP2, VNC, ICA, and SSH/Telnet). |
| | Windows, Mac OS X, and limited Linux OS support. |

**Table 10-2** *Application Access Methods*

| Method | Advantages/Disadvantages |
|---|---|
| Smart tunnel | Allows application access for remote users through the SSL VPN tunnel. |
| | Requires client applications to be locally installed. |
| | Does not require local administrator access. |
| | Local application settings do not need to be modified. |
| | Higher number of TCP applications supported than port forwarding. However, applications requiring dynamic port support require a VPN client or AnyConnect connection. |
| | Supports Windows and Mac OS X. |

Before you can deploy application access to your SSL VPN users, you need to determine the appropriate method for deployment based on the following details about their computing environment:

- What OS are they using (for example, Windows XP, Fedora Core 9, or Mac OS X)?

- Which applications will they need to access?

- What location are they using to connect from (home on a PC, on a company-owned laptop, or at an Internet cafe)?

- Do they have the applications locally installed on their PC?

- Do they have local administrative access to the machine

After assessing the client's environment against these details, compare the information gathered to the available solutions (as listed in Table 10-2) to decide which application-access solution to use.

For example, you have been asked by the marketing manager to allow his staff to use Outlook when logged in to the SSL VPN. Between what you already know about the existing environment and the information he has given us, you have the following details:

- **Group name:** Marketing

- **Application:** Outlook

- **What they use to access the SSL VPN:** Company-provided laptops. Users typically connect from their home ADSL or cable connections but might occasionally connect from a public Wi-Fi point.

- **OS:** Windows

- **Users have local admin access:** No

- **Is Outlook currently installed on each machine:** Yes

You can now determine which application suit the Marketing team's needs. Figured it out yet? The answer is smart tunnels.

You can use Figure 10-1 as a guide through the process of determining the solution to provide. This process starts by asking which operating system the user uses.

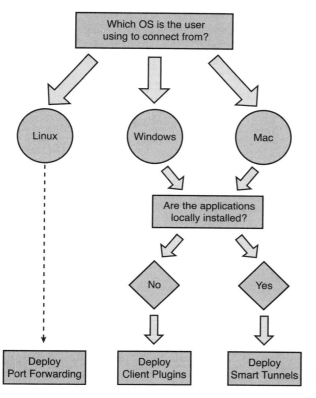

**Figure 10-1**   *Choose Your Application Deployment Solution*

## Application Access Through Port Forwarding

We have explored the various options to deploy application access to your users through the SSL VPN. Now we examine how each method operates, is configured, and is verified.

This section begins by looking at application access using port forwarding. Port forwarding was the first method of application access deployed by Cisco for SSL VPNs. Like any technology, it can be a great solution to all of your problems when it is launched, but there is always room for improvement, as you will see later when we discuss client-server plugins and smart tunnels.

Port forwarding operates this way: The ASA admin (you) first creates a new port forwarding list and entry consisting of a name, the local forwarded port on the client machine, the remote/application server name, the application server's port, and a description. The port forwarding list is then made available through a Java applet that automatically opens when the user logs in to the SSL VPN portal or clicks the Application Access pane from within the portal and chooses Start Application Access.

Upon starting application access, a Java applet is downloaded to the client, and an entry is created in the local hosts file of the user's PC, which contains the application server's name and the local machine's loopback address. The application in use (for example, Outlook) must be configured to send its traffic via the local port as configured in the port forwarding entry on the ASA. With the Java applet open, all traffic originating from Outlook is sent via the SSL tunnel to the ASA. The ASA then establishes a TCP session with the destination server and relays any application data between the client and server, as shown in Figure 10-2.

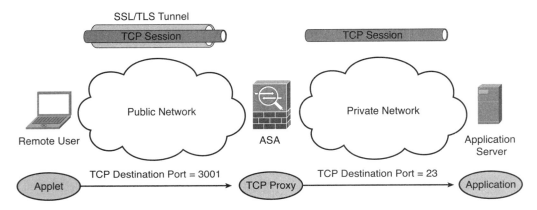

**Figure 10-2** *Port Forwarding Process*

The port forwarding applet can operate with simple applications that run on static TCP ports. However, this allows clients to use familiar applications that are already installed on their laptop/PC. The port settings of the application must also be changed to use those configured on the ASA. For example, if the administrator had created a new port forwarding entry with the remote port 23 and local port 3001, users would have had to modify their application to use port 3001 for Telnet purposes.

One of the main disadvantages to using the port forwarding solution is that remote clients require local administrator access on the machine from which they are connecting. This is because to the local hosts file has to be modified when entering an entry for the remote server. Unfortunately, because of the strict security requirements users often face when using a corporate laptop or PC, it is unlikely that a user will be granted these rights, and this requirement also prevents the user from connecting via a public or shared machine.

When the port forwarding solution is used, remote users face several drawbacks, which have ultimately led to it now being regarded as legacy:

■ As mentioned earlier, local administrative access is required for modification of the hosts file.

■ The application must be installed on the local machine.

■ The application's port settings must be changed by the user for the application to be able to send data via the SSL tunnel.

■ Only simple TCP applications are supported.

Although port forwarding is now a legacy method of remote application access, for the exam, it is still important to understand both its purpose and configuration. It is also good to understand any past technologies that have led to the ones in current use.

### Configuring Port Forwarding Using the ASDM

Configuring and deploying port forwarding for application use involves several tasks. You can deploy access to a Telnet server for remote users, which they can access by clicking a link within the portal area, and automatic deployment of the port forwarding applet.

Begin by navigating in the Adaptive Security Device Manger (ASDM) to **Configuration > Remote Access VPN > Clientless SSL VPN Access > Portal > Port Forwarding**. Depending on your device, there should be no port forwarding entries listed in the Port Forwarding window. Create one by clicking **Add**. As shown in Figure 10-3, the Edit Port Forwarding List dialog opens.

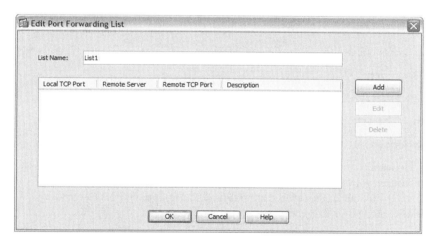

**Figure 10-3**   *Edit Port Forwarding List Window*

Begin creating application entries that remote users can access by giving the Port Forwarding List a name. For this example, we name the list **List1**. However, you might want to give yours a more memorable or meaningful name during deployment because it is used later to add the list to a group policy. (Remember, list names cannot contain spaces.) After naming the list, click **Add**, which takes you to the Add Port Forwarding Entry dialog shown in Figure 10-4.

Enter the following information using the four fields in the window:

- **Local TCP Port:** The listening TCP port on the remote user's machine

- **Remote Server:** The application server's name on the trusted network

- **Remote TCP Port:** The listening TCP port on the application server

- **Description:** An optional field where you can enter an informative note for the remote user

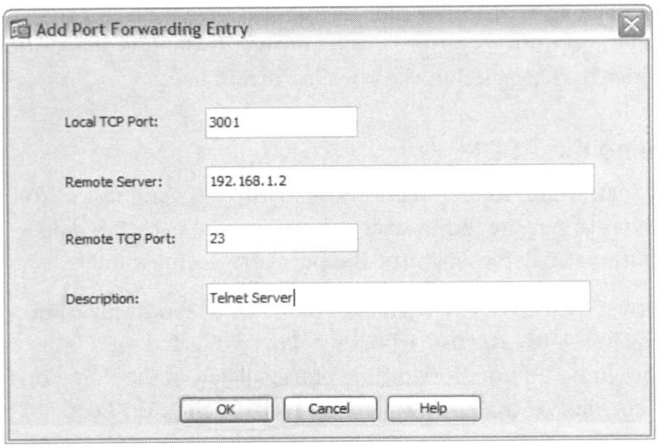

**Figure 10-4** *Add Port Forwarding Entry Dialog*

For the example, we entered the following information:

■ **Local TCP Port:** 3001

■ **Remote Server:** 192.168.1.2

■ **Remote TCP Port:** 23

■ **Description:** Telnet Server

With the information entered, click **OK** and you are returned to the Add Forwarding List window with your new port forwarding entry in the list. If you have no other port forwarding entries to add, click **OK** and you are returned to the original Port Forwarding window (displayed in Figure 10-5), where you can see that the list now appears.

After successfully creating a Port Forwarding list, you can assign it to your remote users. Port forwarding lists can be assigned to users either through group policy objects, Dynamic Access Policies (DAP), or directly within their user configuration. For this example, we make the port forwarding list available to all users through the use of the default group policy object (DfltGrpPolicy). We do this by navigating to **Configuration > Remote Access VPN > Clientless SSL VPN Access > Group Policies** and choosing the group policy and clicking **Edit**. When the Edit Internal Group Policy: <policy name> window will appears, we choose **Portal** from the menu on the left, as shown in Figure 10-6.

You are given the option of selecting and assigning various URL, smart tunnel, and port forwarding entries, and other settings for users. For this example, choose the port forwarding list created earlier from the port forwarding list drop-down. If you want the port forwarding applet to automatically start upon the user logging in to the portal, choose the **Auto Applet Download** option. However, for this example, we navigate through the portal to enable it. You are also given the option of assigning a name to the applet, which can help your users to identify the application when it is running (for example, Outlook Email Access). For this example, use the default name **Application Access**, and then click **OK**.

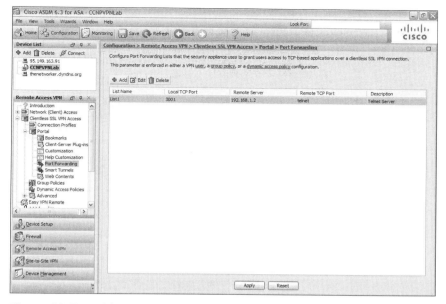

**Figure 10-5**   *Add Port Forwarding List Entries*

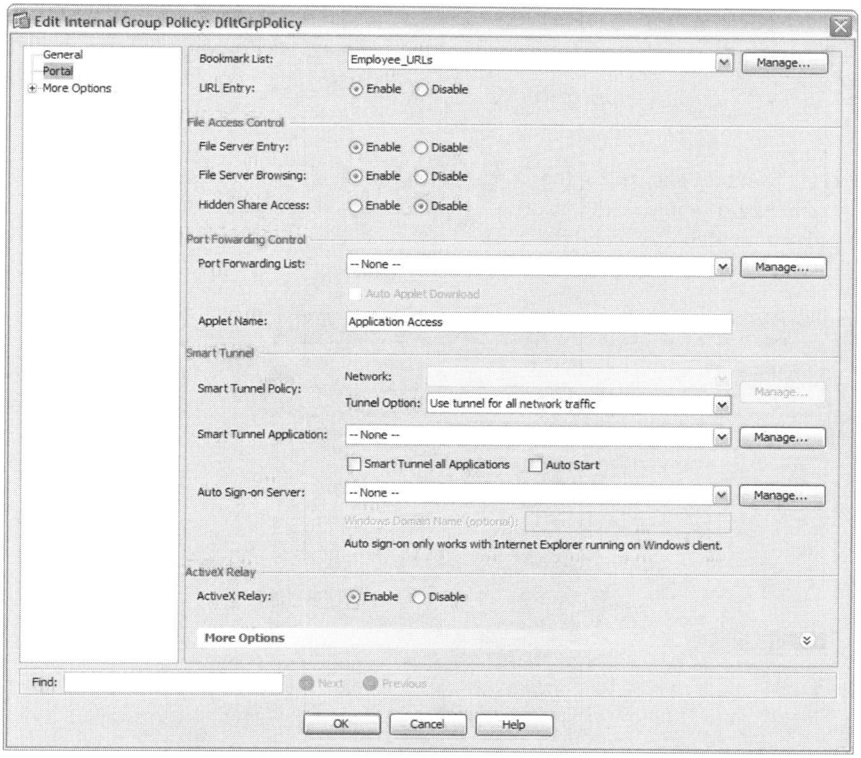

**Figure 10-6**   *Edit Group Policy Window*

We can now test the application-access applet from the SSL VPN portal page. Log in to the SSL VPN using the employee1 account created earlier. From the menu on the left, click the **Application Access** button and are presented with the Application Access window, including the button to start access and a brief help guide, as shown in Figure 10-7.

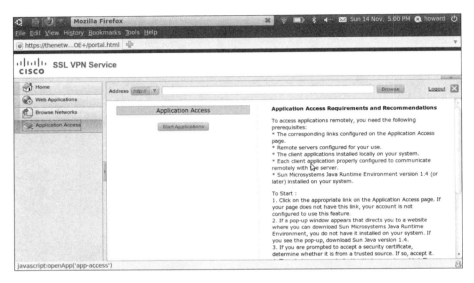

**Figure 10-7** *SSL VPN Portal Application Access Pane*

After selecting **Start Applications**, the Java applet loads, as shown in Figure 10-8. In the Java applet, we are presented with a list of the applications that have been set up for port forwarding, with the details we entered earlier.

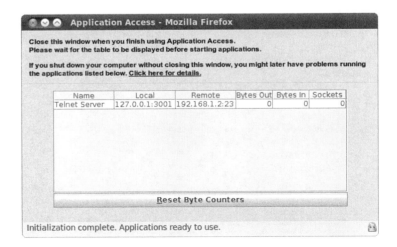

**Figure 10-8** *Portal Application Access Window*

We are now ready to connect to the Telnet server. If the Java applet does not load successfully, check that the client machine has the Java plug-in installed and enabled for the user's browser. If the applet does load but no applications are listed, there might be a port or permissions error. At this point, make sure the remote client has local administrative access on the PC and that the client port within your configuration is not already in use on the remote user's machine.

As shown in Figure 10-9, we open a Telnet connection to our local loopback address and the port configured for port forwarding. We are now connected and ready to work. (Note that for a production environment, you usually connect to the server name because the ASA would have entered this into the hosts file.)

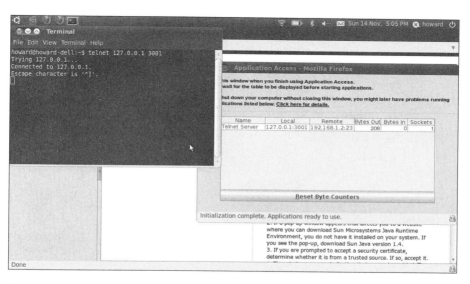

**Figure 10-9**  *Connect to the Local Port for Application Access*

## Application Access Using Client-Server Plug-Ins

Client-server plug-ins are one of the preferred methods of application access when using SSL VPNs, mainly due to their support of the ubiquitous model that SSL VPNs are supposed to provide to users: connect from anywhere using anything. One of the greatest benefits of using client-server plug-ins over the smart tunnel or port forwarding solutions is that clients can have application access without having the full (fat) client application installed on the PC they are connecting from. This is a great benefit to users who are always out and about connecting via different machines and methods where access to the installed applications might not always be available (for example, from an Internet cafe).

One limitation to using client-server plug-ins relates to the nature of plug-ins themselves. They are a thin-client application designed to give the users easy access. But this might come at a compromise, because of the lack of functionality when compared to a full installation.

Plug-ins can be downloaded directly from Cisco.com and are imported into your ASA's flash. Currently, the following plug-ins are available for download:

■    SSH/Telnet Client

■    Citrix ICA Client

■    Remote Desktop (RDP) Client (used for Windows 2000 Pro, Server, and XP)

■    Remote Desktop 2 (RDP2) Client (used for Windows Vista, 7, and Server 2003 and 2008)

■    VNC Client

Plug-ins operate directly within the remote user's browser, and their application traffic is sent and received through the SSL VPN tunnel to the ASA. The ASA carries out the same actions as it does for port forwarding (creates a TCP connection between itself and the application server), and then sends and receives application traffic from the server to the remote user and vice versa, as shown in Figure 10-10.

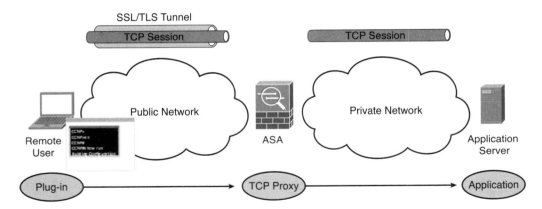

**Figure 10-10**    *Application Plug-In Process*

One of the drawbacks of client-server plug-ins is the lack of them. At the moment, however, the applications required for a user to be able to make a connection to a remote server do exist (for example, using RDP, RDP2, or Citrix ICA), and the user can run the additional or custom applications within the terminal. As time passes and demand grows, more plug-ins may become available for remote users, although the lack of functionality in comparison to the full-client installation might be their downfall.

### Configuring Client-Server Plug-In Access Using the ASDM

Installing and deploying client-server plug-ins for remote users to access from within the SSL VPN portal is a five-step process:

**Step 1.**    Download the plug-in JAR files from Cisco.com.

**Step 2.**    Import the plug-in JAR files into the ASA's flash memory using the ASDM or CLI.

**Step 3.**   Configure a bookmark list or use an existing one and create a new bookmark using the plug-in prefix. (For example, the VNC plug-in uses a prefix of vnc://.)

**Step 4.**   (Optional) Define plug-in parameters to customize the user experience or connection type. (This step is usually carried out during bookmark creation. However, it is important and therefore requires its own step.)

**Step 5.**   Connect to a remote server using the application plug-in bookmark for access and experience verification.

**Note:**   In the case of the Citrix ICA (and possibly future plug-ins), the file type is a ZIP file instead of the common JAR file. However, the import process shown here is the same for each file type whether using the ASDM or CLI.

As you can see, the configuration and verification process is pretty straightforward. In fact, probably the most time-consuming process is waiting for the plug-in files to download from Cisco.com and importing them into the ASA's flash. Because you have already seen the required configuration for bookmarks in earlier discussions, Step 3 will be familiar. It is similar to the process used earlier, except for selecting the application-specific prefix rather than the HTTP, HTTPS, CIFS, and FTP prefixes available by default.

A CCO account on Cisco.com is required to be able to log in and download the plug-ins. Navigate to the following URL: http://www.cisco.com/cisco/software/navigator.html.

This page provides a list of available images, plug-ins, and other software for the ASA. As mentioned previously, the plug-ins require only guest access to download. If you want to download any other files (for example, ASA BIN images), you must have or register for privileged access. As shown in Figure 10-11, scroll down the page and locate the available plug-in files.

Depending on your environment, you might want to download only one or all of them. For this example, we imported all of them for portal-illustration reasons. However, we only cover the installation of one here. (I am not cruel enough to make you sit through the individual screens for the import of each file.)

To begin the example, we have downloaded a plug-in file (in this case, the vnc-plugin.jar file). To import this into the ASA's flash for use in our SSL VPN, navigate in the ASDM to **Configuration > Remote Access VPN > Clientless SSL VPN Access > Portal > Client-Server Plug-Ins** and click **Import**.

The Import Client-Server Plug-In window appears, as shown in Figure 10-12, and from there you can choose the plug-in you are importing and the location you are importing it from:

- Local Computer

- Flash File System

- Remote Server (FTP, TFTP, HTTP)

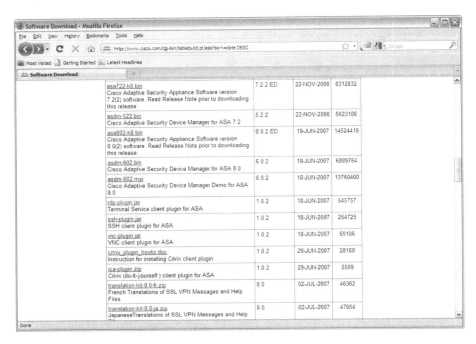

**Figure 10-11**  *Download Available Plug-Ins from Cisco.com*

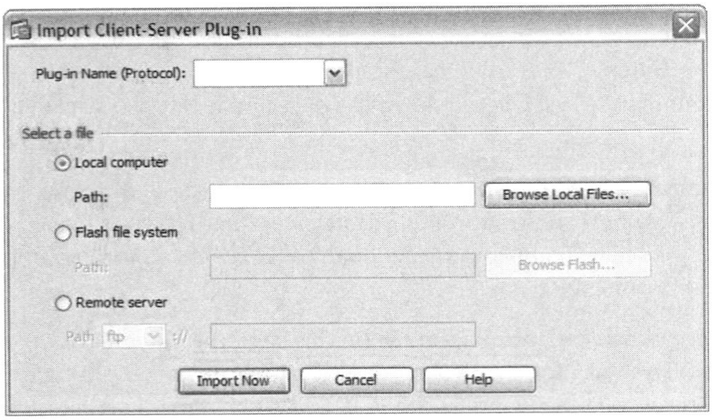

**Figure 10-12**  *Plug-In Import Process*

For this example, we select **VNC** for the plug-in name and enter the path to the destination file on the local computer. We then click **Import Now** and receive a pop-up dialog confirming the plug-in has been installed. We continue this process for all the plug-in files we have downloaded. All the plug-ins we have installed are listed in the Client-Server Plug-In pane, as shown in Figure 10-13.

You can also import plug-in files using the CLI with the command shown in Example 10-1:

```
import webvpn plug-in protocol plugin type file location URL
```

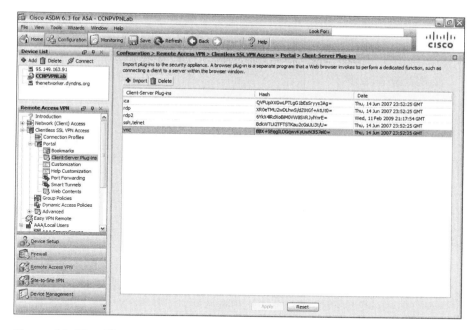

**Figure 10-13**  *Client-Server Plug-In Pane*

**Example 10-1**  *Transfer and Import the Plug-In File*

```
CCNP#
CCNP# import webvpn plug-in protocol vnc tftp://192.168.50.5/vnc-plugin.jar
!!!!!!!!!!!!!!!!!!!!!!!!!!!!!!!!!!!!!!!!!!!!!!!!!!!!!!!!!!!!!!!!!!!!!!!!!!!!!!!
!!!!!!!!!!!!!!!!!!!!!!!!!!!!!!!!!!!!!!!!!!!!!!!!!!!!!!!!!!!!!!!!!!!!!!!!!!!!!!!
!!!!!!!!!!!!!!!!!!!!!!!!!!!!!!!!!!!!!!!!!!!!!!!!!!!!!!!!!!!!!!!!!!!!!!!!!!!!!!!
!!!!!!!!!!!!!!!!!!!!!!!!!!!!!!!!!!!!!!!!!!!!!!!!!!!!!!!!!!!!!!!!!!!!!!!!!!!!!!!
!!!!!!!!!!!!!!!!!!!!!!!!!!!!!!!!!!!!!!!!!!!!!!!!!!!!!!!!!!!!!!!!!!!!!!!!!!!!!!!
!!!!!!!!!!!!!!!!!!!!!!!!!!!!!!!!!!!!!!!!!!!!!!!!!!!!!!!!!!!!!!!!!!!!!!!!!!!!!!!
!!!!!!!!!!!!!!!!!!!!!!!!!!!!!!!!!!!!!!!
CCNP#
```

After successful import of the plug-in files, you can now create the bookmark that users can use to access an application server and assign it to a bookmark list.

To create a new bookmark, navigate to **Configuration > Remote Access VPN > Clientless SSL VPN Access > Portal > Bookmarks**. For this example, we use the existing Employee_URLs bookmark list (created in Chapter 9) for this exercise. Choose the bookmark list and click **Edit**. In the Edit Bookmark List dialog, click **Add** to create a new one.

As displayed in Figure 10-14, in the Add Bookmark dialog, we enter the information required to create our new VNC bookmark. From the URL drop-down, we choose **VNC** (the prefix), and then click **OK**.

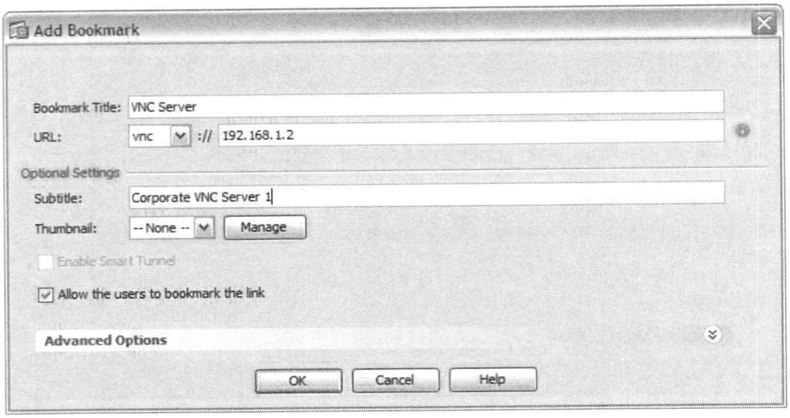

**Figure 10-14**   *Create New Bookmark Entry for Plug-In Operation*

We can now log in to the profile and inspect any changes that may have occurred due to the addition of the plug-ins. Because we have created our bookmark within a predefined bookmark list that is already applied to our default group policy, we can test access using the bookmark without having to carry out any further configuration. However, depending on your deployment at the time, you might require the addition of a new or custom bookmark list for a specific group or user.

As shown in Figure 10-15, upon logging in to the SSL VPN portal using the employee1 user, you can immediately see new buttons in the menu on the left and a new VNC Bookmarks section on the portal home page, with the bookmark created earlier listed underneath.

Each plug-in is given its own menu icon and link to ease access and navigation for remote users. As you take your time to navigate around the new menus available, also notice that the address bar prefix along the top of the window will also change, indicating that remote users also have the opportunity to enter a server name directly (unless we remove the option for them to do so).

As mentioned earlier, you can customize the majority of a plug-ins actions and environment by the addition of parameters to the end of the bookmark file you create. I have left this part for discussion until now because configuring the options at this stage can save you a lot of time digging through and searching for the various documentation files that may be available for each plug-in.

As you navigate through the portal after the addition of any plug-ins, you will also notice that each file shows its own help information on the right side of the respective pane. The majority of the plug-ins available have a brief guide on what the application is and its basic use, and you will see the various parameters that are listed for it.

For example, the help available for the RDP plug-in lists the parameters you can use to customize the user connection experience, as shown in Example 10-2.

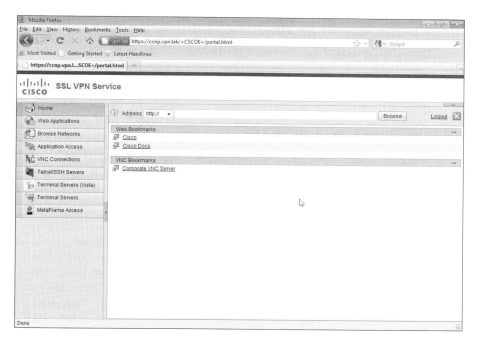

**Figure 10-15**  *The Addition of Plug-In Menus to Our Default SSL VPN Portal*

**Example 10-2**  *SSL VPN RDP Plug-In Available Parameters*

```
server:port/?Parameter1=value&Parameter2=value&Parameter3=value

You may enter the parameters in any order, however, do not enter all of them. We
  recommend entering the geometry parameter.

bpp=integer - Color depth in the popup window to be opened. The value is the
  number of bits per pixel to reserve for specifying color. Enter 8, 16, 24, or 32.

command=string - Working directory.

console=yes - Connect to console.

debug_hex=yes - Show bytes sent and received.

debug_key=yes - Show scan code sent for each key pressed.

debug_level=string - Severity of debug output to log. Enter DEBUG, INFO, WARN,
  ERROR, or FATAL.

domain=string - Logon domain.

geometry=widthxheight - Specifies the width and height in pixels of the popup
  window to be opened.

hostname=string - Client host name.

keymap=string - Keyboard mapping file name for terminal server.

password=string - Password to log on to the server. The password displays in the
  text box as you type it; use only with care and make sure no one is observing.
  Otherwise, wait for the password prompt instead of entering this parameter.

port=integer - RDP port number. The default RDP port number is 3389.

rdp4=yes - Enables use of RDP Version 4.

shell=string - Shell.

username=string - Username to log on to the server.
```

```
The following example specifies the size of the popup window and the bits per
  pixel:
myserver/?geometry=1024x786&bpp=16
```

Now that you know where to easily find the parameter information, you can use this to further customize your application bookmarks if you want to enhance your remote user's experience when using the SSL VPN.

It is strongly recommended, however, that unless you are interested in allowing your users to be able to define their own connections to internal servers using the parameters they choose, remove the help file contents and address bar. You can find further information about how to do so in Chapter 11, "Customizing the Clientless Portal."

To test the VNC plug-in and the bookmark we created earlier, we choose the bookmark on the home page, shown in Figure 10-15. Shortly after, we are prompted to enter the local VNC password for the server we are connecting to. (This is configured and stored locally on the server. For more information about the installation and configuration of the VNC program on a server, visit http://www.realvnc.com.) If you have used VNC to connect to a server or client desktop before, you will notice the familiar options that are available on the local installation are also available by accessing the Options menu in the window (for example, desktop sharing and compression). As shown in Figure 10-16, we are also given the option to record our session for later review to the local PC we are connecting from.

**Figure 10-16**  *VNC Plug-In Connection Authentication*

We enter our password and click **OK**, and then shortly afterward, a window to the server appears, as shown in Figure 10-17, where we can continue to work on existing documents or use locally installed applications for troubleshooting or complete a number of other tasks.

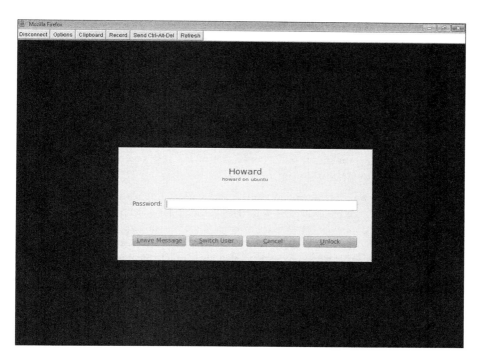

**Figure 10-17**    *Remote VNC Connection to Server Desktop Through Your SSL VPN*

## Application Access Through Smart Tunnels

Smart tunnels are the next in the evolution of application access. With smart tunnels, the requirement for a local user to have administrative rights on the client machine has now gone, the user no longer has to reconfigure his local application settings to forward sessions to local loopback and preconfigured port, and the list of applications supported is more extensive. (Note that this is limited to Winsock2 clients only; Microsoft Outlook MAPI is not currently supported.)

Essentially, the operation of forwarding application traffic through the SSL VPN tunnel remains the same as with port forwarding and client-server plug-ins: Upon receiving the client application traffic, the ASA performs a proxy condition, and after creating a local TCP connection between itself and the application server, forwards the information to it.

The noticeable advantage smart tunnels have over client-server plug-ins is the speed in which the application operates over the tunnel (it is primarily a Java thing, as you may have noticed), and the client can make use of the full feature list available for the application. However, as with port forwarding, the drawback is that the application has to be locally installed on the remote user's PC. Therefore (and also for security reasons), smart tunnels are generally deployed to users on company- or employee-owned PCs/laptops and not those connecting from a public machine.

Smart tunnels can be implemented into an existing or new SSL VPN connection using the following two methods:

**Key Topic**

- **Smart tunnel lists:** Similar to bookmark lists created in the earlier example, you must first create a list and then associate smart tunnel applications.

- **Bookmarks:** As mentioned in Chapter 9, when creating a bookmark list you have the option to Enable Smart Tunnel. You can check this option for web-enabled applications, allowing users to automatically start the smart tunnel process upon bookmark selection.

We discuss both options for smart tunnel configuration because you might be presented with either of them during the exam.

Smart tunnels operate by listening for and interacting with an application process on the remote user's machine. For example, in Figure 10-18, the application process used by Microsoft's remote desktop viewer (mstsc.exe) is listened for, and any application data originating from it is sent by the smart tunnel applet to the ASA and forwarded to the trusted application server. The smart tunnel itself is a small Java applet that silently runs upon user execution of a bookmark or upon selection of the option to start smart tunnel application access.

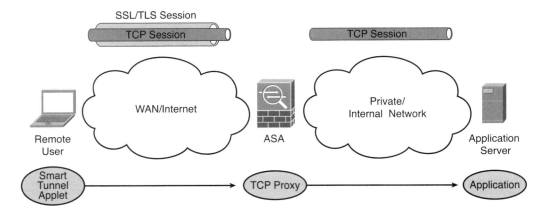

**Figure 10-18** *Smart Tunnel Operation*

It is important to note that when enabling the smart tunnel option within a bookmark (the second option mentioned earlier), if the bookmark is a web URL (for example, www.cisco.com), this will cause the smart tunnel to listen for and send any traffic from the web browser's process (for example, iexplore.exe) through the SSL tunnel. This also means that if you have multiple instances of the browser open, there will be multiple processes with the same name running, causing all browser traffic (for the watched browser anyway) to traverse the SSL tunnel. Despite unnecessarily using the available resources on the ASA for all of your web traffic, this also means the browser sessions that are not holding the window to the SSL VPN portal will also be affected by any web access control lists (WACL) or other restrictions you might have in place.

## Configuring Smart Tunnel Access Using the ASDM

We can now start configuring our smart tunnel. In this example, we run through the process of implementing a basic smart tunnel list that contains a VNC application entry. When configured, we log in using our test employee1 account and verify connectivity to a remote server.

Not unlike other sample configuration tasks we have carried out so far, the implementation of smart tunnels is pretty straightforward for both scenarios. This is largely because the intuitive layout of the ASDM, with all configuration options more or less in the same place. The graphical user interface (GUI) can at times put other vendor approaches to shame. However, the configuration tasks through the CLI are also straightforward enough to complete in a few commands.

As is the case with bookmark lists, we start the configuration scenario by creating a new smart tunnel list. As with bookmark lists, you can also configure many smart tunnels within a list, and it is important to bear in mind that only one smart tunnel list can be applied to a group or user policy. If you have multiple applications that require smart tunnel access, it is recommended to place them within the same list.

In the ASDM, navigate to **Configuration > Remote Access VPN > Clientless SSL VPN Access > Portal > Smart Tunnels** and click **Add**. In the Add Smart Tunnel List window, for this example we name the list **Smart List 1**, and then create the smart tunnel by clicking **Add** on the right side. In the Add Smart Tunnel Entry window, we are given the options described in Table 10-3 to configure.

**Table 10-3**  *Add Smart Tunnel Entry Configuration Options*

| Field | Options |
| --- | --- |
| Application ID | Enter the name you want to give to this smart tunnel entry for user information. |
| OS | Choose your OS from the drop-down box (Windows or Mac). |
| Process Name | Enter the Windows executable process name, or if Mac is selected, enter the full path to the application file on the remote computer. |
| Hash | An optional field that can be used to enter the SHA-1 hash of the application process file to check for application integrity. Currently, this is supported only when working with Windows machines. |

As shown in Figure 10-19, we enter the following details for our smart tunnel to work with our remote client's VNC viewer process, and then click **OK** and **OK** again to save the tunnel entry and the smart tunnel list:

■ **Application ID:** VNC

■ **OS:** Windows

■ **Process Name:** vncviewer.exe

■ **Hash:** Left blank

Now we can assign them to our users. As mentioned earlier, you can assign a list to either a group or user policy. However, for this example, we assign the list to our default group policy (DfltGrpPolicy), as we have with past settings.

We navigate in the ASDM to **Configuration > Remote Access VPN > Clientless SSL VPN > Group Policies**, select the default group policy from the list, and click **Edit** to open the configuration window.

We choose the **Portal** option from the menu on the left, and the pane appears on the right, as shown in Figure 10-20. You should recognize this pane; we used it to select our bookmark port forwarding lists earlier.

We choose our smart tunnel list from the Smart Tunnel Application drop-down under the Smart Tunnel section of the pane. For now, we leave the Auto Start option unchecked. The Auto Sign-On feature will be explored in later chapters when we cover SSO and authentication. When selected, click **OK**, and that is it! We have configured and applied our first smart tunnel entry.

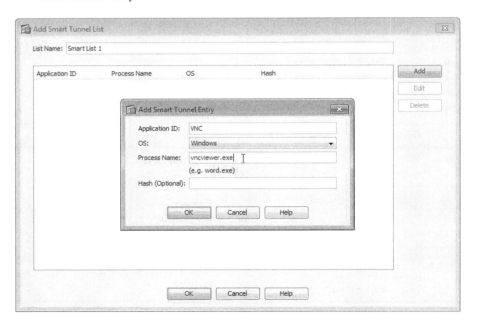

**Figure 10-19** *Smart Tunnel Configuration*

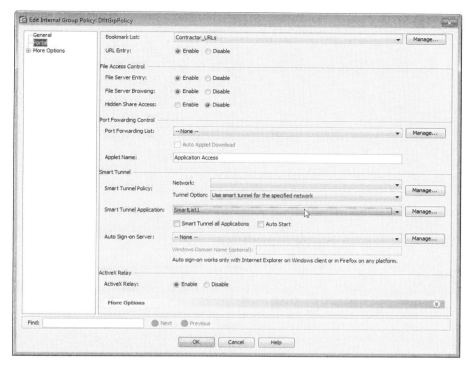

**Figure 10-20**   *Smart Tunnel Addition to Group Policy*

Now it is time to test the smart tunnel and make sure we can use our locally installed VNC application to access our remote server.

We begin by logging in to the portal again using our test user employee1 and clicking the **Application Access** button in the menu on the left. You should notice now a new button has appeared: Smart Tunnels. Figure 10-21 shows the applications that can be used through our tunnel. (In this case, it is the VNC smart tunnel entry created earlier.)

When we click the **Start Smart Tunnel** button, the Java application is loaded and the window is hidden to allow for a "silent operation." We click the **VNC** icon on our local Programs menu. As shown in Figure 10-22, we entered the remote address (server's local address) of the server. We also checked the **Details** option that appears within the SSL VPN portal pane after clicking the **Start** button to display the amount of data using the connection.

In Figure 10-23, we have clicked **OK** and entered the password when prompted by VNC. The VNC window has opened, displaying a view of the remote server. We can verify the smart tunnel is being used for communication because the Kbytes Sent and Received counters are increasing within the portal.

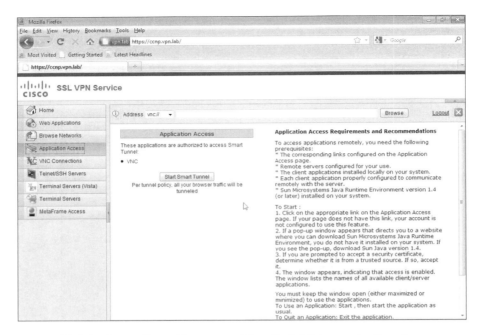

**Figure 10-21**   *Smart Tunnel Button and Details Addition to the Portal*

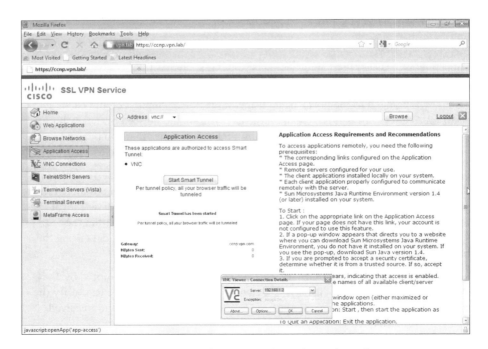

**Figure 10-22**   *Start Smart Tunnel Access and Load Local Application*

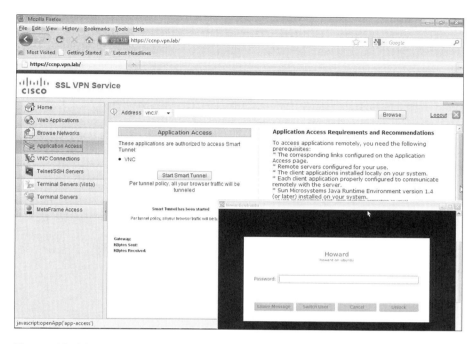

**Figure 10-23**   *Connect to Remote Server Using Smart Tunnel*

# Configuring SSL/TLS Proxies

The ASA allows for the configuration of various proxy parameters for secure email and use of an internal proxy server for additional security or web/content filtering.

## Email Proxy

An email proxy can be configured on the ASA device to enable the secure communications of POP3S, IMAP4S, and SMTPS protocols, much like HTTP and HTTPS, by sending their application/control data across a Secure Sockets Layer/Transport Layer Security (SSL/TLS)-authenticated tunnel.

The three mail protocols listed here (POP3S, IMAP4S, and SMTPS) have their own RFC documents that describe the implementation of secure connectivity:

- **POP3S, IMAP4S:** RFC 2595

- **SMTPS:** RFC 2487

To configure the ASA as an email proxy, navigate in the ADSM to **Configuration > Remote Access VPN > Advanced > E-Mail Proxy**. You are given the following menu options. Each of them is used to configure the relevant information required:

- Access E-Mail Proxy

- Default Servers

- AAA

- Authentication

- Delimiters

By default, the email proxy is not enabled on the ASA. However, you can enable it on a per-protocol and per-interface basis. (For example, the Access E-Mail Proxy window lists the interfaces that are available.) If you choose the inside interface and click **Edit** button on the right side of the window, you are presented with the interface name you are currently configuring the protocols for, followed by the protocols POP3S, IMAP4S, and SMTPS, which you can enable. You are also given the option to allow the protocol configuration in this window to be applied to all interfaces on the ASA device (internal, external, and so on).

In the Default Servers pane, you can specify the IP addresses used for each service, followed by the individual protocol ports the ASA will be listening on for sessions. You can also limit nonauthenticated sessions for denial-of-service (DoS) attack mitigation purposes. By default, the session limit for nonauthenticated clients is 20 per protocol. The port numbers used for each service are as listed:

- **POP3S:** 995

- **IMAP4S:** 993

- **SMTP:** 988

Depending on your own environment, you might want to leave the configured ports at their default values shown here or modify them to use custom values for additional security purposes.

The next three tabs are used to define the AAA and the location of the connecting user's username/password within each protocol's control data. You can select the authentication, authorization, and accounting (AAA) group you want to use for per-protocol authentication reasons; the type of authentication in place per protocol (for example, AAA, piggyback HTTPS, or certificates); and the delimiter to aid the ASA in locating the username, password, and server within each protocol's control data. For example, your mail client or server implementation might use the following format for a username, password, and server string: user:pass@server. Using delimiters, you can tell the ASA the separating character (: @ /) between each authentication field.

Although not as familiar, piggyback HTTPS authentication is fairly simple to understand. With piggyback HTTPS authentication, the user needs to have the SSL VPN session established before connecting to the email server. If SSL VPN and email username/passwords are different, it needs to provide both, separated by the VPN delimiter configured, VPN credentials being used only to verify that the SSL VPN session is established for the respective user. If the session is not established, user access to the email server is not allowed.

Due to a Simple Mail Transfer Protocol (SMTP) flaw, if piggyback authentication is used with SMTP, an attacker can potentially send spam email messages using any name and using a legitimate user account. It happens when the attacker spoofs the IP address and the

VPN name of the legitimate user. For this reason, consider using IMAP4 or POP3 for piggyback authentication or alternatively certificate authentication for SMTP.

## Internal HTTP and HTTPS Proxy

Internal HTTP and HTTPS proxy servers can be configured for clientless SSL VPN users to send their requests and receive responses through. If I am client1, and my proxy server and ASA are ASA1 and proxy1, respectively, the following happens with request and response data traveling from and to my browser through the SSL tunnel:

**client1 > ASA1 > proxy1 > Application Server > proxy1 > ASA1 > client1**

Security administrators and corporations usually configure and set all their internal clients' browser sessions to use an internal proxy server for authentication, accounting, and filtering services. By configuring the proxy server settings on the ASA device, you can maintain the corporate internal security policy on the user's company laptop/device when it is taken out of the office and connected to the SSL VPN.

You can configure the internal proxy servers on the ASA by navigating to **Configuration > Remote Access VPN > Clientless SSL VPN Access > Advanced > Proxies**.

In the Proxies pane, you have the option to select HTTP or HTTPS. When one is selected, the fields for the relevant configuration details appear automatically in the pane. For example, the fields described in Table 10-4 are available when you check the HTTP option.

**Table 10-4**  *HTTP/HTTPS Proxy Configuration Parameters*

| Field | Value |
| --- | --- |
| Proxy Server | Enter the internal proxy server name or IP address. |
| Port | Enter the port used by the proxy server to send requests to (default is 80 or 443 for HTTPS). |
| Exception Address List | An optional field allowing you to enter server names, IP addresses of fully qualified domain names (FQDN) that should be excluded from traffic sent to this proxy server (similar to a proxy bypass list). |
| User Name | Optional field if your proxy server requires authentication. |
| Password | Optional field if your proxy server requires authentication. |
| Use Proxy Auto-Config (PAC) File to Automatically Choose the Appropriate Proxy Server | Specify the URL to a predefined PAC file used for client browser autoconfiguration. |

# Troubleshooting Advanced Application Access

When troubleshooting application access through a clientless SSL VPN session, first make sure the user has established a connection between his or her device and the ASA. When you have confirmed that a connection exists or the problem the user is experiencing is not due to session establishment, you can troubleshoot application-specific settings, a process that can be divided into two categories:

■   Troubleshooting session establishment

■   Troubleshooting application access

For the purposes of this chapter, we focus only on troubleshooting application access. If you require further information when troubleshooting common VPN session-establishment errors, see the "Troubleshooting a Basic Clientless SSL VPN" section in Chapter 9.

## Troubleshooting Application Access

When troubleshooting application access through an SSL VPN solution, the key is to locate where the error might be occurring. Your aim should be to narrow down the particular errors being experienced to one of the following areas (where possible):

■   Client

■   SSL VPN appliance

■   Server

## Client

When troubleshooting application access, most problems you will encounter result from misconfiguration or a missing component on the client device. For example, when troubleshooting application access through port forwarding, you must do the following before a successful client application session can function:

**Step 1.**    Confirm the application required is installed locally.

**Step 2.**    Confirm the local application settings are set to the correct values required for the port forwarding configuration.

**Step 3.**    Ensure the local port configured within the port forwarding applet is unique and not in use on the client. (You can use the netstat tool available for Windows, Linux, and Mac to complete these step.)

**Step 4.**    Confirm the user has local administrative rights.

When troubleshooting problems that may exist on the client device, the following points are also important to consider:

■   **Client Java Runtime Environment (JRE):** Java errors are also a common problem encountered on a client device. More often than not, clients will have an outdated copy of the JRE installed for their particular browser. If they cannot see the Java icon on their taskbar, there is every possibility that Java has not been installed. In this case, try downloading and installing the latest copy of Java specific to the operating system from www.java.com.

- **Client antivirus or firewall:** The client might have a local antivirus or firewall running that may need an exception or rule addition to allow for the Java and application components to run correctly.

- **Client browser settings:** Windows Vista (or, in general, Microsoft IE) users, for example, might need to add the URL used for the SSL VPN to their trusted sites, if not automatically prompted, to allow for application/local machine access through the browser interface. Also, check for pop-up blockers that might be running, which may prevent additional windows needed by the SSL VPN from opening correctly.

## ASA/VPN Termination Appliance

When troubleshooting a problem with the ASA, you must first determine

- Is the problem affecting all users trying to use the service?

- Is the error occurring only with a particular service?

- Is another administrator currently modifying the device's configuration or are you in the middle of a scheduled change window?

If you can narrow down the problem to a particular service, it is significantly easier to delve deeper into the problem and troubleshoot specific issues that might be the cause. For example:

- If using a client-server plug-in list, have the plug-in destination server and details been configured correctly?

- Check any attributes configured for the particular plug-in. Are they valid attributes? Do they have the wrong values? Are there known client-side errors with particular attributes?

You can find most of the plug-in attribute information in the help file specific to the particular plug-in.

If you have deployed smart tunnels to allow your users a connection to an internal server, check the settings between the remote client device and the smart tunnel configuration:

- Does the client have the application locally installed?

- Can they verify (using Windows Task Manager) that the process name matches that configured within the smart tunnel entry?

- Is the user connecting from a Mac or Windows machine, and is the tunnel configuration available for that OS?

- Can you verify that the local path to the destination program is the same as that configured within the ASA if the user is connecting from a Mac?

In addition to the various file parameters, paths, and ASDM configuration elements of the troubleshooting process you can check, you can view the current VPN and SSL VPN specific tunnel/session information from the CLI using the following commands:

- **show vpn-sessiondb detail**

- **show vpn-sessiondb detail webvpn**

Example 10-3 shows the output presented after running **show vpn-sessiondb detail** on the ASA.

**Example 10-3**    show vpn-sessiondb detail *Output*

```
CCNP# show vpn-sessiondb detail
-------------------------------------------------------------------------
VPN Session Summary
-------------------------------------------------------------------------
 Active : Cumulative : Peak Concur : Inactive
 --------------------------------------------------
AnyConnect Client : 0 : 40 : 2 : 0
 SSL/TLS/DTLS : 0 : 40 : 2 : 0
Clientless VPN : 0 : 19 : 1
 Browser : 0 : 19 : 1
IKEv1 IPsec/L2TP IPsec : 0 : 9 : 1
-------------------------------------------------------------------------
Total Active and Inactive : 0 Total Cumulative : 68
Device Total VPN Capacity : 25
Device Load : 0%
-------------------------------------------------------------------------


-------------------------------------------------------------------------
Tunnels Summary
-------------------------------------------------------------------------
 Active : Cumulative : Peak Concurrent
 --------------------------------------------
IKEv1 : 0 : 9 : 1
IPsecOverUDP : 0 : 9 : 1
Clientless : 0 : 23 : 2
AnyConnect-Parent : 0 : 36 : 2
SSL-Tunnel : 0 : 38 : 2
DTLS-Tunnel : 0 : 10 : 1
-------------------------------------------------------------------------
Totals : 0 : 125
-------------------------------------------------------------------------
```

## Application/Web Server

Unless the application you are allowing access to through the SSL VPN is a new implementation, application-access errors caused by the server hosting them might not be the cause. For example, unless created specifically for the SSL VPN environment, applications running on internal servers are usually also made available to internal users on the LAN, and any errors with a server are commonly reported to the appropriate team.

However, if you are the administrator of the server or have the appropriate access to troubleshoot, it is worth going through the basics. For example, does the server have power? Is the application available on the server? Can you make a connection internally? Check using tools such as ping, netstat, and so on for the correct availability or open ports.

If the application is hosted on a remote server or the ASA device is in a remote facility, you move into the area of troubleshooting connectivity between the ASA's site and application server's site. For example, is there a site-to-site VPN between them? Is it currently established, and can you pass traffic through it?

The troubleshooting discussion here is far from exhaustive. However, this information should give you a reasonable starting point to locate the cause of the problem and move on to more specific troubleshooting techniques for the particular area/configuration.

# Exam Preparation Tasks

As mentioned in the section "How to Use This Book" in the Introduction, you have a couple of choices for exam preparation: the memory tables in Appendix C, Chapter 23, "Final Exam Preparation," and the exam simulation questions on the CD-ROM.

## Review All Key Topics

Review the most important topics in the chapter, noted with the Key Topic icon in the outer margin of the page. Table 10-5 lists a reference of these key topics and the page numbers on which each is found.

**Table 10-5**   *Key Topics*

| Key Topic Element | Description | Page |
|---|---|---|
| Table | Access methods | 341 |
| Bulleted List | Client-server plug-ins | 350 |
| Topic | Configuring client-server plug-in access using the ASDM | 350 |
| Bulleted List | Smart tunnel implementation methods | 358 |
| Topic | Configuring smart tunnel access using the ASDM | 359 |
| Bulleted List | Email proxy common service ports | 364 |
| Topic | Troubleshooting application access | 366 |

## Complete Tables and Lists from Memory

Print a copy of Appendix C, "Memory Tables" (found on the CD), or at least the section for this chapter, and complete the tables and lists from memory. Appendix D, "Memory Tables Answer Key," also on the CD, includes completed tables and lists to check your work.

## Define Key Terms

Define the following key terms from this chapter, and check your answers in the glossary:

email proxy, plug-in, port forwarding applet, proxy auto-configuration file (PAC), proxy server, smart tunnel list

This chapter covers the following subjects:

- **Basic Portal Layout Configuration:** In this section, we discuss how to successfully customize the look and feel of your SSL VPN portal area to match that of your corporate or custom scheme. We also discuss the procedures required to successfully implement a different user experience/environment based on the group policies assigned to them.

- **Outside-the-Box Portal Customization:** In this section, we review advanced customization options.

- **Portal Localization:** In this section, we discuss the localization features you have when deploying an SSL VPN to a global or geographically dispersed user base.

- **Getting Portal Help:** In this section, we review the tasks required to obtain and install the portal help files for our remote users.

- **AnyConnect Portal Integration:** In this section, we review the integration of the SSL VPN portal with AnyConnect SSL VPN client.

- **Clientless SSL VPN Advanced Authentication:** In this section, we provide a brief review of the various authentication options that are available for your SSL VPN, along with digital certificates, AAA, and so on.

- **Using an External and Internal CA for Clientless Access:** In this section, we provide a brief overview of CA options, local and remote CA configuration options, and certificate mappings.

- **Clientless VPN Double Authentication:** In this section, we review the implementation of the double authentication process using token or certificate authentication, along with AD or local user accounts.

- **Deploying Clientless SSL VPN Single Sign-On:** In this section, we discuss the SSO process and provide an overview of the SiteMinder and SAML configuration requirements.

- **Troubleshooting SSO and PKI Integration:** In this section, we discuss the various steps available for the troubleshooting of SSO and PKI common problems you may encounter.

## CHAPTER 11

# Customizing the Clientless Portal

An important part of deploying a Secure Sockets Layer (SSL) virtual private network (VPN) solution is customization. After all, businesses often have a logo or color scheme used throughout the company on various pieces of documentation, assets, or even their buildings. It is not only pleasing to the eye and important for the company image to be able to extend this scheme to your VPN portal, but it can also help your remote users to identify who they are connected to and the portal resources they require quickly. An international business may choose to deploy the same VPN solution to staff worldwide. To simplify the deployment, we have the option of selecting localization features and custom help files.

The available authentication schemes are also important to understand and deploy. Unlike the traditional IPsec VPN deployment, SSL VPNs are designed with ubiquitous access in mind, so you need to be especially wary when designing and implementing a suitable authentication scheme. Many corporations choose to implement a two-factor authentication scheme using one-time passwords or certificates and a user's familiar corporate logon details.

## "Do I Know This Already?" Quiz

The "Do I Know This Already?" quiz helps you determine your level of knowledge on this chapter's topics before you begin. Table 11-1 details the major topics discussed in this chapter and their corresponding quiz sections.

**Table 11-1**  *"Do I Know This Already?" Section-to-Question Mapping*

| Foundation Topics Section | Questions |
| --- | --- |
| Clientless SSL VPN Advanced Authentication | 1 |
| Using and External and Internal CA for Clientless Access | 2 |
| Basic Portal Layout Configuration | 3–6 |

1. When configuring an authentication scheme, which three options are available?

   a. Static passwords

   b. Digital certificates

   c. LDAP

   d. Double authentication

2. When preparing to deploy a PKI authentication scheme, which two methods are available for CA use?

   a. Internal

   b. Inside

   c. External

   d. Microsoft ISA

   e. Outside

3. What are the available methods for portal customization? (Choose two.)

   a. CLI

   b. ASDM

   c. Full manual configuration

   d. SNMP

4. By default, which four languages are available for localization?

   a. EN - English

   b. DE - German

   c. FR - French

   d. RU - Russian

   e. JA - Japanese

5. In which ASDM location can you enable the onscreen keyboard?

   a. Configuration > Remote Access VPN > Clientless SSL VPN Access > Portal > Customization

   b. Configuration > Remote Access VPN > Clientless SSL VPN Access > Advanced

   c. Configuration > Remote Access VPN > Clientless SSL VPN Access > Portal > Web Contents

   d. Monitoring > VPN > Sessions

6. Which of the following sections are not available panels for portal customization?

   a. Title panel

   b. Toolbar

   c. Applications

   d. Bookmarks

# Foundation Topics

## Basic Portal Layout Configuration

When given the task of customizing our SSL VPN portal, you have two options available to carry out the task:

■   ASDM basic customization

■   Full manual customization

We review the process of carrying out a basic customization task using the Adaptive Security Device Manager (ASDM). Later, in the "Outside the Box Portal Configuration" section, we review the available methods of manual customization.

The customization option you choose will depend on the level of granularity and customization you require. Customization through the ASDM is based on predefined areas and sections of the profile pages that you can easily modify by changing the color and text and uploading and inserting logos. If you choose to fully customize the portal without the use of the ASDM, you can upload your own HTML files and code.

Regardless of the customization method chosen, you can modify the look and feel of the following pages for your users:

**Key Topic**

■   Logon page

■   Portal page

■   Logout page

When complete, your customization settings can be applied directly to a user, group, or connection profile, allowing you to modify the user environment based on the current location or access method.

The customization tasks within the ASDM are carried out using the Customization pane at **Configure > Remote Access VPN > Clientless SSL VPN Access > Portal > Customization**. Within this window, you can view a list of the currently configured customization objects and immediately start the customization process by enabling the onscreen keyboard.

The onscreen keyboard is a Java-based keyboard that can be used to prevent potential keylogger software access to any credentials the user might be required to enter. This is an especially useful feature if your remote users are known to operate from publicly available computers or devices that you have no control over. The onscreen keyboard can be configured to pop up either during the logon page or each time a user is required to provide authentication parameters (in Username and Password fields) when working within the SSL VPN portal. You have the following options within the ASDM Customization pane to control the behavior of the keyboard:

■   Do Not Show the OnScreen Keyboard (Default)

■   Show Only for the Logon Page

■   Show for All Portal Pages Requiring Authentication

If you find a large number of remote users are accessing your SSL VPN from publicly available devices or home computers that your organization cannot effectively control, it is recommended to enable the onscreen keyboard for at least the logon page.

When approaching the portal configuration, you can either create a new customization object or modify the default DfltCustomization object that is currently applied to all pages. Regardless of which option you choose, you can preview any changes you make before you apply them to the device.

For this task, you carry out the configuration of a new customization object. Start by clicking **Add**. In the Add Customization Object window, you must first give the object a name. For our sample configuration, we have entered the name CorpCustom1, as shown in Figure 11-1.

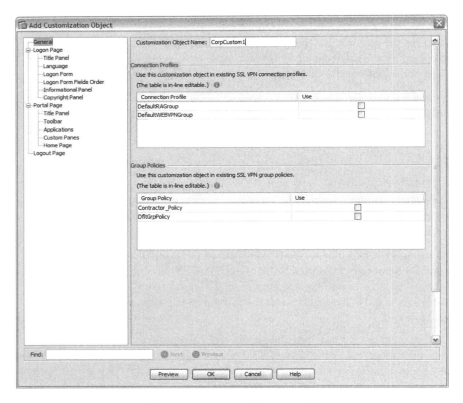

**Figure 11-1**    *ASDM Add Customization Object Window*

In addition to entering a name, you can use the General pane to select either the connection profile or the group policy to which you want to apply the customization object. Note that although not available from this pane, portal customization can be applied also at the user level. Within your own environment, you might have many connection profiles or group policies available. However, for this particular example, we are going to apply our object to the DfltGrpPolicy group policy object.

After entering a name for your customization object and selecting the group policy object to which you want it applied, you can review the customization options available within the remaining areas of the Add Customization Object window.

Three main categories are available for customization within the Add Customization Object window:

- Logon page

- Portal page

- Logout page

## Logon Page Customization

When fully expanded, the following sections exist for logon page customization (although this might vary depending on the Adaptive Security Appliance [ASA] running image and ASDM running image you're using):

- Title Panel

- Language

- Logon Form

- Logon Form Fields Order

- Informational Panel

- Copyright Panel

On the main logon page pane, you can select the option to either customize the logon page using the parameters you enter into the ASDM and indirectly modify predefined components or select a custom logon page that you might have created offline. The advanced configuration of the portal is discussed later in the "Out of the Box Configuration" section. Within this pane, you can also enter a new title you want displayed in the browser title bar instead of the default title SSL VPN Service. Corporations often enter the company name here for easy identification by the user.

When selecting the Title panel section, the first option you are presented with is to remove the title panel from the logon page or leave the default of it being visible to users. This is the panel shown in Figure 11-2. You can also change the default Cisco logo to our own logo or image, change the default SSL VPN Service text to our own title or welcome message, and modify the font weight, size, and color, and background color.

The Language pane allows us to enable the optional language selector so that users can choose their preference from a drop-down list. By default, this option is disabled. To enable it, just check the box. The ASA typically has four languages preinstalled:

- **EN:** English (current default fallback language if errors occur)

- **JA:** Japanese

- **FR:** French

- **RU:** Russian

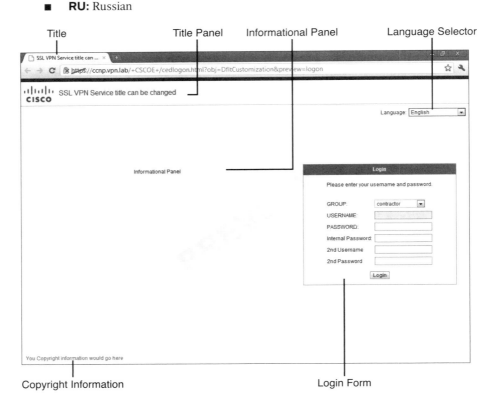

**Figure 11-2**   *SSL VPN Logon Page Customization Areas*

In the Logon Form pane, you can customize the color, title, informational message, and, most important, the form fields and their descriptions. This can be useful if you use a nonstandard authentication scheme or secondary/double authentication scheme, allowing you to rename the fields (that is, password can become pin number). You can order the fields in the next pane, Logon Form Fields Order, by moving the location of the available form fields displayed up or down in relation to each other.

The Informational Panel pane, disabled by default, allows you to add a new panel either to the left or right of our logon form. It is used to enter your own information message or logon instructions to our users. You are also given the option to add an image to the panel and change its position to be above or below our message text.

Finally, the Copyright panel, disabled by default, allows you to enter any copyright information you want displayed on the page. This is positioned toward the bottom left of the page, as shown in Figure 11-2.

## Portal Page Customization

When fully expanded, the following sections exist for portal page customization:

- Title panel

- Toolbar

- Applications

- Custom panes

- Home page

On the main portal pane, you can enter a new title that we want displayed in the browser title bar, rather than the default title SSL VPN Service.

On the Title panel, you have the same options as the Logon Title panel. For example, you can remove the title panel from the logon page or leave it visible to users (the default), change the default Cisco logo to that of our own logo or image, change the default SSL VPN Service text to our own title or message, and choose the font weight, size, and color, and background color.

In the Toolbar pane, you can change the default labels/text for the address bar, Browse button, or Logout prompt. You can even choose to remove the toolbar altogether.

The Applications pane lists the applications available through the SSL VPN (that is, VNC, RDP, and so on) and allows you to remove them, change their names, or hide/disable the navigation panel entirely.

The Custom Panes option allows you to add your own columns and rows to the default portal layout. You can then choose to add your custom content to the new columns and rows. For example (shown in Figure 11-3), we have added an RSS feed.

Finally, in the Home Page pane, you can add your own intranet or other page link to the portal for user access.

## Logout Page Customization

For the logout page, shown in Figure 11-4, you can customize all text color, size, and weight. You can also modify the title bar to match the design of your logon and portal pages. You can also remove the Logon button and add or change the text displayed to users on successfully logging out of the SSL VPN.

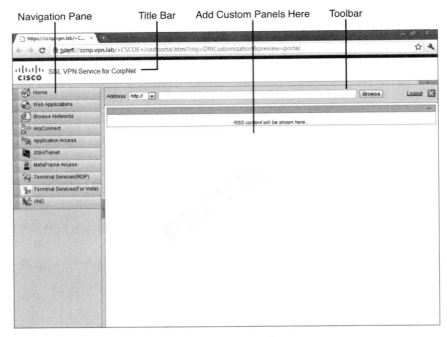

**Figure 11-3** *Portal Pane Customization Panels*

**Figure 11-4** *SSL VPN Logout Page*

# Outside-the-Box Portal Configuration

As mentioned earlier, you are given two options for customization of the SSL VPN logon, portal, and logout pages: either using the ASDM's predefined pages or uploading your own pages that we have created offline.

Commonly, companies upload their own versions of SSL VPN portal pages for one of these reasons:

- To publish a detailed design to match those of an existing intranet, website, or theme.

- They require changes to pages where predefined elements might not been implemented or available.

- A large number of changes have been made, and it is easier to edit the pages offline instead of using the ASDM.

Regardless of why you upload your own versions of the portal pages, it is important to at least know how to do so for the purposes of the exam.

Using the ASDM, you can upload custom content (images, pages, and so on) for later use by navigating to **Configuration > Remote Access VPN > Clientless SSL VPN Access > Portal > Web Contents**. You can then view and edit your content and upload by clicking the **Import** button. When choosing to import new content, you are given the option of uploading from the local machine or a remote FTP, HTTP, or TFTP server, or using a file on the ASA's flash that you might have uploaded earlier. You can also specify whether the content you upload can be viewed with or without having to first be authenticated by logging on to the SSL VPN.

# Portal Localization

As mentioned earlier, it is possible to allow users to determine the portal localization based on their selection of a language from the language drop-down menu.

The ASA manages the task of localization with the use of translation tables. These tables hold the localization information or language editable fields required for each pane or section of the portal pages, client/server plug-ins, Secure Desktop, and AnyConnect client page. Translation tables are then grouped by application or location into functional domains. There are currently eleven translation domains configured that can be edited. Each by default has the following preconfigured languages:

- **EN:** English

- **JA:** Japanese

- **FR:** French

- **RU:** Russian

Table 11-2 lists the available translation domains and their functional areas or translation tables that are affected when translation is applied to the domain.

**Table 11-2** *ASA Translation Domains and Functional Areas*

| Translation Domain | Functional Areas |
|---|---|
| AnyConnect | Messages/text displayed on the AnyConnect user interface |
| CSD | Messages/text displayed for the Cisco Secure Desktop (CSD) |
| Customization | All customizable and default messages on the portal, logon, and logout pages |
| Keepout | "Access denied" messages |
| PortForwarder | Port forwarding user/informational messages |
| url-list | URL bookmarks configured within bookmark lists and displayed on the portal page |
| Webvpn | All noncustomizable Layer 7, AAA, and portal messages |
| Plugin-ica | Citrix ICA plug-in messages |
| Plugin-rdp | RDP (Remote Desktop Protocol) messages |
| Plugin-telnet/ plugin-ssh | SSH or Telnet plug-in messages |
| Plugin-vnc | VNC plug-in messages |

As you might have noticed, each plug-in, when installed, includes its own translation file and therefore has its own translation domain. The translation domains that apply to ASA portal content have their own translation files that are included with the ASA software.

To configure localization for a connection, group, or user, you must complete three steps:

1. Create a new translation table or edit an existing one.
2. Enable the language selection drop-down menu.
3. Add to or edit the available languages displayed within the language selection menu.

Before additional languages can be entered into the drop-down list for user selection, you must first create the translation table for the language you want to import.

You can create a new translation table by one of these methods:

■ Use one of the available template files from the bottom of the Language Localization pane.

■ Edit one of the existing translation table files by first exporting it, editing the file offline, and importing it again.

■ Add a new table within the ASDM using the buttons from the top of the pane, as shown in Figure 11-5.

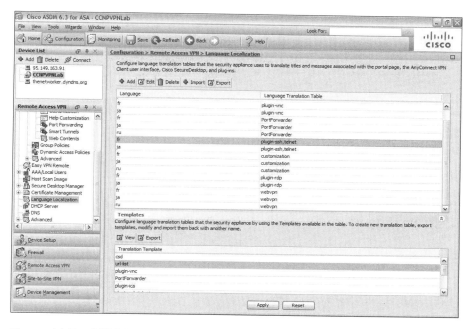

**Figure 11-5**  *ASDM Language Localization Pane*

The translation tables are saved in the form of an XML file and include the following fields:

- **Msgid:** English translation of the message

- **Msgstr:** The translated version of the message

Figure 11-6 displays the Edit Language Localization Entry window, to give you an idea of the translation table file format.

To edit the translation table, click the **Save to File** button and choose where you want to save the file on your computer. When it has finished downloading, open the file within a text editor and proceed to change the translation file for the language you require. When you finish editing the file, click the **Import** button within the Language Localization pane, and then select the language you are importing (from the available list), the translation domain into which you're importing the translation table, and the path to the file.

As shown in Figure 11-7, we are importing a custom translation table entry for the German language. We started by selecting **DE** (the language or country code) from the drop-down list, and we then selected the domain we are importing the translation table into. For this example, we selected the customization domain and entered the local path to our file. With this information entered, we then click the **Import Now** button. After a few seconds, the import process should complete, and a message indicating that a successful import has taken place will display.

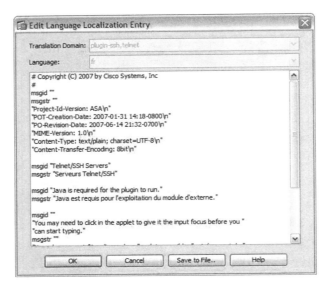

**Figure 11-6** *ASDM Edit Translation Table Entry*

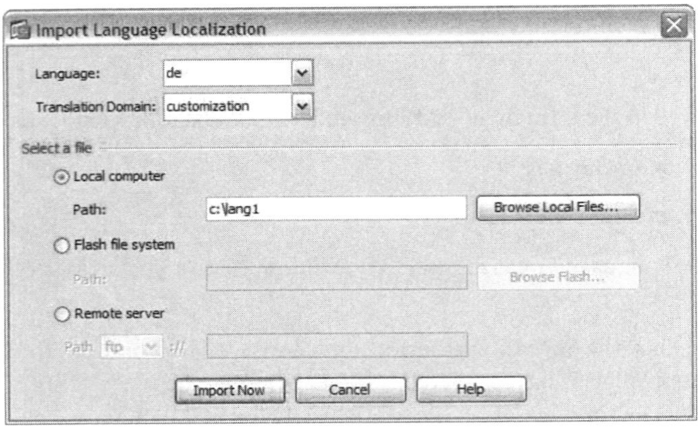

**Figure 11-7** *Import New Translation Table Entry*

After importing a new translation table entry, you can continue the localization process and allow your users to select this language by enabling the Language Selection pane.

As discussed earlier, you can enable the Language Selection pane by navigating to **Configuration > Remote Access VPN > Clientless SSL VPN Access > Portal > Customization**. Here you select your customization object from the list (for this example, we are editing the default object) and click **Edit**.

Within the Edit Customization Object window that opens, open the **Logon Page > Language** area, where you are first presented with an option box that allows you to turn the Language Selection pane on or off (which is deselected by default).

With your Language Selection pane on, you can add to the available languages list by clicking **Add**. When the Add Language window appears, select your new language from the drop-down list, and then enter a name for the language that will display to the remote user. When complete, click **OK**.

Figure 11-8 displays the configuration required to add the German language entry for the sample translation table created earlier.

Now that you have added the required language(s) to the list of those available to the remote user, you can verify the changes have been made successfully by navigating to your SSL VPN logon page. As shown in the right corner of Figure 11-9, you can now select a language (and see the imported language on the list).

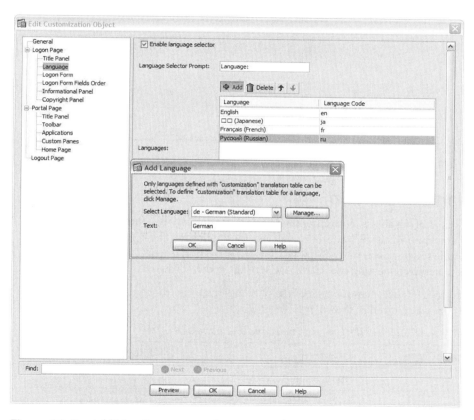

**Figure 11-8**  *Add New Language to Language Selection Pane*

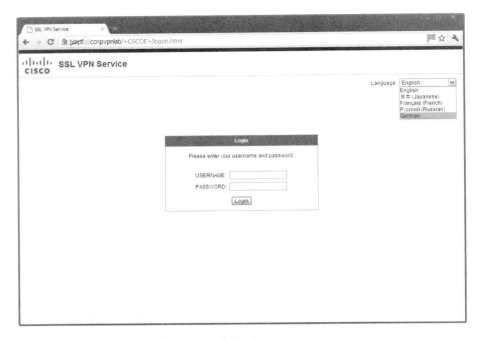

**Figure 11-9**  *Logon Page Language Selection*

# Getting Portal Help

As well as being able to customize the SSL VPN portal design, content, and localization, you can import help files in other languages for your users. The help file language that is available to your users for each application or for the portal areas can be customized, based on the connecting users language settings in their browser.

Cisco supplies help files for each of the plug-ins and portal panels that require user input. They are categorized as shown in Table 11-3.

**Table 11-3**  *ASA Help File Types, Panels, and Filenames*

| Application Type | Panel | Filename |
| --- | --- | --- |
| Standard | Application Access | App-access-hlp.inc |
| Standard | Browse Networks | File-access-hlp.inc |
| Standard | AnyConnect Client | Net-access-hlp.inc |
| Standard | Web Access | Web-access-hlp.inc |
| Plug-in | Citrix Metaframe Access | Ica-hlp.inc |
| Plug-in | Terminal Services | Rdp-hlp.inc |
| Plug-in | Telnet/SSH Services | Ssh/telnet-hlp.inc |
| Plug-in | VNC Connections | Vnc-hlp.inc |

New or custom help files can be uploaded to your ASA for use on each of the panels or application types shown in Table 11-3. It is also possible to download the currently installed help files for modification offline and then re-import them when you have finished your customization.

Existing help files can be downloaded by entering the direct path to them within your browser after first logging on to the SSL VPN. When prompted, click the **Save As** button to save them to a location on your computer. For example, to download the app-access-hlp.inc file, you enter the following URL into a web browser (after first logging on):

https://ASA_IP_Address/+CSCOE+/help/en/app-access-hlp.inc or
https://ASA_FQDN/+CSCOE+/help/en/app-access-hlp.inc

The /en/ directory used within the URL would need to be changed, depending on the language files you want to edit or import. For example, to edit the French language version of a file, the /en/ must be changed to /fr/.

# AnyConnect Portal Integration

The Cisco AnyConnect client can be integrated into your existing SSL VPN portal, and a new application button will become available to remote users within the portal navigation pane.

When the AnyConnect link is clicked by a remote user, one of two actions can occur (depending on whether the remote user already has the client software installed):

- If installed, the AnyConnect software launches and proceeds to connect.

- If not installed, the user is presented with the Cisco AnyConnect VPN Client WebLaunch page, and the software attempts to verify the platform/OS the remote user is connecting from, any ActiveX support, and whether Java has been installed and is active. When the verification procedures have completed, the AnyConnect client attempts to install on the remote user's machine. If the installation is unsuccessful, the remote user is presented with a link to the installation file (if previously uploaded to the ASA) for his OS for manual installation. However, if the installation is successful, the software proceeds to connect.

After the AnyConnect client has been enabled on the interface and within the relevant group policy, the application button appears in the user's portal window. You can customize the logon behavior of the SSL VPN either per user or per group within the group policy settings for automatic download and installation of the AnyConnect client, or to be directed to the portal home page (default) if, for example, the AnyConnect client is not required by the user.

In the Edit Internal Group Policy window, shown in Figure 11-10, you can set a Post Logon Setting, giving users a choice over the action that occurs after they have successfully logged on and a timeout if they cannot make up their mind within a certain number of seconds, or leaving the option at the default of not allowing users to choose. What happens, whether the user can choose or not, depends on the Post Logon Selection you choose. By default, the option is selected to redirect remote users to the SSL VPN portal home page. However, you can change this to enable the automatic download and install the AnyConnect client.

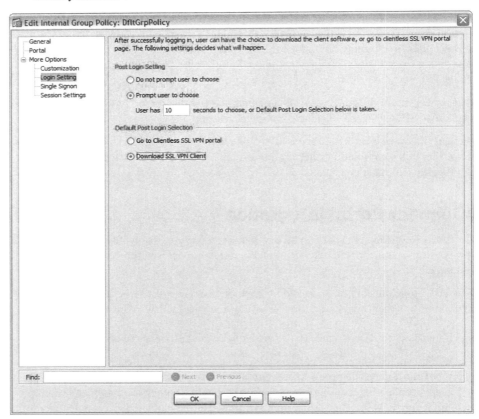

**Figure 11-10**  *SSL VPN Portal Post-Login Parameters*

The action you decide to take ultimately depends on your remote user's environment. Because you can change the previously discussed options based on the user's own account settings or assigned group policy object, you have a great deal of scope when it comes to customizing the environment and type of connection the user is presented upon logon.

With the AnyConnect WebLaunch enabled, as shown in Figure 11-11, when remote users click the AnyConnect link from the navigation panel and click the Start AnyConnect button on the following portal page, they are presented with the WebLaunch portal, where they are guided through the client installation and connection processes.

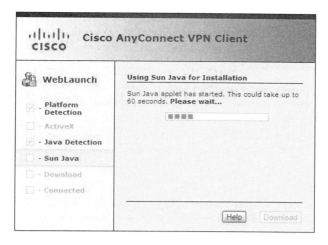

**Figure 11-11** *Cisco AnyConnect VPN Client WebLaunch*

# Clientless SSL VPN Advanced Authentication

So far, as we have progressed through the earlier chapters of this book, we have discussed the various integration and deployment options you can make available to remote users. In most cases, the basic authentication schemes that can be deployed (for example, local authentication) may be a choice for a small business or satellite deployment. However, when you start to consider larger deployment scenarios, or being able to extend or build on your existing internal security policies, you require more advanced authentication options. With options such as LDAP, RADIUS, and TACACS+ authentication, you can integrate the authentication process with Public Key Infrastructure (PKI) and introduce the use of certificates for client authentication and server (ASA) authentication. You can also deploy a double authentication scenario if, for example, you have opted for use of RSA tokens or any other token solution that integrates via RADIUS, such as CryptoCard.

Furthermore, if you have extended your internal authentication scheme to your SSL VPN deployment, you can allow your users to log on using their existing internal credentials. With the use of Single Sign-On (SSO), users might never need to be prompted again for their credentials when accessing internal resources through the SSL VPN.

When you approach the subject of securing your SSL VPN deployment, it is important to note that authentication occurs as a two-stage process:

■ **Server authentication:** The ASA is authenticated by the remote user/client.

■ **Client authentication:** The remote user is authenticated by the ASA.

Server authentication during SSL VPN tunnel negotiation typically occurs with the use of digital certificates, and depending on the deployment scenario, you have three choices when it comes to configuring them:

■ Self-signed certificate

■ Public certificate authority (CA)-issued certificate

■ Internal CA-issued certificate

Self-signed certificates are recommended only for small or test deployments. One of the main disadvantages of using them is that remote users receive a certificate warning from a browser whenever they navigate to the SSL VPN pages. This, unfortunately, does not inspire confidence when trying to assure users of your identity.

Certificates issued by a public CA are typically installed with all public-facing SSL deployment scenarios, whether they are placed on a web server for secure entry of user details or an SSL VPN deployment for securing user access to company resources. Remote users can verify the authenticity of the server they are connecting to, because the majority of commercial CA root server certificates are usually installed on and trusted by client browsers.

The third option you have is to use an internal, company-owned CA and requiring employees to have the CA certificate imported into their local devices Trusted Root Certificate Authorities. This solves the warning problem for them, but not for outside users (for example, contractors or consultants who do not have the CA certificate installed).

The following are typical authentication options for client authentication:

- **Static passwords:** Static passwords can be used either with local user authentication on the ASA or via an external authentication, authorization, and accounting (AAA) server. Generally, static passwords are used for temporary authentication procedures. However, an SSL VPN deployment scenario could offer different access based on the user authentication. For example, static passwords would be used for guest or low-level access, and a more robust authentication scheme could be in place for higher-level or application access.

- **Digital certificates:** As you have seen in our discussion of the SSL/TLS tunnel negotiation between server and host, the client can also send its own certificate file to the server for purposes of client authentication. You have two options for the deployment of client certificate authentication: using the local CA server on the ASA or the certificates issued by a remote (public/commercial) CA server.

- **Double authentication:** Through the use of double authentication, you can ensure that remote users are given a more robust way of being authenticated. Typical uses of double authentication are client certificates and static passwords, or OTP (one-time password) (for example, RSA tokens and static passwords).

When planning to deploy an advanced authentication scheme, consider these three things:

- **Security:** What level of security do you require for your SSL VPN deployment? Are you considering multiple security levels or different groups? How secure is the authentication scheme you are planning to deploy, and what security benefits do you derive by deploying such a scheme?

- **Scalability:** What special factors must you consider when deploying your security scheme? Will every client require a certificate file or OTP token? How will the certificates or tokens be distributed? Will users be able to choose or change their static passwords? Will the introduction of multiple authentication methods cause deployment problems with a geographically dispersed user base?

- **Integration:** Can the authentication scheme be integrated with existing authentication methods or database types?

These points are not, of course, an exhaustive list. However, they indicate the type of information you might require when planning for a new authentication scheme.

# Using an External and Internal CA for Clientless Access

As you have already seen, during the SSL tunnel negotiation phases, the server sends the client a copy of its own digital certificate for authentication purposes. During the same process, the server can also request a copy of the client certificate file, and the client would then, if it has one available, send a copy of its own certificate so that the server can verify the client.

You are given two options when deploying certificates for the purposes of client authentication: You can either use the internal CA that can be enabled and configured on the ASA to generate your own certificate files and distribute them to clients, or you can use an external/commercial CA for certificate generation.

The main advantage of using an external CA over an internal CA is the widespread public root CA support from browser manufacturers can mean a certificate purchased from them will be trusted by a client browser and not display any warning errors to remote users trying to connect.

When you enable the ASA as a local CA server, you lose the failover functionality. You cannot deploy both local CA and failover at the same time, although, for example, in IOS boxes, PKI HA is supported.

Table 11-4 lists some of the common advantages and disadvantages of using an internal CA or an external CA.

**Table 11-4** *Advantages and Disadvantages of Internal or External CAs*

| Application/Task | External CA | Internal CA |
| --- | --- | --- |
| Certificate generation and deployment | The responsibility of certificate generation and deployment is down to the external CA. | The responsibility of certificate generation and deployment is down to the internal CA. |
| Certificate trust | External certificates are automatically trusted by common Internet browsers and generally trusted by partners/guests. | Internal certificates are generally not accepted by partners or guests to a company. Browser trust depends on internal root CA certificates being imported. |
| Cost | A cost is usually involved per certificate file generated unless bulk deployment packages are available. | There is no cost involved with certificate generation when using an internal CA. |

**Table 11-4**   *Advantages and Disadvantages of Internal or External CAs*

| Application/Task | External CA | Internal CA |
| --- | --- | --- |
| Scalability/future growth | External CAs are usually worldwide trusted authorities with all necessary resources in place to manage multiple or a larger number of certificate requests. | Cost might be an issue when expanding an internal CA deployment because any future servers might have to be purchased. New root CA certificates must be imported in all client browsers. |
| Available resources | External CAs are experts in their field and employ key staff for the purpose of certificate generation/management. | In-house staff might need to undergo training, or new staff might need to be employed because of a rise in workload (depending on the size of your deployment). |
| Manageability/ flexibility | We are limited to what we can or cannot achieve or the speed of deployment with external CAs because they are a separate company in their own right. | We have the flexibility with internal CA deployment to be able to scale up or down to meet our needs at our own pace in our own timeframe. |
| Integration | External CAs are usually only used for certificate generation and authentication and cannot be integrated into other internal applications or deployments | Internal CAs, depending on your deployment, may be used for other purposes or integration with third-party databases or products (for example, Microsoft's Active Directory). |

Whether you choose to deploy an internal or external CA depends your own deployment situation and environment, because each method has its advantages. When deploying certificates for client authentication in a small business, cost might be the overriding factor, and an external CA solution is not as feasible to implement as an internal CA. However, for enterprise deployments, you generally use an external CA because of the overall scale and deployment overhead involved with issuing certificates to each of your users.

External CAs, certificate signing request (CSR) generation, and certificate import using the ASDM were all discussed in Chapter 9, "Deploying a Clientless VPN Solution," in the "Basic Clientless SSL VPN Solution" section. Review that section for information about external CAs if required.

The ASA enables us to configure its own internal CA for the use of certificate deployment and authentication. To start using the internal CA, you must first enter the information specific to your deployment (for example, the key sizes you want used, the issuer name, and certificate lifetime). All these options and more can be found by navigating to **Configure > Remote Access VPN > Certificate Management > Local Certificate Authority > CA Server**, as shown in Figure 11-12.

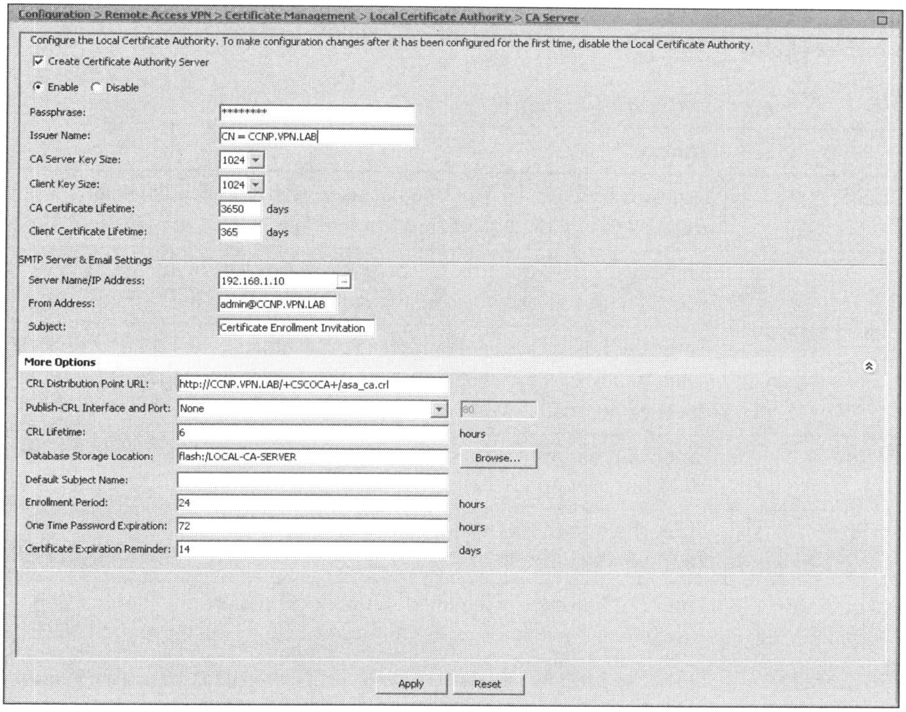

**Figure 11-12**   *ASDM CA Server Configuration Pane*

To start configuring the server, you must first create it. You do this by checking the **Create Certificate Authority Server** check box toward the top of the CA Server pane.

You can edit all the parameters below this option box. Check the **Enable** radio button and click **Apply** to push configuration to the ASA and bring the CA server to life. Once the CA server has been activated, configuration parameters related strictly to the CA (SMTP server address is an exception, for example) are no longer configurable/editable and are dimmed to minimize any production environment impact during server operation. To modify CA parameters, you must first remove the CA from the system by clicking the newly created **Delete Certificate Authority Server** button.

**Note:**   Before the CA server can be enabled, you must enter a passphrase in the CA Server pane. The passphrase can be any password of your choice, but must be a minimum of eight characters in length. Also note that *enabled* here means activated and is not related to the Enable radio button but to the Apply button. To configure the passphrase, you must click **Enable**.

Table 11-5 lists the available fields you can modify to customize the local CA server for your own deployment.

**Table 11-5**  *CA Server Configuration Fields and Values*

| Field | Value |
| --- | --- |
| Enable/Disable | Disabled by default. Must be in this state if you need to make changes to any of the configuration values. |
| Passphrase | Mandatory field used to enter the password for the local CA keystore. The password must be 7 characters in length. |
| Issuer Name | Enter the hostname or IP address you want to be used for the issuer value in any certificates generated. By default, this is the ASA IP address or hostname (where configured). |
| CA Server Key Size | Enter the minimum key size the server will use (512, 768, 1024, or 2048 bits, default 1024). |
| Client Key Size | Enter the minimum key size used by clients (512, 768, 1024, or 2048 bits, default 1024). |
| CA Certificate Lifetime | Enter the lifetime of the local CA root certificate file (default 3650 days). |
| Client Certificate Lifetime | Enter the lifetime of issued client certificate files (default 365 days). |
| SMTP Server Name/IP Address | Enter the name or IP address of the SMTP server used to send Enrollment invitations through. |
| From Address | Enter the email address you want to use to send enrollment invitations from (default admin@asa-domain-name). |
| Subject | Enter the subject for enrollment certificate emails (default Certificate Enrollment Invitation). |
| CRL Distribution Point URL | Default http://ASA Hostname/+CSCOCA+/asa_ca.crl. |
| Publish-CRL Interface and Port | Enter the interface and port to use for the CRL publishing. |
| CRL Lifetime | Enter the lifetime for the CRL (default 6 hours). |
| Database Storage Location | Enter the path and filename of the database stored on the ASA flash. |
| Default Subject Name | Enter the default subject name to be used in issued certificates and appended to the user name. |
| Enrollment Period | Enter the time period for enrollment purposes (default 24 hours). |

**Table 11-5**   *CA Server Configuration Fields and Values*

| Field | Value |
|---|---|
| One-Time Password Expiration | Default 72 hours. |
| Certificate Expiration Reminder | Enter the value in days used to mark the reminder value for emails sent to certificate owners about expiration deadlines (default 14 days). |

After you have created the CA server, the option to create it is removed, and instead a button to delete the CA server is placed at the bottom of the pane. If you select the option to delete the server, all configurations, key pairs, and certificate files generated by the server are removed, and you cannot re-create or import them.

After enabling the CA server, you can add users to the database for certificate creation. In the ASDM, navigate to **Configuration > Remote Access VPN > Certificate Management > Local Certificate Authority > Manage User Database**. If you navigate to this pane without first enabling the CA server, the pane disappears and you cannot view/edit/add/delete users from the database.

By default, the local CA database contains no users, so you need to add some. You do this by clicking the **Add** button. In the new Add User window, enter the following details:

- **Username:** The user's name.

- **Email ID:** The user's email address where the enrollment invitation will be sent.

- **Subject (DN String):** The String of user information that will be entered into the Subject field of the certificate. The available attributes we can add are as follows:
  - Common Name (CN)
  - Department (OU)
  - Company name (O)
  - Country (C)
  - State (St)
  - Location (L)
  - Email address (EA)

- **Allow Enrollment:** Allows users to fulfill their certificate enrollment online without administrator manual intervention (selected by default).

When you have entered all the information you have available, click the **Add User** button. To allow the user to complete the process, select the **Email OTP** button within the Manage User Database pane, and an enrollment invitation will be sent to the email address you entered into the user's Email ID field, along with an OTP for authentication.

If you check your user's mailbox (or he or she might prefer to check it instead), the user should have received an email with the subject Reminder: Certificate Enrollment Invitation and the following text in the body of the email (see Example 11-1).

**Example 11-1**    *Enrollment Invitation - Instructions Received*

```
You have been granted access to enroll for a certificate.

The credentials below can be used to obtain your certificate.
  Username: employee1
  One-time Password: B3DC9569C6572F1A
  Enrollment is allowed until: 07:50:36 UTC Mon Nov 22 2010


NOTE: The one-time password is also used as the passphrase to unlock the
certificate file.


Please visit the following site to obtain your certificate:

https://<asa hostname>/+CSCOCA+/enroll.html


You may be asked to verify the fingerprint/thumbprint of the CA certificate
during installation of the certificates. The fingerprint/thumbprint
should be:
    MD5: F39470FE 493EC3C1 210416D2 42F4B0CB
  SHA1: A8BC57F3 CBE92751 961DEFF6 2A09AA5F 58E72A80
```

Now your users can click the link included in the email and visit it to download their password. To confirm their identity, they must first enter their username and the OTP received in the email, as shown in Figure 11-13.

After entering their credentials, users click the **Submit** button and are automatically asked whether they want to save or open the certificate file. If users choose the option to Save the certificate file, and are on a device running a Microsoft Windows OS, they need to double-click the certificate file to start the Certificate Import Wizard, and then follow the wizard through each step until the certificate has been imported successfully. If your users are running MAC OS X, they can add a new certificate file to an existing or new keychain by using the KeyChain Access program located in **Applications > Utilities**. To import your new certificate using Ubuntu, copy the saved certificate file to the /etc/ssl/certs directory. However, if your users are running another version of Linux, consult the relevant documentation for that OS.

After issuing certificates to your users, you can manage them within the Manage User Certificates pane of the ASDM, found by navigating to **Configuration > Remote Access VPN > Certificate Management > Local Certificate Authority > Manage User Certificates**. As you can see in Figure 11-14, our example user is now listed in the pane along with his certificate's serial number and the current status (revoked or not revoked).

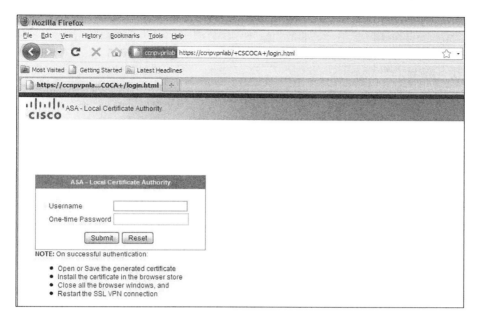

**Figure 11-13**   *Local CA Web Certificate Download Portal*

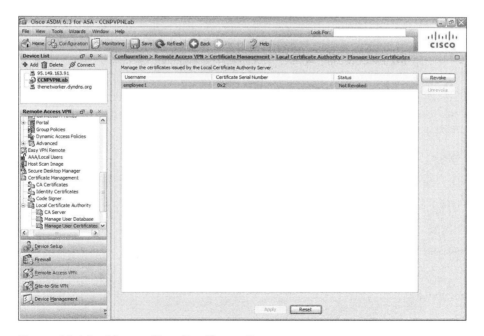

**Figure 11-14**   *Manage User Certificates Pane*

You are also given two options: You can revoke the user certificate if, for example, the user has left the company or if the certificate data becomes invalid (for example, a department or name changes and the user needs a new certificate to be generated). You can also unrevoke the certificate, allowing the user to use it for authentication procedures once again. The option of being able to revoke and unrevoke a certificate gives you a great deal of flexibility. For example, if you rehire the same contractors or temporary staff, each time they arrive you can unrevoke the certificate, and when they leave at the end of the contract, you can revoke the certificate until needed again.

As you saw during the user account creation stage, you can enter certificate-specific attributes (for example, the department and company name). When using client certificates for authentication, the ASA can use this information to determine the connection profile assigned to the user on connecting.

This behavior is achieved via certificate to connection profile maps. You can configure the available certificate maps by navigating to **Configure > Remote Access VPN > Advanced > Certificate to SSL VPN Connection Profile Maps**. This pane has two sections where we define the settings of our certificate maps:

- Certificate to Connection Profile Maps
- Mapping Criteria

To configure mapping criteria, you must first create a certificate matching rule under the Certificate to Connection Profile Maps section. You can either select the default match rule if no other exists or create a new one. When creating a new match rule, enter a name for it and give the rule a priority between 1 and 65535, with higher-priority (lower-value) rules chosen first in the list. After entering the priority, select the connection profile you want this rule, when matched, to apply to. The potential connection profiles are presented as a drop-down list.

You can now add the rules used to specify the matching certificate criteria that will be used in the matching rule we created. In the Matching Rule Criterion window, you can select fields within the certificate, including the following:

- **CN:** Common name
- **O:** Company
- **OU:** Department
- **EA:** Email address
- **SN:** Surname

After selecting the certificate field you want to match, select an operand. These include the following:

- Equals
- Contains
- Does Not Contain
- Does Not Equal

Now enter a value you want your rule to look for in the specified field and click **OK**. Your finished rule will have a form similar to the following:

OU - Equals - Sales

You can define as many rules as you need within your matching rule. However, all rules must match (or not, in the case of Does Not operands) before the selected connection profile will be applied.

# Clientless SSL VPN Double Authentication

As mentioned earlier, many options are available when considering the deployment of a new authentication scheme for your users. One of the most common deployment scenarios for an SSL VPN solution is the use of a double authentication scheme.

The ASA can support up to three simultaneous authentication methods that must all succeed before a user is successfully authenticated. It is, however, more common for corporations to only use two authentication methods when accessing internal resources remotely.

The three authentication methods available are as follows:

- AAA authentication server (primary authentication stage)

- AAA authentication server (secondary authentication stage)

- Client certificate authentication (can be used alongside either the primary or secondary authentication stages or on its own)

As you saw earlier in the "Using an External or Internal CA for Certificate Authentication" section, during the user account creation phase in the local CA user database, you entered the information into the account form that would be used for certificate generation. The username is automatically entered into the CN field of the client certificate and can be retrieved by the ASA to automatically populate the Username field on the logon page.

You can also specify whether the username entered for the first authentication stage will be used for the second. In this case, the ASA enables you to indicate this and automatically copies the username and removes the second Username field from the logon page.

To configure the use of double authentication, you must first decide whether you are using AAA server groups, client certificates, or both. You then need to enable the authentication methods required per connection profile, as shown toward the top of Figure 11-15.

For the purposes of this example, we configure both double AAA and certificate authentication by first navigating to **Configure > Remote Access VPN > Clientless SSL VPN Access > Connection Profiles > Connection Profile**. In the Basic pane of the Edit Clientless SSL VPN Connection Profile window, select the **Both** option. Note that if you are using, for example, Microsoft Active Directory credentials and an RSA SecurID token for authentication purposes, you would select only AAA after creating the relevant AAA groups. We have also selected our AAA server group below the method selection buttons to indicate we will be using the LOCAL authentication database.

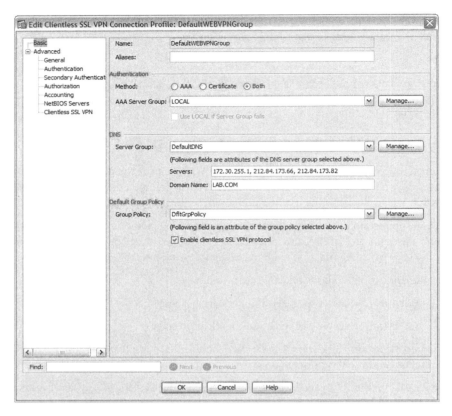

**Figure 11-15**   *Enable Your Chosen Authentication Methods*

Now you can select the stage in the authentication process at which the defined methods will be used. You also review manipulating the received data to minimize the amount of information the user might have to enter into the logon form. Typically, you use a different AAA server group per authentication stage. However, for the purposes of this example, and shown in Figure 11-16, we have selected the LOCAL group for each stage (primary and secondary). See Figure 11-17 for the reference to the LOCAL group as the secondary authentication stage.

As shown in Figure 11-16, we have now moved to the Authentication pane of the Advanced menu for the connection profile settings. In this pane, you can select interface-specific AAA server groups. (This is not required for the configuration to work because we have selected the LOCAL AAA server group in the last stage regardless of the interface. However, we have selected an internal/inside and external/outside server group for illustration purposes.)

Within this pane, you can also select the option to prefill the username logon field with the username stored in the client certificate. You can choose a primary and secondary field that will be checked (in order of priority) for the existence of a username. You can then select the option of using the entire DN certificate field contents as the username or upload and assign a custom script you might have created for username extraction. You can also choose to hide the username field from the user.

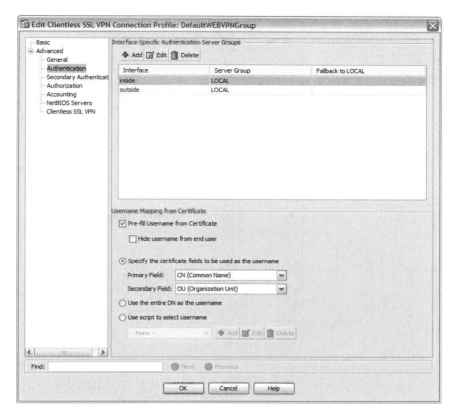

**Figure 11-16**  *Primary Authentication Parameters and Options*

For this example, we have chosen the option to prefill the username from the certificate field and have told the ASA to first look at the CN field of the certificate for the username. If it does not exist, the ASA looks at the OU field instead.

You can now configure the secondary authentication method. Begin by selecting the **Secondary Authentication** option from the Advanced menu on the left of the window, as shown in Figure 11-17.

Select the secondary authentication server from the drop-down list. Optionally, you can click the **Manage** button if you need to create a new server group. If you had selected a group other than LOCAL, the Use LOCAL If Server Group Fails check box becomes available as a fallback option.

For this example, we selected **Use Primary Username** because we are using LOCAL authentication twice. By us selecting this option, the ASA also hides the secondary Username field from the SSL VPN logon page, because there is no longer any need for it. Choosing to use the username dims the certificate options at the bottom of the pane. The options in this case are the same as those given in the earlier Authentication pane.

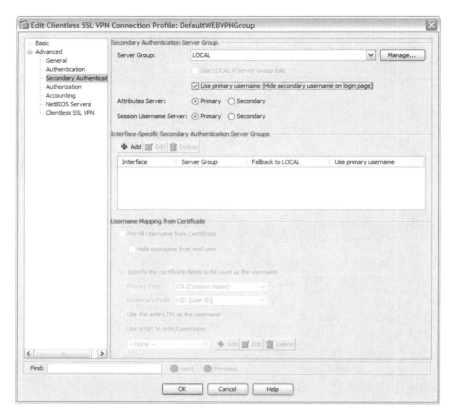

**Figure 11-17** *Secondary Authentication Parameters and Options*

Below the Secondary Authentication Server Group configuration, you can select interface-specific AAA server groups. If you choose to use a RADIUS server or the LOCAL authentication database for external-facing users and an Active Directory server for internal users, for example, you can do so using this section.

As a result of our sample configuration, users are now required to have a client certificate installed and must enter a primary and secondary password. The Username field, as shown in Figure 11-18, has already been prefilled with the one found within the certificate files CN field. If the client does not have the necessary client certificate installed, they will be presented with a link that takes them to the ASA's local CA portal page to download one (shown in the earlier section covering internal CA installation and configuration).

**Figure 11-18**   *SSL VPN Logon Page with Double Authentication and Prefilled Username*

# Deploying Clientless SSL VPN Single Sign-On

Single Sign-On (SSO) can remove the need for users to have to reenter their authentication credentials when accessing internal resources after first logging on successfully to the SSL VPN. SSO is achieved by the ASA taking the role of an authentication proxy between the remote user and the server. After users submit their credentials at the SSL VPN logon page, the ASA sends the details onto the authentication/application server, and if authenticated successfully, the server returns a cookie. The ASA then uses this cookie for all future authentication parameters that the client may be prompted for when accessing resources.

The ASA device supports two SSO server types: CA SiteMinder and SAML post. However, it can also support the use of HTTP Forms POST, HTTP Basic, NTLMv1, or FTP protocols defined for simplified auto-sign-on purposes if no internal SSO scheme currently exists.

SSO servers are defined within the **Configure > Remote Access VPN > Clientless SSL VPN Access > Advanced > Single Signon Servers** pane of the ASDM. To enter the details of a new SSO server, click **Add**, and within the Add SSO Server window, enter a name for the server and select the authentication type (either SiteMinder or SAML Post).

If we select SiteMinder, you can enter the details described in Table 11-6.

**Table 11-6** *Available Fields for SSO SiteMinder Server Configuration*

| Field | Purpose |
| --- | --- |
| URL | Select HTTP or HTTPS and enter the full URL to the authentication server. |
| Secret Key | Enter the password used to authenticate your requests from the ASA to the server entered in the earlier field. |
| Maximum Retries | Enter the number of times the ASA should attempt to send its authentication requests to the server (default 3). |
| Request Time-out | Enter the amount of time in seconds the ASA should wait between communication retries with your SSO server (default 5). |

If you choose SAML Post as your authentication type, you are presented with the fields described in Table 11-7.

**Table 11-7** *Available Fields for SSO SAML Post Server Configuration*

| Field | Purpose |
| --- | --- |
| Assertion URL | Select HTTP or HTTPS and enter the full URL to the authentication server. |
| Issuer | Enter the full name of the authentication issuer. |
| Certificate | Select from a drop-down list a certificate to use for authentication of the ASA device on issuing requests to the server. |
| Maximum Retries | Enter the number of times the ASA should attempt to send its authentication requests to the server (default 3). |
| Request Time-out | Enter the amount of time in seconds the ASA should wait between communication retries with your SSO server (default 5). |

After defining an SSO server, you can then choose to enforce configured parameters for either a single user or a group of users within a group policy.

For this example, we review the group policy settings by navigating to **Configuration > Remote Access VPN > Clientless SSL VPN Access > Group Policies** and editing the default group policy object.

In the Edit Internal Group Policy window on the menu on the left, expand **More Options > Single Signon.** By default, the group policy settings inherit the SSO settings of the Dflt-GrpPolicy policy. (Remember, we are editing the default policy.) However, if you need to specify an SSO server for an administrator-added group policy, deselect the **Inherit** option and select an earlier defined SSO server from the list of those available within the drop-down menu.

If you do not have an already defined SSO policy in your organization, you can configure auto-sign-on servers that allow you to specify the use of HTTP, NTLMv1, or FTP server credentials.

Start by unchecking the Inherit box (this option is available only on manually administrator added group policies) and clicking **Add**. The Add Auto Signon Entry window, displayed in Figure 11-19, appears.

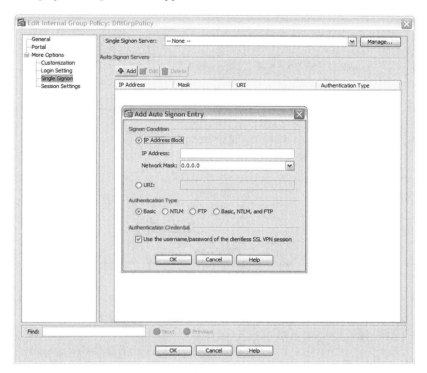

**Figure 11-19** *Group Policy Add Auto Signon Entry*

You can specify a range of server IP addresses or a single server IP address or enter the URI to a server for which you want auto sign-on to occur. You can also specify the type of authentication the server will be using: Basic (HTTP), NTLM, FTP, or all three.

At the bottom of the window, you can choose whether the ASA should use the authentication credentials entered by the user at the logon page for auto sign-on. If you uncheck the box, you can specify a different username or password by either manually entering the credentials or by using POST variables either taken from other areas of the ASA configuration or other fields available to the user on the logon page. The available macros for username substitution are as listed in Table 11-8.

**Table 11-8** *Available Macros for Username Entry*

| Macro | Purpose |
| --- | --- |
| CSCO_WEBVPN_USERNAME | Username from the SSL VPN logon page. |
| CSCO_WEBVPN_CONNECTION_PROFILE | Connection profile alias. |
| CSCO_WEBVPN_MACRO1 | Radius LDAP VSA attribute. |
| CSCO_WEBVPN_MACRO2 | Radius LDAP VSA attribute. |

**Table 11-8** *Available Macros for Username Entry*

| Macro | Purpose |
|---|---|
| CSCO_WEBVPN_PRIMARY_USERNAME | Only available if double authentication has been configured. This is the primary username from the logon page. |
| CSCO_WEBVPN_SECONDARY_USERNAME | Only available if double authentication has been configured. This is the secondary username from the logon page. |

If authentication is taking place on a domain, the username macros here can be specified within the form **<domain>\<macro name>**.

You can also specify user passwords by macro substitution using one of the available macros listed in Table 11-9.

**Table 11-9** *Available Macros for Password Entry*

| Macro | Purpose |
|---|---|
| CSCO_WEBVPN_PASSWORD | Password from the SSL VPN logon page. |
| CSCO_WEBVPN_INTERNAL_PASSWORD | Internal password from the SSL VPN logon page. |
| CSCO_WEBVPN_PRIMARY_PASSWORD | Only available if double authentication has been configured. This is the primary password from the logon page. |
| CSCO_WEBVPN_SECONDARY_PASSWORD | Only available if double authentication has been configured. This is the secondary password from the logon page. |

When you have finished entering in the available information for auto-sign-on or SSO server definition within the user's group policy, click **OK** to complete the operation.

**Note:** It is important that auto sign-on be enabled only for those servers that require authentication and use the authentication parameters saved by the ASA for the user connection. For example, if the ASA is sending NTLM authentication parameters to the internal server SERVER1 that has been configured to use HTTP POST for authentication purposes, authentication will fail, and the user will not be prompted for other credentials.

## Troubleshooting PKI and SSO Integration

As with any authentication scheme, problems can occur. Although the majority of them result from user or server error or configuration, some problems may derive from ASA configuration. And although troubleshooting client certificate authentication might involve external certificate and PKI component issues, we focus here on problems caused by the configuration of the ASA's internal CA.

As you configure and manage the CA, you are responsible for the issuing, revocation, validity, and overall deployment of client certificates used for authentication purposes. One upside to owning or managing the internal CA is that you can troubleshoot any certificate problems directly on the device without the hassles of working through a third party.

Five common points to client certificate authentication can be used for troubleshooting purposes. These points, outlined in Figure 11-20, help determine the root cause of any particular problem.

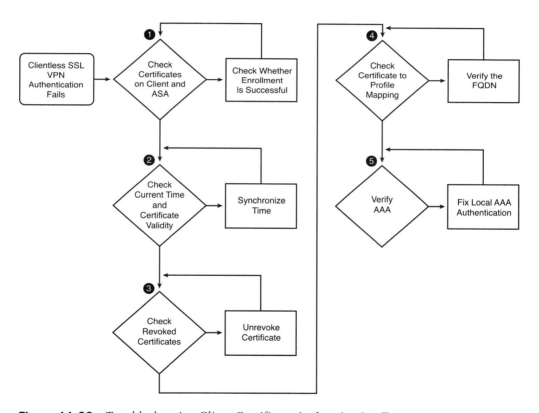

**Figure 11-20**   *Troubleshooting Client Certificate Authentication Errors*

**Step 1.**    First check that the certificates have been installed correctly on the client. After all, the client, if a certificate is not present, will receive a "certificate not found" error on the web page and a link to the appropriate page for them to be able to download one.

**Step 2.**   After you have confirmed that the certificate has been successfully installed on the client machine, check the validity of the installed certificate. If the certificate is being reported as invalid, check the validity time stored within the certificate, and also check to make sure the client and ASA clocks are synchronized.

**Step 3.**   Confirm that the certificate has not been revoked. If it has been (and depending on the reason), you might need to unrevoke it from within the certificate management pane, found at **Configuration > Remote Access VPN > Certificate Management > Local Certificate Authority > Manage User Certificates.**

**Step 4.**   If the user is receiving an incorrect connection profile, this might be due to an incorrectly configured certificate to connection profile map. Check for configured certificate mapping rules within **Configure > Remote Access VPN > Advanced > Certificate to SSL VPN Connection Profile Maps.**

**Step 5.**   Check AAA configuration on the server to determine whether certificate-based authentication parameters are configured to provide details or work alongside AAA authentication.

The vast majority of certificate errors can be explained by either a client-side error message or by information shown on the available log entries, or by viewing the real-time monitor available at **Monitor > Logging > Real-Time Log Viewer.**

When troubleshooting, it is common to choose the default debugging level, because this will give us the largest amount of information available about a device. However, it is important to bear in mind that enabling debugging in a production environment can impact performance for all users connected to and through the device.

Figure 11-21 displays the debugging results we have collected when testing a user connection that has been reported to be working incorrectly when accessing the SSL VPN device. From the sample debugging output shown, we can determine that the certificate has been reported as invalid because of the certificate's validity time lapsing. If, after checking the certificate file, you determine that the date shown is still valid, check the date and time settings on the ASA.

In a similar way to certificates, SSO errors can result from user error or server configuration or the ASA. Because we are now moving the process of authentication between the ASA and server and removing the user from the equation, we can rule out the majority of user errors (if successful logon authentication has first taken place for the SSL VPN) and troubleshoot the cause on the ASA device or server.

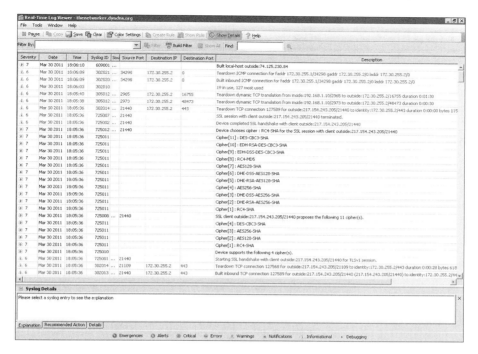

**Figure 11-21**  *Real-Time Log Viewer Debugging Output*

One of the most common reasons for SSO errors is the organization using different authentication schemes internally. As discussed earlier, after authentication has been completed successfully by the ASA and server on behalf of the user, the server returns an authentication cookie, which is stored by the ASA for future server authentication requests. If the server that requires authentication has a different username or password for the user or uses a different authentication protocol than that is configured for the SSO profile on the ASA, however, authentication fails. The user is not prompted for additional logon details.

The same can also occur if a server has not been set up to authenticate users accessing its resources. The ASA continues to wait for an authentication request to occur, resulting in the client being unable to access the requested resources.

Within **Monitor > Logging > Real-Time Log Viewer,** you can find most of the information you need to solve the problem. In addition, the server failing the authentication attempts usually holds valuable logging information that can aid your troubleshooting process.

## Exam Preparation Tasks

As mentioned in the section "How to Use This Book" in the Introduction, you have a couple of choices for exam preparation: the memory tables in Appendix C, Chapter 23, "Final Exam Preparation," and the exam simulation questions on the CD-ROM.

## Review All Key Topics

Review the most important topics in the chapter, noted with the Key Topic icon in the outer margin of the page. Table 11-10 lists a reference of these key topics and the page numbers on which each is found.

**Table 11-10**   *Key Topics*

| Key Topic Element | Description | Page |
|---|---|---|
| Topic | Customization areas | 375 |
| Table | Translation domains and functional areas | 382 |
| Table | Help customization | 386 |
| Bulleted List | Client authentication types | 390 |
| Topic | SSL VPN double authentication | 399 |
| Topic | SSO server types | 403 |
| Step List | Internal CA troubleshooting | 407 |

## Complete Tables and Lists from Memory

Print a copy of Appendix C, "Memory Tables" (found on the CD), or at least the section for this chapter, and complete the tables and lists from memory. Appendix D, "Memory Tables Answer Key," also on the CD, includes completed tables and lists to check your work.

## Define Key Terms

Define the following key terms from this chapter and check your answers in the glossary:

Single Sign-On (SSO), Certificate authority (CA), Public Key Infrastructure (PKI), Macro substitution

This chapter covers the following subjects:

■ **Configuration Procedures, Deployment Strategies, and Information Gathering:** In this section, we discuss the information required for a basic DAP deployment and the additional user local AAA and endpoint attributes available.

■ **DAP Record Aggregation:** In this section, we review the configuration procedures outlined in earlier sections and discuss the differences between policy configuration and deployment for local and remote users.

■ **Troubleshooting DAP Deployment:** In this section, we review how to troubleshoot errors you might encounter following DAP deployment.

## CHAPTER 12

# Advanced Authorization Using Dynamic Access Policies

In previous chapters, we reviewed the customization and deployment of a clientless Secure Sockets Layer virtual private network (SSL VPN) to users via group policy objects as a container to store the available resource, application, and customization attributes. We then discussed the assignment of group policy objects directly to users or connection objects.

Dynamic Access Policies (DAP) provide a higher level of granularity when assigning object access to users or groups through the matching of specific authentication, authorization, and accounting (AAA) attributes and endpoint attributes (for example, the existence of particular local files or Registry settings). DAP is not restricted to just clientless SSL VPN. It can be applied to all remote-access VPN connection types. Most important, DAP policy evaluation is enabled by default starting with ASA Version 8.0.

In this chapter, we also look at the available Adaptive Security Device Manager (ASDM) and command-line interface (CLI) methods used for troubleshooting and verification purposes.

## "Do I Know This Already?" Quiz

The "Do I Know This Already?" quiz helps you determine your level of knowledge on this chapter's topics before you begin. Table 12-1 details the major topics discussed in this chapter and their corresponding quiz sections.

**Table 12-1**  *"Do I Know This Already?" Section-to-Question Mapping*

| Foundation Topics Section | Questions |
| --- | --- |
| Configuration Procedures, Deployment Strategies, and Information Gathering | 1, 2, 4, 6, 7 |
| DAP Record Aggregation | 3 |
| Troubleshooting DAP Deployment | 5 |

1. Where within the ASDM would you create a new clientless SSL VPN DAP?

   a. Configuration > Remote Access VPN > Clientless SSL VPN Access > Dynamic Access Policies

   b. Configuration > Remote Access VPN > Network (Client) Access > Dynamic Access Policies

   c. Configuration > Remote Access VPN > Clientless SSL VPN Access > Group Policies

   d. Configuration > Remote Access VPN > Clientless SSL VPN Access > Advanced

2. Which of the following DAP endpoint attributes *do not* require installation of the CSD? (Choose all that apply.)

   a. Application

   b. Antivirus

   c. Antispyware

   d. NAC

   e. Policy

3. When aggregating the following DAP records SalesPolicy Priority = 20, EmployeePolicy = 30, which policy takes precedence?

   a. SalesPolicy

   b. EmployeePolicy

4. What is the priority of the default DAP policy?

   a. 100

   b. 65535

   c. 0

   d. 1

   e. 10

5. When troubleshooting DAP, which ASDM feature enables you to perform a test of your policy deployment?

   a. debug dap trace

   b. Real-Time Monitor

   c. Test Dynamic Access Policy Feature

   d. ASA

**6.** When examining the default DAP policy, which attributes can be modified?

   **a.** User AAA attributes

   **b.** Endpoint attributes

   **c.** CSD attributes

   **d.** None

**7.** You configure user attributes within a DAP, a group policy object, and directly to the user account. What is the correct order (assuming a match of the user attributes occurs) in which these objects are applied to a remote user?

   **a.** User > group policy > DAP

   **b.** DAP > user > group policy

   **c.** Group policy > user > DAP

   **d.** User > DAP > group policy

# Foundation Topics

# Configuration Procedures, Deployment Strategies, and Information Gathering

Often, when allowing remote user access to resources, you face the challenge of controlling their access rights based on their current environment. For instance, you might have a remote sales user who connects from his company laptop at home in the morning and then connects using the same account from an Internet cafe later in the day.

With growing demand for remote application and internal resource access, and the challenges you face with your remote users connecting from unsecure environments, you require a way to assess the potential for security risks and apply the relevant procedures and policies before the user can be granted the access they require.

Dynamic Access Policies help you to do so, by enabling you to check for certain parameters, either applied to the local user account or to the device they are connecting from. You can then base your policy decisions on the results obtained. This provides you with a much greater level of control and granularity over attribute assignment to your users than group policy objects can provide. For example, you now have the tools to find out which groups your users are assigned to and the connection type they can use based on their current location.

DAPs are a result of the merging of one or more configured Dynamic Access Records created during the user connection. Each Dynamic Access Record is given a name and priority between 0 and 2147483647 (with 0 being the lower priority) and holds a collection of attributes for user assignment, based on one or both of the following criteria:

■   User AAA attributes

■   Endpoint attributes (posture evaluation)

You can configure multiple user AAA attributes from one of the following three AAA attribute types:

■   Cisco

■   Lightweight Directory Access Protocol (LDAP)

■   RADIUS

You can match any, all, or none of these attributes.

Similar to user AAA attributes, multiple endpoint attributes can also be configured for policy-matching purposes. Checking endpoint attributes is also called posture evaluation. Typical posture evaluation attributes include user antivirus definition checks and local firewall settings inspection. However, the type of connection and whether Cisco Secure Desktop (CSD) has been configured and loaded can determine the type of attributes you might be able to check for.

A default policy of DfltAccessPolicy exists in the DAP list with a priority of 0, and the at-tributes to be assigned can be edited within this policy. However, you cannot add or edit user AAA and endpoint attributes for matching purposes because the policy is the last in the list and is applied to all users (who have not been previously matched in earlier poli-cies). In comparison with normal group policies, which are first configured by the admin-istrator at the global level but inactive until manually mapped to certain connection profiles or specific users, DAPs are configured only at the global level and become active immediately, applying to all the matched VPN sessions.

In addition to dynamically building a policy profile, the DAP overrides any default or as-signed user and group policies, based on the existence of the same attributes, because of the ASA's policy-inheritance behavior.

Policy inheritance enables you to apply attributes to users specifically or globally based on the inheritance model. Because DAPs provide the greatest level of control over user policy assignment, they are placed at the top of the policy inheritance "tree," and the lesser assignment methods are applied below, as shown in Figure 12-1.

Key
Topic

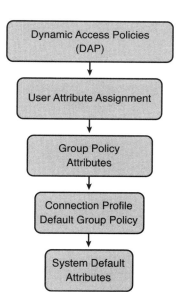

**Figure 12-1**   *User Attribute Assignment Hierarchy*

DAP attributes are assigned to a user first. Then, any user attributes are assigned after a successful login attempt. These are followed by group policy attributes, then the attrib-utes configured within the group policy assigned to the particular connection profile, and finally the system default settings.

If there are any unique attributes in the other attribute assignment methods below DAP, they are merged with the DAP attributes and applied to the user, allowing you, for exam-ple, to specify a global bookmark list or web access control list (ACL) applied to all users of a particular connection profile or group policy.

If there are conflicting attributes between assignment methods, however, the higher method in the hierarchy (or most specific) is applied to the user. For example, if port forwarding list A is defined in a DAP and a port forwarding list B is defined in a group policy, the DAP settings take precedence, and port forwarding list A is applied (but only if the user's AAA attributes and device settings are matched by the particular DAP).

The attributes configured within each DAP are stored in an Extensible Markup Language (XML) file on the ASA's flash, called dap.xml. The XML file can be downloaded from the ASA, modified offline, and re-uploaded. However, the recommended configuration method is through the ASDM, and for the purposes of the exam we focus on this method only. Because of the XML format, as in the case of creating bookmarks, CLI configuration for DAPs is not supported. Example 12-1 shows the basic dap.xml file contents.

**Example 12-1**    *Sample dap.xml file Contents*

```
<?xml version="1.0" encoding="UTF-8" standalone="yes"?>
<dapRecordList>
<dapRecord>
<dapName>
<value>DAP1</value>
</dapName>
<dapViewsRelation>
<value>and</value>
</dapViewsRelation>
<dapBasicView>
<dapSelection>
<dapPolicy>
<value>match-any</value>
</dapPolicy>
<attr>
<name>aaa.ldap.memberOf</name>
<value>sales</value>
<operation>EQ</operation>
<type>caseless</type>
</attr>
</dapSelection>
</dapBasicView>
</dapRecord>
</dapRecordList>
```

DAPs are configured using the ASDM within the Dynamic Access Policies window, found by navigating to **Configuration > Remote Access VPN > Clientless SSL VPN > Dynamic Access Policies**. By default, only the DfltAccessPolicy is listed in the window, as shown in Figure 12-2.

DAPs can be applied to both clientless SSL VPNs and client-based VPNs. However, in this chapter, we focus only on the configuration required for clientless SSL VPNs. If you are interested in learning more about DAP configuration when deploying client-based VPN access methods, you can find more information in the earlier chapters in the discussions about AnyConnect.

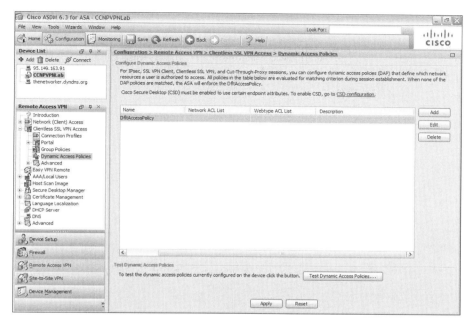

**Figure 12-2**  *ASDM Dynamic Access Policies Window*

To deploy a DAP, we must complete five steps:

**Step 1.**     Create a DAP.

**Step 2.**     Specify user AAA attributes for match purposes.

**Step 3.**     Specify endpoint attributes for match purposes.

**Step 4.**     Configure authorization parameters.

**Step 5.**     Configure authorization parameters for the default DAP.

### Create a DAP

In the Dynamic Access Policy window, click **Add**, and the Add Dynamic Access Policy dialog opens, as shown in Figure 12-3.

### Specify User AAA Attributes

As mentioned earlier, DAP complements native AAA authorization services by overriding them with a limited set of AAA attributes that can be used to select the appropriate DAP record or records used for the particular connection. You can match on user AAA attributes, endpoint attributes, or a combination of both.

To enter a user attribute, begin by clicking **Add** next to the User Attribute section of the window. Then select **Cisco**, **LDAP**, or **RADIUS** for the attribute type.

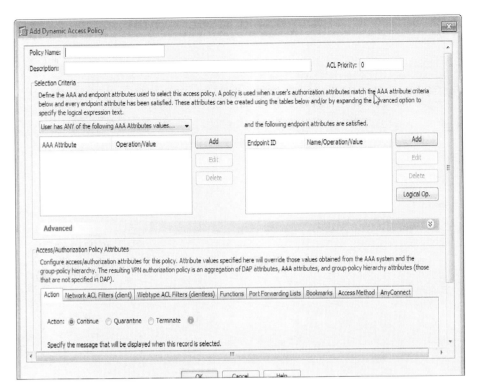

**Figure 12-3**    *Add Dynamic Policy Dialog*

When choosing to match against user Cisco AAA authorization attributes, you are given the following attribute types. Each can either be equal or not equal (= or !=) to the values you specify:

■    Group policy name

■    Assigned IP address

■    Connection profile

■    Username

If you choose to match against LDAP or RADIUS AAA attributes, however, you are given a much larger range of parameters to choose from. For example, you might use the LDAP attribute **memberOf** with a value of **engineering**, which enables you to match against any users who are members of the engineering Active Directory (AD) security group.

Because internal authorization policies often allow a user to be a member of multiple internal groups (for example, remote staff, engineering, or IT), you can also check whether the user belongs to multiple groups when evaluating user AAA attributes by creating multiple LDAP **memberOf** criteria, thus enhancing the level of granularity and your control over policy assignments.

## Specify Endpoint Attributes

To configure endpoint attributes as match criteria, click the **Add** button next to the Endpoint Attribute section of the window. At that point, the Add Endpoint Attribute dialog opens, as shown in Figure 12-4.

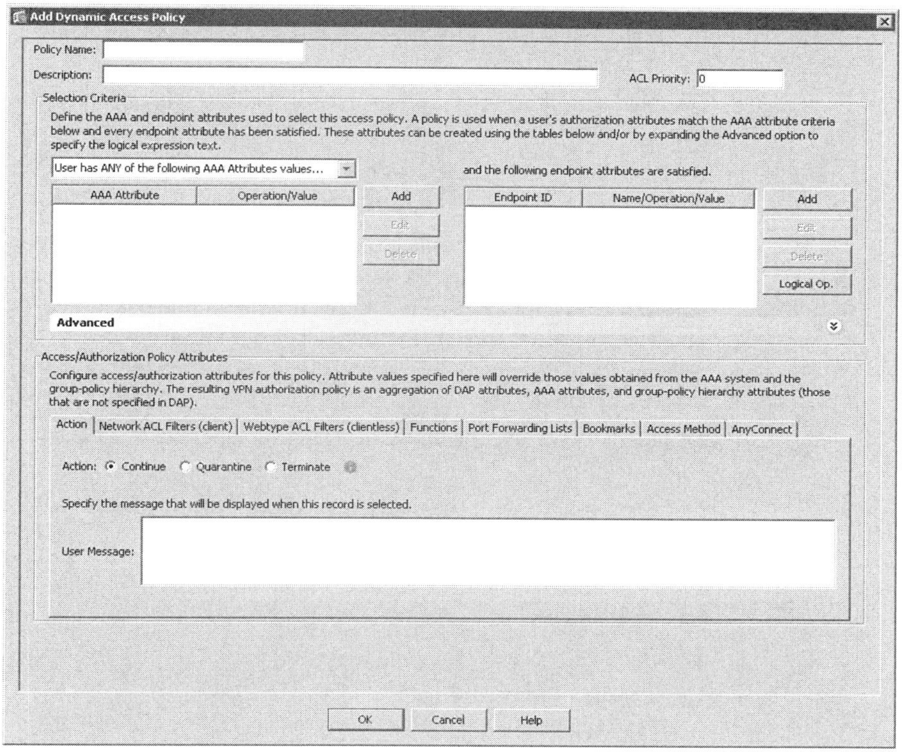

**Figure 12-4**   *DAP Add Endpoint Attribute Dialog*

A lot of what you can choose when selecting endpoint attribute criteria within this dialog depends on whether CSD is enabled. For the purposes of this example, we have enabled CSD (a process discussed in the next chapter). If CSD has not been enabled yet, however, and you try to select an endpoint attribute that requires it, the ASDM presents an error, and you cannot provide any configuration details for it.

Table 12-2 shows the available attributes and their configurable values and any DAP or NAC configuration requirements for a particular attribute.

**Table 12-2**  *DAP Endpoint Attribute Configuration Types and Values*

| Type | Values |
|------|--------|
| Anti-Spyware (CSD required) | **Enabled:** Enables you to check for the existence of local antispyware software. You can specify the vendor, enter a product description string to search for, check whether the installed version is less than, equal to, or greater than that required by your internal security policies (options <, <=, =, =>, >), and also check when the software was last updated. |
| | **Disabled:** Check whether antispyware is installed but currently disabled. |
| | **Not Installed:** Select if the match should occur if the remote device does not currently have any antispyware software installed. |
| Anti-Virus (CSD required) | **Enabled:** Enables you to check for the existence of local antivirus software. You can specify the vendor, enter a product description string to search for, check whether the installed version is less than, equal to, or greater than that required by your internal security policies (options <, <=, =, =>, >), and also check when the software was last updated. |
| | **Disabled:** Check whether antivirus is installed but currently disabled. |
| | **Not Installed:** Select if the match should occur if the remote device does not currently have any antivirus software installed. |
| Application | Check the connection type is either equal or not equal (=, !=) to one of the following; |
| | Clientless |
| | Cut-Through-Proxy |
| | AnyConnect |
| | IPsec |
| | L2TP |
| File (CSD required) | Check for the existence or nonexistence of a file on the connecting device by selecting one of the following: |
| | Exists |
| | Does Not Exist |
| | You then enter the filename into the Endpoint ID field. You can also check for the last update of the file within or greater than a number of days and check the checksum value of the file against that entered in the criteria. |

**Table 12-2**  *DAP Endpoint Attribute Configuration Types and Values*

| Type | Values |
| --- | --- |
| Device (CSD required) | Check for one or more host-specific values, as follows:<br>Host Name<br>Mac Address<br>Port Number<br>Privacy Protection (None/Cache Cleaner/CSD)<br>Version of Secure Desktop<br>Version of Endpoint Assessment |
| NAC | Check for the value equal or not equal (=, !=) to the current posture assessment reported by a Network Access Control (NAC) appliance or program. |
| Operating System (CSD required) | Check for the connecting device's operating system and current build and, where available, the patch level. Available operating systems are as follows:<br>iPhone iOS<br>Windows Vista<br>Windows XP<br>Windows Server 2003<br>Windows 7<br>Windows Mobile<br>Mac OS X<br>Linux |
| Personal Firewall (CSD required) | **Enabled:** Enables you to check for the existence of a local firewall. You can specify the vendor, enter a product description string to search for, and check whether the installed version is less than, equal to, or greater than that required by your internal security policies (options <, <=, =, =>, >).<br>**Disabled:** Match if the local firewall is currently disabled.<br>**Not Installed:** Select if the match should occur if the remote device does not currently have any firewall software installed. |
| Policy (CSD required) | Match against the current value of the CSD policy, Managed or Un-Managed. (CSD is covered in detail in Chapter 13, "Clientless SSL VPN with Cisco Secure Desktop.") |
| Process (CSD required) | Check whether a local process on the remote device does or does not exist. |
| Registry (CSD required) | Check for the existence or nonexistence of a local Registry value on a remote Windows device. |

As you can see from Table 12-3, many options are available for endpoint assessment or posture evaluation purposes. However, because of the level of access to the remote device required, you have very little available for configuration unless CSD is enabled first.

In addition to selecting one of the available endpoint attributes from the list shown earlier, you can manually create and copy and paste your own logical expressions for AAA and endpoint assessment attribute matching into the ASDM configuration Advanced box that appears when you click the **Advanced** link under the User AAA and Endpoint Attribute sections. However, you can only use scripts created with the Lua programming language, the only one supported by the ASA. Lua scripts are beyond the scope of this book and the exam. If you want more information, however, you can click the **Guide** button from within the DAP window next to the Lua Script section to view syntax and configuration examples. You can also find more information about Lua at www.lua.org.

In the Advanced window, you can select the action the ASA will take when a combination of user AAA, endpoint attributes, and your script have been configured. The available actions are AND and OR. If the AND option is selected, the attribute types and values configured AND those of your script must match. If OR is selected, either the configured attributes OR your script (depending on which is matched) will apply.

Example 12-2 shows a Lua script. This particular script checks for the existence of a local antivirus program on the remote device through the help of hostscan included with the CSD image. If none exists, the user receives an error message.

**Example 12-2**  *LUA Script for Local Antivirus Installed Check*

```
(CheckAndMsg(EVAL(endpoint.av["NortonAV"].exists, "EQ", "false"),"Your Norton AV was
found but the active component of it was not enabled", nil) or
CheckAndMsg(EVAL(endpoint.av["NortonAV"].exists, "NE", "true"),"Norton AV was
not found on your computer", nil) )
```

## Configure Authorization Parameters

After specifying the match criteria, you can select the appropriate authorization parameters in the form of resources or actions that will become available to the user if your configured attributes do indeed match those of their user account or connecting device attributes. The authorization parameters are made available through eight tabs, specific to each attribute type configured within the DAP window below the User AAA and Endpoint Attribute Criteria sections. Each tab, along with its contained parameters, is listed in Table 12-3.

**Table 12-3** *DAP Policy Authorization Parameters*

| Tab | Purpose |
|---|---|
| Action | **Continue:** Enables us to authorize the user and allow access to the SSL VPN. Basically, it applies policy attributes to the session. |
| | **Quarantine:** We prevent the users from progressing to the VPN portal and place them into a quarantine area until certain NAC (user or device) attributes have been satisfied; that is, the virus definition file has been updated, the personal firewall has been enabled, and so on. After remediation is done, the user needs to reconnect and hopefully match on a DAP record with "continue" action, allowing him regular resource access. |
| | **Terminate:** Disallow access to the SSL VPN and stop the user session here. |
| | **User Message:** Enter a message that will be displayed to the user within a yellow box at the top of the portal page. (If messages have been configured in multiple DAPs and users are subject to more than one DAP, applicable messages are displayed to them.) |
| Network ACL Filters (Client) | Choose from a defined list of preconfigured ACLs or create a new one to be applied to the user (only takes effect when connected using AnyConnect). |
| Webtype ACL Filters (Clientless) | Choose from a defined list of preconfigured WACLs or create a new one to be applied to the user (only takes effect for clientless sessions). |
| Functions | Allow or deny access to one or more functional areas within the VPN portal area: |
| | **File Server Browsing** - Default Allowed |
| | **File Server Entry** - Default Allowed |
| | **HTTP Proxy** - Default Allowed |
| | **URL Entry** - Default Allowed |
| | For each of these, we can use Enable, Disable, or Unchanged. Whereas the first two are obvious, the last one means inherit settings from a group policy. |
| Port Forwarding Lists | Choose one from a list of preconfigured port forwarding lists or create a new one for this DAP. We can also choose to set the port forwarding behavior to begin as soon as the user has logged in using the autostart option within this tab. |
| Bookmarks | Choose one from a list of preconfigured bookmarks lists or create a new one for this DAP. |
| Access Method | Choose the access method that applies to this DAP from one of the following: |
| | **Unchanged** (Allow all connection types) |
| | **AnyConnect Client** |
| | **Web-Portal** |
| | **Both-default-web-portal** |
| | **Both-default-AnyConnect Client** |

Key Topic

**Table 12-3**  *DAP Policy Authorization Parameters*

| Tab | Purpose |
|---|---|
| AnyConnect | Within this tab, we can choose to either disable the Always-On feature of the AnyConnect client, use the Always-On settings within the configured AnyConnect client, or leave the current setting as Unchanged. The default is Unchanged, so the behavior depends on the settings configured for Always-On in your client profiles or group policy objects. |

## Configure Authorization Parameters for the Default DAP

The DfltAccessPolicy is the last policy in the DAP record order. It provides a default set of parameters and attributes for SSL VPN access for those users who do not match any attributes you might have checked for in earlier (higher) policies. Because the policy is a system default configuration item, you cannot remove it, change its priority to a higher value than the current 0, or add user AAA or endpoint attributes for match purposes. (If there were any, this would defeat the purpose of the catchall nature of the default policy.) You can, however, change the properties or attributes that are assigned to remote users through the policy, as shown in Figure 12-5.

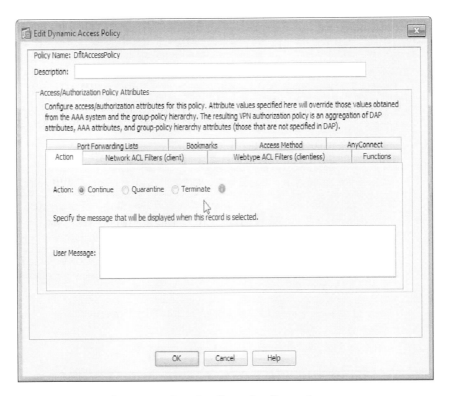

**Figure 12-5**  *DfltAccessPolicy Attribute Configuration*

# DAP Record Aggregation

DAP record aggregation is the result of configured match conditions in two or more DAPs matching those of the user AAA or endpoint attributes. The results can vary based on the priorities of the DAPs being aggregated and the actions that are configured within them. DAP records, unlike ACLs, do not finish processing and apply the action as soon as a match is found. Instead, all DAP records (except for the DfltAccessPolicy) are checked against the session, and any authorization attributes that result from the matching records are cumulated.

If multiple DAPs containing bookmarks or network/webtype access lists are aggregated, for example, the resulting actions are the concatenation of the bookmark lists and access lists. The resources (that is, the bookmarks) from each list are also ordered based on the priority of the DAP. Therefore, you need to make sure if you have multiple DAP records configured to use the Priority field to place the specific entries you want to see first at the top.

If a remote user is matched against multiple DAPs that have differing authorization actions configured, however, the DAP with a terminate action takes precedence. In the example shown in Figure 12-6, whether or not the employee DAP with a continue action has the higher priority, terminate takes precedence and is the action applied to the session, regardless of the DAP priority.

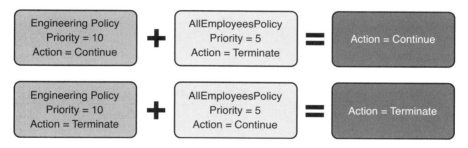

**Figure 12-6**    *DAP Aggregation Action Based on Policy Priority*

Figure 12-6 shows the action selected based on the resulting priority of two aggregated DAP records.

Aggregation is not just limited to the policy action determination. Any bookmark lists and ACLs are aggregated and listed in order of ACL priority. In the example in Figure 12-6, if the EngineerPolicy DAP contained a bookmark list of EngineerList and the AllEmployeesPolicy DAP contained a bookmark list of EmployeesList, the result of aggregating the two DAPs would be the bookmarks listed from the top of the portal page in the order of EngineerList-to-EmployeesList.

If multiple DAP records are matched, and these have functions like port forwarding, file server browsing, file server entry, HTTP proxy, and URL entry (be it conflicting or not), the end result does not have priority, and the following rules apply:

1. If for the same function at least one DAP has its value set to Auto-Start, the resulting action is Auto-Start.

2. If for the same function at least one DAP has its value set to Enable and no DAP has its value set to Auto-Start, the resulting action is Enable.

3. If for the same function at least one DAP has its value set to Disable and no DAP has its value set to Auto-Start or Enable, the resulting action is Disable.

4. Otherwise, the resulting action is the default of Unchanged, which means to inherit values from the group policy that applies to the session.

If multiple DAP records are matched, and these have port forwarding lists configured, these are concatenated, order being done based on the ACL priority, but not necessarily because of this. Because DAP records are automatically ordered top-down based on the ACL priority, this is the order in which ASA processes it for concatenating port forwarding lists.

If multiple DAP records are matched and conflicting access methods are configured, the resulting action is as outlined in Table 12-4.

**Table 12-4**  *DAP Policy Authorization Conflicts*

| AnyConnect Client | Web-Portal | Both-default-Web-portal | Both-default-AnyConnect Client | Aggregation Result |
|---|---|---|---|---|
| | | | X | Both-default-AnyConnect Client |
| | | X | | Both-default-Web-Portal |
| | | X | X | Both-default-Web-Portal |
| | X | | | Web-Portal |
| | X | | X | Both-default-AnyConnect Client |
| | X | X | | Both-default-Web-Portal |
| | X | X | X | Both-default-Web-Portal |
| X | | | | AnyConnect Client |
| X | | | X | Both-default-AnyConnect Client |
| X | | X | | Both-default-Web-Portal |

**Table 12-4**   *DAP Policy Authorization Conflicts*

| AnyConnect Client | Web-Portal | Both-default-Web-portal | Both-default-AnyConnect Client | Aggregation Result |
|---|---|---|---|---|
| X | | X | | Both-default-Web-Portal |
| X | | X | | Both-default-Web-Portal |
| X | X | | X | Both-default-AnyConnect Client |
| X | X | X | | Both-default-Web-Portal |
| X | X | X | X | Both-default-Web-Portal |

In the following example, we walk through how to create two DAP records called SalesPolicy and AllEmployeesPolicy. After creating them and our employee1 user logs in, the authorization parameters from both records will be aggregated.

To start, we access the Configure Dynamic Access Policies window (as used in our earlier examples when discussing the available DAP attributes and settings) by navigating to **Configure > Remote Access VPN > Clientless SSL VPN > Dynamic Access Policies**. We click **Add** on the right side and are presented with the Add Dynamic Access Policy dialog.

We begin the DAP configuration by entering the name for our policy. In this case, as we are configuring the DAP for our Sales users, we call the policy **SalesPolicy**. We leave the Description field blank, and because we want this particular policy to take precedence over any other policies the user might match below it, we enter a priority of **100**.

We then define the user AAA attributes we match for when evaluating the attributes of a remote user establishing a connection. For this example, we have defined a Cisco attribute that checks for the specific username employee1 (cisco.username). We have also specified an endpoint application attribute that must match the client's connection type of clientless. Both of these parameters must match those of our connecting remote user before the DAP authorization attributes are applied.

We then assign the Sales_URL's bookmark list to the Bookmarks tab of the Authorization Attributes section of the window. The bookmark list contains two bookmarks specific to the sales group: Sales Intranet Home Page and the Customer Account Database internal site. Our configuration at the end of this task is shown in Figure 12-7.

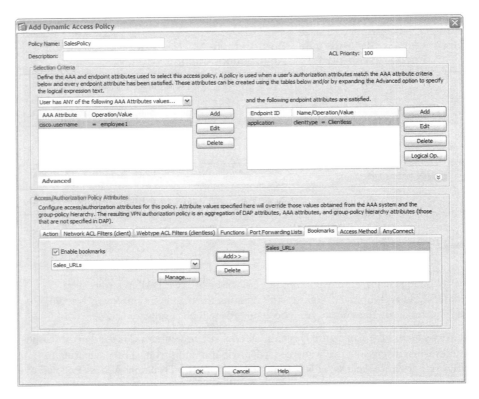

**Figure 12-7**   *SalesPolicy DAP Configuration*

Now that we have created our SalesPolicy DAP, we can create our second DAP, AllEmployeesPolicy. As shown in Figure 12-8, the DAP priority has been set as **10**, indicating this particular DAP is lower in the policy hierarchy compared to our earlier created SalesPolicy. We match on any user connecting via the DefaultWEBVPNGroup connection profile by selecting the user Cisco AAA cisco.tunnel attribute and specifying the bookmark list EmployeeURLs should be applied to any user matched using the specified attributes.

Now that we have configured both of our DAPs, we can test the actions applied to our connecting user employee1. The resulting action should be the aggregation of our two policies and our user being presented with both the SalesURLs and EmployeeURLs specified bookmark lists. These should also be ordered from the top of the portal page by the DAP priorities configured (in this case, SalesURLs then EmployeeURLs).

As shown in Figure 12-9, after our employee1 user has successfully logged in, the aggregation of our two DAPs has resulted in both the SalesURLs (the top two URLs in the list) and EmployeeURLs bookmark lists being added to their portal home page and Web Applications tab.

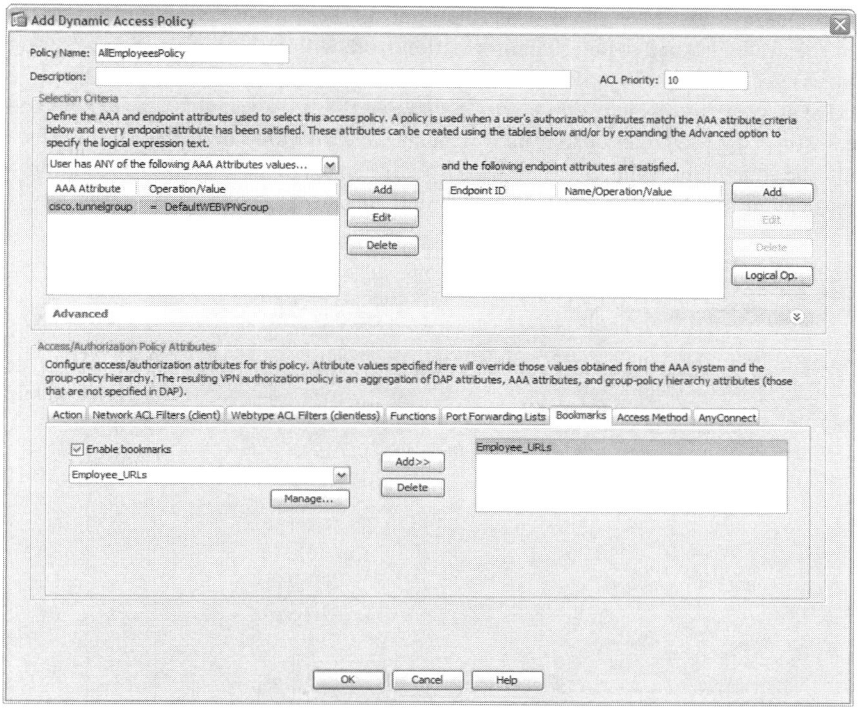

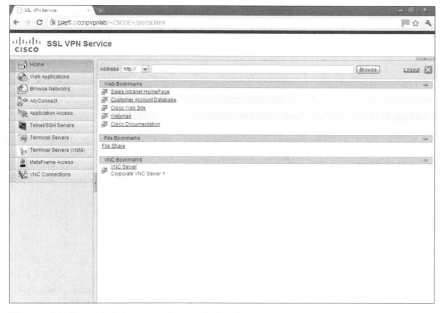

**Figure 12-8**   *AllEmployeesPolicy DAP Configuration*

**Figure 12-9**   *DAP Aggregation and Deployment*

You can also confirm the correct DAP operations and applications have taken place by looking at the available DAP debugging information from within the **Monitoring > Syslog > RealTime** viewer pane of the ASDM. For the earlier example, we can determine from the ASDM syslog entries displayed in Figure 12-10 that the ASA has been able to find and match against the user AAA and endpoint attributes we configured in both of our DAPs. As a result, the fourth line highlighted in the output indicates the selection and resulting aggregation of our two DAP records SalesPolicy and AllEmployeesPolicy.

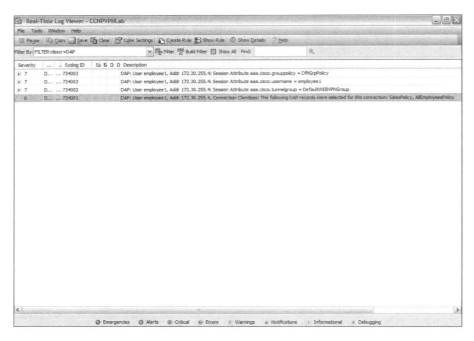

**Figure 12-10** *Successful DAP Operation and Application Verification*

# Troubleshooting DAP Deployment

When troubleshooting DAP deployment scenarios, three main tools are available:

■ ASDM test feature

■ ASA logging

■ DAP debugging

### ASDM Test Feature

One of the great features offered by the ASDM is the ability to test your DAP deployment against the specific AAA attributes you enter. For example, to test the deployment of your configured DAP records, navigate to Dynamic Access Policies window (**Configuration > Remote Access VPN > Clientless SSL VPN Access > Dynamic Access Policies**). Then click the **Test Dynamic Access Policies** button toward the bottom of the window.

In the Test Dynamic Access Policies window, shown in Figure 12-11, you can enter specific user AAA attributes or endpoint attributes to test the deployment of your DAPs. When you enter your attribute information and click the **Test** button, the results of your test display within the Test Result section. In Figure 12-11, we entered the Cisco username (cisco.username) user AAA attribute with a value of **employee1** and the application endpoint attribute with a value of **IPSec**. By entering these two attribute values, we are telling the ASA to test our match criteria within any configured DAPs for a user with the username employee1 connecting in through an IPsec connection.

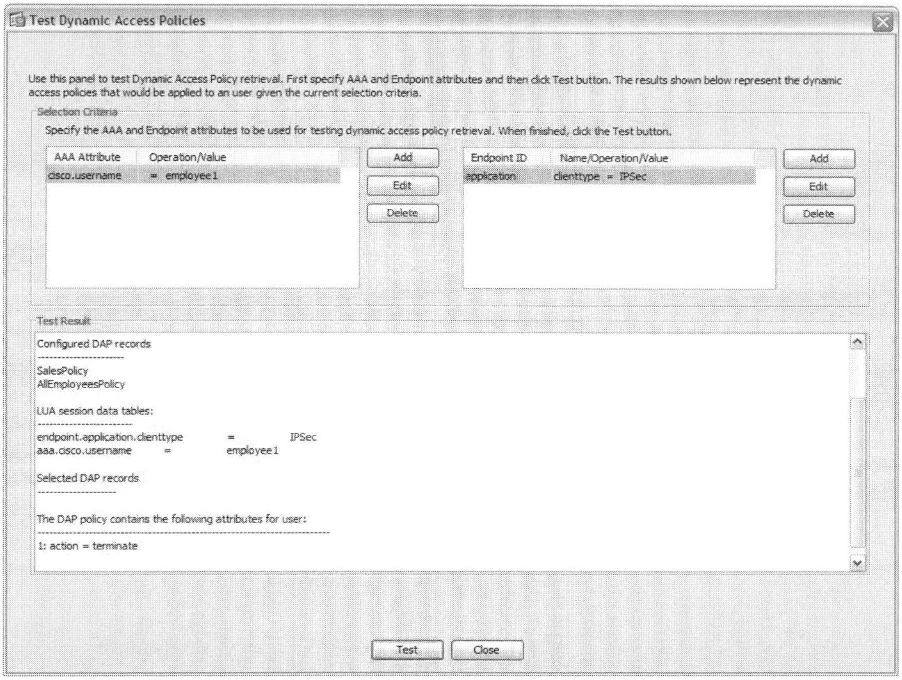

**Figure 12-11**   *ASDM DAP Test Feature, Default Policy Match*

The results of our test indicate that the connecting user did not match any specified DAP records and instead matched that of the default DAP (DfltAccessPolicy) record. Because we have set the action for our default DAP to terminate, the connection the attributes applied is as follows:

1: action = terminate

Although the DfltAccessPolicy has a default action of continue, which allows any connections that do not match any configured DAP records, it is common practice to modify the action to terminate, thus acting like a **deny any** at the end of an ACL and restricting any connections that do not match your configured policies from previous DAP records.

If we revisit the test configuration we entered for the employee1 user and change the endpoint attribute to Clientless rather than IPSec, however, as shown in Figure 12-12, the results we receive indicate the user is now matched by the SalesPolicy DAP, and the following actions are applied:

1: url-list = Sales_URLs

2: action = continue

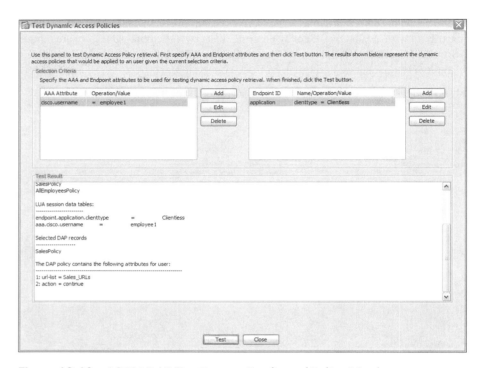

**Figure 12-12** *ASDM DAP Test Feature, Configured Policy Match*

## ASA Logging

As previously discussed in earlier chapters, with the ASDM, you have access to monitoring and debugging information that can prove invaluable during the troubleshooting process.

To view the available logging, you can choose to view the saved items in the current ASA buffer (limited to the current buffer size) or view log information in real time using the real-time log viewer. Regardless of which option you choose, both can be accessed in the ASDM by navigating to **Monitoring > Logging**.

In addition to the ASDM logging windows, you can enable logging when working through the CLI. If you have ever configured logging on a Cisco switch or router, you will notice the process is fairly similar when working on an ASA. Example 12-3 shows the available logging levels that can be referenced by number (1–7) or name, informational warnings, and debugging, followed by the required configuration for the ASA to send all informational log messages to our terminal.

**Example 12-3**  *Enable ASA Logging to the Monitor/Terminal Window*

```
CCNP(config)# logging monitor ?

configure mode commands/options:
  <0-7>           Enter syslog level (0 - 7)
  WORD            Specify the name of logging list
  alerts          Immediate action needed       (severity=1)
  critical        Critical conditions           (severity=2)
  debugging       Debugging messages            (severity=7)
  emergencies     System is unusable            (severity=0)
  errors          Error conditions              (severity=3)
  informational   Informational messages        (severity=6)
  notifications   Normal but significant conditions (severity=5)
  warnings        Warning conditions            (severity=4)
CCNP(config)# logging monitor informational
```

## DAP Debugging

You can use the ASDM real-time log viewer to display the available debugging information. The same results can also be achieved when working within the CLI environment.

To enable DAP debugging from the CLI, enter the **debug dap** {**errors** | **trace**} command within privileged Exec mode, depending on the current level of information you require. However, if you are interested in viewing the full DAP operation in progress, the **debug dap trace** command is recommended. To disable the **debug** command, use the command **no debug dap** {**errors** | **trace**}. If you use the **errors** keyword with this command, you can view all the DAP processing errors that might occur. If you use the **Trace** keyword, however, you receive a full DAP function trace, including a much larger level of detail in your output.

Example 12-4 displays verification that the **debug** command has been applied, and then the available DAP debug trace output when the employee1 user successfully logged in to the SSL VPN portal. The shaded line within the example indicates the two sample DAPs configured earlier (AllEmployeesPolicy and SalesPolicy) have been aggregated and applied to employee1.

**Example 12-4**  *ASA CLI* **debug dap trace** *Command Output*

```
CCNP# show debug
debug dap trace enabled at level 1
CCNP#
CCNP# DAP_TRACE: DAP_open: CAE6D368
DAP_TRACE: Username: employee1, aaa.cisco.grouppolicy = DfltGrpPolicy
DAP_TRACE: Username: employee1, aaa.cisco.username = employee1
DAP_TRACE: Username: employee1, aaa.cisco.tunnelgroup = DefaultWEBVPNGroup
DAP_TRACE: dap_add_to_lua_tree:aaa["cisco"]["grouppolicy"]="DfltGrpPolicy"
DAP_TRACE: dap_add_to_lua_tree:aaa["cisco"]["username"]="employee1"
```

```
DAP_TRACE: dap_add_to_lua_tree:aaa["cisco"]["tunnelgroup"]="DefaultWEBVPNGroup"
DAP_TRACE: dap_add_to_lua_tree:endpoint["application"]["clienttype"]="Clientless"
DAP_TRACE: Username: employee1, Selected DAPs: ,AllEmployeesPolicy,SalesPolicy
DAP_TRACE: dap_request: memory usage = 33%
DAP_TRACE: dap_process_selected_daps: selected 2 records
DAP_TRACE: Username: employee1, dap_aggregate_attr: rec_count = 2
DAP_TRACE: Username: employee1, dap_comma_str_fcn: [Sales_URLs] 10 128
DAP_TRACE: Username: employee1, dap_comma_str_fcn: [Sales_URLs,Employee_URLs] 24 128
```

# Exam Preparation Tasks

As mentioned in the section "How to Use This Book" in the Introduction, you have a couple of choices for exam preparation: the memory tables in Appendix C, Chapter 23, "Final Exam Preparation," and the exam simulation questions on the CD-ROM.

## Review All Key Topics

Review the most important topics in the chapter, noted with the Key Topic icon in the outer margin of the page. Table 12-5 lists a reference of these key topics and the page numbers on which each is found.

**Table 12-5** *Key Topics*

| Key Topic Element | Description | Page |
| --- | --- | --- |
| Topic | Policy inheritance | 417 |
| Step List | DAP deployment preparation | 419 |
| Topic | DAP creation | 419 |
| Table | DAP authorization parameters | 425 |
| Topic | DAP aggregation | 427 |
| Topic | Troubleshooting DAP deployment | 432 |

## Complete Tables and Lists from Memory

Print a copy of Appendix C, "Memory Tables" (found on the CD), or at least the section for this chapter, and complete the tables and lists from memory. Appendix D, "Memory Tables Answer Key," also on the CD, includes completed tables and lists to check your work.

## Define Key Terms

Define the following key terms from this chapter, and check your answers in the glossary:

AAA, CSD, DAP

This chapter covers the following subjects:

- **CSD Overview and Configuration:** In this section, we discuss the Cisco Secure Desktop environment and look at the basic procedures required for successful implementation.

- **Configure Prelogin Criteria:** In this section, we review the flow-based environment available for prelogin attribute assessment within the ASDM and provide configuration examples and examine the results of each.

- **Host Endpoint Assessment:** In this section, we review the basic and advanced endpoint assessment host scan feature along with the licensing requirements and scan features made available on activation.

- **Authorization Through DAP:** In this section, we discuss the CSD integration with DAPs.

- **Troubleshooting CSD:** In this section, we review the common troubleshooting procedures available to us when working with a CSD deployment.

## CHAPTER 13

# Clientless SSL VPN with Cisco Secure Desktop

When deploying a clientless Secure Sockets Layer virtual private network (SSL VPN) solution for remote users, guests, and customers to access our resources, you run the risk of those users connecting from devices that are not under your direct control or that contain potentially harmful software such as keyloggers. Therefore, you must be able to provide them with a secure local environment while they are accessing your resources, and after they have completed their work and closed the connection, also be able to remove any cached settings or credentials that might have been used during their connection, to prevent replay or session-based attacks, identity theft, and so on.

Meet the Cisco Secure Desktop (CSD), built specifically for these purposes. By deploying CSD to your users, you can perform checks such as prescan (that is, before they log in), provide a secure local environment and remote connection, and encrypt local and remote files, manage local and remote resource access, and when users finish, remove all trace of their working on the specific device until they connect again.

This chapter runs through the configuration items required for the scenarios just described and looks at how to integrate the CSD with Dynamic Access Policies (DAP) (discussed in Chapter 12, "Advanced Authorization Using Dynamic Access Policies") for advanced policy deployment and to manage access to a local user's device and resources and allow them secure access to any files created or edited during a CSD session.

## "Do I Know This Already?" Quiz

The "Do I Know This Already?" quiz helps you determine your level of knowledge on this chapter's topics before you begin. Table 13-1 details the major topics discussed in this chapter and their corresponding quiz sections.

**Table 13-1** *"Do I Know This Already?" Section-to-Question Mapping*

| Foundation Topics Section | Questions |
| --- | --- |
| Cisco Secure Desktop Overview and Configuration | 1, 5 |
| Host Endpoint Assessment | 2, 4 |
| Configure Prelogin Criteria | 3, 6 |

**1.** How many phases are involved in a successful user CSD session?

   **a.** 1
   **b.** 2
   **c.** 3
   **d.** 4

**2.** Which of the following are valid host scan applications and extensions? (Choose all that apply.)

   **a.** Basic Host Scan
   **b.** Advanced Endpoint Assessment
   **c.** Basic Endpoint Assessment
   **d.** Endpoint Assessment

**3.** What is the default inactivity timeout in minutes for a user Vault session?

   **a.** 5
   **b.** 3
   **c.** 10
   **d.** 30

**4.** Which host scan extension provides remediation?

   **a.** Basic Host Scan
   **b.** Endpoint Assessment
   **c.** Advanced Endpoint Assessment
   **d.** DAP
   **e.** NAC

**5.** Which privilege level is required for ActiveX installation of CSD from a clientless SSL VPN connection?

   **a.** Guest
   **b.** Administrator
   **c.** Power User
   **d.** Backup Operator

**6.** Which of these are not valid Prelogin Assessment criteria? (Choose all that apply.)

   **a.** Certificate attributes
   **b.** Local file
   **c.** OS version
   **d.** OS patch level

# Foundation Topics

## Cisco Secure Desktop Overview and Configuration

In the vast majority of the chapters up to this point, we have discussed the threats you potentially open your organizations to when allowing users access to your company resources. The very nature of an SSL VPN is to provide remote users with ubiquitous access, that being "anywhere from anything," and unfortunately, the additional flexibility your remote users and organizations benefit from can cause your security engineers to quake in their boots at the very thought of a user connecting into their secure environment from a public Internet cafe PC.

Fear not, however, because you have been provided with the tools required to build a detailed picture of the environment from which your users are connecting and tailor their connection experience and settings based on the image you derive.

When preparing to deploy Secure Desktop access to your users, there are three stages of a user connection, where the answers you receive dictate the policy attributes you can then deploy:

- **Before the SSL VPN session:** More commonly known as the prelogin stage, during this time you evaluate the user's current environment and key variables associated with from where they are connecting; for example, the device type, OS, Registry settings, the owner (that is, is it a company-owned device), and installed software such as antivirus or firewall.

- **During the SSL VPN session:** The user's connection experience during this stage is based on the prelogin criteria matched and subsequent settings applied. You need to be aware of the level of security protecting your remote users; for example, is their data protected? Are they subject to keylogging software or malware attacks? Should any documents created be stored for later use during future connection attempts?

- **After the SSL VPN session:** This stage is particularly important if your remote users are connecting from publicly accessible devices, such as an Internet cafe. You must be able to remove all user settings, stored passwords, cached credentials, and so on from the device to prevent session-replay attacks or identity theft (to name a few). However, you can also leave the Secure Desktop installed on the remote device, if you want your remote users to be able to save time and not have to download and install the software again during subsequent connection attempts.

The actions described here for all three stages are carried out by a number of features that are available individually or in combination. Together they are collectively known as Cisco Secure Desktop (CSD). The individual modules and features available are as follows:

- Prelogin Assessment

- Host Scan

- Secure Desktop (Vault)

- Cache Cleaner

- Keystroke Logger Detection

- Integration with DAP

- Host Emulation Detection

- Windows Mobile Device Management

- Standalone installation packages

- CSD Manual Launch

### Prelogin Assessment

The Prelogin Assessment enables you to check a device before the user has logged in to the SSL VPN for OS version, Windows Registry keys, the existence of specific local files, certificates, and specific attributes within an IP address. Figure 13-1 displays a basic Prelogin Assessment policy deployed. The graphical user interface (GUI) has laid out the steps taken, and subsequent failure or success actions depending on a match within the policy, in an intuitive and easy-to-follow flow diagram.

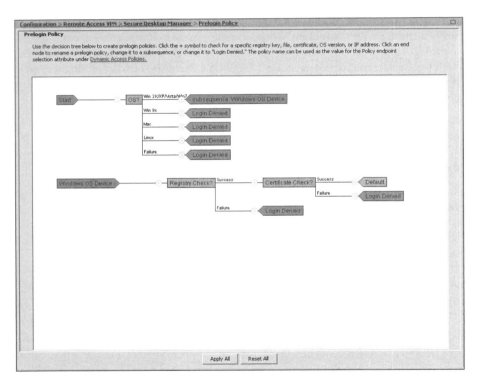

**Figure 13-1** *CSD Prelogin Assessment*

## Host Scan

Three types of host scans are available:

- Basic Host Scan
- Endpoint Assessment
- Advanced Endpoint Assessment

The Basic Host Scan is used automatically by the Adaptive Security Appliance (ASA) for internal functions and for simple policy decisions to be able to take place (for example, which version of OS and patch level is the remote user's device running). You can select custom basic scan parameters to further customize the user experience or policy decision; for example, whether the machine has a specific Registry key or local file or even a particular local process running.

Endpoint Assessment extensions can be enabled that allow you to check the user's device for installed antivirus, personal firewall and definition or patch levels, and so on.

To further customize the user experience and policy behavior, you can also purchase an additional license to enable Advanced Endpoint Assessment extensions that allow you not only to check for locally installed antivirus and personal firewall software, definitions, and patch levels, but also allow you to perform remediation. If the software you are checking for is not found on the remote user's device, you can automatically install or update it.

## Secure Desktop (Vault)

The Vault is a secure partition on the remote user's device that is created during CSD installation and before login, which then provides a Secure Desktop area that a user accesses when using CSD. You can customize the Secure Desktop experience by modifying the available programs and settings applied to them. For example, are they allowed to switch between secure and nonsecure (local) desktops? Are they able to access anything other than a web browser?

## Cache Cleaner

Cache Cleaner is an alternative to Secure Desktop that is commonly deployed to operating systems that are unsupported by the Secure Desktop. The Cache Cleaner can run on Windows, Linux, or Mac devices and operates by clearing the user's browser cache (including any stored passwords, downloaded files, and so on) on termination of the session either through the user logging out or the VPN session timing out. The Cache Cleaner can operate in one of two modes. The amount of cache information removed depends on the mode configured:

- Clear the Whole Cache (IE Only)
- Clear the Current Session Cache

When configured to clear only the current session cache after a minute of the user initially logging in to the VPN, Cache Cleaner takes a snapshot of the current browser cache. Later, when the VPN is disconnected, the Cache Cleaner removes all browser cache information and attempts to restore the snapshot taken at the beginning of the session.

### Keystroke Logger Detection

Keystroke Logger detection, when enabled, downloads to the user's machine and scans it for any known or suspected keystroke logging software applications that might have been installed on the user's machine. The Keystroke Logger can be configured with a list of known applications that might or might not have been approved by the Administrator. If any software has been located that is not approved, the user may be prompted with a list of the application names that have been located and asked to approve them, or the VPN can be configured to terminate.

The Keystroke Logger can detect both User and Kernel mode software keystroke loggers. However, it cannot detect the presence of hardware keystroke loggers. The module can run on Windows 32-bit devices and requires the local user to have administrative privileges before it can continue,

### Integration with DAP

As covered in Chapter 12, CSD is heavily integrated into the DAP policy selection and assignment procedures. When you choose to perform posture assessment, the OS version and patch level are determined by the Basic Host Scan. However, you can also retrieve advanced settings, such as the antivirus vendor and status, local firewall, and so on, performed by the Endpoint Assessment and Advanced Endpoint Assessment extensions, and thus base your policy decisions and assignments on the results received.

### Host Emulation Detection

CSD can detect whether your remote user's SSL VPN session has originated from within a virtual machine environment, and it enables you to base your policy decision on the results received; for example, you might want to restrict access to remote users who are connecting to your organization using an OS within a virtual machine.

### Windows Mobile Device Management

When you deploy the AnyConnect client to remote devices, additional posture checks can be performed by the Host Scan module that is specific to mobile devices.

### Standalone Installation Packages

As well as being able to automatically deploy the CSD package to remote users during a login attempt, it is also possible to download standalone versions of the various CSD packages (OS specific) for manual or company-wide automatic installation. However, any manually installed CSD packages cannot be automatically uninstalled from the user's machine if configured to do so on the ASA.

### CSD Manual Launch

Once CSD is installed locally on the user's device, it is possible for the user to open the CSD software and automatically start a clientless SSL VPN session without the need for Java or ActiveX controls.

As discussed earlier, three phases occur (before, during, and after a remote user's SSL VPN session). The first phase occurs after the user has navigated to the SSL VPN portal URL. If CSD has been enabled for the particular connection profile they are connecting to (determined by the alias entered), they are presented with the Cisco Secure Desktop WebLaunch page, as displayed in Figure 13-2.

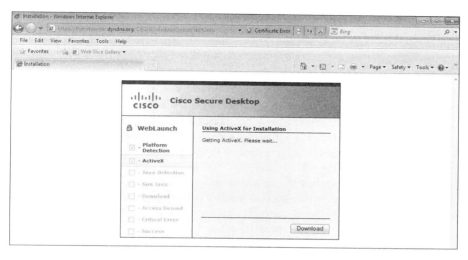

**Figure 13-2**    *Cisco Secure Desktop WebLaunch*

After the WebLaunch page is presented, the second two stages occur:

Key
Topic

■    The OS Detection module is launched for detection of the remote device's OS.

■    The Host Scan module is downloaded and installed.

The installation and running of these modules takes care of the Prelogin Assessment phase. These modules gather the information you require for your prelogin policy assignment (for example, which OS is installed on a remote user's device, or whether their antivirus is running with the most up-to-date definitions installed). These settings are all determined by the Host Scan parameters you have defined, along with the prelogin policy you have configured (which is explained in further detail in the next section).

After the initial Prelogin Assessment, the ASA should have determined whether login is denied or allowed, matched the CSD policy applied to the user, and determined whether the user will be using the Vault (Secure Desktop) or Cache Cleaner.

Depending on the policy that has been applied to them at this stage, you can check whether the connecting user is doing so from a virtual machine and for any keylogging software that might have been intentionally or inadvertently installed on the remote device. You can specify a list of approved or "safe" keylogging software that can be ignored by the CSD or Cache Cleaner. However, if keylogging software is encountered and is not on the approved list (or you haven't specified a list), the CSD will not install. After the host emulation and keylogging software checks have been performed and passed, the Vault (Secure Desktop) or Cache Cleaner applications download and install on the remote device.

### Secure Desktop (Vault)

You can customize the user experience received when working within the Secure Desktop by allowing or denying access to local resources, programs, and files.

### Cache Cleaner

As mentioned earlier, the Cache Cleaner program typically runs on a device that is incapable of running the Secure Desktop; for example, a Mac, Linux, or Windows 7 device. When it starts, the Cache Cleaner closes all open browser windows and re-opens one that all secure SSL VPN communication will take place through. After the user has finished the session and logs out, the Cache Cleaner removes all history, cookies, and saved passwords, allowing for other people to use the device in the future without the risk of recovering any of the previous user's data. One of the main downsides with the Cache Cleaner program is seen when a connected user opens a second browser window. Unfortunately, the Cache Cleaner monitors only the previously opened window. Therefore, users must be educated that for the security of their data, the original browser window used to log in should be the only one used during their SSL VPN session.

After the Vault or Cache Cleaner has been installed and is running, the user is now presented with the familiar login page for the SSL VPN and can begin or continue an SSL VPN session. After authentication, any DAP records, group policies, and user settings become active. When users finish their session and log out, or the inactivity timer expires, the configured settings are applied (for example, to remove the CSD installation from the remote device or leave it installed for future use, run an application, provide the user access to their Vault again, and allow them to save settings). These settings are configured in the prelogin policy that had been applied to the user at the beginning of the connection (before login).

These descriptions represent only a subset of the features and policy options that can be applied to connecting users and their devices. However, they all follow the same process when connecting and disconnecting from the SSL VPN. The following points summarize the prelogin to post-login steps taken:

- The user navigates to or enters the URL to access the SSL VPN.
- The OS detection module is downloaded, runs, and reports back the device's OS and patch level to the ASA.
- The Host Scan module is downloaded and runs on the client device for additional policy matching criteria such as Registry, process, or file scan.
- Based on the OS detection and Host Scan module information, the prelogin policy is matched and applied to the user, or connection is denied.
- If the connection is allowed, the remote machine is being checked for keystroke logger and host emulation.
- Depending on the prelogin policy applied, the Vault or Cache Cleaner downloads and installs on the user's device.

- The user is presented with the familiar login screen and enters his or her details for authentication.

- After successful authentication, any matching DAP records and group and user policies are applied.

- The user continues to his or her SSL VPN session and begins to work.

- The user has finished with the SSL VPN session and logs out, the inactivity or idle timer expires.

- The post-login or "end of session" settings are applied. (For example, cache data is removed, files are deleted, and the Vault or Cache Cleaner is uninstalled.)

## CSD Supported Browsers, Operating Systems, and Credentials

Before you can enable and deploy CSD and configure the prelogin policies that will apply to remote users, you must first assess the possible and common environments they might be connecting from. Based on the results you gather, you can determine groups of users with the same or similar settings and examine the environments that are available to them.

The following tables list the supported operating systems, required user privilege levels, and supported browsers as of CSD Version 3.5. Table 13-2 begins with the operating systems supported by CSD.

**Table 13-2**   *CSD Supported Operating Systems*

Key Topic

| Operating System | Prelogin Assessment | Host Scan | Vault | Cache Cleaner (32-Bit Browsers Only) | Keystroke Logger Detection | Host Emulation Detection |
|---|---|---|---|---|---|---|
| Windows XP SP2 x64 (64 bit) | | X | | X | | |
| Windows XP SP2 and SP3 x86 (32 bit) | X | X | X | X | X | X |
| Windows Vista x86 (32 bit) and x64 (64 bit) | X | X | X Requires KB935855 | X | X Requires KB935855 | X Requires KB935855 |
| Windows 7 x86 (32 bit) and x64 (64 bit) | X | X | | X | | |
| Windows Mobile 6.0, 6.1, 6.1.4, and 6.5 | X | X | | X | | |

**Table 13-2**  *CSD Supported Operating Systems*

| Operating System | Prelogin Assessment | Host Scan | Vault | Cache Cleaner (32-Bit Browsers Only) | Keystroke Logger Detection | Host Emulation Detection |
|---|---|---|---|---|---|---|
| Mac OS X 10.6, 10.6.1, 10.6.2x86 (32 bit), and x64 (64 bit) | X | X | | X | | |
| Mac OS X 10.5.x x86 (32 bit) and x64 (64 bit) | X | X | | X | | |
| Red Hat Enterprise Linux 3 x86 (32 bit) and x64 (64 bit) biarch | X | X˙ | | X˙˙ | | |
| Red Hat Enterprise Linux 4 x86 (32 bit) and x64 (64 bit) biarch | X | X* | | X** | | |
| Fedora Core 4 and later x86 (32 bit) and x64 (64 bit) biarch | X | X* | | X** | | |
| Ubuntu | X | X | | X | | |

˙32-bit and 64-bit biarch Linux operating systems (that is, 64-bit operating systems that can run 32-bit code) require the 32-bit versions of these libraries to run Host Scan: libxml2, libcurl (with openssl support), openssl, glibc 2.3.2 or later, and libz.

˙˙32-bit and 64-bit biarch Linux operating systems (that is, 64-bit operating systems that can run 32-bit code) require the 32-bit versions of these libraries to run Cache Cleaner: libxml2, libcurl (with openssl support), openssl, glibc 2.3.2 or later, and libz.

Depending on the installation method chosen for the Secure Desktop, the local account privileges required by the remote users on their device can differ. Table 13-3 lists the installation options available for remote users and their corresponding privilege levels required when using the AnyConnect Secure Mobility Client. Table 13-4 lists the installation options available when using a clientless SSL VPN connection.

**Table 13-3**  *CSD Privilege Levels Required for Installation with AnyConnect Client*

Key
Topic

|  | AnyConnect Client Installed | AnyConnect Client and CSD Install Together | Executable File |
|---|---|---|---|
| Administrative privileges required? | No | Yes | Yes |

**Table 13-4**  *CSD Privilege Levels Required for Installation During Clientless SSL VPN*

|  | ActiveX | Microsoft JVM | Sun JVM | Executable File |
|---|---|---|---|---|
| Administrative privileges | Yes | Yes | No | Yes |

As you can see from these tables, there are a few CSD installation options available to your remote users. When the AnyConnect client is already installed, the CSD installation is similar to that of updating the existing AnyConnect installation, so there is no requirement for administrative privileges on the local machine. However, if the AnyConnect client is not installed and the two are installed together, the local administrative rights are required. CSD alone cannot be used for full tunneling. Therefore, there is no need in using the executable file without the AnyConnect client if a full tunnel is required.

When initiating a clientless SSL VPN connection along with the CSD, administrative privileges are required for both the ActiveX and Microsoft Java Virtual Machine (JVM) installation options. However, because the Sun JVM is given the appropriate permissions, it handles its own security and therefore doesn't require local administrative privileges for CSD installations. The executable file method is intended for users who do not have ActiveX or Java installed or enabled on their connecting device. The user can select the option to download the csd.exe file (the file extension changes depending on the OS), and once installed can type in the URL to the SSL VPN appliance when prompted. However, the initial installation requires administrative privileges.

Table 13-5 lists the supported browsers when using CSD for Host Scan, Cache Cleaner, Secure Desktop, WebLaunch, and Prelogin Assessment modules to be able to run. The relevant browser security or advanced options must be selected to enable ActiveX controls or Java, and browsers must support Extensible Markup Language (XML) parsing options. Also note that Host Scan and Cache Cleaner do not support 64-bit versions of Internet Explorer.

**Table 13-5**  *CSD Prelogin Assessment and Host Scan Module Supported Browsers*

|  | Prelogin Assessment | Host Scan |
|---|---|---|
| Internet Explorer 6 | Yes | Yes |
| Internet Explorer 7 | Yes | Yes |
| Mozilla Firefox 3.0.x | Yes | Yes |
| Safari 3.2.1 | Yes | Yes |

### Enabling Cisco Secure Desktop on the ASA

The process of enabling CSD on an ASA is pretty straightforward and begins by obtaining the latest CSD PKG file from Cisco.com. After you have obtained a copy of the CSD package, upload it to the ASA's flash so that you can enable it. You can do so by navigating within the ASDM to either **Configuration > Remote Access VPN > Secure Desktop Manager > Setup** and pressing the **Upload File** button (illustrated in Figure 13-3), or navigating to **Tools > File Management** and using the file transfer menus to upload the PKG file from your local PC to the ASA.

**Figure 13-3**   *ASDM Uploading the CSD Image*

After you have uploaded the necessary PKG file, you can then enable the CSD by choosing **Enable Secure Desktop**. After doing so and saving your local configuration to flash, the CSD menu options become available on the left side of the screen below the original setup menu, as shown in Figure 13-4.

You can now carry out the configuration of your CSD customization, prelogin and postlogin options and policies. Note that all CSD-related configurations are stored also in XML format, on flash in the disk0:/sdesktop/data.xml path. When enabled, CSD reads the configuration from this file if it exists; otherwise, it creates it.

To customize the environment for your remote users, use the Secure Desktop Customization panel, found by navigating to **Configuration > Remote Access VPN > Secure Desktop Manager > Secure Desktop Customization**.

You are immediately greeted with the Customization window, as displayed in Figure 13-5, where you can change the CSD text color, banners, and Secure Desktop background by uploading your own images.

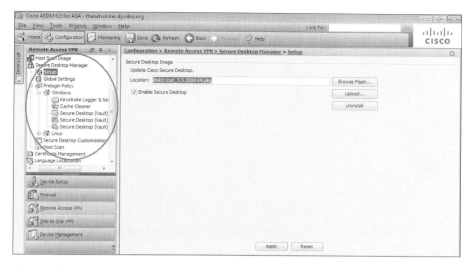

**Figure 13-4**  *ASDM Enable CSD*

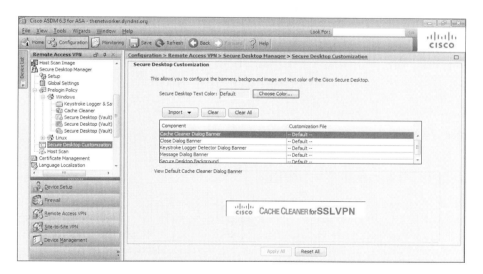

**Figure 13-5**  *ASDM CSD Customization*

CSD can be enabled per connection profile, allowing you to apply CSD prelogin policies to only those users who are, for example, home workers or remote engineers. To make use of this setting, the remote user must navigate to the specific group URL of the SSL VPN connection. The option to disable the CSD can be found within the connection profile settings at **Configuration > Remote Access VPN > Clientless SSL VPN Access > Connection Profiles.** Select the connection profile for which you want to disable CSD shown in the list of available profiles and choose **Edit.** In the Edit Clientless SSL VPN Connection Profile window, navigate to **Advanced > Clientless SSL VPN**, and toward the bottom of the window, choose **Do Not Run CSD**, as shown in Figure 13-6. Note that the connection profile is required to have a group URL applied if one does not exist already.

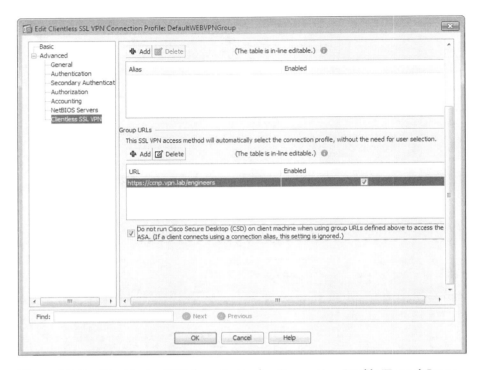

**Figure 13-6**  *Disable the CSD for a Particular Connection Profile/Tunnel Group*

 ## Configure Prelogin Criteria

Now that you have enabled the CSD package and taken a look at the customization and connection/tunnel options available, you can examine the prelogin configuration options and policies. The prelogin criteria you select can dictate the experience that your users receive through their SSL VPN connection. You can map the selection and match criteria using the intuitive flow-based GUI of the prelogin policy window, available at **Configuration > Remote Access VPN > Secure Desktop Manager > Prelogin Policy**.

By default, only one policy is configured (named default) for use with the CSD prelogin criteria. However, you can add more as you go or as your circumstances require. Figure 13-7 displays the initial Prelogin Policy window.

Based on the current actions defined within the default Prelogin Policy window, CSD installs on all remote users who connect to the SSL VPN, but you can change this behavior to deny all users instead. However, depending on your environment, you might want to change this behavior. For example, it is recommended practice to deploy CSD or Vault access to home users or users with corporate devices. However, for guests and remote users connecting from public machines, Cache Cleaner should be used instead.

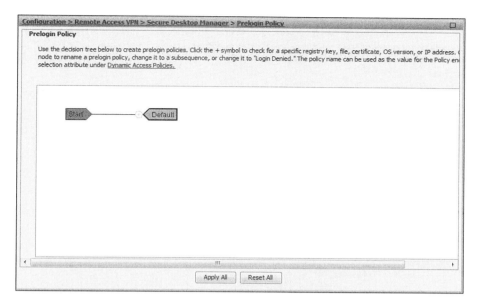

**Figure 13-7**   *CSD Prelogin Policy Window*

You are given a few options within the prelogin policy that can enable you to determine whether a remote user is connecting from a corporate-owned device, a public device, or other device:

■   **Registry Check:** You can check for a specific key within the Windows Registry.

■   **File Check:** You can check for the existence of a particular local file on the user's device.

■   **Certificate Check:** If your organization takes advantage of an internal or external Public Key Infrastructure (PKI) infrastructure, you can check for certain fields and values within certificates that have been deployed to users or devices. However, note that this is not a cryptographic check. It cannot guarantee that the certificate is issued by a certain certificate authority, but only verifies existence of a certificate and certain attributes within it.

■   **OS Check:** You can check for a particular OS running on a user's device.

■   **IP Address Check:** You can check for a specific IP address or subnet that a remote user is connecting from.

For this example, start by dividing users based on the OS they are using on the device they are connecting from. You can do so by selecting the plus (+) symbol shown between the Start and Default Policy in the flow diagram, shown in Figure 13-8. You are then presented with the available policy criteria against which you can match a user's settings and environment; for this example, we select **OS Check** from the list and then **Add**.

As you can see in Figure 13-9, as soon as we have added the OS Check, we are presented with a new set of branches in our flow diagram, which list the available operating systems we can match against and the result (either allow or deny the user to connect).

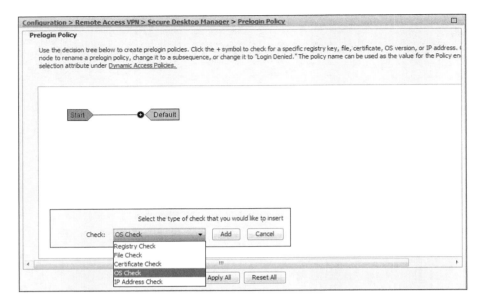

**Figure 13-8** *Insert a New Match Criteria into the CSD Prelogin Policy*

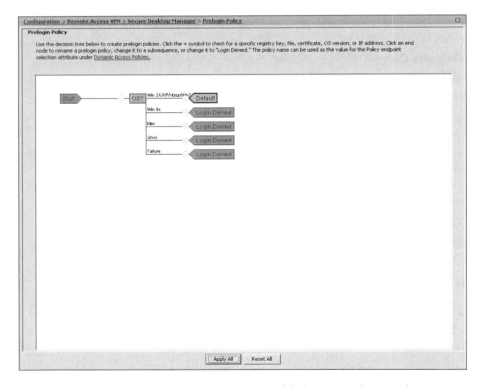

**Figure 13-9** *Additional OS Check Branches Added to the Prelogin Policy*

Using the preceding example, you can start to modify the environment your remote users receive, based on the prelogin criteria they match (that is, the OS their device is running).

You can see in Figure 13-9 the example policy denies all operating systems apart from Windows 2000/XP/Vista. However, you can change this to also allow Linux users to connect. Double-click the current **Login Denied** policy decision next to Linux, and you are presented with a new window giving you the following options:

- Login Denied
- Policy
- Subsequence

By selecting **Policy**, you can create a new prelogin policy or assign matching users to an existing one (only the Default prelogin policy exists at the moment). If a policy by the name you have entered does not already exist, you can type in the name and click **Update**. A new branch is added to the CSD ASDM menu on the left under Prelogin Policy, containing the Keystroke Logger, Cache Cleaner, and Vault options you can customize for matching users of this policy.

If you select **Subsequence**, you can extend the flow diagram and, subsequently, the policy for this group of users who have matched the preceding criteria, basically adding more endpoint checks. You can once again add a label for the policy subsequence. This can be either a new or existing policy.

For this example, we change the login denied action for Linux users to instead apply the Linux policy we will create. We also change the name of the Default policy currently applied to our Windows OS users by double-clicking the Default flow action applied to them and changing the displayed label to **Windows**. As shown in Figure 13-10, two policies now appear in the menu on the left: Windows and Linux.

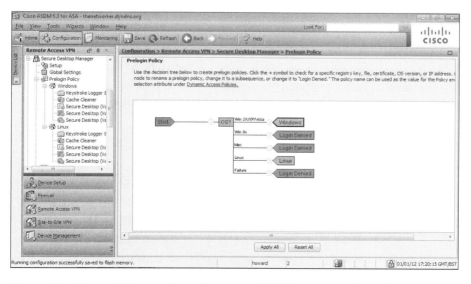

**Figure 13-10**  *Addition and Modification of CSD Prelogin Policy Elements*

Now that a basic prelogin policy has been set to match for Windows or Linux, all other users or OS types will be denied and will receive an "Access Denied" message on the CSD WebLaunch page, informing the users to contact their administrator. To continue the example, now extend the policy by selecting the plus (+) and the Windows policy action that is applied to users and adding the action **File Check**. For now, we use the default actions of the user having to have a local file of example.dat in the root of his or her C: drive. You can, however, change this particular option to match only if a file does not exist, is a particular version, or has a checksum that matches a specific value youenter. As shown in Figure 13-11, after clicking the **Update** button, the tree has been extended for Windows OS users, and additional Success or Failure branches have been added, with the success applying the original Windows policy.

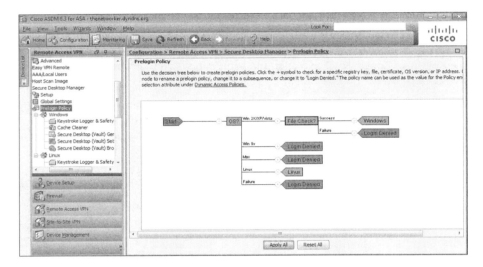

**Figure 13-11**   *Create an Additional Match Criteria for Prelogin Policy Assignment*

With the prelogin policy complete, you can now take a look at and configure the resulting policies that will be applied to Windows and Linux users. As shown in Figure 13-11, you are given the following menu items per policy for the user environment and end-of-session customization:

- Keystroke Logger and Safety Checks

- Cache Cleaner

- Secure Desktop (Vault) General

- Secure Desktop (Vault) Settings

- Secure Desktop (Vault) Browser

Before you proceed to configure these menu settings, however, you must choose whether your users will receive the Vault or Cache Cleaner on policy application. This is achieved by selecting the root of the policy object within the menu displayed (that is, Windows or

Linux). You have the option of selecting Secure Desktop (Vault) or Cache Cleaner. You can, however, leave both deselected and only subject your users to Host Scan checks if this is required by your environment. Note that you can select only one option, not both together. If you select Secure Desktop, and it cannot be installed on remote system but Cache Cleaner can, Cache Cleaner is installed instead, although unchecked.

## Keystroke Logger and Safety Checks

Within the Keystroke Logger and Safety Checks window, we are given the option to check the user devices for keystroke logging software they might have installed. The resulting action if any are found is to deny the connection and prevent the further installation of any CSD or Cache Cleaner modules. However, if your corporation has sanctioned the use of particular keystroke logging software (for example, used for internal auditing), it is possible to add the name of the logging application for this to be bypassed and thus allowed. Note that this detects/protects against software keyloggers, not hardware ones. You are also given the option to turn on host emulation checking. (That is, is the host connecting from within a virtual machine?) By default, the action Allow is applied to any user connecting from a virtual machine. However, this can be changed by selecting **Always Deny Access If Running Within Emulation**.

## Cache Cleaner

Within the Cache Cleaner window, we are given the following options:

- **Launch Hidden URL After Installation:** Along with an accompanying text field for you to be able to enter the URL, this option is sometimes used if your corporation uses session logging utilities.

- **Show Success Message at the End of Successful Installation (Windows Only):** This option, if selected, displays a message to the user after the Cache Cleaner module has installed.

- **Launch Cleanup upon Timeout Based on Inactivity:** By default, this option is selected and set to 5 minutes. Therefore, after 5 minutes of inactivity, the user is disconnected, logged out, and the browser window closed (where available). Network inactivity is related to the idle timeout (also called traffic timer), which is configurable in the Group Policy section. It is important to note that if either timer expires, it will terminate the session.

- **Launch Cleanup upon Closing of All Browser Instances or SSL VPN Connections:** Starts cache cleanup process when all browser windows are closed or the session is closed.

- **Disable Cancel Button (Windows Only):** Select this option if you want to remove the option to cancel Cache Cleaner actions from the user.

- **Clean the Whole Cache in Addition to the Current Session Cache (IE Only):** As mentioned earlier, the Cache Cleaner by default watches only for session data on the current browser window opened during connection establishment (for example, Internet Explorer users). However, this option can be selected to remove the whole cache after they have finished their connection, including files, browsing history, and passwords retained before the session began.

■ **Secure Delete:** Select the number of times the Cache Cleaner will attempt to remove items from the cache on the user exiting or their session timing out, using a U.S. Department of Defense (DoD) sanitation algorithm. By default, this is set to 3. However, you can set it to a value between 1 and 27.

### Secure Desktop (Vault) General

Within this window, you can specify the general settings that apply to your Secure Desktop (Vault) users before during and after their connection. You have the following options:

■ **Enable Switching Between Secure Desktop (Vault) and Local Desktop:** This option is selected by default to allow access to both desktops. You can, however, restrict users to only allow them access to the Secure Desktop during their session, thus further securing their session. However, in situations where a user might need to respond to a prompt or gain access to a local application, access to both the secure desktop (Vault) and unsecured (local) desktop might be required.

■ **Enable Vault Reuse:** If you select this option, your users can save the settings from the current Secure Desktop session and access them again when reconnecting the SSL VPN in the future. If the option is selected, the user is prompted to create a password for the first time. On subsequent connection attempts from the same PC, the user is asked to reenter this password.

■ **Suggest Application Uninstall on Secure Desktop Closing:** If you select this option, the user is prompted to either remove or keep the installed Secure Desktop software used during this session. This might save time and be useful for home users who do not want to have to install and remove the software each time they connect

■ **Force Application Uninstall on Secure Desktop Closing:** If selected, this option disallows users to choose if they will keep the software installed, and instead removes it without intervention

■ **Enable Secure Desktop (Vault) Inactivity Timeout:** Selected by default, after 5 minutes of inactivity, Secure Desktop is automatically closed.

■ **Enable Secure Desktop (Vault) Inactivity Timeout Audio Alert:** This option works together with the previous inactivity timer setting.

■ **Open the Following URL After the Secure Desktop (Vault) Closes:** As it says, this option can allow you to open a URL after the CSD session has closed (for example, a survey, questionnaire, or specific corporate script).

■ **Secure Delete:** Select the number of times the Secure Desktop will attempt to remove items on users exiting or their session timing out; by default, this is set to 3. However, you can set it to a value between 1 and 27.

■ **Launch the Following Application After Installation:** Select this option if your users have access to a locally installed corporate program or a diagnostic/logging program.

## Secure Desktop (Vault) Settings

Within this window, you can select the options that dictate what your connected users can or cannot access during their connection:

■ **Restrict Application Usage:** By default, the user is given access to the installed web browser only. However, by selecting this option, you can select the applications that are available to your users within their web browser on Secure Desktop (that is, browser helpers). Figure 13-12 displays the current list of available browser helpers at this time. You can also optionally insert a hash of the program file that can be checked on its use. This hash limits the ability of the user to use other applications.

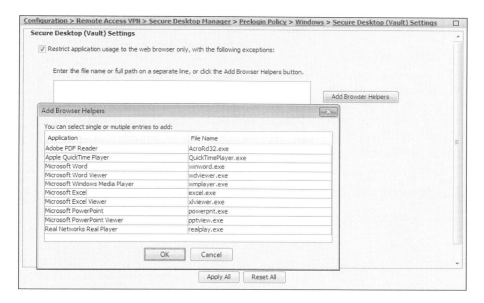

**Figure 13-12**  *Available Browser Helper Applications*

■ **Disable Access to Network Drives and Network Folders:** By default, this option is selected. However, if your users require access to network shares and so on while connected to the SSL VPN, deselect this option.

■ **Disable Access to Removable Drives and Removable Folders:** Select this option if you want to prevent users from being able to access USB or removable media. This will, for example, prevent users from copying internal resources onto them or reduce the risk of malware and viruses from entering the user's session and the network if present on his or her removable hardware. A subitem exists for this option for enabling or disabling encryption of files on removable drives. If the user is legitimately copying files from your corporate environment onto removable media, make sure this option is disabled. However, to increase security and to prevent the loss of internal data, select this option.

■ **Disable Registry Modification:** Typically, Registry modification is conducted by the installation of a program or running of a script. Select this option to prevent any virus or malware from saving or modifying settings within the Registry if users have inadvertently downloaded or accessed something they shouldn't have.

- **Disable Command Prompt Access:** Select this option if you do not want your remote users to be able to have command prompt access during their SSL VPN session.

- **Disable Printing:** Select this option if you want to prevent your remote users from being able to print your corporation's internal data.

- **Allow Email Applications to Work Transparently:** If selected, this option allows the user to use email applications when using Secure Desktop and prevent the deletion of their email by the Secure Desktop on session termination. Currently, supported email applications are Outlook Express, Outlook, Eudora, and Lotus Notes.

### Secure Desktop (Vault) Browser

Within this window, you can customize the user browser settings for the duration of their SSL VPN session. You can achieve this by modifying the home page or adding bookmarks/favorites. This can be a great tool to use when providing users with a familiar environment for them to access. For example, if your organization internally uses group policies to add internal or company resources to the bookmarks list, you can mirror these settings for remote users.

# Host Endpoint Assessment

As mentioned earlier, three different types of Host Scan are available:

- Basic Host Scan

- Host Scan Endpoint Assessment extensions

- Advanced Endpoint Assessment

The Basic Host Scan checks for and provides information to the ASA for further policy decision making and assignment. This is typically OS and patch level information. However, it is possible to add custom criteria to scan for by navigating to **Configuration > Remote Access VPN > Secure Desktop Manager > Host Scan**, as shown in Figure 13-13.

In the Host Scan window, you can add your custom scan criteria. By selecting **Add** from the right side of the window, you can add one or more of the following criteria:

- **Registry Scan:** Check for a particular Registry key and value on the local machine.

- **File Scan:** Check for a local file by name.

- **Process Scan:** Check for a running process name on the local machine—for example, winword.exe.

The example in Figure 13-3 has configured Host Scan to look specifically for the file test.txt within the root of the users C:\ drive. Toward the bottom of the window, notice the highlighted Endpoint Assessment extension. Select this option to allow the Host Scan module to scan for well-known antivirus, personal firewall, and anti-spyware programs.

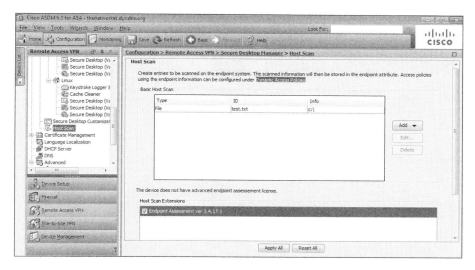

**Figure 13-13**  *CSD Host Scan Custom Criteria*

The information about any applications located on the remote user's system is reported back to the ASA for further policy assignment through DAPs.

The Advanced Endpoint Assessment is available through the purchase of an additional license from Cisco, and as soon as you have installed the license through **Configuration > Device Management > Licenses,** the extension becomes available to select within the Host Scan Extensions panel. When selected, this option allows for remediation and for scanning for installed antivirus software that you can upgrade or install automatically with the Advanced Assessment module.

As well as remediation, the Advanced Endpoint Assessment enables you to enforce rules or exceptions within personal firewall and anti-spyware programs. Based on the success or failure of the remediation attempts, you can allow or deny the user connection. This feature can be compared to a lightweight implementation of NAC (Network Access Control, which is used to perform posture assessment against a user's device and optionally perform remediation before granting network access).

## Authorization Through DAPs

As you saw in the earlier chapter covering DAP deployment, a number of policy elements require the installation of CSD before the profile settings can be configured (for example, antivirus, local files, and personal firewall). The Host Scan and Endpoint Assessment extensions, when enabled, can be used alongside DAP by first scanning for endpoint criteria and sending the results of their scan back to the ASA for policy retrieval and assignment based on configured DAP endpoint attributes.

As you can see in Figure 13-14, within the DAP policy a policy has been created to check for the user connection type (clientless) (to make sure they do not have 360Safe.com's Ant-Spyware program installed), the existence of the Microsoft Windows Firewall and whether it is running, and also that McAfee Managed VirusScan is installed and running. These endpoint attributes are unavailable to us if the CSD has been disabled.

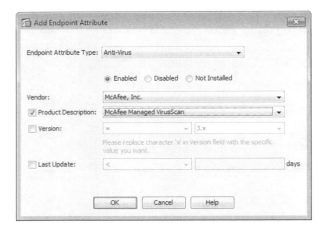

**Figure 13-14**  *ASDM DAP Endpoint Attribute Configuration*

The following endpoint attributes are available for configuration and subsequent matching based on the CSD being previously enabled (see Table 13-6).

**Table 13-6**   *Available DAP Endpoint Attribute Criteria with CSD Enabled*

| Endpoint Attribute | Purpose |
| --- | --- |
| Anti-spyware | Requires CSD and checks for an installed, enabled, or disabled anti-spyware program from an extensive list of well-known programs. |
| | Choose the vendor, product ID, version, and last update time and date. |
| Anti-virus | Requires CSD and checks for an installed, enabled or disabled anti-virus program from an extensive list of well-known programs. |
| | Choose the vendor, product ID, version, and last update time and date. |
| Device | Requires CSD and checks for a match on the following: |
| | Host name |
| | MAC address |
| | Port number |
| | Privacy protection |
| | Version of CSD installed |
| | Version of Endpoint Assessment |

**Table 13-6** *Available DAP Endpoint Attribute Criteria with CSD Enabled*

| Endpoint Attribute | Purpose |
| --- | --- |
| Personal firewall | Requires CSD and checks for an installed, enabled, or disabled personal firewall program from an extensive list of well-known programs. |
| | Choose the vendor, product ID, and version. |
| Policy | Requires CSD and checks for name of the applied CSD policy. |
| Process | Requires CSD and checks for a process that does or does not exist based on your criteria. |
| Registry | Requires CSD and checks for a Registry entry that does or does not exist based on your criteria. |
| | Specify the type, value, and case of the Registry entry. |

# Troubleshooting Cisco Secure Desktop

In the previous sections, we covered the basic elements and configuration required for a successful CSD installation. We have looked at the Prelogin Assessment tree-based GUI and various policy options that are available to you for policy assignment, Host Scan elements, and configuration with DAP. Now armed with this information, we are ready to take a look at some common troubleshooting tasks you might face when deploying CSD for secure access into an environment.

One of the most common reasons for policy assignments or Prelogin Assessments to fail is local authentication or browser settings. It is imperative that the user has the correct ActiveX or Java settings enabled for the modules to be able to run and install. It is also important to note that a user must have local administrative privileges unless installing through a clientless VPN and using the Sun Java virtual machine. However, it is more likely that users will connect from many different locations and device types via SSL VPN. For this reason alone, you can determine how important it is to prepare a full assessment of your current environment before deploying CSD access. This assessment minimizes the disruption and downtime your users might otherwise experience.

Secure Sockets Layer/Transport Layer Security (SSL/TLS) are commonly enabled on a connecting user's browser by default. However, it is worth checking with your users to see whether they can browse to HTTPS-enabled sites. Connectivity errors or problems might also be the cause of a user being unable to access your SSL VPN. The familiar tools to use when troubleshooting client connectivity include the following:

- Ping by fully qualified domain name (FQDN) or IP address if name resolution is not functional.

- Traceroute to verify where possibly connectivity is blocked in the path.

- NSLookup to check on FQDN to IP address resolution.

After troubleshooting client connectivity and confirming the user can access your SSL VPN appliance, you can determine further possible causes with CSD by inspecting the Windows Event Viewer application logs, shown in Figure 13-15.

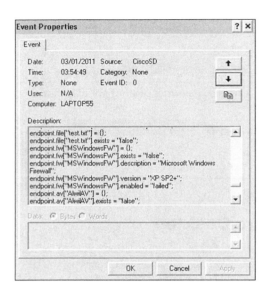

**Figure 13-15** *CSD Endpoint Information: Windows Event Viewer*

The remote device's Event Viewer information shown here displays the results gathered by the Host Scan and Endpoint Assessment modules after downloading and running. You can view a comprehensive list of all settings searched for and found using the modules, such as OS version and patch level, the KB files installed, service pack, any local files or Registry keys it has been configured to search for, personal firewall, and antivirus. The Event Viewer logs in Figure 13-15 report the Endpoint Assessment scan located a personal firewall, the name of the firewall is Microsoft Windows Firewall, and the version is XPSP2+. However, it is disabled. If the policy had called for the remote user's personal firewall to be enabled, the Prelogin Assessment would have failed, causing the connecting user to receive an "Access Denied" message within the CSD WebLaunch window.

ADSM logging and Event Viewer can also help you troubleshoot and debug. You can specify the amount of information that is logged by CSD during its operation by navigating to **Configuration > Remote Access VPN > Secure Desktop Manager > Global Settings** within the ASDM, where you have the following logging-level options to choose from:

■ **Errors:** Logs events that prevent CSD operation

■ **Warnings:** Logs events that prevent optimal CSD operation

■ **Information:** Logs events that describe the state, configuration, and operation of the CSD

■ **Debugging:** Full logging of all CSD events

# Exam Preparation Tasks

As mentioned in the section "How to Use This Book" in the Introduction, you have a couple of choices for exam preparation: the memory tables in Appendix C, Chapter 23, "Final Exam Preparation," and the exam simulation questions on the CD-ROM.

## Review All Key Topics

Review the most important topics in the chapter, noted with the Key Topic icon in the outer margin of the page. Table 13-7 lists a reference of these key topics and the page numbers on which each is found.

**Table 13-7**  *Key Topics*

| Key Topic Element | Description | Page |
|---|---|---|
| Bulleted List | CSD phases | 441 |
| Topic | Prelogin Assessment criteria and options | 442 |
| Bulleted List | CSD module detection and assessment stages | 445 |
| Table | CSD supported OS | 447 |
| Table | CSD required credentials | 449 |
| Topic | Enabling Secure Desktop on the ASA | 450 |
| Topic | Configuring prelogin criteria | 452 |
| Topic | Host Endpoint Assessment | 460 |
| Topic | Troubleshooting client CSD installation with event viewer | 464 |

## Complete Tables and Lists from Memory

Print a copy of Appendix C, "Memory Tables" (found on the CD), or at least the section for this chapter, and complete the tables and lists from memory. Appendix D, "Memory Tables Answer Key," also on the CD, includes completed tables and lists to check your work.

## Define Key Terms

Define the following key terms from this chapter, and check your answers in the glossary:

CSD, DAP, Host Scan, Prelogin Assessment, Vault

This chapter covers the following subjects:

■ **High-Availability Deployment Information and Common Strategies:** In this section, we discuss the important information you need to understand before and while deploying performance enhancements or failover.

■ **Content Caching for Optimization:** In this section, we review the available content caching methods for the ASA and how we configure them to aid in our users experience and our VPN performance.

■ **Clientless SSL VPN Load Sharing Using an External Load Balancer:** In this section, we review the implementation of stateless HA and the performance increase that can be achieved by using an external load balancer.

■ **Clustering and VCA Configuration for Clientless SSL VPN:** In this section, we discuss the VPN load balancing (clustering) operation and configuration.

■ **Troubleshooting Load Balancing and Clustering:** In this section, we review the common troubleshooting procedures available to us when working with SSL VPN load balancing and clustering deployment.

## CHAPTER 14

# Clientless SSL VPN High-Availability and Performance Options

When deploying a clientless Secure Sockets Layer virtual private network (SSL VPN) solution for remote users, you must ensure the availability of the service for them to be able to connect from anywhere, anytime, with minimal loss of service. In this chapter, we review the various options available for achieving high availability (HA) within an SSL VPN environment and the steps you can take to minimize and performance impact you might encounter when the number of users or resources you serve grows.

Most of the information within this chapter serves as a review of Chapter 8, "AnyConnect High Availability and Performance." However, as you read on, you'll be able to distinguish the differences between the options available for both client and clientless SSL VPNs.

## "Do I Know This Already?" Quiz

The "Do I Know This Already?" quiz helps you determine your level of knowledge on this chapter's topics before you begin. Table 14-1 details the major topics discussed in this chapter and their corresponding quiz sections.

**Table 14-1** *"Do I Know This Already?" Section-to-Question Mapping*

| Foundation Topics Section | Questions |
| --- | --- |
| High-Availability Deployment Information and Common Strategies | 1, 3, 4, 6 |
| Clustering Configuration for Clientless SSL VPN | 2, 5 |

1. When choosing a high-availability solution for your VPN deployment, which one will provide your remote client users with continuous connectivity following a failover?

   a. VPN load balancing

   b. Stateful

   c. Redundant VPN peering

   d. Stateless

**2.** Which of the following are required on all members for a basic cluster? (Choose all that apply.)

    **a.** VIP

    **b.** TCP port

    **c.** UDP port

    **d.** ICMP

**3.** When choosing from the available HA and load-balancing methods, which one from the following requires matching hardware and software on each device?

    **a.** Clustering

    **b.** VPN load balancing

    **c.** Active/standby failover

    **d.** Redundant peering

**4.** Which of the following cannot provide HA or load balancing for VPN connectivity?

    **a.** Redundant peering

    **b.** Active/active failover

    **c.** Active/standby failover

    **d.** Clustering

    **e.** Load balancing using an external ACE

**5.** What is the default priority for a VPN cluster member?

    **a.** 1

    **b.** 5

    **c.** 10

    **d.** 100

**6.** Which of the following HA methods are not supported by clientless VPN connections?

    **a.** Redundant peering

    **b.** Clustering

    **c.** Active/standby failover

    **d.** Load balancing using an external ACE

# Foundation Topics

# High-Availability Deployment Information and Common Strategies

As you have already seen in earlier chapters covering HA and performance, various methods are available to us depending on the desired results. We begin here with a quick review of the methods available and their key differences, and then examine which are the greatest benefit to us when planning an HA solution for a clientless SSL VPN deployment.

## Failover

Since the days of the PIX, the failover option has been available. However, failover no longer requires a dedicated failover license to be installed on one of the units, because they can now negotiate the license between them. For failover configuration, the Adaptive Security Appliance (ASA) units must be identical in hardware and software versions. Two types of failover configuration can be achieved with the ASA: active/active and active/standby.

## Active/Active

As the name suggests, both ASA devices are enabled and inspecting traffic simultaneously, allowing for a much greater percentage of available resources for deployment. However, active/active configuration does not provide any support for any type of VPN deployment because ASA needs to run in Multiple Context mode, so we will not spend any further time looking at this option.

## Active/Standby

In this configuration, one ASA device is active and passing/inspecting traffic while the other is in standby, monitoring the state of the other until the time comes when it must take the active role (that is, when the current active device is restarted or becomes unavailable). There are two configuration options when using active/standby failover:

- **Stateful:** Stateful configuration allows existing VPN sessions and tunnels to stay up even when a failover has occurred and the connecting clients and sites are now entering through the previous standby device. The current connection "states" are synchronized between devices across a dedicated stateful connection between the two ASAs or by using the existing failover interfaces. The following clientless SSL VPN objects are *not* supported with stateful failover:

  - Smart tunnels

  - Port forwarding

  - Plug-ins

  - Java applets

  - IPv6 clientless or AnyConnect sessions

  - Citrix authentication

■ **Stateless:** Stateless configuration supports HA in as much as during a failover the standby device assumes the active role. However, it does not support any stateful behavior, meaning all sessions and connections have to be reestablished after a failover has occurred. All ASA models support stateful failover except for the ASA 5505, which supports only stateless failover. Also, all models support by default failover without any licensing, except for ASA 5505 and ASA5510, which require Security Plus licensing.

**Note:**   In both cases (stateful or stateless), the usernames, passwords, and keys are exchanged between devices in clear text. Therefore, it is highly recommended to enter a shared key used for encryption purposes when configuring failover, especially if the failover connection is not directly between the two ASAs but through a switch.

## VPN Load Balancing (Clustering)

Clustering can allow us to take advantage of the performance and HA benefits gained by having multiple devices share the load between them. The overall operation depends on one of the ASA devices becoming a "master" responsible for configuration synchronization and sending new remote client sessions to the least-loaded devices.

## External Load Balancing

This method requires an external load balancer (for example, an ACE 4710 appliance or module in a 6500/7600 switch/router). The Access Control Engine (ACE) will have a public-facing IP address configured, known as a VIP (virtual IP address). You can have several ASAs behind the ACE and configured as real servers. The ACE, on receiving a request for the VIP, forwards it to one of the real servers (ASAs) it has configured.

## Redundant VPN Peering

Both the IPsec VPN client and AnyConnect client allow for multiple VPN server (ASA) addresses to be configured. In the event of the primary ASA failing, the clients try to connect to the next available address in their list of configured addresses. Redundant VPN peering and the use of dead-peer detection (DPD) for peer detection and keepalive purposes are discussed in greater detail in Chapter 8 and Chapter 19, "High Availability and Performance for Easy VPN."

When deploying clientless SSL VPN and active/standby failover scenario, remember that all Extensible Markup Language (XML)-created files on flash (for example, Dynamic Access Policy [DAP] policies, Cisco Secure Desktop [CSD] configurations, and bookmarks) are not automatically replicated to the standby unit. This means for each change made on the active unit, which implies modifications on XML files, you need to manually export these XML files from the active unit flash and import it on standby unit flash.

If users require their application access to remain active during a failover of the VPN devices, you should consider deploying a client-based VPN using either the AnyConnect or IPsec clients, which can take advantage of stateful failover. This method is preferred because of the lack of support for clientless SSL VPN application access methods during a failover. However, as you have seen in earlier chapters, when using active/standby failover, users' clientless connections remain after a failover between devices, although by deploying this failover method, you are required to have the same hardware platforms and software versions on our ASA devices. It is also worth noting that active/standby failover does not support load sharing/balancing between the ASAs. Therefore, if you require only HA, this method is ideal. However, if you require connections to be shared or balanced among your available devices, it is recommended to deploy a method such as clustering or to use an external load balancer.

Clustering, or VPN load balancing, is a popular method of deploying HA to clientless SSL VPN users. Although this particular method does not offer stateful failover between devices, you can deploy an HA and load-sharing solution among devices with different hardware and software revisions, and as you saw in Chapter 8, the AnyConnect client can use DPD for failover reasons. Table 14-2 summarizes the available HA and performance methods.

**Table 14-2** *Advantages and Limitations of Available HA Methods*

Key Topic

| Method | Advantages | Limitations |
|---|---|---|
| Active/standby failover | Can offer stateful or stateless methods. Stateful operation is required to prevent session reestablishment during or after a failover. | No load sharing or balancing occurs between devices. Only one device is active at a time. Lack of support for clientless SSL VPN applications. |
| VPN load balancing (clustering) | Allows for the load between devices to be shared among them based on the "least-used" device receiving the latest connection attempt. Differing hardware and software revisions can be used. Native, built-in ASA feature. | Cannot provide stateful failover. |
| Load balancing using an external load balancer | Allows for the load between devices to be shared among them. You have greater flexibility in choosing load-balancing algorithms than clustering. Differing hardware and software revisions can be used. | Cannot provide stateful failover. No active failover between devices. Clients must reconnect to the next available device after being disconnected. |
| Redundant VPN servers | Allows for connections to be shared among available devices based on clients using different VPN server addresses. Differing hardware and software revisions can be used. | No active failover detection. Clients must use DPD for peer detection. Connections are not stateful. Clientless SSL VPN cannot use this method. |

## Content Caching for Optimization

Key
Topic

As you have seen, there are a number of HA and load-sharing methods that enable you to increase or make greater use of the devices you have. However, one of the most popular methods used in clientless SSL VPN deployments is content caching.

Content caching is a built-in function on the ASA that allows for us to cache content that is commonly used during an SSL VPN session. There are a few options when enabling content caching on the ASA. By default, caching is disabled. However, when enabled, it proceeds to automatically cache rewritten content.

You can configure content caching within the ASDM by navigating to **Configure > Remote Access VPN > Clientless SSL VPN Access > Advanced > Content Cache**, as shown in Figure 14-1.

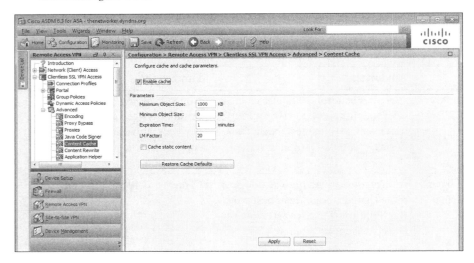

**Figure 14-1**  *SSL VPN Content Caching Configuration*

From this window, the configuration fields, listed in Table 14-3, can be enabled or modified.

**Table 14-3**  *ASDM Available Content Cache Fields and Values*

| Field | Value |
| --- | --- |
| Enable Cache | Disabled by default. Select this to enable caching of rewritten content. |
| Maximum Object Size | Enter the maximum size of an individual document or item you will allow to be cached. Values can be between 0 KB and 10,000 KB (default 1,000 KB). The ASA measures objects based on their original length before rewrite or compression has taken place. |

**Table 14-3**  *ASDM Available Content Cache Fields and Values*

| Field | Value |
|---|---|
| Minimum Object Size | Enter the minimum size of an individual document or item you will allow to be cached. Values can be between 0 KB and 10,000 KB (default 0 KB). The ASA measures objects based on their original length before rewrite or compression has taken place. |
| Expiration Time | Enter the amount of time in minutes between 0 and 900 before cached content expires (default 1 minute). |
| LM Factor | Enter a value between 0 and 100 (default 20) if the ASA encounters content that does not contain a specific server set expiry time. However, it does contain a last modified time. The ASA estimates the age of the content by multiplying the received last modified time by the LM Factor. If you set the LM Factor value to 0, the content is revalidated immediately. |
| Cache Static Content | Select this option to enable the ASA to cache content (that is, flat files, images, or PDFs) that would not be rewritten. |
| Restore Cache Defaults | Click this button and accept the warning to remove your cache settings and restore the default values. |

## Clientless SSL VPN Load Sharing Using an External Load Balancer

You can achieve a performance increase and stateless HA with the implementation of an external load balancer (for example, an ACE 4710 appliance or module in a 6500/7600 switch/router). You would typically implement this design, illustrated in Figure 14-2, if your ASA devices are running different hardware or software levels between them with the result that built-in failover features of the ASA are becoming unavailable.

In this configuration, the ACE appliance has a VIP configured. You can have several ASAs behind the ACE and configured as real servers. Upon receiving a request for the VIP, the ACE forwards it to one of the real servers (ASAs) it has configured. Which ASA receives the request depends on the type of load-balancing algorithm you have configured on the ACE. By default, the behavior is round-robin, meaning if there were three ASAs connected and three clients sending requests to the VIP address, the ACE would send client request one to ASA-A, client request two to ASA-B, and client request three to ASA-C.

Because there is no session awareness (stateless behavior) between the ASA devices in this scenario, you must configure the ACE appliance to forward any future or ongoing requests to the same ASA device it had already connected to. This is known as sticky behavior due to the client session "sticking" to the same ASA device and not being distributed to the available devices.

The ACE is also able to provide end-to-end SSL termination whereby the remote users connect to the VIP configured on the load balancer and are presented with the Public Key Infrastructure (PKI) certificate that has been configured/created for the ACE appliance.

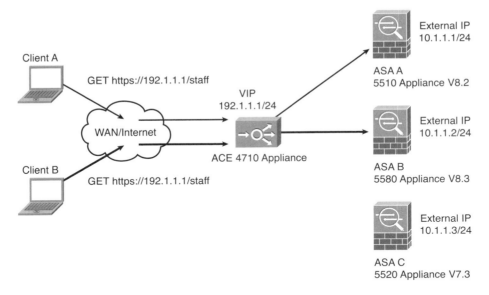

**Figure 14-2**   *Clientless SSL VPN Load Sharing Using an External Load Balancer*

After setting up the Hypertext Transfer Protocol Secure (HTTPS) connection between itself and the client, the ACE creates an HTTPS connection between itself and the destination ASA device, based on the certificate and crypto details it receives and negotiates with the ASA. From this point on in the conversation between the remote client, ACE, and ASA, the client sends HTTPS data to the ACE encrypted with the public key it received, along with the ACE's certificate. The ACE, using its private key and session information, decrypts the data and then directs the data to the appropriate ASA based on existing session (sticky) information or the next ASA chosen by the load-balancing algorithm (if this is a new session). Before transmission, the ACE reencrypts the data using the HTTPS session information it has negotiated with the ASA device and forwards the packet.

## Clustering Configuration for Clientless SSL VPN

If you do not want to use an external load balancer, or do not have one available within your organization for load-sharing purposes, an alternative method of implementing a stateless high-availability scheme is to use the built-in clustering (VPN load balancing) feature.

HA clustering (or VPN load balancing, as it is more commonly known) can be used to divide our remote clients' SSL VPN sessions between our ASA devices without the need for duplicate hardware, software, or an intermediate load balancer (ACE). After a failover between devices occurs, any clientless SSL VPN sessions must be re-created. However, if connected using a client with DPD enabled, the client can automatically reconnect to the virtual cluster address (VIP) for session reestablishment.

Clustering, illustrated in Figure 14-3, can be configured only on an ASA 5510 with an installed Security Plus license or an ASA 5520 and higher device. The devices are also required to have an installed 3DES/AES license for operation. If the load-balancing module cannot detect the presence of a 3DES/AES license, it becomes unavailable.

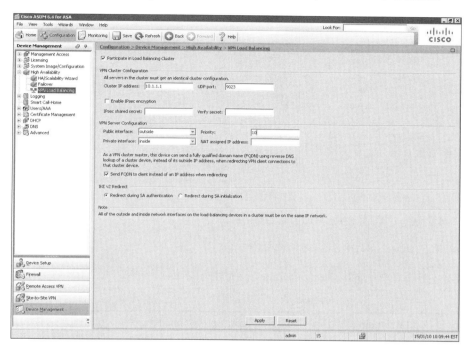

**Figure 14-3**   *VPN Cluster Operation*

The task of load balancing is carried out by the master device, as shown in Figure 14-2. The master device is the first to start up and automatically assumes the role. However, if multiple devices are configured for the same cluster and restarted at the same time, the device with the higher priority wins the election. If at any point during operation the master device becomes unavailable or fails, the cluster member with the highest priority becomes the active master in its place. There is no preempting once the active master has been elected. For example, if an active master already exists for a cluster and a new cluster member with a higher priority is introduced, it cannot take over the role from the active master while it is still available.

The configuration required to create a cluster and add members is straightforward. All members of the same cluster must have an identical virtual cluster IP address, UDP port, and IPsec encryption key (used to encrypt messages between active members), and each device's public and private interfaces must be on the same network.

Figure 14-4 displays the load balancing (VPN cluster) configuration window available within the ASDM at **Configuration > Remote Access VPN > Load Balancing**.

**Figure 14-4** *ASDM VPN Cluster Configuration*

The configurable fields are defined in Table 14-4.

**Table 14-4** *ASDM VPN Cluster Configurable Fields and Values*

| Field | Value |
|---|---|
| Participate in Load Balancing Cluster* | Disabled by default. Before this device can join an active cluster or become the master of a new one, you must select this option. |
| Cluster IP Address* | Enter the virtual cluster IP address to be used by this cluster. All members of the cluster must have the same address configured. |
| UDP Port* | Enter the UDP port used for cluster member communication. This port must be unused on the network (default 9023). |
| Enable IPsec Encryption* | For messages between cluster members to be encrypted instead of sent in plain text, select this option. |
| IPsec Shared Secret* | Enter the shared secret that will be used by each cluster member to encrypt the messages between them. |
| Verify Secret* | Enter the secret from the preceding step again to confirm your entry. |
| Public Interface | Select from the drop-down list your public/external-facing interface. Cluster member interfaces must be on the same network. |
| Priority | Enter the priority value 1 to 10 for this device used for master negotiations. The higher value wins (default 10). |

**Table 14-4**  *ASDM VPN Cluster Configurable Fields and Values*

| Field | Value |
|---|---|
| Private Interface | Select from the drop-down list your private/internal-facing interface. Cluster member interfaces must be on the same network. |
| NAT Assigned IP Address | Enter the IP address the device is being NAT-ed to. If you are not using a NAT on your network, leave this field blank. |
| Send FQDN to Client Instead of an IP Address When Redirecting | By default, the cluster master sends the IP address of a cluster member to a connecting user/client when redirecting. However, if using certificates, the master can be configured to send the FQDN after performing a reverse Domain Name System (DNS) lookup of the cluster member it is redirecting to. |

**Note:**  *These values must match on each cluster member before successful operation can commence.

## Troubleshooting Load Balancing and Clustering

To begin troubleshooting client connectivity to your ASA cluster, start with the familiar tools:

- Ping

- Traceroute

- NSLookup

If the problem experienced is due to the cluster members being unable to communicate with each other, or if you suspect a configuration error on one or more of the cluster devices, ensure that you have the required topology and all the correct information on each cluster member for successful operation.

Each cluster member's internal and external interface must be connected to the same network. (That is, they should all have an IP address belonging to the same internal and external subnet.)

When you have verified that the devices are on the same network, check your configuration on and between the devices. At a minimum, each device must have the following matching configuration:

- Participate in load balancing cluster: Enabled

- Virtual cluster IP address (VIP)

- UDP port

If IPsec has been configured for the encryption of messages between devices, make sure on each cluster device that IPsec encryption has been enabled. Enter and reenter the shared secret on the new device (or all if none of them can communicate).

Ensure that your public and private interfaces have been selected as the correct physical interfaces on the device (that is, Public - Outside, Private - Inside).

Finally, check each device for the correct certificates. If certificates are being used by your cluster members, each should have the following loaded on them:

■ Device-specific certificate

■ Unified Communications Certificate (UCC) or wildcard certificate imported from the master

Navigate to **Monitoring > VPN > Cluster Loads** within the ASDM to see each of your configured devices within the pane.

You can use the flow diagram in Figure 14-5 as a guide when troubleshooting a clustering configuration.

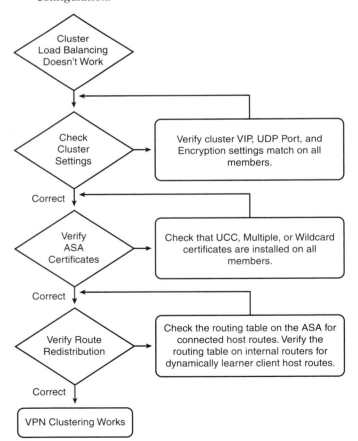

**Figure 14-5**  *Troubleshooting SSL VPN Clustering*

# Exam Preparation Tasks

As mentioned in the section "How to Use This Book" in the Introduction, you have a couple of choices for exam preparation: the memory tables in Appendix C, Chapter 23, "Final Exam Preparation," and the exam simulation questions on the CD-ROM.

## Review All Key Topics

Review the most important topics in the chapter, noted with the Key Topic icon in the outer margin of the page. Table 14-5 lists a reference of these key topics and the page numbers on which each is found.

**Table 14-5** *Key Topics*

| Key Topic Element | Description | Page |
|---|---|---|
| Table | Advantages and limitations of available HA methods | 471 |
| Topic | Content caching for optimization | 472 |
| Table | Cluster configuration information | 476 |
| Topic | Troubleshooting load balancing and clustering | 477 |

## Complete Tables and Lists from Memory

Print a copy of Appendix C, "Memory Tables" (found on the CD), or at least the section for this chapter, and complete the tables and lists from memory. Appendix D, "Memory Tables Answer Key," also on the CD, includes completed tables and lists to check your work.

## Define Key Terms

Define the following key terms from this chapter and check your answers in the glossary:

active/standby, cluster, master, stateful, VIP

This chapter covers the following subjects:

- **IPsec Review:** In this section, we review the IPsec protocols and operation required for a successful VPN connection.

- **Cisco VPN Client Features:** In this section, we discuss the available features of the client software and the supported device operating systems.

- **Client Software Installation and Basic Configuration:** In this section, we discuss the installation of the client software on a Microsoft Windows 7 device and walk through the steps required to implement a basic VPN connection.

- **Advanced Profile Settings:** In this section, we discuss PCF configuration files and the advanced options available when customizing the client for our remote users and OEM use.

- **VPN Client Software GUI Customization:** In this section, we discuss further customizing the client GUI for our remote user experience.

- **Troubleshooting VPN Client Connectivity:** In this section, we cover how to troubleshoot connectivity errors.

## CHAPTER 15

# Deploying and Managing the Cisco VPN Client

Despite the introduction of Secure Sockets Layer virtual private networks (SSL VPN), the Cisco IPsec VPN client remains one of the most common applications used by corporate remote workers to connect into their office environment. The client enables remote workers to seamlessly continue working from their location over any IP-enabled network, just as if they were in the office.

By the end of this chapter, you will understand and be able to explain how to install and configure the Cisco VPN client and how to troubleshoot common connectivity issues.

As discussed in Chapter 1, "Evaluation of the ASA Architecture," and Chapter 3, "Any-Connect Remote-Access VPN Solution," two versions of Internet Key Exchange (IKE) are now supported by the Adaptive Security Appliance (ASA) starting from Version 8.4: IKEv1 and IKEv2. The discussions about IKE within this chapter refer only to IKEv1 because the Cisco IPsec VPN currently offers support only for IKEv1. There are no current plans to add support for IKEv2 to the IPsec client.

## "Do I Know This Already?" Quiz

The "Do I Know This Already?" quiz helps you determine your level of knowledge on this chapter's topics before you begin. Table 15-1 details the major topics discussed in this chapter and their corresponding quiz sections.

**Table 15-1**  *"Do I Know This Already?" Section-to-Question Mapping*

| Foundation Topics Section | Questions |
|---|---|
| Advanced Profile Settings | 1 |
| IPsec Review | 2, 3, 4, 5 |
| Client Software Installation and Basic Configuration | 6 |

1. Which files are used for holding connection entry information?

   a. TXT

   b. PCF

   c. CSV

   d. MDB

**2.** Which of the following can AH provide for an IPsec connection? (Choose all that apply.)

   **a.** Authentication

   **b.** Encryption

   **c.** Integrity

   **d.** Anti-replay

**3.** How many IKEv1 phases are considered mandatory?

   **a.** 2

   **b.** 3

   **c.** 4

   **d.** 5

**4.** During IKEv1 Phase 1 SA creation, which modes are available for operation? (Choose all that apply.)

   **a.** Main mode

   **b.** Quick mode

   **c.** Aggressive mode

   **d.** Violent mode

   **e.** Simple mode

**5.** Which mode is available only for IKE v1 Phase 2 operation?

   **a.** Main mode

   **b.** Quick mode

   **c.** Aggressive mode

   **d.** Simple mode

**6.** What is the recommended value when setting the MTU for a connection?

   **a.** 576

   **b.** 1500

   **c.** 1300

   **d.** 1518

# Foundation Topics

## IPsec Review

No discussion about IPsec VPN connectivity, remote or otherwise, would be complete without a review of the protocols that make the process of creating a successful connection possible.

As discussed in earlier chapters, the term *VPN* can be used for any type of private network connection. (For example, VLANs are a type of VPN connection.) However, many people automatically associate a VPN with the use of IPsec because of its widespread deployment, and the associated marketing of VPNs that has supported this assumption.

IPsec is composed of a collection of underlying protocols that together provide the overall operation of parameter negotiation, connection establishment, tunnel maintenance, data transmission, and connection teardown.

The four main functions provided by IPsec are as follows:

Key Topic

■   Integrity

■   Encryption

■   Authentication

■   Anti-replay

Although the process of encrypting (and therefore, hiding) data is often assumed with IPsec operation, all functions just listed are optional and are carried out by a specific protocol.

Three protocols are used in the IPsec architecture to provide key exchange, integrity, encryption, authentication, and anti-replay:

■   IKEv1 is used by IPsec for the exchange of parameters used for key negotiation and the exchange of the derived authentication keys.

■   ESP (Encapsulating Security Payload) provides a framework for the data integrity, encryption, authentication, and anti-replay functions of an IPsec VPN.

■   AH (Authentication Header) provides a framework for the data integrity, authentication, and anti-reply functions. (No encryption is provided when using AH.)

### IKEv1

IKEv1 operates using UDP port 500 and provides a framework for the parameter negotiation and key exchange between VPN peers for the correct establishment of a security association (SA).

However, the actual processes of key exchange and parameter negotiation are carried out by two protocols used by IKEv1:

■   ISAKMP (Internet Security Association and Key Management Protocol)

■   Oakley

ISAKMP takes care of parameter negotiation between peers (for example, Diffie-Hellman [DH] groups, lifetimes, encryption [if required], and authentication). The process of negotiating these parameters between peers is required for the successful establishment of SAs. After an SA has been established, ISAKMP defines the procedures followed for correct maintenance and removal of the SA.

Oakley provides the key-exchange function between peers using the Diffie-Hellman protocol. Diffie-Hellman is an asynchronous protocol, meaning each peer uses its own set of keys for communications establishment and operation between peers. However, the keys are never exchanged, providing a much higher level of security than synchronous protocols that require both peers to use the same keys for operation. After both peers have established their shared communication path, they can proceed to exchange the keys used by the various synchronous protocols for authentication and encryption purposes.

**Note:**   You will often find the terms *ISAKMP* and *IKE* used interchangeably in earlier versions of ASA (pre 8.4) and IOS to reference IKEv1 functions and parameters. However, as discussed Chapter 1 and Chapter 3, when working with ASA 8.4 and later, any references to IKE now include the respective version number.

Two mandatory IKEv1 phases must be followed by each peer before a communications tunnel can be established between them and they are ready for successful data transmission:

- **IKEv1 Phase 1:** During this phase, both peers negotiate parameters (integrity and encryption algorithms, authentication methods) to set up a secure and authenticated tunnel. This is also called a management channel, because no user data is flowing through it (and it is actually a bidirectional IKE SA). Its sole scope is to handle secure Phase 2 negotiations. It is called bidirectional because both peers use only one session key to secure both incoming and outgoing traffic. Peer authentication can be carried out by one of the following methods:

  - Pre-shared keys
  - Digital certificates (Both this and one-time passwords [OTP] are for Phase 1.5 and optional.)

- **IKEv1 Phase 2:** This second mandatory phase uses the negotiated parameters in Phase 1 for secure IPsec SA creation. However, unlike the single bidirectional SA created within Phase 1, the IPsec SAs are unidirectional, meaning a different session key is used for each direction, (one for inbound, or decrypted, traffic, and one for outbound, or encrypted traffic). This is applicable for any administrator-configured source-destination network pair. Therefore, you might end up with four unidirectional IPsec SAs if you have two source-destination network pairs defined in your policy.

IKEv1 uses either IKEv1 Main mode or IKEv1 Aggressive mode in Phase 1 to carry out the actions required to build a bidirectional tunnel. It then uses IKEv1 Quick mode for Phase 2 operations.

IKEv1 Main mode (Phase 1) uses three pairs of messages (making six in total) between peers:

- **Pair 1 consists of the IKEv1 security policies configured on the device:** One peer (initiator) begins by sending one or more IKEv1 policies, and the receiving peer responds (responder) with its choice from the policies.

- **Pair 2 includes Diffie-Hellman Public Key Exchange:** Diffie-Hellman creates shared secret keys using the agreed upon DH group/algorithm exchanged in pair 1 and encrypts nonces (a randomly generated number) that begin life by first being exchanged between peers. They are then encrypted by the receiving peer and sent back to the sender and decrypted using the generated keys.

- **Pair 3 is used for ISAKMP authentication:** Each peer is authenticated and their identity validated by the other using pre-shared keys or digital certificates. These packets and all others exchanged from now on during the negotiations are encrypted and authenticated using the policies exchanged and agreed upon in pair 2.

IKEv1 Aggressive mode (Phase 1) uses just three messages rather than the six used with Main mode. The same information is exchanged between peers. However, the process is abbreviated by carrying out the following actions:

- The initiator sends DH groups signed nonces, identity information, IKEv1 policies, and so on.

- The responder authenticates the packet and sends back accepted IKEv1 policies, nonces, key material, and an identification hash that are required to complete the exchange.

- The initiator authenticates the responder's packet and sends the authentication hash.

**Note:**   Of the two available modes, Main mode is the preferred due to the lack of encryption used between hosts in Aggressive mode. Due to this, Aggressive mode makes it possible for an attacker to sniff the packets and discover peer identity information. Aggressive mode is used by default on ASA's because of the slower operation of Main mode.

IKEv1 Quick mode (Phase 2) IKEv1 transform sets used for IPsec policy negotiation and unidirectional SA creation are exchanged between peers. Regardless of the parameters/attributes you selected within a transform set, the same five pieces of information are always sent:

- IPsec encryption algorithm (DES, 3DES, AES)

- IPsec authentication algorithm (MD5, SHA-1)

- IPsec protocol (AH or ESP)

- IPsec SA lifetime (seconds or kilobytes)

- IPsec mode (Tunnel, Transport)

An optional X-Auth (Extended Authentication) phase can also take place after successful Phase 1 SA creation. X-Auth carries out the process of end host/device authentication before a user can use the VPN connection. Be careful not to confuse this optional step with the peer authentication carried out within IKEv1 Phase 1. The difference is IKEv1 Phase 1 carries out the authentication of the VPN peers used to terminate each end of the SA, whereas X-Auth is used for the authentication of users or devices that will be transmitting and receiving data across the established VPN tunnel. This phase can occur in remote-access or Easy VPN scenarios but not in site-to-site VPNs. X-Auth authentication can be achieved by using either of the following:

- Static username and passwords

- OTP

### AH and ESP

Both AH and ESP operate at the transport layer and, as a result, have their own IP protocol numbers for protocol identification carried out by devices in the VPN path. (The protocol numbers assigned are 51 and 50, respectively.) As mentioned earlier, ESP can provide the optional encryption function for data traversing the VPN connection. Therefore, ESP is the preferred choice for use with IPsec. The data encryption function provided by ESP is carried out by one of the following symmetric key algorithms:

- Digital Encryption Standard (DES)

- Triple DES (3DES)

- Advanced Encryption Standard (AES) (preferred)

The origin authentication, provided by both AH and ESP, can be carried out by one of the following hash algorithms:

- Message Digest 5 (MD5)

- Secure Hash (SHA)

AH is unavailable for use on the ASA because of the lack of an encryption option. Therefore, when configuring a VPN, only ESP is available to us.

Because ESP and AH operate at the transport layer, as illustrated in Figure 15-1, the original host and destination IP addresses remain in the packet throughout the network, exposing them to potential attackers of the VPN connection. However, which IPsec mode (either Transport or Tunnel) is chosen determines the amount of the original packet to be hidden.

As shown here, in both AH and ESP Transport mode, the original IP addresses remain untouched and are visible to potential attackers. However, when operating within Tunnel mode, the AH and ESP headers are placed after the original IP header, and a new IP header is added. This header contains the IP addresses of the VPN endpoints (ASA, PIX, concentrator, or router), which are public IP addresses and contain no information, thus allowing an attacker to determine any valuable information about the internal network. ASA, as a VPN tunnel endpoint, supports only Tunnel mode. This is also the case for Cisco routers running IOS. However, this restriction applies only to native IPsec functionality when Transport mode is supported on IOS routers (for example, when generic routing encapsulation [GRE] tunneling is used along with IPsec, but not on the ASA, which does not support GRE termination).

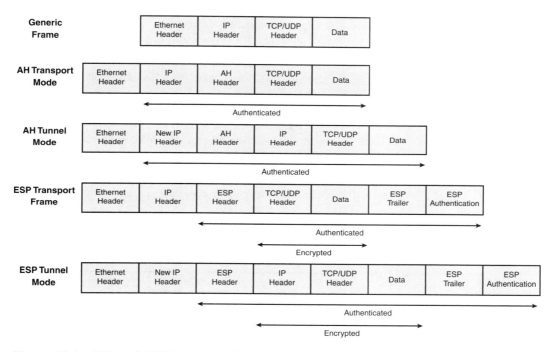

**Figure 15-1**   *ESP and AH Transport and Tunnel Frame Formats*

A feature often used with remote-access IPsec VPNs, which you will see more of later, is NAT Traversal (NAT-T). As you might have noticed already, NAT and Port Address Translation (PAT) play a large and important role in many organizations and general Internet connectivity. The original idea behind NAT was to provide a temporary solution to the growing decline in available IPv4 addresses. However, many organizations have also seen the benefit of using NAT/PAT to mask/hide the IP address information of the internal network from external attackers. Also, home users and small to medium business (SMB) remote users typically use NAT and PAT to translate many internal hosts or devices to only one or two public IP addresses. However, if you take a look at the frame formats in Figure 15-1 again, you will notice the TCP/UDP header information is either encrypted, authenticated, or both. Unfortunately, this does not work too well with PAT, because the original port information is required for the NAT device to be able to modify the port used. To resolve this problem, a similar approach to adding a new IP header can be taken by adding a new transport header.

AH cannot operate with NAT-T, because changing the authenticated IP address in the outer header will break the integrity check when the packet reaches the remote VPN endpoint, unlike ESP, which does not perform authentication of the outer header, thus allowing for the IP address to be changed without breaking communications.

For ESP to pass across PAT devices on Cisco ASA, the following options are available:

■   Standard-based NAT Traversal (NAT-T), which encapsulates ESP into UDP port 4500 only if NAT/PAT device is detected along the path between the two VPN endpoints. This method is supported for all IPsec VPN types, but only in Tunnel mode.

■   Cisco proprietary User Datagram Protocol (UDP) or TCP encapsulation, which always encapsulates ESP into UDP or TCP, even though no NAT/PAT device exists along the path. If UDP encapsulation is being used, IKEv1 negotiation still uses UDP port 500, but ESP is encapsulated into UDP. (By default, port 10000 is used.) With TCP encapsulation, both IKE and ESP are encapsulated into TCP, and by default, port 10000 is used. This method is available only for remote-access IPsec VPNs in Tunnel mode.

Figure 15-2 shows the resulting packet format with the addition of the new TCP or UDP transport layer headers that can be added for NAT-T operation.

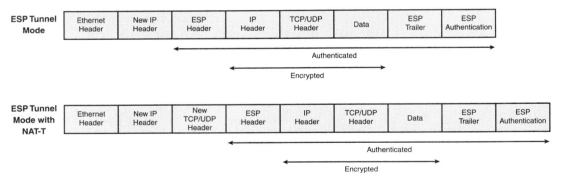

**Figure 15-2**   *ESP and ESP with NAT-T Frame Format*

**Note:**   For further and in-depth coverage of the encryption and hash algorithms provided within an IPsec VPN, review Chapter 1.

# Cisco IPsec VPN Client Features

Now that we have reviewed the basics of the operations and protocols required for the creation of an IPsec VPN tunnel, we can move on to the IPsec VPN client. The IPsec VPN client performs the peer operations required for the correct establishment of an IPsec tunnel with a VPN headend. The headend functions are commonly carried out by one of the following devices: ASA, VPN concentrator, or Cisco IOS router, providing access to corporate resources for authenticated users through the established tunnel.

The Cisco IPsec VPN client has been made available as a separate download for the following operating systems:

■   Microsoft Windows 2000, XP, Vista, 7 (both 32-bit and 64-bit versions)

■   Linux (Intel)

■   Solaris UltraSPARC 32 bit and 64 bit

■   Mac OS X 10.4 and 10.5

It is also compatible for use with the following Cisco products that have been configured to assume the role of the VPN peer or headend:

■   Cisco IOS software-based platforms 12.2(8)T and later

■   Cisco ASA 5500 series appliances Version 7.0 and later

■   Cisco PIX security appliance software Version 6.0 and later

■   Cisco 7600/6500 IPsec VPN Services module and Cisco IPsec VPN SPA (Shared Port Adapter) using 12.2SX and later

■   Cisco VPN 3000 Concentrator

Tables 15-2, 15-3, and 15-4 also list the available features and any protocol support the Cisco VPN client offers. Although this might not be a key element of the information required for the CCNP Security VPN exam, it is worthwhile knowing what the VPN client is capable of when you are preparing to deploy a remote-access VPN solution in a real environment.

**Table 15-2**   *General Functions Available in the Cisco VPN Client*

| Functions | Details |
| --- | --- |
| Connection types supported | Internet-attached Ethernet, async serial PPP |
| Protocol support | IP/IPsec |
| User authentication methods available | RADIUS, TACACS+, RSA SecurID, VPN Server local authentication, PKI, Smart Cards, Microsoft Active Directory |
| General features | Online help, event logging, NAT Transparency, optional MTU size setting, support for dynamic Domain Name System (DNS), virtual adapter, VPN client application programming interface (API), and so on |
| Firewall | Support for firewalls, centralized protection policy, stateful firewall, Internet Control Message Protocol (ICMP) permission |

**Table 15-2**   *General Functions Available in the Cisco VPN Client*

| Functions | Details |
|---|---|
| IPsec | ISAKMP, IKE keepalives, split tunneling, split DNS support, LZS data compression, single SA |
| Troubleshooting | Multiple logging levels available for local event and connection logging |

**Table 15-3**   *Windows Features Supported by the Cisco VPN Client*

| Features | Details |
|---|---|
| Password Expiration | Support for internal password policies. That is, users may be required to change their Windows domain password every 30 days. If this occurs during the time they are attempting to log in to the VPN, the client prompts them to enter a new password and confirm it. |
| Start Before Logon | This is an important feature for users with roaming profiles that may require network access during their login to their local machine. The VPN client can be configured to start before the user logs in to Windows, allowing the client to initiate a connection to the network before logging in locally. |
| Automatic VPN Disconnect on Logoff | The software enables you to disable or enable the automatic disconnection of the VPN connection if the user chooses to log off from his or her local machine. |

**Table 15-4**   *Cisco VPN Client Supported IPsec Attributes*

| IPsec Attribute | Details |
|---|---|
| Main and Aggressive mode | Available IKE Phase 1 methods |
| Authentication algorithms | HMAC MD5<br>HMAC SHA-1 |
| Peer authentication modes | Pre-shared keys<br>Mutual group authentication<br>X.509 digital certificates |
| Diffie-Hellman groups | Group 1 768-bit Prime Modulus<br>Group 2 1024-bit Prime Modulus<br>Group 5 1536-bit Prime Modulus |
| X-Auth | Support for IKE user authentication (optional IKE Phase 1.5) |

**Table 15-4**   *Cisco VPN Client Supported IPsec Attributes*

| IPsec Attribute | Details |
| --- | --- |
| Tunnel encapsulation modes | IPsec over UDP |
| | IPsec over TCP |
| | NAT-T IPsec over UDP/4500 |

**Note:**   For up-to-date product information and features supported by the Cisco IPsec VPN client, go to Cisco.com and see the Cisco VPN client data sheets located at **Products & Services, Security, Cisco VPN Client, Product Literature, Data Sheets.**

# IPsec Client Software Installation and Basic Configuration

The process of installing the Cisco VPN client can be carried out manually by using the Installation Wizard or automatically by deploying the available MSI file to Microsoft Windows devices using a group policy.

Installation begins by obtaining a copy of the VPN client. A copy of the client is shipped along with any purchased ASA or VPN Concentrator 3000 device (with the exception of the ASA 5505). Customers with a valid service contract and account may also download the latest copy of the VPN client from the Cisco.com website.

After you have obtained a copy of the software, continue the process of installation by unzipping the packaged files and double-clicking the setup.exe file. After a few moments, the Welcome screen appears, as shown in Figure 15-3.

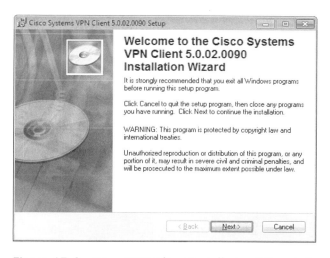

**Figure 15-3**   *IPsec VPN Client Installation Wizard: Screen 1*

Read through the information on the Welcome screen and click **Next** to continue to the client software license agreement, shown in Figure 15-4.

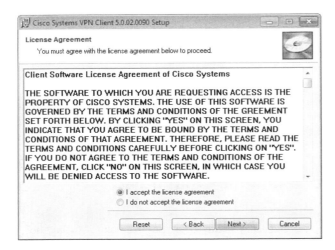

**Figure 15-4**   *IPsec VPN Client Installation Wizard: Screen 2*

You are given a chance to review the license agreement. Upon agreement, click the I Accept the License Agreement radio button, as shown in Figure 15-5, and then click **Next**.

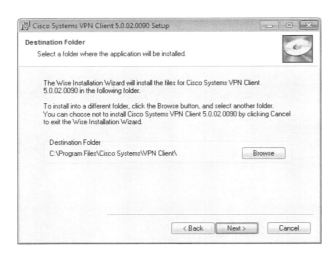

**Figure 15-5**   *IPsec VPN Client Installation Wizard: Screen 3*

The third screen, shown in Figure 15-6, enables you to choose the destination path the files will be installed to. Unless you have a specific destination to use, it is best to keep the default path and click **Next**.

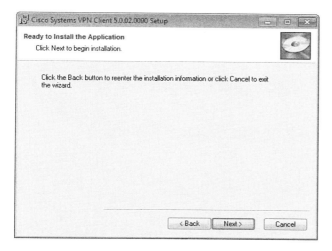

**Figure 15-6**  *IPsec VPN Client Installation Wizard: Screen 4*

As shown in Figure 15-7, the wizard now moves on to copy the required files and install the necessary applications and services for the program to operate.

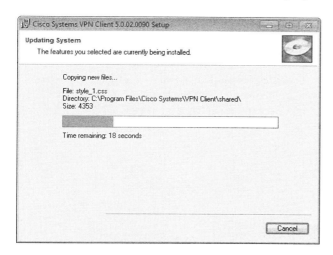

**Figure 15-7**  *IPsec VPN Client Installation Wizard: Screen 5*

When the process has finished, the Successfully Installed window opens, as shown in Figure 15-8. Click **Finish** to close the wizard, and when prompted, restart your device.

Success! The VPN client is now installed. On a Windows machine, navigate to **Start > All Programs > Cisco Systems VPN** to see the following items have been installed:

- Help
- Set MTU
- VPN client

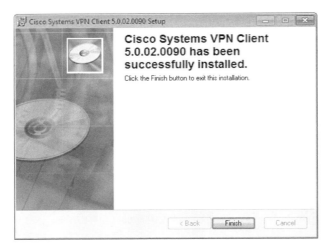

**Figure 15-8**   *IPsec VPN Client Installation Wizard: Screen 6*

Clicking Help opens a browser-based help menu, which provides configuration and troubleshooting guidance.

Set MTU enables you to choose from the available interfaces on the device and set a specific maximum transmission unit (MTU) value. The recommended value is 1300 bytes, as shown in Figure 15-9. You might need to modify the MTU value to minimize any fragmentation that may occur due to the increase in packet size with the additional headers IPsec use requires. Fragmented packets are commonly blocked on firewalls and routers, causing your user's VPN connection to fail. Note that at the install moment, the VPN client automatically modifies the MTU to 1300 for all your interfaces.

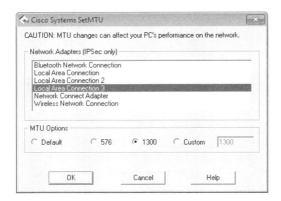

**Figure 15-9**   *Set MTU Application Window*

Now you can explore the VPN client. You are first presented with the Connection Entries panel, shown in Figure 15-10.

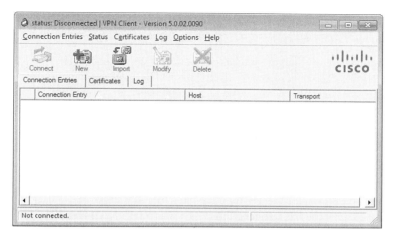

**Figure 15-10**  *Cisco IPsec VPN Client Window*

As shown in Figure 15-10, six menu items are present; the following paragraphs provide an explanation for each tab.

### Connection Entries

The Connection Entries tab is presented by default. This menu item contains buttons that enable you to connect, create a new connection, import an existing connection or connections from a PCF file, modify an existing connection, or remove connections from the list.

### Status

Within the Status menu item, you can see any notifications you might receive during the connection and statistics about protected routes (traffic sent over the VPN tunnel), tunnel negotiation details, and data statistics.

### Certificates

Within the Certificates menu item, you can manage your machine certificates for authentication purposes. You must use this area of the VPN client if you are using Public Key Infrastructure (PKI) for peer-authentication purposes. You can also use this tab to enroll with an existing certificate authority (CA) using the Certificate Enrollment Wizard. This can prove useful if your organization does not make use of the auto-enrollment or automatic certificate distribution services of an internal or external CA.

### Log

We take another look at the Log menu later in this chapter. Briefly, in this menu, you can enable logging, specify the log levels per function (that is, IKE, IPsec, Firewall, and so on), and view the Log Window.

### Options

In the Options menu, you can launch an application upon successful establishment of a VPN session.

### Help

Using the Help menu, you can inspect the VPN client version.

To create a new Connection Entry, begin by selecting the Connection Entries tab, also shown in Figure 15-10, and then select New. The following sections discuss the information required in the Create New VPN Connection Entry window that opens on a tab-by-tab basis.

### Create New VPN Connection Entry, Main Window

Enter the following information for the identification of your VPN connection and a successful connection attempt to occur:

- **Connection name:** This is a local name for the connection that your remote users can use to easily identify the VPN connection if they have multiple connections.

- **Description:** You can help your remote users further by entering a description for the connection here (for example, remote connection to the head office).

- **Host:** Enter the IP address or hostname of the remote VPN endpoint device (the VPN gateway in the case of a VPN client).

### Authentication Tab

You will be using one of three types of authentication: group authentication, certificate authentication, or mutual group authentication (both group and certificates). You need this information before you can proceed any further because, depending on your choice, certain options in the VPN client become unavailable. (For example, if you select Certificate Authentication, the Group Authentication fields dim and become uneditable.) After you have determined the type of authentication you are using, you can collect the remaining information required for your connection. For this example, we select Group Authentication. So, we need the following information:

- **Group name:** The connection profile name created on the ASA

- **Password:** The pre-shared-key configured in the connection profile of the ASA

If you select Certificate Authentication, you need the identity certificate file and the certificate of the root CA (if it is not in the default trusted root CAs of the operating system). For Mutual Authentication, you need only the CA certificate of the entity that issued a certificate to the VPN gateway.

Group and certificate authentication methods are symmetrical; both client and server authenticate each other using the same method. However, the authentication of a remote user with mutual group authentication (also called hybrid authentication) is different:

- The VPN gateway authenticates the client by group password.

- The VPN client then authenticates the VPN gateway by group password. Note that the exchange is digitally signed by the RSA private key of the VPN gateway.

For the purposes of this example, we selected Group Authentication and entered our details for group name **ccnpvpnlab** and our password **security**.

## Transport Tab

As mentioned earlier, NAT-T is used to overcome the use of NAT/PAT with a VPN. By default, the use of UDP 4500 for NAT-T is automatically selected. However, you can choose to use Cisco's UDP/TCP and specify the port to be used. If you select TCP, the port number must match on both ends for successful communication. In the unlikely event that your remote user is not sitting behind a NAT device, you can uncheck **Enable Transparent Tunneling**. However, it is recommended to leave this option checked.

You can also check the Local LAN Access option, also known as split tunneling. This option must be configured on the ASA or other VPN device you are connecting to. Enable the use of split tunneling if your users require access to resources on their local LAN (for example, printers and remote drives). For security reasons, most organizations deny the use of split tunneling because of the security holes it can introduce into a network.

## Backup Servers Tab

If you have more than one VPN device available for your remote users to connect to for failover reasons, you can enter them on a priority basis. (Devices at the top of the list are used before devices at the bottom.) If the Enable Backup Servers option is checked and the VPN client cannot connect to the preferred device, the VPN client tries to connect to the devices listed within this tab until a connection is established (or it runs out of devices to try). However, this setting can be disabled upon successful VPN connection by the VPN gateway, because otherwise, the VPN gateway might overwrite the list of backup servers.

## Dial-Up Tab

On this tab, you can specify whether the VPN client should try to establish a dialup connection, using either the built-in Microsoft dialup networking or a third-party application. If this option has been checked, the dial-up connection automatically begins connecting when a user double-clicks the connection entry in the list or chooses to connect. Upon successful connection, the client proceeds to establish the VPN connection.

Figure 15-11 shows the parameters we entered for our example VPN connection entry. All other options were left at their default values.

After saving the connection entry (by clicking the **Save** button), you can establish the VPN connection by highlighting the entry in the list and clicking **Connect**. When the VPN connection is successfully established, you should be able to see the VPN client Closed Padlock (locked) icon within the list of icons on the taskbar, as shown in Figure 15-12. You can also view the statistics for the connection by right-clicking the **padlock** icon and choosing **Statistics**. The window displayed in the center of Figure 15-12 opens, allowing you to view the number of bytes and packets sent and received, along with the connection information (for example, headend name and time connected). This can prove to be a useful tool when troubleshooting, as discussed later in this chapter.

You can disconnect from the VPN connection by one of two methods: You can right-click the padlock icon and choose **Disconnect**, or select the connection entry within the VPN client and choose **Disconnect**. The padlock icon then changes to that of an unlocked/open padlock.

**Figure 15-11** *IPsec VPN Client Connection Entry with Group Authentication*

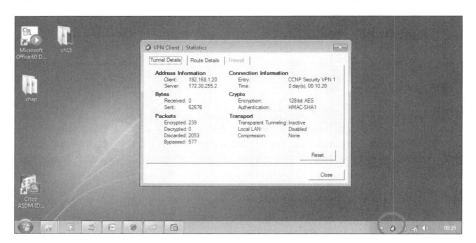

**Figure 15-12** *IPsec VPN Client Successful Connection*

# Advanced Profile Settings

When you create a connection entry, the information entered is stored in a PCF file used by the VPN client. By default, all PCF filenames match the connection entry and are located in C:\Program Files\Cisco Systems\VPN Client\Profiles. (For a non-Windows OS, the location is /etc/CiscoSystemsVPNClient/Profiles.)

The configuration parameters within the PCF file are kept in clear text, allowing for the information to be modified offline (outside of the VPN client software), except for the group and user passwords. This can come in handy when you have a large number of remote users who use the same connection entry. You can create a new PCF file and modify the contents based on the connection information required, and you can then distribute the PCF file to users or make it available for download from a publicly available but secure area of a website or intranet.

Example 15-1 shows the contents of a PCF file.

**Example 15-1** *Cisco VPN Client PCF File Contents*

```
[main]
Description=
Host=ccnp.vpn.lab
AuthType=1
GroupName=ccnpvpnlab
GroupPwd=
enc_GroupPwd=DC68293E270386B05559370C08DD50877E7324C336023546F49
4EAB7D0DC589858C6F9F1B671AE15266387D313D916E3D790AC3ADB528895
EnableISPConnect=0
ISPConnectType=0
ISPConnect=
ISPPhonebook=
ISPCommand=
Username=
SaveUserPassword=0
UserPassword=
enc_UserPassword=
NTDomain=
EnableBackup=0
BackupServer=
EnableMSLogon=1
MSLogonType=0
EnableNat=1
TunnelingMode=0
TcpTunnelingPort=10000
CertStore=0
CertName=
CertPath=
CertSubjectName=
CertSerialHash=00000000000000000000000000000000
SendCertChain=0
PeerTimeout=90
EnableLocalLAN=0
```

The field names in the PCF file are fairly intuitive and have been grouped together in their own sections, as follows:

- Group Authentication
    - GroupName
    - GroupPWD

- Dial-Up
  - EnableISPConnect
  - ISPConnectType
  - ISPConnect
  - ISPPhonebook
  - ISPCommand

The majority of the parameters available in the PCF file are also available for configuration within the VPN client. However, Table 15-5 lists those that are available only within the PCF file.

**Table 15-5**   *Configuration Items Available Only Within the PCF File*

| Parameter | Value |
| --- | --- |
| encGroupPwd | Binary data represented as alphanumeric text |
| encUserPassword | Binary data represented as alphanumeric text |
| SaveUserPassword | 0 - Default, users unable to save their password locally<br>1 - Save the user password locally |
| VerifyCertDN | Include any certificate DN values of both subject and issuer. |
| DH Group | 1, 2, or 5 |
| SDIUserHardwareToken | 0 - Default value Yes use RSA SoftID<br>1 - No Ignore "RSA SoftID Software" installed on the PC |
| EnableSplitDNS | 0 - No<br>1 - Yes (Default) |
| UseLegacyIKEPort | 0 - Turn off legacy setting and use cTCP dynamic ports<br>1 - Keep the legacy IKE ports 500/4500 (default) |
| ForceNetLogin | Windows only<br>0, 1, 2, 3 used to control netlogin |
| ForceNatT | 0 - Default (Off)<br>1 - ForceNatT - Negotiate NatT when available |

In addition to creating and deploying custom PCF files for remote users, you can customize the VPN client experience itself. As discussed in the next section, you can upload your own images to the VPN client directory, thereby customizing the user graphical user interface (GUI) experience. You can also set items and configuration parameters to Read-Only mode, therefore disabling any user modifications within the GUI.

The customization of the VPN client GUI environment depends on the parameters within the vpnclient.ini file. This file is located, by default, in the following locations:

- **Windows:** C:\Program Files\Cisco Systems\VPN Client\

- **Non-Windows OS:** .../etc/CiscoSystemsVPNClient/

Example 15-2 shows the contents of the vpnclient.ini file.

**Example 15-2**   *Default Vpnclient.ini file with DefaultConnectionEntry Parameter*

```
[main]
ClientLanguage=
[GUI]
ShowCACerts=1
WindowWidth=600
WindowHeight=330
WindowX=227
WindowY=115
VisibleTab=0
ConnectionAttribute=0
AdvancedView=1
LogWindowWidth=0
LogWindowHeight=0
LogWindowX=0
LogWindowY=0
DefaultConnectionEntry=CCNP Security VPN 1
```

This example gives you a basic idea about the format and parameters you can modify within the vpnclient.ini file. Each section is preceded by its own title within square brackets, [ ], with the parameters following. Also in the example, you can see a new entry has been created for the default connection entry CCNP Security VPN 1. If you have multiple connection entries, you can change this value to the name of a preferred one.

Example 15-3 includes more parameters that may be entered to further customize your user's experience. In this example, Autoinitiation has been entered, which means the VPN client will start before the user has logged in to her device. Logging for IPsec and IKE have both been enabled with levels 3 and 1, respectively. After the user logs in, the application launcher opens the program located in C:\apps\appname.exe.

The file further customizes the GUI environment by minimizing the client upon connection, making the overall VPN client smaller when maximized, and presenting the user with the Advanced view (allowing the user to view all items within the VPN client window). Example 15-3 shows this expanded vpnclient.ini file.

**Example 15-3**   *Expanded vpnclient.ini file with Additional Parameters*

```
[main]
RunAtLogon=0
EnableLog=1
```

```
DialerDisconnect=1
AutoInitiationEnable=1
AutoInitiationRetryInterval=1
AutoInitiationRetryLimit=50
AutoInitiationList=techsupport,admin
[LOG.IKE]
LogLevel=1
[LOG.IPSEC]
LogLevel=3
[Application Launcher]
Enable=1
Command=c:\apps\apname.exe
[NetLogin]
Force=1
Wait=10
DefaultMsg=For authorized users only
Separator=**************************************
[GUI]
WindowWidth=578
WindowHeight=367
WindowX=324
WindowY=112
VisibleTab=0
ConnectionAttribute=0
AdvancedView=1
DefaultConnectionEntry=ACME
MinimizeOnConnect=1
UseWindowSettings=1
ShowToolTips=1
ShowConnectHistory=1
AccessibilityOption=1
```

Table 15-6 lists a few of the available vpnclient.ini parameters and their values. To view a list of every parameter that can be entered or modified within the vpnclient.ini file, see the "Cisco VPN Client Administrator Guide" available from www.cisco.com for your specific release of the VPN Client software. Any one of these may be entered into your vpnclient.ini file regardless of your particular OS. However, if you have enabled Windows-specific parameters and copied the file onto a Linux or Mac device, the Windows parameters will be ignored. The same behavior occurs when working with PCF files.

**Table 15-6**   *vpnclient.ini File Parameters and Values*

| INI Parameter (Keyword) | VPN Client Parameter Description | Values | VPN Client GUI Configuration Locations |
|---|---|---|---|
| [main] | Required keyword to identify main section. | [main]<br><br>Enter exactly as shown, as first entry in the file. | Does not appear in GUI |
| DialupWait | Specifies the number of seconds to wait between receiving an IP address from a third-party dialer, such as General Packet Radio Services (GPRS), before initiating an IKE tunnel.<br><br>This grants enough time for the connection to go through on the first attempt. | After the keyword and equal sign, enter the number of seconds to wait.<br><br>For example:<br><br>DialupWait=1<br><br>Default number = 0 | Does not appear in GUI |
| MissingGroup Dialog | Controls the pop-up window warning that occurs when a user tries to connect without setting the group name in a preshared connection. | 0 = (default) Do not show the warning message.<br><br>1 = Show the warning message. | Does not appear in GUI |
| RunAtLogon (Windows only) | Specifies whether to start the VPN client connection before users log on to their Microsoft network. Available only for the Windows NT platform (Windows NT 4.0, Windows 2000, and Windows XP). This feature is sometimes known as the NT Logon feature. | 0 = Disable (default)<br>1 = Enable | Options > Windows Logon Properties, Enable start before logon |

**Table 15-6** *vpnclient.ini File Parameters and Values*

| INI Parameter (Keyword) | VPN Client Parameter Description | Values | VPN Client GUI Configuration Locations |
|---|---|---|---|
| DialerDisconnect= (Windows only) | Determines whether to automatically disconnect upon logging off a Windows NT platform (Windows NT 4.0, Windows 2000, and Windows XP). Disabling this parameter lets the VPN connection remain when the user logs off, allowing that user to log back in without having to establish another connection. | 0 = Disable 1 = Enable (default disconnect on logoff) | Options > Windows Logon Properties, Disconnect VPN connection when logging off |
| EnableLog= | Determines whether to override log settings for the classes that use the logging services. By default, logging is turned on. This parameter lets a user disable logging without having to set the log levels to 0 for each of the classes. By disabling logging, you can improve the performance of the client system. | 0 = Disable 1 = Enable (default) | Log, Enable/Disable |
| StatefulFirewall= (Windows only) | Determines whether the stateful firewall is always on. When enabled, the stateful firewall always-on feature allows no inbound sessions from any network, whether a VPN connection is in effect or not. Also, the firewall is active for both tunneled and non-tunneled traffic. | 0 = Disable (default) 1 = Enable | Options > Stateful Firewall (Always On) |

**Table 15-6**  *vpnclient.ini File Parameters and Values*

| INI Parameter (Keyword) | VPN Client Parameter Description | Values | VPN Client GUI Configuration Locations |
|---|---|---|---|
| StatefulFirewall-AllowICMP (Windows only) | Controls whether Stateful-Firewall (Always On) allows ICMP traffic.<br><br>Some Dynamic Host Control Protocol (DHCP) servers use ICMP pings to detect whether the DHCP client PCs are up so that the lease can be revoked or retained. | 0 = Disable (default)<br>1 = Enable | Does not appear in the GUI |
| AutoInitiation-Enable | Enables auto initiation, which is an automated method for establishing a wireless VPN connection in a LAN environment. Can actually be used for both wired and wireless environments, although it was designed with wireless in mind. | 0 = Disable (default)<br>1 = Enable | Options > Automatic VPN Initiation |
| AutoInitiation Retry-Interval | Specifies the time to wait before retrying auto initiation after a connection attempt failure. The AutoInitiation-RetryIntervalType parameter specifies whether this time is in minutes or seconds. | The default is 1 minute.<br><br>The range is 1 to 10 minutes or 5 to 600 seconds. | Options > Automatic VPN Initiation |
| AutoInitiation Retry-IntervalType | Specifies whether the retry interval is displayed in minutes (the default) or seconds. The default is 0 (minutes). | 0 = minutes (default)<br>1 = seconds | Options > Automatic VPN Initiation |
| AutoInitiation Retry-Limit | Identifies the number of consecutive connection failures before automatic initiation gives up and quits trying to connect. | 1 to 1000<br>Default = 0 (no limit) | N/A |

**Table 15-6**   *vpnclient.ini File Parameters and Values*

| INI Parameter (Keyword) | VPN Client Parameter Description | Values | VPN Client GUI Configuration Locations |
|---|---|---|---|
| AutoInitiation List | Identifies auto initiation-related section names within the vpnclient.ini file. The vpnclient.ini file can contain a maximum of 64 auto initiation list entries. | A list of section names separated by commas (for example, SJWLAN, RTP-WLAN, CHWLAN). | Does not appear in GUI |
| SetMTU (Non-Windows only, 4.8.x and later) | Specifies the value to be used for the MTU while the VPN client is connected. For comparison, Windows uses a default value of 1300. | After the keyword and equal sign, enter the MTU value to be used:<br><br>■ SetMTU=1356 (non-Windows default<br><br>■ SetMTU=1200 (suggested troubleshooting point) | Does not appear in GUI |

Example 15-4 shows a sample configuration of the vpnclient.ini file.

**Example 15-4**   *Cisco VPN Client Log Window Output Example*

```
[main]
AutoInitiationEnable = 1
AutoInitiationRetryInterval = 60
AutoInitiationRetryIntervalType = 1
AutoInitiationRetryLimit = 25
StatefulFirewall = 1
StatefulFirewallAllowICMP = 1
RunAtLogon = 1
DialerDisconnect = 1
```

# VPN Client Software GUI Customization

Now that we have reviewed the available options for customizing the user's connection experience, we can look at the additional customization options to provide users with a program that has been modified to their corporate environment.

You can customize the GUI by swapping the default PNG files with your own. The name of any PNG files you want to include in the VPN client must match those of the default files exactly; otherwise, the client will not recognize them. By default, all image files used by the VPN client are included in the following directory:

- **Windows:** C:\Program Files\Cisco Systems\VPN Client\Resources

- **Non-Windows OS:** .../etc/CiscoSystemsVPNClient/Resources

Table 15-7 describes some of the images that you can replace.

**Table 15-7**   *VPN Client GUI Replaceable Image PNG Files*

| PNG File | Description |
| --- | --- |
| Splash_screen.png | The splash screen that appears for 2 to 5 seconds before the VPN client loads |
| Title_bar.png | The title image to the left of the title bar |
| Logo.png | The organizational logo that is visible when in Advanced mode |
| New_profile.png | The *New* visible when in the Advanced mode |

You can also replace the following padlock icon files, as long as the ICO files use *exactly* the same name:

- Connected.ico

- Disconnected.ico

- Disconnecting.ico

**Note:**   Table 15-7 is not an exhaustive list. To view the names and descriptions of all image files that you may replace, see the "Cisco VPN Client Administrator Guide" at Cisco.com for your version of the client.

# Troubleshooting VPN Client Connectivity

To troubleshoot a remote user's connection to your VPN headend device, you have two main areas to examine:

- VPN head end connectivity and configuration (ASA, PIX, router, concentrator)

- VPN client connectivity and configuration

This discussion assumes that all configuration items on your VPN headend device are correct, the devices have connectivity to the public Internet, and remote users can connect.

As with any troubleshooting task with remote user connectivity, you must first determine whether they are able to gain outside connectivity to the public Internet or at least contact your VPN head device. You can do so by using the troubleshooting tools built in to many popular operating systems:

■   Ping

■   Traceroute

■   NSLookup

It is also worth checking for any locally installed firewall or antivirus products that may not have been automatically configured during or after the VPN client installation. For example, an exception will automatically be created within the Windows Personal Firewall for traffic originating from and traveling to the vpnclient.exe. However, other third-party products might not have carried out this action.

After you have established that your remote user can contact your VPN headend device, you can troubleshoot the VPN connection specifically.

The VPN client, as discussed earlier, can log a vast amount of information locally about a user's connection state and protocol operation, as shown in Figure 15-13.

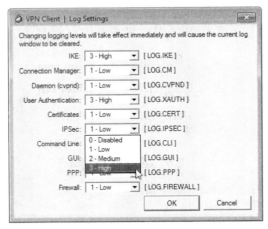

**Figure 15-13**   *Cisco VPN Client Logging Window and Available Log Levels*

As you can see, the logging feature is, by default, in a disabled state (as evident by the Enable icon being visible; if logging was enabled, a Disable icon would be present instead on the Log tab). You can view all logging information within the detachable logging window by clicking the **Log Window** button, and you can specify logging levels 1 (lowest amount of information) to 3 (greatest depth of information) for the following protocols and software modules:

- IKEv1

- Connection Manager

- Daemon (cvpnd)

- User authentication

- Certificates

- IPsec

- Command line

- GUI

- PPP

- Firewall

Furthermore, you can save the Log Window contents to a local file for further examination by a support representative. (For example, a remote user might be asked to enable logging, save the file locally, and email it to his support department for further troubleshooting.)

Example 15-5 is an excerpt from the Log Window during the IKE phase of a VPN connection.

**Example 15-5**   *Cisco VPN Client Log Window Output Example*

```
Cisco Systems VPN Client Version 5.0.02.0090
Copyright (C) 1998-2007 Cisco Systems, Inc. All Rights Reserved.
Client Type(s): Windows, WinNT
Running on: 6.1.7600
Config file directory: C:\Program Files\Cisco Systems\VPN Client\


1 17:11:19.537 01/16/11 Sev=Info/6     IKE/0x6300003B
Attempting to establish a connection with 172.30.255.2.


2 17:11:20.067 01/16/11 Sev=Info/4     IKE/0x63000013
SENDING >>> ISAKMP OAK AG (SA, KE, NON, ID, VID(Xauth), VID(dpd), VID(Frag),
VID(Nat-T), VID(Unity)) to 172.30.255.2


3 17:11:20.083 01/16/11 Sev=Info/4     IPSEC/0x63700008
IPsec driver successfully started


4 17:11:20.083 01/16/11 Sev=Info/4     IPSEC/0x63700014
Deleted all keys
```

```
5 17:11:20.083 01/16/11 Sev=Info/6       IPSEC/0x6370002C
Sent 297 packets, 0 were fragmented.


6 17:11:20.083 01/16/11 Sev=Info/5       IKE/0x6300002F
Received ISAKMP packet: peer = 172.30.255.2


7 17:11:20.083 01/16/11 Sev=Info/4       IKE/0x63000014
RECEIVING <<< ISAKMP OAK AG (SA, KE, NON, ID, HASH, VID(Unity), VID(Xauth),
VID(dpd), VID(Nat-T), NAT-D, NAT-D, VID(Frag), VID(?)) from 172.30.255.2


8 17:11:20.129 01/16/11 Sev=Info/5       IKE/0x63000001
Peer is a Cisco-Unity compliant peer


9 17:11:20.129 01/16/11 Sev=Info/5       IKE/0x63000001
Peer supports XAUTH


10 17:11:20.129 01/16/11 Sev=Info/5       IKE/0x63000001
Peer supports DPD


11 17:11:20.129 01/16/11 Sev=Info/5       IKE/0x63000001
Peer supports NAT-T


12 17:11:20.129 01/16/11 Sev=Info/5       IKE/0x63000001
Peer supports IKE fragmentation payloads


13 17:11:20.176 01/16/11 Sev=Info/6       IKE/0x63000001
IOS Vendor ID Contruction successful


14 17:11:20.192 01/16/11 Sev=Info/4       IKE/0x63000013
SENDING >>> ISAKMP OAK AG *(HASH, NOTIFY:STATUS_INITIAL_CONTACT, NAT-D, NAT-D,
VID(?), VID(Unity)) to 172.30.255.2


15 17:11:20.254 01/16/11 Sev=Info/4       IKE/0x63000083
IKE Port in use - Local Port = 0xDBF0, Remote Port = 0x01F4


16 17:11:20.254 01/16/11 Sev=Info/5       IKE/0x63000072
Automatic NAT Detection Status:
  Remote end is NOT behind a NAT device
This end is NOT behind a NAT device
```

At a glance, you can see the version and client type are presented at the top of the output. For informational purposes, the config file directory has also been included.

The IKE phase has started with a remote client attempting to initiate a connection with the peer 172.30.255.2 (Step 1). The key and session information are successfully sent (Step

2), the IPsec driver is then started (Step 3), and all existing keys are removed for security reasons (Step 4). Step 5 indicates the amount of information sent so far in the process by our client, and in Step 6, the software receives the first ISAKMP packet for Phase 1 negotiation of the parameters sent in Step 2.

In addition to the Log Window, you can also use the Statistics window to aid in your troubleshooting, as shown in Figure 15-14.

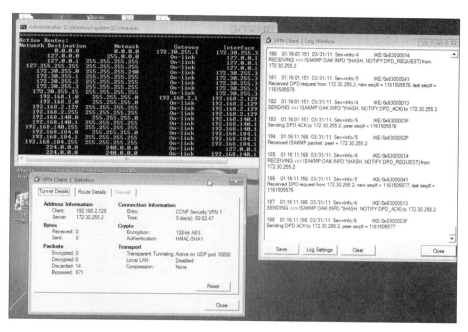

**Figure 15-14**  *Cisco VPN Client Log Window, Statistics Window, and Route Print Output*

With the information displayed in this window, you can determine the number of packets and bytes sent and received the amount of information that has been successfully encrypted and decrypted and any compression algorithms that might be in use during a connection.

If the packet and byte counters you view are not as expected (for example, you do not see any packets appearing to be sent using the VPN), you can further troubleshoot any possible routing issues that might occur because of the existence of split tunneling or local routes that might be taking precedence. You can do so on a Windows machine using the **route print** command and on Linux/Mac machines using the **route -n** command.

## Exam Preparation Tasks

As mentioned in the section "How to Use This Book" in the Introduction, you have a couple of choices for exam preparation: the memory tables in Appendix C, Chapter 23, "Final Exam Preparation," and the exam simulation questions on the CD-ROM.

## Review All Key Topics

Review the most important topics in the chapter, noted with the Key Topic icon in the outer margin of the page. Table 15-8 lists a reference of these key topics and the page numbers on which each is found.

**Table 15-8**  *Key Topics*

| Key Topic Element | Description | Page |
|---|---|---|
| Bulleted List | IPsec review items | 483 |
| Topic | IKE phase review | 484 |
| Topic | IPsec Tunnel and Transport modes | 486 |
| Topic | IPsec client software installation and basic configuration | 491 |
| Topic | Cisco VPN client authentication modes | 496 |
| Topic | Troubleshooting VPN client connectivity: Using the Log Window | 508 |

## Complete Tables and Lists from Memory

Print a copy of Appendix C, "Memory Tables" (found on the CD), or at least the section for this chapter, and complete the tables and lists from memory. Appendix D, "Memory Tables Answer Key," also on the CD, includes completed tables and lists to check your work.

## Define Key Terms

Define the following key terms from this chapter, and check your answers in the glossary:

AH (Authentication Header), asymmetric key protocol, DPD (dead peer detection), ESP (Encapsulating Security Payload), ISAKMP (Internet Security Association and Key Management Protocol), symmetric key protocol

This chapter covers the following subjects:

- **Configuration Procedures, Deployment Procedures, and Information Gathering:** In this section, we discuss what to do before deploying an Easy VPN solution, including gathering the information required for successful configuration and operation.

- **Easy VPN Basic Configuration:** In this section, we review the basic Easy VPN configuration.

- **VPN Client Authentication Using Pre-Shared Keys:** In this section, we review the successful establishment of a VPN connection between an Easy VPN server and a client using pre-shared keys.

- **Using XAUTH for Client Access:** In this section, we review the use of XAUTH for client authentication using the local database.

- **IP Address Allocation Using the VPN Client:** In this section, we review the use of user-specific addressing and local IP pools and the configuration required for successful communication with a remote DHCP server.

- **Controlling Your Environment with Advanced Features:** In this section, we discuss how to further control your remote clients through policy, ACL, and split-tunnel assignment.

- **Troubleshooting a Basic Easy VPN:** In this section, we cover how to troubleshoot a failed VPN client connection.

## CHAPTER 16

# Deploying Easy VPN Solutions

The deployment of an Easy VPN solution can allow your remote clients to connect into your environment using a secure virtual private network (VPN) tunnel, and requires only basic configuration parameters being entered onto your Adaptive Security Appliance (ASA) device. With a basic Easy VPN connection, and depending on the policies configured, you can provide users with a secure tunnel, Internet Key Exchange (IKE), and IPsec policy assignment, IP address and other attribute assignments, along with access to internal resources. This chapter guides you through the steps required to complete a basic Easy VPN configuration and then further customize the configuration to match the settings required for your environment.

## "Do I Know This Already?" Quiz

The "Do I Know This Already?" quiz helps you determine your level of knowledge on this chapter's topics before you begin. Table 16-1 details the major topics discussed in this chapter and their corresponding quiz sections.

**Table 16-1** *"Do I Know This Already?" Section-to-Question Mapping*

| Foundation Topics Section | Questions |
| --- | --- |
| Controlling Your Environment with Advanced Features | 1, 4, 6 |
| Easy VPN Basic Configuration | 2, 5 |
| IP Address Allocation Using the VPN Client | 3 |

1. Which ACL type is used with split-tunneling configuration?

   a. Extended

   b. Standard

2. Which Diffie-Hellman group must be used for a tunnel establishment between an ASA device and the Cisco IPsec VPN client to be successful?

   a. 1

   b. 2

   c. 3

   d. 5

**3.** Which methods are available for client IP address assignment?

- **a.** Authentication servers
- **b.** DHCP
- **c.** Local IP pools
- **d.** Direct user assignment
- **e.** All of the above

**4.** Which is the preferred method of controlling VPN client access to internal resources?

- **a.** Interface ACLs
- **b.** ACL bypass
- **c.** Per-user or per-group ACL

**5.** Which of the following is not required for a basic Easy VPN configuration?

- **a.** ASA outside IP address
- **b.** Configure required routing
- **c.** Interface ACL configuration
- **d.** Preferred IPsec policies

**6.** Which of the following is not classed as an advanced method for controlling VPN client access to resources?

- **a.** ACL bypass
- **b.** Interface ACLs
- **c.** Per-group or per-user ACLs
- **d.** DAP records

# Foundation Topics

## Configuration Procedures, Deployment Procedures, and Information Gathering

The Cisco Easy VPN solution can enable a hardware device or software client to connect to an environment using a minimal IPsec configuration. A central site can push policy information and updates to the connecting device or client, providing a scalable and manageable solution when working with multiple remote sites.

An Easy VPN solution contains the following two components:

- **Easy VPN Remote:** The connecting device, this can be a hardware router (800, 1700, 1800, 1900, 2800, or 3800 series and UBR900), firewall appliance (ASA5505, PIX501, and 506E), or the Cisco IPsec VPN client software. Easy VPN can enable these devices to connect to the Easy VPN Server and receive policy information with as little as an IP address and password configured.

- **Easy VPN Server:** The terminating device, situated at a central site, is capable of running on either a router (800, 1700, 1800, 1900, 2800, 3800, 7200, and 7301 series) or a firewall (Cisco ASA 5500 and PIX appliances). The Easy VPN Server uses the IKE Mode-Config mechanism to push policy attributes—for example, DNS addresses, split tunneling configuration, banners, firewall policies, and so on—to VPN Remote clients each time they connect.

Before approaching the configuration tasks required to deploy an Easy VPN solution, you must first gather the information needed by looking at your current environment and security policies you might already have in place.

Specifically, you need to carry out the following steps for a basic configuration:

- Configure ASA IP addresses
- Configure required routing
- Configure preferred IKEv1 policies
- Configure preferred IPsec policies
- Configure hybrid authentication (optional)
- Configure client settings
- Configure basic access control
- Install and configure the Cisco VPN client software

Table 16-2 describes each of these parameters.

**Table 16-2** *Basic Configuration Parameters and Required Information for Easy VPN*

| Parameter | Description/Value |
|---|---|
| Configure ASA IP addresses | These are the IP addresses that will be applied on an interface facing the internal network (typically the inside or demilitarized zone [DMZ]) to our ASA's external-facing interface (typically the outside interface) for use by our remote clients to communicate with the ASA for VPN tunnel establishment. The external-facing IP address can either be a public routable address or an address assigned from our internal IP addressing plan (typically RFC1918) that might have been subject to a Network Address Translation (NAT) further toward your organization's gateway to the Internet. Regardless of the type of external address used, both must be unused and routable within your environment. |
| Configure required routing | With the outside IP address configured, you can now proceed to configure your routing behavior for the ASA to be able to connect to your remote clients. Depending on your organization's routing behavior and protocols, this might be achieved with a dynamic routing protocol. However, it is common practice to use a static route to your Internet edge router, as it is in the example in this chapter. |
| Configure preferred IKEv1 policies | This step is optional. However, based on your existing policies and the default ASA policies (these are added after enabling ISAKMP on an interface using the Adaptive Security Device Manager [ASDM]), you might need to further customize the various combinations of encryption or authentication parameters and protocols in use. This section also includes the use of peer authentication and whether an extended authentication scheme will be used (for example, XAUTH). |
| Configure preferred IPsec policies | This step is optional. However, based on your requirement to further customize the default ASA policies (these are added after enabling ISAKMP on an interface using the ASDM), you might need to further customize the various combinations of encryption or authentication parameters and protocols in use. |
| Configure hybrid authentication (optional) | You may choose to implement hybrid authentication to prevent the use of man-in-the-middle attacks. By choosing to introduce this step, we provide the client with a way to authenticate the Adaptive Security Appliance (ASA) device through the use of certificates. |
| Configure client settings | As part of your configuration, you must determine and enter the required information that will be applied to connecting clients (for example: IP address pools, the use of internal, external or static assignment, Domain Name System [DNS] servers, and domain suffixes). |

**Table 16-2**  *Basic Configuration Parameters and Required Information for Easy VPN*

| Parameter | Description/Value |
| --- | --- |
| Configure basic access control | You do this through the use of policy assignment and access control lists (ACL). Depending on the resource access you are providing to users, you might or might not want to restrict their movement within your network environment. |
| Install and configure the Cisco IPsec VPN client software | For further information about the installation of the client software and basic parameters required to add a connection, see Chapter 15, "Deploying and Managing the Cisco VPN Client." |

# Easy VPN Basic Configuration

Although the ASDM has many wizards that you can use for VPN and policy configuration, for the exam you must be able to configure a basic VPN configuration without them. Therefore, this section guides you through the various manual configuration procedures without the use of the ASDM wizards.

Key Topic

## ASA IP Addresses

To begin your configuration, you must obtain the IP addresses allowing for successful communication to your ASA device, both from the internal/DMZ network and external/public-facing networks. These addresses must also be unique and routable within and outside of your organization for communication to occur with the ASA and any associated VPN connections.

Figure 16-1 shows the configuration of the outside IP address we use for our example. As mentioned earlier, an internal IP address must also be configured. However, it is assumed you are connecting to the device using the ASDM and already have one applied.

## Configure Required Routing

As previously mentioned, this step might require you to configure a dynamic routing protocol, such as RIP or Open Shortest Path First (OSPF), for correct operation within your environment. However, for the purposes of this example, we configured a static route to our Internet edge router, as shown in Figure 16-2.

## Enable IPsec Connectivity

With the IP addresses and routing configured, you next enable IPsec connectivity on the outside interface. By default, IPsec operation is disabled, so this step is required for correct operation. Note that although the graphical user interface (GUI) says Enable Interfaces for IPsec Access, you are actually enabling IKEv1 processing on the respective interface. IPsec/IKEv1 naming is used interchangeably when configuring IPsec VPNs within the ASDM. Although not technically correct, I guess here when I say Cisco is probably aiming to make configuration through the ASDM possible for people who might not have the technical ability that you and I have, it is possible due to the "marketing hype" that more people have heard of IPsec than have heard of IKEv1. Therefore, it is easier for them to distinguish where a VPN is or is not configured... but that's just my opinion.

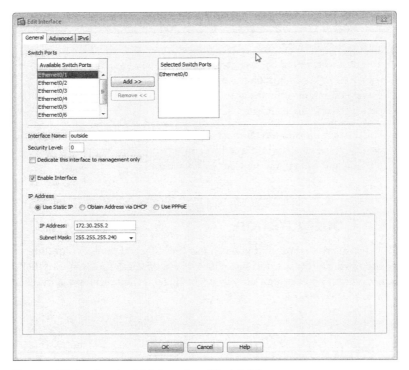

**Figure 16-1** *Apply ASA Interface IPv4 Address*

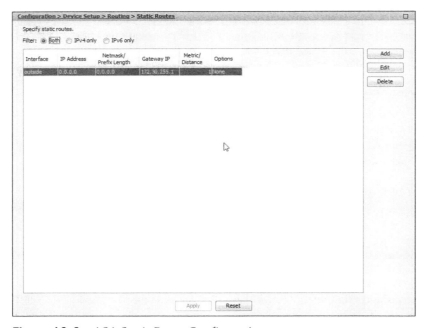

**Figure 16-2** *ASA Static Route Configuration*

Figure 16-3 shows the configuration procedure used to enable IPsec. To complete this operation, navigate in the ASDM to **Configuration > Remote Access VPN > Network (Client) Access > IPsec Connection Profiles**.

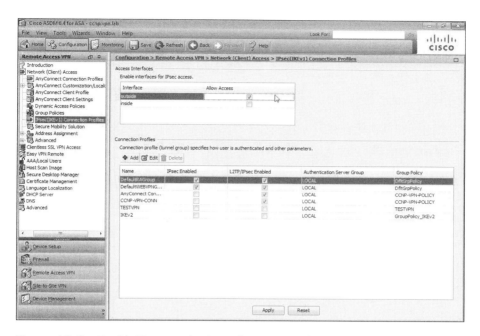

**Figure 16-3**    *Enable IPsec on the Outside ASA Interface*

When you arrive at the correct location, it is just a matter of checking the box next to the outside interface for IPsec to be enabled.

After you have enabled IPsec, a number of actions occur on the ASA device.

For example, ten new IPsec transform sets are created for the authentication and encryption parameter negotiation with clients, and they are listed in order of priority with the top of the list being preferred, as follows (these transform sets cannot be edited or deleted from the ASDM, but once applied to the ASA, they can be edited or deleted from the command-line interface [CLI]):

- ESP-AES-128-SHA

- ESP-AES-128-MD5

- ESP-AES-192-SHA

- ESP-AES-192-MD5

- ESP-AES-256-SHA

- ESP-AES-256-MD5

- ESP-3DES-SHA

- ESP-3DES-MD5

- ESP-DES-SHA

- ESP-DES-MD5

A new IKEv1 policy with priority 5 (preferred) is created with the following parameters:

- **Encryption:** 3DES (Triple Digital Encryption Standard)

- **Hash:** SHA (Secure Hash)

- **DH group:** 2

- **Authentication:** Pre-shared key

- **Lifetime (seconds):** 86400

And a second new IKEv1 policy with priority 10 is created with the following parameters:

- **Encryption:** DES

- **Hash:** SHA

- **DH group:** 2

- **Authentication:** Pre-shared key

- **Lifetime (seconds):** 86400

A new dynamic and static IPsec crypto map is configured with the priority of 65535 (appearing last in the list of any existing maps) and contains the newly created IPsec transform sets just listed. The static crypto map is also applied to the IPsec/IKEv1-enabled interface.

## Configure Preferred IKEv1 and IPsec Policies

As discussed earlier, after enabling IPsec on the outside interface, two new IKE policies and an IPsec policy (crypto map) were created. However, you can tune/modify the configured policies to offer the security parameters required by your environment. For example, many organizations might view the use of a DES policy as a security risk. Therefore, the recommended approach is to remove the policy from the list of those available and configure your own custom policies.

Begin by looking at the IKEv1 policies in place. At the moment, as shown in Figure 16-4, there are two system-configured policies with priorities 5 and 10 (with the lower policy number preferred). To continue the example configuration, navigate to **Configuration > Remote Access VPN > Network (Client) Access > Advanced > IPsec > IKE Policies,** where we remove the policy with priority 10 and create our own custom policy with the following parameters:

- **Priority:** 1. This policy will be preferred over all others in the list.

- **Encryption:** AES-256. This is the highest level of encryption offered by the ASA.

- **Hash:** SHA. It is advisable to use SHA. However, if your organization has a requirement for message digest 5 (MD5) until an upgrade takes place, this option is also available.

- **DH group:** 2 (options 1, 2, 5). Warning: If you are planning to deploy your Easy VPN for the use with remote clients using the Cisco IPsec VPN client, only group 2 is supported.

- **Authentication:** Pre-share. Each end of the VPN connection will use the same pre-shared key for peer authentication.

- **Lifetime (seconds):** Default value of 86400.

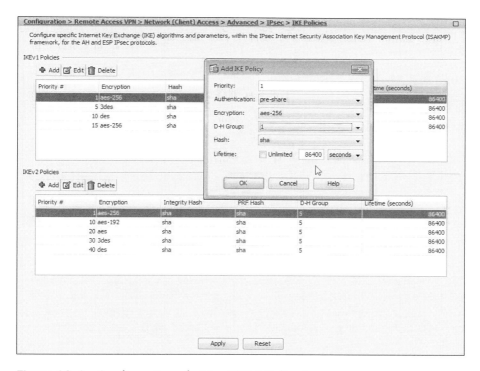

**Figure 16-4**  *Configuration of a New IKEv1 Policy Item*

IKEv1 or ISAKMP policy priority is important because the ASA, on initiating or responding to an IKEv1, behaves as follows: When initiating, it sends all of its IKEv1 policies to the remote VPN gateway for negotiation in the order of their priority, from lowest to highest. The remote endpoint compares all of these (in the order it receives them) with its own policies and stops on the first match.

With our example IKEv1 policy now configured, we move on to tuning the IPsec policy (crypto map) for use with IPsec clients. Begin by navigating to **Configuration > Remote Access VPN > Network (Client) Access > Advanced > IPsec > Crypto Maps**, shown in Figure 16-5.

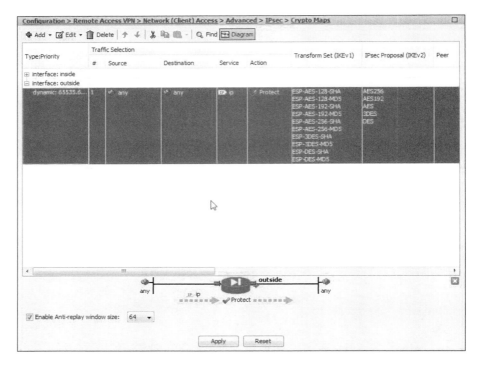

**Figure 16-5**   *IPsec Crypto Map Configuration*

The system created a dynamic IPsec crypto map, with priority 65535 currently configured to send all traffic through the VPN tunnel and offering the ten transform sets (also created earlier) for parameter negotiation with connecting clients. However, note what is not visible here is the fact that this dynamic crypto map is bound to a static crypto map, which is in turn applied on the outside interface. You cannot apply dynamic crypto maps to interfaces.

By default, this crypto map will allow Easy VPN clients to establish a VPN connection with our device.

To create a new IPsec crypto map, click **Add** in the top of the pane beneath the title bar and you are presented with the window shown in Figure 16-6.

In this window, you can specify the configuration parameters outlined in Tables 16-3, 16-4, and 16-5.

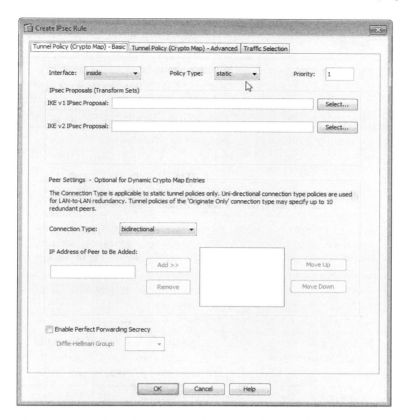

**Figure 16-6**  *IPsec Crypto Map Configuration Window*

**Table 16-3**  *Tunnel Policy (Crypto Map) Basic Tab*

| Field | Value |
|-------|-------|
| Interface | Select from the list of available interfaces this crypto map will apply to (default outside). |
| Policy Type | **Static:** Commonly used with LAN-to-LAN (L2L) tunnels whereby both peers will be configured with the same and complete information because all parameters are known. |
| | **Dynamic:** Allow the ASA to select the preferred settings from those available or configured for parameter negotiation with the client. This policy type is commonly used in remote-access VPN scenarios whereby the IP address of the connecting remote client is unknown, unlike static policies—that is, LAN-to-LAN tunnels where the IP addresses of both endpoints (local and remote) have been preconfigured. |

**Table 16-3**   *Tunnel Policy (Crypto Map) Basic Tab*

| Field | Value |
|---|---|
| Priority | Enter the priority of this crypto map. Values range from 1 to 65535, with 1 being the preferred (first) policy map to be checked for parameter matches. It is common for a dynamic catch-all policy to be given the value of 65535, allowing for more specific policies to be entered below. |
| Transform Sets to Be Added | Choose from the list of available transform sets and move up or down in your collected list to sort into a priority order. Those at the top of the list are sent to the client first. |
| Connection Type | Choose from Bidirectional, Originate Only, or Answer Only. |
| | This option specifies how the ASA will behave when configured with a VPN connection entry. However, these settings only really apply when L2L connections have been configured (static crypto maps). If you have selected Dynamic for the crypto map type earlier, this option disappears and the action of Answer Only is applied. This makes perfect sense, because you cannot initiate a VPN session with someone whose IP address is unknown to you, like a VPN client who can connect from anywhere on the Internet. |
| IP Address of Peer to Be Added | IP address of the remote VPN endpoint, applicable only for static crypto maps. Policies with the Originate Only policy type might have up to 10 backup peers configured for failover reasons. |
| Enable PFS | Disabled by default, this option allows you to specify a DH group type used to derive Phase 2 keying material instead of deriving it from the Phase 1 master key. Basically, it says that for Phase 2, a new DH exchange needs to take place. |

**Table 16-4**   *Tunnel Policy (Crypto Map) Advanced Tab*

| Field | Value |
|---|---|
| Security Association Lifetime Settings Time | Specify the length of time that will pass before a new security association (SA) is negotiated (default is 8 hours). |
| Security Association Lifetime Settings Traffic Volume | Specify the amount of traffic that will pass before a new SA is negotiated. |
| Enable NAT-T | Enabled by default. |
| Enable Reverse Route Injection | Enable the use of reverse route injection for routes to the connecting host to automatically be created and installed into the routing table of the ASA. This is disabled by default. |
| CA Certificate (Static Map Only) | Select the certificate authority (CA) certificate from a list of those configured. |

**Table 16-4**  *Tunnel Policy (Crypto Map) Advanced Tab*

| Field | Value |
|---|---|
| IKE Negotiation Mode (Static Map Only) | Choose the IKE negotiation mode used when initiating a session (the responder always negotiates this), either Main mode, which is the default, or Aggressive mode.<br><br>For Aggressive mode, you can also specify the DH group to be used (default is DH group 2). |

**Table 16-5**  *Traffic Selection Tab*

| Field | Value |
|---|---|
| Action | Choose from Protect or Do Not Protect, to indicate whether the traffic specified will be sent across the VPN tunnel. |
| Source | Choose the source of traffic from configured networks/hosts within the ASA. Source is referred to traffic coming from remote VPN endpoints. |
| Destination | Choose the destination of traffic from configured networks/hosts within the ASA. Destination is referred to traffic destined to resources protected by this ASA. |
| Service | Choose the specific service, if required, for matching traffic. (The default is IP.) If you select a specific service, such as User Datagram Protocol [UDP] or TCP, this will act as a destination service/port in correlation with the previously defined source/destination traffic. |
| Enable Rule | Selected by default. |
| Source Service (TCP or UDP Only) | Choose from a list of predefined TCP or UDP protocols. With this option, if you selected TCP or UDP previously in Service, you can also match on source UDP/TCP ports. However, you must match the protocol TCP/UDP with one from the Service selection. |
| Time Range | Choose from a list of predefined time ranges for which this rule will become active. |

## Client IP Address Assignment

IP address assignment is a mandatory configuration. If this is not configured, the VPN session for remote VPN clients will fail in IKE Phase 1.5, where Push Config takes place and the client is given an IP address and optionally DNS server, domain names, WINS servers, and so on. Although the VPN session may be correctly configured, if the client cannot receive an IP address, the ASA sees the VPN session as not functional and restricts the connection from being successful.

There is no restriction to IP addresses assigned to remote VPN clients. However, these addresses need to be unique within your enterprise and routable, so that when clients access internal resources, traffic can be routed back toward the ASA. The ASA, by default, proxies for IP addresses assigned to VPN clients, because there is no logical/physical interface on the ASA with IP address assigned from the same subnet.

For this example, we created a new internal local pool holding a small number of addresses. We named the address pool **192**. (Had this been a production network, we would have assigned a more meaningful name for quick identification.) In addition, we assigned the 192 address pool to our DefaultRAGroup connection profile.

Figure 16-7 outlines this configuration.

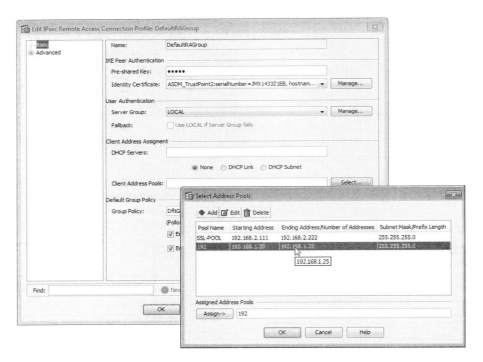

**Figure 16-7**  *Local IP Address Pool Configuration and Assignment to a Connection Profile*

At this point in the example configuration, believe it or not, we have enabled enough to allow an Easy VPN client to establish an IPsec VPN connection with our ASA. However, at the moment, connected clients can access all resources within our internal network, and we are using only group names and pre-shared keys for authentication. In the sections that follow, we discuss the use of pre-shared key configuration, XAUTH implementation, IP address allocation using internal or external servers, and the use of policies to control our client's access to resources.

## VPN Client Authentication Using Pre-Shared Keys

As shown, creating a basic configuration for a client to be able to establish a remote connection to your Easy VPN server (ASA) is pretty straightforward. However, now that we have seen how to create a basic configuration, we can start to explore the details that must further customize and secure our deployment.

A pre-shared key, also known as a group password, is by no means a foolproof authentication method. Static password schemes always inherently suffer from the issue that they are in fact static. That is, they are usually configured at the time of the VPN creation by the security administrator and then forgotten. Let's be honest here: How many of you work in an environment that makes use of IPsec VPNs and can say you change the pre-shared keys on all of your VPN connections once a week, month, or even a year? Unfortunately, this is the case in many environments, mainly due to the administrative burden that is involved with changing the key. It is not too much of a problem if you own the equipment at either end of the connection and only have a small handful of device configurations to modify. However, when you encounter a site with more than 100 VPNs and various third parties that need to be contacted to make sure they too make the configuration changes, you then start to get into the realm of our third parties' own security level agreements (SLA) and scheduled configuration windows. As you can imagine, people do not usually line up to be the one responsible for this task. However, by not changing the keys regularly, you open yourselves up to the forever-looming possibility of an attacker compromising those keys.

If an attacker were to gain access to the group name and pre-shared keys in use on your network, the attacker could initiate a connection into your environment through your ASA device. Many people also assume that by deploying XAUTH, they are protected from this very possibility occurring, because they have now introduced an additional level of authentication. It is true that the use of one-time passwords (OTP) or one-way authentication mechanisms employed by XAUTH can increase the security of your VPN deployment by prompting the user to enter additional information upon connection. However, if an attacker again had gained access to your group name and pre-shared key, the attacker is now technically able to spoof the identity of your legitimate ASA device, causing your remote clients to connect to the attacker rather than your genuine VPN head-end. Once connected, the attacker can prompt for and retrieve the user's XAUTH credentials to store them for later use when accessing our internal resources through its now established VPN to your legitimate ASA device. This kind of attack can occur when your remote clients are unable to validate the identity of the ASA device they are connecting to. However, you can thwart such an attack by implementing a hybrid-style authentication scheme, making use of Public Key Infrastructure (PKI) and certificate assignment to devices. (Chapter 17, "Advanced Authentication and Authorization Using Easy VPN," covers the use of certificates and PKI.)

For now, we return to the subject of configuring pre-shared key authentication for use between our remote clients and ASA device. We begin by creating a custom group policy object that will allow access only to IPsec VPN connections.

All other settings remain at their defaults for now. We create a new connection entry for use by our remote clients and review the pre-shared key entry. This connection entry and group policy is then referred to in later configuration tasks.

The group policy configuration has been carried out by first navigating to **Configuration > Remote Access VPN > Network (Client) Access > Group Policies**. As shown in Figure 16-8, we named it **CCNP-VPN-POLICY**. We unchecked the default **Inherit** option for the tunnel protocol configuration and have selected only IPsec. All other policy attributes have been left at their default values for now.

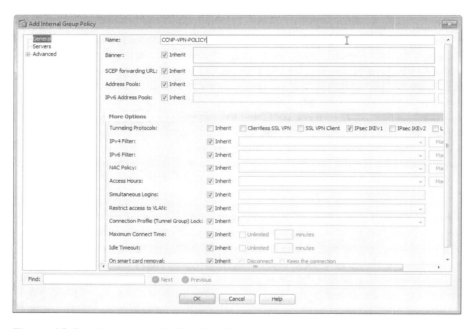

**Figure 16-8**   *IPsec Group Policy Configuration*

After creating the group policy object, we create our custom connection profile (tunnel group) and reference our newly created policy. As shown in Figure 16-9, our new connection profile has been configured with the following parameters:

- **Name:** CCNP-VPN-CONN

- **Pre-Shared Key:** security

- **Server Group:** LOCAL

- **Client Address Pools:** 192 address pool created earlier

- **Group Policy:** CCNP-VPN-POLICY

- **Enable IPsec Protocol:** Checked (Inherited from our Group Policy object)

Now that we have configured the policy and connection profile with the necessary protocols in use for our connection (IPsec) and the pre-shared key that we want to use for authentication purposes between our clients and ASA device, our ASA is ready to accept connections from remote clients.

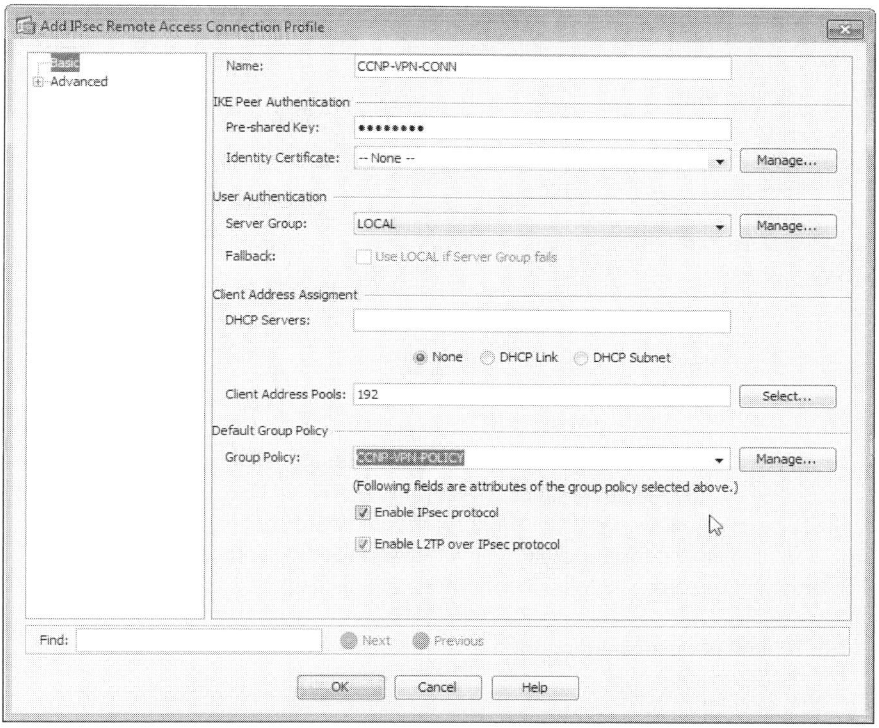

**Figure 16-9**   *Adding an IPsec Connection Profile*

Notice, however, that we cannot view the pre-shared key added. This holds true when viewing the configuration through the CLI, too. Instead, we are presented with asterisks (****). Therefore, if we ever need to validate the saved key, we cannot and run the risk of having to reenter the key (or enter a new one), which could lead to a large amount of administrative overhead if the saved key has in fact been changed by another colleague, and remote clients must now change their saved configuration for a successful connection to establish. However, all hope is not lost, because we can view the saved key, as shown Example 16-1.

**Example 16-1**   *Pre-Shared Key Retrieval*

```
Show run
!
Output Abbreviated
!
tunnel-group CCNP-VPN-CONN ipsec-attributes
pre-shared-key *****
```

```
!
Notice above the key is replaced with asterisks; however, using the following
command we can view the key in clear text, this is due to the keys being hidden by
the cli parser only during their output to the terminal
!
more system:running-config

!
Output Abbreviated
!
tunnel-group CCNP-VPN-CONN ipsec-attributes
pre-shared-key security

!
```

You can produce the same results by viewing the ASA running configuration through the HTTP console, or by downloading the configuration file to a TFTP or FTP server and viewing the file offline. However, if the thought of your pre-shared keys and passwords being stored in the native configuration file in clear text sends you running for the hills, you can overcome this using the following new commands in OS 8.3.1:

- key config-key password-encryption
- password encryption aes

## Using XAUTH for VPN Client Access

As discussed earlier, you can enable the use of XAUTH for additional authentication purposes, resulting in your users being prompted for a username and password during their connection attempt.

In this example, we use the group policy and connection profiles we created in our earlier sections. To configure XAUTH under the IPsec-specific parameters of our connection profile, we navigate to **Configuration > Remote Access VPN > Network (Client) Access > IPsec Connection Profiles**, as shown in Figure 16-10. We then open our connection profile from the list (CCNP-VPN-CONN, created earlier) and click **Edit**.

In the Connection Profile window, we navigate to **Advanced > IPsec > IKE Authentication** and choose **XAUTH (Extended User Authentication)** from the drop-down list. We have also selected the option for the ASA to display an 'Enter your Username and Password' dialog box to the user during authentication. Note that the XAUTH is enabled by default in any new connection profile you create, as it is inherited from the default DefaultRAGroup connection profile.

Next, we create our local user account for us to use when logging in to our VPN connection. We navigate to **Configuration > Device Management > Users/AAA > User Accounts** and click **Add**.

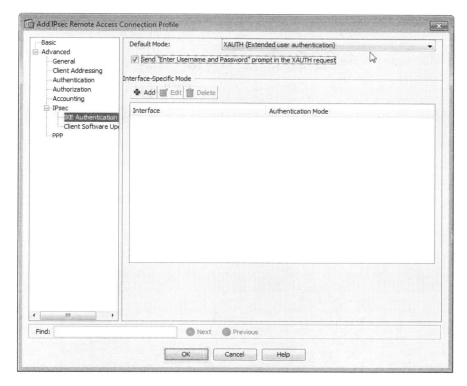

**Figure 16-10**  *Connection Profile XAUTH Configuration*

As shown in Figure 16-11, we entered the name **EzUser1** and the password **security**. We also checked the option of **No ASDM, SSH, Telnet or Console Access** because this user will be used only for the purposes of VPN authentication, and there is no need for the user to log in to the ASA device for any management capacity.

Now, when a user attempts to connect to our ASA device, they receive a prompt for additional authentication parameters, as shown in Figure 16-12. We can now enter the credentials for our new user account (created earlier) for the connection to succeed.

### IP Address Allocation Using the VPN Client

You have a few options available when deciding on an IP address assignment method.

However, before you begin the configuration, you must first tell the ASA which methods should be used, by navigating to **Configuration > Remote Access VPN > Network (Client) Access > Address Assignment > Assignment Policy**, as shown in Figure 16-13.

You have three options to choose from, listed in order of preference for assigning IP addresses to VPN clients:

■ **Use Authentication Server:** Internal and remote authentication, authorization, and accounting (AAA) servers

- **Use DHCP:** An external or internally available Dynamic Host Control Protocol (DHCP) server

- **Use Internal Address Pools:** An internal address pool configured locally on the ASA device.

For this example, we checked the **Use Authentication Server** and **Use Internal Address Pools** options. After checking the option to use internal address pools, you are presented with the option to enable the client reuse of IP addresses. This is similar in operation to DHCP lease times, in that the default timeout for leases is 5 minutes. However, it is worth considering an increase to the default if a few or many of your remote clients suffer from poor-quality connections that require them to reconnect often.

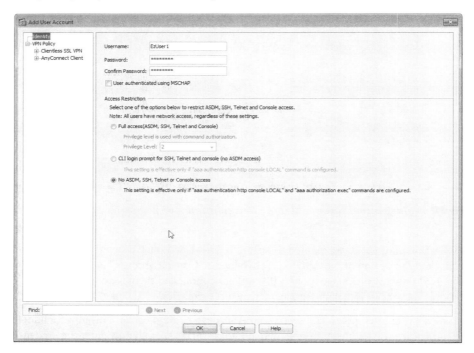

**Figure 16-11** *ASDM Local User Account Creation*

**Figure 16-12** *Cisco VPN Client XAUTH Prompt for Additional Authentication Parameters*

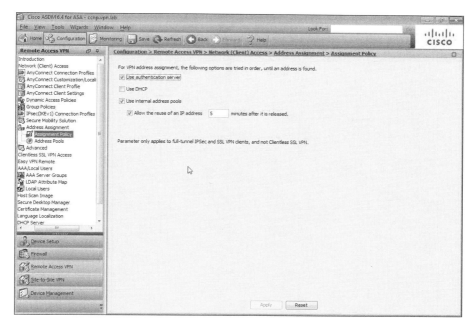

**Figure 16-13**  *IP Assignment Policy Methods*

Direct user assignment of IP addresses allows you to further control the specific addresses your users receive. For example, company directors might have specific internal access (administered with access lists) that might be easier to control if they connect using the same address each time. This also removes the need to create a DHCP reservation on a remote DHCP server, somewhat lessening the administrative burden. However, there are drawbacks to using this scheme: If you have many users into your environment, this will not scale very easily.

To configure the allocation of a specific IP address directly to our user, open the user account configuration window by navigating to **Configuration > Device Management > Users/AAA > User Accounts**. In this window, choose the **VPN Policy** option from the menu. At the bottom, enter a dedicated IP address in the last two fields, as shown in Figure 16-14.

As mentioned earlier, if your VPN deployment is in use by a large number of remote clients, a dedicated IP address assignment policy will not scale well because of the administrative overhead and general manageability. In such a case, consider the use of a DHCP scope containing the available IP addresses that are dynamically assigned to your users.

The ASA enables you to create local address pools, which, depending on your environment, may be allocated to a group of clients either by using a group policy or connection profile. For this example, we use our CCNP-VPN-CONN connection profile because we have only the one connection profile that is configured for IPsec access.

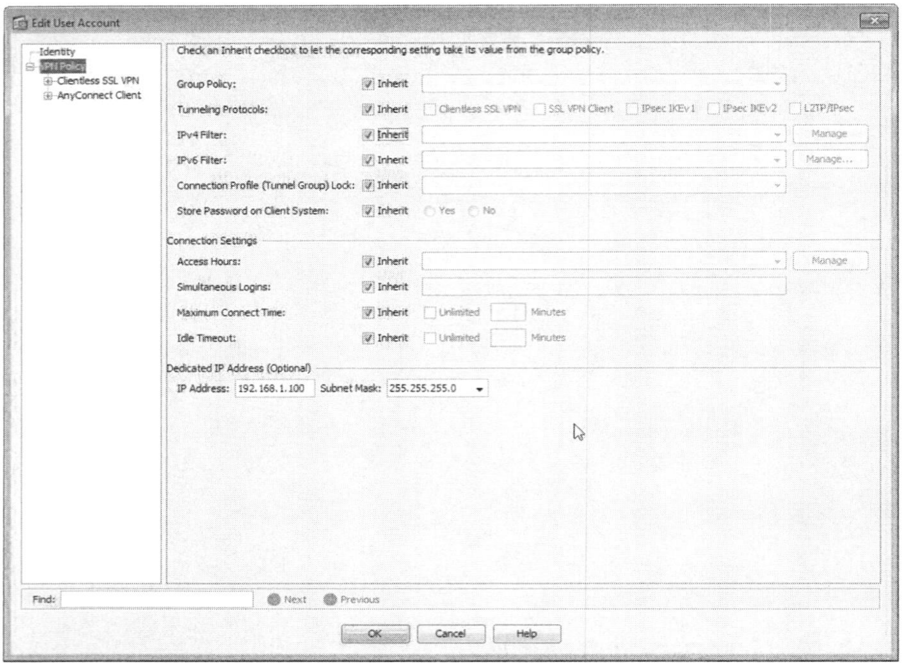

**Figure 16-14**   *User-Dedicated IP Address Assignment*

The first step in assigning an address pool to remote clients is to create one. So, navigate to **Configuration > Remote Access VPN > Network (Client) Access > Address Assignment > Address Pools** and click **Add**.

Figure 16-15 shows the configuration parameters entered for our example address pool, as follows:

■   **Name:** IPSEC-POOL

■   **Starting IP Address:** 192168.1.111

■   **Ending IP Address:** 192.168.1.222

■   **Subnet Mask:** 255.255.255.0

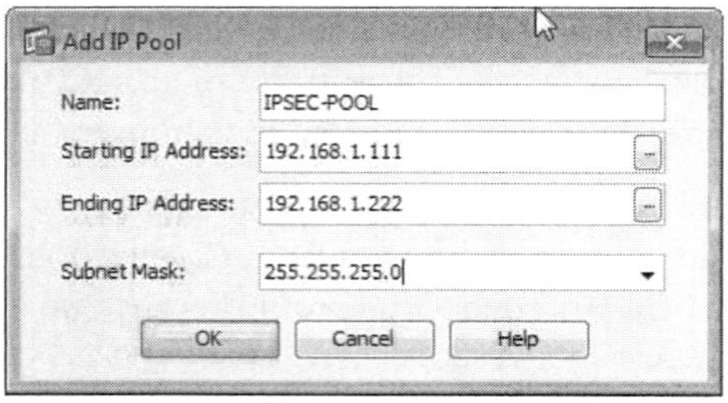

**Figure 16-15**   *IP Address Pool Creation*

After creating an address pool, you can assign it to a connection profile. Begin by opening your chosen connection profile by navigating to **Configuration > Remote Access VPN > Network (Client) Access > IPsec Connection Profiles**, selecting the connection profile from the list, and clicking **Edit**.

Figure 16-16 shows the Connection Profile window and the selection of our example address pool. We select the address pool from the list and click **Add**, and then save our configuration changes.

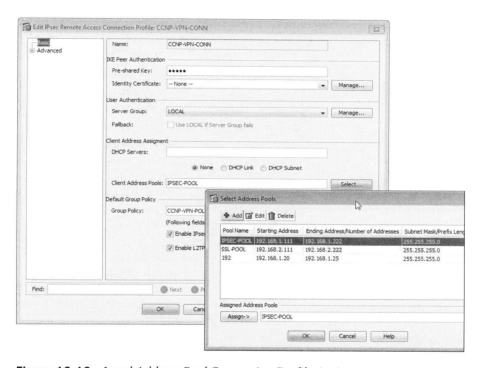

**Figure 16-16**   *Local Address Pool Connection Profile Assignment*

In addition to allocating an IP address to connected clients, it is useful, and in many instances required, to have their DNS server addresses (and optionally a DNS suffix) sent to them. You can fulfill this requirement through the use of group policy objects. Begin by navigating to **Configuration > Remote Access VPN > Network (Client) Access > Group Policies**. Select the group policy object from the list, and click **Edit**. When the group policy object edit window opens, choose the **Servers** menu option on the left, and in the pane on the right, uncheck the option to inherit DNS server settings.

Inside the DNS Servers field, you can enter up to two DNS servers, separated by a comma, space, or semicolon, as shown in the configuration in Figure 16-17.

After you enter your DNS servers, expand the available options by clicking **More Options**. You can now view the Domain field used to enter the DNS suffix that will be applied to your clients. Uncheck the **Inherit** option to edit the field contents and enter the domain suffix in use. Upon connection, your clients will now be assigned an IP address with the default lease time of 5 minutes (300 seconds) and their primary and backup DNS servers and the DNS suffix.

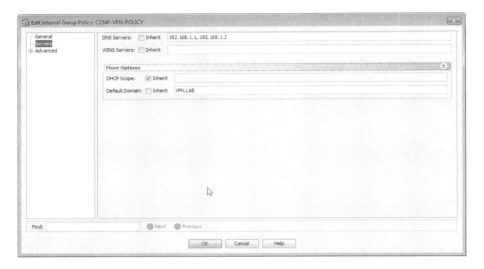

**Figure 16-17**   *User DNS Servers and DNS Suffix Configuration*

## DHCP Configuration

As discussed earlier when enabling the various address assignment features, you are also given the option of using a remote (available externally or internally to your network) DHCP server for address and network information assignment purposes. You can configure this by first enabling the use of DHCP within the available assignment methods. (Refer back Figure 16-13 for the specific configuration steps required.) When you have completed this step, you can then configure the addresses of available DHCP servers for use with your remote clients.

Open the properties window of your specific connection profile by navigating to **Configuration > Remote Access VPN > Network (Client) Access > IPsec Connection Profiles**. Select the connection profile from the available list and click **Edit**.

In the IP Address Assignment section, about midway down in the profile properties pane, enter the addresses of the available DHCP servers. The ASA allows up to ten DHCP server addresses for use by remote clients to be added. Each address is tried in the order entered until a response is received. As per RFC 2131 for DHCP, the ASA sets the giaddr field in DHCP packets it receives from remote users with the IP address of the interface used to communicate with the DHCP server (for example, the inside interface), and then forwards the modified DHCP packets to our DHCP server.

However, this causes your remote users to receive an IP addresses from the directly connected subnet of the ASA. If the DHCP server has the appropriate scope of addresses for that subnet/network configured, this behavior may be undesirable if, for example, you want to have your remote users allocated an IP address from a specific scope that is not already in use on your network. For this to occur, you must configure the ASA to include an IP address from the subnet/network that you require the IP addresses to be allocated from (within the giaddr field of received DHCP packets). Upon receipt of this information, the DHCP server can then provide a remote user with an IP address from the correct scope you have specified.

You can achieve this behavior described (whereby the ASA modifies the giaddr field accordingly) by configuring the DHCP Scope attribute in your group policy objects available, by clicking the **More Options** link in the Servers pane, as shown in Figure 16-17. In the DHCP Scope field, you can enter an IP address from the subnet/network from which you want your remote users to receive addresses. However, it is also important to note that if you create a new DHCP scope for a subnet/network that is not currently in use on your network, you also must add the appropriate routing information onto your network devices to send all packets destined for IP addresses allocated within these networks to the ASA.

## Controlling Your Environment with Advanced Features

So, you have enabled IPsec; configured your connection profiles, group policies, and authentication; and you have even given the connecting clients an IP address and DNS information. Great! They can connect and access everything on your internal network... ah, that does not sound so good anymore, does it?

Controlling the access your remote clients have when connected into your environment is an important piece of the puzzle when deploying a VPN solution. If you do not, you run the risk of your Sales users potentially being able to access your Accounts department information, your support engineers can access important HR records and find out exactly how much the Sales users are earning... and this could make for a very bad day at the office (or out of the office, depending on how you look at it). Luckily, you have a few options available that permit or deny access to certain resources based on who the user is through his or her applied policies:

- **ACL bypass:** Your ASA device can be configured to allow all VPN traffic to bypass any configured interface ACLs, thereby allowing all remote client/site traffic into your environment and gaining full internal resource access. However, implementing this option is recommended only if you are using another method of access control along the internal path to your ASA or within your network. By allowing this option, you are effectively saying, "I trust all VPN traffic entering my network." It is important to note, however, that per-group, per-user, and Dynamic Access Policy (DAP)-assigned ACLs, service policies, and service module redirection are still able to be applied even with ACL bypass enabled.

- **Interface ACLs:** If you disable ACL bypass, you can control client VPN access through the use of interface ACLs. However, this method is recommended only when a comprehensive IP addressing plan has been implemented, resulting in VPN users and groups receiving contiguous ranges of addresses. Otherwise, if the ranges are noncontiguous, you run the risk of a large number of configurations having to be entered if you are applying similar rules or regularly updating the access lists applied to all users and groups.

- **Per-group or per-user ACLs:** This is the recommended approach to controlling remote client access. ACLs can be created and applied dynamically to users or groups through policy assignment methods (that is, group policies/DAPs).

- **Split tunneling:** By default, the ASA tunnels all client traffic through the VPN to itself. However, split-tunneling rules can be configured to restrict or further control the type of traffic sent through the VPN (for example, to increase the performance of user applications that do not require the use of the VPN tunnel). Some organizations choose to allow all remote client Internet traffic to bypass the VPN tunnel and leave the client's device directly through their local Internet connection. However, by enabling such access, we open ourselves up to the potential of any compromised client devices acting as a relay between the trusted and untrusted networks (that is, forwarding unwanted traffic from the local LAN through the VPN tunnel). Organizations also risk losing the ability to filter their remote users' web traffic (which has been the source of many discussions and court battles in the past few years), unless their web filtering is carried out by a publicly available service (for example, an IronPort appliance or filtering organization).

## ACL Bypass Configuration

There are two locations within the ASDM to configure ACL bypass (although this might differ depending on the version of ASDM you are using):

- Configure > Remote Access VPN > Network (Client) Access > Advanced > IPsec > System Options

- Configure > Remote Access VPN > Network (Client) Access > Advanced > SSL VPN > Bypass Interface Access List

Both locations allow the same configuration to be applied. Just select the option presented for this configuration to take effect, as shown in Figure 16-18. Note that ACL bypass is enabled by default.

## Basic Interface ACL Configuration

With the Bypass ACL option turned off, you can configure ACLs to allow VPN client traffic access into your environment within the ASDM by navigating to **Configure > Firewall > Access Rules**. In the Access Rules window, click **Add**, and the Add Access Rule window opens. In this window, you can configure the following parameters:

- **Interface:** Select the appropriate interface from the drop-down list. You typically select the outside interface for this task unless your VPNs are terminating on a different interface.

- **Action:** Permit or Deny. If you are creating a new ACL to allow access, you would need to select the Permit action.

- **Source:** The source address is that of an IP address pool, specific IP address within a pool, or one has been assigned directly to a user.

- **Destination:** Enter the IP address or range of addresses for the internal resources to which you are granting access.

- **Service:** Select the specific service (that is, TCP, UDP, HTTP) to which you are allowing access.

- **Description:** Optionally, add a description to this ACL for informational purposes. Many organizations require the addition of a description or note for internal change management purposes.

- **Enable Logging:** By default, this box is checked to enable logging for this particular ACL entry. However, if you do not want to log any information using this ACL, uncheck the box.

- **Logging Level:** Select the level of logging (that is, how much information and what depth you require to be logged).

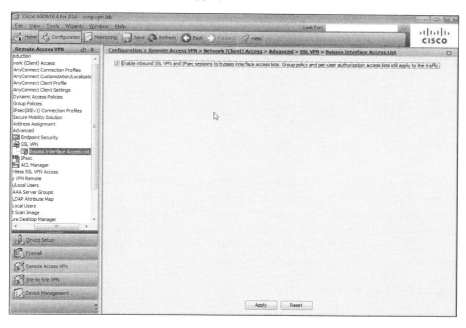

**Figure 16-18** *ACL Bypass Configuration*

If you click **More Options**, you can select to disable the rule, basically making it inactive by unchecking the **Enable Rule** box. You can also specify the source port if above filtering was done for TCP/UDP services, the time range for when this rule is active, and the direction the ACL is applied on the interface (In is the default). For our example, as shown in Figure 16-19, we created a new ACL entry that allows HTTP access from our VPN clients on the 10.10.1.0/28 subnet to the internal web server 192.168.1.10. When configuring rules, the diagram can serve as a useful tool if you have many ACLs configured and need a way to quickly determine the actions, protocols, and addresses that have been configured. The ACL diagram has also been enabled in the ASDM shown in the figure and provides a clear graphical representation of the ACL configuration.

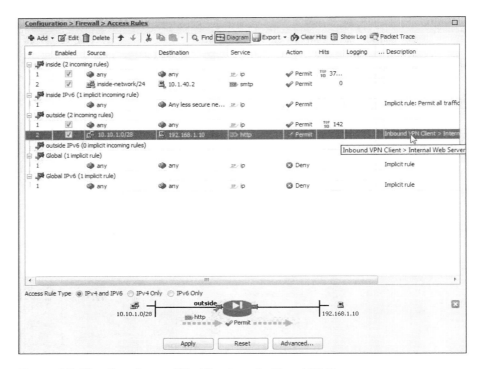

**Figure 16-19**   *Creation and Verification of a New ACL Entry*

When allowing access from VPN clients using ACLs, it is important to be wary of the possibility of non-VPN devices taking advantage of the same ACLs by spoofing the VPN addresses, because both VPN and non-VPN devices will match the configured ACL rules if the same source addresses are being used. A common way to mitigate this kind of attack is to implement ACLs or Unicast Reverse Path Forwarding (uRPF) on the upstream router (next outside hop) directly attached to your ASA.

## Per-Group ACL Configuration

As mentioned earlier, per-group or per-user ACLs are preferred over those applied directly to the interface, mainly because of management and support overhead reasons.

The configuration of an ACL entry, as you will see in a moment, is the same as you saw earlier with regard to interface ACL configuration. However, the difference this time is you are applying our ACL directly to the VPN group policy, allowing you further granularity when it comes to controlling your VPN clients' access to your internal resources.

Begin the configuration task by opening the group policy object you want to apply the ACL to by navigating to **Configuration > Remote Access VPN > Network (Client) Access > Group Policies**, highlighting your chosen group policy object, and clicking **Edit**.

As shown in Figure 16-20, expand **the More Options** section of the Edit Internal Group Policy window and uncheck **Inherit** next to the IPv4 Filter drop-down list. In a production environment, you will more than likely already have ACLs configured on your ASA and available from the drop-down list. However, for the purposes of this example, we have created a new ACL.

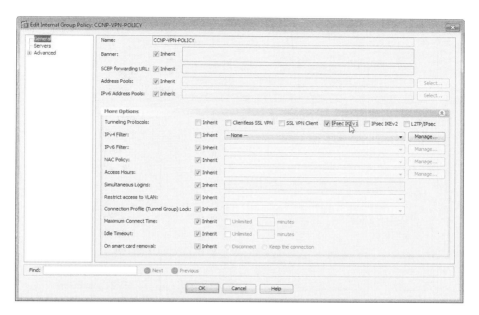

**Figure 16-20**  *Per-Group ACL Configuration: Step 1*

Click **Manage** to the right of the IPv4 Filter drop-down list shown in Figure 16-20, and the ACL Manager window opens, as shown in Figure 16-21.

To create a new access control entry (ACE) containing your chosen access rules, you must first configure an ACL for your ACE to be applied to. In the ACL Manager window, click **Add** and, from the menu, choose **ACL**. In the Add ACL dialog, enter a name for the new ACL and click **OK**. Your new entry appears in the window, and you can create your ACE by highlighting your new ACL, clicking **Add** again, and this time choosing **ACE** from the menu.

For this example in the Add Access Rule dialog, we create the same rule as shown in the "Basic Interface ACL Configuration" section, earlier in this chapter, allowing HTTP access from the VPN client subnet 10.10.1.0/28 to our internal web server 192.168.1.10, and then click **OK**. We can now see our ACL containing our new ACE in the ACL Manager window, shown in Figure 16-21.

After creating an ACL, you can apply it to a group policy. To do so, just select the entry from the group policy IPv4 Filter drop-down list, as shown in Figure 16-22.

## Per-User ACL Configuration

The configuration required for the successful implementation of per-user ACLs is similar to that of the per-group ACL configuration. The only difference, of course, is the ACL is now applied directly to a user account.

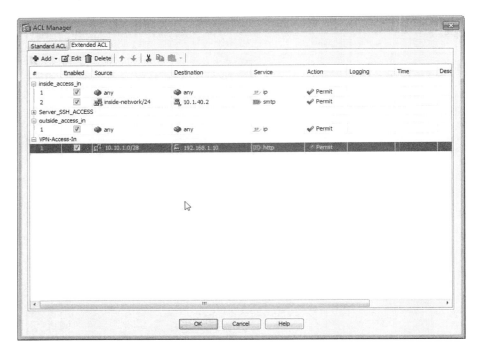

**Figure 16-21**  *Per-Group ACL Configuration: Step 2 (Creating the ACL)*

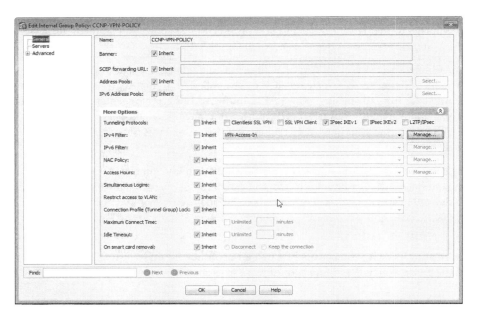

**Figure 16-22**  *Per-Group ACL Configuration: Step 3 (Apply the ACL)*

To configure the local user accounts, navigate to **Configuration > Device Management > Users/AAA > User Accounts**, select the desired user account from the list of those available, and click **Edit**. In the user account properties window, select **VPN Policy** from the menu on the left, uncheck the **Inherit** option next to the IPv4 Filter field, and select the configured ACL. If no ACLs exist, you can click **Manage** to go to the ACL Manager window and create a new one. Figure 16-23 shows the assignment of an IPv4 per-user ACL.

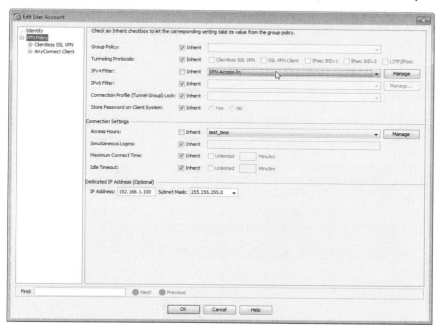

**Figure 16-23**   *Per-User ACL Assignment*

## Split-Tunneling Configuration

Recall that split tunneling enables you to control the traffic that is tunneled through the VPN connection to the ASA and the traffic that will be sent directly by the client device to the local LAN or Internet.

Begin the process of configuring split tunneling by first creating a standard access list entry. (Because you will only be matching one network/subnet/address, there is no need for the advanced source and destination capabilities an extended ACL can give you. Split tunneling actually supports only standard ACLs, and within it, you specify protected resources VPN clients are given access to.)

A standard ACL is configured in the Standard ACL window by navigating to **Configure > Firewall > Advanced > Standard ACL**. Click **Add** at the top of the pane and choose **ACL**. When prompted, enter a name for the new ACL and click **OK**. Back in the Standard ACL window, select the newly created ACL and again click **Add**. This time, choose **ACE** from the menu, and in the Add ACE dialog, leave the default action of **Permit** and add the network range, subnet, or specific IP address followed by the prefix, and then click **OK**. For this example, we entered the internal network 192.168.1.0/24.

The process of assigning a split-tunneling ACL occurs through the use of group policies. Open the group policy object on which to enable split tunneling by first navigating to **Configuration > Remote Access VPN > Network (Client) Access > Group Policies**. Highlight the group policy object in the list and click **Edit**.

In the Edit Internal Group Policy dialog, expand the **Advanced** list in the menu on the left and choose **Split Tunneling** from the list.

In the Split Tunneling pane, uncheck **Inherit** next to the Policy field, and select the desired behavior from the policy drop-down list:

■ **Tunnel All Networks:** Default

■ **Tunnel Network List Below:** Only tunnel the specified networks

■ **Exclude Network List Below:** Tunnel everything but the specified networks

For this example, we selected **Tunnel Network List Below**. To add the network list, we unchecked the **Inherit** option next to the Network List field and select the standard ACL we created earlier from the drop-down list. That is it. We have configured our desired behavior of only tunneling traffic destined to our internal network range through the VPN, and all remaining traffic (that is, Internet) will be sent directly to the destination without going through the VPN. Figure 16-24 shows this configuration.

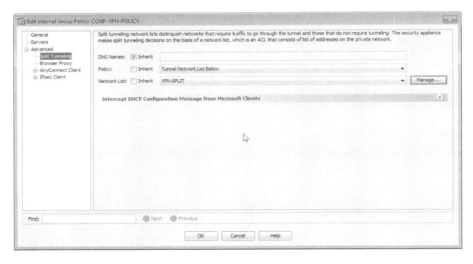

**Figure 16-24**   *Group Policy Split-Tunneling Configuration*

## Troubleshooting a Basic Easy VPN

When troubleshooting VPN connectivity between the Easy VPN server (ASA) and an IPsec client, both devices can be used to obtain further information and progress through the fault-finding process. As discussed in Chapter 15, "Deploying and Managing the Cisco VPN Client," the IPsec VPN client can be configured to log and display a large amount of protocol and process information that is extremely useful when troubleshooting VPN connectivity. The ASA can also provide a vast amount of information through both its internal logging and debugging abilities. It is recommended practice to explore the information gathered by both devices when troubleshooting a problem with VPN connectivity. Note that for simple configuration mismatches, the ASA will be specific enough in its logging, and you may find that enabling debugging for the problem is unnecessary. However, for advanced problems, enabling debugging can provide you with a great deal of detailed information.

You can use the flowchart in Figure 16-25 as a troubleshooting guide when faced with VPN connectivity errors.

Key
Topic

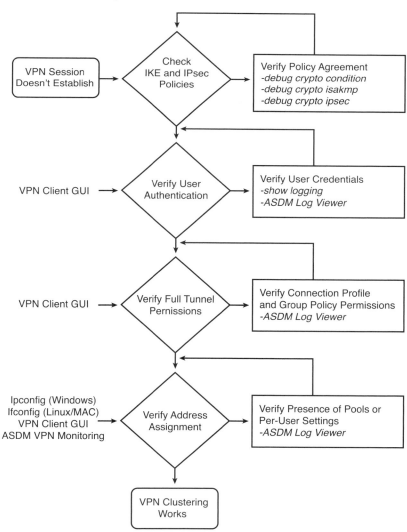

**Figure 16-25**  *Basic Easy VPN Troubleshooting Flowchart*

## Exam Preparation Tasks

As mentioned in the section "How to Use This Book" in the Introduction, you have a couple of choices for exam preparation: the memory tables in Appendix C, Chapter 23, "Final Exam Preparation," and the exam simulation questions on the CD-ROM.

## Review All Key Topics

Review the most important topics in the chapter, noted with the Key Topic icon in the outer margin of the page. Table 16-6 lists a reference of these key topics and the page numbers on which each is found.

**Table 16-6**  *Key Topics*

| Key Topic Element | Description | Page |
|---|---|---|
| Table | Basic information required for Easy VPN configuration | 518 |
| Topic | Easy VPN basic configuration | 519 |
| Bulleted List | Pre-shared authentication configuration | 530 |
| Bulleted List | Available client IP address-allocation methods | 539 |
| Bulleted List | Available methods for controlling VPN client resource access | 540 |
| Topic | Troubleshooting a basic Easy VPN | 547 |

## Complete Tables and Lists from Memory

Print a copy of Appendix C, "Memory Tables" (found on the CD), or at least the section for this chapter, and complete the tables and lists from memory. Appendix D, "Memory Tables Answer Key," also on the CD, includes completed tables and lists to check your work.

## Define Key Terms

Define the following key terms from this chapter and check your answers in the glossary:

ACE (access control entry), ACL (access control list), split tunneling

This chapter covers the following subjects:

■ **Authentication Options and Strategies:** In this section, we review the information discussed in earlier chapters about the use of PKI, digital certificates, and certificate mappings. In addition, we introduce the use of NTP for correct local clock synchronization for the purposes of certificate validation.

■ **Configuring PKI with IPsec Easy VPNs:** In this section, we review the tasks required for PKI configuration used for Easy VPN authentication purposes.

■ **Configuring Certificate Mappings:** In this section, we review the certificate mappings feature for correct certificate choice and presentation to our remote clients.

■ **Provisioning Certificates from a Third-Party CA:** In this section, we discuss the use of a third-party root CA for the purposes of certificate enrollment and generation.

■ **Advanced PKI Deployment Strategies:** In this section, we review the available methods for advanced deployment of digital certificates within your environment with the use of OCSP and CRL.

■ **Troubleshooting Advanced Authentication for Easy VPN:** In this section, we provide a brief overview of some of the common troubleshooting tools available when working with an Easy VPN failure scenario.

## CHAPTER 17

# Advanced Authentication and Authorization Using Easy VPN

As discussed in earlier chapters, the use of digital certificates and Public Key Infrastructure (PKI) is widespread for authentication purposes and heavily implemented within Secure Sockets Layer virtual private network (SSL VPN) deployments. In this chapter, we briefly review the PKI concept and digital certificate method of authentication, and we then explore the information and configuration tasks required for their deployment within an Easy VPN solution.

## "Do I Know This Already?" Quiz

The "Do I Know This Already?" quiz helps you determine your level of knowledge on this chapter's topics before you begin. Table 17-1 details the major topics discussed in this chapter and their corresponding quiz sections.

**Table 17-1** *"Do I Know This Already?" Section-to-Question Mapping*

| Foundation Topics Section | Questions |
| --- | --- |
| Advanced PKI Deployment Strategies | 1, 2, 6 |
| Authentication Options and Strategies | 3, 4 |
| Configuring PKI with IPsec Easy VPNs | 5 |

1. Within which field of a digital certificate used for identity reasons would you commonly find a username?

   a. S

   b. CN

   c. SP

   d. AIA

2. Which of the following are valid certificate revocation list methods? (Choose all that apply.)

   a. OCSP

   b. HTTP

   c. CRL

   d. AAA

**3.** When choosing to implement a one-way certificate-based authentication scheme, which one would you choose?

    **a.** Mutual/hybrid

    **b.** Certificate

    **c.** Pre-shared key

    **d.** XAUTH

**4.** When configuring your ASA to use more than one NTP server, what parameter decides whether one server is used or the other?

    **a.** Priority

    **b.** Preferred

    **c.** Accuracy

    **d.** Trusted key

**5.** True or false: After receiving a digital certificate from a CA, you import it into the Windows certificate store using the wizard; before you can view the certificate in the Cisco IPsec VPN client, you must also manually import the certificate using the VPN client.

    **a.** True

    **b.** False

**6.** When examining a digital certificate for the available OCSP and CRL revocation list locations, which fields would you find the information in?

    **a.** AIA

    **b.** SER

    **c.** CDP

    **d.** CN

# Foundation Topics

## Authentication Options and Strategies

In earlier discussions about a basic Easy VPN deployment, you learned that several authentication options are available. We have already discussed a pre-shared key and XAUTH-based deployment, so in this chapter we continue with a discussion of the two remaining authentication options:

- Mutual/hybrid authentication

- Authentication using digital certificates

Both options require the use of digital certificates. If you recall, digital certificates are used to provide a method of validating the identity of a server, client, or other device. The device's corresponding public key is sent with the certificate.

A certificate is issued by a certificate authority (CA), which may be public (commercial provider) or private (internal), depending on your organization's chosen PKI deployment. Regardless of the type of CA, when a digital certificate is used for the purposes of authentication, the issuing CA must also be trusted by the authenticating device or browser that received the certificate. Otherwise, the certificate will be assumed invalid and the peer unauthenticated. Figure 17-1 shows this process.

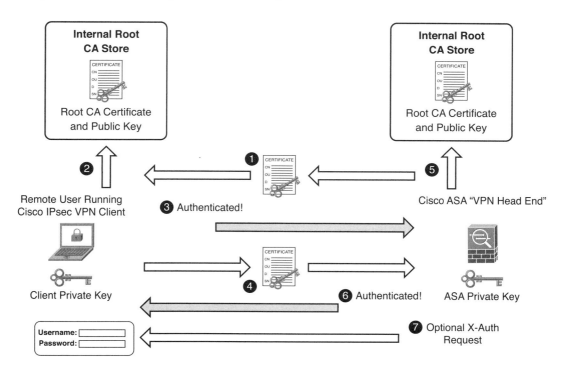

**Figure 17-1**  *Basic Digital Certificate Authentication Process*

Following is an explanation of the steps shown in Figure 17-1:

1. The Adaptive Security Appliance (ASA) has sent a copy of its digital certificate to the IPsec client for authentication purposes. The certificate has been encrypted/digitally signed using the root CA's private key on being issued to the ASA.

2. The IPsec client receives the ASA's certificate, verifies that the root CA's certificate (that issued the ASA's certificate) is in its local trusted root CA store, and decrypts (verifies the signature) the ASA certificate using the stored root CA's public key.

3. The ASA's certificate has been validated using the stored CA information, and the authenticity of the ASA is confirmed.

4. The IPsec client sends a copy of its digital certificate to the ASA for authentication purposes. The certificate has been encrypted/digitally signed using the issuing root CA's private key.

5. The ASA receives the IPsec client's certificate, verifies the issuing root CA's certificate is in its local trusted root CA store, and decrypts (verifies the signature) the clients certificate using the stored root CA's public key.

6. The IPsec client's certificate has been validated using the stored CA information, and the authenticity of the IPsec is confirmed.

7. (Optional) In the case of mutual/hybrid or certificate authentication, the connecting user of the IPsec client can now be prompted for additional authentication information using XAUTH. If XAUTH was disabled on the ASA at the connection profile level, this step does not occur.

You may recall that when a host wants to receive a certificate for the purpose of sending to devices for validation checking, a request is sent to a CA, along with the device's public key from a generated private/public key pair. The process of requesting a certificate from a CA is known as enrollment.

A host can use two methods when enrolling with a CA, depending on the services made available by the CA:

■ **Automatic enrollment (online):** The device may send its information gathered to the CA for the purposes of enrollment to a URL or online script for automatic enrollment purposes.

■ **Manual enrollment (offline):** The device compiles all requested information along with its public key and stores the information in a file offline. This file can be later emailed or uploaded to the CA for processing and validation procedures to take place.

Both the IPsec VPN client and the ASA support automatic and manual enrollment methods.

For the purposes of verifying the validity of digital certificates (among other parameters), the fields Valid From and Valid To are included in the certificate and checked against the receiving device's date and time. Therefore, it is important that the local devices have the correct and accurate time and date information. You can do so by manually setting the clock on each device. However, the accuracy of such a task can be questioned (that is, the source you are using, your ability to set the specific time, and so on). Therefore, the use Network Time Protocol (NTP) is preferred and encouraged for accurate time synchronization of the devices on your network.

To configure NTP on your ASA device, begin by opening the NTP window by navigating to **Configuration > Device Setup > System Time > NTP**.

Click **Add** on the left side, and in the Add NTP Server Configuration window, provide the information shown in Table 17-2.

**Table 17-2** *Add NTP Server Configuration*

| Field | Description |
| --- | --- |
| IP address | Add the IP address of the NTP server. (This may be the IP address of a publicly available NTP server or an internal server on your network.) |
| Interface | Select the interface the server will be contacted through. If no interface is selected, the ASA uses the default route to try to locate the server. |
| Preferred | If you have entered multiple servers and require this one to be preferred over others, select this option. However, depending on the accuracy of the server, if another server's time is more accurate than the preferred, it is used instead. |
| Key Number | Select from the list or enter a number for this authentication key. |
| Trusted | This option must be selected for authentication to work successfully. |
| Key Value | Enter the message digest 5 (MD5) key used by the server for authentication. |
| Re-Enter Key Value | Reenter the MD5 key. |

Figure 17-2 shows the Add NTP Server Configuration dialog and with parameters entered as described here.

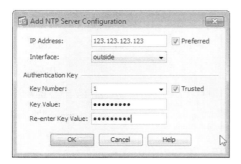

**Figure 17-2** *ASA NTP Server Configuration*

## Configuring PKI with IPsec Easy VPNs

Before your remote users can successfully establish a working VPN connection using certificate-based authentication, you must first enable the use of certificates in two places:

- ASA connection profile (tunnel group)
- IPsec VPN client

The process of enabling certificate-based authentication for IPsec VPNs is largely the same as that for clientless SSL VPNs. Each IPsec connection profile that will be using certificate-based authentication requires an identity certificate to be selected.

To select an identity certificate, navigate in the Adaptive Security Device Manager (ASDM) to **Configuration > Remote Access VPN > Network (Client) Access > IPsec Connection Profiles**, select the connection profile you want to edit from the list, and click **Edit** to open the properties window, as shown in Figure 17-3.

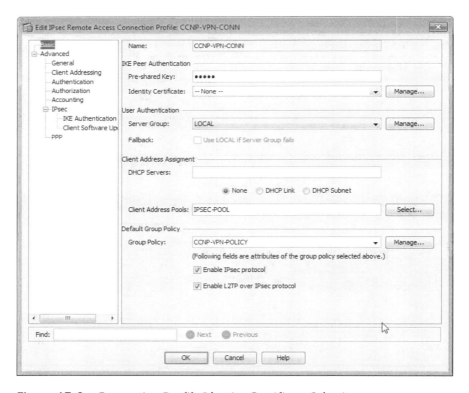

**Figure 17-3**  *Connection Profile Identity Certificate Selection*

If you have an existing identity certificate installed, it is just a matter of selecting the certificate from the drop-down list under the Identity Certificate section. However, if no certificates are installed, then you begin the process of obtaining one by clicking the **Manage** button. The Manage Identify Certificates dialog will open, as shown in Figure 17-4.

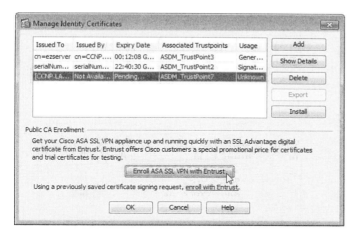

**Figure 17-4**   *ASA Manage Identity Certificates Dialog*

In this dialog, click the option to **Enroll ASA SSL VPN with Entrust** to create a new certificate signing request (CSR). By selecting this option, you are not, however, limited to using Entrust as your certificate provider, as shown in Figure 17-5.

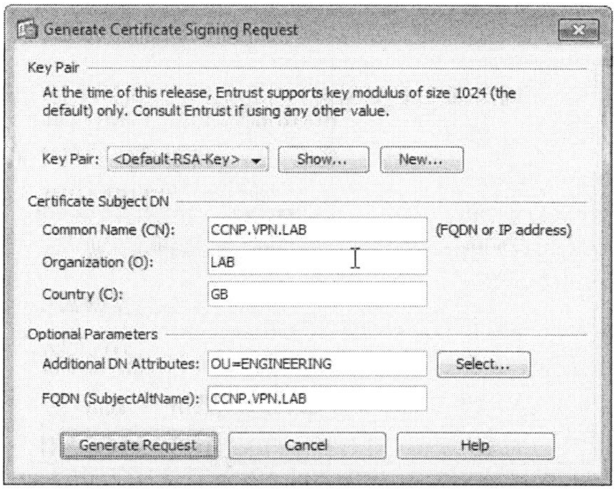

**Figure 17-5**   *Generate a Certificate Signing Request*

When creating a new CSR, you can also create a new key pair, use one you have already created, or select the default pair. In this window, enter the Common Name (CN) for use with the certificate, and optionally the organization, country, fully qualified domain name

(FQDN), and any additional fields you might want to use later for certificate mapping reasons. After the required and optional information is entered, click the **Generate Request** button. You are then presented with the new CSR, as shown in Figure 17-6. You can either save the text to a file for later or offline use or copy the contents of the CSR to your Clipboard and paste it into an online form, used by the majority of online certificate providers. Regardless of your selection to use a public or local CA server, the process of generating a CSR is the same. It is important to note, however, that you will also require the root CA and any intermediate root CA certificates used by the certificate provider installed on your device for the authentication process to succeed.

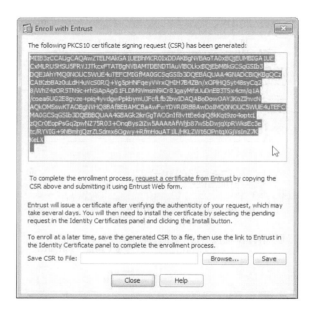

**Figure 17-6**   *New CSR (Enroll with Entrust) Window*

After submitting your new CSR, receiving your identity certificate back, and importing the certificate onto your device, you can select the certificate for use with your connection profile (previously illustrated in Figure 17-3).

The process of configuring an IPsec VPN client to use certificate-based authentication is also straightforward. If an identity certificate and associated root CA certificates are already installed in the local machine's certificate store, the VPN client software loads them automatically upon startup (Windows). These are shown within the certificate's pane and their associated store listed as Microsoft, as shown in Figure 17-7. By default, you cannot view the CA root and intermediate certificates within the VPN client. However, you can change this behavior to make all certificates viewable by choosing the **Show CA/RA Certificates** option from the client's Certificates menu.

If an identity certificate is not yet installed, however, you can create a new CSR for one by clicking **Enroll.** The Certificate Enrollment dialog opens, and you can choose whether this is to be a manual or automatic enrollment, as shown in Figure 17-8.

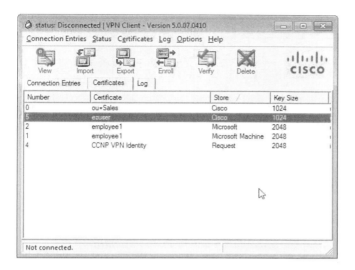

**Figure 17-7**   *Cisco IPsec VPN Client Certificate Store*

**Figure 17-8**   *Cisco IPsec VPN Client Certificate Enrollment Method*

Remember that automatic enrollment involves the process of contacting the server via a specified URL using Simple Certificate Enrollment Protocol (SCEP), whereas manual enrollment involves the creation of a local CSR file for later uploading or emailing to the issuing CA.

When the preferred method for enrollment is chosen, click **Next** and enter any information you have available (or require, in the case of certificate mappings) to populate the various certificate fields. As shown in Figure 17-9, the list is not exhaustive. The only field that is marked as required when enrolling using the IPsec client is the certificate's CN. It is typical with identity certificates used for the purposes of authentication to enter the remote user's username or device name into this field for accounting purposes. However, this may vary depending on your deployment.

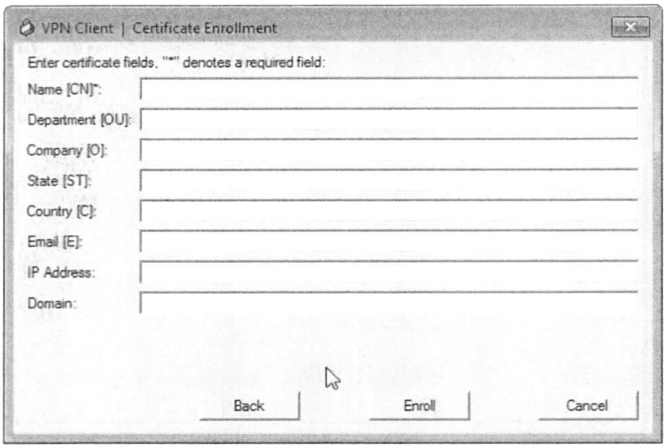

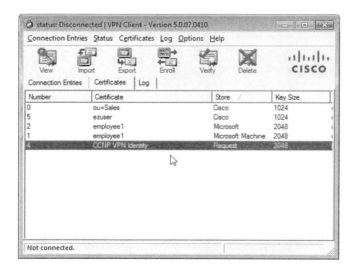

**Figure 17-9**   *Cisco IPsec VPN Client Certificate Enrollment Field Population*

After entering the necessary information into the Enrollment window, click **Enroll**. A dialog box alerts you to the creation of the CSR (if offline is chosen) or the status of the automatic enrollment (denied or successful).

Back on the Certificates tab, you can now see your new identity certificate in the list, and the store is currently identified as Request, as shown in Figure 17-10. Because for this example we have chosen to generate the CSR offline, once we have received the approved certificate file back from the CA, we can import it by clicking **Import**. If there are no errors with the file after the import has completed, the certificate will move from the Request store to the Cisco certificate store.

**Figure 17-10**   *Cisco IPsec VPN Client CSR Pending Certificate Import*

After you have installed your identity certificates and those of your root CA, you must configure the connection entry to use certificate-based authentication.

Select the connection from the available list on the Connection Entries tab and choose **Modify** from the menu bar. In the connection entry properties window that opens, select **Certificate Authentication**. From the drop-down list of available certificates, select your chosen identity certificate for this connection and click **Save**. You should now be able to establish the connection successfully using certificate authentication.

**Note:** Although the configuration shown here is walking you through creating and editing the necessary connection entries and profiles to enable certificate-based authentication, by default, the Internet Key Exchange (IKE) policies (Phase 1) have only been created for use with pre-shared key authentication. To use certificate-based authentication, you must create new IKE policies on your ASA device using the RSA-SIG authentication method.

## Configuring Mutual/Hybrid Authentication

Mutual/hybrid authentication, so named because of the difference in terminology between the IPsec VPN client and the ASA, is carried out using a combination of pre-shared keys and certificates. However, unlike the use of native certificate-based authentication discussed in the preceding section, only the ASA requires an identity certificate to be installed and configured within the connection profile authentication methods.

Although the client does not require its own identity certificate, it does require the certificate of any CA or intermediate CAs that are responsible for issuing the ASA's identity certificate. After retrieving the issuing CA certificates and installing them into its local "trusted root certificate store," the client can validate the authenticity of the received ASA's identity certificate.

As with other authentication methods, the use of XAUTH for user-based authentication is optional, and if required, may also be configured for additional security purposes.

To configure mutual authentication on the IPsec VPN client, the CA root certificate responsible for the ASA's identity certificate must be installed in the device's local certificate store. You can do so by obtaining a local copy of the certificate on the device and clicking **Import** in the IPsec client (and carry out the same action for any additional root certificates that may also have been issued by this CA). In the Connection Entries window, select the connection entry from the list, and in the Properties dialog, as shown in Figure 17-11, click the **Mutual Group Authentication** radio button, enter the valid group name and pre-shared key, and click **Save**.

Configuration for the client is now complete. However, you must also configure your ASA for use with mutual authentication, as follows:

**Step 1.**   Enter the connection profile name (group name).

**Step 2.**   Enter the pre-shared key.

**Step 3.**   Select the identity certificate to use with the connection profile.

**Step 4.**   Enable the use of hybrid XAUTH authentication.

**Figure 17-11**   *Cisco IPsec VPN Client Enabling Mutual Group Authentication*

We have already described the first three steps, so we move directly to enabling hybrid XAUTH. To configure hybrid XAUTH authentication, navigate from the connection profile properties window to **IPsec > IKE Authentication**, as shown in Figure 17-12, change the current default mode from XAUTH (Extended Authentication) to **Hybrid XAUTH**, and click **OK**.

At this point, the configuration will now allow your remote client and ASA to form a successful VPN tunnel between them (depending on the correct pre-shared key and group name being used).

# Configuring Digital Certificate Mappings

As you saw in the chapters covering clientless SSL VPNs, you can select the connection profile a user receives based on specific information you have entered into their identity certificates.

The various fields can be matched by a certificate-to-connection profile map that may be configured with one or more rules that define the fields that match. Therefore, you can use a granular approach when faced with multiple users who might have matching information within the various fields of their identity certificates. In this example, we have two users initiate a new connection to our ASA device (userA and userB). We then have two certificate profile maps that have been configured with the following rules:

- CertificateMAP1
    - Rule1 - Organizational Unit (OU) = Engineering
    - Connection Profile - EngGeneric

- CertificateMAP2
  - Rule1 - Organizational Unit (OU) = Engineering
  - Rule2 - State/Province (SP) = NY
  - Connection Profile EngNY

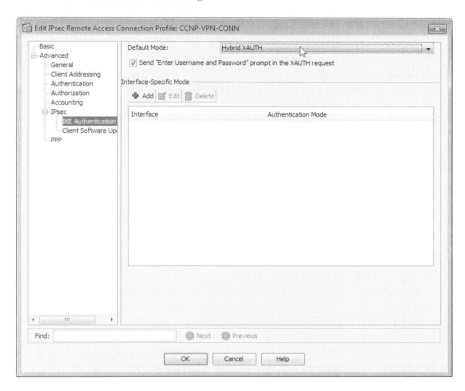

**Figure 17-12**   *Connection Profile Hybrid XAUTH Configuration*

Based on this certificate-to-connection profile mapping information, if userA and userB both have the OU field Engineering in their certificate, they will connect using the EngGeneric connection profile. However, if userB's SP field value is NY and userA's SP field value is NJ, the connection profile EngNY is applied to userB, and EngGeneric to userA.

In addition to creating your own custom certificate mapping profiles, the ASDM enables you to specify criteria used for mapping a connection profile in the way of policies. These are a series of option boxes and can be configured in the Certificate to Connection Profile Maps Policy pane in the following ASDM location: **Configure > Remote Access VPN > Network (Client) Access > Advanced > IPsec > Certificate to Connection Profile Maps > Policy**. In the Policy pane, you are given the following options:

- Use the configured rules to match a certificate to a connection profile. (This option must be selected before any incoming identity certificates are evaluated against your configured mapping rules.)

- Use the certificate OU field to determine the connection profile.

- Use the IKE identity to determine the connection profile.

- Use the peer IP address to determine the connection profile.

- Default connection profile. Select the default connection profile name from the drop-down list of those configured. If none of the points listed match along with any custom certificate maps you have created, the user will be applied this connection profile.

Note that if several or all the options are enabled, the ASA tries to map an incoming VPN session to a connection profile in the order of operation as listed here.

You can also configure the mapping profiles and rules as described here by navigating to **Configure > Remote Access VPN > Network (Client) Access > Advanced > IPsec > Certificate to Connection Profile Maps > Rules.**

Creating a new certificate to connection profile map is a two-step process:

**Step 1.** Create a new map.

Create a new map by clicking **Add** underneath the Certificate to Connection Profile Maps section of the pane. In the window that opens, enter a name for the new map, enter the priority value (anything from 0 to 65535, with the lower number being the higher priority), and choose the connection profile this map will apply to (that is, which connection profile will be applied to the users who match the parameters matched in the rules configured for this policy).

**Step 2.** Create rules and apply them to the new map.

To create a new rule, select the map created in the previous step (or an existing one) and click **Add** in the Mapping Criteria section of the Rules pane. In the Add Certificate Matching Rule Criterion window, you can select from the fields listed in Table 17-3, and enter the values required for a match to occur.

**Table 17-3**  *Create a New Certificate-to-Profile Map Rule*

| Field | Component |
|---|---|
| Subject | —Whole Field— |
| Subject | Country (C) |
| Subject | Common Name (CN) |
| Subject | DN Qualifier (DNQ) |
| Subject | E-mail Address (EA) |
| Subject | Generational Qualifier (GENQ) |
| Subject | Given Name (GN) |
| Subject | Initials (I) |
| Subject | Locality (L) |

**Table 17-3**  *Create a New Certificate-to-Profile Map Rule*

| Field | Component |
| --- | --- |
| Subject | Name (N) |
| Subject | Organization (O) |
| Subject | Organizational Unit (OU) |
| Subject | Serial Number (SER) |
| Subject | Surname (SN) |
| Subject | State/Province (SP) |
| Subject | Title (T) |
| Subject | User ID (UID) |
| Subject | Unstructured Name (UNAME) |
| Subject | IP Address (IP) |
| Subject | Domain Component (DC) |
| Alternative Subject | Custom Value |
| Issuer | —Whole Field— |
| Issuer | Country (C) |
| Issuer | Common Name (CN) |
| Issuer | DN Qualifier (DNQ) |
| Issuer | E-mail Address (EA) |
| Issuer | Generational Qualifier (GENQ) |
| Issuer | Given Name (GN) |
| Issuer | Initials (I) |
| Issuer | Locality (L) |
| Issuer | Name (N) |
| Issuer | Organization (O) |
| Issuer | Organizational Unit (OU) |
| Issuer | Serial Number (SER) |
| Issuer | Surname (SN) |
| Issuer | State/Province (SP) |
| Issuer | Title (T) |
| Issuer | User ID (UID) |

**Table 17-3** *Create a New Certificate-to-Profile Map Rule*

| Field | Component |
|---|---|
| Issuer | Unstructured Name (UNAME) |
| Issuer | IP Address (IP) |
| Issuer | Domain Component (DC) |
| Extended Key Usage | Select Values from |
| | Clientauth |
| | Codesigning |
| | Emailprotection |
| | Ocspsigning |
| | Serverauth |
| | Timestamping |

Rules are given automatic priority levels when configured, with the ordering of the rules from highest priority (lowest number) to lowest priority.

## Provisioning Certificates from a Third-Party CA

This section provides a working example of an IPsec VPN client configured to connect to an ASA device. Both are using the unique identity certificates that have been assigned to them using the local CA configured on the ASA. Note that in the CCNP Security VPN exam course, this particular section of the course uses the Microsoft CA server, which is available only on the Windows Server platforms. However, for certificate enrollment purposes, the majority of CAs follow a process similar to the one described earlier, whether they require a CSR file emailed to them, the contents of the file pasted into an online form, or enrollment via an automatic process.

**Note:** The following information in this section assumes you have already configured the local CA server on the ASA device. If you are unfamiliar with the configuration required for enabling the local CA server, you are encouraged to read Chapter 11, "Customizing the Clientless Portal."

For this example, we begin by creating two users in our local CA server database with the following attributes:

- **Username:** ezuser
- **Email ID:** ezuser@company.com
- **Subject (DN String):** OU=Sales
- **Device/Role:** Cisco IPsec VPN Client
- **Username:** ezserver

- **Email ID:** ezserver@company.com

- **Subject (DN String):** OU=Engineering

- **Device/Role:** ASA Device

After the addition of the users, we select each in turn and click **Email OTP**. This causes the ASA to send each remote user an email (to the email address configured in their user account) via the mail server we entered into the local CA server configuration. The email contains information similar to that shown in Example 17-1.

**Example 17-1**  *Received Enrollment Email from ASA CA Admin*

```
You have been granted access to enroll for a certificate.
The credentials below can be used to obtain your certificate.
 Username: ezuser
 One-time Password: B3DC9569C6572F1A
 Enrollment is allowed until: 07:50:36 UTC Mon Nov 22 2010
NOTE: The one-time password is also used as the passphrase to unlock the
certificate file.
Please visit the following site to obtain your certificate:
https://CCNP.VPN.LAB/+CSCOCA+/enroll.html
You may be asked to verify the fingerprint/thumbprint of the CA certificate
during installation of the certificates. The fingerprint/thumbprint
should be:
 MD5: F39470FE 493EC3C1 210416D2 42F4B0CB
 SHA1: A8BC57F3 CBE92751 961DEFF6 2A09AA5F 58E72A80
```

When the remote user opens the URL as directed, the ASA user enrollment screen appears, as illustrated in Figure 17-13. For purposes of this example, we created a test remote user account in our CA database. Our test user receives an email from the ASA's CA, and we log in to the CA web portal using the link, username, and OTP contained in the email. After clicking **Submit**, we are prompted to save or open our certificate information. For this example, we have saved the certificate to our desktop. The process we have just carried out for our test remote user (ezuser) is the same for any remote users you have set up for certificate enrollment.

We carry out the same actions as earlier for the ezserver user, and now we have the identity certificates we require for authentication. (The certificate information is downloaded from the ASA CA in PKCS#12 format, automatically containing the CA chain [CA root] certificates we require.)

Now that we have our identity certificates, we can carry on with the configuration process and import them onto our devices. To import the certificate for the ezuser user account, we open the Cisco IPsec VPN client, navigate to **Certificates > Import**, and in the Import Certificate window shown in Figure 17-14, select the certificate file on the desktop we saved earlier. We enter the one-time password (OTP) received in the email from the ASA local CA as the passphrase, and then click **Import**. A pop-up window announces the successful import of the certificate information.

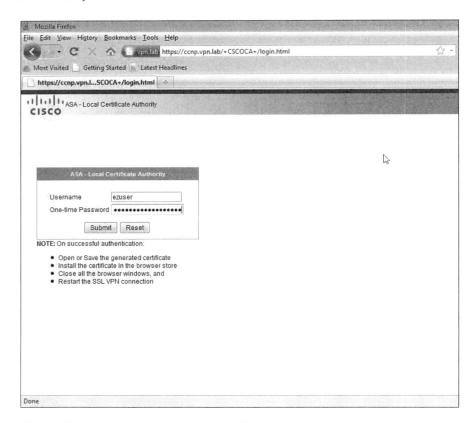

**Figure 17-13**   *ASA Local CA User Enrollment*

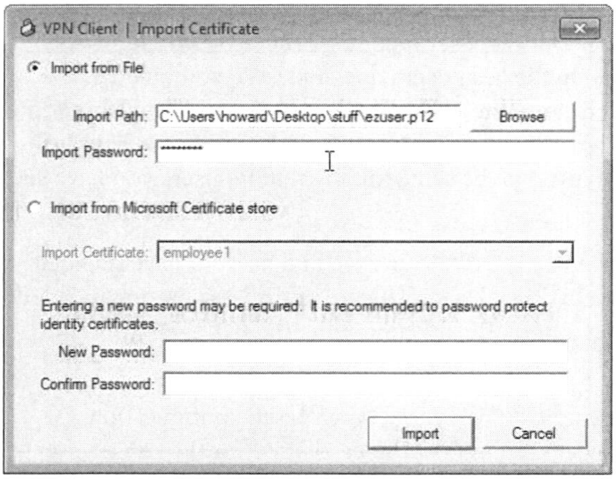

**Figure 17-14**   *Cisco IPsec VPN Client: Import Certificate Window*

After the certificate has been imported successfully into the VPN client's certificate store, we can now use it for authentication with our Easy VPN connection. In the IPsec client, we display the **Connection Entries** tab, select the desired connection entry from the list, and click **Modify** to open the connection entry's Properties window, shown in Figure 17-15.

**Figure 17-15**  *Cisco IPsec VPN Client: Configure Certificate Authentication*

In this window, we select the authentication type as **Certificate Based**, and from the drop-down menu, choose our newly imported identity certificate for the ezuser user account. We then click **Save**.

To import the new identity certificate for the ezserver user account into our ASA's certificate store, we open the Identity Certificates window, found by navigating to **Configure > Remote Access VPN > Certificate Management > Identity Certificates**. We click **Add** and enter a name for the trustpoint. (This is optional; you can choose to keep the default of TrustPoint<next available number>.) Then (similar to the VPN client process earlier), we select the certificate we saved to our desktop earlier, but this time we choose the one for user ezserver. We then enter the OTP included in the original enrollment email for the passphrase, as shown in Figure 17-16.

**Note:**  The local CA certificate, which is actually a self-signed certificate at the moment the local CA was enabled, cannot be used as an identity certificate. The CA certificate is used only to digitally sign certificates to endpoints. This is why you actually need an identity certificate on the ASA itself.

When we finish entering our information, we click **Add Certificate**. We can now use this identity certificate in our connection profile for the purposes of peer authentication.

We start by navigating in the ASDM to **Configure > Remote Access VPN > Network (Client) Access > IPsec Connection Profiles**, select our chosen connection profile from the list, and then click **Edit** to open the Edit Connection Profile dialog.

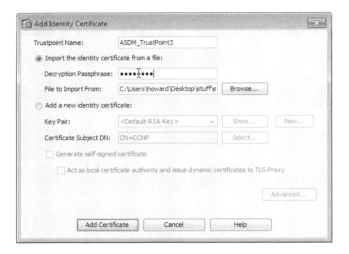

**Figure 17-16**    *ASA ASDM Import Identity Certificate Window*

From the drop-down list of available identity certificates, we select the newly imported certificate from the list and then click **OK**, as shown in Figure 17-17. That is it. We can now establish a VPN tunnel between our client software and ASA using the certificate-based peer authentication scheme.

**Note:**    Whereas identity certificates generated by the local CA will work for peer authentication reasons, on the ASA a self-signed certificate will not. Therefore, if you are testing certificate-based authentication on your ASA device, it is recommended to use the local CA server or a third-party internal or public service. Many public CAs now offer free trial certificates that you can use for such purposes.

# Advanced PKI Deployment Strategies

We have discussed the basic configuration deployments and tasks that must implement them. This section now builds on that information and introduces you to some of the advanced authorization and certificate revocation list (CRL) methods that are available (namely, CRLs, Online Certificate Status Protocol [OCSP], and authentication, authorization, and accounting [AAA]).

A CRL is a list of certificate serial numbers updated periodically and published by a CA. The ASA does not automatically check for a certificate that has been revoked. However, you can configure it to do so using HTTP, Lightweight Directory Access Protocol (LDAP), or SCEP. The CRL location is found in a certificate in the CRL distribution point (CDP) field (for example, URL=http://crl.thawte.com/ThawteSGCCA.crl), and usually the CDP location is available as an attribute within the identity certificate itself.

OCSP is a protocol for retrieving a revocation list using HTTP, and similar to the CRL, it is not checked by the ASA when using the default configuration. However, this can be changed to make the OCSP retrieval mandatory. The OCSP information can be found in the Authority Information Access (AIA) field within a certificate, an example of which is shown in Example 17-2.

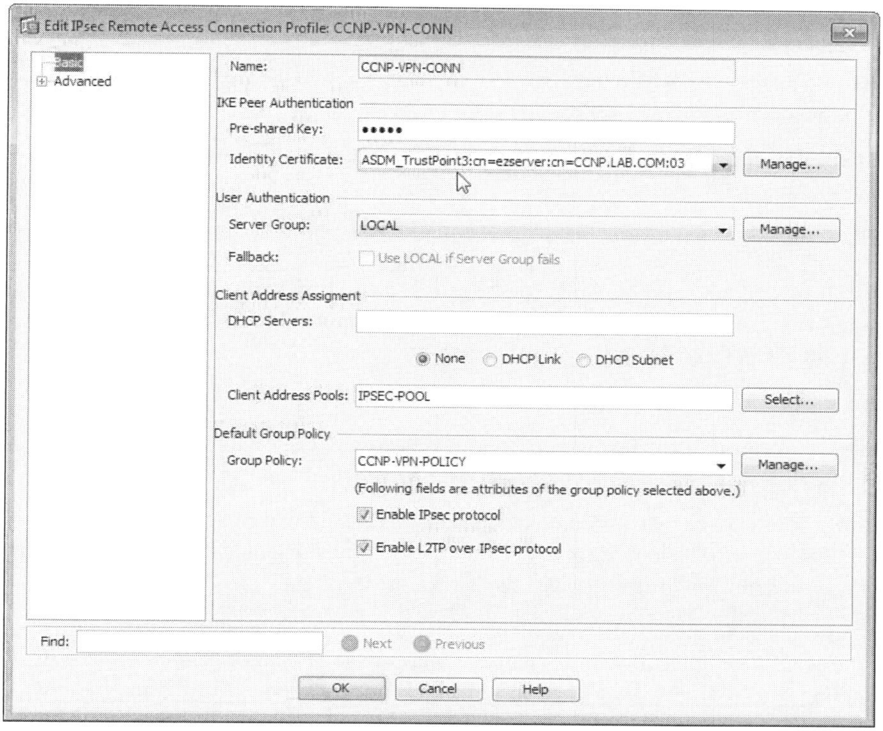

**Figure 17-17**  *ASA ASDM Connection Profile Identity Certificate Selection*

**Example 17-2**  *Digital Certificate AIA Field*

```
[1]Authority Info Access
 Access Method=On-line Certificate Status Protocol (1.3.6.1.5.5.7.48.1)
 Alternative Name:
 URL=http://ocsp.thawte.com
[2]Authority Info Access
 Access Method=Certification Authority Issuer (1.3.6.1.5.5.7.48.2)
 Alternative Name:
 URL=http://www.thawte.com/repository/Thawte_SGC_CA.crt
```

AAA can be carried out by an external RADIUS server (for example, Cisco Access Control Server [ACS]). With AAA, you can control user certificate authorization by disabling, enabling, or removing a user account. When the ASA device receives a user certificate, it forwards the username in a predefined field and a generic password (used for all users) to the RADIUS server for authorization.

These methods should be used in the following priority:

- **AAA:** Preferred. Use if you have access to an external RADIUS server and are also using downloadable access lists and so on.

- **OCSP:** Recommended for use if you do not have access to an AAA server but have an available OCSP server.

- **CRL:** Use only as a last resort if the preceding two methods are unavailable for use.

The CRL and OCSP retrieval methods can be selected and optional settings configured within the CA certificate, located at **Configuration > Remote Access VPN > Certificate Management > CA Certificates**.

Select your CA certificate from the list and click **Edit**.

To enable the retrieval of the revocation list and subsequent checking, you must first enable the function by checking **Check Certificates for Revocation**.

Next, select your chosen revocation methods. For this example, we have selected CRL. However, if you were to select both, the first method in the list would be used, and only if an error is returned would the second in the list be used.

We have also checked the option to allow the certificate to be considered valid if for any reason the certificate revocation information is unavailable or cannot be checked, as shown in Figure 17-18. Note that when this option is not checked, if configured methods OCPS and CRL are not functional or remote servers are not available, the certificate cannot be validated and the VPN session is terminated. So, this option is a failsafe, which still allows VPN sessions to establish even if you temporarily cannot verify the validity of the remote peer certificate.

You now need to specify the location of the revocation list. As mentioned earlier, this information is within the CDP certificate field. However, you can also specify URLs if you want to use them, as shown in Figure 17-19.

In addition to the location of the revocation list, you can choose the protocols that can be used to retrieve the list. You can use LDAP, HTTP, or SCEP, or a combination of all three, as shown in Figure 17-20. For this example, we chose to use HTTP only. Your choice of protocol for CRL retrieval is related to the URLs you configure in the earlier CRL Retrieval Location tab. When adding a URL, you are given the protocol choice of either HTTP or LDAP. However, if you choose HTTP, this will also be used for SCEP if chosen as a retrieval protocol.

To use AAA for the purposes of authorization, a generic or common password needs to be specified that will be used, along with the predefined fields for usernames when checking the accounts held on an external RADIUS server.

To begin, you must first enter the common password in the RADIUS server properties, located at **Configuration > Remote Access VPN > AAA/Local Users > AAA Server Groups**. Select the configured group and the server you want to edit from the pane below (or click **Add** to create a new server entry). In the Add AAA Server dialog, enter the common password, as shown in Figure 17-21.

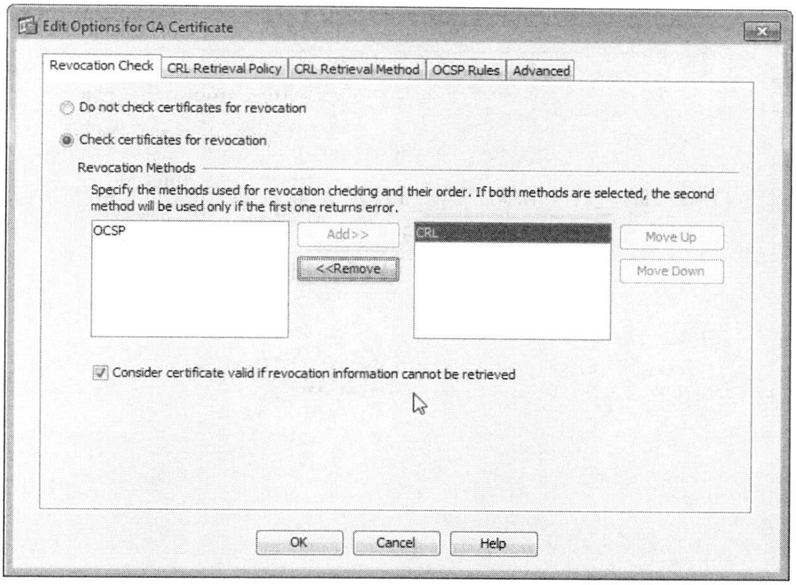

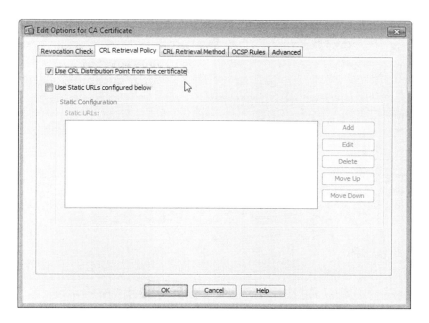

**Figure 17-18**  *CA Revocation Check Methods*

**Figure 17-19**  *CA CRL Retrieval Location*

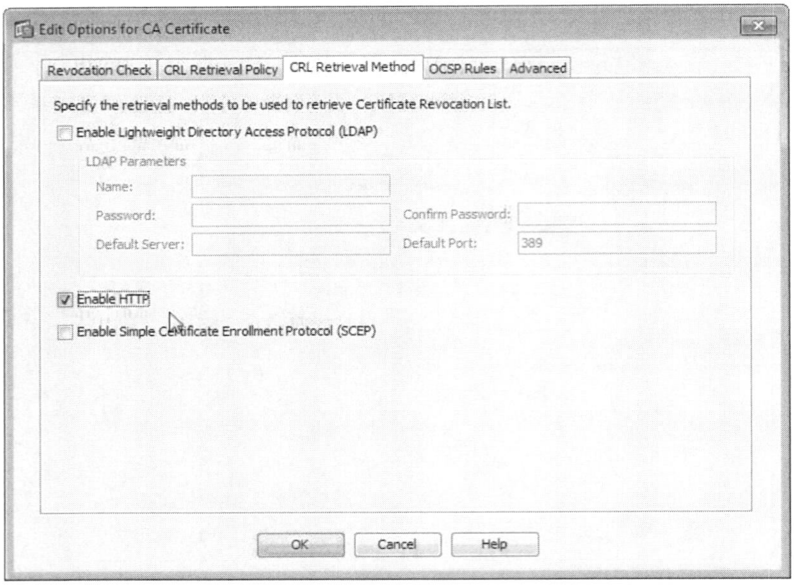

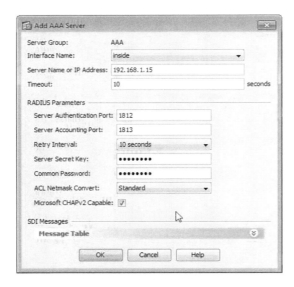

**Figure 17-20**    *CA CRL Retrieval Method*

**Figure 17-21**    *Entering the Common User Password in the Add AAA Server Dialog*

You can now assign the AAA group to a connection profile for advanced authorization purposes and choose the predefined fields used to supply the username information, as shown in Figure 17-22.

Within Figure 17-22, we selected our AAA server group (aptly named AAA) and checked the **Users Must Exist in the Authorization Database to Connect** check box beneath the drop-down list to force the user to be configured in the AAA server database. Otherwise, authorization will fail immediately.

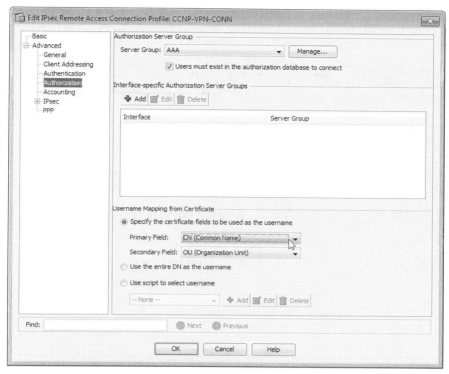

**Figure 17-22**   *IPsec Connection Profile Advanced Authorization Parameters*

In the Username Mapping from Certificate section, we chose the default values of using the Common Name (CN) field as the primary field and the Organizational Unit (OU) field as the secondary field, from which the username information will be supplied. However, you can select from a number of defined fields (for example, Name [N], Surname [SN]), depending on the individual deployment.

## Troubleshooting Advanced Authentication for Easy VPN

When approaching the task of troubleshooting any deployment, it is first important to make sure you understand the underlying technology and protocol operations that combine to provide the successful (or not, as the case may be) parameter negotiation and tunnel establishment. Therefore, if you are unsure which phase of a connection you are looking at, revisit the IPsec and IKE information discussed earlier in this book.

The devices used (for example, the VPN client and ASA) can provide you with a large amount of information that can prove to be useful when troubleshooting a problem. The following is a brief list of the tools available to you:

■   Cisco IPsec VPN client logging facility and window

■   ASA internal logging buffer

■   ASA real-time logging console

■   ASA **debug** commands

In addition to this list, you can send Simple Network Messaging Protocol (SNMP) and syslog information to a remote server that can be later used for troubleshooting purposes.

For example, an engineer has configured certificate authentication on his ASA device and his remote IPsec VPN client. However, after several minutes of trying to establish, it is clear the connection is not working, and the error message he receives on the VPN client is "Remote peer is no longer responding." The information in the ASA's Real-Time Log Viewer, as shown in Figure 17-23, provides an indication of where the fault lies.

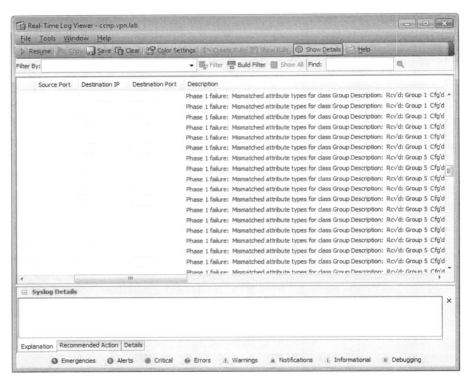

**Figure 17-23**   *Cisco IPsec VPN Client Error Message and ASA Real-Time Log Viewer*

By examining the Real-Time Log Viewer output, you can decipher that our ASA does not have the necessary IKE policies available. As you can see further down in the list, all others have been tried but no match has been found. This is common when certificate-based authentication has been enabled within the connection profile on the ASA, but the default IKE policies used to negotiate the necessary Phase 1 information are configured only for pre-shared key information. In this instance, we have used the information to add a new IKE policy using AES-256, SHA, or RSA-SIG authentication with the default lifetimes. Afterward, the IPsec client can now connect successfully.

# Exam Preparation Tasks

As mentioned in the section "How to Use This Book" in the Introduction, you have a couple of choices for exam preparation: the memory tables in Appendix C, Chapter 23, "Final Exam Preparation," and the exam simulation questions on the CD-ROM.

## Review All Key Topics

Review the most important topics in the chapter, noted with the Key Topic icon in the outer margin of the page. Table 17-4 lists a reference of these key topics and the page numbers on which each is found.

**Table 17-4**   *Key Topics*

| Key Topic Element | Description | Page |
|---|---|---|
| Bulleted List | Authentication options and strategies | 553 |
| Topic | Configuring PKI with IPsec VPNs | 556 |
| Topic | Discussing certificate mapping operation | 562 |
| Topic | Advanced PKI deployment strategies | 570 |

## Complete Tables and Lists from Memory

Print a copy of Appendix C, "Memory Tables" (found on the CD), or at least the section for this chapter, and complete the tables and lists from memory. Appendix D, "Memory Tables Answer Key," also on the CD, includes completed tables and lists to check your work.

## Define Key Terms

Define the following key terms from this chapter and check your answers in the glossary:

AAA (authentication, authorization, and accounting), AIA (Authority Information Access), CA (certificate authority), CN (Common Name), CRL (certificate revocation list), mutual group authentication, OCSP (Online Certificate Status Protocol)

This chapter covers the following subjects:

- **Configuration Procedures, Deployment Strategies, and Information Gathering:** In this section, things to consider when deciding whether to deploy an internal AAA server for authorization.

- **Configuring Local and Remote Group Policies:** In this section, we discuss the differences between ASA local and remote group policies and the configuration required on the ASA for the deployment of each.

- **Accounting Methods for Operational Information:** In this section, we review the accounting methods available on the ASA for connection and user information gathering.

## CHAPTER 18

# Advanced Easy VPN Authorization

In earlier chapters, you learned how to plan for and configure the various authentication mechanisms available on the Adaptive Security Appliance (ASA) to allow remote users access into your environment. Now that you have given them access, you need to control and account for it.

The information in this chapter will enable you to prepare for the deployment of an advanced authorization scheme for your remote users, allowing you to control the level of access granted to them based on such information as their internal department, username, IP address, and so on, using the familiar local group policies that are configured on the ASA device. This chapter also introduces you to remote group policies, their configuration on the ASA, and their remote server requirements.

After we explore the various ways to authorize remote users into your environment, we then move on to review the accounting methods available on the ASA device that enable us to track the success or failure of specific authorization settings and connections.

## "Do I Know This Already?" Quiz

The "Do I Know This Already?" quiz helps you determine your level of knowledge on this chapter's topics before you begin. Table 18-1 details the major topics discussed in this chapter and their corresponding quiz sections.

**Table 18-1** *"Do I Know This Already?" Section-to-Question Mapping*

| Foundation Topics Section | Questions |
|---|---|
| Configuring Local and Remote Group Policies | 1, 2, 3, 4 |
| Accounting methods for Operational Information | 5, 6, 7 |

1. Which of the following are available group policy types on the ASA? (Choose all that apply.)

    a. Internal

    b. External

    c. Active

    d. Standby

**2.** Which of the following are legitimate ways to assign a group policy? (Choose all that apply.)

   **a.**   DAP

   **b.**   Direct user assignment

   **c.**   Connection profile

   **d.**   AAA

**3.** In what format are the attributes stored in an external group policy?

   **a.**   Text files

   **b.**   A/V pairs

   **c.**   CSV files

   **d.**   XML files

**4.** Which of the following remote user types are external group policy objects available on? (Choose all that apply.)

   **a.**   LDAP

   **b.**   TACACS+

   **c.**   SDI

   **d.**   RADIUS

**5.** By default, where is ASA syslog information stored?

   **a.**   External syslog server

   **b.**   Internal syslog server

   **c.**   NetFlow collection service

   **d.**   ASA internal buffer

**6.** When configuring an AAA server on the ASA, which communication protocol when configured allows for secure (SSL/TLS) communication between the AAA server and the ASA?

   **a.**   UDP

   **b.**   SCEP

   **c.**   SMTP

   **d.**   TCP

**7.** Which of the following are available actions used for NetFlow flow information creation? (Choose all that apply.)

   **a.**   Created

   **b.**   Denied

   **c.**   Torn down

   **d.**   Dropped

# Foundation Topics

## Configuration Procedures, Deployment Strategies, and Information Gathering

The role of authorization in any virtual private network (VPN) deployment is an important one. With it, you can control which of your remote users can or cannot access corporate servers, email, financial and personnel records, and even the Internet. However, not only can you control the level of access each remote user has in your corporate environment, you can also control the user's connection experience through maximum connection times, timeout settings, simultaneous logins, portal customization, and so on.

You can restrict or allow access to specific internal resources from remote users using the available policy options on the Adaptive Security Appliance (ASA) device, whether you allow full access from all of your remote users to all of your internal resources (really not recommended) or, as shown in Figure 18-1, you provide remote users access to only the internal resources they require (for example, Client A can access the corporate finance server and file server but not the corporate email server, but Client B can access the corporate email server and file server but not the corporate finance server). Specifically, this chapter focuses on the role of group policies for user authorization purposes, and as you will see in the next section, you can assign IPv4 and IPv6 access lists in group policy objects that allow or deny access to internal servers for a particular group, access hours, maximum connection time, and so on.

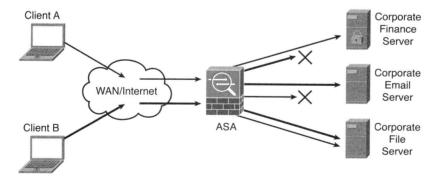

**Figure 18-1**   *ASA Authorizing (or Not) Remote Users*

In addition to the available authorization attributes that can be applied by local group policies to our remote users, you can extend the role of authorization to a remote (internal) AAA server. After the remote user has been authenticated, the remote AAA server is queried for the authorization attributes that should be applied to this session.

## Configuring Local and Remote Group Policies

Via group policies, you can assign attributes to users and groups based on their individual user account, group membership, or the connection profile used to connect to the ASA device.

Using group policy objects, you can define the following user authorization settings (and many more, as discussed momentarily):

■ Set the maximum connection time applied to remote users before they are required to carry out the connection process and reauthenticate.

■ Control the number of simultaneous logins that can be made using the particular user account.

■ Restrict access only to the internal resources and subnets using IPv4 and IPv6 filters (access control lists [ACL]).

■ Define the networks used for split tunneling.

■ Control our remote user access hours (the time they can and cannot log in).

You can configure two types of group policy objects. The location of the policy attributes contained in them dictates the type of policy it is:

■ **Local group policies** (also known as internal group policies) are policy objects that have been configured locally on the ASA along with the attributes they contain. They are assigned either to local users directly (local user accounts configured on the ASA) or in connection profiles.

■ **Remote group policies** (also known as external group policies) are applied either to remote users or groups. The attributes contained in a remote group policy are configured on a remote (typically internal) authentication, authorization, and accounting (AAA) server (for example, RADIUS or Lightweight Directory Access Protocol [LDAP]) in the form of A/V (attribute/value) pairs. However, the remote group policy container (name) must also be configured on the ASA device, although authorization **attributes** are imported from the AAA server.

Local and remote group policies are both configured on the ASA in **Configuration > Remote Access VPN > Network (Client) Access > Group Policies**. You begin by clicking **Add**. Then, in the Add menu, click either Internal Group Policy or External Group Policy. For this example, as shown in Figure 18-2, we clicked **Add > Add External Group Policy**.

In the Add External Group Policy window, enter the following details:

■ **Name:** Enter a name for the group policy object. This will be the actual username used by the ASA to authenticates to the RADIUS server.

■ **Server Group:** Choose an existing AAA server group or create a new one.

■ **Password:** Enter a password to be used for authentication with the internal AAA servers. This will be the password of the previously defined username (group policy name).

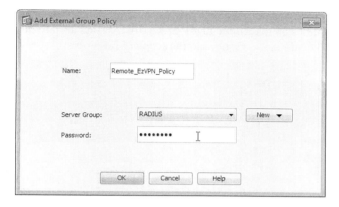

**Figure 18-2**  *External Group Policy Configuration*

The group policy object is then used as a container for the A/V attributes received from the internal AAA server.

If you want to create a new AAA server group instead of selecting an existing one, you just choose **New > New RADIUS Server Group** or **New > New LDAP Server Group** in the Add External Group Policy window. After choosing the appropriate server group type to create, enter the following information into the Add AAA Server Group window:

- **Server Group:** Enter a name for the server group.

- **Protocol:** Uneditable. This displays either RADIUS or LDAP depending on your chosen group.

- **Accounting Mode:** Choose either Simultaneous (the ASA sends accounting data to all servers in the group) or Single (the ASA sends accounting data to only one server); this option is not available for LDAP server groups.

- **Reactivation Mode:** Choose either Depletion (servers that have failed in the group are only reactivated when all other servers in the group are inactive) or Timed (failed servers are reactivated after 30 seconds). If Depletion mode is chosen, you can also modify the dead timer (default 10 minutes), which is time that elapses between disabling the last server in the group and the reenabling of all servers.

- **Max Failed Attempts:** Enter the maximum number of attempts that will be used to connect to a server configured in the server group until declaring it dead (default is 3).

- **Enable Interim Accounting Update:** Choose this option to enable multisession accounting for both AnyConnect and clientless Secure Sockets Layer (SSL) VPNs.

- **VPN3K Compatibility:** Choose Do Not Merge (to disable merging of RADIUS downloadable ACLs with received A/V pair ACLs), Place the Downloadable ACL After the Cisco AV Pair ACL, or Place the downloadable ACL Before the Cisco AV Pair ACL.

After creating your new AAA server group, you then need to add AAA servers to it in the AAA Server Groups window (**Configuration > Remote Access VPN > AAA/Local Users**

**> AAA Server Groups**), as shown in Figure 18-3. Note that for this configuration to be fully usable and valid, configurations on the remote LDAP or RADIUS servers need to be performed. (LDAP and RADIUS configuration is beyond the scope of this book.)

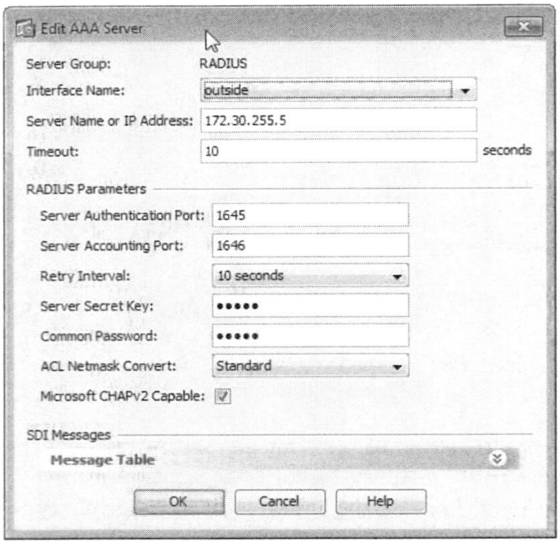

**Figure 18-3**  *AAA Server Configuration*

After clicking **Add > Add Internal Group Policy**, the Add Internal Group Policy window opens, as shown in Figure 18-4. As you can see, many more options are available for this configuration, because all attributes of the group policy are configured and stored on the ASA. Begin by giving the policy a name, which is the only mandatory attribute required when configuring a new policy. All other attributes are inherited from the default group policy object (DfltGrpPolicy).

Table 18-2 lists the General window fields and values that you can use to configure the remaining general attributes you want to set explicitly. Note that before configuration is possible, you must uncheck the respective field's **Inherit** option.

**Table 18-2**  *Internal Group Policy General Attributes*

| Field | Value |
|-------|-------|
| Banner | Enter a banner that will be displayed to users as they attempt to connect to the VPN. |
| SCEP Forwarding URL | Enter the URL that users of this group policy will use to automatically request digital certificates (if using certificate-based authentication). |
| Address Pools | Choose an IP address pool from the list. An IP address will be assigned to users for use during their connection. |

**Table 18-2**  *Internal Group Policy General Attributes*

| Field | Value |
|---|---|
| IPv6 Address Pools | Select an IPv6 address pool from the list. An IP address will be assigned to users for use during their connection. |
| Tunneling Protocols | Choose from the available tunneling protocols that this group policy object will apply to. |
| IPv4 Filter | Select an IPv4 ACL from the list to restrict network access during the user's connection to only the networks/hosts the user requires. |
| IPv6 Filter | Choose an IPv6 ACL from the list to restrict network access during the user's connection to only the networks/hosts the user requires. |
| NAC Policy | Select a Network Access Control (NAC) policy from the list of those configured. The NAC policy is used to perform posture assessment and validation for the connecting user. |
| Access Hours | Choose a time-based ACL from the list of those available if you only allow access to this connection during specific times (for example, regular business hours). |
| Simultaneous Logins | Enter the number of simultaneous logins that can appear for this user account (default is 3). |
| Restrict Access to VLAN (5505 Only) | Choose the only VLAN (Inside, Outside, DMZ) you will allow this connecting user access to. |
| Connection Profile (Tunnel Group) Lock | Choose the connection profile from the list. This group policy object will be assigned to the user if the user is connected via selected connection profile. |
| Maximum Connect Time | Choose either Unlimited or enter the number of minutes the user is allowed to be connected before being automatically disconnected (default is Unlimited). |
| Idle Timeout | Choose either Unlimited or enter the number of minutes the user's connection can be idle before being automatically disconnected (default is 30 minutes). |
| On Smart Card Removal | Choose the option to either keep the user's connection connected or disconnect the connection upon the user removing his or her smartcard. |

After setting the specific general attributes required in your local group policy, you can assign the policy either directly to a local user account or globally to all users of a connection in the connection profile's properties.

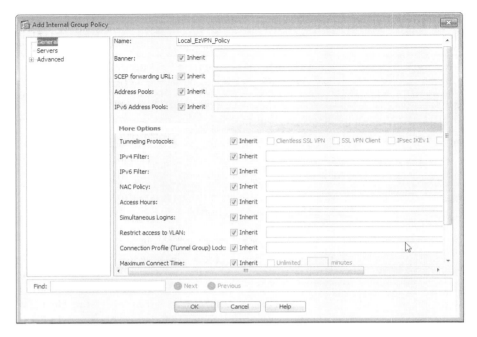

**Figure 18-4**    *Internal Group Policy Configuration*

## Assigning a Group Policy to a Local User Account

Begin this task by opening your user's account properties in **Configuration > Remote Access VPN > AAA/Local Users > User Accounts**. In the User Accounts window, choose the local user account to apply the group policy object to and click **Edit**.

As shown in Figure 18-5, in the Edit User Account window that opens, we choose **VPN Policy** from the menu on the left and uncheck the **Inherit** check box next to the Group Policy section. Using the drop-down list, we then choose the group policy object we want applied to the user account.

## Assigning a Group Policy to a Connection Profile

You can assign a group policy object to a connection profile in the connection profile properties, available at **Configuration > Remote Access VPN > Network (Client) Access > IPsec (IKEv1) Connection Profiles**. Select the connection profile to assign the group policy object to from the list and click **Edit**.

In the Edit IPsec Remote Access Connection Profile <name> window, using the drop-down list in the Default Group Policy section of the window, select the group policy object to be applied, as shown in Figure 18-6.

In addition to the more general properties that can be assigned using a group policy object, you can assign advanced properties (for example, split-tunneling exceptions and rules).

The configuration in Figure 18-7 shows the split-tunneling properties located in the **Advanced > Split Tunneling** section of the **Edit Internal Group Policy - <name>** window.

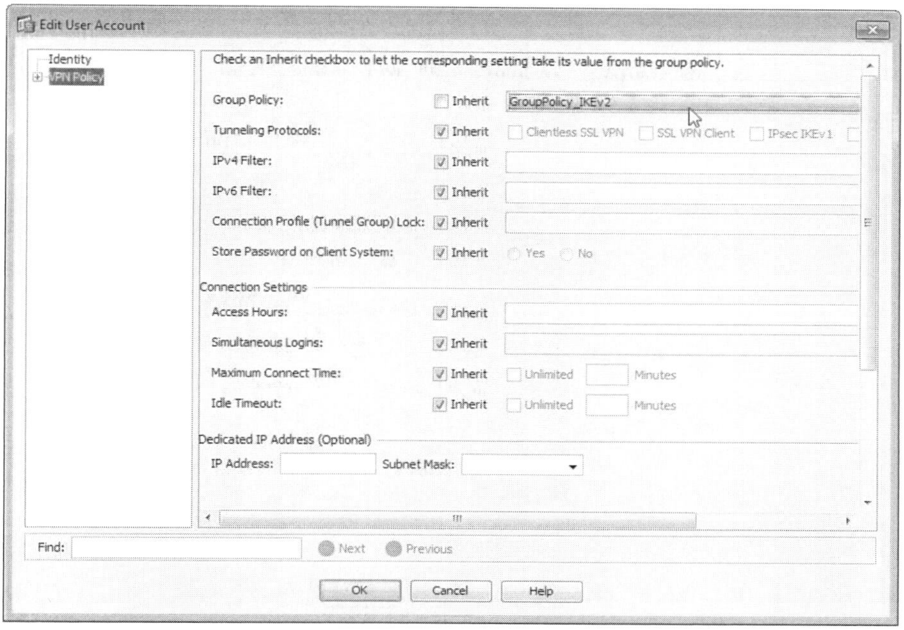

**Figure 18-5**   *Assigning a Group Policy Directly to a User*

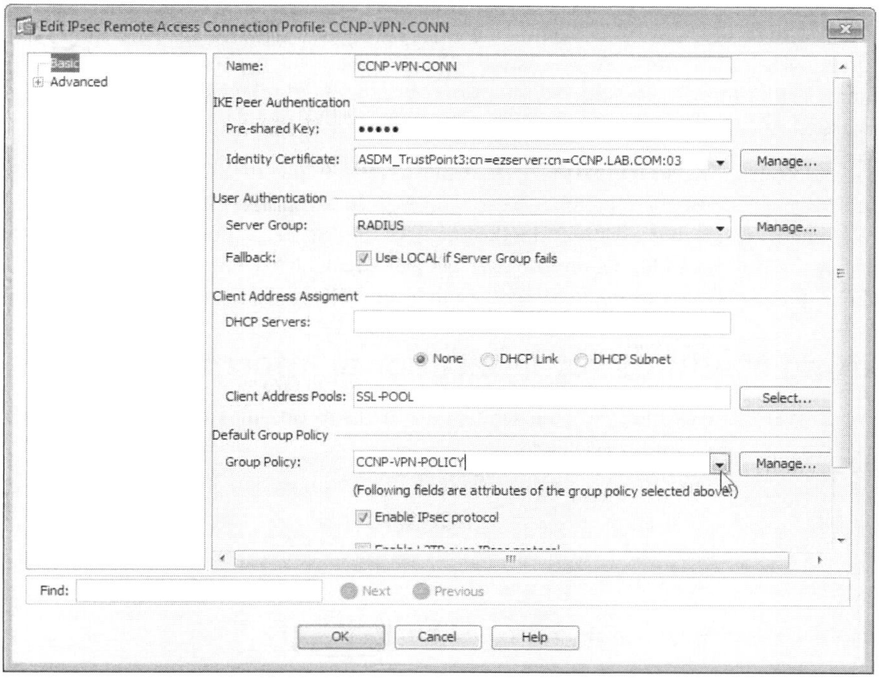

**Figure 18-6**   *Assigning a Group Policy to a Connection Profile*

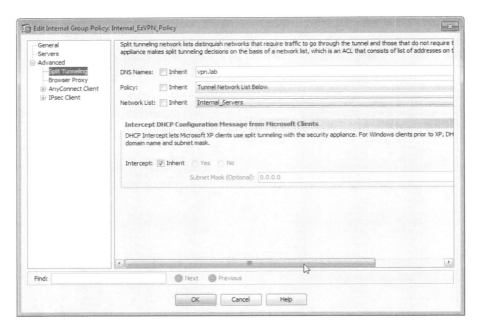

**Figure 18-7**    *Group Policy Split-Tunneling Configuration*

For this example, we added the domain name vpn.lab as a Domain Name System (DNS) name, indicating to the Easy VPN clients that any requests for DNS information for hosts in this domain should be tunneled (for example, secretfiles.vpn.lab). In addition to our DNS names configuration, we selected the option to tunnel only the list specified in the preconfigured ACL Internal_Servers by using the Policy and Network List fields.

The configuration shown in Figure 18-7 will result in DNS requests for devices in the domain name vpn.lab, or traffic matching that of the ACL Internal_Servers, to be sent by Easy VPN clients through the VPN tunnel to the ASA and on to the corporate network. All other traffic (for example, the remote user device's local LAN or Internet data) will travel directly to the destination instead of through the VPN tunnel.

## Accounting Methods for Operational Information

You have at your disposal the following logging mechanisms on the ASA to monitor remote user activity and connection state:

- Syslog

- NetFlow 9

- RADIUS accounting

- Simple Network Management Protocol (SNMP)

Syslog can provide a large amount of information for statistics-based analysis or information regarding the current ASA's health and the status of our remote connections. In addition to being able to send syslog (debugging, informational, and so on) information to remote servers for offline inspection, you can choose to store it in a local buffer on the ASA for later viewing when working on the device.

Figure 18-8 shows the Logging Setup window available via **Configuration > Device Management > Logging > Logging Setup**. To enable logging, just check the **Enable Logging** check box. You can also optionally include debugging information when troubleshooting a feature/error on the ASA by checking the **Send Debug Messages as Syslogs** check box.

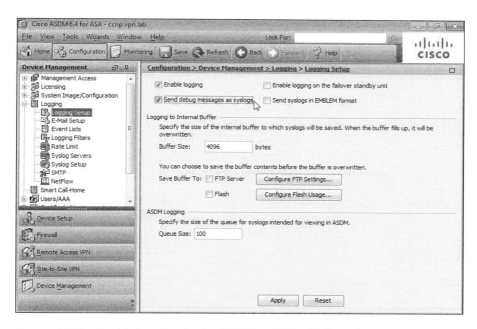

**Figure 18-8**   *Enable Logging in the ASDM and Specify Location*

In the Logging Setup window, you can also enable logging on the failover device if you are running two ASAs in a hardware failover pair, and you can select to send your syslog information in EMBLEM format. (This is required if you are running CiscoWorks software as applications. For example, RME [Resource Manager Essentials] processes syslog information in EMBLEM format.) In addition to these options, in the Logging to Internal Buffer section of the window, you can increase or decrease the size of the internal buffer used to store the logging information (default is 4096 bytes) on the ASA. The internal buffer is a rolling log, meaning as soon as it becomes full, any new information starts to overwrite the older information in the buffer. For example, if your ASA device is logging a large amount of information while you are trying to troubleshoot an error, it is worthwhile to increase the size of the logging buffer to prevent the information you might require being overwritten before you have had a chance to look at it. In this section, you can also configure the ASA to store the buffer information in a file on the ASA's flash device or upload it to an FTP server when it reaches a specific size. This can also prevent your valuable log information from being overwritten. In the final section of the window, you can select the amount of information that is written to the Adaptive Security Device Manager (ASDM) log viewer (visible on the home page). The default is 100 messages.

After you have enabled logging on the ASA device, you can configure the remote servers to which the ASA will send its generated syslogs in **Configuration > Device Management > Logging > Syslog Servers**.

Figure 18-9 shows the Syslog Servers window and the Add Syslog Server window that opens when you click **Add**. In the Add Syslog Server window, select the interface your server is available on, enter the IP address of the server, and select either TCP or UDP (default) and the port (514 by default). In addition, you can select the option to send the messages to this server using the Cisco EMBLEM format (only available with UDP) or to enable secure syslog by encapsulating the syslog data in Secure Sockets Layer (SSL) or Transport Layer Security (TLS). (This option is available only when using TCP for communications between the ASA and server.)

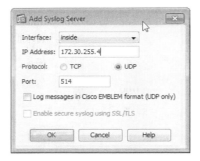

**Figure 18-9**    *Creating a New Syslog Entry*

After you have entered your syslog servers, you need to then specify the level of logging information that will be sent to our syslog server. In **Configuration > Device Management > Logging > Logging Filters**, you can choose from the following:

- Emergencies
- Alerts
- Critical
- Errors
- Warnings
- Notifications
- Informational
- Debugging

As shown in Figure 18-10, you can choose the level of logging per function on the ASA. For example, you might want to send informational messages to the console but debugging information to the ASA's internal buffer.

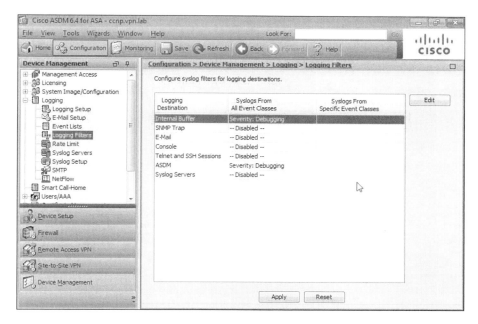

**Figure 18-10**   *Choose the Logging Level Per Function*

And that's it! Well... not quite. At the moment, enough options have been selected and enough information entered for the ASA to be able to log to the internal buffer, syslog, and servers. Now you can start to get really granular with the control you have over syslog information. For example, if you are interested in only a particular log message or set of messages, you can create a filter in the Event Lists window. After creating a filter, you can select this in the Logging Filters window instead of selecting a predefined logging level.

You can optionally rate limit the number of log messages sent per second per logging level, or even per log message, in the Rate Limit window. You can set up a dedicated facility per logging level, if you want to view or filter the different logging levels easily on our syslog server. And in the E-Mail Setup and SMTP windows, you can set up the parameters and options used to send syslog information to a recipient via email.

You can view logging information held in the ASA's internal buffer in **Monitoring > Logging > Log Buffer**. Choose the logging level you are interested in viewing and click **View**. Figure 18-11 shows an example of the log buffer contents in the internal logging buffer.

## NetFlow 9

NetFlow logging can enable information to be viewed on a flow-by-flow basis based on Layer 3 and Layer 4 information of a conversation. Unlike sending information to a collector in tuple format (which can lead to limitations in the amount of information sent in any one packet, like its predecessor NetFlow 5), NetFlow 9 uses a template-based method of transferring information to a server running the NetFlow collector service. The template is sent to the server at specific intervals (30 minutes) and is used to format the information it receives from the ASA.

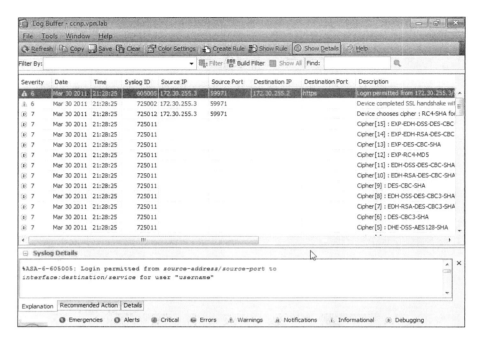

**Figure 18-11**  *ASA Internal Log Buffer*

The ASA can send NetFlow 9 information to a server running the NetFlow 9 collector service (all other versions are incompatible) based on the following packet-flow actions occurring:

■  Created

■  Denied

■  Torn down

Figure 18-12 shows the configuration of NetFlow on the ASA device.

In the NetFlow window (**Configuration > Device Management > Logging > NetFlow**), you can enter a value in minutes for the interval used to send the Version 9 template to the collection service running on your remote server (default 30). Optionally, you can choose to delay the sending of flow-creation events by a specific time you enter in seconds (which can help minimize the amount of information sent at any one time if, for example, a lot of flows are created at once on the ASA device). You also enter your flow collector's (server) IP address, the interface they are available on, and the UDP port that will be used for the communication of NetFlow information to them. After entering this information, you can then specify the type of event for which NetFlow information is sent to the servers. As shown in Figure 18-12, three events can cause the information to be sent. You can specify the event using a service policy that, if you recall from earlier chapters, you have already seen when used to create quality of service (QoS) policies on the ASA.

However, unlike QoS policies, NetFlow policies can be applied only globally, not per in-terface. By default, the ASA has an existing default service policy that is applied globally to the ASA. However, you are unable to edit this in the ASDM, so you must create a new global service policy and either use an access list to define the IP addresses for which your NetFlow flow information will be generated or use the class-default class of our policy.

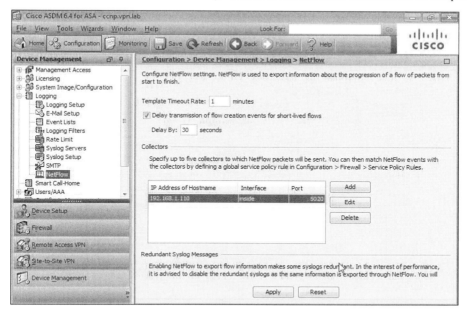

**Figure 18-12**   *ASA NetFlow Configuration*

In this example, we create a new global service policy and use the class-default class to match all traffic for NetFlow flow information. We begin by opening the service policy in the Service Policy Rules window (**Configuration > Firewall > Service Policy Rules**) and clicking **Add**. We then choose **Add Service Policy Rule**. In the Add Service Policy Rule Wizard - Service Policy window, we choose **Global - Applies to All Interfaces** and click **Next**.

On the next screen, Add Service Policy Rule Wizard - Traffic Classification Wizard, we choose the **Use Class-Default as the Traffic Class** and click **Next**.

Then, in the Add Service Policy Rule Wizard - Rule Actions window, we open the **NetFlow** tab. On this tab, we click **Add**. In the new Add Flow Event window that opens, as shown in Figure 18-13, we choose the event that will trigger the sending of NetFlow information from the Flow Event Type drop-down box and check the box next to the host for which we want to enable this rule. Finally, we click **OK** and **Finish** to apply our new rule.

## RADIUS VPN Accounting

RADIUS accounting information can be enabled so that your support representatives can interrogate the RADIUS logging information to see whether a VPN connection has succeeded or failed (and if failed, why).

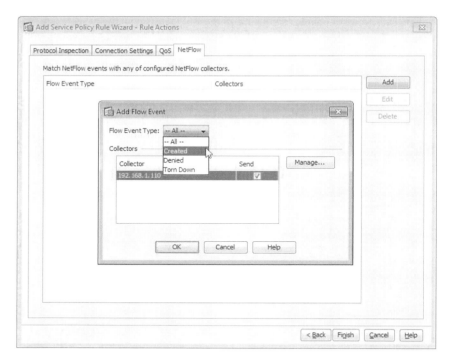

**Figure 18-13**    *ASA NetFlow Service Policy Configuration*

To enable RADIUS accounting in a connection profile, as shown in Figure 18-14, navigate to **Configuration > Remote Access VPN > Network (Client) Access > IPsec (IKEv1) Connection Profiles**. Choose your connection profile from the list and click **Edit**. In the Edit IPsec Remote Access Connection Profile: <name> window, choose **Advanced > Accounting** from the menu on the left. In the Accounting window, from the drop-down list choose the RADIUS server group that contains the RADIUS servers to which the ASA will be sending its accounting information. You can also create a new server group by clicking **Manage** if no groups are currently available.

After configuring RADIUS accounting servers in a connection profile, you can inspect the received RADIUS accounting information on your RADIUS server implementation using the various logging options that are available.

## SNMP

The ASA can support access for device and statistical interrogation using SNMP Version 1, Version 2c, and Version 3. Many texts and books already explain the differences between these versions, so to save you from reading it all again, this discussion assumes that you know enough about SNMP already to have made the decision that if version 3 is available on a device, you use version 3 to access it.

You configure the various SNMP options (traps, location, global community string, and hosts) in **Configuration > Device Management > Management Access > SNMP**, as shown in Figure 18-15.

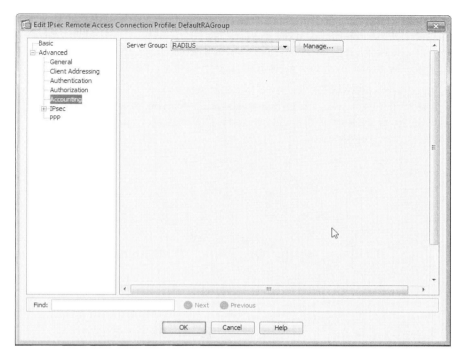

**Figure 18-14**   *IKEv1 Connection Profile RADIUS Accounting Configuration*

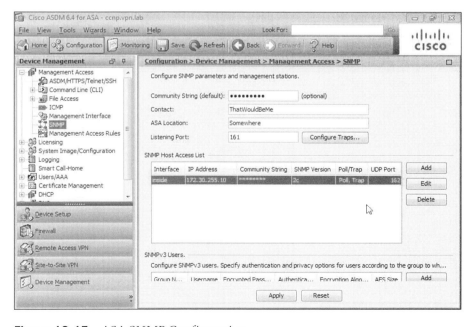

**Figure 18-15**   *ASA SNMP Configuration*

In the SNMP window, you can configure all the familiar options for the protocol, such as the community string, contact, location, and listening port (UDP 161 by default). You can configure the criteria for trap information to be sent by clicking **Configure Traps** and choosing from the available options in the SNMP Trap Configuration window that opens.

In addition, in the SNMP window, in the SNMP Host Access List section, you can explicitly enter the addresses of your servers that will be accessing your ASA device. You can also create the users and groups that will be used for SNMPv3 access in the SNMPv3 Users section of the window.

# Exam Preparation Tasks

As mentioned in the section "How to Use This Book" in the Introduction, you have a couple of choices for exam preparation: the memory tables in Appendix C, Chapter 23, "Final Exam Preparation," and the exam simulation questions on the CD-ROM.

## Review All Key Topics

Review the most important topics in the chapter, noted with the Key Topic icon in the outer margin of the page. Table 18-3 lists a reference of these key topics and the page numbers on which each is found.

**Table 18-3**   *Key Topics*

| Key Topic Element | Description | Page |
|---|---|---|
| Bulleted List | Group policy types | 582 |
| Sub-Topic | Assigning a group policy to a user account | 586 |
| Sub-Topic | Assigning a group policy to a connection profile | 586 |
| Bulleted List | Available accounting methods | 588 |
| Bulleted List | Available logging levels | 590 |
| Bulleted List | NetFlow flow-creation actions | 592 |

## Complete Tables and Lists from Memory

Print a copy of Appendix C, "Memory Tables" (found on the CD), or at least the section for this chapter, and complete the tables and lists from memory. Appendix D, "Memory Tables Answer Key," also on the CD, includes completed tables and lists to check your work.

## Define Key Terms

Define the following key terms from this chapter, and check your answers in the glossary:

external group policy, internal group policy, NetFlow, SNMP (Simple Network Management Protocol)

This chapter covers the following subjects:

- **Configuration Procedures, Deployment Strategies, and Information Gathering:** In this section, we review the HA methods available for Easy VPN connections and their operation.

- **Easy VPN Client HA and Failover:** In this section, we discuss the failover methods available for a VPN client connection to the Easy VPN server.

- **Hardware-Based Failover with VPNs:** In this section, we review the configuration steps required for deploying a hardware-based active/standby failover solution.

- **Clustering Configuration for Easy VPN:** In this section, we review the implementation of VPN clustering on the ASA device.

- **Troubleshooting Device HA and Clustering:** In this section, we discuss the troubleshooting procedures we can follow using the tools available to us.

# CHAPTER 19

# High Availability and Performance for Easy VPN

With the deployment of a virtual private network (VPN) service, you can offer familiar resources to users outside their office environment. These users expect the same level of uptime and service as they receive on the LAN. Therefore, when deploying VPN services, you must provide high availability (HA). By the end of this chapter, you will be able to understand and configure the available HA methods that are provided to an IPsec client. You will also be able to configure Adaptive Security Appliance (ASA) built-in functions to provide stateful failover to in addition to the introduction of an external load balancer for service enhancement. This chapter also expands on material covered earlier by exploring the differences between the options available for particular VPN deployments.

## "Do I Know This Already?" Quiz

The "Do I Know This Already?" quiz helps you determine your level of knowledge on this chapter's topics before you begin. Table 19-1 details the major topics discussed in this chapter and their corresponding quiz sections.

Table 19-1  *"Do I Know This Already?" Section-to-Question Mapping*

| Foundation Topics Section | Questions |
| --- | --- |
| Configuration Procedures, Deployment Strategies, and Information Gathering | 1, 2 |
| Easy VPN Client HA and Failover | 4, 6, 9 |
| Hardware-Based Failover with VPNs | 3, 7, 8, 10 |
| Clustering Configuration for Easy VPN | 5 |

1. When deploying an active/standby failover solution for HA requirements, which should you configure to prevent the use of an ASA answering an ARP request with the BIA for its physical interface?

   a. DPD

   b. VMAC

   c. ARP

   d. Interface Monitoring

**2.** Which of the following are available for use when deploying a stateful HA solution for Easy VPN? (Choose all that apply.)

   **a.** Active/active failover

   **b.** Redundant peering

   **c.** VPN clustering

   **d.** Active/standby failover

**3.** By default, how many interfaces must be in any state other than UP for a failover to occur?

   **a.** 1

   **b.** 2

   **c.** 3

   **d.** 250

**4.** When deploying an HA or VPN load-sharing configuration using the IPsec VPN client software, which method is available?

   **a.** Redundant peering

   **b.** Active/active failover

   **c.** Active/standby failover

   **d.** VPN clustering

**5.** What is the minimum number of cluster members before a cluster can become operational?

   **a.** 1

   **b.** 5

   **c.** 10

   **d.** 100

**6.** Which of the following protocols are used for the periodic keepalives sent between IKE peers during periods of inactivity?

   **a.** IPsec

   **b.** ICMP

   **c.** DPD

   **d.** UDP

**7.** What type of packet is sent by a peer across a failover link to detect the operational state of a peer device?

   **a.** DPD

   **b.** Hello

   **c.** ACK

   **d.** GoodBye

**8.** Which of the following are available interface types that can be used for a stateful failover link between peers?

   **a.** Any unused physical interface

   **b.** The existing failover interface

   **c.** An existing -network interface

   **d.** All of the above

**9.** By default, after how many DPD R_U_THERE packets sent without receiving a DPD_R_U_THERE_ACK response is a peer declared down and a session deleted?

   **a.** 3

   **b.** 4

   **c.** 5

   **d.** 6

**10.** What is the default number of seconds before a monitored interface availability status is changed causing a failover to occur?

   **a.** 10

   **b.** 30

   **c.** 500

   **d.** 25

## Foundation Topics

## Configuration Procedures, Deployment Strategies, and Information Gathering

When preparing to introduce HA to improve service for your remote users, it is important to determine the overall level of service you want to achieve and the resources you have available. For example, do your users require their sessions to stay up and active during a device failure event? Does your internal budget allow for the procurement of additional devices, if required, to achieve HA?

The following is a brief list of the failover methods available using the ASA, VPN client software, or external hardware:

- **Failover:** An internal mechanism provided by the ASA and can be configured in one of two modes, depending on the environment in which you want to deploy it:

  - **Active/active:** As the name suggests, both ASA devices are enabled and inspecting traffic simultaneously, allowing for a much greater percentage of available resources for deployment. However, active/active configuration does not provide support for any type of VPN deployment, so we do not spend any more time looking at this option.

  - **Active/standby:** In this configuration, one ASA device is active and passing/inspecting traffic while the other is on standby, monitoring the state of the other until it must take the active role (that is, until the current active device is restarted or becomes unavailable).

    These failover methods require the use of identical hardware and software version, which might (unless you have a spare ASA device sitting around) require the purchase of additional hardware.

- **VPN clustering:** Another method of failover offered by the ASA. However, this is more of a performance benefit than failover. If a failover occurs, connected users must reestablish their connection, at which point their session is directed to another member of the cluster by the active cluster master.

- **Redundant peering:** The Cisco IPsec VPN client can store up to ten different peer IP addresses for the use as backup servers. During a failover condition, the IPsec client software attempts to connect to the next available peer in the list of those configured.

- **External load balancing:** This method requires an external load balancer (for example, an ACE 4710 appliance or module in a 6500/7600 switch/router). The Application Control Engine (ACE) will have a public-facing IP address configured, known as a VIP (virtual IP address). You can have several ASAs behind the ACE and configured as real servers; on receiving a request for the VIP, the ACE forwards it to one of the real servers (ASAs) it has configured.

HA can be categorized into one of two types:

- Stateful

- Stateless

By *stateful*, we mean the operation of keeping existing connections alive and up during a failover situation. This method is by far the most popular choice and is provided natively by the ASA in active/standby failover mode. However, as mentioned earlier, if you are configuring the built-in failover method available on the ASA, you must use identical software and hardware devices. At present, this is the only stateful failover solution available to the ASA for use with VPNs.

*Stateless*, as you have probably guessed already, is a type of HA that does not enable keeping a user's existing connection open. However, depending on the HA method deployed, this type of failover can provide the designer with a greater level of scope. After all, methods are available that do not require identical hardware/software. Be aware, however, that the use of the ASA's failover method still requires the ASA pair to have identical hardware and software versions installed.

Table 19-2 (also shown in earlier chapters covering HA) summarizes the available methods.

**Table 19-2**   *Advantages and Limitations of Available HA Methods*

| Method | Advantages | Limitations |
|---|---|---|
| Active/standby failover | Can offer stateful or stateless methods. Stateful operation is required to prevent session reestablishment during or after a failover. | No load sharing or balancing occurs between devices. Only one device is active at a time. Lack of support for clientless Secure Sockets Layer (SSL) VPN applications. Requires identical hardware and software versions. |
| VPN load balancing (clustering) | Allows for the load between devices to be shared among them based on the "least used" device receiving the latest connection attempt. Differing hardware and software revisions can be used. Native, built-in ASA feature. | Cannot provide stateful failover. |
| Load balancing using an external load balancer | Allows for the load between devices to be shared among them. We have greater flexibility in choosing load-balancing algorithms than clustering. Differing hardware and software revisions can be used. | Cannot provide stateful failover. No active failover between devices. Clients must reconnect to the next available device after being disconnected. |

**Table 19-2**  *Advantages and Limitations of Available HA Methods*

| Method | Advantages | Limitations |
| --- | --- | --- |
| Redundant VPN servers | Allows for connections to be shared among available devices based on clients using different VPN server addresses.<br><br>Differing hardware and software revisions can be used. | No active failover detection. Clients must use dead peer detection (DPD) for peer-availability detection.<br><br>Connections are not stateful.<br><br>Clientless SSL VPN cannot use this method. |

Given a set of requirements, you should now have an idea of the appropriate method of HA. For example:

■   If you require the operation of stateful HA, the only solution currently available is ASA active/standby failover.

■   However, if you require VPN connections to be shared among the available equipment you have and do not require the implementation of a stateful solution, you can deploy VPN clustering directly on the ASA devices. This will manage the available devices and automatically share the incoming connections between them.

■   If your ASA devices include the use of those with a lower software level that might not have the VPN clustering option available, you can use an external load balancer and achieve the load-balancing behavior using the available features (for example, sticky sessions, round robin, and so on).

■   If you want to share the incoming VPN connections between available devices but do so by configuration applied on your VPN clients, you can use redundant peering within the client software. You could also go as far as to install the available VPN head-end device addresses in a different order, based on the client's group membership, and so on.

# Easy VPN Client HA and Failover

The IPsec VPN client software allows for the configuration of up to ten backup servers for use when the primary VPN head-end is unavailable. The client can detect the availability of the VPN head-end during the initial connection phase, and also by using dead peer detection (DPD).

DPD is simply a method of sending periodic keepalives during periods of inactivity. The default inactivity time for a group is 300 seconds. Therefore, if a connection is idle for 300 seconds, the client or ASA (depending on which end has DPD enabled and whose timer elapses first) sends a DPD R_U_THERE packet. Upon receipt of the DPD packet, the device or software should send back a DPD R_U_THERE_ACK. If the remote peer is unavailable, however, the sending device continues to send R_U_THERE packets every keepalive period (by default, this is 2 seconds) until it has sent four and received no reply. At this point, the connection is torn down. Example 19-1 shows the DPD operation during an established connection using the IPsec VPN client.

**Example 19-1**   *DPD Operation During an IPsec Connection*

```
1     20:20:48.701  01/24/11  Sev=Info/4    IKE/0x63000013
SENDING >>> ISAKMP OAK INFO *(HASH, NOTIFY:DPD_REQUEST) to 172.30.255.2


2     20:20:48.701  01/24/11  Sev=Info/6    IKE/0x6300003D
Sending DPD request to 172.30.255.2, our seq# = 3329592955


3     20:20:48.701  01/24/11  Sev=Info/5    IKE/0x6300002F
Received ISAKMP packet: peer = 172.30.255.2


4     20:20:48.701  01/24/11  Sev=Info/4    IKE/0x63000014
RECEIVING <<< ISAKMP OAK INFO *(HASH, NOTIFY:DPD_ACK) from 172.30.255.2


5     20:20:48.701  01/24/11  Sev=Info/5    IKE/0x63000040
Received DPD ACK from 172.30.255.2, seq# received = 3329592955, seq# expected =
3329592955
```

Figure 19-1 displays the Backup Servers tab in the IPsec VPN client. To access this, select the connection entry from the list shown in the Connection Entries tab. In the Properties window, select the **Backup Servers** tab.

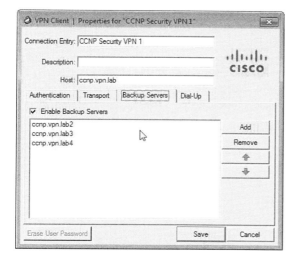

**Figure 19-1**   *Cisco IPsec VPN Client: Connection Entry Properties, Backup Servers*

You first select **Enable Backup Servers**, and then click **Add** to enter the IP address or hostname of the available peer device.

You can enter up to ten peers in the Backup Server list. They are each used in order from the top of the list to the bottom. If there is a particular peer address you want preferred over the others, select the entry in the list and use the arrow buttons on the right side to re-order them. Although you can specify backup servers directly in the IPsec VPN client, you have the option to push backup server information on first successful connection from the ASA. In the group policy attached to the connection profile, navigate to **Advanced > IPsec Client > IPsec Backup Servers**, where you have the following options:

■ Keep Client Configuration (default) specifies to keep whatever configuration was done on the client side in the Backup Servers section.

■ Backup Servers Below specifies the backup server configuration from the client be overwritten with configured servers from the ASA.

■ Clear Client Configuration specifies to just clear any backup server configuration that exists on the client.

## Hardware-Based Failover with VPNs

Active/standby failover consists of two ASAs connected using a dedicated failover link. The link can be any of the unused Ethernet interfaces on the ASA. However, note that no network traffic is passed across this link because it is used for the purposes of failover control messages only. It is recommended practice to use an Ethernet connection between the two devices that both connect into a switch. You can, however, use a crossover connection if a switch is unavailable. Bear in mind that if the failover interface fails on one of the devices in the failover pair, and you have a direct connection between them, both interfaces are caused to fail, which can make it difficult to narrow down which device the problem has occurred on.

In configuring the failover mode for stateful operation, it is recommended to use a dedicated Ethernet connection for stateful information to be passed between devices. Although it is recommended, the use of a dedicated Ethernet connection is not required. For example, if you do not have the relevant interfaces available, you can use the failover link or a connection used for network traffic (not recommended). If you attempt to configure a regular data interface also as the stateful link, you may still proceed but will also receive a warning telling you this is not the recommended practice.

The following information is sent across the failover link by both devices:

■ State (active or standby)

■ Keepalives (hellos)

■ Network link status

■ MAC address exchange

■ Configuration synchronization and initial replication

Table 19.3 describes license requirements that govern whether the use of failover is available.

**Table 19-3**  *ASA Hardware-Based Failover License Requirements*

| ASA Model | License Required |
| --- | --- |
| ASA 5505˙ | Security Plus |
| ASA 5510 | Security Plus |
| All remaining models | Base License |

˙Stateful failover is not supported on the ASA 5505 device.

As you saw earlier, the devices must have identical hardware and software before being able to use failover between them. They must also be running in the same mode (for example, Routed, Transparent, or Multiple Context modes).

There are three stages to configuring a failover pair for active/standby operation:

- Configure the primary ASA device for failover.
- Configure the secondary ASA device for failover.
- Configure optional active/standby failover settings.

To configure failover, navigate in the ASDM to **Configuration > Device Management > High Availability > Failover**.

In this pane, described in Table 19-4, enter the specific configuration information required for failover operation.

**Table 19-4**   *ASDM Failover Configuration Items*

| Field | Value |
|---|---|
| Enable Failover | Check this box to enable failover. |
| Use 32-Hexadecimal Character Key and Shared Key | Enter the shared key that will be used by each device to create the encryption key used on the failover link. The key can be 1 to 64 alphanumeric characters in length. However, if you have selected the option to enable the use of a 32-hexadecimal character key, enter the 32-character hex key into the Shared Key field. |
| *LAN Failover* | |
| Interface | Select an available/unused interface from the drop-down list for the use as the failover link. |
| Logical Name | Enter a name for the interface. |
| Active IP | Enter the IP address of this device that will be used for communication across the failover link. |
| Subnet Mask | Enter the subnet mask that corresponds to the Active IP address configured. |
| Standby IP | Enter the IP address of the second ASA device that will be contactable using the failover link. |
| Preferred Role | Select the preferred role for this device, either Primary or Standby. If Primary is selected, this device will be the preferred unit for the active firewall status. However, if the standby unit comes up from a reboot/power on before the active one, it will resume the role of the active firewall. Note that active/standby configuration is not preemptive. |

**Table 19-4**   *ASDM Failover Configuration Items*

| Field | Value |
|---|---|
| *(Optional) State Failover* | |
| Interface<br><br>(Select if stateful HA operation is required.) | Select the interface from the list available. This need not be a physically separate interface from the LAN failover connection. However, it is recommended. If you select the same interface as the failover one, there is no need to supply IP addressing information, only logical nameif. |
| Logical Name | Enter the name for this connection. |
| Active IP | Enter the IP address used by this device for communication across the stateful link, but only if the stateful link is not the same as the failover link. |
| Subnet Mask | Enter the subnet mask that corresponds to the active IP address on the stateful link. |
| Standby IP | Enter the IP address used by the secondary device for communication across the stateful link. |
| Enable HTTP Replication | Check this box if you want to enable the replication of HTTP connection states between the active and standby devices. |

Figure 19-2 shows an ASDM Failover pane configuration example.

After entering the configuration parameters required for failover, and (optionally) configuring the details required for stateful operation, click **Apply**. A dialog box, shown in Figure 19-3, asks for the IP address of the secondary ASA device and whether the configuration replication should commence now between the two devices.

Before you proceed, the standby device must be configured following the steps listed for the primary device. However, the relevant active, standby IP address information must be reversed and the correct role (standby) for this device selected based on the configuration details entered and selected on the other device.

After you have configured the standby device to match that of the primary, select **Yes** to enable the configuration replication between devices. During this stage, the running configuration of the standby device is wiped of all content apart from the failover-specific commands. The configuration from the active device is then copied across the failover link and applied to the standby device. Note the following about a failover configuration:

■  Once failover is configured and a relationship established between the two boxes, no configuration changes are done on the standby unit, only on the active one. Any configuration changes done on the standby will lead failover to fail, because units no longer have configurations synchronized. Remember that the entire configuration is replicated from active to standby.

■  The active role is not tied to the primary role. The active device is the one forwarding traffic, but the active device can be either the primary or secondary box.

- If you do not configure a virtual MAC address (VMAC, which we cover later in this chapter), the primary device's unit IP and MAC addresses are used. The exception here is when both units are down and the secondary unit boots first. In this case, the primary's unit IP addresses is used but the secondary's MAC addresses is used.

- Secondary IP, also known as standby IP, is used only for the boxes to detect failures when a monitored interface goes down, or to gain management access to the secondary unit. These IPs are never used to forward data traffic.

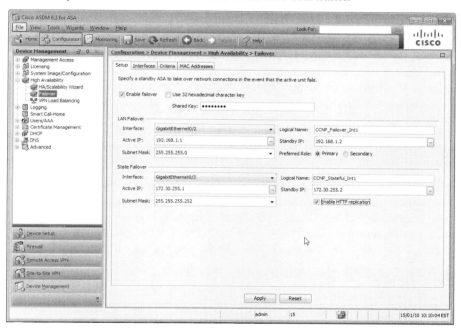

**Figure 19-2**  *ASDM Active/Standby Failover Configuration*

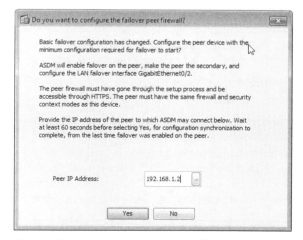

**Figure 19-3**  *ASDM Active/Standby Failover Secondary Device Configuration*

### Configure Optional Active/Standby Failover Settings

So far, the configuration reviewed in the previous sections has enabled a basic failover solution with stateful operation. You can enter information using the various optional settings to improve the service that has been deployed. For example, at the moment, the units in the example failover pair are using their own BIA (burned-in addresses) and are both up and running. Therefore, when a client or other device sends an Address Resolution Protocol (ARP) for the corresponding Layer 2 address for the active unit IP address, they will receive the primary unit's own MAC address (BIA). This can cause user traffic and sessions to be dropped if, for example, during a maintenance window you took both units down and the secondary unit had come up before the primary unit and taken over the role of the active unit. In this case, because the secondary unit does not see the primary, it takes over the role of active and use its own MAC addresses (BIA), because it does not know the MAC addresses of the primary unit (but does know the primary unit's IP addresses). Clients and infrastructure devices continue to have an ARP mapping between the primary's unit IP address pointing to the primary's unit MAC address, which at this moment does not replicate the reality. Even more, when the primary unit boots, the secondary unit obtains the MAC addresses from the primary unit, which again can cause network traffic disruption.

You can solve this problem by entering VMACs that will be shared among the devices and sent to the users rather than the device-specific BIAs. VMACs are configured in the MAC Addresses tab in the ASDM's failover menu by clicking **Add**. In the Add Interface Mac Address window, shown in Figure 19-4, select the interface for which the new VMAC will apply and enter the hexadecimal VMAC for both the active and standby units.

**Figure 19-4** *ASDM Failover VMAC Configuration Window*

As you generally configure VMAC information to improve the service your users receive during a failover condition, you can also enable or disable the interfaces monitored for failover conditions to either occur or remain stable, thereby minimizing any potential disruption to users. For example, if a management interface moves to a down state, you might not necessarily want a failover condition to occur. However, if one critical interface moves into a down state, you might want to fail the active unit over to the standby unit immediately.

Interface monitoring can be disabled for each interface. You accomplish this by navigating to the Interfaces pane and deselecting the relevant interface from the list shown. By default, all physical interfaces are monitored (with the exception of subinterfaces). A monitored interface can have one of the following statuses:

- **Unknown:** Initial status. This status can also mean the status cannot be determined.

- **Normal:** The interface is receiving traffic.

- **Testing:** Hello messages are not heard on the interface for five poll times.

- **Link Down:** The interface or VLAN is administratively down.

- **No Link:** The physical link for the interface is down.

- **Failed:** No traffic is received on the interface, yet traffic is heard on the peer interface.

To further control the rate of failover based on interface states and keepalives, you can modify the configuration present on the Criteria tab, as shown in Figure 19-5.

Table 19-5 lists the fields and information that you can enter on the Criteria tab.

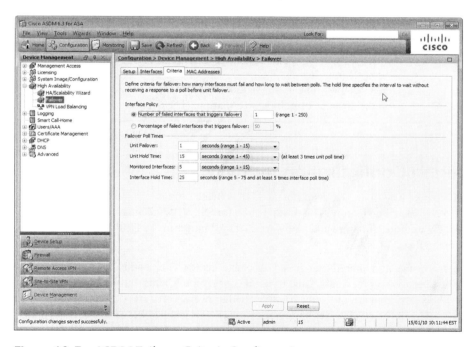

**Figure 19-5**  *ASDM Failover Criteria Configuration*

Key Topic

**Table 19-5** *Active/Standby Failover Criteria Configuration*

| Field | Values |
|---|---|
| Number of Failed Interfaces That Triggers Failover Or Percentage of Failed Interfaces That Triggers a Failover | By default, the number of interfaces that may cause a failover condition if any state other than UP is set to 1. You can, however, change this to a value that meets the needs of your organizations HA policy (up to 250 interfaces). If you prefer the failover occurrence be due to a percentage of the available interfaces being down or unavailable, select this option and enter your required value. |
| Unit Failover | Enter the number of seconds (1–15) or milliseconds (200–999) between failover hellos sent between peers. (The default is 1 second.) |
| Unit Hold Time | Enter the number of seconds (1–45) or milliseconds (800–999) between the absence of hellos before a failover occurs, at least 3 times the unit poll time. (The default is 1 second.) |
| Monitored Interfaces | Enter the number of seconds (1–15) or milliseconds (500–999) between interface polls for the purpose of monitoring. (The default is 5 seconds.) |
| Interface Hold Time | Enter the number of seconds (5–75 and at least 5 times the configured interface poll time) before a monitored interfaces state is changed based on the absence of polling information. (The default is 25 seconds.) |

## Clustering Configuration for Easy VPN

An alternative way to implement a stateless HA scheme is to use the built-in clustering (VPN load-balancing) feature. This is supported for SSL VPN (client and clientless) and Easy VPN Remote (software and hardware clients), but not for L2TP, PPTP, L2TP/IPsec, or site-to-site IPsec VPN.

For performance and limited (stateless) HA, clustering (or VPN load balancing, as it is more commonly known) can be used to divide our remote clients' Easy VPN sessions between ASA devices without having to duplicate hardware, software, or intermediate load balancers (ACE). After a failover has occurred, if DPD is enabled between the client and server, the client can automatically reconnect to the virtual cluster address (VIP) for session reestablishment. However, if keepalives/DPD are not enabled, the remote client must create a new session to the VIP address.

Clustering can be configured on an ASA 5510 only with an installed Security Plus license, or an ASA 5520 and later device. The devices are also required to have an installed Triple Data Encryption Standard/Advanced Encryption Standard (3DES/AES) license for operation.

If the load-balancing module cannot detect the presence of a 3DES/AES license, it becomes unavailable.

Figure 19-6 illustrates the behavior of VPN clustering when configured on three devices. One ASA acts as the master, directing the incoming requests to the remaining ASA devices in the cluster.

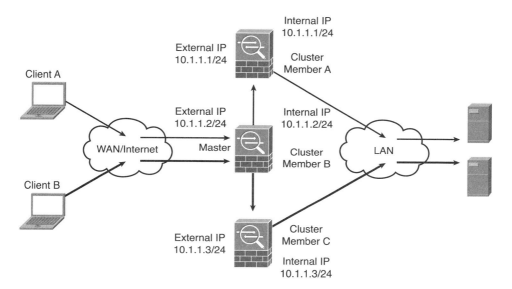

**Figure 19-6**  *VPN Cluster Operation*

The task of load balancing is carried out by the master device. The master device is the first to start up and automatically assumes the role. However, if multiple devices are configured for the same cluster and restarted at the same time, the device with the higher priority wins the election. If at any point during operation the master device becomes unavailable or fails, the cluster member with the next highest priority becomes the active master in its place. There is no preempting once the active master has been elected. For example, if an active master already exists for a cluster and a new cluster member with a higher priority is introduced, it cannot take over the role from the active master while it is still available.

The configuration required to create a cluster and add members is straightforward: All members of the same cluster must have an identical virtual cluster IP address, UDP port, and IPsec encryption key (used to encrypt messages between active members), and each device's public and private interfaces must be on the same network with each other.

Figure 19-7 displays the load balancing (VPN cluster) configuration window, which you can access in the ASDM by navigating to **Configuration > Remote Access VPN > Load Balancing**.

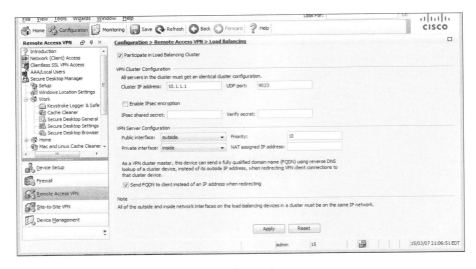

**Figure 19-7**   *ASDM VPN Cluster Configuration*

Table 19-6 lists the configuration fields and descriptions found on the Load Balancing pane.

**Table 19-6**   *ASDM VPN Cluster Configurable Fields and Values*

| Field | Value |
| --- | --- |
| Participate in Load Balancing Cluster* | Disabled by default. Before this device can join an active cluster or become the master of a new one, you must select this option. |
| Cluster IP Address* | Enter the virtual cluster IP address to be used by this cluster. All members of the cluster must have the same address configured, and this address must be within the same subnet as the device IP address configured on the interface. |
| UDP Port* | Enter the UDP port used for cluster member communication. This port must be unused on the network. (The default is 9023.) |
| Enable IPsec Encryption* | For messages between cluster members to be encrypted instead of sent in plain text, select this option. |
| IPsec Shared Secret* | Enter the shared secret that will be used by each cluster member to encrypt the messages between them. |
| Verify Secret* | Enter the shared secret from the preceding step again to confirm your entry. |
| Public Interface | Select from the drop-down list your public/external-facing interface. Cluster member interfaces must be on the same network. |

**Table 19-6**  *ASDM VPN Cluster Configurable Fields and Values*

| Field | Value |
| --- | --- |
| Priority | Enter the priority value 1–10 for this device used for master negotiations. The higher value wins. (The default is 5.) |
| Private Interface | Select from the drop-down list your private/internal-facing interface. Cluster member interfaces must be on the same network. |
| NAT Assigned IP Address | Enter the IP address the device is being NAT-ed to. If you are not using Network Address Translation (NAT) on your network, leave this field blank. |
| Send FQDN to Client Instead of an IP Address When Redirecting | By default, the cluster master sends the IP address of a cluster member to a connecting user/client when redirecting. However, if using certificates, the master can be configured to send the fully qualified domain name (FQDN) after performing a reverse Domain Name System (DNS) lookup of the cluster member it is redirecting to. |

**Note:**  *These values must match on each cluster member before successful operation can commence.

# Troubleshooting Device Failover and Clustering

When troubleshooting device failover, you can start by checking the status of the failover configuration in the ASDM by navigating to **Monitoring > Properties > Failover > Status**. As shown in Figure 19-8, this window displays the failover criteria, the failover interface, and the current active unit.

In this window, you can also reload the standby device, reset the current failover state, and force the device to take the active or standby role if you need to take the current active device out of operation for further troubleshooting.

If you suspect degradation of performance is due to the number of sessions, available bandwidth, or open connections to your device (for example, if you suspect a denial or distributed denial-of-service [DoS/DDoS] attack might be occurring), you can view the current connection and failover Xmit and Receive queues by viewing the appropriate graphs by navigating to **Monitoring > Properties > Failover > Graphs**. As with other troubleshooting sections, you should use both the real-time monitor and ASA's internal logging buffer to inspect any alarms or alerts that may be occurring due to physical or (depending on your configuration) logical interfaces being down or inactive.

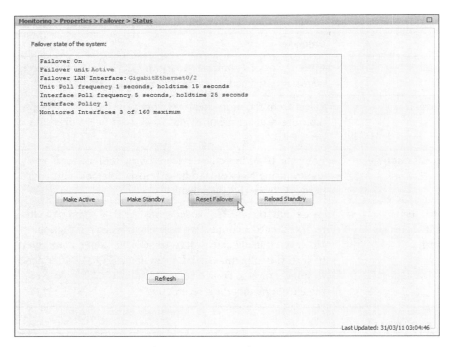

```
Monitoring > Properties > Failover > Status                                    □

  Failover state of the system:

     Failover On
     Failover unit Active
     Failover LAN Interface: GigabitEthernet0/2
     Unit Poll frequency 1 seconds, holdtime 15 seconds
     Interface Poll frequency 5 seconds, holdtime 25 seconds
     Interface Policy 1
     Monitored Interfaces 3 of 160 maximum




         Make Active      Make Standby      Reset Failover      Reload Standby



                            Refresh

                                                 Last Updated: 31/03/11 03:04:46
```

**Figure 19-8**   *ASDM Failover Status Window*

If an active/active situation has inadvertently occurred, check for any cabling or switch configuration errors along the path between the two ASA devices. For example, if a failover interface on one ASA has been placed into an incorrect VLAN during operation, the failover hold times will expire on both devices. However, the interfaces and their states will still remain up, resulting in the two devices both taking the role of the active device. Note that this scenario can happen only if the failover link fails at startup, resulting in both units becoming active. If the failover link fails during operation, the failover link is marked as failed on the standby unit, which remains in the standby state. If you suspect such a situation, check the current failover status to determine whether this has occurred. Examine the failover role displayed, fix the connection or intermediate device error if required, and restart the standby device to resume normal operation.

To begin troubleshooting client connectivity to your ASA cluster, it is advisable to start with the familiar tools:

- Ping

- Traceroute

- NSLookup

If the problem experienced is due to the cluster members being unable to communicate with each other, or possibly a configuration error on one or more of the cluster devices, check to make sure you have the required topology and all the correct information on each cluster member for successful operation.

Each cluster member's internal and external interface must be connected to the same network. (That is, they should all have an IP address belonging to the same internal and external subnet.)

When you have verified the devices are on the same network, you can proceed to check the configuration on and between the devices. At a minimum, each device must have the following matching configuration:

- Participate in Load Balancing Cluster: Enabled

- Virtual cluster IP address (VIP)

- UDP port

If IPsec has been configured for the encryption of messages between devices, you must make sure on each cluster device that IPsec encryption has been enabled, and then enter and reenter the shared secret on the new device (or All, if none of them can communicate).

Ensure that the public and private interfaces have been selected as the correct physical interfaces on the device (that is, public - outside, private - inside).

Finally, check each device for the correct certificates. If certificates are being used by cluster members, each should have the following loaded on them:

- Device-specific certificate

- Unified Communications Certificate (UCC) or wildcard certificate imported from the master

Navigate to **Monitoring > VPN > Cluster Loads** within the ASDM to view each of the configured devices within the pane.

You can use the flow diagram in Figure 19-9 as a guide when troubleshooting a cluster configuration.

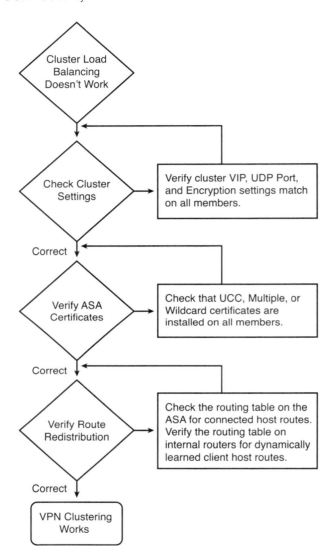

**Figure 19-9**   *Troubleshooting ASA VPN Clustering*

## Exam Preparation Tasks

As mentioned in the section "How to Use This Book" in the Introduction, you have a couple of choices for exam preparation: the memory tables in Appendix C, Chapter 23, "Final Exam Preparation," and the exam simulation questions on the CD-ROM.

## Review All Key Topics

Review the most important topics in the chapter, noted with the Key Topic icon in the outer margin of the page. Table 19-7 lists a reference of these key topics and the page numbers on which each is found.

**Table 19-7**   *Key Topics*

| Key Topic Element | Description | Page |
|---|---|---|
| Table | Available HA and load-balancing methods | 603 |
| Table | Failover configuration | 607 |
| Table | Active/standby failover criteria | 612 |
| Table | VPN cluster configuration | 614 |

## Complete Tables and Lists from Memory

Print a copy of Appendix C, "Memory Tables" (found on the CD), or at least the section for this chapter, and complete the tables and lists from memory. Appendix D, "Memory Tables Answer Key," also on the CD, includes completed tables and lists to check your work.

## Define Key Terms

Define the following key terms from this chapter and check your answers in the glossary:

ACE, BIA, Hello packet, Hold Time, Stateful, Stateless, VMAC

This chapter covers the following subjects:

- **Easy VPN Remote Hardware Client Overview:** This section discusses the available operation of the Easy VPN hardware client available on the Cisco ASA 5505 device.

- **Configuring a Basic Easy VPN Remote Client Using the ASA 5505:** This section discusses the procedures involved in performing a basic Easy VPN Remote configuration on an ASA 5505 device.

- **Configuring Advanced Easy VPN Remote Client Settings for the ASA 5505:** This section reviews the advanced settings available on an ASA 5505 when configured as an Easy VPN remote, and discusses the configuration required on both the ASA 5505 device and the VPN head-end device.

- **Troubleshooting the ASA 5505 Easy VPN Remote Hardware Client:** This section reviews the available tools on the ASA 5505 device we can use to help us verify the operation of an Easy VPN client connection.

## CHAPTER 20

# Easy VPN Operation Using the ASA 5505 as a Hardware Client

We move on from our discussion of the Easy VPN Server capabilities of the Adaptive Security Appliance (ASA) product family and concentrate now on the hardware client functionality offered only by the ASA 5505 device. This places the ASA 5505 as a perfect device for SOHO (small office/home office) deployment or environments that require a large amount of remote-site connectivity. By completing the configuration required to enable the ASA 5505 as an Easy VPN remote client, the complexity and local support that may have been required at a remote site are removed, allowing the end users behind the device to use the negotiated IPsec virtual private network (VPN) for secure connectivity into their regional or central HQ office.

## "Do I Know This Already?" Quiz

The "Do I Know This Already?" quiz helps you determine your level of knowledge on this chapter's topics before you begin. Table 20-1 details the major topics discussed in this chapter and their corresponding quiz sections.

**Table 20-1** *"Do I Know This Already?" Section-to-Question Mapping*

| Foundation Topics Section | Questions |
| --- | --- |
| Easy VPN Hardware Remote Client Overview | 6 |
| Configure a Basic Easy VPN Remote Client Using the ASA 5505 | 2, 5 |
| Configuring Advanced Easy VPN Remote Client Settings for the ASA 5505 | 1, 3, 4, 6 |

1. When deploying an advanced authentication scheme that requires each user at the remote site to enter authentication parameters before tunnel access is granted, which option would you choose for your deployment?

   a. SUA

   b. Unit Authentication

   c. IUA

   d. X-Auth

**2.** Which of the following are available authentication methods used between the Easy VPN Remote client and server for tunnel establishment? (Choose all that apply.)

   **a.**  Pre-shared keys

   **b.**  RSA SecurId

   **c.**  X.509 certificates

   **d.**  RSA certificates

**3.** Which advanced hardware client feature can be enabled to allow a Cisco Aironet access point at the remote site to contact a RADIUS server at the VPN head-end site when Easy VPN advanced authentication methods have been deployed?

   **a.**  Device Pass-Through

   **b.**  LEAP Bypass

   **c.**  Network Extension mode

   **d.**  Client mode

**4.** When preparing to allow a Cisco IP phone unauthenticated access to a VPN head-end site without having to authenticate first, which two items require configuration and details of the phone to be entered?

   **a.**  VPN head-end group policy object

   **b.**  VPN head-end connection profile

   **c.**  Cisco Easy VPN Remote client MAC exemption list

   **d.**  Cisco Easy VPN Remote client firewall rules

**5.** What is the minimum number of configuration steps required for a basic Easy VPN Remote client to set up a tunnel?

   **a.**  3

   **b.**  4

   **c.**  5

   **d.**  None (because it is an automatic process)

**6.** Which of the following are valid modes of operation when configuring the Easy VPN Remote client device?

   **a.**  Client mode

   **b.**  Network Extension mode

   **c.**  Remote mode

   **d.**  Local mode

# Foundation Topics

## Easy VPN Remote Hardware Client Overview

The Easy VPN chapters up to this point have covered the configuration steps required to enable a basic and advanced Easy VPN Server deployment on the ASA using the Cisco IPsec VPN client as an example of a remote client. This chapter concentrates solely on the role an ASA 5505 device can take as an Easy VPN hardware client (also known as an Easy VPN Remote endpoint).

Throughout the ASA product family, the role of an Easy VPN remote hardware client is available on only an ASA 5505, due largely to its design, which is based around the use for SOHO and remote-branch deployments. The ASA 5505 can also operate as an Easy VPN server. There is no default mode of operation, however, because either Server or Client mode can be used on the device. Do note, however, that the two cannot operate together.

In addition to the ASA 5505 device, the following devices can fulfill the role of an Easy VPN remote client:

Key Topic

■   PIX 501/506E

■   800, 1800, 1900, 2800, 2900, 3800, 3900 series Integrated Services Routers (ISR)

■   uBR 900 series routers

When choosing to deploy ASA 5505 as a hardware Easy VPN remote client, you have two modes of operation to choose from, depending on the environment into which you are introducing your remote site:

■   Client mode

■   Network Extension mode

### Client Mode

In Client mode, the end devices within the remote client's network (ASA 5505 client's inside hosts) are hidden from the head-end site by the implementation of automatic Network/Port Address Translation (NAT/PAT) rules. As clients of the remote site contact resources using the Easy VPN connection, the ASA 5505 automatically creates the necessary NAT and PAT translations using the IP address associated with the ASA's outside interface. Therefore, the only IP address that is presented to the head-end site by the remote site is that of the remote client device.

In addition to the NAT/PAT entries, the ASA 5505 creates the necessary access control lists (ACL) that are required for the appropriate traffic to be matched and sent across the VPN tunnel to the head-end device.

The ASA hardware client also supports the use of split tunneling when configured on the head-end device. This provides for the use of resources on the local LAN, and enables the use of direct Internet access from the remote client's site without the need to send all traffic through the VPN tunnel.

Figure 20-1 displays the operation of an ASA 5505 Easy VPN hardware client when running in Client mode.

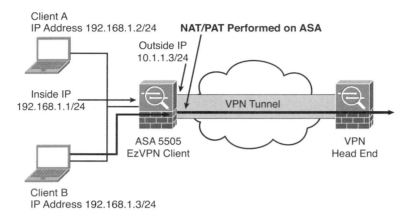

**Figure 20-1**   *ASA 5505 Easy VPN Remote Endpoint Client Mode*

## Network Extension Mode

Network Extension mode (NEM) does not perform any outgoing NAT or PAT. Therefore, it allows for the end devices within the remote site to be contacted directly. The client devices are assigned individual IP addresses for use across the VPN tunnel, as shown in Figure 20-2.

The use of split tunneling is also supported when using NEM. It is deployed to the remote client by the head-end device's configured group policies.

NEM is typically deployed for the use of direct end-user device access and site-to-site access between the remote client site and the VPN head-end site, or the remote client site and another remote site.

When there is a requirement for a remote client site to contact another remote site through their established VPN tunnels, the use of the **same-security-traffic permit intra-interface** command is required on the VPN head-end device. As packets in this design are sent and received to and from remote sites on the same interface of the VPN head-end device (effectively creating a "hairpin" situation), the **same-security-traffic permit intra-interface** command permits this behavior to occur. This design is commonly referred to as a hub-and-spoke network, with the VPN head-end carrying out the role of the hub and the remote sites carrying out the role of the spokes. It is also important to remember when configuring the ACLs to define your VPN's interesting traffic (traffic that will be matched and sent through the VPN tunnel to the remote network) to include the subnets of all remote sites where access is required from the Easy VPN remote client site you are configuring.

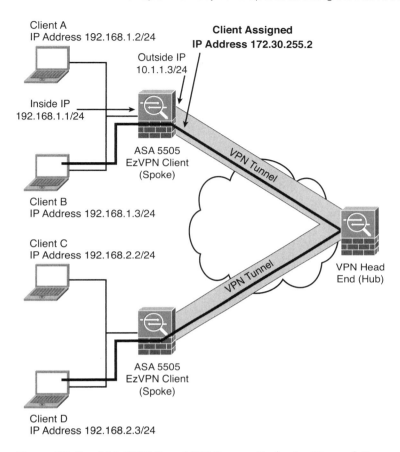

**Figure 20-2**  *ASA 5505 Easy VPN Remote Endpoint Network Extension Mode*

## Configuring a Basic Easy VPN Remote Client Using the ASA 5505

This section covers the Easy VPN remote client configuration required on an ASA 5505 device. However, it is assumed that the required configuration steps have been carried out on another ASA or other VPN termination device for the deployment of an Easy VPN server.

To begin, access the Easy VPN Remote pane within the ASDM by navigating to **Configuration > Remote Access VPN > Easy VPN Remote**, shown in Figure 20-3.

You must perform four steps to complete the configuration with the minimal required information:

1. Enable Easy VPN Remote.
2. Select the operational mode of either Client or Network Extension.
3. Select the authentication scheme.

**4.** Enter the addresses of the Easy VPN server.

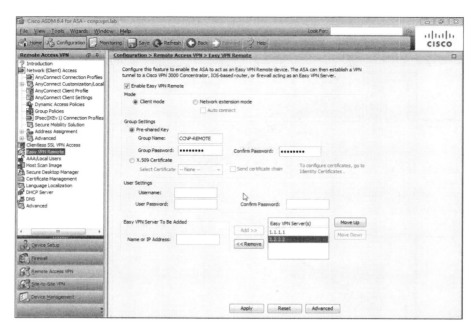

**Figure 20-3**  *ASDM Easy VPN Remote Configuration*

For this example, we have entered the following details for our configuration.

We begin by selecting **Enable Easy VPN Remote** to enable the hardware client function and select **Pre-Shared Key** authentication using the following details:

■  **Group Name:** CCNP-REMOTE

■  **Group Password:** Security

If we select X.509 certificate authentication, we can select one of our existing identity certificates from the drop-down list that appears or import a new certificate by clicking the Identity Certificates link. If we leave the selected certificate as None, our ASA device will attempt to use RSA certificates for authentication purposes.

We then enter the following Easy VPN server IP addresses: **1.1.1.1** and **2.2.2.2**. The server IP addresses are tried in order from the top of the list to the bottom. So, if our first server (1.1.1.1) is unavailable, our client tries to initiate a connection to the second (2.2.2.2) instead. You can change server-use order by selecting the appropriate server from the list and clicking the **Move Up** or **Move Down** buttons.

# Configuring Advanced Easy VPN Remote Client Settings for the ASA 5505

You can optionally configure four advanced settings on the ASA 5505 hardware client. This section describes these available settings and their respective configuration and any additional configuration that is required on the VPN head-end device for their operation to be successful.

The following are the advanced settings you can configure:

■   X-Auth and Device Authentication

■   Remote Management

■   NAT Transparency

■   Device Pass-Through

## X-Auth and Device Authentication

All authentication options within this section are configured in the applied group policy object on the VPN head-end device. However, for the authentication to be successful and depending on the type of authentication that has been enabled, you need to enter user credentials onto the remote ASA device. Otherwise, the individual users on the remote site are prompted for authentication credentials.

The available authentication options that can be incorporated into your remote client Easy VPN deployment include the following:

■   No X-Auth

■   Unit Authentication (Automatic X-Auth)

■   Secure Unit Authentication

■   Individual User Authentication

By default, no X-Auth authentication is applied to a remote VPN connection. Therefore, after entering the initial group authentication (consisting of a group name, pre-shared key, or certificate), the ASA is not required to supply any additional authentication credentials during VPN tunnel initiation. For the connection to be successful when the ASA is the head-end, X-Auth needs to be disabled in the connection profile at the head-end, as well, because on the ASA X-Auth is enabled by default within each configured connection profile.

Unit Authentication (Automatic X-Auth) occurs each time the VPN connection is initiated. The required username and password are preconfigured on the connecting ASA device, negating the requirement for a user or administrator to actively enter authentication credentials each time a new VPN tunnel is established. The username and password are saved in the User Settings section of the Easy VPN Remote pane, as shown in Figure 20-4.

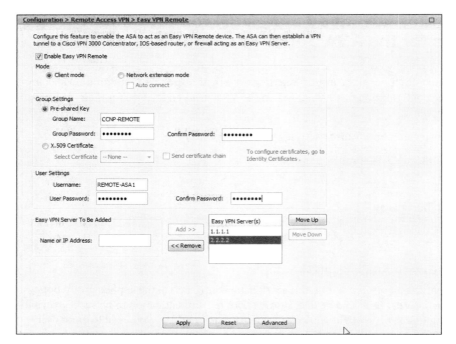

**Figure 20-4**  *ASA Easy VPN Remote Automatic X-Auth Credentials*

Secure Unit Authentication (SUA), also known as Interactive Unit Authentication, is enabled by the policy pushed down to the client from the Easy VPN server. Each time a VPN connection is initiated, the user is required to authenticate the ASA before a successful connection is established. Due to the policy push by the Easy VPN server, any preconfigured authentication parameters on the ASA 5505 are ignored. When SUA is disabled and Hardware Remote works in Network Extension mode, the VPN session is automatically initiated. When SUA is disabled and Hardware Remote works in Client mode, the VPN session is automatically initiated only if interesting traffic (to be protected) is detected. Of course, the VPN session can be manually initiated from the ASA command-line interface (CLI) with the command **vpnclient connect**. For SUA to work, credentials need to be supplied via a web browser. The simplest way to accomplish this is to instruct a user to initiate a web browser session to a protected resource. At this moment, the hardware remote redirects the user to a local login page to supply a username and password, used by SUA to complete the authentication process and bring the tunnel up. Once authenticated, if the initiated URL is valid, the user is redirected to the accessed resource.

Individual User Authentication (IUA) requires each user at the remote site to authenticate before being granted access to the VPN tunnel. User authentication is carried out by HTTP redirection on the ASA 5505 client device if one of the following is true:

■   No pre-authentication parameters have been configured and SUA is not enabled.

■   IUA is enabled on the VPN server head-end.

For user authentication to be carried out, the remote clients must open a web browser session, at which point they are prompted to enter the credentials. The problem with SUA is that once the tunnel is up, anyone (authenticated or not) can send traffic through the tunnel. With IUA, you can force all users to authenticate. The Hardware Remote keeps track of authenticated clients based on the IP/MAC address pair.

SUA and IUA are both enabled based on the group policy settings configured on the VPN head-end and applied to the remote client device. To configure each of these settings, navigate to **Configure > Remote Access VPN > Network (Client) Access > Group Policies** and open the appropriate group policy object on the Easy VPN server device. Select the group policy and click **Edit**.

In the group policy object, expand the menu on the left side to **Advanced > IPsec Client > Hardware Client**. To enable SUA, uncheck **Inherit** next to Require Interactive Client Authentication and check **Enable**, as shown in Figure 20-5.

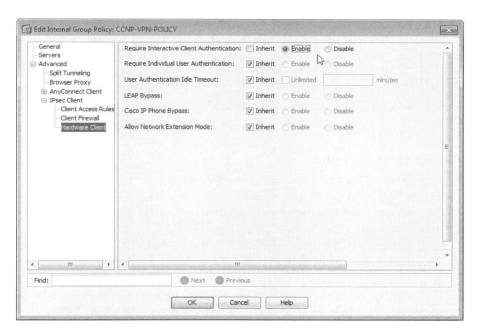

**Figure 20-5**   *Easy VPN Server, Enable SUA*

If you require the use of IUA instead, uncheck **Inherit** next to Require Individual User Authentication and optionally enter an idle timeout value for re-authentication purposes, as shown in Figure 20-6.

## Remote Management

Two options are available to enable remote management of the Easy VPN remote client ASA's outside interface from administrators located at the head-end site (behind the Easy VPN Server ASA). Our two options using the ASDM Easy VPN remote advanced configuration are Enable Tunneled Management and Clear Tunneled Management.

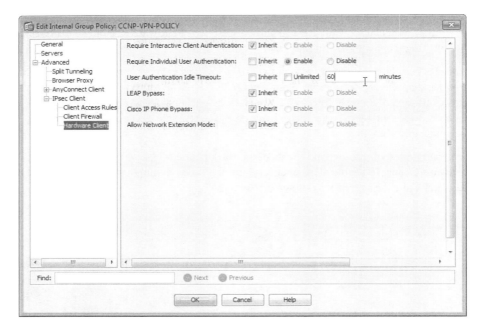

**Figure 20-6**  *Easy VPN Server, Enable IUA*

## Enable Tunneled Management

If the Enable Tunneled Management check box is checked, each session from a management station to the ASA device is tunneled through its own automatically generated IPsec tunnel. The ASA remote client device requires the IP addresses of each individual management station or network/subnet to be entered in the Advanced Easy VPN Properties dialog (shown in Figure 20-7). However, management access through this method is possible only to the remote ASA's outside interface. The management of the remote ASA through the inside interfaces is restricted to inside clients only.

To enable tunneled management, open the Advanced Easy VPN client Properties dialog within the ASDM by navigating to **Configure > Remote Access VPN > Easy VPN Remote > Advanced**.

As shown in Figure 20-7, in the Tunneled Management section of the Advanced dialog, check the **Enable Tunneled Management** box and enter the IP addresses and subnet masks of any management stations at the VPN head-end site that require management access to this ASA device.

## Clear Tunneled Management

You can check the **Clear Tunnel Management** check box (within the Advanced Easy VPN Properties dialog) if you do not want the management connections from head-end office clients to the remote ASA to be automatically tunneled. If you check this box, the normal routing process is followed for clients to be able to access the remote ASA device. This option is recommended if a NAT device is within the path between the VPN head-end device and the ASA remote device.

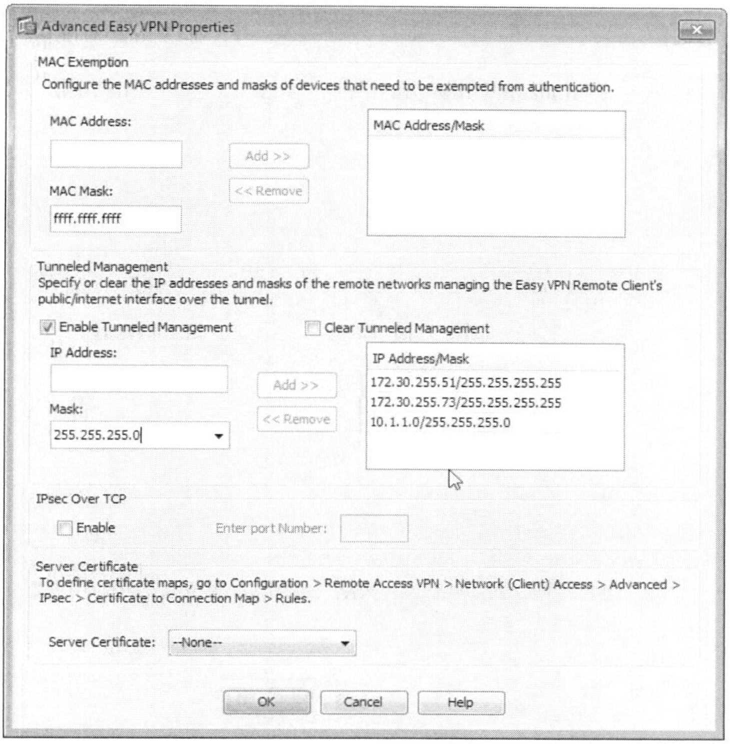

**Figure 20-7**    *ASA Easy VPN Remote Client Enable Tunneled Management Access*

## NAT Traversal

NAT Traversal is enabled by default by using UDP and assigning port number 4500. The object of NAT Traversal, as you can probably guess from the name, is to allow for successful communication between two IPsec hosts for tunnel negotiation purposes when a NAT/PAT device is in the path of communication.

The initial problem that arises with having a PAT device within the path is when the Encapsulating Security Payload (ESP) protocol is used by IPsec for packet encapsulation. ESP is an IP protocol that does not by default use TCP or UDP for transport purposes. It is connectionless by nature, and therefore, the ESP packets contain no port information that can be used by a PAT device to build a translation. Cisco can use both the NAT-T standard and a proprietary method to encapsulate IPsec packets within a UDP datagram to enable the successful transmission when traversing a PAT device. However, some organizations' firewall policies do not allow UDP inbound access to their organization, so an option to use TCP instead of UDP had to be added to get around this problem.

As shown in Figure 20-8, you can enable TCP by navigating to the same Advanced dialog used earlier (**Configure > Remote Access VPN > Easy VPN Remote > Advanced**). Once there, just check the **Enable** check box in the IPsec Over TCP section and enter a port number between 1 and 65535. Unlike UDP, when using TCP, you must specify the port and match on both the VPN head-end and the Easy VPN Remote devices.

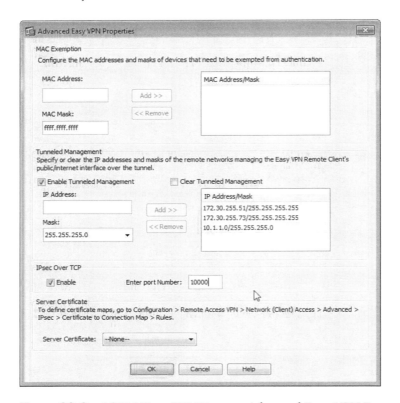

**Figure 20-8** *ASDM Easy VPN Remote, Advanced Easy VPN Properties, Enable TCP NAT Traversal*

## Device Pass-Through

To accompany the implementation of any IUA authentication that might have been configured, you can also configure the option to allow certain devices to pass through without having to authenticate. This is helpful because many devices do not provide authentication details when prompted (for example, IP phones, printers, and wireless access points).

The configuration to enable the authentication bypass of certain devices is carried out on both the group policy applied to the client using the VPN head-end device and the Easy VPN Remote device. As shown in Figure 20-9, on the VPN head-end device, select the appropriate group policy from **Configuration > Remote Access VPN > Network (Client) Access > Group Policies** and click **Edit**. Within the Edit Internal Group Policy dialog, use the menu on the left side to navigate to **Advanced > IPsec Client > Hardware Client**, uncheck the **Inherit** check box next to Cisco IP Phone Bypass, and click the **Enable** button.

Doing this enables the Authentication Bypass feature, but it works only if the hardware client functions in Network Extension mode. Optionally, if you have autonomous Cisco Aironet wireless access points located in your remote office, you might also want to enable the LEAP Bypass option to allow the head-end for wireless clients using LEAP authentication to bypass the authentication process. This works for both Client and

Network Extension mode, and LEAP authentication packets will travel through the tunnel only to a RADIUS server on ports 1645 or 1812. Note that this is only for the process of users authenticating to the wireless infrastructure. Afterward, each user still needs to authenticate because of the IUA.

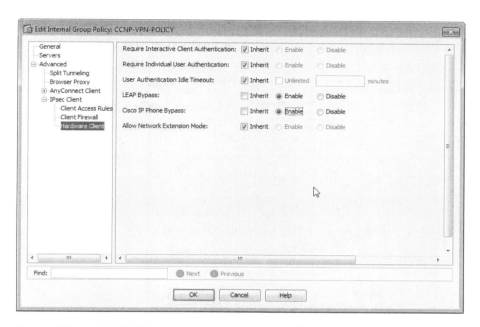

**Figure 20-9**   *ASDM Edit Internal Group Policy, Allow Device Pass-Through*

After enabling device pass-through on the VPN head-end, you also need to complete the configuration on the Easy VPN Remote client. Open the Advanced menu located via **Configuration > Remote Access VPN > Easy VPN Remote > Advanced**, and then, as shown in Figure 20-10, enter the MAC addresses per device (or range of MAC addresses that require the use of device pass-through). As shown in Figure 20-10, we have entered the MAC address for a Cisco IP phone with the mask FFFF.FFFF.FFFF, to allow this specific address only within the MAC Exemption section of the Advanced dialog. Whereas a mask of FFFF.FFFF.FFFF matches only the specified MAC, a mask of 0000.0000.0000 matches no MAC address, and a mask of FFFF.FF00.0000 matches all devices made by the same manufacturer.

# Troubleshooting the ASA 5505 Easy VPN Remote Hardware Client

When troubleshooting an Easy VPN connection, follow the same rules as discussed in earlier chapters. For example, make sure the required connectivity exists between the client and server and use the available tools such as ping, traceroute, and NSLookup. (The role of NSLookup is mentioned here based on a connection entry created using the hostname of a device.) For troubleshooting the Easy VPN Remote device specifically, some additional tools and commands can be of great use before, during, and after a connection attempt.

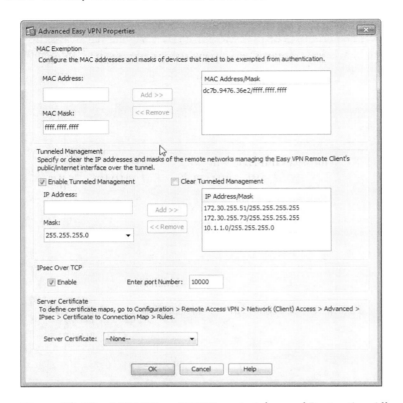

**Figure 20-10**  *ASDM Easy VPN Remote Advanced Properties, Allow Device Pass-Through*

You can begin by looking at the VPN Connection Status panel in the ASDM. This can indicate the current connection status and the various parameters configured (for example, split tunnel network lists, backup servers, authentication schemes in use). In addition, you can view the current full Easy VPN remote configuration within this window and, if required, copy and paste it into an email/web form for further troubleshooting by corporate site support personnel.

You can also control the connection status from this pane by either choosing to disconnect an already established tunnel or forcing the connection of a disconnected tunnel, as shown in Figure 20-11. You can access the Connection Status pane via **Monitoring > VPN > Easy VPN Client > VPN Connection Status**.

The ASDM also has graph functions that enable you to check the status of a connection. To access the graphs, navigate to **Monitoring > VPN > VPN Connection Graphs > IPsec Tunnels**. As shown in Figure 20-12, we have selected both IPsec Active Tunnels and IKE Active Tunnels for graph purposes.

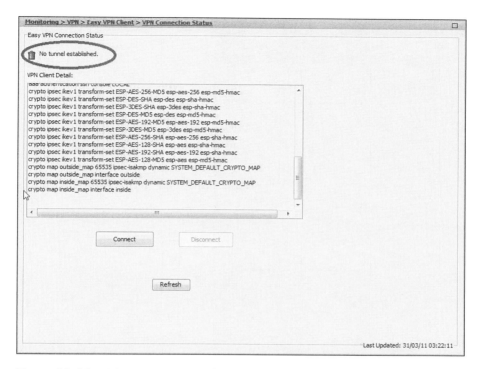

**Figure 20-11**   *ASDM Easy VPN Client, Connection Status Pane*

After clicking the **Show Graphs** button at the bottom of the pane, you are presented with the current connection status. What you are looking for in these graphs is a steady line next to the number of expected sessions you have open (in the case of the Easy VPN Remote client, this is one). As you can also see in Figure 20-12, we have the expected number of active connections on our Easy VPN Remote client (one).

You can access further information using the following **debug** commands from the command-line interface (CLI):

■   **debug crypto isakmp**

■   **debug crypto ipsec**

These commands provide you with a great deal of information involved in the connection establishment, policy negotiation, and peer authentication process within their respective IKE phases (IKE Phase 1 and IKE Phase 2).

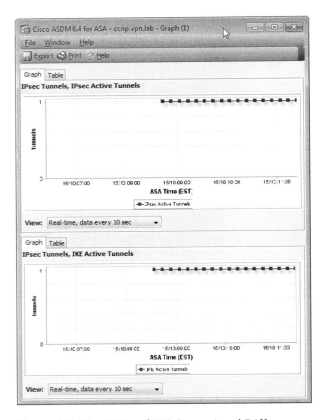

**Figure 20-12**   *IDS and IPS Operational Differences*

## Exam Preparation Tasks

As mentioned in the section "How to Use This Book" in the Introduction, you have a couple of choices for exam preparation: the memory tables in Appendix C, Chapter 23, "Final Exam Preparation," and the exam simulation questions on the CD-ROM.

## Review All Key Topics

Review the most important topics in the chapter, noted with the Key Topic icon in the outer margin of the page. Table 20-2 lists a reference of these key topics and the page numbers on which each is found.

**Table 20-2**  *Key Topics*

| Key Topic Element | Description | Page |
|---|---|---|
| Bulleted List | Easy VPN Remote-supported hardware platforms | 623 |
| List | Basic Easy VPN Remote configuration | 625 |
| Topic | X-Auth and device authentication | 627 |
| Topic | Device Pass-Through | 632 |

## Complete Tables and Lists from Memory

Print a copy of Appendix C, "Memory Tables" (found on the CD), or at least the section for this chapter, and complete the tables and lists from memory. Appendix D, "Memory Tables Answer Key," also on the CD, includes completed tables and lists to check your work.

## Define Key Terms

Define the following key terms from this chapter and check your answers in the glossary:

Device Pass-Through, IUA, SUA

This chapter covers the following subjects:

■ **Configuration Procedures, Deployment Strategies, and Information Gathering:** In this section, we review the common deployment methods and designs that are used for IPsec site-to-site VPNs and the information we require for a basic VPN deployment.

■ **Configuring a Basic IPsec Site-to-Site VPN:** In this section, we discuss how to configure a successful deployment between two sites using the ASDM.

■ **Configuring Advanced Authentication for IPsec Site-to-Site VPNs:** In this section, we cover the role of PKI when deployed for peer authentication reasons instead of pre-shared keys, and take a look at the configuration necessary for a successful connection attempt to occur.

■ **Troubleshooting an IPsec Site-to-Site VPN:** In this section, we review the available tools in the ASDM that enable us to verify and troubleshoot our site-to-site VPN connectivity.

## CHAPTER 21

# Deploying IPsec Site-to-Site VPNs

In the earlier chapters, we discussed and configured various virtual private network (VPN) deployment methods that allow remote users access to your central office resources, either through a software or hardware IPsec VPN client and client or clientless Secure Sockets Layer (SSL) VPN. However, site-to-site VPNs have been around and have become popular since the days when organizations had to make use of private connections. These were commonly deployed between themselves and a remote site using either dedicated physical lines or virtual circuits provisioned by a service provider in their network.

With the introduction of the Internet and subsequent surge in businesses becoming IP enabled, the IPsec site-to-site VPN allowed organizations to quickly provision secure connectivity to remote and partner offices at a dramatically lower cost than dedicated physical connections, with the additional flexibility of having greater control and visibility of the connection (unlike third-party provisioned virtual circuits).

In this chapter, we look at a few of the available and common deployment scenarios that have been used by organizations to allow secure connectivity between sites. We then review the information required to configure a basic site-to-site VPN connection. The first scenario uses pre-shared key peer authentication. The second uses the advanced method of Public Key Infrastructure (PKI) certificates.

## "Do I Know This Already?" Quiz

The "Do I Know This Already?" quiz helps you determine your level of knowledge on this chapter's topics before you begin. Table 21-1 details the major topics discussed in this chapter and their corresponding quiz sections.

**Table 21-1** *"Do I Know This Already?" Section-to-Question Mapping*

| Foundation Topics Section | Questions |
| --- | --- |
| Configuration Procedures, Deployment Strategies, and Information Gathering | 1, 2, 3 |
| Configuring a Basic IPsec Site-to-Site VPN | 4, 5, 6 |
| Configuring Advanced Authentication for IPsec Site-to-Site VPNs | 8 |
| Troubleshooting an IPsec Site-to-Site VPN | 7 |

1. When deploying an IPsec site-to-site VPN, what is the recommended method of peer authentication from a security perspective?

   a.  Pre-shared keys

   b.  Digital certificates

   c.  Biometrics

   d.  OTP

2. During which phase does peer authentication occur?

   a.  1

   b.  2

   c.  1.5

   d.  5

3. Which of the following are available Diffie-Hellman groups for use on the ASA? (Choose all that apply.)

   a.  1

   b.  2

   c.  5

   d.  7

4. How many methods exist for IPsec site-to-site VPN configuration using the ASDM?

   a.  1

   b.  2

   c.  3

   d.  None

5. By default, which ASA interface in the ASDM is enabled for IPsec operation?

   a.  Inside

   b.  Outside

   c.  DMZ

   d.  Management

   e.  None

6. When configuring an IPsec site-to-site VPN, where are your available authentication options stored?

   a.  Connection profile

   b.  ISAKMP policy

   c.  Tunnel group

   d.  Group policy

**7.** You have configured your IKEv1 policies and have confirmed that your site-to-site VPN tunnel is established and operational. However, your hosts are unable to access resources on the remote network. What is the most likely cause of this problem?

   **a.** Interface ACLs

   **b.** NAT

   **c.** Crypto ACLs

   **d.** Routing

   **e.** All of the above

**8.** When configuring peer authentication using digital certificates, what can you choose to send the root CA and intermediate CA certificates to the peer?

   **a.** Briefcase

   **b.** Certificate chain

   **c.** Certificate link

   **d.** Certificate rope

## Foundation Topics

# Configuration Procedures, Deployment Strategies, and Information Gathering

As discussed in earlier chapters, you can deploy a number of VPN solutions using the Adaptive Security Appliance (ASA). However, for secure connectivity between sites or for multiple remote users in the same location, the remote-access VPN deployments you have seen do not scale well. When facing this scenario, the preferred choice is to use an IPsec site-to-site VPN. In this deployment, each site has an ASA device configured with the appropriate information for tunnel creation.

The process of secure tunnel creation is carried out by parameter negotiation and authentication using the same Internet Key Exchange Version 1 (IKEv1), Internet Security Association and Key Management Protocol (ISAKMP), Oakley, Encapsulating Security Payload (ESP), and Authentication Header (AH) protocols we have already discussed. Before a connection is initiated, you must first configure the ASA with the IP addresses you trust at each end of the connection (or as is more popularly known, the interesting traffic). As shown in Figure 21-1, the tunnel-initiation process begins if the ASA device receives traffic from a local device that is intended for a device at a configured remote site that matches our interesting traffic definition.

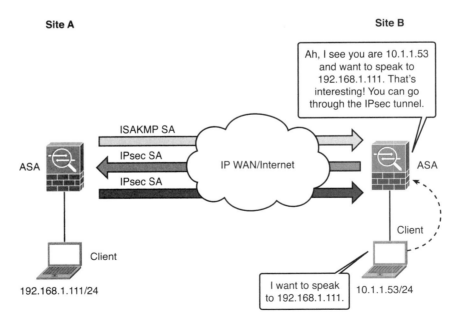

**Figure 21-1**  *IPsec Site-to-Site VPN Connectivity*

Recall that during IKEv1 Phase 1, a bidirectional security association (SA) is created between peers for the purpose of policy negotiation and key exchange for IKEv1 Phase 2 operation, and for the successful creation of unidirectional SAs by each peer. It is during Phase 1 that your peers are authenticated, either using pre-shared keys or digital certificates.

In a basic or small VPN deployment, pre-shared keys are commonly deployed because of the requirement for simplicity, ease of management, and cost (overruling the decision to implement an internal PKI solution or purchase digital certificates from an external provider). However, as the number of site-to-site VPNs grows, the use of pre-shared keys for peer authentication does not scale well and can quickly become a large headache for management. Therefore, the use of digital certificates in this environment is preferred.

IPsec site-to-site VPNs are deployed for many reasons, such as enabling secure connectivity to remote offices, partner sites, and third-party support companies. However, many organizations also use them as a means of WAN backup connectivity (for example, customers that may have many interconnected sites using a private Multiprotocol Label Switching [MPLS] or service provider WAN, which provides a backup connection to the Internet over which an IPsec tunnel has been configured). During a failure of the WAN circuit, the site-to-site traffic is rerouted across the IPsec tunnel. There is also a cost benefit with this scenario, as Internet connections are fairly inexpensive, so the customer does not have to pay their WAN provider for two expensive dedicated circuits, one of which will be seldom used unless a failure of the primary occurs.

As with any solution, you must select the appropriate device that will scale well with your current and future deployment needs. Table 21-2 lists the available ASA platforms and their respective VPN performance statistics.

**Table 21-2**  *ASA IPsec Site-to-Site VPN Capacity and Performance Information*

| Model | AES or 3DES Available Throughput | Concurrent IPsec Peers | VPN Cluster |
|---|---|---|---|
| ASA 5505 (Base License) | 100 Mbps | 10 | No |
| ASA 5505 (Security Plus) | 100 Mbps | 25 | No |
| ASA 5510 | 170 Mbps | 250 | Yes (Security Plus) |
| ASA 5520 | 225 Mbps | 750 | Yes |
| ASA 5540 | 325 Mbps | 5000 | Yes |
| ASA 5550 | 425 Mbps | 5000 | Yes |
| ASA 5580-20 | 1 Gbps | 10,000 | Yes |
| ASA 5580-40 | 1 Gbps | 10,000 | Yes |
| ASA 5585-X SSP-10 | 1 Gbps | 5,000 | Yes |

**Table 21-2**   *ASA IPsec Site-to-Site VPN Capacity and Performance Information*

| Model | AES or 3DES Available Throughput | Concurrent IPsec Peers | VPN Cluster |
|---|---|---|---|
| ASA 5585-X SSP-20 | 2 Gbps | 10,000 | Yes |
| ASA 5585-X SSP-40 | 3 Gbps | 10,000 | Yes |
| ASA 5585-X SSP-60 | 5 Gbps | 10,000 | Yes |

The following lists the information required and that must be configured before a basic IPsec site-to-site connection and the relevant phases and respective operations can take place. The sections that follow provide further information for the two IKEv1 phases, respectively:

■ **Interesting traffic:** The local and remote devices/subnets that will require access to each other through the tunnel must be defined on each ASA device for a connection to initialize.

■ **IKEv1 Phase 1:** Peer Authentication schemes, authentication, encryption, lifetimes, and Diffie Hellman groups.

■ **IKEv1 Phase 2:** IPsec authentication, encryption, SA lifetimes, modes, encapsulation, and so on.

# IKEv1 Phase 1

For this phase, you need to choose and configure the appropriate IKEv1 parameters that will be used for policy negotiation between sites. The information contained in these consists of the following:

■ Peer authentication scheme (pre-shared keys or digital certificates)

■ Authentication (MD5 or SHA-1)

■ Encryption (DES, 3DES, AES)

■ Tunnel lifetime in seconds from 120 to 2147483647

■ Diffie-Hellman groups (1, 2, or 5)

IKEv1 Phase 1 operates in one of two modes: Main mode or Aggressive mode. Depending on the mode chosen, either six or three messages are exchanged. Except for remote-access IPsec VPNs with pre-shared key authentication, where the ASA uses Aggressive mode, it will negotiate and use Main mode. Although Main mode offers identity protection, when used with pre-shared key authentication it needs to know the peer's pre-shared key prior to knowledge of its identity. For these reasons, Main mode does not fit in environments where the IP address does not identify the peer, such as Easy VPN Remote. In Aggressive mode, identities are exchanged in the first two messages.

IKEv1 Main mode uses three pairs of messages (making six in total) between peers:

- **Pair 1 consists of the IKEv1 security policies configured:** One peer (initiator) begins by sending one or more policies, including the Diffie-Hellman. The receiving peer responds (responder) with its choice from the proposals.

- **Diffie-Hellman Key Exchange:** Diffie-Hellman creates shared secret keys using the agreed on Diffie-Hellman group/algorithm and encrypts nonces (a randomly generated number) that begin life by first being exchanged between peers, are then encrypted by the receiving peer, sent back to the sender, and decrypted using the generated keys.

- **Authentication:** Each peer is authenticated by the other by using pre-shared keys, digital certificates, and so on. These packets (and all others exchanged during the negotiations) are encrypted using the methods agreed on in the proposals exchanged earlier.

IKEv1 Aggressive mode uses only three messages rather than the six used with Main mode. The same information is exchanged between peers. However, the process is abbreviated by carrying out the following actions:

- The initiator sends Diffie-Hellman, signed nonces, identity information, IKEv1 policies, and so forth.

- The responder authenticates the packet and sends back IKEv1 policies, nonces, key material, and identification parameters that are required to complete the exchange.

- The initiator authenticates the responder's packet and replies, confirming the exchange.

**Note:** Out of the two available modes, Main mode is the preferred because of the lack of encryption used between hosts in Aggressive mode, which makes it possible for an attacker to sniff the packets and discover peer identity information. Both modes are enabled by default on ASA, and Aggressive mode can even be disabled globally, which will prohibit Easy VPN with pre-shared key (PSK) to be successfully established.

After successful policy negotiation, key exchange, and peer authentication, a bidirectional SA is created between peers.

# IKEv1 Phase 2 (Quick Mode)

For this phase, you need to specify our IPsec transform sets used for policy negotiation and unidirectional SA's creation. Regardless of the parameters/attributes you have selected, the same five pieces of information are always sent:

- IPsec encryption algorithm (DES, 3DES, AES).

- IPsec authentication algorithm (MD5, SHA-1).

- IPsec encapsulation protocol (AH or ESP). (Note, however, that AH is no longer supported on ASA Version 7.0 and later.)

- IPsec SA lifetime (seconds or kilobytes)

- IPsec mode (Tunnel, Transport)

The Diffie-Hellman process is carried out again using new nonces exchanged between peers. If Perfect Forward Security (PFS) is disabled (default), the encryption session keys generated are based on the master key derived during Phase 1's Diffie-Hellman process. However, if PFS is enabled, new shared keys should be generated for use with Diffie-Hellman, and the ones created during Phase 1 are not used.

With the process complete, at least a unidirectional SA is generated by each peer. Therefore, each peer will have at least two SAs, one for the inbound direction and one for the outbound direction. SAs are used locally by each peer to reference the relevant information used for secure communications in internal databases. Note that Phase 2 SAs are unidirectional in nature. Each SA, inbound and outbound, has its own session encryption key, but Phase 1 SAs are unidirectional because they use only one session encryption key. Each SA has three parameters:

- Destination IP address

- SPI (security parameter index)

- IPsec protocol in use (ESP or AH)

Two databases are used for each interface to store SAs and policy information by each peer. These are the SAD (Security Association Database) and the SPA (Security Policy Database). The two databases each hold different information but are used together to determine whether a packet belongs to a VPN (is interesting) and the corresponding encryption and authentication information to use.

Each peer maintains a SAD for each direction of traffic on each interface. The SAD holds information such as the SPI, secret keys, IPsec profile for this SA, IPsec mode (Tunnel or Transport), Peer address, lifetime (seconds or kilobytes), and sequence counters.

The SPD holds policy information, interesting traffic information, and SPIs.

During the configuration of an IPsec site-to-site VPN tunnel, as soon as the crypto map has been applied to an interface, the two databases are created for that interface. If at any point the crypto map is modified or removed, the database information is updated, and any current connections are dropped.

Depending on the direction of a packet, either the SPD or SAD is checked for a packet's SA details first. For example, an outbound packet traveling through an interface with an applied crypto map is first examined against the SPD for a match. If the packets source/destination IP addresses are that of an "interesting" flow, the packet is assigned to an SA and the details from SAD are checked for and applied next. However, if the packet is that of an incoming direction, the SPI in either the AH or ESP header is used to determine the corresponding entry in the SAD first. Afterward, the SPD is consulted for policy (decryption/authentication) information and so on.

If at any point in the process an SA has not been located for the incoming or outgoing packet, a site-to-site tunnel is initiated, using IKEv1.

# Configuring a Basic IPsec Site-to-Site VPN

After the necessary keys and SAs have been created, you must establish the following information to proceed with your configuration to ultimately enable you to send and receive traffic through the encrypted site-to-site VPN tunnel:

- IKEv1 policies used (3DES, AES, MD5, SHA, lifetime, Diffie-Hellman group)

- IPsec policies/transform sets used (3DES, AES, MD5, SHA, lifetime, Diffie-Hellman group)

- Authentication type (pre-shared keys, digital certificates)

- Peer addresses (the publicly accessible IP addresses of each ASA device)

- Local and remote identity (the interesting traffic at each site requiring access to each other)

As soon as you have this information, you can begin your configuration. We use pre-shared keys for this example because we are covering only the configuration of a basic site-to-site VPN. However, digital certificates can also be configured for peer-authentication purposes, as you will see later in this chapter.

The deployment of a basic site-to-site VPN can be accomplished in three steps:

**Step 1.**    Configure basic peer authentication. Enable IKEv1 on the interface and configure pre-shared keys and IKEv1 policies.

**Step 2.**    Configure transmission protection. Configure IPsec transform sets, peer addresses, and local and remote identity (interesting traffic).

**Step 3.**    Verify communication through the encrypted tunnel.

In addition to the various options and information required for configuration of your VPN, you have three choices when it comes to configuration:

- IPsec VPN Wizard

- Site-to-site VPN connection profiles

- Site-to-site VPN Advanced menus

For this example, we complete the configuration using the Advanced menus to enable you to see the available configuration items in a step-by-step manner. Then we take a look at the connection profile configuration, where we can enter all details required for our VPN using the one window. (Note that the use of the VPN Wizard is not covered in this book.)

Key Topic

## Configure Basic Peer Authentication

As you learned in the preceding section, the first step required for a basic site-to-site VPN deployment is configuring basic peer authentication. The following sections provide explanations and examples of the information required and how to enter this into your configuration to accomplish this task.

## Enable IKEv1 on the Interface

Begin the configuration by enabling IKEv1 on the interface your VPN connections will be established to and from. First navigate to **Configuration > Site-to-Site VPN > Advanced > IKE Parameters**. By default, the external interface is selected, as shown in Figure 21-2. Unless your particular configuration uses a different interface for VPNs (for example, the demilitarized zone [DMZ]), there is no need to change this.

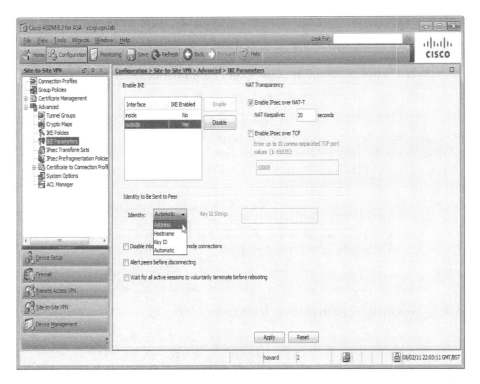

**Figure 21-2**    *ASDM Site-to-Site VPN: Enable IKEv1 on the Outside ASA Interface*

In the Parameters window, you can specify the identity that will be sent by this device. For example, will the interface IP address be sent to the remote peer, the hostname, or key ID? By default, this is set to Automatic. The use of Automatic is recommended when you have a mixture of pre-shared key and digital certificate authentication. The ASA will automatically use its IP address as its identity for pre-shared key authentication and its fully qualified domain name (FQDN) as its identity for digital certificate authentication.

## Configure IKEv1 Policies

Next, configure your IKEv1 policies in IKEv1 **Configuration > Site-to-Site VPN > Advanced > IKE Policies**. As shown in Figure 21-3, you already have policies configured by default. These are set up with the most common options for configuration. However, if you require a custom policy, you can create one by clicking **Add** in the IKEv1 Policies section. In the Add IKE Policy dialog, enter a priority for the new policy. Policies are sent in order of priority from lowest number to highest. Therefore, if the policy needs to be sent to the connecting peer before all others, it should have a lower number than any others configured. Then choose peer authentication method, encryption algorithm, authentication hash, Diffie-Hellman group, and lifetime settings, and then click **OK**.

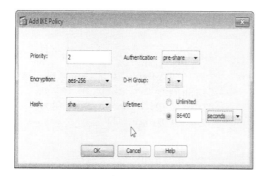

**Figure 21-3**  *ASDM Site-to-Site VPN: Create Our IKE Policy*

### Configure Pre-Shared Keys

In the next step, create the tunnel group in **Configuration > Site-to-Site VPN > Advanced > Tunnel Groups**, as shown in Figure 21-4.

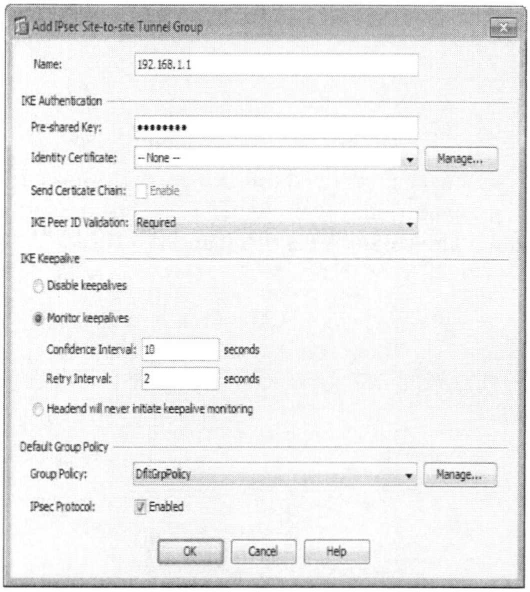

**Figure 21-4**  *ASDM Site-to-Site VPN: Create Tunnel Group*

For our example configuration, we entered the tunnel name as the peer IP address and the pre-shared key. At this stage in the configuration, all other details in this dialog can be left at their default values.

## Configure Transmission Protection

This section discusses and shows examples of the information required to configure the general IPsec settings, transform sets, and define interesting traffic for our site-to-site VPN to be successfully established.

### Select Transform Set and VPN Peer

With the interface selected and IKEv1 parameters set up, you can now move on to configuring IPsec (Phase 2) transform sets and peer address information. Begin by navigating to **Configuration > Site-to-Site VPN > Advanced > Crypto Maps**. In the Crypto Maps window, click **Add**, and in the Edit IPsec Rule dialog, shown in Figure 21-5, you must select or enter the following information:

- The interface to which our crypto map will be applied.

- The IPsec transform sets that will be used. (For this example, we selected a few of the defaults for our basic VPN.)

- The Connection type:

  - **Bidirectional:** The connection can be initiated by this peer or the remote peer.

  - **Originate-Only:** Only this peer can initiate a connection and will ignore any initiation requests from remote peers.

  - **Answer-Only:** This peer will listen for initiation requests from a remote peer but will not initiate the connection itself.

- Enter the IP address of the remote peer.

- Optionally, select the use of PFS and the corresponding Diffie-Hellman group to use.

As mentioned earlier, for this example we selected a predefined transform set. However, if you require a custom transform set for your connection, you can enter a new one or modify one of the default sets in **Configuration > Site-to-Site VPN > Advanced > IPsec Transform Sets**.

As shown in Figure 21-6, you can create a new set by clicking **Add**. In the Add Transform Set dialog, enter a name and select the IPsec mode (Tunnel or Transport), the ESP encryption algorithm (DES, 3DES, AES-128, AES-192, AES-256, or None), and the ESP authentication hash algorithm (MD5, SHA, or None).

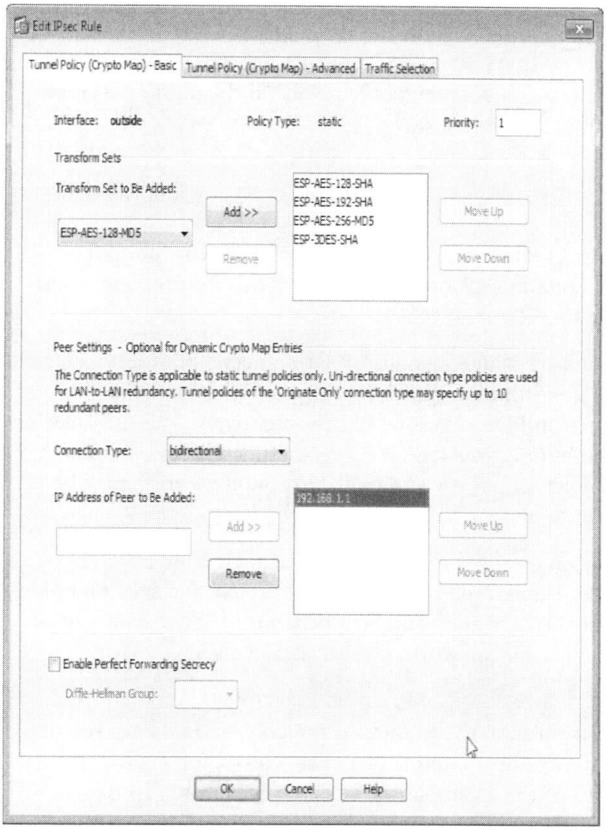

**Figure 21-5**   *ASDM Site-to-Site VPN: Configure the Crypto Map*

**Figure 21-6**   *Create Custom IPsec Transform Sets*

**Note:**    Although our previous discussions focused on the IPsec protocols (ESP or AH), the AH protocol has been removed from the PIX and ASA for many reasons, including its inability to work with a Network Address Translation (NAT) device in the path of communications.

### Define Interesting Traffic

In this next step, enter the interesting traffic that will be matched and sent through the VPN tunnel to the remote site for communication. You can enter this information using the same Edit IPsec Rule in the Traffic Selection tab.

On this tab, you can select preconfigured source and destination network object groups containing the subnets or specific hosts that require access through the tunnel or you can enter them manually into the Source and Destination fields, respectively. This information must match at the remote peer end but be reversed for a successful connection to establish. You can also select a specific service or protocol that these subnets/hosts may be using to access resources through the tunnel.

In the More Options section, you can disable or enable the traffic selection criteria you have entered, specify a TCP or User Datagram Protocol (UDP) service, and select a predefined time range access control list (ACL) if, for example, you want to allow access to or from these specific subnets/hosts only during work hours or in the evening.

As shown in Figure 21-7, we entered our source and destination subnets and identified they will be using TCP applications through the tunnel. Although we could have restricted this further to a specific service (for example, Simple Network Messaging Protocol [SMTP] or HTTP), for the purposes of this example, we selected the entire protocol allowing all TCP services.

And that is it. At this stage you have entered enough information for a basic IPsec site-to-site VPN connection. If the IKEv1 policies, IPsec transform sets, and pre-shared keys match, and the remote peer enters your ASA's public IP address into the crypto map (IPsec Rule window), it will be successfully connected. It is also important to remember that your interesting traffic definitions must include the same hosts/subnets for both destination and source. As mentioned earlier, the interesting traffic configured on peer should be reversed when configured on the corresponding remote peer.

So far, the configuration has been carried out using just one of the three available configuration methods: the Advanced menu in the Adaptive Security Device Manager (ASDM). However, there is a simpler way to define all of our VPN connection information: using the Tunnel Group/Connection Profile window.

As shown in Figure 21-8, we have begun the configuration by first creating a new connection profile by opening the Add Site-to-Site Connection Profile dialog in the ASDM Connection Profiles window by navigating to **Configuration > Site-to-Site VPN > Connection Profiles** and clicking **Add**.

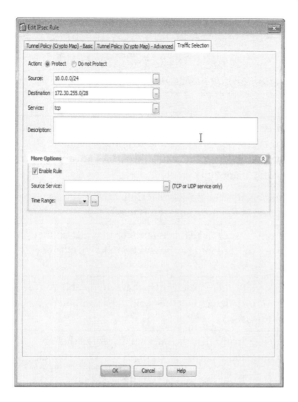

**Figure 21-7**    *ASDM Site-to-Site VPN: Configure the Crypto Map (Interesting Traffic Definition)*

**Figure 21-8**    *Add IPsec Site-to-Site VPN: Connection Profile Window*

Table 21-3 lists the available configuration values and corresponding values you can enter in this window.

Key
Topic

**Table 21-3** *Add IPsec Site-to-Site Connection Profile Fields and Values*

| Field | Value |
|---|---|
| Peer IP Address | Enter the peer IP address in this field. You also have the option to define whether the peer uses a static IP address (default). If unchecked, the field becomes unavailable and we are able to add a connection entry name only. |
| Connection Name | (Optional) Enter a name for this connection. By default, the peer IP address entered in the previous step is used. |
| Interface | Choose one from a list of available interfaces that our connection will be using for inbound/outbound connectivity (tunnel termination). |
| Protected Networks (IP Address Type) | Here you define your interesting traffic that will be able to traverse the VPN tunnel. Select whether your hosts will be using IPv4 or IPv6 addresses. |
| Protected Networks (Local Network) | Enter here or select from a list the internal networks that are able to access the remote networks through the VPN tunnel. |
| Protected Networks (Remote Networks) | Enter here or select from the list the remote hosts/subnets our inside hosts/subnets will be accessing through the VPN tunnel. |
| Group Policy Name | Select the group policy object that will apply to this connection profile. Optionally, select the use IKEv1 and or IKEv2 for this connection profile by checking either Enable IKEv1 or Enable IKEv2, respectively. (By default, the protocols enabled are copied from the group policy settings.) |
| IKEv1 Settings - Pre-Shared Key | If you are using pre-shared key authentication for this connection, enter the pre-shared key into this field. |
| IKEv1 Settings - Device Certificate | If you are using certificate-based authentication for this connection, choose the identity certificate from the drop-down list that will be used for this device. Alternatively, click the **Manage** button to be able to add, edit, or remove the installed identity certificates. |
| IKEv1 Settings - IKE Policy | Select your proposals from the list of those configured or add new ones for the use of Phase 1 (IKEv1) parameters. |
| IKEv1 Settings IPsec Proposal | Select your proposals from the list of those configured or add new ones for the use of Phase 2 (IPsec) parameters. |

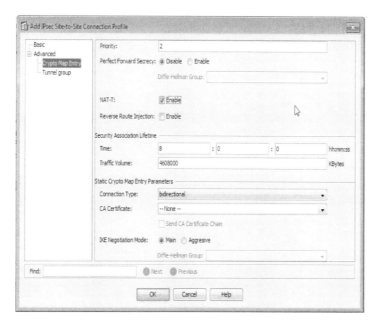

**Figure 21-9**  *Add IPsec Site-to-Site VPN Connection Profile: Advanced (Crypto Map Entry)*

You can further customize your site-to-site VPN connection by opening the crypto map properties that are available in the Advanced menu of the Connection Profile window, shown in Figure 21-9. In this pane, you can modify the priority assigned to your profile. If you require this connection entry to be used above a dynamic one that has also been created, for example, you can also enable PFS, NAT Traversal (NAT-T), and reverse route injection (RRI). RRI, for example, allows for the subnets used by your remote sites to be entered into your ASA's routing table on successful connection. These routes can be advertised to other internal network equipment by configuring dynamic routing protocols on your ASA devices.

Also in this window, you can specify the SA lifetime based on time or traffic volume (if both are specified, the one that expires first takes precedence), select the connection type (bidirectional and so on), select the CA certificate if using digital certificates for peer-authentication purposes, and select the IKEv1 negotiation mode (either Main [default] or Aggressive). If Aggressive is chosen, you cannot select a new Diffie-Hellman group for shared key negotiations.

In the next Advanced menu (Tunnel Group), shown in Figure 21-10, you can modify the certificate settings, such as requiring the peer ID to be validated against the details entered in the provided digital certificate, enabling or disabling keepalives (dead peer detection [DPD]) between our peers, and selecting a group policy that can be applied to this connection.

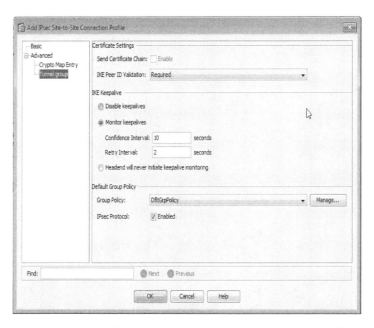

**Figure 21-10**   *Add IPsec Site-to-Site VPN Connection Profile: Advanced (Tunnel Group)*

## Configure Advanced Authentication for IPsec Site-to-Site VPNs

So, as you saw in the preceding section, the configuration required for a basic IPsec site-to-site VPN is pretty straightforward. As mentioned previously, however, while the use of pre-shared keys for peer authentication purposes can work well for small deployments, as the number of tunnels configured on our devices grow, the management of such a deployment can become unmanageable. Therefore, we now look at the preferred method of peer authentication: digital certificates.

You have already seen the implementation of PKI in the earlier AnyConnect, clientless SSL VPN, and Easy VPN chapters, so there is no need to cover old ground again. However, if you are interested in reviewing the steps required for the successful enrollment and import of a CA certificate, revisit these chapters.

Recall that you can manage the internal CA certificates and root CA certificates that have been successfully imported in the Identity Certificates and CA Certificates areas of the ASDM. These can be accessed by navigating to **Configuration > Site-to-Site VPN > Certificate Management**.

As shown in Figure 21-11, the available CA certificates are listed in the Identity Certificates pane, along with their expiration date, the configured trustpoint, their usage options, and the CA name that issued them. You can view the specific certificate details by selecting one of the imported certificates from the list shown and clicking **Show Details** on the right side of the window.

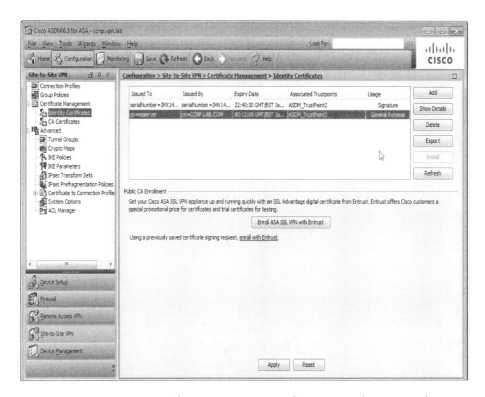

**Figure 21-11**  *ASDM Certificate Management, Identity Certificates Window*

If no certificates are listed, you can enroll for a new one by clicking the **Enroll ASA SSL VPN with Entrust** button or importing an already saved certificate file by clicking **Add** on the right side of the window.

By choosing the option to **Enroll/Create a New CSR**, you are also able to create a new key pair, which is required for the subsequent transmission of our ASA's public key in the certificate.

It is also important to make sure that you have the corresponding root CA and any intermediate root CAs that may be used for the authentication of digital certificates. If the relevant remote peers' root CA certificates have not been imported into your ASA's certificate store, peer authentication will fail, and your IPsec VPN tunnel will not establish.

**Note:**  Although selecting the option to enroll with Entrust might be a little confusing if you want to create a CSR and use a different third-party CA, fear not, because you are still able to do this in the window that opens after you choose this option.

The process of configuring a site-to-site VPN when using PKI/digital certificates for the purposes of peer authentication follows the same steps as basic configuration. However, in this particular case, instead of entering a pre-shared key in our Connection Profile or Tunnel Group window, select the relevant certificate from the list of those available. Figure 21-12 shows the selection of the certificate file we will be using for peer authentication in our IPsec connection. If we do not have any certificate files available, we could click **Manage**. Doing so opens the Manage Identity Certificates dialog box and allows us to perform all the tasks available in the Identity Certificates window mentioned earlier.

**Figure 21-12**  *IPsec Site-to-Site Connection Profile: Peer PKI Authentication*

After selecting the certificate for use, you can then select the root CA certificate you have installed, along with the option to send the full certificate chain (**Root CA Certificate > Intermediate Root CA Certificate > Peer Identity Certificate**), allowing for the receiving peer to successfully authenticate us. The selection of the root CA certificate and certificate chain options are carried out in the **Advanced > Crypto Map** area of the Connection Profile window. As you can see in Figure 21-13, we selected our root CA certificate and chose the option to send the certificate chain.

With the configuration applied, we have now successfully carried out the steps required to enable peer authentication using digital certificates/PKI.

You can further customize the behavior defined by the use of digital certificates using certificate-to-connection profile mappings. As covered in earlier chapters, the rules and containing maps that you configure can allow you to automatically select the appropriate connection profile that your connecting peers will use, based on the criteria in their digital certificate. Note that the order listed earlier is the order in which the ASA tries to match the incoming VPN session to a connection profile name. You can use the following naming conventions when creating the connection profile:

■   Any string. For example, if you use certificate-to-connection profile maps, it is possible to match the configured attributes in the peer's presented certificate and associate the VPN session to a connection profile based on configured rules. This option is disabled by default and is used only for digital certificate authentication.

■ The OU attribute from remote's peer identity certificate (only used for digital certificate authentication).

■ The IKEv1 identity used by the remote peer. ASA, by default, uses its FQDN as identity for digital certificate authentication and its IP address of the VPN terminating interface for pre-shared key authentication.

■ The peer's IP address, from the VPN terminating interface. This works for both pre-shared key and digital certificate authentication and acts as a gateway of last resort.

To enable the use of your configured certificate to connection maps, you can add them to the policy criteria that is automatically checked against a connecting peers certificate, by navigating to **Configuration > Site-to-Site VPN > Advanced > Certificate to Connection Profile Maps > Policy**, as shown in Figure 21-14. Then select the top option in the list to **Use the Configured Rules to Match a Certificate to a Connection Profile** (ours). Without this option selected, all mapping rules that you create will not be used by the ASA.

To create the necessary maps and their associated rules for the selection of your connection profile for connecting peers, navigate to **Configuration > Site-to-Site VPN > Advanced > Certificate to Connection Profile Maps > Rules** and click **Add** in the Certificate to Connection Profile Maps section of the window. In the Add Certificate Matching Rule dialog, give the map a name, a priority (lowest preferred), and select the connection profile you want it to map to from the list of those available.

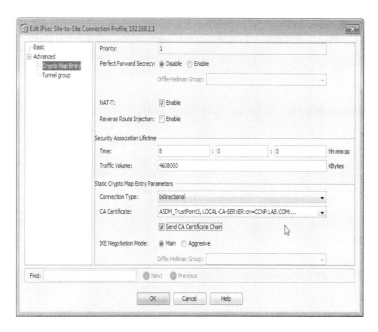

**Figure 21-13** *IPsec Site-to-Site Connection Profile: Advanced (Crypto Map Entry)*

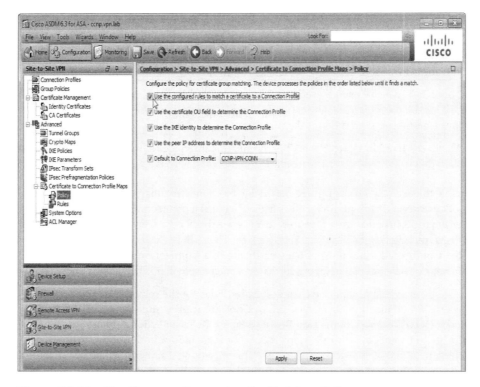

**Figure 21-14**   *Certificate-to-Connection Profile Maps Policy*

As shown in Figure 21-15, we have configured our new map with the following details:

■ **Name:** IPsecCCNPVPN

■ **Priority:** 10

■ **Mapped to Connection Profile:** 192.168.1.1 (the name given to our connection profile earlier)

**Figure 21-15**   *Certificate-to-Connection Profile Maps Matching Rule Configuration*

After creating the certificate map, you can configure the rules with attributes that will be checked against the incoming peer certificates and will result in the connection profile being selected when a match occurs.

You carry out the configuration for this task by first selecting a certificate map from the list available, and then clicking **Add** in the Mapping Criteria section of the window.

In the Add Certificate Matching Rule Criterion window, you can select the various fields that are carried in a digital certificate and enter the corresponding value that you want your rule to match on. For example, as shown in Figure 21-16, our rule has been configured as follows:

- **Field:** Subject

- **Component:** Common Name (CN)

- **Operator:** Equals

- **Value:** remote vpn peer

Now if our connecting peer presents us with its digital certificate that contains the Common Name (CN) value we are looking for (remote vpn peer), the result will be that our connection profile 192.168.1.1 will be used to establish the VPN session. Otherwise, if no match occurs, the ASA will proceed further and try to determine the connection profile based on the other options available.

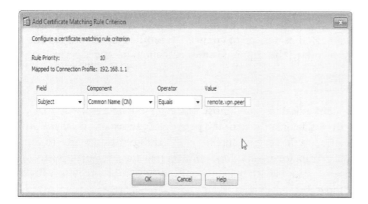

**Figure 21-16**  *Certificate-to-Connection Profile Maps Rule Criterion Configuration*

# Troubleshooting an IPsec Site-to-Site VPN Connection

Having two IKEv1 tunnel creation phases allows you to apply a phased approach to troubleshooting an IPsec site-to-site VPN connection. To troubleshoot a connection error between your ASA and a remote peer, follow these steps.

## Tunnel Not Establishing: Phase 1

- Is ISAKMP enabled on the correct interface? Check your ISAKMP configuration to make sure you have enabled ISAKMP on the outside interface in **Configuration > Site-to-Site VPN > Advanced > IKE Parameters**. Also check for any ACLs applied to the incoming interface of your device, and make sure the necessary ports/protocols have been allowed through (for example, AH IP protocol 50, ESP IP protocol 51, IKEv1 UDP 500, and NAT-T UDP 4500).

- Are the appropriate ISAKMP policies available? Check your ISAKMP policies to make sure that you have the appropriate encryption, authentication methods, hash, and Diffie-Hellman groups available. Lifetimes do not need to match at each end for Phase 1 to complete successfully because this is negotiated and the lowest value from ones configured in both ends are used. You can check ISAKMP policies at **Configuration > Site-to-Site VPN > Advanced > IKE Policies**.

- Do you have the correct authentication parameters? If you are using pre-shared key authentication, make sure that both your ASA and the remote end have the correct pre-shared key configured. If using digital certificates, check for the validity of your certificates and that of your peers. Make sure they are in the correct date/time to be used, their serial numbers are not on any of the CAs' published certificate revocation lists (CRL), the hostnames configured in the certificates match those configured on the peer devices, and that each end has the appropriate CA root and intermediate certificates in their local certificate stores.

- Make sure traffic you want to go through the tunnel is routed over the interface where crypto map is applied, so the crypto process gets triggered.

- Make sure the connection profile name can be matched by the ASA used algorithm discussed earlier. If you created certificate to connection profile maps, make sure attributes used in rules have indeed the required values in the remote's peer certificate.

## Tunnel Not Establishing: Phase 2

- Are your IPsec policies configured to match those of the remote peer? Check your available IPsec transform sets against those of the peer device to make sure that both are offering acceptable policies that can be agreed on in **Configuration > Site-to-Site VPN > Advanced > IPsec Transform Sets**. Also confirm that the available transform sets have been configured in your crypto map at **Configuration > Site-to-Site VPN > Advanced > Crypto Maps**.

- Make sure the crypto ACL (one which defines interesting traffic) is configured in mirror on the two VPN endpoints—for example, ASA1 Network 1 allowed to Network 2, ASA2 Network 2 allowed to Network 1.

## Traffic Not Passing Through Your Tunnel

A few reasons why your devices might not be able to reach those at the remote end through the tunnel include the following:

- **Interesting traffic/ACLs:** Check the local and remote network information that has been entered for your interesting traffic. Have the appropriate subnets/hosts been allowed? Do the ACLs match in reverse order at each end of the connection (for example, ASA1 Network 1 allowed to Network 2, ASA2 Network 2 allowed to Network 1).

■ **Local NAT:** Make sure that any traffic that has been marked as interesting is configured to bypass any NAT rules for packets traveling out of the destination interface toward the remote network.

If you want traffic that travels over the tunnel to be NAT'ed, make sure you configured the crypto ACL to match on the NAT'ed subnets, because from the order-of-operation point of view, NAT takes place before the crypto process.

■ **NAT-T:** Is there a NAT device in the path of your tunnel? NAT-T works during the connection phase to report whether there is or is not a NAT device in the path between the tunnel endpoints. If NAT-T has been disabled, your networks at each end will not be able to communicate with each other, because ESP is not NAT aware and will be dropped along the path.

■ **Routing:** Are the appropriate routes in place on each of the devices at either end of the tunnel? If not, your ASA or the remote device may not be able to direct packets to the remote subnets through the tunnel, and they might be subject to a default route.

■ **RRI:** Do you have any internal routes advertised in the Interior Gateway Protocol (IGP) of your network? If any devices in your network do not have a specific route for the remote network via your ASA device, they may be sending the traffic to their default route or another destination.

■ **ACLs:** Is your IPsec traffic subject to the same interface ACLs as incoming packets? If so, you might want to bypass the ACLs for IPsec traffic or allow through the appropriate packets.

As with any troubleshooting scenario, the statistics, debugging, and syslog information provided by the ASDM can be a great resource when troubleshooting a connection:

■ The IKE/IPsec statistics are located in **Monitoring > VPN Statistics > Global IKE/IPsec Statistics** and can be used to monitor any failures that may be occurring (for example, dropped packets, authentication, and hash failures). From here, if we notice a large number of a particular type of failure, we can use the debugging tools to further investigate the cause.

■ The Real-Time Log Viewer enables you to view debugging information for in-depth and detailed analysis of a problem. As you have seen in earlier troubleshooting discussions, the Real-Time Log Viewer can be opened by navigating to **Monitoring > Logging > Real Time Log Viewer**. Select the appropriate level of logging information you want to receive and click **View**. Be prepared, however, for a large amount of information to appear if you have selected debugging and have a particularly busy/large network. It is generally not recommended to enable debugging on a production environment (or at least during business hours) without supervision from a Cisco Technical Assistance Center (TAC) engineer.

# Exam Preparation Tasks

As mentioned in the section "How to Use This Book" in the Introduction, you have a couple of choices for exam preparation: the memory tables in Appendix C, Chapter 23, "Final Exam Preparation," and the exam simulation questions on the CD-ROM.

## Review All Key Topics

Review the most important topics in the chapter, noted with the Key Topic icon in the outer margin of the page. Table 21-4 lists a reference of these key topics and the page numbers on which each is found.

**Table 21-4**  *Key Topics*

| Key Topic Element | Description | Page |
|---|---|---|
| Table | ASA capacity and performance information | 643 |
| Topic | IKEv1 phases | 645 |
| Topic | Configuring a basic IPsec site-to-site VPN connection | 647 |
| Table | IPsec connection profile fields and information | 654 |
| Topic | Certificate to connection profile mapping configuration | 658 |

## Complete Tables and Lists from Memory

Print a copy of Appendix C, "Memory Tables" (found on the CD), or at least the section for this chapter, and complete the tables and lists from memory. Appendix D, "Memory Tables Answer Key," also on the CD, includes completed tables and lists to check your work.

## Define Key Terms

Define the following key terms from this chapter, and check your answers in the glossary:

ESP (Encapsulating Security Payload), IKEv1, RRI (reverse route injection)

This chapter covers the following subjects:

- **Configuration Procedures, Deployment Strategies, and Information Gathering:** In this section, we cover how to tune performance across your site-to-site VPN tunnel and how to deploy high availability.

- **High Assurance with QoS:** In this section, we discuss QoS methods and review a basic QoS deployment for voice traffic prioritization using the ASDM.

- **Deploying Redundant Peering for Site-to-Site VPNs:** In this section, we review the operation of redundant peering and work through a basic configuration required for redundant peering deployment using the ASDM.

- **Site-to-Site VPN Redundancy Using Routing:** In this section, we review the configuration of redundancy between two IPsec VPN tunnels using OSPF as our dynamic routing protocol.

- **Hardware-Based Failover with VPNs:** In this section, we discuss the active/standby failover method available for HA and how to configure it.

- **Troubleshooting HA Deployment:** In this section, we discuss tools in the ASDM that enable you to verify and troubleshoot an HA configuration.

## CHAPTER 22

# High Availability and Performance Strategies for IPsec Site-to-Site VPNs

This chapter builds on the preceding chapter (which covered IPsec site-to-site VPN deployment) and explains how you can deploy high availability (HA) between multiple peers and connections. This chapter also covers various QoS methods and their basic deployment for the prioritization of voice traffic traveling through your IPsec site-to-site VPN tunnel.

## "Do I Know This Already?" Quiz

The "Do I Know This Already?" quiz helps you determine your level of knowledge on this chapter's topics before you begin. Table 22-1 details the major topics discussed in this chapter and their corresponding quiz sections.

**Table 22-1** *"Do I Know This Already?" Section-to-Question Mapping*

| Foundation Topics Section | Questions |
| --- | --- |
| Configuration Procedures, Deployment Strategies, and Information Gathering | 1 |
| High Assurance with QoS | 2, 3, 4 |
| Site-to-Site VPN Redundancy Using Routing | 5, 6 |
| Hardware-Based Failover with VPNs | 7, 8 |

1. When deploying an HA solution for VPN, which method can provide you with stateful failover?

   a. Active/active failover

   b. Active/standby failover

   c. Redundant peering

   d. Redundancy with routing

2. How many configuration elements are required for a successful QoS deployment using the MQC?

   a. 1

   b. 2

   c. 3

   d. 4

3. When configuring QoS policies, at which stage do you configure your classification criteria?

   a. Policy maps

   b. Class maps

   c. Service policy

   d. Rate limiting

4. When deciding to rate limit the amount of traffic passing through your ASA's 10/100 interface to 3 Mb, but any out-of-profile traffic must be buffered and not dropped, which type of bandwidth management would you deploy?

   a. Shaping

   b. Policing

5. True or false: When you are configuring OSPF to form a neighborship between your ASA devices, your ASA-facing interfaces must be in the same area.

   a. True

   b. False

6. True or false: When you are configuring OSPF between neighboring ASA devices, the OSPF process ID must match.

   a. True

   b. False

7. True or false: When you are configuring an active/standby failover pair, the stateful interface must use a separate physical interface.

   a. True

   b. False

8. When you are configuring active/standby failover, which of the following is not a required step for successful operation?

   a. Configure failover interfaces

   b. Configure standby peer interface addresses

   c. Select failover criteria

   d. Configure interface virtual MAC addresses

# Foundation Topics

## Configuration Procedures, Deployment Strategies, and Information Gathering

As mentioned in earlier chapters when discussing the deployment of failover and HA, a number of methods are available. This is also true for IPsec site-to-site virtual private network (VPN) tunnels. However, in addition to HA, you can apply quality-of-service (QoS) policies to traffic traveling through your VPN tunnel for the purposes of prioritization, policing, and queuing.

As with any HA and performance-improvement deployment, it is important to first gauge the level of HA you require. For example, do you require your users' VPN tunnels to stay up and connected during a failover? Or do you only require the availability of multiple VPN endpoints that during a failover can be used to terminate a new VPN connection from your device?

Depending on your answers to these questions, you will have a good indication of the HA method you require, based on the available methods and the level of redundancy they offer. Table 22-2 reviews the available HA methods and their respective benefits and limitations.

**Table 22-2**  *ASA HA Methods*

Key Topic

| Method | Benefits/Limitations |
|---|---|
| Active/standby failover | VPN tunnels remain up during a failover event, and session state is maintained (stateful). |
| | Cannot provide load balancing/load sharing of VPN connections between devices. |
| | Identical hardware and software is required on devices in the failover pair. |
| | Easiest HA method to deploy. |
| Redundant peering | Can provide multiple ASA device addresses for VPN termination during a failover. |
| | Cannot provide stateful failover. |
| | Can provide manual load sharing by placing available devices in a different order of priority. |
| Routing redundancy | Can provide for the failover to another device/tunnel using the existence of multiple routes and different costs/metrics. |
| | Cannot provide stateful failover. |
| | Hardware and software can be of different types/levels. |

After reviewing the information in Table 22-2, you can make a better decision about which failover/load-sharing method might meet your expectations for an HA deployment based on the requirements you have been given. For example, if you require stateful failover and your VPN tunnels to remain active during a failover event, you must use active/standby failover.

Or, if you only require that during a failover, your VPN tunnel is reestablished using the next-available device or a secondary tunnel, you can choose redundant peering or to deploy a dynamic routing protocol between your VPN peers and manipulate the protocol metrics to achieve the desired routing behavior.

The deployment of each method is discussed in greater detail in the following sections.

## High Assurance with QoS

So far, we have been reviewing ways to enable load sharing and HA when deploying a VPN solution. However, this section describes what happens when packets are sent through a VPN tunnel that require service differentiation and a higher priority than others.

QoS can be configured for just that: It enables you to differentiate between multiple traffic flows traveling through your VPN tunnel and provide them with a different level of service based on their endpoint information, packet markings, application type, and so on.

When approaching the task of configuring QoS using the command-line interface (CLI) on the Adaptive Security Appliance (ASA), you use the Modular Policy Framework (MPF) terminology, which is similar in functionality to Modular QoS CLI (MQC) from Cisco routers. Through a combination of class maps, policy maps, and service policies, you can match the traffic you want to apply a service to (class maps), apply the service you want to the traffic matched in the previous step (policy maps), and apply your new rules to an interface or globally (service policy).

The following methods are QoS actions that can be applied to traffic traveling through a VPN on the ASA:

- **Policing:** You can apply policing to incoming or outgoing traffic, globally or per interface. Policing can allow you to rate limit the amount of traffic sent and received through an interface (for example, if you are connected using a 10-Mb interface but all traffic must not exceed 2 Mb). Traffic that exceeds the limit imposed via policing may either be dropped or transmitted, depending on your overall QoS strategy. In the VPN context, policing is available only for IPsec site-to-site and remote-access tunnels, and not for a Secure Sockets Layer (SSL) VPN, be it client or clientless.

- **Shaping:** You can apply shaping to outgoing traffic using the class-default class only, because the ASA requires all traffic to be matched for traffic shaping and cannot be applied per interface. This makes traffic shaping unavailable for VPN tunnels because (as discussed later) to apply QoS to VPN tunnels, you need a specific command inside a class map, which is **match tunnel-group**, and this is not supported in class-default.

  Shaping, similar to policing, can enable you to rate limit the amount of traffic sent through an interface. However, unlike policing, instead of dropping out of profile traffic (exceeding the bandwidth limit you have set), the shaper places the packets into a buffer to achieve smoothing of a traffic flow to match the limit imposed. Note that traffic shaping is not supported on the ASA 5580.

■ **Low-latency queuing (LLQ):** LLQ enables you to prioritize some packets/flows over others. For example, if you have voice and email traffic using the same connection, you can tell the ASA to always send the voice traffic ahead of the email traffic (give it priority). LLQ is available for both IPsec and SSL VPN tunnels.

By default, all traffic sent and received through the ASA, regardless of the application type, is classed as best effort. However, this can cause problems when delay-sensitive applications (for example, voice and video applications, which typically send small packets at a constant rate) have to wait for other application data (for example, email or FTP, which typically send larger packet sizes or periodically burst large amounts of data at a time) to be sent during periods of congestion.

You can overcome this problem by implementing LLQ in your environment and assigning delay-sensitive (voice) packets to a priority queue. Any voice packets traveling through the interface to which your QoS policy is applied will then be prioritized and sent before other applications, resulting in a smooth flow of packets.

LLQ is a combination of the older priority queuing (PQ) method and class-based weighted fair queuing (CBWFQ), which you usually see configured on a router used in a QoS deployment. However, unlike the older PQ, where each matching packet is given priority and sent before any others (which might result in queue starvation), LLQ resolves this problem by giving priority to selected traffic but at a policed rate. However, note that CBWFQ is not available on the ASA with MPF. This term is used here just to better explain the behavior.

When configuring QoS using the MPF on the CLI, you generally implement things in the following order:

Key
Topic

■ **Class map configuration:** Select the traffic to which you want to apply your QoS actions.

■ **Policy map configuration:** Apply your chosen QoS actions to the traffic selected in the class map defined earlier.

■ **Service policy configuration:** Apply your QoS matching and associated actions to an interface or globally.

However, when configuring QoS using the ASDM, although you still achieve the same results, the order of configuration is changed, as follows:

■ Service policy configuration

■ Class map configuration

■ Policy map configuration

Figure 22-1 illustrates the ordered steps taken to configure QoS using the ASDM and CLI and their relationship.

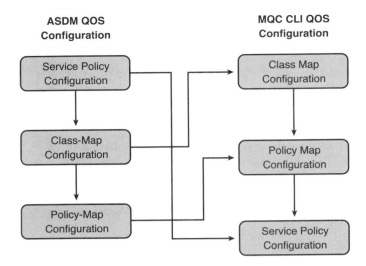

**Figure 22-1**   *ASDM and IOS MQC QoS Configuration Comparison*

## Basic ASDM QoS Configuration

For our example configuration that follows, we have the following requirements:

■   Voice packets must be prioritized over all others.

■   All traffic must be policed to 2 MB.

We begin our configuration by navigating in the Adaptive Security Device Manager (ASDM) to **Configuration > Firewall > Service Policy Rules**.

By default, no QoS policies are applied. Therefore, we must add a new one by clicking **Add** at the top of the pane. The Add Service Policy Rule Wizard - Service Policy window will open, as shown in Figure 22-2.

We select the interface that our service policy will be applied to and give it a name. (Make sure the selected interface is the one terminating VPN tunnels if you want QoS policies to apply to VPN traffic.) In this example, we use CCNP-VPN-QoS-Policy. We then click **Next** and, as shown in Figure 22-3, we are asked to select the criteria that our packets will be matched against.

To meet our requirements, we have selected **Tunnel Group** because the traffic we will be matching will travel through our VPN tunnel and IP differentiated services codepoint (DSCP). On the next screen, we select our VPN tunnel group from the drop-down list. However, if we did not have one available, we could select **Manage** to create a new one. In that case, if we were to match only the tunnel group in the preceding screen, without the DSCP, we could also select the second match criteria to be Match Flow Destination IP Address. (Criteria used to define a flow is the destination IP address, and all traffic going to a unique destination IP address is considered a flow.) With this selection, the end result is that the policy action is applied to each flow instead of the entire class of traffic.

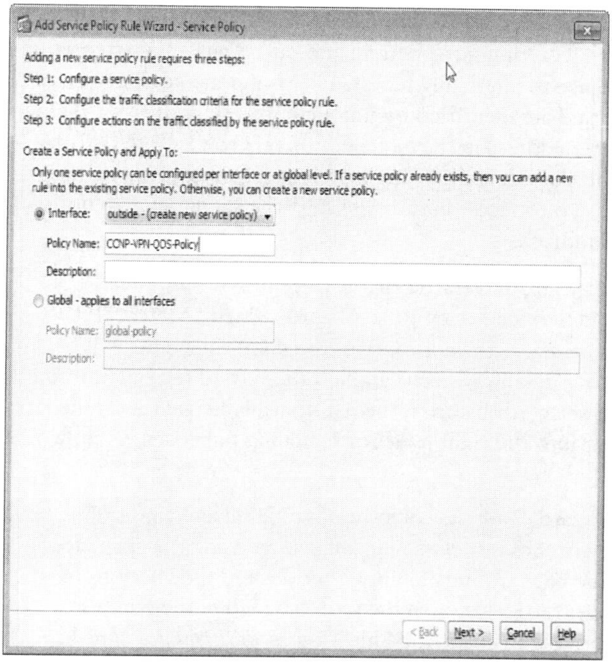

**Figure 22-2**   *ASDM QoS Service Policy Configuration*

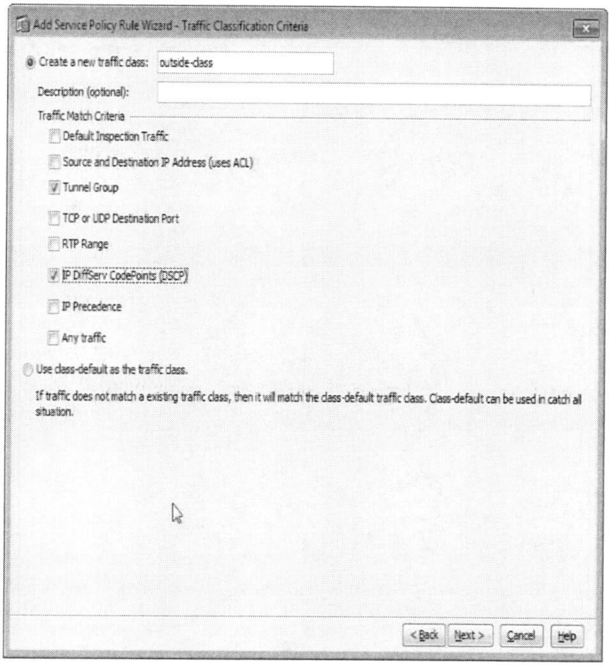

**Figure 22-3**   *ASDM QoS Service Policy Configuration: Class-Map*

With policing in mind, for site-to-site IPsec VPNs, this does not make any difference, because there is only one destination IP address: the remote end of the tunnel. For remote-access VPN tunnels, though, because theoretically remote clients initiate sessions from different places around the globe and are identified by unique public IP addresses, the policed rate is applicable per user/peer address in the matched tunnel group. Note that in a user-configured class map, not the class-default, if you match on a tunnel group, you cannot even configure policing unless you specify in the class map the second match option to be **match flow ip destination-address**.

We have now selected our tunnel group, and traffic that is traveling through our VPN tunnel will be matched. In the Add Service Policy Rule Wizard - Traffic Match, IP Diffserv CodePoint (DSCP) window, we select the appropriate IP DSCP value that will be used to match our voice packets. By default, voice is applied the Expedited Forwarding (EF) (46) DSCP value, so we have selected this from the list of available values on the left and selected the option to move it into the right pane for matching purposes, as shown in Figure 22-4.

In the Add Service Policy Rule Wizard - Rule Actions window, we select QoS actions that will be applied to the traffic that matches our class map we just created. This step effectively creates the policy map in the background. To apply our desired QoS actions for the prioritization of the matched voice traffic, we open the **QoS** tab, and in the window shown in Figure 22-5, we check **Enable Priority for This Flow**, and then click **Finish**.

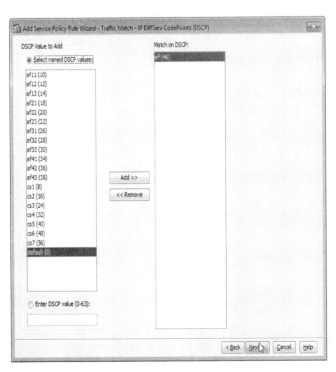

**Figure 22-4**   *ASDM QoS Service Policy Configuration: Class Map Continued*

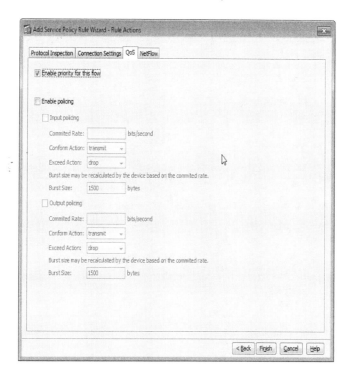

**Figure 22-5**   *ASDM QoS Service Policy Configuration: Policy Map Configuration*

**Note:**   So far, our QoS configuration has depended on matching packets that have already been tagged within our network. For example, any voice packets matched on the ASA with IP DSCP 46 would have previously been matched and marked earlier within the network path for them to have the DSCP 46 applied. It is generally recommended that QoS markings be applied as close to the traffic source as possible (that is, either marked by the phone itself or on the receiving access switch port).

To achieve the remaining actions of our desired QoS policy, we must follow the same steps again to enable the selection of all traffic and policing it to 2 Mb.

We begin the rest of our configuration by clicking **Add** in the Service Policy Rules pane. Then, in the Add Service Policy Rule Wizard shown in Figure 22-6, from the Interface drop-down list, select the outside interface, which will automatically select our service policy created earlier. (You can have only one service policy applied per ASA interface.)

In the Add Service Policy Rule Wizard - Traffic Classification Criteria window, we select the default class map (class-default) for traffic selection. The default class map is configured automatically at the end of every policy map and acts as a catchall policy. Therefore, any remaining traffic that does not match our custom class maps will be matched using the default class map class-default, as shown in Figure 22-7.

Key
Topic

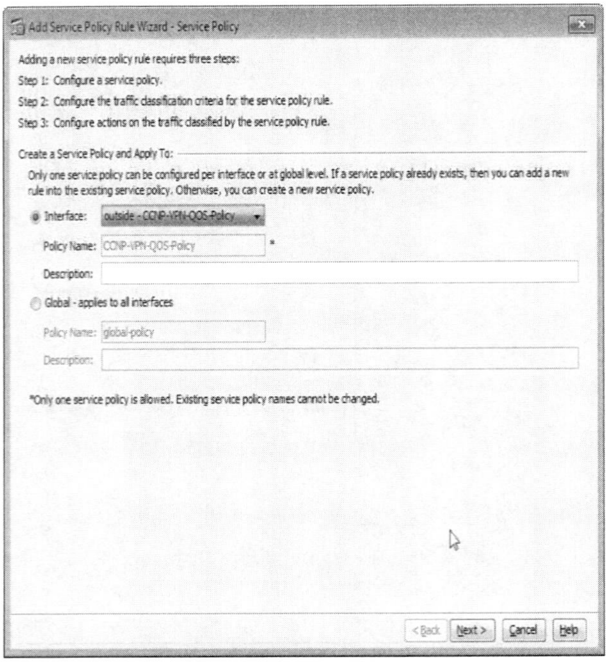

**Figure 22-6**   *ASDM QoS Service Policy Configuration: Service Policy Selection*

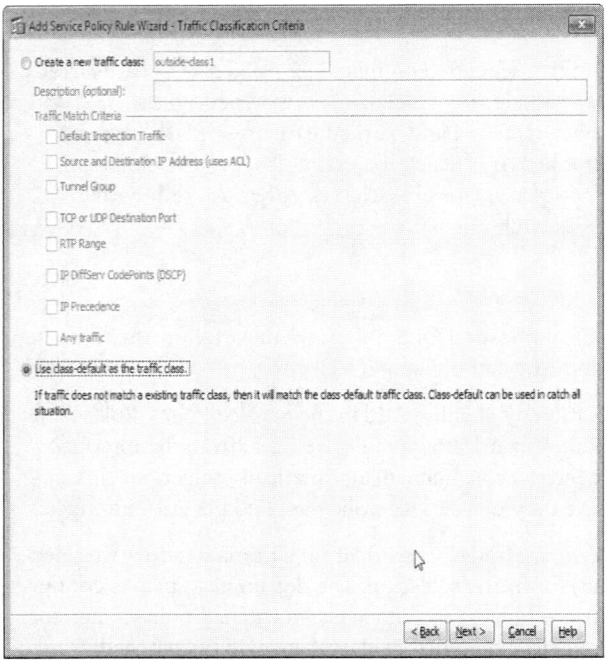

**Figure 22-7**   *ASDM QoS Service Policy Configuration: Default Traffic Class Selection*

Now that we have selected the class map that will match all remaining traffic, we can configure our policing that will apply to it. In the Add Service Policy Rule Wizard - Rule Actions window, we display the **QoS** tab and from the list of available options and check **Enable Policing** and then **Outbound Policing**, because for this example, we will be policing all remaining traffic to 2-Mb Outbound.

We enter the following details for our configuration, as shown in Figure 22-8:

- **Committed Rate (bps):** 2000000

- **Conform Action:** Transmit

- **Exceed Action:** Drop

- **Burst Size:** Left at default, 1500

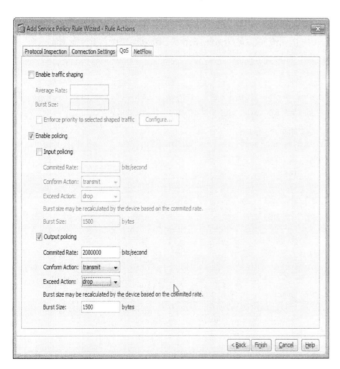

**Figure 22-8**   *ASDM QoS Service Policy Configuration: Policy Map Policing*

And that is it for our example QoS configuration. We have successfully enabled the prioritization for voice traffic traveling through our VPN tunnel and policed all remaining traffic to 2 Mb. Any traffic in the 2-Mb limit will be sent. However, any out-of-profile traffic that exceeds the 2 Mb will be dropped.

You can view the resulting actions and configuration of QoS policies in the Service Policy Rules window. To further guide your understanding, click **Diagram** in this window to see a visual representation of the configuration.

# Deploying Redundant Peering for Site-to-Site VPNs

Just as a basic failover deployment can be achieved using redundant peering with the Cisco IPsec VPN client and the Easy VPN client, basic failover deployment can also be achieved for IPsec site-to-site VPNs.

Although this method of failover does not provide for stateful session maintenance, it is an easy way to enable failover for users if our primary ASA becomes unavailable. If we use dead peer detection (DPD), our remote ASA device can detect when a failover of the primary device occurs and attempt a connection to a back up server that has been configured.

You can enter your backup ASA devices on a peer in the crypto map configuration. Open the Edit IPsec Rule dialog by navigating to **Configuration > Site-to-Site VPN > Advanced > Crypto Maps,** where you select the correct crypto map from the list of those available and click **Edit.**

In the Edit IPsec Rule window that opens in the Peer Settings section, you can enter the IP addresses of any additional peers/backup servers, as shown in Figure 22-9.

**Figure 22-9**   *IPsec Site-to-Site VPN Redundant Peer Configuration*

During a failover, a new VPN session is established with the backup peer IP once the primary peer is no longer available/reachable based on configured DPD settings. However, once the primary peer is again reachable, there is no preemption (that is, a new session will not automatically be established with the primary VPN peer).

Now that you have entered your redundant peers, you can optionally tune DPD timeouts to either speed up or slow down the detection of a communication problem between peers.

You configure DPD timeouts in the tunnel group configuration located in **Configuration > IPsec Site-to-Site VPN > Advanced > Tunnel Groups**, shown in Figure 22-10. Check the option to **Monitor Keepalives** and in the Confidence Interval field, enter the amount of time in seconds for this peer to wait until it starts to send DPD packets because of tunnel inactivity (sort of an idle timer). The retry interval can be used to specify the amount of time in seconds between DPD packets being sent to a peer device.

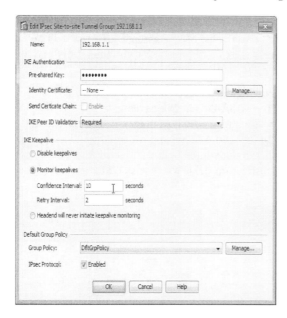

**Figure 22-10**   *IPsec Site-to-Site VPN Redundant Peer: Optional DPD Settings*

## Site-to-Site VPN Redundancy Using Routing

If you have multiple devices with VPN tunnels configured for failover purposes, you can route between them by using either a dynamic routing protocol or static routes. For a small deployment, it might be common for a floating static route toward the client destinations to be used or even associated with a track, using the IOS IP service level agreement (SLA) feature.

However, for a large organization with multiple internal routers and equipment, the static routing method does not scale well. Therefore, you must use a dynamic routing protocol to manage the distribution of routes to remote subnets and manipulate the metrics of this protocol to allow you to manage the direction that traffic takes.

For this scenario to work, you must configure a dynamic routing protocol on the ASA and between peers for routes to be advertised to remote sites and vice versa. Unlike the configuration on a router that hosts an IPsec tunnel, you do not require our Open Shortest Path First (OSPF) packets to be sent through the tunnel using an additional generic routing encapsulation (GRE) tunnel. As an example, you have two ASA devices in your local site, each of which has a VPN tunnel established to the remote site. OSPF will be configured on both ASA devices, and each device will peer with the remote site ASA and internal routes for propagation of remote subnets throughout your routers. In the following configuration example, we discuss the steps required to enable OSPF and peering between the local and remote ASA. We show only one ASA device configuration, because the steps required on both devices are the same, apart from the manual cost increase on the secondary ASA interface, which is discussed in the example.

We begin our configuration by adding OSPF to the list of interesting traffic that will be allowed to travel through our VPN. This task is required for OSPF to function between our peers, neighborships to be established, and routing tables to be populated.

An additional ACE can be added to our existing crypto access control list (ACL). However, this must also be carried out on the peer ASA/device. We navigate to **Configuration> IPsec Site-to-Site VPN > Advanced >ACL Manager**, select our existing ACL from the list, and click **Add > ACE**. In the Add ACE dialog, we enter the outside/public-facing IP address of our ASA in the Source field and the outside/public-facing IP address of the remote ASA in the Destination field. We choose **OSPF** as the service and click **OK**. Figure 22-11 shows this configuration.

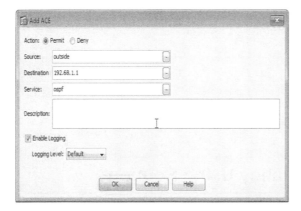

**Figure 22-11**   *IPsec ACE Entry: Add OSPF as Interesting Traffic*

Next, we enable the OSPF process on our ASA device by navigating to **Configuration>Device Setup > Routing > OSPF > Setup**, shown in Figure 22-12. In this window, we enable OSPF Process 1 and enter a number for the process ID. This number is used only locally and is not required to match on both ends of the connection, although you might find it easier for troubleshooting to give both ASAs the same process ID.

Now that we have enabled our OSPF process, we need to tell the ASA which networks it will be advertising. For this example, we enter both the internal and remote subnets, as shown in Figure 22-13. The configuration of our OSPF networks is carried out in **Configuration>Device Setup > Routing > OSPF > Setup > Area/Networks**. When we click **Add**, the Add OSPF Area dialog opens.

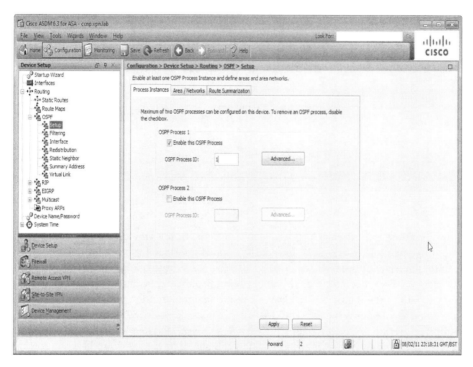

**Figure 22-12**   *Enable OSPF Process on Your ASA Device*

In this dialog, as you can also see in Figure 22-13, we entered the following information:

- **Area ID:** 1 (This must be the same on either end of your VPN.)
- **Area Type:** Normal
- **Area Networks:** 172.30.255.0/28 and 10.0.0.0/24
- **Authentication:** None

**Figure 22-13**   *Create OSPF Area and Advertised Networks*

We now configure our interface properties in **Configuration > Device Setup > Routing > OSPF > Interface > Properties**. We select the outside interface from the list and click **Edit**. In the Interface Properties window, we use the OSPF network type of point-to-point non-broadcast, so we need to begin by unchecking **Broadcast**, because this device is our secondary path to the remote network. We need to manipulate the OSPF cost of the interface by entering a larger value into the Cost field. This task is carried out on this device only, and our second ASA device uses the default value of 10. Therefore, the path toward the remote network through our second device will have a lower metric and be preferred by our internal routers.

Figure 22-14 shows our configuration for this task.

Now that we have changed the default OSPF interface behavior of broadcast to nonbroadcast, we need to manually enter the address of our OSPF neighbor (remote peer) because they will no longer be able to automatically build a neighbor relationship. (The disabling of broadcast also disables multicast and breaks the default behavior of dynamically discovering neighbors using the OSPF multicast address 224.0.0.5.)

We enter our neighbor IP address by navigating to **Configuration > Device Setup > Routing > OSPF > Static Neighbor** and clicking **Add** to create a new one. In the Add OSPF Neighbor Entry dialog, shown in Figure 22-15, we choose our OSPF process ID from the drop-down list, enter our neighbor's outside IP address, and select the interface over which we will be contacting this neighbor (outside). After entering these details, we click **OK**.

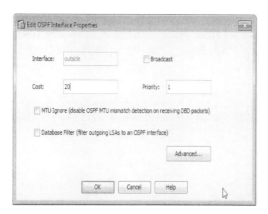

**Figure 22-14**  *Modify OSPF Interface Network Type and OSPF Interface Cost (Secondary)*

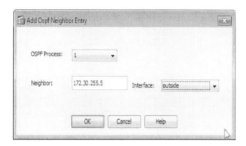

**Figure 22-15**  *Static OSPF Neighbor Entry*

That is it, as far as our example goes. However, if you were configuring this deployment for a production network, you would also need to enable the OSPF process on the internal interfaces of your ASA and configure the relevant areas and networks to be advertised. After carrying out these actions, you are then ready to set up a neighbor relationship with your internal routing equipment and begin advertising routes to them. Note that the functionality of using OSPF directly over IPsec without any sort of tunneling mechanism like GRE is available only on the ASA. Another exception from the normal behavior of OSPF is the fact that peers do not share the same subnet, which usually prohibits OSPF neighborship forming.

## Hardware-Based Failover with VPNs

As discussed in the opening section of this chapter, many HA options are available for both IPsec and SSL VPNs. Your overall requirements will dictate the failover/HA method you deploy.

For example, the active/standby failover method is the only one that supports stateful session failover. Therefore, if a failover occurs, the VPN tunnels to your remote sites remain active and your users do not have to reopen applications and such.

For this deployment, the devices must be of the same model and running the same software release. There must also be a dedicated failover interface/connection and optionally a dedicated connection used for stateful session information, as shown in Figure 22-16.

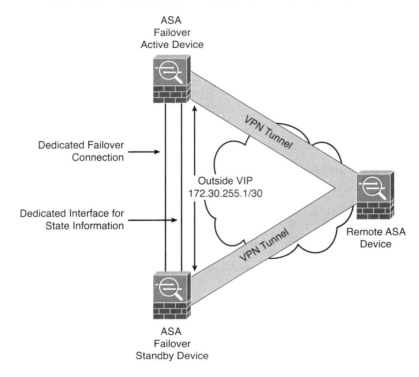

**Figure 22-16**   *ASA Hardware Failover Pair Configuration*

There are three mandatory and one optional step for configuring active/standby failover:

**Step 1.**    Configure LAN failover interfaces.

**Step 2.**    Configure standby addresses on interfaces used for traffic forwarding.

**Step 3.**    Define failover criteria.

**Optional**    Configure nondefault MAC addresses.

### Configure LAN Failover Interfaces

In this step, select the interfaces that will be used for your failover deployment and, optionally, the stateful connection. You can select the same interface for both roles. However, it is recommended to use separate physical interfaces because of the large amount of information that might be sent across the stateful link, if on your ASA device you have interfaces with different physical speeds. For example, if you are using 100-Mb interfaces for forwarding, your stateful link should also be a 100-Mb interface. However, if you are using 1-Gb interfaces for forwarding, your stateful link should also be a 1-Gb link.

During this step, you also define the active and standby IP addresses that will be used between the two devices on both the failover and optional stateful link, and configure the role of the device—for example, primary or secondary (active or standby, respectively, in normal circumstances, although any box can be the active unit).

Figure 22-17 shows our configuration and the details we entered to enable failover and our stateful connection. We entered our configuration details in **Configuration > Device Management > High Availability > Failover**.

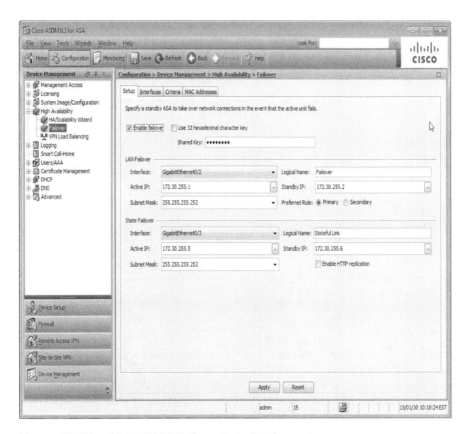

**Figure 22-17** *ASA ASDM Failover Pair Configuration*

## Configure Standby Addresses on Interfaces Used for Traffic Forwarding

In this next step, configure the standby IP addresses that will be used by your peer ASA device using the Interfaces tab of the Failover window, as shown in Figure 22-18.

**Figure 22-18** *ASA ASDM Failover Standby IP Address Configuration*

## Define Failover Criteria

To finish the failover configuration, you can specify the criteria that will actually cause the devices to fail over between active and standby units. A failover can occur based on a number of interfaces being in a down or unknown state. By default, a failover occurs if only one interface is in any state other than up. However, this can be changed to either a number between 1 and 250 or a percentage of overall interfaces.

As shown in Figure 22-19, we have decided to go with the default values for this configuration example.

## Configure Nondefault Mac Addresses

After completing the three mandatory steps required for a basic failover configuration, you have the option to configure virtual MAC (VMAC) addresses that will be used to represent your interfaces responsible for forwarding. This step is optional. However, it is recommended because of the potential downtime that might result if a standby/secondary device were ever to become available before the primary/active. This was explained in detail in Chapter 19, "High Availability and Performance for Easy VPN."

**Figure 22-19**   *ASA ASDM Failover Criteria*

VMACs can be configured in the MAC Addresses tab of the ASDM Failover window. You start by clicking the **Add** button (by default, none are configured). Then, in the Edit Interface Mac Addresses window, select each of the interfaces responsible for forwarding. You enter both the active interface MAC address and the interface MAC address of the standby device, and you continue this operation for each interface available, as shown in Figure 22-20.

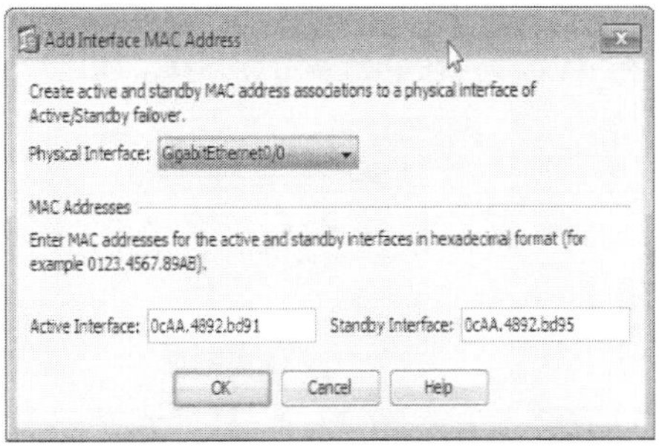

**Figure 22-20**   *ASA ASDM Failover VMAC Configuration*

## Troubleshooting HA Deployment

As with the majority of features available for configuration using the ASDM, you have a large number of tools that can provide statistics and connectivity information to help you troubleshoot your HA deployment.

For example, when troubleshooting a failover deployment, you can quickly view your failover status by navigating to **Monitoring > Properties > Failover > Status**. Figure 22-21 shows the information available in that window.

**Figure 22-21**   *ASDM Active/Standby Failover Status*

In this window, you can also reload the standby device, reset the current failover state, and force the device to take the active or standby role if you need to take the current active device out of operation for further troubleshooting.

If degradation of performance might be due to the number of sessions or open connections to the device (for example, if it is possible that a denial-of-service/distributed DoS [DoS/DDoS] attack might be occurring), you can view the current connection and failover Xmit and Receive queues by selecting the appropriate graphs available and opening them in the **Monitoring > Properties > Failover > Graphs** section of the ASDM.

As with other troubleshooting sections, the use of the real-time monitor and ASA's internal logging buffer are recommended for inspection of any alarms or alerts that might be occurring because physical or (depending on configuration) logical interfaces are down or inactive.

If an active/active situation has inadvertently occurred, check for any cabling or switch configuration errors along the path between the two ASA devices. For example, if a failover interface on one ASA had been placed into an incorrect VLAN during operation, the failover holdtimes will expire on both devices. However, the interfaces and their states will still remain up, resulting in the two devices both taking the role of the active device. Note that this scenario can happen only if the failover link fails at machine startup, resulting in both units becoming active. If the failover link fails during operation, the failover link is marked as failed on the standby unit, which remains in the standby state.

If such a situation might be occurring, you can check the current failover status to see whether this has occurred by examining the failover role displayed. In this instance, you can fix the connection or intermediate device error and restart the standby device to resume normal operation. Note that in this scenario, if VMACs were not configured, it is possible that devices on the directly connected subnets of the ASA use the secondary's ASA MAC address as a Layer 3 to Layer 2 mapping for ASA's primary IP address. Because this is not functional, you might need to manually clear the Address Resolution Protocol (ARP) cache on directly connected devices to resume normal network operation, even though you have restarted the secondary box.

## Exam Preparation Tasks

As mentioned in the section "How to Use This Book" in the Introduction, you have a couple of choices for exam preparation: the memory tables in Appendix C, Chapter 23, "Final Exam Preparation," and the exam simulation questions on the CD-ROM.

## Review All Key Topics

Review the most important topics in the chapter, noted with the Key Topic icon in the outer margin of the page. Table 22-3 lists a reference of these key topics and the page numbers on which each is found.

**Table 22-3**  *Key Topics*

| Key Topic Element | Description | Page |
|---|---|---|
| Table | Available HA methods and their benefits/limitations | 669 |
| Topic | QoS configuration building blocks | 671 |
| Topic | QoS class-default operation | 675 |
| Topic | Failover with routing | 679 |
| Topic | Failover VMAC configuration | 686 |

## Complete Tables and Lists from Memory

Print a copy of Appendix C, "Memory Tables" (found on the CD), or at least the section for this chapter, and complete the tables and lists from memory. Appendix D, "Memory Tables Answer Key," also on the CD, includes completed tables and lists to check your work.

## Define Key Terms

Define the following key terms from this chapter, and check your answers in the glossary:

class map, MPF (Modular Policy Framework), policing, policy map, service policy, shaping, VMAC (Virtual MAC address)

## CHAPTER 23

# Final Exam Preparation

The first 22 chapters of this book cover the technologies, protocols, design concepts, and considerations necessary to prepare for the 642-647 CCNP Security VPN exam. Although these chapters supply the detailed information, most people need more preparation than just reading the first 22 chapters of this book. This chapter details a set of tools and a study plan to help you complete your preparation for the exams.

This short chapter has two main sections. The first section lists the exam preparation tools useful at this point in the study process. The second section lists a suggested study plan now that you have completed all the earlier chapters in this book.

**Note:** Note that Appendix C, "Memory Tables," and Appendix D, "Memory Tables Answer Key," exist as soft-copy appendixes on the CD included at the back of this book.

## Tools for Final Preparation

This section lists some information about the available tools and how to access the tools.

### Pearson Cert Practice Test Engine and Questions on the CD

The CD at the back of this book includes the Pearson Cert Practice Test engine—software that displays and grades a set of exam-realistic multiple-choice questions. Using the Pearson Cert Practice Test engine, you can either study by going through the questions in Study mode or take a simulated (timed) CCNP Security VPN exam.

The installation process requires two major steps. The CD at the back of this book has a recent copy of the Pearson Cert Practice Test engine. The practice exam—the database of CCNP Security VPN exam questions—is not on the CD.

**Note:** The cardboard CD case at the back of this book includes the CD and a piece of paper. The paper lists the activation key for the practice exam associated with this book. *Do not lose the activation key*. On the opposite side of the paper from the activation code is a unique, one-time-use coupon code for the purchase of the *CCNP Security VPN Official Cert Guide, Premium Edition*.

## Install the Software from the CD

The software installation process is pretty straightforward as compared to other software installation processes. To be complete, the following steps outline the installation process:

**Step 1.**    Insert the CD into your PC.

**Step 2.**    The software that automatically runs is the Cisco Press software to access and use all CD-based features, including the exam engine and the CD-only appendixes. From the main menu, click the option to **Install the Exam Engine**.

**Step 3.**    Respond to window prompts as with any typical software installation process.

The installation process gives you the option to activate your exam with the activation code supplied on the paper in the CD sleeve. This process requires that you establish a Pearson website login. You will need this login to activate the exam, so please do register when prompted. If you already have a Pearson website login, there is no need to register again. Just use your existing login.

## Activate and Download the Practice Exam

Once the exam engine is installed, you should then activate the exam associated with this book (if you did not do so during the installation process), as follows:

**Step 1.**    Start the Pearson Cert Practice Test (PCPT) software from the Windows Start menu or from your desktop shortcut icon.

**Step 2.**    To activate and download the exam associated with this book, from the **My Products** or **Tools** tab, select the **Activate** button.

**Step 3.**    On the next screen, enter the activation key from paper inside the cardboard CD holder at the back of the book. After doing so, click the **Activate** button.

**Step 4.**    The activation process downloads the practice exam. Click **Next**, and then click **Finish**.

When the activation process completes, the My Products tab should list your new exam. If you do not see the exam, make sure you have selected the **My Products** tab on the menu. At this point, the software and practice exam are ready to use. Just select the exam and click the **Use** button.

To update a particular exam you have already activated and downloaded, open the **Tools** tab and click the **Update Products** button. Updating your exams ensures you have the latest changes and updates to the exam data.

If you want to check for updates to the Pearson Cert Practice Test engine software, open the **Tools** tab and click the **Update Application** button. Doing so ensures you are running the latest version of the software engine.

## Activating Other Exams

The exam software installation process, and the registration process, has to happen only once. Then, for each new exam, only a few steps are required. For instance, if you buy another new Cisco Press Official Cert Guide or Pearson IT Certification Cert Guide, extract the activation code from the CD sleeve at the back of that book—you don't even need the CD at this point. From there, all you have to do is start the exam engine (if not still up and running), and perform steps 2 through 4 from the previous list.

### Premium Edition

In addition to the free practice exam provided on the CD-ROM, you can purchase additional exams with expanded functionality directly from Pearson IT Certification. The Premium Edition of this title contains an additional two full practice exams and an eBook (in both PDF and ePub format). In addition, the Premium Edition title also has remediation for each question to the specific part of the eBook that relates to that question.

Because you have purchased the print version of this title, you can purchase the Premium Edition at a deep discount. There is a coupon code in the CD sleeve that contains a one-time-use code and instructions for where you can purchase the Premium Edition.

To view the premium edition product page, go to www.informit.com/title/9780132748360.

## The Cisco Learning Network

Cisco provides a wide variety of CCNP preparation tools at a Cisco Systems website called the Cisco Learning Network. This site includes a large variety of exam preparation tools, including sample questions, forums on each Cisco exam, learning video games, and information about each exam.

To reach the Cisco Learning Network, go to www.cisco.com/go/learnnetspace, or just search for "Cisco Learning Network." You must use the login you created at Cisco.com. If you do not have such a login, you can register for free. To register, simply go to Cisco.com, click **Register** at the top of the page, and supply some information.

## Memory Tables

Like most Official Cert Guides from Cisco Press, this book purposefully organizes information into tables and lists for easier study and review. Rereading these tables can prove to be very useful before the exam. However, it is easy to skim over the tables without paying attention to every detail, especially when you remember having seen the table's contents when reading the chapter.

Instead of just reading the tables in the various chapters, you can use another review tool that this book's Appendixes C and D provide. Appendix C lists partially completed versions of many of the tables from the book. You can open Appendix C (a PDF on the CD that comes with this book) and print the appendix. For review, you can attempt to complete the tables. This exercise can help you focus on the review. It also exercises the memory connectors in your brain, plus it makes you think about the information without as much information, which forces a little more contemplation about the facts.

Appendix D, also a PDF located on the CD, lists the completed tables to check yourself. You can also just refer to the tables as printed in the book.

## Suggested Plan for Final Review/Study

This section lists a suggested study plan from the point at which you finish reading through Chapter 22 until you take the 642-647 CCNP Security VPN exam. Certainly, you can ignore this plan, use it as is, or just take suggestions from it.

The plan consists of four steps:

**Step 1.** Review key topics and DIKTA questions:

You can use the table that lists the key topics in each chapter or just flip the pages looking for key topics. Also, reviewing the "Do I Know This Already?" questions from the beginning of the chapter can be helpful for review.

**Step 2.** Complete memory tables:

Open Appendix C on the CD and print the entire appendix, or print the tables by major part. Then complete the tables.

**Step 3.** Subnetting practice:

If you can no longer do subnetting well and quickly, without a subnetting calculator, take some time to get better and faster before going to take the 642-647 CCNP Security VPN exam.

**Step 4.** Use the Pearson Cert Practice Test engine to practice:

The Pearson Cert Practice Test engine on the CD can be used to study using a bank of unique exam-realistic questions available only with this book.

### Using the Exam Engine

The Pearson Cert Practice Test engine on the CD includes a database of questions created specifically for this book. The Pearson Cert Practice Test engine can be used either in Study mode or Practice Exam mode, as follows:

- **Study mode:** Study mode is most useful when you want to use the questions for learning and practicing. In Study mode, you can select options like randomizing the order of the questions and answers, automatically viewing answers to the questions as you go, testing on specific topics, and many other options.

- **Practice Exam mode:** This mode presents questions in a timed environment, providing you with a more realistic experience. It also restricts your ability to see your score as you progress through the exam and view answers to questions as you are taking the exam. These timed exams not only allow you to study for the actual 642-647 CCNP Security VPN exam, they also help you simulate the time pressure that can occur when taking the actual exam.

When doing your final preparation, you can use Study mode, Practice Exam mode, or both. However, after you have seen each question a couple of times, you will likely start to remember the questions, and the usefulness of the exam database might go down. So, consider the following options when using the exam engine:

- Use this question database for review. Use Study mode to study the questions by chapter, just as with the other final review steps listed in this chapter. Plan on getting another exam (possibly from the Premium Edition) if you want to take additional simulated exams.

- Save the question database, not using it for review during your review of each book part. Save it until the end so that you will not have seen the questions before. Then, use Practice Exam mode to simulate the exam.

Picking the correct mode from the exam engine's user interface is pretty obvious. The following steps show how to move to the screen from which to select Study or Practice Exam mode:

**Step 1.**   Open the **My Products** tab if you are not already at that screen.

**Step 2.**   Select the exam you want to use from the list of available exams.

**Step 3.**   Click the **Use** button.

The engine then displays a window from which you can choose Study mode or Practice Exam mode. When in Study mode, you can further choose the book chapters, limiting the questions to those explained in the specified chapters of the book.

## Summary

The tools and suggestions listed in this chapter are designed with one goal in mind: to help you develop the skills required to pass the 642-647 CCNP Security VPN exam. This book has been developed from the beginning to not just tell you the facts, but to help you learn how to apply the facts. No matter what your experience level is leading up to when you take the exams, it is our hope that the broad range of preparation tools, and even the structure of the book, helps you pass the exam with ease.

# Answers to the "Do I Know This Already?" Quizzes

## Chapter 1

**1.** A, B, and D
**2.** A and D
**3.** B
**4.** B
**5.** B
**6.** A
**7.** A, C, and D
**8.** D
**9.** C

## Chapter 2

**1.** D
**2.** A
**3.** A, B, and C
**4.** B, C, and D
**5.** A and B
**6.** A and D

## Chapter 3

**1.** B and C
**2.** C
**3.** A
**4.** B
**5.** A, B, and C
**6.** C
**7.** A, B, and C
**8.** B
**9.** B
**10.** B
**11.** C
**12.** B

## Chapter 4

**1.** B and C
**2.** B
**3.** A, C, and D
**4.** C
**5.** A
**6.** B
**7.** A

## Chapter 5

**1.** A and B
**2.** A, C, and D
**3.** C and D
**4.** A, B, D, and E
**5.** A and D
**6.** B

## Chapter 6

**1.** A, B, and D
**2.** A and C
**3.** B and D
**4.** F
**5.** A
**6.** A and B

## Chapter 7

**1.** A, B, and C
**2.** C
**3.** D
**4.** C
**5.** B
**6.** A and C
**7.** A
**8.** A, B, C, and D

## Chapter 8

**1.** B
**2.** B
**3.** D
**4.** C
**5.** C
**6.** D

## Chapter 9

**1.** B and D
**2.** C
**3.** E
**4.** D
**5.** A and C
**6.** D
**7.** A, C, D, and E
**8.** C
**9.** C, E, and F
**10.** D

## Chapter 10

**1.** A and D
**2.** A, B, D, E, and G
**3.** C, E, and F
**4.** A
**5.** A, C, and D
**6.** B
**7.** D
**8.** A and C
**9.** C
**10.** A and D

## Chapter 11

**1.** A, B, and D
**2.** A and C
**3.** B and C
**4.** A, C, D, and E
**5.** A
**6.** D

## Chapter 12

**1.** A
**2.** A and D
**3.** B
**4.** C
**5.** C
**6.** D
**7.** B

## Chapter 13

**1.** C
**2.** A, B, and D
**3.** D
**4.** C
**5.** B
**6.** D

## Chapter 14

**1.** B
**2.** A and C
**3.** C
**4.** B
**5.** C
**6.** A

## Chapter 15

**1.** B
**2.** A, C, and D
**3.** A
**4.** A and C
**5.** B
**6.** C

## Chapter 16

**1.** B
**2.** B
**3.** E
**4.** C
**5.** C
**6.** D

## Chapter 17

1. B
2. A and C
3. A
4. C
5. B
6. A and C

## Chapter 18

1. A and B
2. B and C
3. B
4. A and D
5. D
6. D
7. A, B, and C

## Chapter 19

1. B
2. D
3. A
4. A
5. A
6. C
7. B
8. D
9. B
10. D

## Chapter 20

1. C
2. A, C, and D
3. B
4. A and C
5. B
6. A and B

## Chapter 21

1. B
2. A
3. A, B, and C
4. C
5. B
6. C
7. E
8. B

## Chapter 22

1. B
2. C
3. B
4. A
5. A
6. B
7. B
8. D

# 642-647 CCNP Security VPN Exam Updates, Version 1.0

Over time, reader feedback allows Cisco Press to gauge which topics give our readers the most problems when taking the exams. To assist readers, authors may create new materials clarifying and expanding on those troublesome exam topics. This additional content about the exam will be posted as a PDF document on this book's companion website, at http://www.ciscopress.com/title/9781587142567.

This appendix is intended to provide you with updated information if Cisco makes minor modifications to the exam on which this book is based. When Cisco releases an entirely new exam, the changes are usually too extensive to provide in a simple update appendix. In those cases, you need to consult the new edition of the book for the updated content.

This appendix attempts to fill the void that occurs with any print book. In particular, this appendix does the following:

- Mentions technical items that might not have been mentioned elsewhere in the book

- Covers new topics if Cisco adds new content to the exam over time

- Provides a way to get up-to-the-minute current information about content for the exam

## Always Get the Latest at the Companion Website

You are reading the version of this appendix that was available when your book was printed. However, given that the main purpose of this appendix is to be a living, changing document, it is important that you look for the latest version online at the book's companion website. To do so:

**Step 1.**   Browse to http://www.ciscopress.com/title/9781587142567.

**Step 2.**   Select the **Updates** option under the More Information box.

**Step 3.**   Download the latest Appendix B document.

**Note:**   The downloaded document has a version number. Comparing the version of this print Appendix B (Version 1.0) with the latest online version of this appendix, you should do the following:

■   **Same version:** Ignore the PDF that you downloaded from the companion website.

■   **Website has a later version:** Ignore this Appendix B in your book and read only the latest version that you downloaded from the companion website.

If there is no appendix posted on the book's website, that simply means there have been no updates to post and Version 1.0 is still the latest version.

## Technical Content

The current version of this appendix does not contain any additional technical coverage.

# Glossary

**AAA** Authentication, Authorization, and Accounting. Provides a framework for granting or denying user access, rights within the network, and associated information held for their activities.

**AAA(LOCAL)** The local user database of the ASA device used to store user accounts and associated attributes.

**ACE** Access Control Entry. Contains access control parameters and actions.

**ACE** The Cisco Application Control Engine can be either a standalone device or a 7600/6500 module. Regardless of the physical configuration, the device provides high-level load balancing services.

**ACL** Access Control List; used to permit or deny packets into or out of the ASA device. Contains one or more ACEs.

**Active/Standby** Failover method providing HA.

**AH** Authentication Header. A protocol used within IPsec operation for the successful authentication, anti-replay, and integrity parameter management.

**AIA** Authority Information Access. A field within a digital certificate used to store the online OCSP URL and parameters.

**APCF** XML file used by an Application Helper to determine the when, how, and what resources of an application need to be modified for correct display or operation.

**asymmetric key protocol** Protocols within this category use different keys at each end of the conversation typically used for the secure transport of symmetric keys.

**BIA** The MAC address applied to a physical interface by the manufacturer.

**bookmark list** An ordered list of URLs for user access to defined resources.

**CA** Certificate authority. A public organization or internal server responsible for the overall PKI implementation in use by your organization.

**Cache Cleaner** An alternative to the Vault allowing for the full or partial removal of cached user information upon termination of their VPN connection.

**certificate authority (CA)** The entity or server responsible for the generation, revocation, and deployment of digital certificates.

**CIFS** Common Internet File System. A protocol used for file and folder access within a network.

**class-map**    Used in a QoS deployment to hold parameters and criteria for matching packets.

**cluster**    A method providing load balancing between VPN devices based upon the least-loaded device.

**clustering**    A stateless HA method provided by two or more ASA devices. One ASA is delegated the role of master responsible for directing user connections to cluster ASA members based on load.

**CN**    Common Name. A field within a digital certificate commonly populated with the username if used for identity authentication or the FQDN of a peer.

**Code Signing**    A method used by program developers to secure the integrity of a program by attaching a computed signature for the checks to be carried out by the receiving client.

**connection profile**    A VPN protocol-specific connection object and container for connection-specific parameters and attributes.

**content rewrite engine**    The internal component of the ASA used for the rewrite of URL and objects returned to the client browser after a request.

**CRL**    Certificate revocation list. Issued by a CA containing an up-to-date list of certificate serial numbers for certificates that have been issued but revoked.

**CSD**    Cisco Secure Desktop. Provides a secure remote environment for user connectivity.

**CSR**    Certificate Signing Request. A file generated by a host for the purposes of requesting a digital certificate from a CA (Certificate Authority).

**DAP**    Dynamic Access Policy. Used for the assignment of policy parameters and actions based on user AAA and machine posture validation attributes.

**DART**    Diagnosis and Reporting tool. An optional module used to collect a large amount of information from the AnyConnect logs, installed software, modules, and overall environment.

**device pass-through**    Allows for devices on the remote site that are unable to participate in authentication to access network resources without having to authenticate.

**digital signature**    Hash value generated by a protocol such as SHA or MD5 and assigned to a file or application for integrity check purposes.

**DNS**    Domain Name System. Used to provide a mapping of IP addresses to names on a network.

**DPD**    Dead Peer Detection. Used as a keepalive function between a VPN client and server used for the purposes of failover and DTLS fallback.

**DTLS**    Datagram Transport Layer Security. An implementation of the TLS protocol using the UDP transport protocol for the purposes of transmitting delay-sensitive data.

**email proxy**    A function provided by the ASA to facilitate the secure connection of common mail protocols POP3S, IMAP4S, and SMTPS.

**ESP**    Encapsulating Security Payload. A protocol used within IPsec operation for the successful authentication, anti-replay, integrity, and encryption parameter management.

**external group policy**   A group policy object configured on the ASA whose attributes are held on an external AAA server in the form of RADIUS or LDAP attribute/value (A/V) pairs.

**group policy**   Policy object container used to store VPN portal objects and settings.

**hello packet**   Periodic packets sent between hosts to check the status of a device and/or connection.

**hold time**   The length of time from when a host sends a hello packet until it is received.

**Host Scan**   Posture Assessment module for attribute gathering and remediation.

**IKEv1**   A protocol that operates using UDP port 500 and is used as a framework for underlying protocols and their negotiations for successful tunnel establishment.

**internal group policy**   A locally configured group policy whose attributes are stored on the ASA device used for the purposes of connection profile- or user-specific policy attribute assignments.

**ISAKMP**   Internet Security Association and Key Management Protocol. Used by IKE for key and SA parameter negotiation.

**IUA**   Interactive User Authentication. When configured in the applied VPN head-end group policy, requires the users on the remote device network to individually authenticate before network access is granted through the tunnel.

**LDAP**   Lightweight Directory Access Protocol. A common protocol used to query for parameters and objects from a directory containing user and other similar objects.

**LLQ**   Low Latency Queuing. Allows for the prioritization of defined application data but policed to a predefined rate.

**macro substitution**   Allows the use of predefined or POST data for authentication and customization purposes.

**master**   The VPN device responsible for redirecting requests among cluster members. The master is elected based on priority or the first active device in the cluster.

**MPF**   Modular Policy Framework. A command-line framework used to configure and hold all QOS elements among other functionalities.

**mutual group authentication**   A method of authentication used to provide an additional level of security when deploying a VPN connection using pre-shared key peer authentication. The head end can be configured to present an identity certificate to the remote user.

**NAM**   Network Access Manager. An optional AnyConnect module allowing for the management of remote user wired and wireless connectivity.

**NetFlow**   A Cisco technology that creates accounting data in the form of flow information based on Layer 3 and Layer 4 packet information.

**OCSP**   Online Certificate Status Protocol. A recommended revocation list retrieval protocol, commonly operating over HTTP.

**PKI**   Public Key Infrastructure. The overall framework governing the standards and operations of a digital certificate deployment.

**plug-in**   A thin client Java-based version of an application typically used for remote access purposes.

**policing**   A method of rate-limiting traffic sent through or coming into an interface, with out-of-profile traffic usually dropped.

**policy-map**   Used in a QoS deployment to apply chosen QoS settings to those packets matched using a class-map.

**port forwarding applet**   Java applet used to configure the local client settings in preparation for application access.

**Posture Assignment module**   An optional AnyConnect module that contains the Host Scan image, Keystroke Logger Detection, Cache Cleaner, and Host Emulation Detections applications.

**Prelogin Assessment**   The phase before a user login, allowing for policy assignment based on device and connecting environment attributes.

**proxy auto-configuration file (PAC)**   An administratively defined or automatically generated file used to automate the configuration of proxy server parameters.

**proxy server**   An internal or external server for the use of forwarding requests and responses between source and destination.

**Public Key Infrastructure (PKI)**   The standards and protocols that encompass the process of digital certificate deployment and functional areas.

**Resource Mask**   A user-defined parameter used by the ASA to determine valid content for rewrite operations.

**RRI**   Reverse route injection. Can enable the installation of routes into the ASA local routing table for a remote site subnet, and these in turn can be advertised in a network using an IGP.

**SBL**   Start Before Login. An AnyConnect module responsible for allowing the user to connect to a VPN before logging in to the machine.

**service policy**   Used in a QoS deployment to apply the policy map at the interface or global level, basically activating the chosen QoS settings.

**shaping**   A method of limiting the rate of traffic sent through an interface and buffering any out-of-profile traffic for later sending to achieve a result close to the configured CIR.

**single sign-on (SSO)**   The use of a single authentication cookie or credential type for successive authentication requests.

**smart tunnel list**   A software list containing all smart tunnel entries configured for a particular group or user.

**SNMP**   Simple Network Management Protocol. Standards-based protocol used to provide device and statistical information to servers.

**split tunneling**   A method of controlling which traffic is tunneled through the VPN or sent directly to the destination.

**stateful**   A method of sharing session information between devices to provide for continuing communication following a failover.

**stateless**   A method of failover or load-balancing HA configuration that does not provide for the synchronization of session information between devices.

**SUA**   Secure Unit Authentication. When configured, requires the ASA to authenticate using non-preconfigured parameters before the tunnel setup can continue.

**symmetric key protocol**   Protocols within this category use the same keys at each end of the conversation for encryption/authentication reasons.

**Telemetry module**   An optional AnyConnect module allowing for the tracking of user, system, and API calls made to locate the origin of viruses, worms, and so on.

**Vault**   Secure Desktop partition applied to a remote user for higher local and endpoint security.

**VIP**   Virtual IP address shared between all members within a VPN cluster. Clients direct their requests to this IP address and the master receives them, and then redirects to the least-loaded device.

**VMAC**   A shared virtual MAC address between ASA devices in a hardware failover configuration.

**web ACL**   A web-specific access control list used to permit or deny access to specific URLs (HTTP, HTTPS, ICA, VNC, and so on).

**Web Security module**   An optional AnyConnect module allowing for the use of ScanSafe remote-filtering services.

**XML**   Extensible Markup Language. A lightweight markup format typically used to store objects and settings for fast access rather than using a database.

# Index

# O

Object NAT, configuring ASA, 18

obtaining portal help (clientless SSL VPN), 386-387

operating systems, CSD support, 447-449

OSCP (Online Certificate Status Protocol), 152-155

clientless SSL VPN deployment, 297-301

# P

packet processing, ASA, 28-29

Pearson Cert Practice Test Engine, 696-697

peering VPNs, 252-253, 470-471

IPsec site-to-site VPNs, 678-679

per-user connection profile lock, 54

physical topologies for SSL VPN deployment, 289-292

PKI

advanced deployment strategies, 570-575

Cisco Easy VPN solution, configuring, 556-561

membership, establishing for clientless SSL VPN deployment, 294

SSO integration, troubleshooting, 406-409

policies

DAPs

*attributes, 417-418*

*configuring, 213-215, 418-426*

*CSD, authorization, 461-463*

*debugging, 435-436*

*record aggregation, 427-432*

*testing, 432-434*

*troubleshooting, 432-436*

group policies, 56-59

*AnyConnect Secure Mobility Client, 199-207*

*ASA, configuring, 582-588*

*assigning to AnyConnect Secure Mobility Client, 100-104*

*clientless SSL VPN deployment, access control, 323-327*

*external group policies, configuring, 60-69*

hierarchical policy model, 50

prelogin policies (CSD), configuring, 234-237

policing, 670

port forwarding, application access for clientless SSL VPN deployment, 343-349

portal (clientless SSL VPN)

AnyConnect Secure Mobility Client integration, 387-388

help, obtaining, 386-387

layout, configuring, 375-379

localization, configuring, 381-385

post-login phase, remote users, 49

Posture Assessment module, 231

practice exam

CD, installing, 694

downloading, 694

Prelogin Assessment module (CSD), 225-226

prelogin criteria, configuring CSD, 452-460

prelogin phase, remote users, 49

prelogin policies (CSD), configuring, 234-237

preparing for exam, 696-697

pre-shared keys, configuring Cisco Easy VPN solution, 529-532

provisioning

certificates as local CA, 126-134

certificates from third-party CA, 139-150, 566-570

# ciscopress.com: Your Cisco Certification and Networking Learning Resource

Subscribe to the monthly Cisco Press newsletter to be the first to learn about new releases and special promotions.

Visit **ciscopress.com/newsletters.**

While you are visiting, check out the offerings available at your finger tips.

–Free Podcasts from experts:
  · OnNetworking
  · OnCertification
  · OnSecurity

**Podcasts**

View them at **ciscopress.com/podcasts.**

–Read the latest author **articles** and **sample chapters** at ciscopress.com/articles.

–Bookmark the Certification Reference Guide available through our partner site at **informit.com/certguide.**

Connect with Cisco Press authors and editors via Facebook and Twitter, visit **informit.com/socialconnect.**

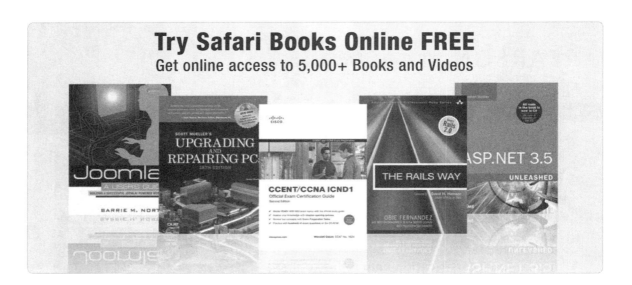

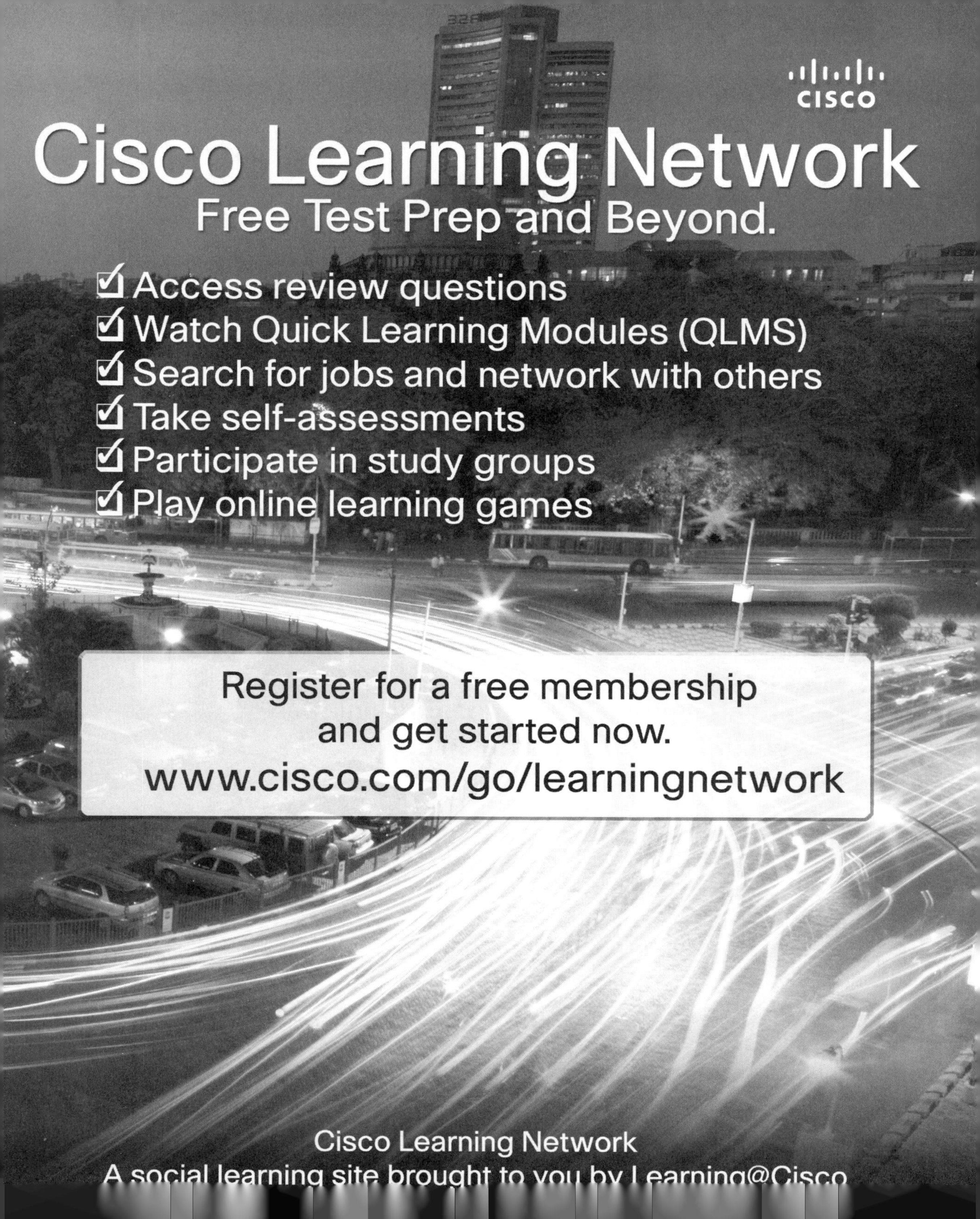
CISCO
Cisco Learning Network
Free Test Prep and Beyond.
Access review questions
Watch Quick Learning Modules (QLMS)
Search for jobs and network with others
Take self-assessments
Participate in study groups
Play online learning games
Register for a free membership
and get started now.
www.cisco.com/go/learningnetwork
Cisco Learning Network
A social learning site brought to you by Learning@Cisco

# FREE Online Edition

Your purchase of **CCNP Security VPN 642-647 Official Cert Guide** includes access to a free online edition for 45 days through the Safari Books Online subscription service. Nearly every Cisco Press book is available online through Safari Books Online, along with more than 5,000 other technical books and videos from publishers such as Addison-Wesley Professional, Exam Cram, IBM Press, O'Reilly, Prentice Hall, Que, and Sams.

**SAFARI BOOKS ONLINE** allows you to search for a specific answer, cut and paste code, download chapters, and stay current with emerging technologies.

## Activate your FREE Online Edition at
## www.informit.com/safarifree

> **STEP 1:** Enter the coupon code: IUEOVFA

> **STEP 2:** New Safari users, complete the brief registration form.
> Safari subscribers, just log in.

If you have difficulty registering on Safari or accessing the online edition, please e-mail customer-service@safaribooksonline.com